DATA STRUCTURES
USING PASCAL

PRENTICE-HALL SOFTWARE SERIES
Brian W. Kernighan, advisor

DATA STRUCTURES USING PASCAL

AARON M. TENENBAUM

MOSHE J. AUGENSTEIN

Department of Computer and Information Science
Brooklyn College
City University of New York

PRENTICE-HALL, INC., ENGLEWOOD CLIFFS, NEW JERSEY 07632

Library of Congress Cataloging in Publication Data

Tenenbaum, Aaron M.
   Data structures using Pascal.

   (Prentice-Hall software series)
   Bibliography: p.
   Includes index.
   1. Data structures (Computer science) 2. Pascal
(Computer program language) I. Augenstein, Moshe
(date), joint author. II. Title. III. Series.
QA76.9.D35T46   001.64'2   80-21570
ISBN 0-13-196501-8

Printed in the United States of America

10 9 8 7 6 5 4 3

Editorial/production supervision and interior design: Nancy Milnamow
Cover design: Jorge Hernandez
Manufacturing buyer: Joyce Levatino

Prentice-Hall International, Inc., *London*
Prentice-Hall of Australia Pty. Limited, *Sydney*
Prentice-Hall of Canada, Ltd., *Toronto*
Prentice-Hall of India Private Limited, *New Delhi*
Prentice-Hall of Japan, Inc., *Tokyo*
Prentice-Hall of Southeast Asia Pte. Ltd., *Singapore*
Whitehall Books Limited, *Wellington, New Zealand*

To my daughter, Sara Tova

A. T.

To my sons, Menachem, Yakov and Elchonon

M. A.

Contents

Preface

This text is designed for a two-semester course in data structures and programming. For several years, we have taught a course in data structures to students who have had a semester course in high-level language programming and a semester course in assembly language programming. We found that a considerable amount of time was spent in teaching programming techniques because the students had not had sufficient exposure to programming and were unable to implement abstract structures on their own. The brighter students eventually caught on to what was being done. The weaker students never did. Based on this experience, we have reached the firm conviction that a first course in data structures must go hand in hand with a second course in programming. This text is a product of that conviction.

The text introduces abstract concepts, shows how those concepts are useful in problem solving and then shows how the abstractions can be made concrete by using a programming language. Equal emphasis is placed on both the abstract and the concrete versions of a concept, so that the student learns about the concept itself, its implementation, and its application.

The language used in this text is Pascal. Pascal is well-suited to such a course since it contains the control structures necessary to make programs readable and allows basic data structures such as stacks, linked lists, and trees to be implemented in a variety of ways. This allows the student to appreciate the choices and tradeoffs which face a programmer in a real situation. The only prerequisite for students using this text is a one-semester course in programming. Students who have had a course in programming using such languages as FORTRAN or PL/I can use this text together with one of the elementary Pascal texts listed in the bibliography. Chapter 1 and the Appendix also provide information necessary for such students to acquaint themselves with Pascal.

Chapter 1 is an introduction to data structures. Section 1.1 introduces the concept of an abstract data structure and the concept of an implementation. Sections 1.2 and 1.3 introduce arrays and records in Pascal. The implementations of these two data structures as well as their applications are covered.

Chapter 2 discusses stacks and their Pascal implementation. Since this is the first new data structure introduced, considerable discussion of the pitfalls of implementing such a structure is included. Section 2.3 introduces postfix, prefix, and infix notations.

Chapter 3 covers recursion, its applications, and its implementation. Chapter 4 introduces queues and linked lists and their implementations using an array of available nodes.

Chapter 5 discusses Pascal dynamic storage and the implementation of stacks, queues, and linked lists using dynamic storage.

Chapter 6 discusses trees and Chapter 7 introduces graphs.

Chapter 8 covers sorting and Chapter 9 covers searching.

The Appendix discusses a number of topics related to the Pascal language and its usage which are relevant to data structures. Some students may have encountered some of these topics in an introductory Pascal course, but many have not. The instructor can assign sections of the Appendix as independent reading or can integrate them into the body of the course.

At the end of the text, we have included a large bibliography with each entry classified by the appropriate topic, chapter, or section of the text.

A one-semester course in data structures consists of Section 1.1, Chapters 2–6, and Chapters 8 and 9. Parts of Chapters 3, 6, 8, and 9 may be omitted if time is pressing.

The text is suitable for course I1 of Curriculum 68 (*Communications of the ACM*, March 1968), courses UC1 and UC8 of the Undergraduate Programs in Information Systems (*Communications of the ACM*, Dec. 1973) and course CS2 and parts of courses CS7 and CS13 of Curriculum 78 (*Communications of the ACM*, March 1979). In particular, the text covers parts or all of topics P1, P2, P3, P4, P5, S2, D1, D2, D3, and D6 of Curriculum 78.

Algorithms are presented as intermediaries between English language descriptions and Pascal programs. They are written in Pascal style interspersed with English. These algorithms allow the reader to focus on the method used to solve a problem without concern about declaration of variables and the peculiarities of a real language. In transforming an algorithm into a program, we introduce these issues and point out the pitfalls which accompany them.

The indentation pattern used for Pascal programs and algorithms is based on a format suggested by Peterson (*SIGPLAN Notices*, December 1977) and which we have found to be quite useful. We also adopt the convention of indicating in a comment the construct being terminated by occurrences of the keyword *end*. Together with the indentation pattern, this is a valuable tool in improving program comprehensibility. We distinguish between algorithms and programs by presenting the former in italics and the latter in roman.

Most of the concepts in the text are illustrated by several examples. Some of these examples are important topics in their own right (e.g., postfix notation, multi-word arithmetic, etc.) and may be treated as such. Other examples illustrate different implementation techniques (such as sequential storage of trees). The instructor is free to cover as many or as few of these examples as he or she wishes. Examples may also be assigned to students as independent reading. It is anticipated that an instructor will be unable to cover all the examples in sufficient detail within the confines of a one- or two-semester course. We feel that, at the stage of a student's development for which the text is designed, it is more important to cover several examples in great detail than to cover a broad range of topics cursorily.

All the programs and algorithms in this text have been tested and debugged. We wish to thank Kai Ming Lee and Professor Allen J. Schreier for their invaluable assistance in this task. Their zeal for the task was above and beyond the call of duty and their suggestions were always valuable. Of course, any errors that remain are the sole responsibility of the authors.

The exercises vary widely in type and difficulty. Some are drill exercises to ensure comprehension of topics in the text. Others involve modifications of programs or algorithms presented in the text. Still others introduce new concepts and are quite challenging. Often, a group of successive exercises includes the complete development of a new topic which can be used as the basis for a term project or an additional lecture. The instructor should use caution in assigning exercises so that an assignment is suitable to the student's level. We consider it imperative for students to be assigned several (from five to twelve, depending on difficulty) programming projects per semester. The exercises contain several projects of this type. The instructor may find a great many additional exercises and projects in the Exercise Manual of our earlier text, *Data Structures and PL/I Programming*. Although many of the exercises in that manual are presented using PL/I, they can readily be recast in a Pascal setting. The *Exercise Manual for Data Structures and PL/I Programming* is available from the publisher.

We have attempted to use "standard" Pascal, as specified in the *Pascal Manual and Report* and in the third working draft of the proposed BSI/ISO standard. We have tried to use no feature about which these two sources differ and have attempted to use the strictest possible assumptions about implementation-dependent features, or have noted the use of such features. (The primary exception to this is the occasional use of a packed array of a subrange of characters as an argument to the *write* procedure.) You should, of course, warn your students about any idiosyncracies of the particular compiler which they are using. As the manuscript was being edited, a subsequent version of the Pascal standard proposal was published (see *SIGPLAN Notices*, April 1980) which includes the capability of allowing the bounds of an array parameter to be determined during run-time. We do not know whether or how soon this feature will be adopted, or how soon Pascal compilers which include this feature will be produced. Because of this, we have included material on this new feature as it is currently being proposed in Section 5 of the Appendix and have added references to that section at the few places where the feature was relevant.

Itchy Goldbrenner, Simon Krischer, and Carl Markowitz spent many hours typing and correcting the original manuscript. Their cooperation and patience as we continually made up and changed our minds about additions and deletions are most sincerely appreciated. Carl Markowitz and Allen J. Schreier should be singled out for their extraordinary enthusiasm and dedication in all phases of the book's production. Kai Ming Lee is commended for his thoroughness and dedication.

We would also like to thank J. Barone, D. Bieber, A. Ciappina, J. Davis, R. Gerard, T. Goldfinger, W. Lee, G. Markowitz, D. Rybstein, G. Schechter, R. Teich, D. Zaslowsky, and B. Zusin for their invaluable assistance.

The staff of the City University Computer Center deserves special mention. They were extremely helpful in assisting us in using the excellent facilities of the Center. The same can be said of the staff of the Brooklyn College Computer Center.

We would like to thank the editors and staff at Prentice-Hall and especially the reviewers for their helpful comments and suggestions.

Finally, we thank our wives, Miriam Tenenbaum and Gail Augenstein, for their advice and encouragement during the long and arduous task of producing such a book.

Aaron Tenenbaum
Moshe Augenstein

1 Introduction to Data Structures

A computer is a machine that manipulates information. The study of computer science includes the study of how information is organized in a computer, how it can be manipulated, and how it can be utilized. Thus it is exceedingly important for a student of computer science to understand the concepts of information organization and manipulation in order to continue study of the field.

1. INFORMATION AND MEANING

If computer science is fundamentally the study of information, the first question that arises is: What is information? Unfortunately, although the concept of information is the bedrock of the entire field, this question cannot be answered precisely. In this sense, the concept of information in computer science is similar to the concepts of point, line, and plane in geometry—they are all undefined terms about which statements can be made but which cannot be explained in terms of more elementary concepts.

In geometry, it is possible to talk about the length of a line despite the fact that the concept of a line itself is undefined. The length of a line is a measure of quantity. Similarly, in computer science, we can measure quantities of information. The basic unit of information is the *bit*, whose value asserts one of two mutually exclusive possibilities. For example, if a light switch can be in one of two positions but not in both simultaneously, the fact that it is either in the "on" position or the "off" position is one bit of information. If a device can be in more than two possible states, the fact that it is in a particular state is more than one bit of information. For example, if a dial has eight possible positions, the fact that it is in position 4 rules out seven other possibilities, whereas the fact that a light switch is on rules out only one other possibility.

Another way of thinking of this phenomenon is as follows. Suppose that we had only two-way switches but could use as many of them as we needed. How many such switches would be necessary to represent a dial with eight

1

Switch 1

OFF

ON

(a) One switch (two possibilities).

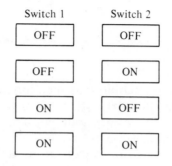

Switch 1   Switch 2

OFF   OFF

OFF   ON

ON   OFF

ON   ON

(b) Two switches (four possibilities).

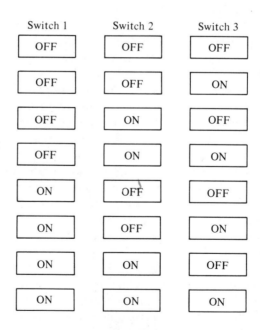

Switch 1   Switch 2   Switch 3

OFF   OFF   OFF

OFF   OFF   ON

OFF   ON   OFF

OFF   ON   ON

ON   OFF   OFF

ON   OFF   ON

ON   ON   OFF

ON   ON   ON

(c) Three switches (eight possibilities).

Figure 1.1.1

positions? Clearly, one switch can represent only two positions (see Figure 1.1.1a). Two switches can represent four different positions (Figure 1.1.1b) and three switches are required to represent eight different positions (Figure 1.1.1c). In general, n switches can represent 2^n different possibilities.

The binary digits 0 and 1 are used to represent the two possible states of a particular bit (in fact, the word "bit" is a contraction of the words "binary digit"). Given n bits, a string of n 1s and 0s is used to represent their settings. For example, the string 101011 represents six switches, the first of which is "on" (1), the second of which is "off" (0), the third on, the fourth off, and the fifth and sixth on.

We have seen that 3 bits are sufficient to represent eight possibilities. The eight possible configurations of these 3 bits (000, 001, 010, 011, 100, 101, 110, and 111) can be used to represent the integers 0 through 7. However, there is nothing intrinsic about these bit settings which implies that a particular setting represents a particular integer. Any assignment of integer values to bit settings is equally valid as long as no two integers are assigned to the same bit setting. Once such an assignment has been made, a particular bit setting can be unambiguously interpreted as a specific integer. Let us examine several widely used methods for interpreting bit settings as integers.

Binary and Decimal Integers

The most widely used method for interpreting bit settings as nonnegative integers is the *binary number system*. In this system each bit position represents a power of 2. The rightmost bit position represents 2^0, which equals 1; the next position to the left represents 2^1, which is 2; the next bit position represents 2^2, which is 4; and so on. An integer is represented as a sum of powers of 2. A string of all 0s represents the number 0. If a 1 appears in a particular bit position, the power of 2 represented by that bit position is included in the sum, but if a 0 appears, that power of 2 is not included in the sum. For example, the group of bits 00100110 has 1s in positions 1, 2, and 5 (counting from right to left with the rightmost position counted as position 0). Thus 00100110 represents the integer $2^1 + 2^2 + 2^5 = 2 + 4 + 32 = 38$. Under this interpretation, any string of bits of length n represents a unique nonnegative integer between 0 and $2^n - 1$, and any nonnegative integer between 0 and $2^n - 1$ can be represented by a unique string of bits of length n.

There are two widely used methods for representing negative binary numbers. In the first method, called *ones-complement notation*, a negative number is represented by changing each bit in its absolute value to the opposite bit setting. For example, since 00100110 represents 38, 11011001 is used to represent -38. This means that the first bit of a number is no longer used to represent a power of 2, but is reserved for the sign of the number. A bit string starting with a 0 represents a positive number, while a bit string starting with a 1 represents a negative number. Given n bits, the range of numbers that can be represented is $-2^{n-1} + 1$ (a 1 followed by

$n-1$ 0s) to $2^{n-1} - 1$ (a 0 followed by $n-1$ 1s). Note that under this representation, there are two representations for the number 0: a "positive 0" consisting of all 0s, and a "negative 0" consisting of all 1s.

The second method of representing negative binary numbers is called *twos-complement notation*. In this notation, 1 is added to the ones-complement representation of a negative number. For example, since 11011001 represents -38 in ones-complement notation, 11011010 is used to represent -38 in twos-complement notation. Given n bits, the range of numbers that can be represented is -2^{n-1} (a 1 followed by $n - 1$ 0s) to $2^{n-1} - 1$ (a 0 followed by $n - 1$ 1s). Note that -2^{n-1} can be represented in twos-complement notation but not in ones-complement notation. However, its absolute value 2^{n-1} cannot be represented in either notation using n bits. Note also that there is only one representation for the number 0 using n bits in twos-complement notation. To see this, consider 0 using 8 bits: 00000000. The ones complement is 11111111, which is "negative 0" in that notation. Adding one to produce the twos-complement form yields 100000000, which is 9 bits long. Since only 8 bits are allowed, the leftmost bit (or "overflow") is discarded, leaving 00000000 as minus 0.

The binary number system is by no means the only method by which bits can be used to represent integers. For example, a string of bits may be used to represent integers in the decimal number system, as follows. Four bits can be used to represent a decimal digit between 0 and 9 in the binary notation described above. A string of bits of arbitrary length may be divided into consecutive sets of 4 bits, where each set represents a decimal digit. The string then represents the number that is formed by those decimal digits in conventional decimal notation. For example, in this system, the bit string 00100110 is separated into two strings of 4 bits each: 0010 and 0110. The first of these represents the decimal digit 2 and the second represents the decimal digit 6, so that the entire string represents the integer 26. This representation is called *binary-coded decimal*.

One important feature of the binary-coded decimal representation of nonnegative integers is that not all bit strings are valid representations of a decimal integer. Four bits can be used to represent one of 16 different possibilities since there are 16 possible states for a set of 4 bits. However, in the binary-coded decimal integer representation, only 10 of those 16 possibilities are used. That is, codes such as 1010 and 1100 whose binary values are 10 or larger are invalid in a binary-coded decimal number.

Real Numbers

The usual method used by computers to represent real numbers is floating-point notation. There are many varieties of floating-point notation and each has individual characteristics. The key concept is that a real number is represented by a number, called a *mantissa*, times a *base* raised to an integer power, called an *exponent*. The base is usually fixed and the mantissa and exponent vary to represent different real numbers. For example, if the base is fixed at 10, the number 387.53 could be represented as 38,753 times 10 to the -2 power. (Recall that 10^{-2} is .01.) The mantissa is 38753 and the exponent is -2. Other possible representations are $.38753 \times 10^3$ and 387.53×10^0. We choose the representation in which the mantissa is an integer with no trailing zeros.

In the floating-point notation that we describe (which is not necessarily implemented on any particular machine exactly as described), a real number is represented by a 32-bit string consisting of a 24-bit mantissa followed by an 8-bit exponent. The base is fixed at 10. Both the mantissa and the exponent are twos-complement binary integers. For example, the 24-bit binary representation of 38753 is 000000001001011101100001 and the 8-bit twos-complement binary representation of -2 is 11111110, so the representation of 387.53 is 00000000100101110110000111111110.

Other real numbers and their floating-point representations are:

0	00000000000000000000000000000000
100	00000000000000000000000100000010
.5	00000000000000000000010111111111
.000005	00000000000000000000010111111010
12000	00000000000000000000110000000011
-387.53	11111111011010001001111111111110
-12000	11111111111111111111010000000011

The advantage of floating-point notation is that it can be used to represent numbers with extremely large or extremely small absolute values. For example, in the notation presented above, the largest number that can be represented is $(2^{23} - 1) \times 10^{127}$, which is a very large number indeed. The smallest positive number that can be represented is 10^{-128}, which is quite small. The limiting factor on the precision to which numbers can be represented on a particular machine is the number of significant binary digits in the mantissa. Not every number between the largest and the smallest can be represented. Our representation allows only 23 significant bits. Thus a number such as 10 million and one, which requires 24 significant binary digits in the mantissa, would have to be approximated by 10 million (1×10^7), which requires only one significant digit.

Character Strings

As we all know, information is not always interpreted numerically. Items such as names, job titles, and addresses must also be represented in some fashion within a computer. To enable the representation of such non-numeric objects, still another method of interpreting bit strings is necessary. Such information is usually represented in character string form. For example, in some computers, the eight bits 00100110 are used to represent the character '&'. A different eight-bit pattern is used to represent the character 'A', another to represent 'B', another to represent 'C' and still another for each character that has a representation in a particular machine. A Russian machine uses bit patterns to represent Russian characters; an Israeli machine uses bit patterns to represent Hebrew characters. (In fact, the characters being used are transparent to the machine; the character set can be changed by using a different print chain on the printer.) If 8 bits are used to represent a character, up to 256 different characters can be represented, since there are 256 different 8-bit patterns. If the string 11000000 is used to represent the character 'A' and 11000001 is used to represent the character 'B', the character string 'AB' would be represented by the bit string 1100000011000001. In general, a character string *str* is represented by the concatenation of the bit strings that represent the individual characters of *str*.

As in the case of integers, there is nothing intrinsic about a particular bit string which makes it suitable for representing a specific character. The assignment of bit strings to characters may be entirely arbitrary, but it must be adhered to consistently. It may be that some convenient rule is used in assigning bit strings to characters. For example, two bit strings may be assigned to two letters so that the one with a smaller binary value is assigned to the letter that comes earlier in the alphabet. However, such a rule is merely a convenience; it is not mandated by any intrinsic relation between characters and bit strings. In fact, computers even differ over the number of bits used to represent a character. Some computers use 7 bits (and therefore allow only up to 128 possible characters), some use 8 (up to 256 characters), and some use 10 (up to 1024 possible characters). The number of bits necessary to represent a character in a particular computer is called the *byte size* and a group of bits of that number is called a *byte*.

Note that using 8 bits to represent a character means that 256 possible characters can be represented. It is not very often that one finds a computer which uses so many different characters (although it is conceivable for a computer to include upper- and lowercase letters, special characters, italics, boldface, and other type characters), so that many of the 8-bit codes are not used to represent characters.

Thus we see that information itself has no meaning. Any meaning can be assigned to a particular bit pattern as long as it is done consistently. It is the interpretation of a bit pattern that gives it meaning. For example, the bit string 00100110 can be interpreted as the number 38 (binary), the number 26 (binary-coded decimal), or the character '&'. A method of interpreting a bit pattern is often called a *data type*. We have presented several data types: binary integers, binary-coded decimal nonnegative integers, real numbers, and character strings. The key questions are how to determine what data types are available to interpret bit patterns and which data type to use in interpreting a particular bit pattern.

Hardware and Software

The *memory* (also called *storage* or *core*) of a computer is simply a group of bits (switches). At any instant of the computer's operation any particular bit in memory is either 0 or 1 (off or on). The setting of a bit is called its *value* or its *contents*.

CHAP. 1: INTRODUCTION TO DATA STRUCTURES

The bits in a computer memory are grouped together into larger units such as bytes. In some computers, several bytes are grouped together into units called *words*. Each such unit (byte or word, depending on the machine) is assigned an *address*, which is a name identifying a particular unit among all the units in memory. This address is usually numeric, so that we may speak of byte 746 or word 937. An address is often called a *location*, and the contents of a location are the values of the bits that make up the unit at that location.

Every computer has a set of "native" data types. This means that it is constructed with a mechanism for manipulating bit patterns in a way that is consistent with the objects they represent. For example, suppose that a computer contains an instruction to add two binary integers and place that sum at a given location in memory for subsequent use. Then there is a mechanism built into the computer to:

1. Extract operand bit patterns from two given locations.
2. Produce a third bit pattern, representing the binary integer that is the sum of the two binary integers represented by the two operands.
3. Store the resultant bit pattern at a given location.

The computer "knows" to interpret the bit patterns at the given locations as binary integers because the hardware which executes that particular instruction is designed to do so. This is akin to a light "knowing" to be on when the switch is in a particular position.

If the same machine also has an instruction to add two real numbers, there is a separate built-in mechanism to interpret operands as real numbers. Two distinct instructions are necessary for the two operations, and each instruction carries within itself an implicit identification of the types of its operands as well as their explicit locations.

Therefore, it is the programmer's responsibility to know which data type is contained in each location that is used. It is the programmer's responsibility to choose between using an integer or real addition instruction to obtain the sum of two numbers.

A high-level programming language aids in this task considerably. For example, if a Pascal programmer declares

```
var x,y: integer;
    a,b: real;
```

space is reserved at four locations for four different numbers. These four locations may be referenced by the *identifiers* $x, y, a,$ and b. An identifier is used instead of a numerical address to refer to a particular memory location because of its convenience for the programmer. The contents of the locations reserved for x and y will be interpreted as integers, and the contents of a and b will be interpreted as real numbers. The compiler responsible for translating Pascal programs into machine language will translate the "+" in the statement

```
x := x + y
```

into integer addition and will translate the "+" in the statement

$$a := a + b$$

into real addition. An operator such as "+" is really a *generic* operator because it has several different meanings, depending on its context. The compiler relieves the programmer of specifying the type of addition that must be performed by examining the context and using the appropriate version.

It is important to recognize the key role played by declarations in a high-level language. It is by means of declarations that the programmer specifies how the contents of the computer memory are to be interpreted by the program. In doing this, a declaration specifies how much memory is needed for a particular entity, how the contents of that memory are to be interpreted, and other vital details. Declarations also specify to the compiler exactly what is meant by the operation symbols which are subsequently used.

The Concept of Implementation

Thus far, we have been viewing data types as a method of interpreting the memory contents of a computer. The set of native data types which a particular computer can support is determined by the functions that have been wired into its hardware. However, we can view the concept of "data type" from a completely different perspective—not in terms of what a computer can do, but in terms of what the user wants done. For example, if a human being wishes to obtain the sum of two integers, he or she does not care very much about the detailed mechanism by which that sum will be obtained. The person is interested in manipulating the mathematical concept of an "integer," not in manipulating hardware bits. The hardware of the computer may be used to represent an integer and is useful only insofar as the representation is successful.

Once the concept of "data type" is divorced from the hardware capabilities of the computer, there are a limitless number of data types that can be considered. A data type is an abstract concept defined by a set of logical properties. Once such an abstract data type is defined and the legal operations involving that type are specified, we may *implement* that data type (or a close approximation to it). An implementation may be a *hardware implementation*, in which the circuitry necessary to perform the required operations is designed and constructed as part of a computer. Or it may be a *software implementation*, in which a program consisting of already existing hardware instructions is written to interpret bit strings in the desired fashion and to perform the required operations. Thus a software implementation includes a specification of how an object of the new data type is represented by objects of previously existing data types, as well as a specification of how such an object is manipulated in conformance with the operations that have been defined for it. Throughout the remainder of this text, the term "implementation" is used to mean "software implementation."

AN EXAMPLE

Let us illustrate these concepts with an example. Suppose that the hardware of a computer contains an instruction

MOVE (SOURCE,DEST,*length*)

which copies a character string of *length* bytes from an address specified by SOURCE to an address specified by DEST. We present hardware instructions and locations using uppercase letters. The length must be specified by an integer, and for that reason we indicate it with lowercase letters. SOURCE and DEST can be specified by identifiers that represent storage locations. An example of this instruction is MOVE(A,B,3), which copies the three bytes starting at location A to the three bytes starting at location B.

Note the different roles played by the identifiers A and B in this operation. The first operand of the MOVE instruction is the contents of the location specified by the identifier A. The second operand, however, is not the contents of location B, since these contents are irrelevant to the execution of the instruction. Rather, the location itself is the operand, since the location specifies the destination of the character string. Although an identifier always stands for a location, it is common for an identifier to be used to reference the contents of that location. It is always apparent from the context whether an identifier is referencing a location or its contents. The identifier appearing as the first operand of a MOVE instruction refers to the contents of memory, whereas the identifier appearing as the second operand refers to a location.

We also assume that the computer hardware contains the usual arithmetic and branching instructions, which we indicate by using Pascal-like notation. For example, the instruction

$$Z := X + Y$$

interprets the contents of the bytes at locations X and Y as binary integers, adds them, and inserts the binary representation of their sum into the byte at location Z. (We do not operate on integers greater than one byte in length, and we ignore the possibility of overflow.) Here again, X and Y are used to reference memory contents and Z is used to reference a memory location, but the proper interpretation is clear from the context.

Sometimes, it is desirable to add a quantity to an address to obtain another address. For example, if A is a location in memory, we might want to reference the location 4 bytes beyond A. We cannot refer to this location as A+4 because that notation is reserved for the integer contents of location A plus four. We therefore introduce the notation A[4] to refer to this location. We also introduce the notation A[X] to refer to the address given by adding the binary integer contents of the byte at X to the address A.

The MOVE instruction requires the programmer to specify the length of the string to be copied. Thus it deals with an operand that is a fixed-length character string (i.e., the length of the string must be known). A fixed-length string and a byte-sized binary integer may be considered native data types of that particular machine.

Suppose that we wished to implement varying-length character strings on this machine. That is, we want to enable programmers to use an instruction

$$MOVEVAR(SOURCE, DEST)$$

to move a character string from location SOURCE to location DEST without being required to specify any length.

In order to implement this new data type, we must first decide on how it is to be represented in the memory of the machine and then indicate how that representation is to be manipulated. Clearly, it is necessary to know how many bytes must be moved in order to execute this instruction. Since the MOVEVAR operation does not specify this number, the number must be contained within the representation of the character string itself. A varying-length character string of length l may be represented by a contiguous set of $l + 1$ bytes ($l < 256$). The first byte contains the binary representation of the length l and the remaining bytes contain the representations of the characters in the string. Representations of three such strings are illustrated in Figure 1.1.2. [Note that the digits 5 and 9 in these figures do not stand for the bit patterns representing the characters '5' and '9' but rather for the patterns 00000101 and 00001001 (assuming eight bits to a byte), which represent the integers five and nine. Similarly, 14 in Figure 1.1.2c stands for the bit pattern 00001110.]

The program to implement the MOVEVAR operation can be written as follows (I is an auxiliary memory location):

```
MOVE(SOURCE, DEST, 1);
for I := 1 to DEST
    do MOVE(SOURCE[I], DEST[I], 1)
```

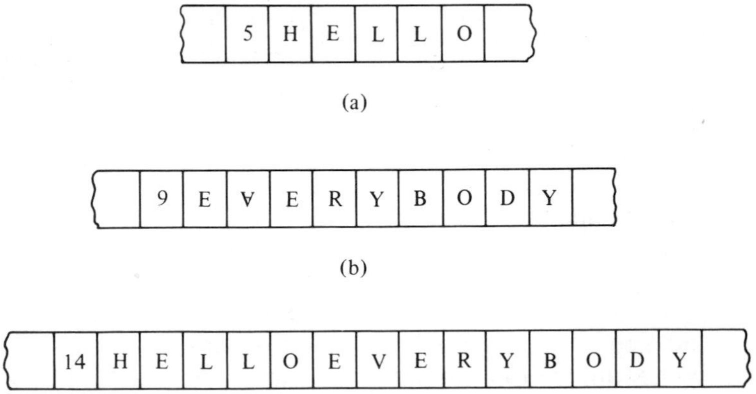

(a)

(b)

(c)

Figure 1.1.2 Varying-length character strings.

Similarly, we can implement an operation CONCATVAR(C1,C2,C3) to concatenate two varying-length character strings at locations C1 and C2 and place the result at C3. Figure 1.1.2c illustrates the concatenation of the two strings in Figure 1.1.2a and b:

```
{     move the length      }
Z:= C1+C2;
MOVE(Z,C3,1);
{ move the first string      }
for I:= 1 to C1
    do MOVE(C1[I],C3[I],1);
{ move the second string   }
for I:= 1 to C2
    do begin
           X:= C1+I;
           MOVE(C2[I],C3[X],1)
        end {for...do begin}
```

However, once the operation MOVEVAR has been defined, CONCATVAR can be implemented using MOVEVAR as follows:

```
MOVEVAR(C2,C3[C1]); {    move the second string     }
MOVEVAR(C1,C3);      {      move the first string     }
Z:= C1+C2;           { update the length of the result }
MOVE(Z,C3,1)
```

Figure 1.1.3 illustrates phases of this operation on the strings of Figure 1.1.2. Although this latter version is shorter, it is not really more efficient, since all the instructions used in implementing MOVEVAR are performed each time that MOVEVAR is used.

The statement Z:=C1+C2 in both of the foregoing algorithms is of particular interest. The addition instruction operates independently of the use of its operands (in this case, parts of varying-length character strings). The instruction is designed to treat its operands as single-byte integers regardless of any other use that the programmer has for them. Similarly, the reference to C3[C1] is to the location whose address is given by adding the contents of the byte at location C1 to the address C3. Thus the byte at C1 is treated as holding a binary integer, although it is also the start of a varying-length character string. This illustrates the fact that a data type is a method of treating the contents of memory, and that those contents have no intrinsic meaning.

Note that this representation of varying-length character strings allows only strings whose length is less than or equal to the largest binary integer that fits into a single byte. If a byte is eight bits, this means that the largest such string is 255 (which is $2^8 - 1$) characters long. To allow for longer strings, a different representation must be chosen and a new set of programs must be written. If we use this representation of varying-length character strings, the concatenation operation is invalid if the resulting string is more

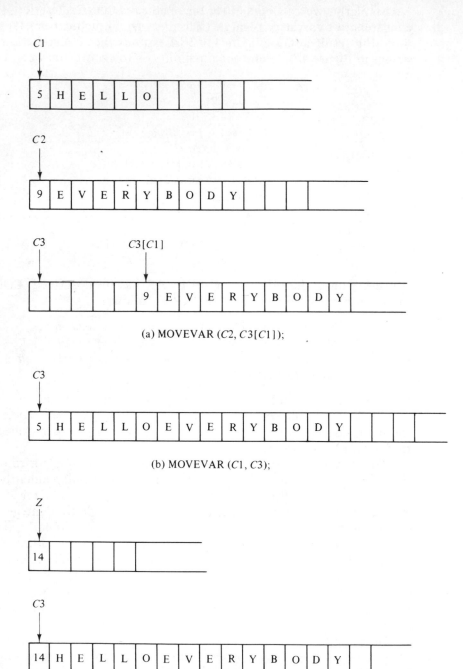

(a) MOVEVAR $(C2, C3[C1])$;

(b) MOVEVAR $(C1, C3)$;

(c) $Z := C1 + C2$; MOVE $(Z, C3, 1)$;

Figure 1.1.3 The CONCATVAR operation.

than 255 characters long. Since the result of such an operation is undefined, there are a wide variety of actions that an implementor can take if that operation is attempted. One possibility is to use only the first 255 characters of the result. Another possibility is to ignore the operation entirely and not move anything to the result field. There is also a choice of printing a warning message or of assuming that the user wants to achieve whatever result the implementor decides on.

Once a representation has been chosen for objects of a particular data type and routines have been written to operate on those representations, the programmer is free to use that data type to solve problems. The original hardware of the machine plus the programs for implementing more complex data types than those provided by the hardware can be thought of as a "better" machine than the one consisting of the hardware alone. The programmer of the original machine need not worry about how the computer is designed and what circuitry is being used to execute each instruction. He or she need only know what instructions are available and how those instructions can be used. Similarly, the programmer who uses the "extended" machine (which consists of hardware and software) need not be concerned with the details of how various data types are implemented. All the programmer needs to know is how they can be manipulated.

Data Types in Pascal

A type definition in Pascal specifies two things. First, it specifies the amount of storage that must be set aside for objects declared with that type. For example, a variable of type *integer* must have enough space to hold the largest possible integer value, whereas a variable of type *boolean* needs only a single bit. Second, it specifies how data represented by strings of bits are to be interpreted. The same bits at a specific storage location can be interpreted as an integer or a real number, yielding two completely different numeric values. For a discussion of the scalar data types available in Pascal, see Section 1 of the Appendix.

A variable declaration specifies that storage be set aside for an object of the specified type and that the object at that storage location can be referenced with the specified variable identifier.

A Pascal programmer can think of the Pascal language as defining a new machine with its own capabilities, data types, and operations. The user can state a problem solution in terms of the more useful Pascal constructs rather than in terms of lower-level machine language constructs. Thus problems can be solved more easily because a larger set of tools is available.

The study of data structures therefore involves two complementary goals. The first goal is to identify and develop useful mathematical entities and operations and to determine what classes of problems can be solved by using those entities and operations. The second goal is to determine representations for those abstract entities and to implement the abstract operations on those concrete representations. The first of these goals views a high-level data type as a tool that can be used to solve other problems, whereas the second views the implementation of such a data type as a problem to be solved using already existing data types. In determining representations for abstract entities, we must be careful to specify what facilities are available for constructing such representations. For example, it must be stated whether the full Pascal language is available or if we are restricted to the hardware facilities of a particular machine.

In the next two sections we examine several data structures that already exist in Pascal—the array, the set, and the record. We describe the facilities that are available in Pascal for utilizing these structures. We also focus on the abstract definitions of these data structures and how they can be useful in problem solving. Finally, we examine how they could be implemented if Pascal were not available (although a Pascal programmer can simply use the data structures as defined in the language without being concerned with most of these implementation details).

In the remainder of the book, we develop more complex data types and show their usefulness in problem solving. We also show how to implement these data types using the data types that are already available in Pascal. Since the problems that arise in the course of attempting to implement high-level data structures are quite complex, this will also allow us to investigate the Pascal language more thoroughly and to gain valuable experience in the use of that language.

Often, no implementation, hardware or software, can model a mathematical concept completely. For example, it is impossible to represent arbitrarily large integers on a computer, because the size of such a machine's memory is finite. Thus it is not the data type "integer," which is represented by the hardware but rather the data type "integer between x and y," where x and y are the smallest and largest integers representable by that machine.

It is important to recognize the limitations of a particular implementation. Often, it will be possible to present several implementations of the same data type, each with its own strengths and weaknesses. One particular implementation may be better than another for a specific application and the programmer must be aware of the possible trade-offs that might be involved.

One important consideration in any implementation is its efficiency. In fact, the reason that the high-level data types which we discuss are not built into Pascal is the significant overhead that they would entail. There are languages of significantly higher level than Pascal which have many of these data types already built into them, but many of them are highly inefficient and are therefore not in widespread use.

Efficiency is usually measured by two factors: time and space. If a particular application is heavily dependent on manipulating high-level data structures, the speed at which those manipulations can be performed will be the major determinant of the speed of the entire application. Similarly, if a program uses a large number of such structures, an implementation that uses an inordinate amount of space to represent the data structure will be impractical. Unfortunately, there is usually a trade-off between these two efficiencies, so that an implementation that is fast uses more storage than one which is slow. The choice of implementation in such a case involves a careful evaluation of the trade-offs among the various possibilities.

EXERCISES 1. In the text, an analogy is made between the length of a line and the number of bits of information in a bit string. In what ways is this analogy inadequate?

2. Determine what hardware data types are available on the computer at your particular installation and what operations can be performed on them.

3. Prove that there are 2^n different settings for n two-way switches. Suppose that we wanted to have m settings. How many switches would be necessary?

4. Interpret the following bit settings as binary positive integers, binary integers in twos-complement notation, and binary-coded decimal integers. If a setting cannot be interpreted as a binary-coded decimal integer, explain why.

   (a) 10011001   (b) 1001   (c) 000100010001
   (d) 01110111   (e) 01010101   (f) 100000010101

5. Write Pascal routines *add*, *subtract*, and *multiply* that read two strings of 0s and 1s representing binary nonnegative integers and print the string representing their sum, difference, and product, respectively.

6. Assume a ternary computer in which the basic unit of memory is a "trit" (ternary digit) rather than a bit. Such a trit can have three possible settings (0, 1, and 2) rather than just two (0 and 1). Show how nonnegative integers can be represented in ternary notation using such trits by a method analogous to binary notation using bits. Is there any nonnegative integer which can be represented using ternary notation and trits that cannot be represented using binary notation and bits? Are there any which can be represented using bits that cannot be represented using trits? Why are binary computers more common than ternary computers?

7. Write a Pascal program to read a string of 0s and 1s representing a positive integer in binary and to print a string of 0s, 1s, and 2s representing the same number in ternary notation (see Exercise 6). Write another Pascal program to read a ternary number and print the equivalent in binary.

2. ARRAYS AND SETS IN PASCAL

In this section and the next we examine several data structures which are an invaluable part of the Pascal language. We see how to use these structures and how they can be implemented. These structures are *composite* or *structured* types; that is, they are made up of simpler data types which exist in the language. The study of these structures involves an analysis of how the simple structures combine to form the composite and how to extract a specific component from the composite. We expect that you have already seen these data structures in an introductory Pascal programming course and that you are aware of how they are defined and used in Pascal. In these sections, therefore, we will not dwell on the many details associated with these structures but instead will highlight those features that are interesting from a data structure point of view.

The first of these data types is the *array*. The simplest form of an array is a *one-dimensional array*, which may be defined abstractly as a finite, ordered set of homogeneous elements. By "finite" we mean that there is a specific number of elements in the array. This number may be large or small, but it must exist. By "ordered" we mean that the elements of the array are arranged so that there is a first, second, third, and so on. By "homogeneous" we mean that all the elements in the array must be of the same type. For example, an array may contain all integers or all characters but may not contain both.

However, specifying the form of a data structure does not yet completely describe the structure. We must also specify how the structure is accessed. An array has two data types associated with it. The first type, called the *base type* (or *component type*) of the array, is the type of the elements, or components, of the array. For example, we can have an array of integers, or reals, or even of arrays. The second type, called the *index type* of the array, is the type of the values used to access individual elements of the array. For example, the Pascal declaration

var a: array [1..100] of integer;

specifies that *a* is an array whose base type is *integer* and whose index type is the subrange type 1..100. The declarations

type fruittype = (apple, orange, pear, banana);
       season = (winter, spring, summer, fall);
var   ripe: **array** [fruittype] of season;

specify that *ripe* is an array whose base type is *season* and whose index type is *fruittype*.

The two basic operations that access an array are *extraction* and *storing*. The extraction operation is a function that accepts an array *a* and an element of its index type *i* and returns an element of the array's base type. In Pascal, the result of this operation is denoted by the expression $a[i]$. The storing operation accepts an array *a*, an element of its index type *i*, and an element of its base type *x*. In Pascal, this operation is denoted by the assignment statement $a[i]:=x$. This operation is defined by the rule that after this assignment statement has been executed, the value of $a[i]$ is *x*. Before a value has been assigned to an element of the array, its value is undefined and a reference to it in an expression is illegal.

The index type of an array may be any ordinal type and the base type may be any valid Pascal type. (For a definition of ordinal types and the *ord* function, see Section 1 of the Appendix.) Although *integer* is prohibited as a base type by many Pascal implementations, a subrange of the *integer* type is permitted and is most useful. The smallest element of an array's index type is called its *lower bound* and the highest element is called its *upper bound*. If l is the lower bound of an array and u is the upper bound, the number of elements in the array, called its *range*, is given by $ord(u)-ord(l)+1$.

For example, in the array a declared above, the lower bound is 1, the upper bound is 100, and the range is $ord(100)-ord(1)+1$, which equals $100 - 1 + 1$, which is 100. In the array *ripe*, the lower bound is *apple*, the upper bound is *banana*, and the range is $ord(banana)-ord(apple)+1$, which equals $3 - 0 + 1$, or 4. The four elements of *ripe* are *ripe*[*apple*], *ripe*[*orange*], *ripe*[*pear*], and *ripe*[*banana*].

An important feature of a Pascal array is that its upper bound, lower bound, and range are fixed at the time a program is written. They cannot be changed without modifying the program. The size of a Pascal array cannot change during a program's execution. One very useful technique is to declare a bound as a constant identifier, so that the work required to modify the size of an array is minimized. For example, consider the following program segment to declare and initialize an array:

```
var i: 1..100;
     a: array [1..100] of integer;
begin
     for i:= 1 to 100
         do a[i]:= 0;
```

In order to change the array to a larger (or smaller) size, the constant 100 must be changed in three places: twice in the declarations and once in the *for* statement. Consider the following equivalent alternative:

```
const numelts = 100;
var i: 1..numelts;
     a: array [1..numelts] of integer;
begin
     for i:= 1 to numelts
         do a[i]:= 0;
```

Now, only a single change in the constant definition is needed to change the upper bound. Still another suggestion for improving the modifiability of the program would be to introduce a new type identifier, *indextype*, as follows:

```
const numelts = 100;
type indextype = 1..numelts;
var i: indextype;
     a: array [indextype] of integer;
begin
     for i:= 1 to numelts
         do a[i]:= 0;
```

By explicitly defining the index type and declaring all variables used as indexes to be of that type, you will detect the error of using an illegal index value earlier (at the time that the variable is assigned an illegal value rather than at the time that it is used as an index). It is also common for several arrays in a program to have the same index type. By defining that type explicitly, it is possible to modify the size of all the arrays with a single change in the index type definition. See Section 2 of the Appendix for a discussion of the use of one-dimensional arrays.

There is a special kind of array in Pascal called a *packed* array which may be used to save space. The details of how such an array is used and implemented are presented in Section 3 of the Appendix, which the reader is encouraged to review. For now, however, we merely indicate that an array *a* can be declared as packed by a declaration such as

var a: **packed array** [1..10] of integer;

Such an array may be used exactly as any other array (with slight exceptions, as noted in Section 3 of the Appendix). As we shall see later, the Pascal language requires some arrays to be declared as packed in certain contexts.

Implementing One-dimensional Arrays

A one-dimensional array can be easily implemented. Let us first consider arrays whose index types are subranges of integers. The Pascal declaration

var b: **array** [1..100] of integer;

reserves 100 successive memory locations, each large enough to contain a single integer. The address of the first of these locations is called the *base address* of the array *b* and is denoted by $base(b)$. Suppose that the size of each individual element of the array is *esize*. Then a reference to the element $b[1]$ is to the element at location $base(b)$, a reference to $b[2]$ is to the element at $base(b) + esize$, and a reference to $b[3]$ is to the element $base(b) + 2*esize$. In general, a reference to $b[i]$ is to the element at location $base(b) + (i-1)*esize$. Thus it is possible to reference any element in the array, given its index.

To implement an array declared with a lower bound other than 1, there is one minor change in the formula for computing the address of an element. For example, if the array *c* is declared by

var c: **array** [10..100] of integer;

then $base(c)$ refers to the location of $c[10]$ which is the first element of the array *c*, $c[11]$ is at location $base(c) + esize$, $c[12]$ at $base(c) + 2*esize$, and $c[i]$ is at location $base(c) + (i-10)*esize$. In general, if *l* is the integer lower bound of an array *d*, then $d[i]$ is located at $base(d) + (i-l)*esize$.

The foregoing formulas can be modified easily for an array whose index type is not a subrange of the integers. If *l* is the lower bound of the array *e*, the position of $e[i]$ in the array is $ord(i)-ord(l)+1$. Thus $e[l]$ is in position $ord(l)-ord(l)+1$, which is the first position; $e[succ(l)]$ is in position $ord(succ(l))-ord(l)+1$, which is the second position; and so on. Therefore, the location of $e[i]$ is given by $base(e)+(ord(i)-ord(l))*esize$. When *i* is an integer, $ord(i)=i$, so that this formula holds generally for arrays with any index type including integer subranges. Note, however, that the Pascal programmer can use arrays without being concerned with these implementation details. The Pascal system automatically computes the appropriate location for each array reference.

In Pascal, all elements of an array have the same fixed, predetermined size. Some programming languages, however, allow arrays of objects of differing sizes. For example, a language might allow arrays of varying character strings. In such cases, the method described above cannot be used to implement the array. This is because this method of calculating the address of a specific element of the array depends upon knowing the fixed size *esize* of each preceding element. If not all the elements have the same size, a different implementation must be used.

One method of implementing an array of varying-sized elements is to reserve a contiguous set of memory locations, each of which holds an address. The contents of each such memory location is the address of the varying-length array element in some other portion of memory. For example, Figure 1.2.1a illustrates an array of five varying-length character strings under this implementation. The arrows in that diagram indicate addresses of other portions of memory. The character 'ƀ' indicates a blank.

Since the length of each address is fixed, the location of the address of a particular element can be computed in the same way that the location of a fixed-length element was computed in the previous examples. Once this location is known, its contents can be used to determine the location of the actual array element. This, of course, adds an extra level of indirection to referencing an array element by involving an extra memory reference, which in turn decreases efficiency. However, this is a small price to pay for the convenience of being able to maintain such an array.

A similar method for implementing an array of varying-sized elements is to keep all fixed-length portions of the elements in the contiguous array area, in addition to keeping the address of the varying-length portion in the contiguous area. For example, in the implementation of varying-length character strings presented in the previous section, each such string contains a fixed-length portion (a one-byte-length field) and a variable-length portion (the character string itself). One implementation of an array of varying-length character strings keeps the length of the string together with the address, as shown in Figure 1.2.1b. The advantage of this method is that those parts of an element that are of fixed length can be examined without an extra memory reference. For example, a function to determine the current length of a varying-length character string can be implemented with a single memory lookup. The fixed-length information for an array element of varying length which is stored in the contiguous memory area of the array is often called a *header*.

Character Strings

A *string* is defined in Pascal as a packed array of characters whose lower bound is 1. A string constant is denoted by any set of characters included

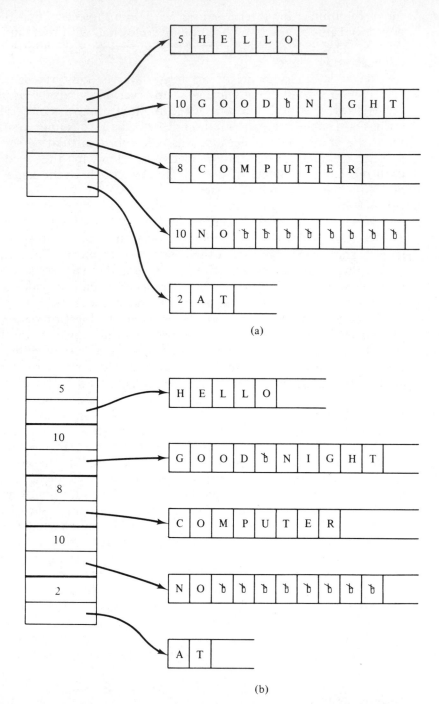

Figure 1.2.1 Two implementations of an array of varying length strings.

CHAP. 1: INTRODUCTION TO DATA STRUCTURES

in single quote marks. A single quote within a string constant is denoted by two consecutive single quotes. Each such string constant represents an array whose lower bound is 1 and whose upper bound, or *length*, is the number of characters in the string. For example, the string *'hello there'* is a packed array of 11 characters (the blank counts as a character), and *'i don''t know'* is a packed array of 12 characters (the two quotes represent the single quote character).

We may define a string type explicitly, as in

type string = **packed array** [1..80] **of** char;

Note that any variable of type *string* has a fixed length of 80. The length of a string cannot vary during a program execution. This is sometimes extremely annoying. For example, if we declared

var s: string;

and wished to assign the string *'hello'* to *s*, the statement

s:= 'hello'

would be invalid. The reason for this is that the type of *s* is *packed array* [1..80] *of char*, whereas the type of *'hello'* is *packed array* [1..5] *of char*. Thus the two objects have different types, and one cannot be assigned to the other. Seventy-five blanks would have to follow the letters *hello* in order to make the assignment valid. One solution to this problem is to define a new type by

type shortstr = **packed array**[1..10] **of** char;

and write a procedure *assign* as follows:

```
procedure assign(ss: shortstr; var s: string);
var i: 1..80;
begin
    for i:= 1 to 10
        do s[i]:= ss[i];
    for i:= 11 to 80
        do s[i]:= ' '
end {procedure assign};
```

Then we could assign the string *'hello'* to *s* as follows:

```
var ss: shortstr;
    s: string;
begin
    ss:= 'hello . . . . . '
    assign(ss,s)
```

Note the five blanks used to pad *'hello'* to a length of 10.

(Some versions of Pascal, such as UCSD Pascal, allow the assignment of a short string to a long string variable. In UCSD Pascal, the type *string* is predefined as *packed array* [1..80] *of char*. Shorter string types such as *packed array* [1..10] *of char* are also predefined, as in *string* [10]. If *s* is of type *string*, the assignment statement

s:= 'hello'

is perfectly valid in UCSD Pascal. The length of a string may vary depending on its current value. However, these features are nonstandard.)

The comparison operators may be used to compare two packed character arrays. For example, if *s1*='hello' and *s2*='helio', the expression *s1*>*s2* has the value *true* because *hello* comes later in alphabetic order than *helio*. The comparison proceeds character by character until a character in one string is not equal to the corresponding character of the second. If that character in the first string follows the character in the second string in the ordering of characters on the particular machine being used, the first string is greater than the second; otherwise, the first string is less than the second. If all the characters are equal, the two strings are equal. Pascal requires that two strings being compared have equal length, but some nonstandard compilers permit comparison of strings of different lengths.

Another special provision made for strings is that they can be passed as arguments to the *write* and *writeln* procedures for text files. This allows printing an entire message in a single call to one of these procedures. However, an unpacked array of characters may not be passed to these procedures.

Under compilers that implement all arrays of characters as packed arrays, any array of characters may be used as a string even if it is not explicitly declared packed. That is, it can be the target of an assignment statement from a string constant, it can appear as an operand of a comparison, and it can be passed as an argument to *write* and *writeln*. Similarly, under many such compilers, an element of a character array (whether or not declared packed) can be passed as a variable parameter to a function or procedure. However, these features are nonstandard. A Pascal programmer should know how character arrays are handled by the compilers available and which Pascal rules and exceptions apply.

According to the definition of a Pascal string, a variable such as *number*, declared by

var number: **packed array** [1..10] **of** '0'..'9';

is not a string, because its base type is '0'..'9' rather than *char*. Therefore, it cannot be assigned a string value and cannot appear as an argument to the procedures *write* and *writeln*. However, many Pascal compilers do treat such a variable as a string. We will occasionally use such a variable as an argument to *write* and *writeln*, but the reader should be aware that this is a minor extension to standard Pascal.

Character String Operations

A string in Pascal has a fixed length. However, we can treat a string as having a varying length if we choose to ignore all trailing blanks. Under such a system, the string '*hello*   ' may be considered to have a length of five, since all the remaining characters are blanks. Of course, embedded blanks do count, so that a string such as '*a   b*' with two blanks between the *a* and the *b* has a length of four. The declaration of a string variable would then define only the maximum length of a string; its actual length would be the declared length minus the number of trailing blanks. It is important to note that this method of implementing varying-length character strings does not represent an addition or a change in the Pascal language, but only a new method of using the language in a specific way.

To illustrate the use of such strings, let us present Pascal routines to implement some primitive operations on varying-length character strings. For all these routines, we assume the global declarations

```
const strsize = 80;
type string = packed array [1..strsize] of char;
```

The first routine is a function to find the current length of a string interpreted as a varying-length character string:

```
function length(s: string): integer;
var i: integer;
    found: boolean;
begin
     i:= strsize;
     found:= false;
     while (i > 0) and (not found)
          do begin
                    if s[i] <> ' '
                         then found:= true
                         else i:= i-1
          end {while...do begin};
     length:= i
end { function length};
```

The second routine is a function that accepts two strings as parameters. The function returns an integer which indicates the starting location of the first occurrence of the second parameter string within the first parameter string. If the second string does not exist within the first, 0 is returned.

```
function pos(s1,s2: string): integer;
var i,j,len1,len2: integer;
    found,finis: boolean;
begin
     len1:= length(s1);
     len2:= length(s2);
     i:= 0;
     found:= false;
```

```
          while (i+len2 <= len1) and (not found)
             do begin
                         finis:= false;
                         j:= 1;
                         while (j <= len2) and (not finis)
                             do if s1[i+j] = s2[j]
                                    then j:= j+1
                                    else finis:= true;
                      if j > len2
                         then found:= true
                         else i:= i+1
                   end {while...do begin};
          if found
             then pos:= i+1
             else pos:= 0
       end {function pos};
```

(UCSD Pascal provides both *length* and *pos* as built-in functions for strings.)
  Another common operation on strings is concatenation. The result of concatenating two strings is a third string, consisting of the characters of the first followed by the characters of the second. The following procedure sets *s3* to the concatenation of *s1* and *s2*.

```
       procedure concat(s1,s2: string; var s3: string);
       var len1,len2,len3,i: integer;
       begin
            len1:= length(s1);
            len2:= length(s2);
            len3:= len1 + len2;
            if len3 > strsize
               then writeln('error - strings are too long')
               else begin
                         s3:= s1;
                         for i:= len1+1 to strsize
                             do s3[i]:= s2[i-len1]
                   end {else begin}
       end {procedure concat};
```

(UCSD Pascal contains *concat* as a built-in function accepting any number of strings as input and returning their concatenation. We have written *concat* as a procedure since a function in Pascal may not return an array. UCSD Pascal exempts certain built-in functions, including *concat*, from this restriction.)
  The last operation we present on strings is the substring operation. *substr*($s1,i,j,s2$) sets the string *s2* to the *j* characters beginning at *s1*[*i*]. If fewer than *j* characters remain in *s1*, *s2* is padded with blanks.

```
procedure substr(s1: string; i,j: integer; var s2: string);
var k,limit: integer;
begin
    if i+j-1 <= strsize
       then limit:= i+j-1
       else limit:= strsize;
    for k:= i to limit
        do s2[k-i+1]:= s1[k];
    for k:= limit-i+2 to strsize
        do s2[k]:= ' '
end {procedure substr};
```

(UCSD Pascal contains a built-in function similar to *substr*, called *copy*, which returns a substring of a given string. UCSD Pascal also contains two other built-in string routines: *insert*, to insert one string into the middle of another; and *delete*, to remove a portion of a string.)

While the routines we have presented give us the capability of implementing varying-length character strings, there is one basic flaw with the representation that we have chosen. Under our representation, trailing blanks are not significant. Very often, it is desirable to include trailing blanks as part of a character string. For example, given a long character string, we might wish to break the string into words separated by blanks. The *pos* function, however, cannot be used to locate a blank in a string. As another example, consider extracting the first six characters from the string *'today is a nice day'* using *substr*. The resultant string will have a length of only five characters. In the next section we see how varying-length character strings can be represented to include trailing blanks.

Varying-sized Arrays and Pascal

The amount of work necessary to provide for varying-length character strings in Pascal is clearly excessive. This is symptomatic of a generally recognized problem with the Pascal language. The size of an array in a Pascal program must be known at compile time. There is no way to change the size of an array during the program's execution. If the number of elements needed in a particular situation depends on the input, the Pascal programmer must estimate the maximum number that will ever be required and declare an array of that size. If the program is used repetitively in a production environment, it will eventually be presented with input for which the estimate is not large enough and will fail. On the other hand, in most cases the estimate is a gross exaggeration and all the extra space in the array is wasted. Unfortunately, there is no remedy for this situation in Pascal, because the language does not allow the size of an array to be determined dynamically during execution. There is a data structure that can be used instead of an array in situations where the number of elements varies dramatically from run to run. This data structure is a linked list and will be examined in Chapters 4 and 5.

Two-dimensional Arrays

The component type of an array can be another array. For example, we may define

type matrix = array[1..3] of array[1..5] of integer;

This defines a new array type containing three elements. Each of these elements is itself an array containing five integers. This definition may be abbreviated to

type matrix = array[1..3, 1..5] of integer;

Figure 1.2.2a illustrates an array declared by

var a: matrix;

An element of this array is accessed by specifying two indices—a row number and a column number. For example, the darkened element in Figure 1.2.2a

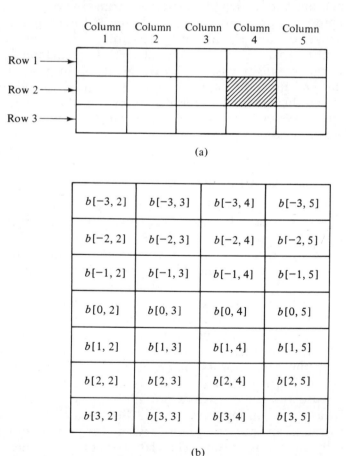

(a)

(b)

Figure 1.2.2 Two-dimensional arrays.

is in row 2 and column 4 and may be referenced as $a[2][4]$ or as $a[2,4]$. Note that $a[2]$ refers to the entire row 2, but there is no equivalent way to reference an entire column. Figure 1.2.2b illustrates an array declared by

var b: **array** $[-3..3, 2..5]$ **of** integer;

and names each element of the array. Such an array is called a *two-dimensional* array. The number of rows or columns is equal to the upper bound minus the lower bound plus 1. This number is called the *range* of the dimension. In the array a above, the range of the first dimension is $3 - 1 + 1$, which is 3, and the range of the second dimension is $5 - 1 + 1$, which is 5. Thus the array a has three rows and five columns. In the array b, the number of rows is $3 - (-3) + 1 = 7$ and the number of columns is $5 - 2 + 1 = 4$. The number of elements in a two-dimensional array is equal to the product of the number of rows and the number of columns. Thus the array a contains $3 \times 5 = 15$ elements and the array b contains $7 \times 4 = 28$ elements. If the index type of either dimension is not an integer subrange, the range of that dimension equals the number of elements in that index type. This can be computed as *ord* of the upper bound, minus *ord* of the lower bound, plus 1.

A two-dimensional array clearly illustrates the differences between a *logical* and a *physical* view of data. A two-dimensional array is a logical data structure which is useful in programming and problem solving. For example, such an array is useful in describing an object that is physically two-dimensional, such as a map or a checkerboard. It is also useful in organizing a set of values that are dependent upon two inputs. For example, a program for a department store that has 20 branches, each of which sells 30 items, might include a two-dimensional array declared by

var sales: **array** $[1..20, 1..30]$ **of** real;

Each element $sales[i,j]$ represents the amount of item j sold in branch i.

However, although it is convenient for the programmer to think of the elements of such an array as being organized in a two-dimensional table (and programming languages do indeed include facilities for treating them as a two-dimensional array), the hardware of most computers has no such facilities. An array must be stored in the memory of a computer and that memory is usually linear. By this we mean that the memory of a computer is essentially a one-dimensional array. A single address (which may be viewed as a subscript of a one-dimensional array) is used to retrieve a particular item from memory. In order to implement a two-dimensional array, it is necessary to develop a method of ordering its elements in a linear fashion and of transforming a two-dimensional reference to the linear representation.

One method of representing a two-dimensional array in memory is the *row-major* representation. Under this representation, the first row of the array occupies the first set of memory locations reserved for the array, the second row occupies the next set, and so on. There may also be several locations at the start of the physical array which serve as a header and which contain the upper and lower bounds of the two dimensions. (This header should not be confused with the headers discussed earlier. This header is for the entire array, whereas the headers mentioned earlier are headers for the individual array elements.) Figure 1.2.3 illustrates the row major representation of the two-dimensional array *b* declared above and illustrated in Figure 1.2.2b. Alternatively, the header need not be contiguous to the array elements, but could instead contain the address of the first element of the array. Additionally, if the elements of the two-dimensional array are variable-length objects, the elements of the contiguous area could themselves contain the addresses of those objects in a form similar to those of Figure 1.2.1 for linear arrays.

Let us suppose that a two-dimensional array with integer index types is stored in row-major sequence, as in Figure 1.2.3, and let us suppose that, for an array *ar*, *base(ar)* is the address of the first element of the array. That is, if *ar* is declared by

var ar: array [l1..u1, l2..u2] of integer;

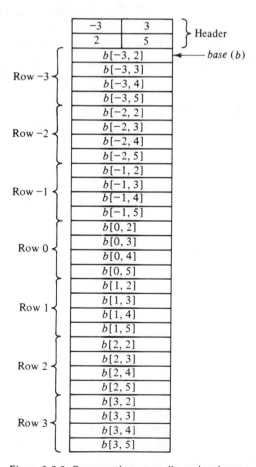

Figure 1.2.3 Representing a two-dimensional array.

where $l1$, $u1$, $l2$, and $u2$ are the integer lower and upper bounds, then $base(ar)$ is the address of $ar[l1,l2]$. For example, for the array a of Figure 1.2.2a, $base(a)$ is the address of $a[1,1]$, and for the array b of Figure 1.2.2b, $base(b)$ is the address of $b[-3,2]$. Let us define $r2$ (the range of the second dimension) as $u2-l2+1$. We also assume that $esize$ is the size of each element in the array. Let us calculate the address of an arbitrary element, $ar[i1,i2]$. Since the element is in row $i1$, its address can be calculated by computing the address of the first element of row $i1$ and adding the quantity $(i2-l2)*esize$ (this quantity represents how far into row $i1$ the element at column $i2$ is). But in order to reach the first element of row $i1$ (which is the element $ar[i1,l2]$), it is necessary to pass through $i1-l1$ complete rows, each of which contains $r2$ elements (since there is one element from each column in each row), so that the address of the first element of row $i1$ is at $base(ar)+(i1-l1)*r2*esize$. Therefore, the address of $ar[i1,i2]$ is at

$$base(ar) + [(i1 - l1)*r2 + (i2 - l2)]*esize$$

As an example, consider the array b of Figure 1.2.2b, whose representation is illustrated in Figure 1.2.3. In this array, $l1=-3$, $u1=3$, $l2=2$, and $u2=5$, so that $base(b)$ is the address of $b[-3,2]$ and $r2$ equals 4. Let us also suppose that each element of the array requires a single unit of storage, so that $esize$ equals 1. (This is not necessarily true, since b was declared as an array of integers and an integer may need more than one unit of memory on a particular machine. For simplicity, however, we accept this assumption.) Then the location of $b[0,4]$ may be computed as follows. To reach row 0, we must skip over rows -3, -2, and -1. Each of those rows contains four elements, consisting of one memory location each. Thus the first element of row zero (which is $b[0,2]$) is 12 elements past the address of $b[-3,2]$, which is $base(b)$. The element $b[0,4]$ is two elements past $b[0,2]$. Use of this formula yields the address of $b[0,4]$ as

$$base(b) + [(0 - (-3))*4 + (4 - 2)]*1$$

which is

$$base(b) + 12 + 2 = base(b) + 14$$

You may confirm the fact that $b[0,4]$ is 14 units past $base(b)$ in Figure 1.2.3.

The formula for the location of an element of a two-dimensional array is easily modified to accommodate noninteger ranges as index types. $i1, i2, l1, u1, l2,$ and $u2$ are all members of the index types. $r2$, the range of the second dimension, is now defined as the integer $ord(u2)-ord(l2)+1$. $i1, i2, l1,$ and $l2$ are replaced in the formula by $ord(i1), ord(i2), ord(l1),$ and $ord(l2)$. This yields

$$base(ar) + [(ord(i1) - ord(l1))*r2 + (ord(i2) - ord(l2))]*esize$$

as the location of $ar(i1,i2)$.

Multidimensional Arrays

Pascal also allows arrays with more than two dimensions. For example, a three-dimensional array may be declared by

$$\text{var } c: \textbf{array}[3..5, 1..2, 1..4] \textbf{ of } \text{integer};$$

which is equivalent to

$$\text{var } c: \textbf{array}[3..5] \textbf{ of array}[1..2] \textbf{ of array}[1..4] \textbf{ of } \text{integer};$$

and is illustrated in Figure 1.2.4a. An element of this array is specified by three subscripts such as $c[4][1][3]$ or $c[4,1,3]$. The first subscript specifies a plane number, the second subscript a row number, and the third a column number. Such an array is useful when a value is determined by three inputs. For example, an array of temperatures might be indexed by latitude, longitude, and altitude.

For obvious reasons, the geometric analogy breaks down when we go beyond three dimensions. However, Pascal does allow an arbitrary number of dimensions. For example, a six-dimensional array may be declared by

$$\text{var } d: \textbf{array}[1..7, 1..15, 1..3, -2..2, 1..8, 5..6] \textbf{ of } \text{integer};$$

Referencing an element of this array would require six subscripts, such as $d[3,14,1,-1,7,6]$. The number of different subscripts which are allowed in a particular position (the range of a particular dimension) equals the upper bound of that dimension, minus its lower bound, plus 1. The number of elements in an array is the product of the ranges of all its dimensions. For example, the array c above contains $(5 - 3 + 1) \times (2 - 1 + 1) \times (4 - 1 + 1) = 3 \times 2 \times 4 = 24$ elements; the array d contains $7 \times 15 \times 3 \times 5 \times 8 \times 2 = 25,200$ elements.

The row-major representation of arrays can be extended to arrays of more than two dimensions. Figure 1.2.4b illustrates the representation of the array c of Figure 1.2.4a. The elements of the six-dimensional array d described above are ordered as follows:

$$d[1, 1, 1, -2, 1, 5]$$
$$d[1, 1, 1, -2, 1, 6]$$
$$d[1, 1, 1, -2, 2, 5]$$
$$d[1, 1, 1, -2, 2, 6]$$
$$d[1, 1, 1, -2, 3, 5]$$
$$\cdots$$
$$\cdots$$
$$d[7, 15, 3, 2, 6, 5]$$
$$d[7, 15, 3, 2, 6, 6]$$
$$d[7, 15, 3, 2, 7, 5]$$
$$d[7, 15, 3, 2, 7, 6]$$
$$d[7, 15, 3, 2, 8, 5]$$
$$d[7, 15, 3, 2, 8, 6]$$

CHAP. 1: INTRODUCTION TO DATA STRUCTURES

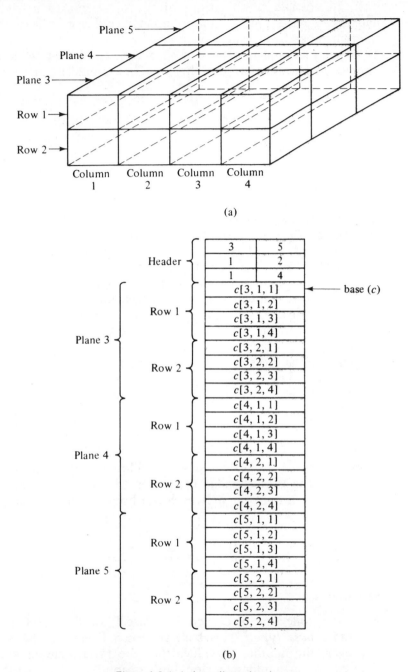

(a)

(b)

Figure 1.2.4 A three-dimensional array.

That is, the last subscript varies most rapidly and a subscript is not increased until all possible combinations of the subscripts to its right have been exhausted. This is similar to an odometer (mileage indicator) of a car, where the rightmost digit changes most rapidly.

What mechanism is needed to access an element of an arbitrary multidimensional array? Suppose that *ar* is an *n*-dimensional array declared by

$$\text{var ar: \textbf{array}}[l_1..u_1, l_2..u_2, ..., l_n..u_n] \text{ of integer;}$$

which is stored in row-major order. Each element of *ar* is assumed to occupy *esize* storage locations and *base*(*ar*) is defined as the address of the first element of the array (which is $ar[l_1, l_2, ..., l_n]$). r_i is defined as $u_i - l_i + 1$ for all i between 1 and n. Then in order to access the element

$$ar[i_1, i_2, ..., i_n]$$

it is first necessary to pass through $(i_1 - l_1)$ complete "hyperplanes," each consisting of $r_2 * r_3 * ... * r_n$ elements, to reach the first element of *ar* whose first subscript is i_1. Then it is necessary to pass through an additional $(i_2 - l_2)$ groups of $r_3 * r_4 * ... * r_n$ elements in order to reach the first element of *ar* whose first two subscripts are i_1 and i_2, respectively. A similar process must be carried out through the other dimensions until the first element whose first $n - 1$ subscripts match those of the desired element is reached. Finally, it is necessary to pass through $(i_n - l_n)$ additional elements to reach the element desired.

Thus the address of $ar[i_1, i_2, ..., i_n]$ may be written as $base(ar) + esize *$ $[(i_1 - l_1) * r_2 * ... * r_n + (i_2 - l_2) * r_3 * ... * r_n + ... + (i_{n-1} - l_{n-1}) * r_n + (i_n - l_n)]$, which can be evaluated more efficiently by using the equivalent formula

$$base(ar) + esize * [i_n - l_n + r_n * (i_{n-1} - l_{n-1} + r_{n-1} * (...$$

$$... + r_3 * (i_2 - l_2 + r_2 * (i_1 - l_1))...))]$$

This formula may be evaluated by the following algorithm, which computes the address of the array element and places it into *addr* (assuming that arrays *i*, *l*, and *r* of size *n* hold the indices, lower bounds, and the ranges, respectively):

```
offset := 0;
for j := 1 to n
    do offset := r[j] * offset + (i[j] - l[j]);
addr := base(ar) + esize * offset
```

Sets in Pascal

A *set* is a collection of objects. In Pascal, all the objects in a set must be of the same *base type*. This base type can be any scalar or subrange type. However, the number of values that the type includes can be severely restricted by an implementation. For example, every Pascal implementation would permit a declaration such as

$$\text{var x: \textbf{set of} } 1..10;$$

The base type of the set x is the subrange type 1..10, which includes only 10 values. However, a declaration such as

var y: set of 1..100;

may be invalid in a Pascal implementation that allows fewer than 100 values in the base type of a set. We will shortly examine the reasons for this restriction. Note that the base type of a Pascal set may not be a composite type such as an array or another set.

A set can be specified by enumerating its elements in brackets. An example of this is the following program segment:

```
type days = (sun, mon, tues, wed, thur, fri, sat);
     dayset = set of days;
var  weekdays,weekend: dayset;
begin
     weekdays:= [mon, tues, wed, thur, fri];
     weekend:= [sun, sat]
```

It is also permissible to use a subrange to specify a group of set elements. For example, the variable *weekdays* could have been initialized as follows:

weekdays:= [mon..fri]

All values of type *days* between the values *mon* and *fri* are elements of *weekdays*. The two ways of specifying set elements can be mixed, as in [1..4, 6, 9..11, 14..20], which contains 15 elements. The set with no elements is called the *empty set* and is denoted by [ ].

[The restriction on the number of elements in the base type of a set often causes a problem in enumerating elements of a set. For example, one popular Pascal compiler permits up to 60 elements in the base type of a set. Under this compiler, the set [1,100] is illegal, although it contains only two elements. The reason for this is that the type of such a set must be *set of* 1..100 and the base type 1..100 contains too many values. In fact, it might be the case that even the set [99,100] is illegal. Despite the fact that a base type of 99..100 or even 51..110 would make such a set valid, the compiler may assume that any enumerated set containing integers has a base type 1..60, so that any set containing an integer larger than 60 is invalid.

This problem is also prevalent in sets containing characters. The type *set of char* may be prohibited because the number of characters of type *char* is greater than the maximum allowable in the base type of a set. This may imply that such useful sets as ['0'..'9'] or ['a'..'z'] are invalid. (In any case, the subrange 'a'..'z' may include characters which are not letters, although the subrange '0'..'9' includes only digits.)

A Pascal programmer should determine the maximum number of values allowed in the base type of a set by the compiler being used and the implications of that number on enumerated sets.]

Operations on Sets

If a and b are sets, their *union* is a new set which contains every element that is in a or b. In Pascal, the union of two sets a and b is written as $a+b$. The *intersection* of two sets a and b is a new set containing every element that is in both a and b. In Pascal, the intersection of a and b is written $a*b$. The *difference* of two sets, a and b, is a new set containing every element of a that is not in b. In Pascal, the difference of a and b is written as $a-b$. Note that $a-b$ is not equal to $b-a$. The base types of the two operands of the union, intersection, and difference operators must be either identical, or subranges of the same type, in which case the types are said to be *compatible*. However, some Pascal compilers prohibit operands whose base types are not identical.

As an illustration of these three operations, consider the integer sets $a=[1..5]$, $b=[1,3,5,7,9]$, and $c=[2,4,6,8]$. Make sure you understand why each of the following expressions has the value indicated:

$$a+b = [1..5, 7, 9] \qquad b+c = [1..9]$$

$$a*b = [1, 3, 5] \qquad b*c = [\ ]$$

$$a-b = [2, 4] \qquad b-a = [7, 9]$$

$$b-c = b \qquad c-b = c$$

There are also four comparison operators defined on sets. $a = b$ is *true* if every element of a is an element of b and every element of b is an element of a; otherwise, it is *false*. $a <= b$ is *true* if every element of a is an element of b; otherwise, it is *false*. $a >= b$ is *true* if every element of b is an element of a; otherwise, it is *false*. If $a >= b$ is *true* (which is the same as saying that $b <= a$ is *true*), then set a *contains* set b (or, equivalently, set b *is contained in* set a). $a <> b$ is *true* if there is an element in one of the two sets that is not in the other; otherwise, $a <> b$ is *false*. As is the case with union, intersection, and difference, these operations may be applied in Pascal only to two sets of compatible base type.

Referring to the sets a, b, and c defined above, make sure you understand why each of the following boolean expressions has the value indicated:

$$(a >= b) = false \qquad (b+c >= a) = true$$

$$(a-c <= b) = true \qquad ((b+c)*a = a) = true$$

$$(b*c <> [\ ]) = false \qquad (a-b = c) = false$$

Note that the set operators +, *, and – have precedence over the set comparison operators =, <=, >=, and <>. Note also that the set operator * takes precedence over the set operators + and –, so that $(b+c) * a$ is not the same as $b + c*a$. All other mixtures of set operators are evaluated by performing the leftmost operation first.

The final set operation determines whether an object is an element of a set. x *in* s, where x is an object of the base type of the set s, is *true* if x is an element of s, and *false* otherwise. The *in* operator is at the same precedence level as the other comparison operators.

Implementation of a Set

Many peculiarities of sets in Pascal become clearer by looking at their implementation. Given the base type B of a set type T, any set of type T may be specified by its *characteristic function*. This function is defined for all values of type B. Given a set s of type T, the characteristic function of s, called c, is defined as follows. If b is of type B, then $c(b)$ is 0 if b is not in s and is 1 if b is in s. For example, suppose that B is the type 1..10, so that T is the type *set of* 1..10. Suppose also that s is a variable of type T and that the value of s is [1..3, 5, 9, 10]. Then the characteristic function of s is as follows:

$$c(1) = 1 \quad c(4) = 0 \quad c(7) = 0 \quad c(10) = 1$$

$$c(2) = 1 \quad c(5) = 1 \quad c(8) = 0$$

$$c(3) = 1 \quad c(6) = 0 \quad c(9) = 1$$

The characteristic function of every element in the set is 1 and of every element not in the set is 0.

The most convenient way to represent a single characteristic function value is by a single bit. The most convenient way to represent the entire characteristic function is by a string of bits, one for each element in the base type of the set type. In the example above, where the base type is 1..10, a string of 10 bits is needed. For the set [1..3, 5, 9, 10], the characteristic bit string is 1110100011. A 1 appears in every position, corresponding to an element of the set. The characteristic bit string of the set [2, 4, 6, 8] is 0101010100, the string of the set [1, 2, 5, 9] is 1100100010, the string of [1..10] is 1111111111, and the string of [ ] is 0000000000. Every set on a given base type corresponds to one and only one characteristic bit string.

One of the reasons that a characteristic bit string is a useful method for representing a set is the ease with which the set operations can be performed using that method. Given two bit strings, $b1$ and $b2$, of the same length, their *disjunction* is the bit string of that length which contains a 1 in every position in which either $b1$ or $b2$ (or both) contains a 1. For example, if $b1$=0101010100 and $b2$=1100100010, their disjunction is 1101110110. (Note that disjunction is a natural extension of the boolean *or* operation, where if 1 represents *true* and 0 represents *false*, the disjunction of two bits is the *or*ing of the two boolean values they represent.) The disjunction of two characteristic bit strings representing two sets is the characteristic bit string of the union of those two sets. For example, $b1$=0101010100 represents the set [2, 4, 6, 8], $b2$=1100100010 represents [1, 2, 5, 9], and their disjunction, 1101110110, represents [1, 2, 4, 5, 6, 8, 9], which is the union of [2, 4, 6, 8] and [1, 2, 5, 9]. This fact is not at all surprising when we realize that an element is in a union if it is in either of two sets, and a bit is 1 in a disjunction if it is 1 in either of two bit strings.

Similarly, the *conjunction* of two bit strings, $b1$ and $b2$, is defined as a bit string containing a 1 in every position in which both $b1$ and $b2$ have a 1. For example, if $b1$=0101010100 and $b2$=1100100010, their conjunction is 0100000000. (Note that conjunction is a natural extension of the boolean *and* operation, where if 1 represents *true* and 0 represents *false*, the conjunction of two bits is the *and*ing of the two boolean values they represent.) The conjunction of two strings represents the intersection of the two sets they represent, in the same way that their disjunction represents the union. For example, using $b1$ and $b2$ as above, their conjunction is 0100000000, which represents [2], the intersection of [2, 4, 6, 8] and [1, 2, 5, 9]. Again, this relationship is clear when we realize that an element is in an intersection if it is in both of two sets and a bit is 1 in a conjunction if it is 1 in both of two bit strings.

The *difference* of two bit strings, $b1$ and $b2$, is defined as the bit string containing a 1 in every position in which $b1$ contains a 1 and $b2$ contains a 0. The difference of two bit strings corresponds to the set difference of the two sets they represent. Again using $b1$ and $b2$, their difference is 0001010100, which represents [4, 6, 8], which equals [2, 4, 6, 8] - [1, 2, 5, 9]. (If 1 represents *true* and 0 represents *false*, the difference of two bits representing two boolean values, $x1$ and $x2$, represents the value of $x1$ *and not* $x2$.)

Most computers have hardware instructions (called *logical operations*) to form the conjunction, disjunction, and difference of bit strings. For this reason, representation of sets by bit strings leads to efficient operation on sets. Similarly, comparison operations are easily implemented, because most computers have hardware operations to compare two bit strings for equality. For the set-containment operations ($<=$ and $>=$), the fact that $a <= b$ is *true* if and only if $a*b = a$, and $a >= b$ is *true* if and only if $a*b = b$ leads to the efficient implementation of these operations. The condition x *in* a is equivalent to $[x] <= a$, so this operation can also be implemented efficiently.

The reason for many restrictions on the use of sets in Pascal now becomes apparent. The limitation on the number of elements in the base type of a set stems from the maximum length of bit strings on which the logical operations may be performed efficiently. In general, this length varies from machine to machine and is usually related to the number of bits in a machine word. Some implementations allow larger base types by extending the hardware logical operations using software routines. Also, composite types such as arrays, sets, or records are not permitted as the base type of a set, because the possible values of such a composite type are too numerous for efficient implementation of a set by a characteristic bit string.

Similarly, the base types of two sets that participate in a set operation must be compatible in order to allow the same bit position in two bit strings representing the sets to represent the same element of the base types of the two sets.

Choosing Elements from a Set

Because of the Pascal implementation of a set, there are no built-in mechanisms for choosing an arbitrary element from a set or for performing some process for every element of a set. These are extremely useful operations in manipulating sets. Let us see how they can be implemented by Pascal routines.

Assume a set *s* declared as follows:

```
const lowval = ...;
       hival = ...;
type t = lowval..hival;
     stype = set of t;
var s: stype;
```

The function *arb* returns an arbitrary element of *s*. (Actually, *arb* returns the smallest element of *s*, but if we desire any element of the set, it is irrelevant which is returned.)

```
function arb(s: stype): t;
var i: t;
    found: boolean;
begin
    if s = [ ]
        then writeln('the set is empty')
        else begin
                found:= false;
                i:= lowval;
                while (i <= hival) and (not found)
                    do if i in s
                        then begin
                                arb:= i;
                                found:= true
                            end {then begin}
                        else i:= succ(i)
            end {else begin}
end {function arb};
```

Suppose that we wish to apply a routine *process* to every element of *s*. We can do this using the following procedure:

```
procedure procset(s: stype)
var i: t;
begin
    for i:= lowval to hival
        do if i in s
            then process(i)
end {procedure procset};
```

Note that there is no method of processing all the elements of a Pascal set without checking every value in the base type of the set. This is an inefficiency in Pascal set processing.

Another common operation on a set is to find an element *i* in *s* such that some condition on *i* is *true*. Let *cond* be a function defined for all values of type *t* which returns a boolean value. Then a function to return an element *i* of *s* for which *cond* (*i*) is *true* may be written as follows:

```
function find(s: stype): t;
var i: t;
    found, completed: boolean;
begin
    found := false;
    completed := false;
    i := lowval;
    while (not completed) and (not found)
        do if (i in s) and cond(i)
            then begin
                    find := i;
                    found := true
                end {then begin}
            else if i < hival
                    then i := succ(i)
                    else completed := true;
    if not found
        then writeln('no such element exists')
end {function find};
```

EXERCISES

1. (a) The *median* of an array of numbers is the element *m* of the array such that half the remaining numbers in the array are greater than or equal to *m* and half are less than or equal to *m*, if the number of elements in the array is odd. If the number of elements is even, the median is the average of the two elements *m*1 and *m*2 such that half the remaining elements are greater than or equal to *m*1 and *m*2, and half the elements are less than or equal to *m*1 and *m*2. Write a Pascal function that accepts an array of numbers and returns the median of the numbers in the array.

   (b) The *mode* of an array of numbers is the number *m* in the array which is repeated most frequently. If several numbers are repeated with equal maximal frequency, there is no mode. Write a Pascal subroutine which accepts an array of numbers and returns the mode or an indication that the mode does not exist.

2. Write a Pascal program to read a group of temperature readings. A reading consists of two numbers, an integer between −90 and 90 representing the latitude at which the reading was taken and the observed temperature at that latitude. Print a table consisting of each latitude and the average temperature at that latitude. If there are no readings at a particular latitude, print *no data* instead of an average. Then print the average temperature in the northern and southern hemispheres (the northern consists of latitudes 1 through 90 and the southern consists of latitudes −1 through −90).

(This average temperature should be computed as the average of the averages, not the average of the original readings.) Also determine which hemisphere is warmer. In making the determination, take the average temperatures in all latitudes of each hemisphere for which there are data for both that latitude and the corresponding latitude in the other hemisphere. (For example, if there are data for latitude 57 but not for latitude −57, the average temperature for latitude 57 should be ignored in determining which hemisphere is warmer.)

3. Write a program for a chain of 20 department stores, each of which sells 10 different items. Every month, each store manager submits a data card for each item, consisting of a branch number (from 1 to 20), an item number (from 1 to 10), and a sales figure (less than $100,000) representing the amount of sales for that item in that branch. However, some managers may not submit cards for some items (e.g., not all items are sold in all branches). You are to write a Pascal program to read these data cards and print a table with 12 columns. The first column should contain the branch numbers from 1 to 20 and the word *total* in the last line. The next 10 columns should contain the sales figures for each of the 10 items for each of the branches, with the total sales of each item in the last line. The last column should contain the total sales of each of the 20 branches for all items, with the grand total sales figure for the chain in the lower right-hand corner. Each column should have an appropriate heading. If no sales were reported for a particular branch and item, assume zero sales. Do not assume that your input is in any particular order.

4. Show how a checkerboard can be represented by a Pascal array. Show how to represent the state of a game of checkers at a particular instant. Write a Pascal routine which inputs an array representing such a checkerboard and prints all possible moves which black can make from that position.

5. Write a routine *printar*(*a*) that accepts an *m* by *n* array *a* of integers and prints the values of the array on several pages as follows. Each page is to contain 50 rows and 20 columns of the array. Along the top of each page, headings COL 1, COL 2, and so on, should be printed, and along the left margin of each page, headings ROW 1, ROW 2, and so on, should be printed. The array should be printed by subarrays. For example, if *a* were a 100 by 100 array, the first page contains $a[1..50, 1..20]$, the second page contains $a[1..50, 21..40]$, the third page contains $a[1..50, 41..60]$, and so on, until the fifth page contains $a[1..50, 81..100]$, the sixth page contains $a[51..100, 1..20]$, and so on. The entire printout occupies 10 pages. If the number of rows is not a multiple of 50, or the number of columns is not a multiple of 20, some pages of the printout should contain fewer than 100 numbers.

6. Assume that each element of an array *a* stored in row-major order occupies four units of storage. If *a* is declared by each of the following, and the address of the first element of *a* is 100, find the address of the indicated array element:

    (a) var a: **array** [1..100] ... ;   address of a[10]
    (b) var a: **array** [10..200] ... ;   address of a[100]
    (c) var a: **array** [−100..1, 1..100] ... ;   address of a[1, 12]
    (d) var a: **array** [1..10, 1..20] ... ;   address of a[1, 1]
    (e) var a: **array** [1..10, 1..20] ... ;   address of a[2, 1]
    (f) var a: **array** [1..10, 1..20] ... ;   address of a[5, 1]
    (g) var a: **array** [1..10, 1..20] ... ;   address of a[1, 10]
    (h) var a: **array** [1..10, 1..20] ... ;   address of a[2, 10]

(i)	var a: **array** [1..10, 1..20] ... ;	address of a[5, 3]
(j)	var a: **array** [1..10, 1..20] ... ;	address of a[10, 20]
(k)	var a: **array** [5..10, 1..20] ... ;	address of a[5, 13]
(l)	var a: **array** [5..10, 1..2] ... ;	address of a[7, 1]
(m)	var a: **array** [5..10, −10..20] ... ;	address of a[5, −5]
(n)	var a: **array** [5..10, −10..20] ... ;	address of a[7, 7]

7. Write a Pascal procedure *listoff* which accepts three one-dimensional array parameters of the same size: *lb*, *ub*, and *sub*. *lb* and *ub* represent the lower and upper bounds of an integer array. For example, if the elements of *lb* are

$$1\ 3\ 1\ 1\ 1$$

and the elements of *ub* are

$$3\ 5\ 10\ 6\ 3$$

then *lb* and *ub* represent an array *a* declared by

var a: **array** [1..3, 3..5, 1..10, 1..6, 1..3] **of** integer;

The elements of *sub* represent subscripts to this array. If *sub* [i] does not lie between *lb* [i] and *ub* [i], all subscripts from the *i*th onward are missing. In the example above, if the elements of *sub* are

$$1\ 3\ 1\ 2\ 0$$

then *sub* represents the expression $a[1,3,1,2]$. The procedure *listoff* should print the offsets from the base of the array *a* represented by *lb* and *ub* of all the elements of *a* that are included in the array (or the offset of the single element if all subscripts are within bounds) represented by *sub*. Assume that the size (*esize*) of each element of *a* is one. In the example above, *listoff* would print the values 4, 5, and 6.

8. (a) A *lower triangular* array *a* is an *n* by *n* array in which $a[i,j]=0$ if $i<j$. What is the maximum number of nonzero elements in such an array? How can these elements be stored sequentially in memory? Develop an algorithm for accessing $a[i,j]$ where $i \geqslant j$. Define an *upper triangular* array in an analogous manner and do the same as described above for such an array.

(b) A *strictly lower triangular array* *a* is an *n* by *n* array in which $a[i,j]=0$ if $i \leqslant j$. Answer the questions of part (a) for such an array.

(c) Let *a* and *b* be two *n* by *n* lower triangular arrays. Show how an *n* by *n*+1 array *c* can be used to contain the nonzero elements of the two arrays. Which elements of *c* represent the elements $a[i,j]$ and $b[i,j]$, respectively?

(d) A *tridiagonal* array *a* is an *n* by *n* array in which $a[i,j]=0$ if the absolute value of $i-j$ is greater than 1. What is the maximum number of nonzero elements in such an array? How can these elements be stored sequentially in memory? Develop an algorithm for accessing $a[i,j]$ if the absolute value of $i-j$ is 1 or less. Do the same for an array *a* in which $a[i,j]=0$ if the absolute value of $i-j$ is greater than k.

9. (a) Show how to represent a set of integers between 1 and *n* by a boolean array in Pascal.

(b) Write Pascal routines to implement the union, intersection, and difference operations and tests for equality, containment, and membership for sets represented by boolean arrays.

(c) Rewrite the routines of part (b) if the sets are represented by packed boolean arrays.

10. Assume the following type definitions and declarations:

$$\textbf{type } basetype = 1..25;$$
$$settype = \textbf{set of } basetype;$$
$$\textbf{var } s1,s2,s3: settype;$$

Write Pascal routines to:

(a) Form the set of all elements that are in $s1$ or $s2$, but not both.
(b) Form the set of all elements that are in a single one of $s1$, $s2$, and $s3$.
(c) Form the set of all elements that are in exactly two of $s1$, $s2$, and $s3$.
(d) Form the set of all elements of type *basetype* that are not in $s1$.
(e) Form the set of all elements of type *basetype* that are not in any of $s1$, $s2$, or $s3$.
(f) Form the set of all elements of type *basetype* that are not in all three sets $s1$, $s2$, and $s3$.

11. Write a Pascal program to create and print the following set s. s contains the integers 1 and 2. s also contains all integers (less than the upper bound u allowed by your compiler for the type $1..u$ as the base type of a set) of the form $3*x + y$, where x and y are distinct elements of s. (That is, s contains 1, 2, 5, 7, 8, 10, 11, 13, 14, 16, 17, ...)

3. RECORDS IN PASCAL

In this section we examine the Pascal data structure called a *record*. A record is a group of items in which each item is identified by its own *field identifier*. For example, a record for a name can be defined by the type definition:

```
type nametype = record
                    first: packed array [1..10] of char;
                    midinit: char;
                    last: packed array [1..20] of char
                end;
```

This definition may now be used to declare a variable such as

```
var myname: nametype;
```

Alternatively, *myname* could have been declared directly as

```
var myname: record
                first: packed array [1..10] of char;
                midinit: char;
                last: packed array [1..20] of char
            end;
```

As in the case of arrays, the two basic operations on records are *extraction* and *storing*. *Fields* of a record are referenced by specifying the variable name followed by the field identifier separated by a period. For example, the middle initial of *myname* could be extracted by

```
mid:= myname.midinit
```

and could be assigned the letter '*j*' by

$$myname.midinit := 'j'$$

We assume that you are familiar with the record from an introductory course. Sections 6 through 12 of the Appendix describe the facilities available in Pascal for defining and using records. In the remainder of this section, we illustrate the use of records in implementing varying-length character strings and contrast the record implementation with the array implementation of the previous section. We also discuss the implementation of records.

Character Strings Using Records

In the preceding section, we presented an implementation of varying-length character strings using arrays. To refresh your memory, a string was represented by a fixed-length array of characters with trailing blanks. All trailing blanks were considered insignificant and not part of the string. There are two drawbacks to that method. First, it is sometimes desirable to include trailing blanks in a string. Second, to determine the length of the string, the trailing blanks must be traversed until the last nonblank position is found. Since finding the length of a string is such a common operation, this method may be too inefficient.

The record type is extremely convenient for defining new data structures, such as varying-length strings. We illustrate its usefulness in this section by defining varying-length character strings using a record type. The technique that we present here will be repeated throughout the book to define new and complex data structures.

A record representing a varying-length character string consists of two fields. One of these fields is an array containing the actual characters of the string, and the other is an integer representing the current length of the string:

```
const strsize = 80;
type string = record
                ch: packed array [1..strsize] of char;
                length: 0..strsize
              end;
```

For example, to represent the string '*john smith*' of length 10 in a string variable *s*, the 10 elements *s.ch* [1] through *s.ch* [10] are set to the 10 characters '*j*' through '*h*', and *s.length* is set to 10. The values of *s.ch* [11] through *s.ch* [*strsize*] are irrelevant to the value of the string. The string '*john smith*   ' with 3 trailing blanks is represented in a string variable *s* by setting *s.ch* [1] through *s.ch* [10] to the 10 characters '*j*' through '*h*', *s.ch* [11], *s.ch* [12], and *s.ch* [13] to blanks, and *s.length* to 13. Under such a scheme, trailing blanks are significant because they are included in the length of the string.

Let us now write routines similar to those of the preceding section for this representation. It is no longer necessary to write a function *length* to determine the length of a string s, since the variable $s.length$ can be used directly. The function $pos(s1,s2)$ accepts two varying-length character strings $s1$ and $s2$ and returns the position of the first occurrence of $s2$ in $s1$ if $s2$ appears as a substring of $s1$. If $s2$ is not a substring of $s1$, then pos returns 0.

```
function pos(s1,s2: string): integer;
var i,j,len1,len2: integer;
    found,finis: boolean;
begin
    len1:= s1.length;
    len2:= s2.length;
    i:= 0;
    found:= false;
    while (i+len2 <= len1) and (not found)
        do begin
            finis:= false;
            j:= 1;
            while ( j <= len2) and (not finis)
                do if s1.ch[i+j] = s2.ch[j]
                        then j:= j + 1
                        else finis:= true;
            if j > len2
                then found:= true
                else i:= i + 1
        end {while...do begin};
    if found
        then pos:= i + 1
        else pos:= 0
end {function pos};
```

The procedure $concat(s1,s2,s3)$ sets $s3$ to the concatenation of $s1$ and $s2$:

```
procedure concat(s1,s2: string; var s3: string);
var len1,len2,len3,i: integer;
begin
    len1:= s1.length;
    len2:= s2.length;
    len3:= len1+len2;
    if len3 > strsize
        then writeln('error - strings are too long')
        else begin
                s3.ch:= s1.ch;
                for i:= len1+1 to len3
                    do s3.ch[i] := s2.ch[i-len1] ;
                s3.length:= len3
            end {else begin}
end {procedure concat};
```

The procedure *substr*(*s1*,*i*,*j*,*s2*) sets the string *s2* to the substring of *s1* of length *j* beginning with the *i*th character. If fewer than *j* characters remain in *s1*, *s2* is padded with blanks.

```
procedure substr(s1: string; i,j: integer; var s2: string);
var k,limit: integer;
begin
    if i+j−1 <= s1.length
        then limit:= i+j−1
        else limit:= s1.length;
    for k:= i to limit
        do s2.ch[k−i+1]:= s1.ch[k];
    for k:= limit−i+2 to j
        do s2.ch[k]:= ' ';
    s2.length:= j
end {procedure substr};
```

Another routine becomes necessary under the record representation of character strings. This is a function to determine if two strings are equal. Under the array representation, the two packed arrays could be tested for equality using the Pascal = operator. However, under the record representation, if *s1* and *s2* are two records representing strings, the arrays *s1.ch* and *s2.ch* might be identical, yet *s1* and *s2* represent different strings. For example, suppose that both *s1.ch*[1] through *s1.ch*[26] and *s2.ch*[1] through *s2.ch*[26] contain the letters of the alphabet (and *s1.ch*[27] through *s1.ch*[*strsize*] and *s2.ch*[27] through *s2.ch*[*strsize*] are blank). If *s1.length* is 4 and *s2.length* is 5, then *s1* represents the string '*abcd*' while *s2* represents '*abcde*', so the strings are unequal. Similarly, if *s1.ch*[1] and *s2.ch*[1] both equal '*a*' and all the remaining characters of both arrays are blanks but *s1.length* is 3 and *s2.length* is 2, then *s1* and *s2* are unequal since *s1* represents '*a* ' with two trailing blanks, while *s2* represents '*a* ' with only one trailing blank. Note that under the array representation of the previous section, the two strings are equal, because trailing blanks are insignificant and both arrays (*s1.ch* and *s2.ch*) represent the string '*a*' of length 1.

It is also possible for the two arrays *s1.ch* and *s2.ch* to be unequal, yet for the two strings to be equal. For example, if *s1.ch* starts with '*abcde...*' and *s2.ch* starts with '*abcdf...*' but *s1.length* and *s2.length* are both 4, both *s1* and *s2* represent the string '*abcd*'.

Thus a function to determine whether two strings are equal is clearly necessary.

```
function equalstr(s1,s2: string): boolean;
var i,len1: integer;
    equal: boolean;
begin
    len1:= s1.length;
    if s2.length <> len1
        then equalstr:= false
```

```
            else begin
                   i:= 1;
                   equal:= true;
                   while (i <= len1) and (equal)
                        do if s1.ch[i] = s2.ch[i]
                              then i:= i + 1
                              else equal:= false;
                   equalstr:= equal
            end {else begin}
      end {function equalstr};
```

Implementing Records

Let us now turn our attention from the application of record types to their implementation. Any type in Pascal may be thought of as a pattern or a template. By this we mean that a type is a method for interpreting a portion of memory. When a variable identifier is declared as being of a certain type, we are saying that the identifier refers to a certain portion of memory and that the contents of that memory are to be interpreted according to the pattern defined by the type. The type specifies both the amount of memory set aside for the variable and the method by which that memory is interpreted.

For example, suppose that under a certain Pascal implementation an integer is represented by 4 bytes, a real number by 8, and a packed array of 10 characters by 10 bytes. Then the variable declarations

```
            var x: integer;
                y: real;
                z: packed array[1..10] of char;
```

specify that 4 bytes of memory be set aside for x, 8 bytes be set aside for y, and 10 bytes for z. Once those bytes are set aside for those variables (which occurs just prior to the program's execution), the names x, y, and z will always refer to those locations. When x is referenced, its 4 bytes will be interpreted as an integer; when y is referenced, its 8 bytes will be interpreted as a real number; and when z is referenced, its 10 bytes will be interpreted as a collection of 10 characters in packed format. Note that the amount of storage set aside for each type and the method by which the contents of memory are interpreted as specific types vary from one machine and Pascal implementation to another. But within a given Pascal implementation, any type always indicates a specific amount of storage and a specific method of interpreting that storage.

Now suppose that we defined a record type by

```
            type rectype = record
                              field1: integer;
                              field2: real;
                              field3: packed array[1..10] of char
                           end;
```

and declared a variable

var r: rectype;

Then the amount of memory specified by the record type is the sum of the storage specified by each of its field types. Thus the space required for the variable r of type *rectype* is the sum of the space required for an integer (4 bytes), a real number (8 bytes), and a packed array of 10 characters (10 bytes). Therefore, 22 bytes are set aside for r. The first 4 of these bytes are interpreted as an integer, the next 8 as a real number, and the last 10 as a packed array of characters. (This is not always true. On some computers, objects of certain types may not begin anywhere in memory but are constrained to start at certain "boundaries," For example, an integer of length 4 bytes may have to start at an address divisible by 4, and a real number of length 8 bytes may have to start at an address divisible by 8. Thus, in our example, if the starting address of r is 200, the integer occupies bytes 200 through 203, but the real number cannot start at byte 204 because that location is not divisible by 8. Thus the real number must start at location 208 and the entire record requires 26, rather than 22, bytes. Bytes 204 through 207 are wasted space.)

For every reference to a field of a record, an address must be calculated. Associated with each field identifier of a record type is an *offset*, which specifies how far beyond the start of the record is the location of that field. In the example described above, the offset of *field*1 is 0, the offset of *field*2 (assuming no boundary restrictions) is 4, and the offset of *field*3 is 12. Associated with each record variable is a base address, which is the location of the start of the memory allocated to that variable. These associations are established by the compiler and are of no concern to the user. In order to calculate the location of a field in a record, the offset of the field identifier is added to the base address of the record variable.

For example, assume that the base address of r is 200. Then what really happens in executing a statement such as

r.field2:= r.field1 + 3.7

is the following. First, the location of $r.field1$ is determined as the base address of r (200) plus the field offset of *field*1 (0), which yields 200. The 4 bytes at locations 200 through 203 are interpreted as an integer. This integer is then converted to a real number, which is then added to the real number 3.7. The result is a real number that takes up 8 bytes. The location of $r.field2$ is then computed as the base address of r (200) plus the field offset of *field*2 (4), which is 204. The 8 bytes 204 through 211 are set to the real number computed in evaluating the expression.

Note that the process of calculating the address of a record component is very similar to that of calculating the address of an array component. In both cases, an offset that depends on the component selector (the field identifier or the subscript value) is added to the base address of the compound structure (the record or the array). In the case of a record, the offset is associated with the field identifier by the type definition, whereas in the case of an array, the offset is calculated based on the value of the subscript.

These two types of addressing (record and array) may be combined. For example, to calculate the address of $r.field3[4]$, we first use record addressing to determine the base address of the array $r.field3$ and then use array addressing to determine the location of the fourth element of that array. The base address of $r.field3$ is given by the base address of r (200) plus the offset of $field3$ (12), which is 212. The address of $r.field3[4]$ is then determined as the base address of $r.field3$ (212) plus 3 (the subscript 4 minus the lower array bound 1) times the size of each element of the array (1), which yields 212 + 3 * 1, or 215.

As a further example, consider another variable rr, declared by

var rr: **array** [1..20] **of** rectype;

rr is an example of an array of records. If the base address of rr is 400, the address of $rr[14].field3[6]$ may be computed as follows. The size of each component of rr is 22, so the location of $rr[14]$ is 400+13*22, which is 686. The base address of $rr[14].field3$ is then 686+12, which is 698. The address of $rr[14].field3[6]$ is therefore 698+5*1, which is 703. (Again, this ignores the possibility of boundary restrictions. For example, although the type *rectype* may require only 22 bytes, each *rectype* may have to start at an address divisible by 4, so that 2 bytes are wasted between each element of rr and its neighbor. If such is the case, the size of each element of rr is really 24, so that the address of $rr[14].field3[6]$ is actually 729 rather than 703.)

Variant Records

Thus far, each record type we have looked at has had fixed fields and a single format. Pascal also allows another type of record, the *variant record*, which permits a record variable to be interpreted in several different ways.

For example, consider an insurance company that offers three kinds of policies: life, auto, and home. A policy number identifies each insurance policy, of whatever kind. For all three types of insurance, it is necessary to have the policyholder's name, address, the amount of the insurance, and the monthly premium payment. For auto and home insurance policies, a deductible amount is needed. For a life insurance policy, the insured's birth date and beneficiary are needed. For an auto insurance policy, a license number, state, model, and year are required. For a homeowner's policy, an indication of the age of the house and the presence of any security precautions are required. A policy record type for such a company may be defined as a variant record. We first define two auxiliary types.

```
type addrtype = record
            streetaddr: packed array [1..50] of char;
            city: packed array [1..10] of char;
            state: packed array [1..2] of char;
            zip: packed array [1..5] of '0'..'9'
        end;
```

```
        type date = record
                      month: 1..12;
                      day: 1..31;
                      year: 0..2000
                  end;
    type policy = record
                      polnumber: integer;
                      name: packed array [1..30] of char;
                      address: addrtype;
                      amount: integer;
                      premium: real;
                      case kind: (life, auto, home) of
                          life: (beneficiary: packed array [1..30] of char;
                                 birthday: date);
                          auto: (autodeduct: integer;
                                 license: packed array [1..10] of char;
                                 state: packed array [1..2] of char;
                                 model: packed array [1..15] of char;
                                 year: 1900..2000);
                          home: (homededuct: integer;
                                 yearbuilt: 1700..2000;
                                 security: (bolts, alarm, dog, watchman, other))
          end;
```

Let us examine the variant type definition more closely. The definition, between the keywords *record* and *end*, consists of two parts: a fixed part and a variant part. The fixed part consists of all field declarations up to the keyword *case*, while the variant part consists of the remainder of the type definition. The fixed part may be omitted, but, if present, must precede the variant part. The variant part may be omitted, but then the record is no longer a variant record.

The variant part begins with the keyword *case*, followed by a field declaration, followed by the keyword *of*. The field of the record declared after the keyword *case* is called a *tag field* and its type is called a *tag type*. The tag type may not be *real* or a compound type. In the record type *policy*, the tag field is *kind* and its tag type is the enumerated type (*life, auto, home*). Following the keyword *of* is a list of variant declarations. Each variant declaration consists of a constant whose type is the tag type (e.g., *auto*), followed by a colon, followed by a parenthesized list of field declarations. The fields declared in a variant declaration are called *variant fields*, while those declared in the fixed part of a record definition are called *fixed fields*. The tag field is also a fixed field. Note that the single keyword *end* ends both the variant part and the entire record definition.

Now that we have examined the syntax of a variant record definition, let us examine its semantics. A variable declared as being of a variant record type t (e.g., *var p:policy*) always contains all the fixed fields of t, including the tag field. Thus it is always valid to reference *p.name* or *p.premium* or *p.kind*. However, the variant fields contained in the value of such a variable depend on the value of its tag field. In the example above, if the value of *p.kind* is *life*, then *p* currently contains variant fields *p.beneficiary* and *p.birthday*, since those are the only fields declared in the variant declaration preceded by the value *life* in the record definition. It is invalid to reference *p.model* or *p.yearbuilt*, while the value of *p.kind* is *life*. Similarly, if the value of *p.kind* is *auto*, we may reference *p.autodeduct*, *p.license*, *p.state*, *p.model*, and *p.year*, but may not reference any other variant field. When the value of a tag field is changed, the variant fields associated with the old value cease to exist and the variant fields associated with the new value come into being with undefined values.

Thus a variant record allows a variable to take on several different "types" at different points in execution. It also allows an array to contain objects of different types. For example, the array *a* declared by

$$\text{var } a: \mathbf{array}\,[1..100] \ \mathbf{of} \ policy;$$

may contain life, auto, and home insurance policies.

Suppose that such an array *a* is declared and it is desired to raise the premiums of all auto insurance policies and all home insurance policies for homes built before 1950 by 5%. This can be done as follows: (Note the use of the *with* statement which is discussed in Sections 9 and 10 of the Appendix.)

```
for i:= 1 to 100
    do with a[i]
        do begin
            case kind of
                auto: premium:= 1.05 * premium;
                home: if yearbuilt < 1950
                        then premium:= 1.05 * premium
            end {case}
        end {with...do begin}
```

A variant of a record may contain no variant fields, in which case the list of variant fields in the variant declaration consists of an open parenthesis followed immediately by a closed parenthesis. For example, a mailing list may contain both home and business addresses. Business addresses may contain a company name and a department, while home addresses do not. We may define

```
type custype = (home, business);
    customer = record
                name: packed array[1..30] of char;
                address: addrtype;
                case kind: custype of
                    home: ( );
                    business: (company, dept: packed array[1..25] of char)
            end;
```

The tag field is used to determine the variant that the record variable is currently assuming. However, it is possible for a tag field to be omitted from the declaration of a record, although the tag type must be included. For example, the following is a definition of such a record:

```
type vrectype = record
                field1: integer;
                case 1..3 of
                    1: (field11,field12: integer);
                    2: ( );
                    3: (field31: char)
            end;
```

No tag field is included, but the variants are specified by the values of the tag type 1..3. Any field of any variant may be referenced at any time. However, that field must be initialized before it can be used meaningfully. Once any field of one variant is referenced, there is no guarantee that the fields of any other variant retain their values.

For example, assume the declaration

```
var v: vrectype;
```

and the statements

```
v.field11:= 7;
v.field12:= 10;
writeln (v.field11,v.field12);
```

These statements utilize the first variant of the record. Now, if we execute

```
v.field31:= 'a';
```

we are utilizing the third variant. If we now again execute

```
writeln(v.field11,v.field12);
```

an error may result, because a different variant (variant 3) was referenced between the initialization and current utilization of the current variant (variant 1).

Implementation of Variant Records

To understand fully the concept of a variant record, it is necessary to examine its implementation. A record type may be regarded as a road map to an area of memory. It defines how the memory is to be interpreted. A variant record type provides several different road maps for the same area of memory, and a tag field value determines which road map is in current use. For example, consider the simple variant record type and variable

```
type vtype = record
             f1: integer;
             f2: real;
```

```
                    case c: (first,second) of
                         first: (f3,f4: integer);
                         second: (f5,f6: real)
            end;
      var v: vtype;
```

Let us again assume an implementation in which an integer requires 4 bytes, and a real number, 8 bytes. Let us also assume that an enumerated type such as (*first*, *second*) uses 4 bytes (although only a single bit is needed). Then the three fixed fields $f1$, $f2$, and c occupy 16 bytes. The fields of the first variant, $f3$ and $f4$, require 8 bytes, while the fields of the second require 16. The memory actually allocated for the variant part of such a record variable is the maximum of the space needed by any single variant. In this case, therefore, 16 bytes are allocated for the variant part of v. Added to the 16 bytes needed for the fixed part, 32 bytes are allocated to v.

The different variants of a variant record overlay each other. In the example above, if space for v is allocated starting at location 100, so that v occupies bytes 100 through 131, the fixed fields $v.f1$, $v.f2$, and $v.c$ occupy bytes 100 through 103, 104 through 111, and 112 through 115, respectively. If the value of the tag field $v.c$ is *first*, bytes 116 through 119 and 120 through 123 are occupied by $v.f3$ and $v.f4$, respectively, while bytes 124 through 131 are unused. If the value of $v.c$ is *second*, bytes 116 through 123 are occupied by $v.f5$ and bytes 124 through 131 are occupied by $v.f6$. That is why only one variant of a record can exist at a single instant. All the variants of a record use the same space and that space can be used by only one of them at a time. The value of the tag field determines how that space is organized.

If no tag field exists, any interpretation of the space for a variant record can be used at any time. For example, assume the definition and declaration

```
      type vtype2 = record
                    f1: integer;
                    f2: real;
                    case (first, second) of
                         first: (f3, f4: integer);
                         second: (f5, f6: real)
            end;
      var v2: vtype2;
```

Then a total of 28 bytes are allocated for $v2$ (12 for the fixed part and 16 for the longest variant part). If $v2$ begins at location 100, a reference to $v2.f1$ is to bytes 100 through 103, a reference to $v2.f2$ is to bytes 104 through 111, a reference to $v2.f3$ is to bytes 112 through 115, a reference to $v2.f4$ is to bytes 116 through 119, a reference to $v2.f5$ is to bytes 112 through 119, and a reference to $v2.f6$ is to bytes 120 through 127. Because there is no tag type, any field may be referenced at any time. However, an assignment to either $v2.f3$ or $v2.f4$ destroys the value of $v2.f5$, since they occupy the same space. Although this does not destroy the value of $v2.f6$

under the particular implementation we have presented, another implementation (e.g., if an integer requires 6 bytes while a real takes up 8, or if an integer and a real both occupy 4) may not be so kind. A Pascal programmer should be writing programs that are implementation-independent, unless he is writing a systems program for a specific implementation. The Pascal language itself (being, by definition, implementation-independent) leaves the values of the fields of all other variants undefined once a field in a particular variant is referenced.

If a variant record does not contain a tag field, there is no way to determine which variant of a record variable is currently in use. The programmer must keep track of the current variant and make sure not to reference a field of a different variant until the values of the current variant are no longer needed. It is therefore always a good idea to include a tag field in a variant record and to keep that field set to its appropriate value.

EXERCISES 1. A *complex number* is one that contains real and imaginary parts, both of which are real numbers. If $c1$ has real and imaginary parts $r1$ and $i1$, respectively, and $c2$ has real and imaginary parts $r2$ and $i2$, respectively, then:

(a) The sum of $c1$ and $c2$ has real part $r1+r2$ and imaginary part $i1+i2$.
(b) The difference of $c1$ and $c2$ has real part $r1-r2$ and imaginary part $i1-i2$.
(c) The product of $c1$ and $c2$ has real part $r1*r2 - i1*i2$ and imaginary part $r1*i2 + r2*i1$.

Implement complex numbers by declaring a record with real and complex parts and write routines to add, subtract, and multiply such complex numbers.

2. Suppose that a real number is represented by a Pascal record such as

```
type realtype = record
                    left: integer;
                    right: 0..maxint
                end;
```

where *left* and *right* represent the digits to the left and right of the decimal point, respectively. If *left* is a negative integer, the represented real number is negative.

(a) Write a routine to input a real number and create a record representing that number.
(b) Write a function that accepts such a record and returns the real number represented by it.
(c) Write routines *add*, *subtract*, and *multiply* that accept two such records and set the value of a third record to represent the number that is the sum, difference, and product, respectively, of the two input records.

3. Assume that an integer needs 4 bytes, a real number needs 8 bytes, an unpacked array of characters takes four times as many bytes as characters in the array, and a packed array takes as many bytes as characters in the array. Assume the following definitions and declarations:

```
        type nametype = record
                            first: packed array [1..12] of char;
                            midinit: char;
                            last: packed array [1..20] of char
                          end;
                person = record
                            name: nametype;
                            birthday: array [1..3] of integer;
                            parents: array [1..2] of nametype;
                            income: real;
                            numchildren: integer;
                            address: array [1..20] of char;
                            city: array [1..10] of char;
                            state: array [1..2] of char
                          end;
        var p: array [1..100] of person;
```

If the starting address of p is 100, what are the starting addresses (in bytes) of each of the following?

(a) p[10]
(b) p[20].name.midinit
(c) p[20].income
(d) p[20].address[5]
(e) p[5].parents[2].last[10]

4. Assuming the space requirements of Exercise 3, what is the starting location of each field of a record variable x declared as in each of the following, if the starting location for x is 100? Assume that an element of an enumerated type requires 4 bytes.

(a) var x: record
```
            f1: real;
            case f2: (a,b,c,d,e) of
                a: (f3,f4: array [1..10] of char);
                b: (f5,f6: record
                              f7: real;
                              f8: integer
                           end);
                c: (f9,f10: packed array [1..20] of char);
                d: (f11,f12: real);
                e: (f13,f14: integer)
        end;
```

(b) var x: record
```
            case f1: 17..19 of
                17: (f2,f3,f4: char);
                18: (f5,f6: integer);
                19: (f7,f8: real)
        end;
```

(c) var x: **record**
          f1: integer;
          case (a,b,c) **of**
            a: (f2,f3: real);
            b: (f4,f5: integer);
            c: (f6,f7: **packed array** [1..20] **of** char)
      end;

5. Write a Pascal procedure to print the value of all current fields in the current value of the record variable *x* declared in Exercise 4(a).

Exercises 6 through 8 refer to material presented in Sections 6 through 12 of the Appendix.

6. Which of the following sets of definitions and declarations are invalid, and why?

(a) **type** x = 1..10;
    var z: **record**
         x: x;
         y: integer
       end;

(b) **procedure** sample(x,y: integer);
    type xtype = 1..10;
    var i,j,x: xtype;

(c) **type** oneten = 1..10;
    function sample(x,y: oneten): oneten;
    type oneten = (one, five, ten);
        rectype = **record**
              one: oneten;
              ten: oneten
          end;

(d) **type** st = **record**
            x: integer;
            y: real
        end;
    var x,y: st;
      st1,st2,st: integer;

(e) **type** xt = 1..10;
    var xt: xt;

(f) **type** rec = **record**
          f1: integer
          case f2: 1..2 **of**
            1: (x,y,z: integer);
            2: (v,w,x: integer)
         end;

(g) **type** rec = **record**
                    f1: integer;
                    f2: **record**
                            f1: integer;
                            f2: real;
                            rec: char
                        end
                end;
        var f1,f2: rec;

7. Assume two arrays, one of student records, the other of employee records. Each student record contains fields for a last name, first name and a grade-point index. Each employee record contains fields for a last name, first name, and salary. Both arrays are ordered in alphabetical order by last name and first name. Two records with the same last name/first name do not appear in the same array. Write a Pascal procedure to give a 10% raise to every employee who has a student record and whose grade-point index is greater than 3.0.

8. Write a procedure as in Exercise 7, but assume that the employee and student records are kept in two ordered external files rather than in two ordered arrays.

2 The Stack

One of the most useful concepts in computer science is that of the stack. In this chapter we examine this deceptively simple data structure and see why it plays such a prominent role in the areas of programming and programming languages. We shall define the abstract concept of a stack and show how that concept can be made into a concrete and valuable tool in problem solving.

1. DEFINITION AND EXAMPLES

A *stack* is an ordered collection of items into which new items may be inserted and from which items may be deleted at one end, called the *top* of the stack.

Let us see what this definition means. Given any two items in a stack, one of them can be thought of as "higher" in the stack than the other. Thus we can picture a stack as in Figure 2.1.1. Item *F* is higher in the stack than all the other items. Item *D* is higher than items *A*, *B*, and *C* but is lower than items *E* and *F*.

You may protest that if Figure 2.1.1 were turned upside down, a very similar picture would result, but *A* rather than *F* would be the highest element. If a stack were a static, unchanging object your objection would be quite correct. However, the definition of a stack provides for insertion and deletion of items, so that a stack is really a dynamic, constantly changing object. Figure 2.1.1 is only a snapshot of a stack at a particular point in its continuing evolution. In order to have a true view of a stack, a motion picture is necessary.

The question therefore arises, how does a stack change? From the definition, note that a single end of the stack must be designated as the stack *top*. New items may be put on top of the stack (in which case the top of the stack moves upward to correspond to the new highest element) or items that are at the top of the stack may be removed (in which case the top of the stack moves downward to correspond to the new highest ele-

56

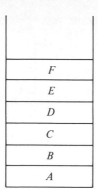

Figure 2.1.1 A stack containing six items.

ment). To answer the question "which way is up?" we must decide which end of the stack is designated as its top—that is, at which end will items be added or deleted? By drawing Figure 2.1.1 so that F is physically higher on the page than all the other items in the stack, we mean to imply that F is the current top element of the stack. If any new items are to be added to the stack, they will be placed on top of F and if any items are to be deleted, F will be the first to be deleted. This is also indicated by the vertical lines which extend past the items of the stack in the direction of the stack top.

Of course, stacks may be drawn in many different ways, as shown in Figure 2.1.2, as long as it is clearly understood which end is the top of the stack. Ordinarily, we will illustrate stacks as in Figure 2.1.1, with the stack top facing the top of the page.

Let us now view a motion picture of a stack to see how it expands and shrinks with the passage of time. Such a picture is given by Figure 2.1.3. In Figure 2.1.3a we see the stack as it existed at the time that the snapshot of Figure 2.1.1 was taken. In Figure 2.1.3b, item G is added to the stack. According to the definition, there is only one place on the stack where it can be placed—on the top. The top element on the stack is now G. As our motion picture progresses through frames (c), (d), and (e), we see items H, I, and J successively added onto the stack. Notice that the last item inserted (in this case J) is at the top of the stack. Beginning with frame (f), however, the stack begins to shrink as first J, then I, H, G, and F are successively removed. At each point, the top element is removed since a deletion can be made only from the top. Item G could not be removed from the stack before items J, I, and H were gone. This illustrates the most important attribute of a stack, that the last element inserted into a stack is the first element deleted. Thus J is deleted before I because J was inserted after I. For this reason a stack is sometimes called a last-in, first-out (or *lifo*) list.

Between frames (j) and (k), the stack has stopped shrinking and begins to expand again as item K is added. However, this expansion is short-lived, as the stack then shrinks to only three items in frame (n).

Note that there is no way to distinguish between frame (a) and frame (i)

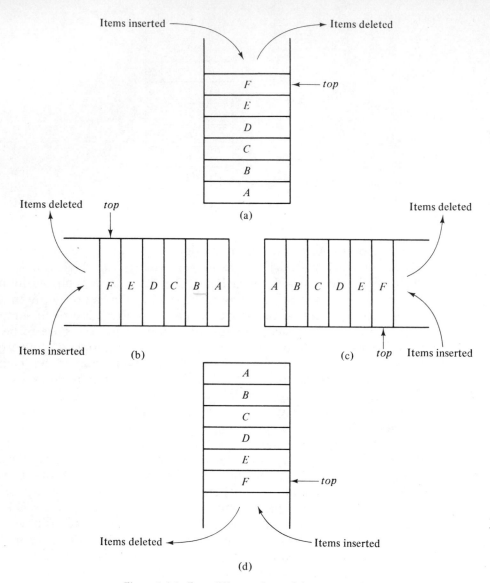

Figure 2.1.2 Four different views of the same stack.

by looking at the stack's state at the two instances. In both cases, the stack contains the identical items in the same order and has the same stack top. No record is kept on the stack of the fact that four items had been inserted and deleted in the meantime. Similarly, there is no way to distinguish between frames (d) and (f) or (j) and (l). If a record is needed of the intermediate items having been on the stack, that record must be kept elsewhere; it does not exist within the stack itself.

In fact, we have actually taken an extended view of what is really observed in a stack. The true picture of a stack is given by a view from the top

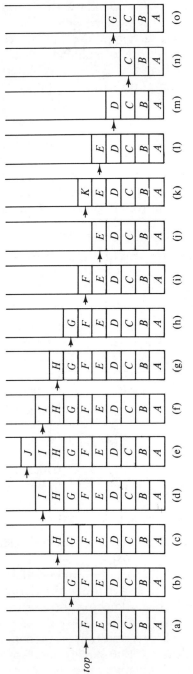

Figure 2.1.3 A motion picture of a stack.

59

looking down, rather than from a side looking in. Thus there is no perceptible difference between frames (h) and (o) in Figure 2.1.3. In each case the element at the top is G. While we know that the stack at (h) and the stack at (o) are not equal, the only way to determine this is to remove all the elements on both stacks and compare them individually. Although we have been looking at cross sections of stacks to make our understanding clearer, you should remember that this is an added liberty and there is no real provision for taking such a picture.

Primitive Operations

The two changes that can be made to a stack are given special names. When an item is added to a stack, it is *pushed* onto the stack. Given a stack s, and an item i, performing the operation $push(s,i)$ is defined as adding the item i to the top of stack s. Similarly, the operation $pop(s)$ removes the top element and returns it as a function value. Thus the assignment operation

$$i := pop(s)$$

removes the element at the top of s and assigns its value to i.

For example, if s is the stack of Figure 2.1.3, we performed the operation $push(s,G)$ in going from frame (a) to frame (b). We then performed, in turn, the operations

push (s,H);	(frame (c))
push (s,I);	(frame (d))
push (s,J);	(frame (e))
pop (s);	(frame (f))
pop (s);	(frame (g))
pop (s);	(frame (h))
pop (s);	(frame (i))
pop (s);	(frame (j))
push (s,K);	(frame (k))
pop (s);	(frame (l))
pop (s);	(frame (m))
pop (s);	(frame (n))
push (s,G)	(frame (o)).

Because of the push operation, which adds elements to a stack, a stack is sometimes called a *pushdown list*.

There is no upper limit on the number of items that may be kept in a stack, because no mention was made in the definition as to how many items are allowed in the collection. Pushing another item onto a stack merely produces a larger collection of items. However, if a stack contains a single item and the stack is popped, the resulting stack contains no items and is called the *empty stack*. Although the *push* operation is applicable to any stack, the *pop* operation cannot be applied to the empty stack because such a stack has no elements to delete. Therefore, before applying the *pop* operator to a stack, we must ensure that the stack is not empty. The operation $empty(s)$

determines whether or not a stack s is empty. If the stack is empty, *empty*(s) returns the value *true*; otherwise, it returns the value *false*.

Another operation that can be performed on a stack is to determine what the top item on a stack is without removing it. This operation is written *stacktop*(s) and returns as its value the top element of stack s. The operation *stacktop*(s) is not really a new operation, because it can be decomposed into a pop and a push.

$$i := stacktop(s)$$

is equivalent to

$$i := pop(s);$$
$$push\ (s,i)$$

Like the operation *pop*, *stacktop* is not defined for an empty stack. The result of an illegal attempt to pop or access an item from an empty stack is called **underflow**. Underflow can be avoided by ensuring that *empty*(s) is *false* before attempting the operation *pop*(s) or *stacktop*(s).

AN EXAMPLE

Now that we have defined a stack and have indicated the operations that can be performed on it, let us see how we may use the stack in problem solving. Suppose that a mathematical expression is given which includes several sets of nested parentheses; for example,

$$7-((X *((X+Y) / (J-3)) + Y) /(4-2.5))$$

and we want to ensure that the parentheses are nested correctly. That is, we want to check that:

1. There are an equal number of right and left parentheses.
2. Every right parenthesis is preceded by a matching left parenthesis.

Expressions such as

$$((A+B) \quad \text{or} \quad A+B($$

would violate condition 1, and

$$)A+B(-C \quad \text{or} \quad (A+B))-(C+D$$

would violate condition 2.

To solve this problem, think of each left parenthesis as opening a scope and each right parenthesis as closing a scope. The **nesting depth** at a particular point in an expression is the number of scopes which have been opened but not yet closed at that point. This is the same as the number of left parentheses encountered whose matching right parentheses have not yet been encountered. Let us define the **parenthesis count** at a particular point in an expression as the number of left parentheses minus the number of right parentheses which have been encountered in scanning the expression from its left end up to that particular point. If the parenthesis count is nonnegative, it is the same as the nesting depth. The two conditions that must hold if the parentheses in an expression are to form an admissible pattern are:

1. The parenthesis count at the end of the expression is 0. This implies that no scopes have been left open or that exactly as many right parentheses as left parentheses have been found.
2. The parenthesis count at each point in the expression is nonnegative. This implies that no right parenthesis has been encountered for which a matching left parenthesis had not previously been encountered.

In Figure 2.1.4, the count at each point in each of the previous five strings is given directly below that point. Since only the first string meets the foregoing two conditions, it is the only one among the five with a correct parentheses pattern.

Let us now change the problem slightly and assume that three different types of scopes exist. These types are indicated by parentheses ((and)), brackets ([and]), and braces ({ and }). A scope ender must be of the same type as its scope opener. Thus strings such as

$$(A+B], \quad [(A+B]), \quad \{A-(B]\}$$

are illegal.

It is necessary to keep track not only of how many scopes have been opened, but also of their types. This information is needed because when a scope ender is encountered, we must know the symbol with which the scope was opened in order to ensure that it is being closed properly.

A stack may be used to keep track of the types of scopes encountered. Whenever a scope opener is encountered, it is pushed onto the stack. Whenever a scope ender is encountered, the stack is examined. If the stack is empty, the scope ender does not have a matching opener, so the string is

```
7 - ( ( X * ( ( X + Y ) / ( J - 3 ) ) + Y ) / ( 4 - 2.5 ) )
0 0 1 2 2 2 3 4 4 4 4 3 3 4 4 4 4 3 2 2 2 1 1 2 2 2   2 1 0


                      ( ( A + B )
                      1 2 2 2 2 1


                      A + B (
                      0 0 0 1


                  )   A   +   B   ( - C
                 -1  -1  -1  -1 0 0 0


              ( A + B )   )   - ( C + D
              1 1 1 1 0  -1  -1 0 0 0 0
```

Figure 2.1.4 Parenthesis count at various points of strings.

invalid. If, however, the stack is nonempty, we pop the stack and check whether the popped item corresponds to the scope ender. If a match occurs, we continue. If it does not, the string is invalid. When the end of the string is reached, we make sure that the stack is empty; otherwise, one or more scopes have been opened which have not been closed making the string invalid. The algorithm for this procedure is outlined below. Figure 2.1.5 shows the state of the stack after reading in parts of the string $\{x+(y-[a+b])*c-[(d+e)]\}/(b-(j-(k-[l-n])))$.

```
valid := true;
Let s := the empty stack;
while (we have not read the entire string) and (valid)
    do begin
            read the next symbol (symb) of the string;
            if symb in [ '(', '[', '{' ] then push (s, symb);
            if symb in [ ')', ']', '}' ]
                then if empty (s)
                        then valid := false
                        else begin
                                i := pop (s);
                                if i is not the matching opener for symb
                                    then valid := false
                            end {else begin}
        end {while...do begin};
    if not empty (s) then valid := false;
    if valid
        then writeln ('the string is valid')
        else writeln ('the string is invalid')
```

Let us see why the solution to this problem calls for the use of a stack. The last scope to be opened must be the first to be closed. This is precisely simulated by a stack where the last element arriving is the first to leave. Each item on the stack represents a scope that has been opened but has not yet been closed. Pushing an item onto the stack corresponds to the opening of a scope and popping an item from the stack corresponds to the closing of a scope, leaving one less scope open.

Notice the correspondence between the number of elements on the stack in this example and the parenthesis count in the previous example. When the stack is empty (parenthesis count =0), and a scope ender is encountered, an attempt is being made to close a scope which has never been opened, so that the parenthesis pattern is invalid. In the first example, this is indicated by a negative parenthesis count and in the second example by an inability to pop the stack. The reason that a simple parenthesis count is inadequate for the second example is that we must keep track of the actual scope openers themselves. This can be done by the use of a stack. Notice also that at any point we examine only the element at the top. The particular configuration of parentheses below the top element is irrelevant when we are examining

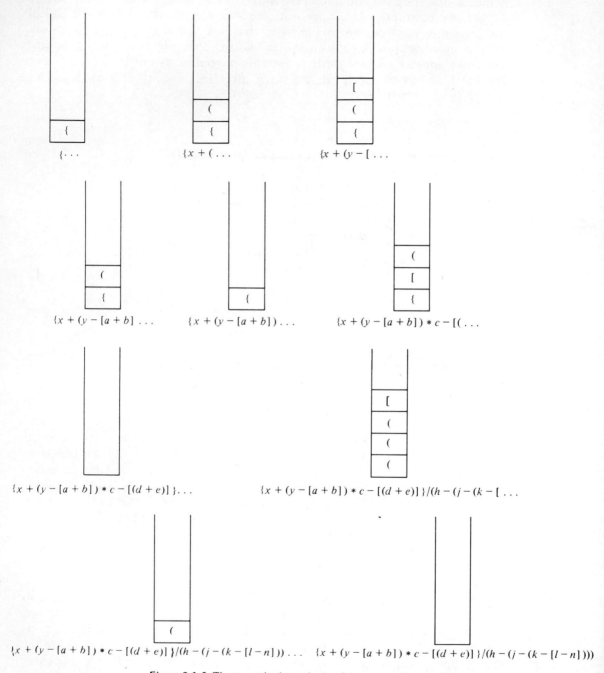

Figure 2.1.5 The parenthesis stack at various stages of processing.

this top element. It is only after the top element has been popped that we concern ourselves with subsequent elements in a stack.

In general, a stack can be used in any situation that calls for a last-in, first-out discipline or displays a nesting pattern. We shall see more examples of the use of stacks in the remaining sections of this chapter and, indeed, throughout the text.

EXERCISES   1. Use the operations *push*, *pop*, *stacktop*, and *empty* to construct operations which do each of the following:

(a) Set i to the second element from the top of the stack, leaving the stack without its top two elements.

(b) Set i to the second element from the top of the stack, leaving the stack unchanged.

(c) Given an integer n, set i to the nth element from the top of the stack, leaving the stack without its top n elements.

(d) Given an integer n, set i to the nth element from the top of the stack, leaving the stack unchanged.

(e) Set i to the bottom element of the stack, leaving the stack empty.

(f) Set i to the bottom element of the stack, leaving the stack unchanged. (*Hint:* Use another, auxiliary stack.)

(g) Set i to the third element from the bottom of the stack.

2. Simulate the action of the algorithm in this section for each of the following strings by showing the contents of the stack at each point.

(a) $(a+b\})$

(b) $\{[a+b] - [(c-d)]$

(c) $(a+b) - \{c+d\} - [f+g]$

(d) $((b) * \{([j+k])\})$

(e) $(((a)))$

3. Write an algorithm to determine if an input character string is of the form

$$x \, \text{C} \, y$$

where x is a string consisting of the letters 'A' and 'B' and where y is the reverse of x (i.e., if x = 'ABABBA', then y must equal 'ABBABA'). At each point you may read only the next character of the string.

4. Write an algorithm to determine if an input character string is of the form

$$a \, \text{D} \, b \, \text{D} \, c \, \text{D} \ldots \text{D} \, z$$

where each string a, b, ..., z is of the form of the string $x \, \text{C} \, y$ defined in Exercise 3. (Thus a string is in the proper form if it consists of any number of such strings separated by the character 'D'.) At each point you may read only the next character of the string.

5. Design an algorithm that does not use a stack which reads a sequence of *push* and *pop* operations and determines whether or not underflow occurs on some *pop* operation. Implement the algorithm as a Pascal program.

6. What set of conditions are necessary and sufficient for a sequence of *push* and *pop* operations on a single stack (initially empty) to leave the stack empty and not to cause

underflow? What set of conditions are necessary for such a sequence to leave a non-empty stack unchanged?

2. REPRESENTING STACKS IN PASCAL

Before programming a problem solution that calls for the use of a stack, we must decide how to represent a stack using the data structures that exist in our programming language. As we shall see, there are several ways to represent a stack in Pascal. We now consider the simplest of these. As the entire book progresses, you will be introduced to other possible representations. Each of them, however, is merely an implementation of the concept introduced in Section 1 of this chapter. Each has its advantages and disadvantages in terms of how close it comes to mirroring the abstract concept of a stack and how much effort must be made by the programmer and the computer in using it.

A stack is an ordered collection of items, and Pascal already contains a data type that is an ordered collection of items—the array. Whenever a problem solution calls for use of a stack, therefore, it is tempting to begin a program by defining a type identifier *stack* to be an array. Unfortunately, however, a stack and an array are two entirely different things. The number of elements in an array is fixed and is determined by the definition of the array. In general, the user cannot change this number. A stack, on the other hand, is fundamentally a dynamic object whose size is constantly changing as items are popped and pushed.

However, although an array cannot be a stack, it can be the home of a stack. That is, an array can be declared with a range that is large enough for the maximum size of the stack. During the course of program execution, the stack will grow and shrink within the space reserved for it. One end of the array will be the fixed bottom of the stack, while the top of the stack will constantly shift as items are popped and pushed. Thus another field is needed which, at each point during program execution, will keep track of the current position of the top of the stack.

A stack in Pascal may therefore be declared as a record containing two objects: an array to hold the elements of the stack, and an integer to indicate the position of the current stack top within the array. This may be done by the declarations

```
const maxstack = 100;
type  stack = record
                 item: array [1..maxstack] of integer;
                 top: 0..maxstack
              end;
var    s: stack;
```

Here we assume that the elements of the stack *s* contained in the array *s.item* are integers and that the stack will at no time contain more than *maxstack* integers. In this example *maxstack* is set to 100. There is, of course, no reason to restrict a stack to contain only integers; *item* could just as easily have been given the type *array* [1..*maxstack*] **of** *real* or *array* [1..*maxstack*] **of** *char*, or whatever other type we might wish to give to the elements of the stack. The field identifier *top*, however, must be declared as an integer between 0 and *maxstack*, because its value represents the position within the array *item* of the topmost stack element. Thus, if the value of *s.top* is 5, there are 5 elements on the stack. These are *s.item*[1], *s.item*[2], *s.item*[3], *s.item*[4], and *s.item*[5]. When the stack is popped, the value of *s.top* must be changed to 4 to indicate that there are now only four elements on the stack and that *s.item*[4] is the top element. On the other hand, if a new object is pushed onto the stack, the value of *s.top* must be increased by 1 to 6 and the new object inserted into *s.item*[6].

The empty stack contains no elements and can therefore be indicated by *top* equaling 0. In order to initialize a stack *s* to the empty state, we may initially execute *s.top*:=0.

To determine, during the course of execution, whether or not a stack is empty, the condition *s.top*=0 may be tested by means of an *if* statement as follows:

```
if s.top=0
    then {    stack is empty    }
    else  { stack is not empty }
```

This test corresponds to the operation *empty*(*s*) which was introduced in Section 1. Alternatively, we may write a function that returns *true* if the stack is empty and *false* if it is not empty. Such a function may be written as follows:

```
function empty (s: stack): boolean;
begin
    if s.top = 0
        then empty := true
        else empty := false
end { function empty };
```

Once this function exists, a test for the empty stack is implemented by the statement

```
if empty(s)
    then {    the stack is empty    }
    else  { the stack is not empty }
```

You may wonder why we bother to define the function *empty* when we could just as easily write *if s.top*=0 each time that we want to test for the empty condition. The answer is that we wish to make our programs more comprehensible and to make the use of a stack independent of its implementation. Once we understand the stack concept, the phrase "*empty*(*s*)" is more meaningful than the phrase "*s.top=0*." If we should later introduce a better implementation of a stack so that "*s.top=0*" becomes meaningless, we would have to change every reference to the field identifier *s.top* throughout our entire program. On the other hand, the phrase "*empty(s)*" would still retain its meaning, since it is an inherent attribute of the stack concept rather than of an implementation of that concept. All that would be required to revise our program to accommodate a new implementation of the stack would be a revision of the definition of the type *stack* in the main program and the rewriting of the function *empty*. Aggregating the set of implementation-dependent trouble spots into small, easily identifiable units is an important method of making a program more understandable and modifiable. This concept is known as *modularization*, in which individual functions are isolated into low-level *modules* whose properties are easily provable. These low-level modules can then be used by more complex routines, which do not have to concern themselves with the details of the low-level modules, only with their function. The complex routines may themselves be viewed as modules by still-higher-level routines, which use them independently of their internal details.

A programmer should always be concerned with the readability of the code he or she produces. Often, a small amount of attention to clarity will save a large amount of time in debugging. Large and medium-size programs will almost never be correct the first time they are run. If precautions are taken at the time that a program is written to ensure that it is easily modifiable and comprehensible, the total time needed to get the program to run correctly will be sharply reduced. For example, the *if* statement in the *empty* function could be replaced by the shorter, more efficient statement

$$\text{empty} := \text{s.top}=0$$

The effect of this statement is precisely equivalent to the longer statement

$$\textbf{if } \text{s.top}=0$$
$$\textbf{then } \text{empty}:=\text{true}$$
$$\textbf{else } \text{empty}:=\text{false}$$

This is because the value of the expression *s.top=0* is *true* if and only if the condition *s.top=0* is true. However, someone else who reads a program will probably be much more comfortable reading the *if* statement. Often, you will find that if you use "tricks" of the language in writing programs, you will be unable to decipher your own programs after putting them aside for a day or two.

To implement the *pop* operation, the possibility of underflow must be taken into account, because the user may inadvertently attempt to pop an element from an empty stack. Of course, such an attempt is illegal and should be avoided. However, if such an attempt should be made, the user should be informed of the underflow condition. We therefore introduce a function *pop*, which consists of the following three actions:

1. If the stack is empty, it prints a warning message and halts execution.
2. It removes the top element from the stack.
3. It returns this element to the calling program.

Note that in Pascal there is no way to halt execution prematurely from within a function such as *pop*. Therefore, we assume the existence of a library procedure *error(str)*, where *str* is a character string. This routine prints the string *str* as an error message and then halts execution. (You may wish to replace the call to *error* by a compound statement consisting of a call to *writeln* and a *goto* the end of your program. In UCSD Pascal, a call to *exit* might replace the *goto*. Note that despite the fact that *error* ends program execution, we place the remainder of the function in an *else* clause in keeping with the "spirit" of Pascal.)

```
function pop (var s: stack): integer;
begin
    if empty(s)
        then error('stack underflow')
        else begin
                pop:= s.item[s.top];
                s.top:= s.top - 1
            end {else begin}
end {function pop};
```

Testing for Exceptional Conditions

Let us look at the *pop* function more closely. If the stack is not empty, the top element of the stack is saved as the returned value. This element is then removed from the stack by the statement $s.top:=s.top-1$. Let us assume that when *pop* is called, $s.top$ equals 87; that is, there are 87 items on the stack. The value of $s.item[87]$ is returned and the value of $s.top$ is changed to 86. Note that $s.item[87]$ still retains its old value; the array $s.item$ remains unchanged by the call to *pop*. However, the stack is changed, because it now contains only 86 elements rather than 87. Recall that an array and a stack are two different objects. The array only provides a home for the stack. The stack itself contains only those elements between the first item of the array and the *top*th element. Thus, reducing the value of $s.top$ by 1 effectively removes an element from the stack. This is true despite the fact that $s.item[87]$ retains its old value.

To use the *pop* function, the programmer can declare $x: integer$ and write

$$x:= pop(s)$$

x will then contain the value popped from the stack. If the intent of the *pop* operation was not to retrieve the element on the top of the stack but only to remove it from the stack, x will not be used again in the program except perhaps to serve once more as the target of a *pop* operation. Of course, the programmer should ensure that the stack is not empty when he or she calls the *pop* operation. If unsure of the state of the stack, the programmer may write

```
if not empty(s)
    then x:= pop(s)
    else { take remedial action }
```

If the programmer unwittingly does call *pop* with an empty stack, the function will print the error message *stack underflow* and execution will halt. Although this is an unfortunate state of affairs, it is far better than what would occur had the *if* statement in the *pop* routine been omitted entirely. In that case, the value of *s.top* would be 0 and an attempt would be made to access the nonexistent element *s.item*[0].

A programmer should always provide for the almost certain possibility of error by including meaningful diagnostics. By doing so, if and when an error does occur, the programmer will be able to pinpoint its source and take corrective action immediately.

However, within the context of a given problem, it may not be necessary to halt execution immediately upon the detection of underflow. Instead, it might be more desirable for the *pop* routine to signal the calling program that an underflow has occurred. Upon detecting this signal, the calling routine can take corrective action. Let us call the procedure that pops the stack and returns an indication as to whether underflow has occurred, *popandtest*.

```
procedure popandtest (var s: stack; var x: integer; var und: boolean);
begin
    if empty(s) then und:= true
        else begin
                und:= false;
                x:= s.item[s.top];
                s.top:= s.top - 1
            end {else begin}
end {procedure popandtest};
```

In the calling program the programmer would write

```
popandtest (s, x, underflow);
if underflow
    then {        take corrective action        }
    else { x is the element popped off the stack }
```

Implementing the *push* Operation

Let us now examine the *push* operation. It seems that this operation should be quite easy to implement using the array representation of a stack. A first attempt at a *push* procedure might be the following:

```
procedure push (var s: stack; x: integer);
begin
      s.top:= s.top + 1;
      s.item[s.top]:= x
end {procedure push};
```

This routine makes room for the item x to be pushed onto the stack by incrementing $s.top$ by 1, and then it inserts x into the array $s.item$.

The procedure directly implements the *push* operation, which was introduced in the preceding section. Yet, as it stands, it is quite incorrect. It allows a subtle error to creep in, caused by using the array representation of the stack. See if you can spot this error before reading further.

Recall that a stack is a dynamic structure that is constantly allowed to grow and shrink and thus change its size. An array, on the other hand, is a fixed object of predetermined size. Thus it is quite conceivable that a stack will outgrow the array that was set aside to contain it. This will occur when the array is full, that is, when the stack contains as many elements as the array—and an attempt is made to push yet another element onto the stack. The result of such an attempt is called an *overflow*.

Assume that the array is full and that the Pascal *push* routine is called. The full array is indicated by the condition $s.top=100$, so that the 100th (and last) element of the array is the current top of the stack. When *push* is called, an attempt is made to increase the value of $s.top$ to 101. Since 101 is outside the subrange $0..100$ which is the type of $s.top$, this attempt will result in an error and produce an appropriate error message. This message is totally meaningless within the context of the original algorithm, because it does not indicate an error in the algorithm but rather in the computer implementation of that algorithm. It would be far more desirable for the programmer to provide for the possibility of overflow and to print out a more meaningful message.

The *push* procedure may therefore be revised so that it reads as follows:

```
procedure push (var s: stack; x: integer);
begin
    if s.top = maxstack
      then error ('stack overflow')
      else begin
               s.top:= s.top + 1;
               s.item[s.top] := x
           end {else begin}
end {procedure push};
```

Here, a check is made to determine whether the array is full before attempting to push another element onto the stack. The array will be full if $s.top=maxstack$.

You should again note that if and when the overflow condition is detected in *push*, execution will halt immediately after the printing of an error message. This action, as in the case of *pop*, may not be the most desirable. It might, in some cases, make more sense for the calling routine to be able to invoke the push operation with the instructions

```
pushandtest (s, x, overflow);
if overflow
    then {Overflow has been detected. x was not }
         {pushed on stack. Take remedial action.}
    else {x was successfully pushed on the stack }
         {            continue processing.        }
```

This will allow the calling program to proceed after the call to *pushandtest* whether or not overflow was detected. The procedure *pushandtest* is left as an exercise for the reader.

It is useful to compare this *push* procedure with the earlier *pop* function. Although the overflow and underflow conditions are handled similarly in the two routines, there is a fundamental difference between them. Underflow indicates that the *pop* operation cannot be performed on the stack and may indicate an error in the algorithm or the data. No other implementation or representation of the stack will cure the underflow condition. Rather, the entire problem must be rethought. (Of course, it is possible that the programmer wishes an underflow to occur as a signal for ending one process and beginning another. However, in such a case, the *popandtest* procedure rather than the *pop* function should be used.)

Overflow, however, is not a condition that is applicable to a stack as an abstract data structure. As we saw in the preceding section, it is always possible to push an element onto a stack because a stack is just an ordered collection and there is no limit to the number of elements such a collection can contain. The possibility of an overflow is introduced when a stack is implemented by an array with only a finite number of elements, thereby prohibiting the growth of the stack beyond that number. It may very well be that the algorithm which the programmer used is correct; he or she just did not anticipate that the stack would become so large. Thus, in some cases, a possible way to correct an overflow condition is to change the value of the constant *maxstack* in the program so that the array field *item* contains more elements. There is no need to change the routines *pop* or *push*, because they refer to whatever data structure was declared for the type *stack* in the program declarations. *push* also refers to the constant *maxstack* rather than the actual value 100.

However, more often than not, an overflow does indicate an error in the program which cannot be attributed to a simple lack of space. The program may be in an infinite loop where things are constantly being pushed onto the stack and nothing is ever popped. Thus the stack will outgrow the array bound no matter how high that bound is set. The programmer should always check that this is not the case before indiscriminately raising the array bound.

Let us now look at our last operation on stacks, *stacktop(s)*, which returns the top element of a stack without removing if from the stack. As we noted in the preceding section, *stacktop* is not really a primitive operation, because it can be decomposed into the two operations:

```
x:= pop(s);
push (s,x)
```

However, this is a rather awkward way to retrieve the top element of a stack. Why not ignore the decomposition noted above and directly retrieve the proper value? Of course, a check for the empty stack and underflow must then be explicitly stated, because the test is no longer handled by a call to *pop*.

We present a Pascal function *stacktop* as follows:

```
function stacktop (s: stack): integer;
begin
    if empty (s)
        then error('stack underflow')
        else stacktop:= s.item[s.top]
end {function stacktop};
```

You may wonder why we bother writing a separate routine *stacktop* when a reference to *s.item*[*s.top*] would serve just as well. There are several reasons for this. First, the routine *stacktop* incorporates a test for underflow, so that no mysterious errors will occur if the stack is empty. Second, it allows the programmer to use a stack without worrying about its internal makeup. Third, if a different implementation of a stack is introduced, the programmer need not comb through all the places where he or she referred to *s.item*[*s.top*] to make those references compatible with the new implementation. The programmer need only change the *stacktop* routine.

Stacks of Differing Types

As we have implemented a stack, a stack can contain only integers. We have noted that a stack of elements of another type may be obtained by altering the type of the *item* field. For example, a stack of real numbers is declared by

```
const maxstack = 100;
type  stack = record
                  item: array[1..maxstack] of real;
                  top: 0..maxstack
              end;
var   s: stack;
```

However, this would require a change to all the routines that manipulate a stack. For example, the function header of *pop* would now become

```
function pop (var s: stack): real;
```

while the procedure header of *push* must be changed to

procedure push (**var** s: stack; x: real);

We would like to specify routines such as *pop* and *push* so that they work regardless of the type of the items on the stack. This can be done very simply in Pascal by introducing a new type *stackitem* and defining a stack in terms of this new type, as follows:

```
type stackitem = integer;
     stack = record
                item: array[1..maxstack] of stackitem;
                top: 0..maxstack
             end;
```

The headers of the *pop* and *push* routines would be

function pop (**var** s: stack): stackitem;

and

procedure push (**var** s: stack; x: stackitem);

The same routines can be used to manipulate a stack of reals by simply changing the type definition of *stackitem* to

type stackitem = real;

No other change is necessary, neither in the type definition of *stack* nor in the stack manipulation routines. Once these routines have been written in this way, they can be used in any program that manipulates stacks. However, some Pascal compilers may require that any variables popped or pushed off the stack must be declared to be of type *stackitem*.

It is also possible to allow the same stack to contain different types of elements by using variant records. For example, to define a stack that can contain integers and characters, we write

```
type stackitem = record
                    case itemtype: (int,ch) of
                        int: (iitem: integer);
                        ch: (citem: char)
                 end {record};
```

No changes need be made to the definition of *stack* or the *push*, *empty*, or *stacktop* routines. However, since a Pascal function may only return a scalar type, we must write a procedure *popsub* to replace the function *pop*. The header for this procedure is

procedure popsub(**var** s: stack; **var** x: stackitem);

We leave the body of the procedure as an exercise for the reader.

Given the foregoing definition for *stackitem*, a program segment to print an item popped off a stack would be

```
var x: stackitem;
    s: stack;

    . . .

popsub(s, x);
case x.itemtype of
    int: write (x.iitem);
    ch: write (x.citem)
end {case}
```

EXERCISES

1. Write Pascal routines that use the routines presented in this chapter to implement the operations of Exercise 2.1.1.

2. Given a sequence of *push* and *pop* operations and an integer representing the size of an array in which a stack is to be implemented, design an algorithm to determine whether or not overflow occurs. The algorithm should not use a stack. Implement the algorithm as a Pascal program.

3. Implement the algorithms of Exercises 2.1.3 and 2.1.4 as Pascal programs.

4. Show how to implement a stack of integers in Pascal by using an array s:*array* $[0..100]$ *of stackitem*, where $s[0]$ is used to contain the index of the top element of the stack and where $s[1]$ through $s[100]$ contain the elements on the stack. Write a declaration and routines *pop*, *push*, *empty*, *popandtest*, *stacktop*, and *pushandtest* for this implementation.

5. Implement a stack in Pascal in which each item on the stack is a varying number of integers. Choose a Pascal data structure for such a stack and design *push* and *pop* routines for it.

6. Consider a language that does not have arrays but does have stacks as a data type. That is, one can declare

   var s: stack;

   and the *push*, *pop*, *popandtest*, and *stacktop* operations are defined. Show how a one-dimensional array can be implemented by using these operations on two stacks.

7. Design a method for keeping two stacks within a single linear array s:*array* $[1..spacesize]$ in such a way that neither stack overflows until all of memory is used and an entire stack is never shifted to a different location within the array. Write Pascal routines *push*1, *push*2, *pop*1, and *pop*2 to manipulate the two stacks. (*Hint*: The two stacks grow toward each other.)

8. The Bashemin Parking Garage contains a single lane which can hold up to 10 cars. There is only a single entrance/exit to the garage at one end of the lane. If a customer arrives to pick up a car that is not nearest the exit, all cars blocking its path are moved out, the customer's car is driven out, and the other cars are restored in the order they were in originally.

   Write a program that processes a group of input lines. Each input line contains an '*a*' for arrival or '*d*' for departure, and a license plate number. Cars are assumed to arrive and depart in the order specified by the input. The program should print a message whenever a car arrives or departs. When a car arrives, the message should specify whether or not there is room for the car in the garage. If there is no room, the car leaves without entering the garage. When a car departs, the message should include the number of times that the car was moved out of the garage to allow other cars to depart.

3. AN EXAMPLE: INFIX, POSTFIX, AND PREFIX

Basic Definitions and Examples

In this section we examine a major application of stacks. Although it is one of the most prominent applications, it is by no means the only one. The reason that we consider this application is that it illustrates so well the different types of stacks and the various operations and functions we have defined upon them. The example is also an important topic of computer science in its own right.

Before proceeding with the algorithms and programs of this section it will be necessary to provide some groundwork. Consider the sum of A and B. We think of applying the *operator* "+" to the *operands* A and B and write the sum as $A+B$. This particular representation is called *infix*. There are two alternative notations for expressing the sum of A and B using the symbols A, B, and +. These are

$$+ A\ B \qquad \text{prefix}$$
$$A\ B + \qquad \text{postfix}$$

The prefixes "pre," "post," and "in" refer to the relative position of the operator with respect to the two operands. In prefix notation the operator precedes the two operands, in postfix notation the operator follows the two operands, and in infix notation the operator is between the two operands. The prefix and postfix notations are not really as awkward to use as they might first appear. For example, if we were using a Pascal function to return the sum of the two arguments a and b, we might invoke it by $add(a, b)$. The operator add precedes the operands a and b.

Let us now consider some additional examples. The evaluation of the expression $A+B*C$, as written in standard infix notation, requires knowledge of which of the two operations, + or *, is to be performed first. In the case of + and * we "know" that multiplication is to be done before addition (in the absence of parentheses to the contrary). Thus $A+B*C$ is to be interpreted as $A+(B*C)$ unless otherwise specified. We say that multiplication takes *precedence* over addition. Suppose that we would now like to rewrite $A+B*C$ in postfix. Applying the rules of precedence, we first convert the portion of the expression that is evaluated first, namely the multiplication. By doing this conversion in stages, we obtain

$A+(B*C)$	parentheses for emphasis
$A+(BC*)$	convert the multiplication
$A(BC*)+$	convert the addition
$ABC*+$	postfix form

CHAP. 2: THE STACK

The only rules to remember during the conversion process is that the operations with highest precedence are converted first and that after a portion of the expression has been converted to postfix it is to be treated as a single operand. Let us now consider the same example with the precedence of operators reversed by the deliberate insertion of parentheses.

$(A+B)*C$	infix form
$(AB+)*C$	convert the addition
$(AB+)C*$	convert the multiplication
$AB+C*$	postfix form

In the example above, the addition was converted before the multiplication because of the parentheses. In going from $(A+B)*C$ to $(AB+)*C$, A and B are the operands and $+$ is the operator. In going from $(AB+)*C$ to $(AB+)C*$, $(AB+)$ and C are the operands and $*$ is the operator. The rules for converting from infix to postfix are simple provided that you know the order of precedence.

We consider five binary operations: addition, subtraction, multiplication, division, and exponentiation. The first four are available in Pascal. The fifth, exponentiation, will be represented by the operator $. The value of the expression $A\$B$ is A raised to the B power, so that $3\$2$ is 9. The other four operations are denoted by the usual operators $+$, $-$, $*$, and $/$. For these binary operators the following is the order of precedence (highest to lowest):

exponentiation
multiplication/division
addition/subtraction

By using parentheses we can override the default precedence.

We give the following additional examples of converting from infix to postfix. Be sure that you understand each of these examples (and can do them on your own) before proceeding to the remainder of this section. We follow the convention that when unparenthesized operators of the same precedence are scanned, the order is assumed to be left to right except in the case of exponentiation, where the order is assumed to be from right to left. Thus $A+B+C$ means $(A+B)+C$ and $A\$B\$C$ means $A\$(B\$C)$.

Infix	Postfix
$A+B$	$AB+$
$A+B-C$	$AB+C-$
$(A+B)*(C-D)$	$AB+CD-*$
$A\$B*C-D+E/F/(G+H)$	$AB\$C*D-EF/GH+/+$
$((A+B)*C-(D-E))\$(F+G)$	$AB+C*DE--FG+\$$
$A-B/(C*D\$E)$	$ABCDE\$*/-$

The precedence rules for converting an expression from infix to prefix are identical. The only change from postfix conversion is that the operator is placed before the operands rather than after them. We present the prefix forms of the foregoing expressions. Again, you should attempt to make the transformations on your own.

Infix	Prefix
$A+B$	$+AB$
$A+B-C$	$-+ABC$
$(A+B)*(C-D)$	$*+AB-CD$
$A\$B*C-D+E/F/(G+H)$	$+-*\$ABCD//EF+GH$
$((A+B)*C-(D-E))\$(F+G)$	$\$-*+ABC-DE+FG$
$A-B/(C*D\$E)$	$-A/B*C\$DE$

Note that the prefix form of a complex expression is not the mirror image of the postfix form, as can be seen from the second of the foregoing examples, $A+B-C$. Henceforth, we shall be concerned with the postfix transformations and will leave to the reader as exercises most of the work involving prefix.

One point immediately obvious about the postfix form of an expression is that it requires no parentheses. Let us consider the two expressions $A+(B*C)$ and $(A+B)*C$. Whereas the parentheses in one of the two expressions are superfluous [by convention $A+B*C = A+(B*C)$], the parentheses in the second expression are necessary to avoid confusion with the first. The postfix forms of these expressions are

Infix	Postfix
$A+(B*C)$	$ABC*+$
$(A+B)*C$	$AB+C*$

There are no parentheses in either of the two transformed expressions. A close look tells us that the order of the operators in the postfix expressions determines the actual order of operations in evaluating the expression, making the use of parentheses unnecessary. In going from infix to postfix we are sacrificing the ability to note at a glance the operands associated with a particular operator. We are gaining, however, an unambiguous form of the original expression without the use of cumbersome parentheses. In fact, you may argue that the postfix form of the original expression might look simpler were it not for the fact that it appears difficult to evaluate. For example, how do we know that if $A=3$, $B=4$, and $C=5$ in the examples above, we have 3 4 5 * + =23 and 3 4 + 5 * =35?

Evaluating a Postfix Expression

The answer to this question lies in the development of an algorithm for evaluating expressions in postfix. Each operator in a postfix string refers to the previous two operands in the string. (Of course, either of these two operands may itself be the result of applying a previous operator.) Suppose that each time we read an operand we push it onto a stack. When we reach an operator, its operands will then be the top two elements on the stack. We can then pop these two elements, perform the indicated operation on them, and push the result on the stack so that it will be available for use as an operand of the next operator. The following algorithm evaluates an expression in postfix using this method.

```
Initialize a stack, opndstk, to be empty;
    {scan the input string reading one element at a}
    {              time into symb              }
while there are more characters in the input string
    do begin
            symb := next input character;
            if symb is an operand
                then push (opndstk, symb)
                else {symb is an operator}
                    begin
                        opnd2 := pop (opndstk);
                        opnd1 := pop (opndstk);
                        value := result of applying symb
                                    to opnd1 and opnd2;
                        push (opndstk, value)
                    end {else begin}
        end {while...do begin};
    result := pop (opndstk)
```

Let us now consider an example. Suppose that we are asked to evaluate the following expression in postfix:

$$6\ 2\ 3\ +\ -\ 3\ 8\ 2\ /\ +\ *\ 2\ \$\ 3\ +$$

We show the contents of the stack *opndstk* and the variables *symb*, *opnd*1, *opnd*2, and *value* after each successive iteration of the loop. The top of *opndstk* is to the right.

symb	opnd1	opnd2	value	opndstk
6				6
2				6,2
3				6,2,3
+	2	3	5	6,5
–	6	5	1	1
3	6	5	1	1,3
8	6	5	1	1,3,8
2	6	5	1	1,3,8,2
/	8	2	4	1,3,4
+	3	4	7	1,7
*	1	7	7	7
2	1	7	7	7,2
$	7	2	49	49
3	7	2	49	49,3
+	49	3	52	52

Let us make some observations about the example above which will aid us in translating the algorithm into a program. As its name implies, *opndstk* is a stack of operands. Each operand is pushed onto the stack when encountered. Therefore, the maximum size of the stack is the number of operands that appear in the input expression. However, in dealing with most postfix expressions the actual size of the stack needed is less than this maximum, because an operator removes operands from the stack. In the previous example the stack never contained more than four elements, despite the fact that eight operands appeared in the postfix expression.

Program to Evaluate a Postfix Expression

We are now prepared to plan a program to evaluate an expression in postfix notation. There are a number of questions we must consider before we can actually write the program. A primary consideration, as in all programs, is to define precisely the form and restrictions, if any, on the input. Usually, the programmer is presented with the form of the input and is required to design a program to accommodate the given data. On the other hand, we are in the fortunate position of being able to choose the form of our input. This enables us to construct a program that is not overburdened with transformation problems that overshadow the actual intent of the routine. Had we been confronted with data in a form that is awkward and cumbersome to work with, we could relegate the transformations to various procedures and use the output of these procedures as input to our primary routine. In the "real world," recognition and transformation of input is a major concern.

Let us assume in this case that each input line is in the form of a string of digits and operator symbols. We assume that operands are single non-negative digits (e.g., 0, 1, 2, ..., 8, 9). For example, an input line might contain 345*+ in the first five columns with the remaining columns left blank. We would like to write a program that reads input lines of this format, as long as there are any remaining, and prints out for each line the original input string and the result of the evaluated expression.

Since the symbols are read as characters, we must find a method to convert the operand·characters to numbers and the operator characters to operations. For example, we must have a method for converting the character '5' to the number 5 and the character '+' to the addition operation. The conversion of a character to an integer can be handled easily in Pascal. If x:*char* is a digit in Pascal, the expression $ord(x) - ord(\text{'0'})$ yields the numerical value of that digit. To convert an operator symbol into the corresponding action, we use a function *oper* which accepts an operator and two operands as input parameters. The header for this function is

function oper(operator: char; op1, op2: real): real;

The function returns the value of the expression obtained by applying the operator to the two operands. The body of the function will be given below.

The body of the main program might be the following. The constant *maxcols* is the number of columns in an input line.

```
program evaluate (input, output);
const maxcols = 80;
type exprtype = array [1..maxcols] of char;
var   expr: exprtype;
      position: 1..maxcols;
function eval (expr: exprtype): real;
          {body of eval goes here}
begin
   while not eof
      do begin
             {process next expression}
             for position:= 1 to maxcols
                do read (expr[position] );
             readln;
             writeln ('original postfix expression is     ');
             for position:= 1 to maxcols
                do write (expr[position] );
             writeln ('value of expression is     ', eval (expr));
             writeln
         end {while...do begin}
end {program evaluate}.
```

(Note that we cannot print the value of *expr* in a single statement because its type is an unpacked, rather than a packed, array. If *exprtype* were defined as a packed array, we could print the value of *expr* with the single statement *write(expr)*. However, under some Pascal compilers, we would then be unable to execute *read(expr[position])* but would have to execute *read(c); expr[position]:=c* instead. Some compilers, however, will allow *write(expr)* even if *expr* is not packed.)

The main part of the program is, of course, the function *eval*, which is presented below. The routine is merely the Pascal implementation of the evaluation algorithm, taking into account the specific environment and format of the input data and calculated outputs. *eval* calls on a function *opnd*, which determines whether or not its argument is an operand.

```
function eval (expr: exprtype): real;
          {eval accepts a postfix expression as input}
          {and returns the value of the expression as}
          {              a real number              }
```

```
const maxstack = maxcols;
type  stack = record
                  item: array[1..maxstack] of real;
                  top: 0..maxstack
              end;
var   opndstk: stack;
      opnd1, opnd2, value: real;
      symb: char;
      position: 1..maxcols;
function pop (var s: stack): real;
    { body of pop }
procedure push (var s: stack; x: real);
    {body of push}
function opnd (symb: char): boolean;
    {body of opnd}
function oper (symb: char; op1,op2: real): real;
    { body of oper }
begin {function eval}
    opndstk.top:= 0;
    position:= 1;
    symb:= expr[position];
    {position indicates the current position in the}
    { expression and symb is the current symbol. }
    {Start scanning symbols until a blank is found}
    while symb <> ' '
        do begin
               if opnd(symb)
                  then begin {operand is found}
                           value:= ord(symb) - ord('0');
                           push(opndstk, value)
                       end {then begin}
                  else begin {operator is found}
                           opnd2:= pop(opndstk);
                           opnd1:= pop(opndstk);
                           value:= oper(symb, opnd1, opnd2);
                           push(opndstk, value)
                       end { else begin };
               if position < maxcols
                  then begin
                           position:= position + 1;
                           symb:= expr[position]
                       end {then begin}
                  else symb:= ' '
           end {while...do begin};
    eval:= pop(opndstk)
end  {function eval};
```

For completeness, we present the functions *opnd* and *oper*. The function *opnd* simply checks if its argument is a digit:

```
function opnd(symb: char): boolean;
begin
    if (ord(symb) >= ord('0')) and (ord(symb) <= ord('9'))
        then opnd:= true
        else opnd:= false
end {function opnd};
```

The function *oper* checks to ensure that its first argument is a valid operator and, if it is, determines the results of its operation on the next two arguments. For exponentiation, we assume the existence of a function *expon*(*op1, op2*: *real*): *real*. The function *oper* uses a set of characters which is not implemented in some Pascal compilers, but it can easily be modified to eliminate this feature.

```
function oper(symb: char; op1,op2: real): real;
function expon(op1, op2: real): real;
    {body of expon}
begin
    if symb in ['+', '*', '-', '/', '$']
        then case symb of
                '+': oper:= op1 + op2;
                '*': oper:= op1 * op2;
                '-': oper:= op1 - op2;
                '/': oper:= op1 / op2;
                '$': oper:= expon(op1,op2)
            end {then case}
        else error ('illegal operator')
end {function oper};
```

Limitations of the Program

Before we leave the program, we should note some of its deficiencies. Understanding what a program cannot do is as important as knowing what it can do. It should be obvious that attempting to use a program to solve a problem for which it was not intended will lead to chaos. Worse still is the case where an attempt is made to solve a problem with an incorrect program only to have the program produce incorrect results, without the slightest trace of an error message. In these cases the programmer has no indication that the results are wrong, and may therefore make faulty judgments based on those results. For this reason, it is important for the programmer to understand the limitations of a program.

A major criticism of this program is that it does nothing in terms of error detection and recovery. If the data on each input line form a correct postfix expression, the program will work. Suppose, however, that one input line has too many operators or operands or that they are not in a proper sequence. These problems could come about as a result of someone innocently using the program on a postfix expression that contains two-digit numbers, yielding an excessive number of operands. Or possibly the user of the program was under the impression that negative numbers could be handled by the program and that they are to be entered with the minus sign, the same sign that is used to represent subtraction. These minus signs will be treated as subtraction operators, resulting in an excess number of operators. Depending on the specific type of error, the computer may take one of several actions (e.g., halt execution, print erroneous results, etc.). Suppose that at the final statement of the program, the stack *opndstk* is not empty. We will get no error messages (because we asked for none) and *eval* will return a numerical value for an expression that was probably incorrectly stated in the first place. Suppose that one of the calls to the *pop* routine raises the *underflow* condition. Since we did not use the *popandtest* routine to pop elements from the stack, our program will stop. This seems unreasonable since faulty data on one line should not prevent the processing of additional lines. By no means are these the only problems that could arise. As exercises, you may wish to write programs that accommodate less restrictive inputs and some others that will test for and detect some of the errors listed above.

Converting an Expression from Infix to Postfix

We have thus far presented routines to evaluate a postfix expression. Although we have discussed a method for transforming infix to postfix, we have not as yet presented an algorithm for doing so. It is to this task that we now direct our attention. Once such an algorithm has been constructed, we will have the capability of reading an infix expression and evaluating it by first converting it to postfix and then evaluating the postfix expression.

In our previous discussion, we mentioned that subexpressions within innermost parentheses must first be converted to postfix, so that they can then be treated as single operands. In this fashion, parentheses can be successively eliminated until the entire expression is converted. The last pair of parentheses to be opened within a group of parentheses encloses the first subexpression within that group to be transformed. This last-in, first-out behavior should immediately suggest the use of a stack.

Consider the two infix expressions $A+B*C$ and $(A+B)*C$ and their respective postfix versions $ABC*+$ and $AB+C*$. In each case the order of the operands is the same as the order of the operands in the original infix expressions. In scanning the first expression, $A+B*C$, the first operand A can be immediately inserted into the postfix expression. Clearly, the + symbol cannot be inserted until after its second operand, which has not yet been scanned, is inserted. Therefore, it must be stored away to be retrieved and inserted in its proper position. When the operand B is scanned, it is inserted immediately after A. Now, however, two operands have been scanned. What prevents the symbol + from being retrieved and inserted? The answer is, of course, the * symbol, which follows and has precedence over +. In the case of the second expression the closing parenthesis indicates that the + operation should be performed first. Remember that in postfix, unlike infix, the operator that appears earlier in the string is the one that is applied first.

Let us assume the existence of a function $prcd(op1, op2: char): boolean$, where $op1$ and $op2$ are characters representing operators. This function returns $true$ if $op1$ has precedence over $op2$ when $op1$ appears to the left of $op2$ in an infix expression without parentheses. $prcd(op1, op2)$ returns $false$ otherwise. For example, $prcd('*','+')$ and $prcd('+','+')$ are $true$ while $prcd('+','*')$ is $false$. Let us now present an outline of an algorithm to convert an infix string without parentheses into a postfix string. Since we are assuming no parentheses in our input string, the only governor of the order in which operators appear in the postfix string is precedence.

```
1    initialize the stack opstk to empty;
2    initialize the postfix string to '';
3    while there are more input symbols
4        do begin
5                read(symb);
6            if symb is an operand
7                then add symb to the postfix string
8                else { the symbol is an operator }
9                    begin
10                       while (not empty(opstk)) and
                                 (prcd(stacktop(opstk),symb))
11                           do begin
12                               topsymb:= pop(opstk);
                                 { topsymb has precedence over }
                                 {  symb so it can be added to  }
                                 {      the postfix string       }
13                               add topsymb to the postfix string
14                           end {while...do begin};
                          {   At this point, either opstk is empty or   }
                          { symb has precedence over stacktop(opstk). }
                          {   We cannot output symb into the postfix   }
                          {      string until we have read the next     }
                          { operator, which may have precedence.  We }
                          {          must therefore store symb          }
15                       push (opstk,symb)
16                   end {else begin}
17            end {while...do begin};
           {   At this point, we have reached the end of the   }
           { string. We must output the operators remaining }
           {      on the stack into the postfix string.        }
18    while not empty(opstk)
19        do begin
20                topsymb:= pop(opstk);
```

```
21            add topsymb to the postfix string
22        end {while…do begin}
```

Simulate the algorithm with such infix strings as '*a*b+c*d*' and '*a+b*cde*' [where '$' represents exponentiation and *prcd*('$','$')=*false*] to convince yourself that it is correct. Note that at each point of the simulation, an operator on the stack has a lower precedence than all the operators above it. This is because the initial empty stack trivially satisfies this condition, and an operator is pushed onto the stack (line 15) only if the operator currently on top of the stack has a lower precedence than the incoming operator.

You should also note the liberty that we have taken in line 10 in forming the condition

$$(not\ empty(opstk))\ and\ (\ prcd(stacktop(opstk), symb))$$

Later in this section, we will explain why such a condition should not be used in an actual program.

What modification must be made to this algorithm to accommodate parentheses? The answer is surprisingly little. When an opening parenthesis is read, it must be pushed onto the stack. This can be done by establishing the convention that *prcd*(*op*,'(')=*false*, for any operator symbol *op* other than a right parenthesis. This ensures that an operator symbol appearing after a left parenthesis will be pushed onto the stack.

When a closing parenthesis is read, all operators up to the first opening parenthesis must be popped from the stack into the postfix string. This can be done by setting *prcd*(*op*,')')=*true* for all operators *op* other than a left parenthesis. When these operators have been popped off the stack and the opening parenthesis is uncovered, special action must be taken. The opening parenthesis must be popped off the stack, and it and the closing parenthesis must be discarded rather than placed in the postfix string or on the stack. Let us set *prcd*('(',')') to *false*. This will ensure that upon reaching an opening parenthesis, the loop beginning at line 10 will be skipped, so that the opening parenthesis will not be inserted into the postfix string. Execution will therefore proceed to line 15. However, since the closing parenthesis should not be pushed onto the stack, line 15 will be replaced with the statement

```
15                    if (empty(opstk)) or (symb <> ')')
                      then push (opstk, symb)
                      else topsymb := pop(opstk)
```

With the foregoing conventions for the *prcd* function and the revision to line 15, the algorithm can be used to convert any infix string to postfix. We summarize the precedence rules for parentheses:

prcd('(',*op*)=*false*	for any operator *op*
prcd(*op*,'(')=*false*	for any operator *op* other than ')'
prcd(*op*,')')=*true*	for any operator *op* other than '('
prcd(')','(')=*undefined*	(an attempt to compare the two indicates an error).

We illustrate this algorithm on some examples:

Ex. 1: $A+B*C$

The contents of *symb*, the postfix string, and *opstk* are shown after scanning each symbol. *opstk* is shown with its top to the right.

	symb	postfix string	opstk
1	A	A	
2	$+$	A	$+$
3	B	AB	$+$
4	$*$	AB	$+*$
5	C	ABC	$+*$
6		$ABC*$	$+$
7		$ABC*+$	

Lines 1, 3, and 5 correspond to the scanning of an operand, so the symbol (*symb*) is immediately placed on the postfix string. In line 2 an operator was scanned and the stack was found to be empty, so the operator is placed on the stack. In line 4 the precedence of the new symbol (*) was greater than the precedence of the symbol on the top of the stack (+), so the new symbol is pushed onto the stack. In steps 6 and 7 the input string was empty, so the stack is popped and its contents placed on the postfix string.

Ex. 2: $(A+B)*C$

symb	postfix string	opstk
$($		$($
A	A	$($
$+$	A	$(+$
B	AB	$(+$
$)$	$AB+$	
$*$	$AB+$	$*$
C	$AB+C$	$*$
	$AB+C*$	

In this example, when the right parenthesis is encountered, the stack is popped until a left parenthesis is encountered, at which point both parentheses are discarded. By using parentheses to force an order of precedence different than the default, the order of appearance of the operators in the postfix string is different than in Example 1. We present an additional example on the next page.

Why does the conversion algorithm seem so involved, whereas the evaluation algorithm seems so simple? The answer is that the former converts from one order of precedence (governed by the *prcd* function and the appearance of parentheses) to the natural order (i.e., the operation to be executed first appears first). Because of the many combinations of elements at the top of the stack (if not empty) and possible incoming symbol, a large

Ex. 3: $((A-(B+C))*D)\$(E+F)$

symb	postfix string	opstk
(		(
(		((
A	A	((
-	A	((-
(	A	((-(
B	AB	((-(
+	AB	((-(+
C	ABC	((-(+
)	ABC+	((-
)	ABC+-	(
*	ABC+-	(*
D	ABC+-D	(*
)	ABC+-D*	
$	ABC+-D*	$
(	ABC+-D*	$(
E	ABC+-D*E	$(
+	ABC+-D*E	$(+
F	ABC+-D*EF	$(+
)	ABC+-D*EF+	$
	ABC+-D*EF+$	

number of statements are necessary to cover each possibility. In the latter algorithm, on the other hand, the operators appear in precisely the order they are to be executed. For this reason the operands can be stacked until an operator is found, at which point the operation is performed immediately.

The motivation behind the conversion algorithm is the desire to output the operators in the order in which they are to be executed. In solving this problem by hand, we could follow vague instructions that require us to convert from the inside out. This works very well for human beings doing a problem with pencil and paper (if they do not become confused or make a mistake). However, when writing a program or an algorithm, we must be more precise in our instructions. We cannot be sure that we have reached the innermost parentheses or the operator with the highest precedence until we have actually scanned all the symbols. At that time, we must backtrack to some previous point.

Rather than backtrack continuously, we make use of the stack to "remember" the operators encountered previously. If an incoming operator is of greater precedence than the one on top of the stack this new operator is pushed onto the stack. This means that when all the elements in the stack are finally popped, this new operator will precede the former top in the postfix string (which is correct, because it has higher precedence). If, on the other hand, the precedence of the new operator is less than that of the top of the stack, the operator at the top of the stack should be executed

88

first. Therefore, the top of the stack is popped and the incoming symbol is compared with the new top, and so on. By including parentheses in our input string, we may override the order of operations. Thus when a left parenthesis is scanned, it is pushed on the stack. When its associated right parenthesis is found, all the operators between the two parentheses are placed on the output string, because they are to be executed before any operators appearing after the parentheses.

Program to Convert an Expression from Infix to Postfix

There are two things that we must do before we actually start writing a program. The first is to define precisely the format of the input and output. The second is to construct, or at least define, those routines that the main routine depends upon. We assume that our input will be strings of characters, one string per input line. The end of the string will be signaled by the occurrence of a blank. For the sake of simplicity, we assume that all operands are single-character letters or digits. All operators and parentheses are represented by themselves and $ represents exponentiation. The output will be an array of characters. These conventions will make the output of the conversion process suitable for the evaluation process provided that all the single-character operands in the initial infix string are digits.

In transforming the conversion algorithm into a program, we make use of several routines. Among these are *empty*, *pop*, *push*, and *popandtest*, all suitably modified so that the elements on the stack are characters. We also make use of the function *opnd*, which returns *true* if its argument is an operand and *false* otherwise. This function must also be slightly modified from the version introduced in the program for the evaluation algorithm so that it recognizes a letter as well as a digit as an operand. These simple modifications are left to the reader.

Similarly, the *prcd* function is left to the reader as an exercise. It accepts two single-character operator symbols as arguments and returns *true* if the first has precedence over the second when it appears to the left of the second in an infix string and *false* otherwise. The function should, of course, incorporate the parentheses conventions which we previously introduced.

Once these auxiliary subroutines and functions have been written, we can write the program that calls a conversion procedure *postfix* and the function *postfix* itself. We assume that the program reads a line containing an expression in infix, calls the routine *postfix*, and prints the original string and the postfix string. The body of the main routine follows:

```
program conv (input, output);
const maxcols = 80;
type exprtype = array [1..maxcols] of char;
var  instring, poststring: exprtype;
     position: 1..maxcols;
```

```
        procedure postfix (infix: exprtype; var out: exprtype);
            {body of postfix}
        begin {program conv}
            while not eof
                do begin {process next expression}
                        for position:= 1 to maxcols
                            do read (instring[position]);
                        readln;
                        write ('infix expression is    ');
                        for position:= 1 to maxcols
                            do write (instring[position]);
                        writeln;
                        postfix (instring, poststring);
                        write ('postfix equivalent is    ');
                        for position:= 1 to maxcols
                            do write (poststring[position]);
                        writeln;
                        writeln
                    end {while...do begin}
        end {program conv}.
```

The postfix routine that implements the conversion appears below.

```
        procedure postfix (infix: exprtype; var out: exprtype);
        const maxstack = maxcols;
        type  stack = record
                            item: array[1..maxstack] of char;
                            top: 0..maxstack
                        end;
        var   opstk: stack;
              position, outlen: 0..maxcols;
              und: boolean;
              symb, topsymb: char;

        function empty (s: stack): boolean;
                { body of empty }

        function opnd (symb: char): boolean;
                { body of opnd }

        function pop (var s: stack): char;
                { body of pop }

        function prcd (op1,op2: char): boolean;
                { body of prcd }

        procedure push (var s: stack; x: char);
                { body of push }

        procedure popandtest (var s: stack; var x: char; var und: boolean);
                { body of popandtest }
```

```
begin {procedure postfix}
      topsymb:= '+';
      opstk.top:= 0; { stack is initially empty }
      { initialize postfix string to blanks }
      for position:= 1 to maxcols
          do out[position]:= ' ';
      position:= 1;
      outlen:= 0;
      { begin scanning symbols until a blank is found }
      symb:= infix[position];
      while symb <> ' '
          do begin
               if opnd(symb)
                   then begin {operand is found}
                            outlen:= outlen + 1;
                            out[outlen]:= symb
                        end {then begin}
                   else begin {operator}
                            popandtest(opstk,topsymb,und);
                            while (not und) and (prcd(topsymb,symb))
                                do begin
                                     outlen:= outlen + 1;
                                     out[outlen]:= topsymb;
                                     popandtest(opstk,topsymb,und)
                                   end {while...do begin};
                            if not und
                                then push(opstk, topsymb);
                            if und or (symb <> ')')
                                then push(opstk, symb)
                                else topsymb:= pop(opstk)
                        end {else begin};
               if position < maxcols
                   then begin
                            position:= position + 1;
                            symb:= infix[position]
                        end {then begin}
                   else symb:= ' '
             end {while...do begin};
      while not empty(opstk)
          do begin
               outlen:= outlen +1;
               out[outlen]:= pop(opstk)
             end {while...do begin}
end {procedure postfix};
```

The program has one major flaw, in that it does not check that the input string is a valid infix expression. In fact, it would be instructive for you to examine the operation of this program when it is presented with a valid postfix string as input. As an exercise you are asked to write a program that checks whether or not an input string is a valid infix expression.

It is useful for you to examine how lines 10 through 14 of the conversion algorithm were implemented. We could not simply code

$$\textbf{while } (\textbf{not } empty(opstk)) \textbf{ and } (prcd(stacktop(opstk),symb))$$

because if *opstk* were empty, *stacktop*(*opstk*) would result in an underflow and halt program execution under those Pascal compilers that evaluate all conditions in any logical expression. Instead, we used *popandtest* to both pop the top element and test for underflow simultaneously. However, if it turns out that the popped element (*topsymb*) has lower precedence than the incoming symbol (*symb*), it must be restored to the stack. That is why we must add the statement

$$\textbf{if not } und \textbf{ then } push(opstk, topsymb)$$

after the inner loop. Such a statement was unnecessary in the algorithm outline, because there the top element of the stack is not popped until it is known that it has higher precedence than the incoming symbol.

One other point to make note of is that *topsymb* is initialized to '+'. The reason that *topsymb* must be initialized is that the statement *popandtest*(*opstk*,*topsymb*,*und*) will be executed upon encountering the first operator. Since *opstk* is initially empty, *topsymb* will not be changed by *popandtest*. If *topsymb* had no initial value, the call to *prcd*(*topsymb*,*symb*) in the *while* statement would result in an error. This will occur in spite of the fact that it is the value of *und* which will govern the algorithm's action in this case rather than the value of *prcd*. By initializing *topsymb* to some value, we are sure that *prcd* will return a value on this call, although that value is irrelevant to further processing. Details such as these can often cause errors in program execution.

We can now write a program to read an infix string and find its numerical value. If the original string consists of single-digit operands with no letter operands, the following program will read the original string and print its value.

```
program convandeval (input,output);
const maxcols = 80;
type exprtype = array [1..80] of char;
var   instring, poststring: exprtype;
      position: 1..maxcols;
      value: real;
procedure postfix (infix: exprtype; var out: exprtype);
         { body of postfix goes here }
function eval (expr: exprtype): real;
         { body of eval goes here }
```

```
begin {program convandeval}
    while not eof
        do begin {process next expression}
            for position:= 1 to maxcols
                do read(instring[position]);
            readln;
            write ('infix expression is      ');
            for position:= 1 to maxcols
                do write (instring[position]);
            writeln;
            postfix (instring, poststring);
            value:= eval(poststring);
            writeln ('value is      ', value)
        end {while...do begin}
    end {program convandeval}.
```

The stack manipulation procedures (*pop*, *push*, etc.) for the stack of character operators (i.e., *opstk*) are internal to *postfix*, whereas the procedures for manipulating the stack of *real* operands (i.e., *opndstk*) are internal to *eval*. This is necessary to avoid any conflict between the two versions of each procedure. Of course, it would be possible to use a stack that can contain both reals or characters by defining a type *stackitem* as a variant record, as described at the end of Section 2. This would allow a single set of the stack manipulation routines to be defined in the main program which could be used by both the conversion and evaluation routines.

Most of our attention in this section has been devoted to transformations involving postfix expressions. The algorithm to convert an infix expression into postfix scans characters from left to right stacking and unstacking as necessary. If it were necessary to convert from infix to prefix, the infix string could be scanned from right to left and the appropriate symbols entered in the prefix string from right to left. Since most algebraic expressions are read from left to right, postfix is a more natural choice.

The programs discussed above are merely indicative of the type of routines one could write to manipulate and evaluate postfix expressions. They are by no means comprehensive or unique. There are many variations of these routines that are equally acceptable. Some of the older high-level language compilers actually used routines such as *eval* and *postfix* to handle algebraic expressions. Since that time, more sophisticated schemes have been developed to handle these problems.

EXERCISES   1. Transform each of the following expressions to prefix and postfix.

    (a) $A+B-C$
    (b) $(A+B)*(C-D)\$E*F$
    (c) $(A+B)*(C\$(D-E)+F)-G$
    (d) $A+(((B-C)*(D-E)+F)/G)\$(H-J)$

2. Transform each of the following prefix expressions to infix.

   (a) +-ABC
   (b) +A-BC
   (c) ++A-*$BCD/+EF*GHI
   (d) +-$ABC*D**EFG

3. Transform each of the following postfix expressions to infix.

   (a) AB+C-
   (b) ABC+-
   (c) AB-C+DEF-+$
   (d) ABCDE-+$*EF*-

4. Apply the evaluation algorithm in the text to evaluate the following postfix expressions. Assume that A = 1, B = 2, and C = 3.

   (a) AB+C-BA+C$-
   (b) ABC+*CBA-+*

5. Modify the routine *eval* to accept as input a character string of operators and operands representing a postfix expression and to create the fully parenthesized infix form of the original postfix. For example, AB+ would be transformed into (A+B) and AB+C- would be transformed into ((A+B)-C).

6. Write a single program combining the features of *eval* and *postfix* to evaluate a string given in infix. You are to use two stacks, one for operands and the other for operators. You should not first convert the infix string to postfix and then evaluate the postfix string, but rather evaluate as you go along.

7. Write a routine *prefix* to accept an input string in infix and create the prefix form of that string, assuming that the string is read from right to left and that the prefix string is created from right to left.

8. Write a Pascal program to convert:

   (a) A prefix string to postfix.
   (b) A postfix string to prefix.
   (c) A prefix string to infix.
   (d) A postfix string to infix.

9. Write a Pascal routine *reduce* that accepts an infix string and forms an equivalent infix string with all superfluous parentheses removed. Can this be done without using a stack?

10. Assume a machine that has a single register and six instructions.

LD	A	which places the operand A into the register
ST	A	which places the contents of the register into the variable A
AD	A	which adds the contents of the variable A to the register
SB	A	which subtracts the contents of the variable A from the register
ML	A	which multiplies the contents of the register by the variable A
DV	A	which divides the contents of the register by the variable A

Write a program that accepts a postfix expression containing single-letter operands and the operators +, -, *, and / and which prints a sequence of instructions to evaluate the expression and leave the result in the register. Use variables of the form *TEMPn* as temporary variables. For example, the postfix expression $ABC*+DE-/$ should yield the printout

```
LD    B
ML    C
ST    TEMP1
LD    A
AD    TEMP1
ST    TEMP2
LD    D
SB    E
ST    TEMP3
LD    TEMP2
DV    TEMP3
ST    TEMP4
```

3 Recursion

This chapter introduces recursion, a programming tool that is one of the most powerful and one of the least understood by beginning students of programming. We define recursion, introduce its use in Pascal, and present several examples. We also examine an implementation of recursion using stacks. The programmer should be aware of how recursion is defined in his particular programming language because the lack of such knowledge will cause errors that may or may not be readily apparent. Finally, we discuss the advantages and disadvantages of using recursion in problem solving.

1. RECURSIVE DEFINITION AND PROCESSES

Many objects in mathematics are defined by presenting a process to produce that object. For example, π is defined as the ratio of the circumference of a circle to its diameter. This is equivalent to the set of instructions: obtain the circumference of a circle and its diameter, divide the former by the latter, and call the result π. Clearly, the process specified must terminate with a definite result.

The Factorial Function

Another example of a definition specified by a process is that of the factorial function, a function that plays an important role in mathematics and statistics. Given a positive integer n, n *factorial* is defined as the product of all integers between n and 1. For example, 5 factorial is equal to $5*4*3*2*1 = 120$ and 3 factorial equals $3*2*1 = 6$. 0 factorial is defined as 1. In mathematics, the exclamation mark (!) is often used to denote the factorial function. We may therefore write the definition of this function as follows:

$$n! = 1 \text{ if } n = 0$$
$$n! = n*(n-1)*(n-2)*\ldots*1 \text{ if } n > 0$$

Note that the three dots are really a shorthand for the product of all the numbers between $n-3$ and 2. In order to avoid this shorthand in the definition of $n!$ we would have to list a formula for $n!$ for each value of n separately, as follows:

$$0! = 1$$
$$1! = 1$$
$$2! = 2*1$$
$$3! = 3*2*1$$
$$4! = 4*3*2*1$$
$$\cdots$$

Of course, we cannot hope to list a formula for the factorial of each integer. In order to avoid any shorthand and to avoid an infinite set of definitions, yet to define the function precisely, we may present an algorithm that accepts a nonnegative integer n and returns the value of $n!$ in a variable *fact*:

```
x := n;
prod := 1;
while x <> 0
    do begin
            prod := x * prod;
            x := x - 1
        end {while...do begin};
fact := prod
```

Such an algorithm is called *iterative* because it calls for the explicit repetition of some process until a certain condition is met. This algorithm can be readily translated into a Pascal function that will return $n!$ when n is input as a parameter. An algorithm may be thought of as a program for an "ideal" machine without any of the practical limitations of a real computer and may therefore be used to define a mathematical function. A Pascal function, however, cannot serve as the definition of the factorial function because of such limitations as precision and the finite size of a real machine.

Let us look more closely at the definition of $n!$, which lists a separate formula for each value of n. We may note, for example, that 4! equals $4*3*2*1$, which equals $4*3!$. In fact, for any $n > 0$, we see that $n!$ equals $n*(n-1)!$. Multiplying n by the product of all integers from $n-1$ to 1 yields the product of all integers from n to 1. We may therefore define

$$0! = 1$$
$$1! = 1*0!$$
$$2! = 2*1!$$
$$3! = 3*2!$$
$$4! = 4*3!$$
$$\cdots$$

or, using the mathematical notation used earlier,

$$n! = 1 \text{ if } n = 0$$
$$n! = n*(n-1)! \text{ if } n > 0$$

This definition may appear quite strange, since it defines the factorial function in terms of itself. This seems to be a circular definition and totally unacceptable until we realize that the mathematical notation is only a concise way of writing out the infinite number of equations necessary to define $n!$ for each n. 0! is defined directly as 1. Once 0! has been defined, defining 1! as 1*0! is not circular at all. Similarly, once 1! has been defined, defining 2! as 2*1! is equally straightforward. It may be argued that the latter notation is more precise than the definition of $n!$ as $n*(n-1)*\ldots*1$ for $n>0$, because it does not resort to three dots to be filled in by the hopefully logical intuition of the reader. Such a definition, which defines an object in terms of a simpler case of itself, is called a *recursive definition*.

Let us see how the recursive definition of the factorial function may be used to evaluate 5!. The definition states that 5! equals 5*4!. Thus before we can evaluate 5!, we must first evaluate 4!. Using the definition once more, we find that 4!=4*3!. Therefore, we must evaluate 3!. Repeating this process, we have that

(1) $5! = 5*4!$
(2) $4! = 4*3!$
(3) $3! = 3*2!$
(4) $2! = 2*1!$
(5) $1! = 1*0!$
(6) $0! = 1$

Each case is reduced to a simpler case until we reach the case of 0!, which is, of course, 1. At line (6) we have a value that is defined directly and not as the factorial of another number. We may therefore backtrack from line (6) to line (1), returning the value computed in one line to evaluate the result of the previous line. This produces

(6') $0! = 1$
(5') $1! = 1*0! = 1*1 = 1$
(4') $2! = 2*1! = 2*1 = 2$
(3') $3! = 3*2! = 3*2 = 6$
(2') $4! = 4*3! = 4*6 = 24$
(1') $5! = 5*4! = 5*24 = 120$

Let us attempt to incorporate this process into an algorithm. Again, we want the algorithm to accept a nonnegative integer n and to return in a variable *fact* the nonnegative integer that is n factorial.

```
1.  if n = 0
2.      then fact := 1
3.      else begin
4.              x := n - 1;
5.              Find the value of x!. Call it y;
6.              fact := n * y
7.      end {else begin}
```

This algorithm exhibits the process used to compute $n!$ by the recursive definition. The key to the algorithm is, of course, line 5, where we are told to "find the value of $x!$". This requires reexecuting the algorithm with input x since the method for computing the factorial function is the algorithm itself. To see that the algorithm will eventually halt, note that at the start of line 5, x equals $n-1$. Each time that the algorithm is executed, its input is one less than the preceding time, so that (since the original input n was a nonnegative integer) 0 will eventually be input to the algorithm. At that point, the algorithm will simply return 1. This value is returned to line 5, which asked for the evaluation of 0!. The multiplication of $y(=1)$ by $n(=1)$ is then executed and the result is returned. This sequence of multiplications and returns continues until the original $n!$ has been evaluated. In the next section, we see how to convert this algorithm into a Pascal program.

Of course, it is much simpler and more straightforward to use the iterative method for evaluation of the factorial function. We present the recursive method as a simple example to introduce recursion, not as a more effective method of solving this particular problem. Indeed, all the problems in this section can be solved more efficiently by iteration. However, later in this chapter and in subsequent chapters, we will come across examples that are more easily solved by recursive methods.

Multiplication of Natural Numbers

Another example of a recursive definition is the definition of multiplication of natural numbers. The product $a*b$, where a and b are positive integers, may be defined as a added to itself b times. This is an iterative definition. An equivalent recursive definition is:

$$a*b = a \text{ if } b = 1$$
$$a*b = a*(b-1)+a \text{ if } b > 1$$

In order to evaluate $6*3$ by this definition, we must first evaluate $6*2$ and then add 6. To evaluate $6*2$, we must first evaluate $6*1$ and add 6. But $6*1$ equals 6 by the first part of the definition. Thus

$$6*3 = 6*2+6 = 6*1+6+6 = 6+6+6 = 18$$

The reader is urged to convert the foregoing definition to a recursive algorithm as a simple exercise.

Note the pattern that exists in recursive definitions. A simple case of the term to be defined is defined explicitly (in the case of the factorial, 0! was defined as 1; in the case of multiplication, $a*1 = a$). The other cases are defined by applying some operation to the result of evaluating a simpler case. Thus $n!$ is defined in terms of $(n-1)!$ and $a*b$ in terms of $a*(b-1)$. Successive simplifications of any particular case must eventually lead to the explicitly defined trivial case. In the case of the factorial function, successively subtracting 1 from n will eventually yield 0. In the case of multiplication, successively subtracting 1 from b will eventually yield 1. If this were not the case, the definition would be invalid. For example, if we defined

$$n! = (n+1)!/(n+1)$$

or

$$a*b = a*(b+1)^-a$$

we would be unable to determine the values of 5! or 6*3. (You are invited to attempt to determine these values using the definitions given above.) This is true despite the fact that the two equations are valid. Continually adding one to n or b does not eventually produce an explicitly defined case. Even if 100! was defined explicitly, how could the value of 101! be determined?

The Fibonacci Sequence

Let us examine a less familiar example. The *Fibonacci sequence* is the sequence of integers

$$0, 1, 1, 2, 3, 5, 8, 13, 21, 34, \ldots$$

Each element in this sequence is the sum of the two preceding elements (e.g., 0+1=1, 1+1=2, 1+2=3, 2+3=5, ...). If we let $fib(0)=0$, $fib(1)=1$, and so on, we may define the Fibonacci sequence by the following recursive definition:

$$fib(n) = n \text{ if } n = 0 \text{ or } 1$$
$$fib(n) = fib(n-2)+fib(n-1) \text{ if } n >= 2$$

To compute $fib(6)$, for example, we may apply the definition recursively to obtain

$fib(6)= fib(4)+fib(5)= fib(2)+fib(3)+fib(5)=$
$fib(0)+fib(1)+fib(3)+fib(5)= 0+1+fib(3)+fib(5)= 1+fib(1)+fib(2)+fib(5)=$
$1+1+fib(0)+fib(1)+fib(5)= 2+0+1+fib(5)= 3+fib(3)+fib(4)=$
$3+fib(1)+fib(2)+fib(4)= 3+1+fib(0)+fib(1)+fib(4)= 4+0+1+fib(2)+fib(3)=$
$5+fib(0)+fib(1)+fib(3)= 5+0+1+fib(1)+fib(2)= 6+1+fib(0)+fib(1)= 7+0+1= 8$

Notice that the recursive definition of the Fibonacci numbers differs from the recursive definitions of the factorial function and multiplication. The recursive definition of fib refers to itself twice. For example, $fib(6)= fib(4)+fib(5)$, so that in computing $fib(6)$, fib must be applied recursively twice. However, part of the computation of $fib(5)$ involves determining $fib(4)$, so that a great deal of computational redundancy occurs in applying the definition. In the example above, $fib(3)$ was computed three separate times. It would have been much more efficient to "remember" the value of $fib(3)$ the first time that it was evaluated and reuse it each time that it was needed. An iterative method of computing $fib(n)$, such as the following, is much more efficient (the result is placed in the variable fib):

```
if n <= 1
    then fib := n
    else begin
            lofib := 0;
            hifib := 1;
            for i := 2 to n
                do begin
                        x := lofib;
                        lofib := hifib;
                        hifib := x + lofib
                end {for...do begin};
            fib := hifib
    end {else begin}
```

Essentially, this algorithm enumerates all the Fibonacci numbers in the successive values of the variable *hifib*.

Compare the number of additions (not including increments of the index variable i) which are performed in computing $fib(6)$ by this algorithm and by using the recursive definition. In the case of the factorial function, the same number of multiplications must be performed in computing $n!$ by the recursive and iterative methods. The same is true of the number of additions in the two methods of computing multiplication. However, in the case of the Fibonacci numbers, the recursive method is far more expensive than the iterative. We shall have more to say about the relative merits of the two methods in a later section.

The Binary Search

You may have received the erroneous impression that recursion is a very handy tool for defining mathematical functions but has no influence in more practical computing activities. The next example will illustrate an application of recursion to one of the most common activities in computing—that of searching.

Consider an array of elements in which objects have been placed in some order. For example, a dictionary or telephone book may be thought of as an array whose entries are in alphabetical order. A company payroll file may be in the order of employees' social security numbers. Suppose that such an array exists and we wish to find a particular element in it. For example, we wish to look up a name in a telephone book, a word in a dictionary, or a particular employee in a personnel file. The process used to find such an entry is called a *search*. Since searching is such a common activity in computing, it is desirable to find an efficient method for performing it. Perhaps the crudest search method is the *sequential* or *linear* search, in which each item of the array is examined in turn and compared to the item being searched for until a match occurs. If the list is unordered and haphazardly constructed, the linear search may be the only way to find anything in it (unless, of course, the list is first rearranged). However, such a method would never be used in looking up a name in a telephone book. Rather, the book is opened to a random page and the names on that page are examined. Since the names are ordered alphabetically, such an examination would determine whether the search should proceed in the first or the second half of the book.

Let us apply this idea to searching an array. If the array contains only one element, the problem is trivial. Otherwise, compare the item being searched for with the item at the middle of the array. If they are equal, the search has been completed successfully. If the middle element is greater than the item being searched for, the search process is repeated in the first half of the array (since if the item appears anywhere, it must appear in the first half); otherwise, the process is repeated in the second half. Note that each time a comparison is made, the number of elements yet to be searched is cut in half. For large arrays, this method is superior to the sequential search, in which each comparison reduces the number of elements yet to be searched by only one. Because of the division of the array to be searched into two equal parts, this search method is called the *binary search*.

Notice that we have quite naturally defined a binary search recursively. If the item being searched for is not equal to the middle element of the array, the instructions are to search a subarray using the same method. Thus the search method is defined in terms of itself with a smaller array as input. We are sure that the process will terminate because the input arrays become smaller and smaller, and the search of a one-element array is defined nonrecursively since the middle element of such an array is its only element.

We now present a recursive algorithm to search a sorted array a for an element x between $a[low]$ and $a[high]$. The algorithm places in a variable *binsrch* an *index* of a such that $a[index] = x$ if such an *index* exists between *low* and *high*. If x is not found in that portion of the array, *binsrch* is set to 0. We assume that *low* and *high* are either both greater or both less than 0, so that there is no element $a[0]$.

```
1    if low > high
2       then binsrch := 0
3       else begin
4              mid := (low+high) div 2;
5              if x = a[mid]
6                 then binsrch := mid
7                 else if x < a[mid]
8                        then search for x in a[low] to a[mid−1]
9                        else search for x in a[mid+1] to a[high]
10         end {else begin}
```

Since the possibility of an unsuccessful search is included (i.e., the element may not exist in the array), the trivial case has been altered somewhat. A search on a one-element array is not defined directly as the appropriate index. Instead, that element is compared to the item being searched for. If

CHAP. 3: RECURSION

the two items are not equal, the search continues in the "first" or "second" half—each of which contains no elements. This case is indicated by the condition $low > high$ and its result is defined directly as 0.

Let us apply this algorithm to an example. Suppose that the array a contains the elements 1, 3, 4, 5, 17, 18, 31, and 33 in that order and we wish to search for 17 (i.e., $x=17$) between item 1 and item 8 (i.e., $low = 1$, $high = 8$). Applying the algorithm, we have

line 1: Is $low > high$? It is not, so execute the *else* clause.

line 4: $mid := (1+8)$ *div* $2 = 4$.

line 5: Is $x = a[4]$? 17 is not equal to 5, so execute the *else* clause.

line 7: Is $x < a[4]$? 17 is not less than 5, so perform the *else* clause at line 9.

line 9: Repeat the algorithm with $low = mid+1 = 5$ and $high = high = 8$ (i.e., search the upper half of the array).

line 1: Is $5 > 8$? No, so execute the *else* clause.

line 4: $mid := (5+8)$ *div* $2 = 6$.

line 5: Is $x = a[6]$? 17 does not equal 18, so execute the *else* clause.

line 7: Is $x < a[6]$? Yes, since $17 < 18$, so execute the *then* clause.

line 8: Repeat the algorithm with $low = low = 5$ and $high = mid - 1 = 5$. We have isolated x between the fifth and the fifth elements of a.

line 1: Is $5 > 5$? No, so execute the *else* clause.

line 4: $mid := (5+5)$ *div* $2 = 5$.

line 5: Since $a[5] = 17$, return 5 as the answer. 17 is indeed the fifth element of the array.

Note the pattern of calls to and returns from the algorithm. A diagram tracing this pattern appears in Figure 3.1.1. The solid arrows indicate the

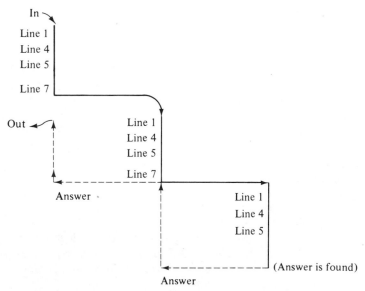

Figure 3.1.1 A diagrammatic representation of the binary search algorithm.

flow of control through the algorithm and the recursive calls. The dotted lines indicate returns. Since there are no steps to be executed in the algorithm after line 8 or 9, the returned result is returned intact to the previous execution. Finally, when control returns to the original execution, the answer is returned to the caller.

Let us examine how the algorithm works in searching for an item that does not appear in the array. Assume the array a as in the previous example and assume that we are searching for $x = 2$.

line 1: Is $low > high$? 1 is not greater than 8, so execute the *else* clause.
line 4: $mid := (1+8)$ *div* $2 = 4$.
line 5: Is $x = a[4]$? 2 does not equal 5, so execute the *else* clause.
line 7: Is $x < a[4]$? Yes, $2 < 5$, so perform the *then* clause.
line 8: Repeat the algorithm with $low = low = 1$ and $high = mid - 1 = 3$. If 2 appears in the array, it must appear between $a[1]$ and $a[3]$ inclusive.
line 1: Is $1 > 3$? No, so execute the *else* clause.
line 4: $mid := (1+3)$ *div* $2 = 2$.
line 5: Is $2 = a[2]$? No, so execute the *else* clause.
line 7: Is $2 < a[2]$? Yes, since $2 < 3$. Perform the *then* clause.
line 8: Repeat the algorithm with $low = low = 1$ and $high = mid - 1 = 1$. If x exists in a, it must be the first element.
line 1: Is $1 > 1$? No, so execute the *else* clause.
line 4: $mid := (1+1)$ *div* $2 = 1$.
line 5: Is $2 = a[1]$? No, so execute the *else* clause.
line 7: Is $2 < a[1]$? 2 is not less than 1, so perform the *else* clause.
line 9: Repeat the algorithm with $low = mid + 1 = 2$ and $high = high = 1$.
line 1: Is $low > high$? 2 is greater than 1, so $binsrch$ is 0. The item 2 does not exist in the array.

Properties of Recursive Definitions or Algorithms

Let us summarize what is involved in a recursive definition or algorithm. One important requirement for a recursive algorithm to be correct is that it not generate an infinite sequence of calls on itself. Clearly, any algorithm that does generate such a sequence will never terminate. For at least one argument or group of arguments, a recursive function f must be defined in terms that do not involve f. There must be a "way out" of the sequence of recursive calls. In the examples of this section the nonrecursive portions of the definitions were

factorial: $0! = 1$
multiplication: $a*1 = a$
Fibonacci seq.: $fib(0) = 0$; $fib(1) = 1$
binary search: **if** $low > high$ **then** $binsrch := 0$
                       if $x = a[mid]$ **then** $binsrch := mid$

Without such a nonrecursive exit, no recursive function can ever be computed. Any instance of a recursive definition or invocation of a recursive algorithm must eventually reduce to some manipulation of one or more simple, nonrecursive cases.

EXERCISES

1. Write an iterative algorithm to evaluate $a * b$ by using addition, where a and b are non-negative integers.

2. Write a recursive definition of $a + b$, where a and b are nonnegative integers, in terms of the Pascal *succ* function.

3. Let a be an array of integers. Present recursive algorithms to compute:
   (a) The maximum element of the array.
   (b) The minimum element of the array.
   (c) The sum of the elements of the array.
   (d) The product of the elements of the array.
   (e) The average of the elements of the array.

4. Evaluate each of the following, using both the iterative and recursive definitions:
   (a) 6!   (b) 9!
   (c) 100 * 3   (d) 6 * 4
   (e) $fib(10)$ (f) $fib(11)$

5. Assume that an array of 10 integers contains the elements

$$1, 3, 7, 15, 21, 22, 36, 78, 95, 106$$

   Use the recursive binary search to find each of the following items in the array
   (a) 1   (b) 20   (c) 36

6. Write an iterative version of the binary search algorithm. (*Hint:* Modifiy the values of *low* and *high* directly.)

7. Ackerman's function is defined recursively on the nonnegative integers as follows:

$$a(m,n) = n+1 \qquad\qquad \text{if } m = 0$$
$$a(m,n) = a(m-1, 1) \qquad \text{if } m \neq 0, n = 0$$
$$a(m,n) = a(m-1, a(m,n-1)) \quad \text{if } m \neq 0, n \neq 0$$

   (a) Using the definition above, show that $a(2,2) = 7$.
   (b) Prove that $a(m,n)$ is defined for all nonnegative integers m and n.
   (c) Can you find an iterative method of computing $a(m,n)$?

8. Count the number of additions necessary to compute $fib(n)$ for $0 \leqslant n \leqslant 10$ by the iterative and recursive methods. Does any pattern emerge?

9. If an array contains n elements, what are the maximum number of recursive calls made by the binary search algorithm?

2. RECURSION IN PASCAL

Factorial in Pascal

The Pascal language allows a programmer to write procedures and functions that call themselves. Such routines are called *recursive*. In order to present

Pascal routines for the algorithms of the preceding section, we first define two global types for the positive and nonnegative integers, respectively:

```
type posint = 1..maxint;
     nonegint = 0..maxint;
```

The recursive algorithm to compute $n!$ may be directly translated into a Pascal function as follows:

```
function fact(n: nonegint): posint;
var x: nonegint;
    y: posint;
begin
    if n = 0
        then fact:= 1
        else begin
                x:= n - 1;
                y:= fact(x);
                fact:= n * y
             end {else begin}
end {function fact};
```

In the statement $y := fact(x)$, the function *fact* calls itself. This is the essential ingredient of a recursive routine. The programmer assumes that the function he is computing has already been written and uses it in its own definition. However, he must ensure that this does not lead to an endless series of calls on itself.

Let us examine the execution of the function shown above when it is called by another program. For example, suppose that the calling program contains the statement

$$\text{write}(fact(4))$$

When the calling routine calls *fact*, the parameter n is set equal to 4. Since n is not 0, x is set equal to 3. At that point, *fact* is called a second time with an argument of 3. Therefore, the block *fact* is reentered and the local variables (x and y) and parameter (n) of the block are reallocated. Since execution has not yet left the first call of *fact*, the first allocation of these variables remains. Thus there are two generations of each of these variables in existence simultaneously. From any point within the second execution of *fact*, only the most recent copy of these variables can be referenced.

In general, each time the function *fact* is entered recursively, a new set of local variables and value parameters is allocated and only this new set may be referenced within that call of *fact*. When a return from *fact* to a point in a previous call takes place, the most recent allocation of these variables is freed and the previous copy is reactivated. This previous copy is the one that was allocated upon the original entry to the previous call and is local to that call.

This description suggests the use of a stack to keep the successive generations of local variables and value parameters. This stack is maintained by the Pascal system and is invisible to the user. Each time that a recursive procedure is entered, a new allocation of its variables is pushed on top of the stack. Any reference to a local variable or parameter is through the current top of the stack. When the procedure returns, the stack is popped, the top allocation is freed, and the previous allocation becomes the current stack top to be used for referencing local variables. This mechanism will be examined more closely in Section 4, but for now, let us see how it is applied in computing the factorial function.

Figure 3.2.1 contains a series of snapshots of the stacks for the variables n, x, and y as execution of the *fact* function proceeds. Initially, the stacks are empty, as illustrated by Figure 3.2.1a. After the first call on *fact* by the calling procedure, the situation is as shown in Figure 3.2.1b, with $n=4$. The

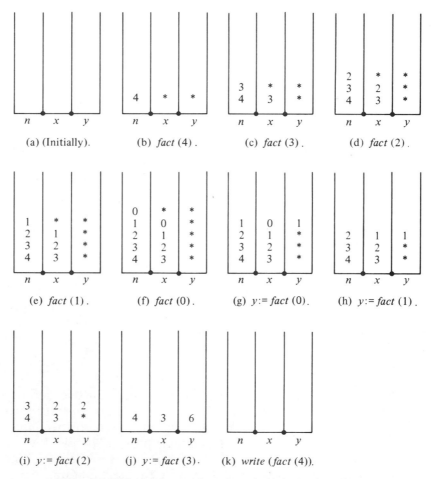

Figure 3.2.1 The stack at various times during execution. (An asterisk indicates an uninitialized value.)

variables x and y are allocated but not initialized. Since n does not equal 0, x is set to 3 and $fact(3)$ is called (Figure 3.2.1c). The new value of n does not equal 0, so x is set to 2 and $fact(2)$ is called (Figure 3.2.1d). This continues until n equals 0 (Figure 3.2.1f). At that point, the value 1 is returned from the call to $fact(0)$. Execution resumes from the point at which $fact(0)$ was called, which is the assignment of the returned value to the copy of y declared in $fact(1)$. This is illustrated by the status of the stack shown in Figure 3.2.1g, where the variables allocated for $fact(0)$ have been freed and y is set to 1.

The statement $fact := n*y$ is then executed, multiplying the top values of n and y to obtain 1, and returning this value to $fact(2)$ (Figure 3.2.1h). This process is repeated twice more, until finally the value of y in $fact(4)$ equals 6 (Figure 3.2.1j). The statement $fact := n*y$ is executed one more time. The product 24 is returned to the calling procedure, where it is printed by the statement

write(fact(4))

Note that each time that a recursive routine returns, it returns to the point immediately following the point from which it was called. Thus the recursive call to $fact(3)$ returns to the assignment of the result to y within $fact(4)$, but the call to $fact(4)$ returns to the *write* statement in the calling routine.

Let us transform some of the other recursive definitions and processes of the previous section into recursive Pascal programs. It is difficult to conceive of a Pascal programmer writing a function to compute the product of two positive integers in terms of addition, since he can simply use an asterisk to perform the multiplication. Nevertheless, such a function can serve as another illustration of recursion in Pascal. Following closely the definition of multiplication in the previous section, we may write

```
function mult(a,b: posint): posint;
begin
    if b = 1
       then mult := a
       else mult := mult(a,b-1) + a
end {function mult};
```

Notice how similar this program is to the recursive definition of the preceding section. We leave it as an exercise for you to trace through the execution of this function when it is called with two positive integers. The use of stacks will be a great aid in this tracing process.

This example illustrates that a recursive function may invoke itself even within a statement assigning a value to the function. Similarly, we could have written the recursive *fact* function more compactly as:

CHAP. 3: RECURSION

```
function fact(n: nonegint): posint;
begin
    if n = 0
        then fact:= 1
        else fact:= n * fact(n-1)
end {function fact};
```

Note the difference between the uses of *fact* on the left and the right side of the assignment in the *else* clause above; the reference to *fact* on the left is to a local variable; the reference to *fact* on the right is a recursive call. This compact version avoids the explicit use of local variables x (to hold the value of $n-1$) and y (to hold the value of $fact(x)$). However, temporary locations are set aside anyway for these two values upon each invocation of the function. These temporaries are treated just as any explicit local variable. Thus in tracing the action of a recursive routine, it may be helpful to declare all temporary variables explicitly. See if it is any easier to trace the following more explicit version of *mult*:

```
function mult (a,b: posint): posint;
var c,d: posint;
begin
    if b = 1
        then mult:= a
        else begin
                c:= b - 1;
                d:= mult(a,c);
                mult:= d + a
            end {else begin}
end {function mult};
```

Another point which should be made is that it is particularly important to check for the validity of input parameters in a recursive routine. In Pascal, this is easily done by using subrange types such as *posint* and *nonegint* to ensure that parameters are within the proper range. If such subranges are not used, recursive routines can be the source of much grief. For example, consider the *fact* routine if the type *integer*, rather than *posint* and *nonegint*, were used in its declaration. Let us examine the execution of *fact* when it is invoked by a statement such as

$$write(fact(-1))$$

Of course, the *fact* function was not designed to produce a meaningful result for negative inputs. However, one of the most important things for a programmer to learn is that a procedure or function will invariably be presented at some time with invalid input and, unless provision is made for such input, the resultant error may be very difficult to trace. For example, when – 1 is passed as a parameter to *fact*, so that $n=-1$, x is set to -2 and -2 is passed to a recursive call on *fact*. Another set of n, x, and y is allocated, n is set to -2, and x becomes -3. This process continues until the program either runs out of time or space or the value of x becomes too small. No message indicating the true cause of the error is produced. If *fact* were originally called with a complicated expression as its argument and the expression erroneously evaluated to a negative number, a programmer might spend hours searching for the cause of his error. The problem can be remedied either by using subranges as we have done, or by revising the *fact* routine to explicitly check its input, as follows:

```
function fact(n: integer): integer;
var x,y: integer;
begin
    if n < 0
        then error('negative argument passed to the factorial function')
        else if n = 0
            then fact:= 1
            else begin
                    x:= n - 1;
                    y:= fact(x);
                    fact:= n * y
                end {else begin}
end {function fact};
```

Similarly, the function *mult* must guard against a nonpositive value in the second parameter.

The Fibonacci Numbers in Pascal

We now turn our attention to the Fibonacci sequence. A Pascal program to compute the nth Fibonacci number can be modeled closely after the recursive definition:

```
function fib(n: nonegint): nonegint;
var x,y: nonegint;
begin
    if n <= 1
        then fib:= n
        else begin
                x:= fib(n-1);
                y:= fib(n-2);
                fib:= x + y
            end {else begin}
end {function fib};
```

Let us trace through the action of the foregoing function in computing the sixth Fibonacci number. You may compare the action of the routine with the manual computation we performed in the last section to compute *fib*(6). The stacking process is illustrated in Figure 3.2.2. When the program is first called, the variables n, x, and y are allocated and n is set to 6 (Figure 3.2.2a). Since $n>1$, $n-1$ is evaluated and *fib* is called recursively. A new set

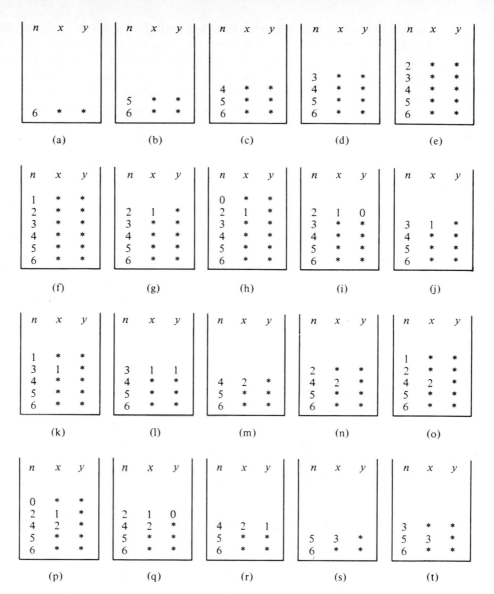

Figure 3.2.2 The recursion stack of the Fibonacci function.

of n, x, and y is allocated and n is set to 5 (Figure 3.2.2b). This process continues (Figures 3.2.2c–f) with each successive value of n equaling one less than its predecessor, until *fib* is called with $n=1$. The sixth call to *fib* returns 1 to its caller, so the fifth allocation of x is set to 1 (Figure 3.2.2g).

The next sequential statement $y:=fib(n-2)$ is then executed. The value of n that is used is the most recently allocated one, which is 2. Thus we again call on *fib* with an argument of 0 (Figure 3.2.2h). The value of 0 is immediately returned so that y in *fib*(2) is set to 0 (Figure 3.2.2i). Note that each recursive call results in a return to the point of call, so that the call of *fib*(1) returns to the assignment to x, while the call of *fib*(0) returns to the assignment to y. The next statement to be executed in *fib*(2) is the statement that assigns $x+y = 1+0 = 1$ to *fib* and then returns to its invoking statement in the generation of the function calculating *fib*(3). This is the assignment to x, so that x in *fib*(3) is given the value *fib*(2) = 1 (Figure 3.2.2j). The process of calling and pushing and returning and popping continues until finally the routine returns for the last time to the main program with the value 8. Figure 3.2.2 shows the stack up to the point where *fib*(5) calls on *fib*(3), so that its value can be assigned to y. The reader is urged to complete the picture by drawing the stack states for the remainder of the program execution.

This program illustrates that a recursive routine may call itself a number of times with different arguments. In fact, as long as a recursive routine uses only local variables, the programmer can use the routine just as he uses any other and assume that it performs its function and produces the desired value. He need not worry about the underlying stacking mechanism.

The Binary Search in Pascal

Let us now present a Pascal program for the binary search. A function to do this would accept an array a and an element x as input and would return the index i in a such that $a[i] = x$, or 0 if no such i existed. Thus the function *binsrch* might be invoked in a statement such as

$$i := \text{binsrch}(a, x)$$

However, in looking at the binary search algorithm of Section 1 as a model for a recursive Pascal routine, we note that two other parameters are passed in the recursive calls. Lines 8 and 9 of that algorithm call for a binary search on only part of the array. Thus, in order for the function to be recursive, the bounds between which the array is to be searched must also be specified. We assume in the subsequent discussion that the following global definitions appear:

```
const maxarraysize = 500;
      maxplus1 = 501; {array size plus one}
type  arraytype = array[1..maxarraysize] of integer;
      index = 0..maxplus1;
```

The routine is written as follows:

```
function binsrch(a: arraytype; x: integer; low, high: index): index;
var mid: index;
begin
    if low > high
        then binsrch := 0
        else begin
                mid := (low+high) div 2;
```

112

```
        if x = a[mid]
            then binsrch:= mid
            else if x < a[mid]
                    then binsrch:= binsrch(a, x, low, mid-1)
                    else  binsrch:= binsrch(a, x, mid+1, high)
            end {else begin}
    end {function binsrch};
```

When *binsrch* is first called from another routine to search for x in an array declared by

$$a: arraytype$$

of which the first n elements are occupied, it is called by the statement

$$i:= binsrch(a, x, 1, n)$$

You are urged to trace the execution of this routine and follow the stacking and unstacking using the example of the preceding section, where a is an array of 8 elements ($n=8$) containing 1, 3, 4, 5, 17, 18, 31, 33 in that order. The value being searched for is 17 ($x=17$). Note that the array a is stacked for each recursive call. The values of *low* and *high* are declared as being in the range 0 to one more than the maximum array size, because if x is less than $a[1]$, *high* is set to zero on the last recursive call and if x is larger than $a[n]$, *low* is set to $n+1$ on the last recursive call.

In the course of tracing through the *binsrch* routine, you may have noticed that the values of the two parameters a and x do not change throughout its execution. Each time that *binsrch* is called, the same array is searched for the same element: it is only the upper and lower bounds of the search that change. It therefore seems wasteful to stack and unstack these two parameters each time that the routine is called recursively. (In addition, since a is a value parameter, it is copied on each call. Of course, a could be made a variable parameter.)

One solution is to allow a and x to be global variables, declared in the calling routine, which includes the function *binsrch* as a subblock. In this case these variables are declared in the surrounding block by

```
        var a: arraytype;
            x: integer;
```

and the header of *binsrch* is replaced by

```
        function binsrch(low,high: index): index;
```

The routine would be called by a statement such as

```
        i:= binsrch(1,n)
```

In this case, all references to a and x are to the single copy which is declared in the outer block but also known in the inner block. This saves the allocation and freeing of multiple copies of these two variables.

However, this solution has some serious drawbacks. The variable x must always be set in the calling routine to the variable whose value is being searched for. Another serious objection is one based on logical and aesthetic design factors. Logically, the two parameters to a search function should be the array that is being searched and the object being searched for, in our case a and x. However, in the current version of *binsrch*, neither of these appears as a parameter. Instead, the two parameters that do appear—the upper and lower bounds—relate to the internal workings of the algorithm and not to the problem specification.

To remedy all these problems, we may rewrite the *binsrch* function as a nonrecursive routine with parameters a and x, which calls on an internal auxiliary recursive routine *auxsrch* with parameters *low* and *high*, as follows:

```
function binsrch (a: arraytype; n: index; x: integer): index;
    function auxsrch (low,high: index): index;
    var mid: index;
    begin {function auxsrch}
        if low > high
            then auxsrch:= 0
            else begin
                    mid:= (low+high) div 2;
                    if x = a[mid]
                        then auxsrch:= mid
                        else if x < a[mid]
                                then auxsrch:= auxsrch (low, mid-1)
                                else auxsrch:= auxsrch (mid+1, high)
                end {else begin}
    end {function auxsrch};
    begin {function binsrch}
        binsrch:= auxsrch(1,n)
    end {function binsrch};
```

Using this scheme, the variables a and x are passed to the binary search routine, as they should be. a and x do not change their values and are not stacked. The work of stacking, unstacking, and altering the values of *low* and *high* is left to the internal recursive routine *auxsrch*. The programmer wishing to make use of *binsrch* in his program need not even be aware of the existence of *low* and *high*. He merely invokes the routine with a statement such as

$$i:= binsrch(a, n, x)$$

Note that the function *binsrch* is not recursive.

Recursive Chains

A recursive procedure need not call itself directly. Rather, it may call itself indirectly, as in the following example:

```
procedure a(formal parameters);        procedure b(formal parameters);
    begin                                   begin
        .                                       .
        .                                       .
        .                                       .
    b(arguments);                           a(arguments);
                                                .
    end {procedure a};                      end {procedure b};
```

In this example procedure *a* calls *b*, which may in turn call *a*, which may again call *b*. Thus both *a* and *b* are recursive, since they indirectly call on themselves. However, the fact that they are recursive is not evident from examining the body of either of the routines individually. The routine *a* seems to be calling a separate routine *b*, and it is impossible to determine, by examining *a* alone, that it will indirectly call itself.

More than two routines may participate in a *recursive chain*. Thus a routine *a* may call *b*, which calls *c*,..., which calls *z*, which calls *a*. Each routine in the chain may potentially call itself and is therefore recursive. Of course, the programmer must ensure that his program does not generate an infinite sequence of recursive calls.

There is one special rule for recursive chains in Pascal. Ordinarily, a function or procedure must be defined before it can be referenced. But if *a* calls *b* and *b* calls *a*, *a* cannot be defined first because it references *b*, but *b* cannot be defined first either because it references *a*. The solution is to define the procedures as follows:

```
procedure b(formal parameters); forward;
procedure a(formal parameters);
        {body of a}
    procedure b;
        {body of b}
```

The keyword *forward* indicates that the body of procedure *b* will be defined subsequently. Since the parameters of *b* have been declared before *a* is defined, the call on *b* within *a* can be compiled correctly. Then after *a* has been defined, the body of *b* is defined. Note that the parameters of *b* are not redeclared in the header when the body of the procedure is defined.

Recursive Definition of Algebraic Expressions

As an example of such a recursive chain, consider the following recursive group of definitions:

1. An *expression* is a *term* followed by a *plus sign* followed by a *term*, or a *term* alone.
2. A *term* is a *factor* followed by an *asterisk* followed by a *factor*, or a *factor* alone.
3. A *factor* is either a *letter* or an *expression* enclosed in *parentheses*.

Before looking at some examples, note that none of the foregoing three items is defined directly in terms of itself. However, each is defined in terms of itself indirectly. An expression is defined in terms of a term, a term in terms of a factor, and a factor in terms of an expression. Similarly, a factor is defined in terms of an expression, which is defined in terms of a term, which is defined in terms of a factor. Thus the entire set of definitions forms a recursive chain.

Let us now give some examples. The simplest form of a factor is a letter. Thus A, B, C, Q, Z, M are all factors. They are also terms, because a term may be a factor alone. They are also expressions, because an expression may be a term alone. Since A is an expression, (A) is a factor and therefore a term as well as an expression. $A+B$ is an example of an expression which is neither a term nor a factor. $(A+B)$, however, is all three. $A*B$ is a term and therefore an expression, but it is not a factor. $A*B+C$ is an expression that is neither a term nor a factor. $A*(B+C)$ is a term and an expression but not a factor.

Each of the examples above is a valid expression. This can be shown by applying the definition of an expression to each of them. Consider, however, the string $A+*B$. It is neither an expression, a term, nor a factor. It would be instructive for you to attempt to apply the definitions of expression, term, and factor to see that none of them describe the string $A+*B$. Similarly, $(A+B*)C$ and $A+B+C$ are not valid expressions according to the definitions given above.

Let us write a program that reads a character string, prints it out, and then prints *valid* if it is a valid expression and *invalid* if it is not. We will use three functions to recognize expressions, terms, and factors, respectively. However, we first present an auxiliary function *getsymb*, which operates on three global variables: *str*, *length*, and *pos*. The first of these variables, *str*, contains the input character string as an array of characters. *length* represents the number of elements of *str* containing characters. The third of these variables, *pos*, is the position in *str* from which we last obtained a character. Upon entry to *getsymb*, *pos* is incremented by 1. If *pos* ≤ *length*, then *getsymb* returns the character at position *pos* of *str*. If *pos* > *length*, then *getsymb* returns a blank.

```
function getsymb: char;
begin
    pos:= pos + 1;
    if pos > length
        then getsymb:= ' '
        else getsymb:= str[pos]
end {function getsymb};
```

The function that recognizes an expression is called *expr*. It, too, has no arguments and uses *str* and *pos* as global variables. It returns *true* if a valid expression begins at position *pos* of *str* and *false* otherwise. It also resets *pos* to the last position of the longest expression it can find. The program also calls a procedure *readstr* that reads a string of characters, placing the string in *str* and its length in *length*. Having described the function *expr* and the procedure *readstr*, we can write the main routine as follows.

```
program findexp(input,output);
const maxstringsize = 100;
      maxplusone = 101;
type  arraychar = array[1..maxstringsize] of char;
      index = 1..maxstringsize;
var str: arraychar;
    length: index;
    pos: 0..maxplusone;
    ok: boolean;
function getsymb: char;
        {body of getsymb goes here}
function factor: boolean; forward;
function term: boolean; forward;
function expr: boolean;
        {  body of expr goes here  }
function factor;
        {  body of factor goes here  }
function term;
        {  body of term goes here  }
procedure readstr(var str: arraychar; var length: index);
        {  body of readstr goes here  }
begin {program findexp}
     readstr(str,length);
     for pos:= 1 to length
        do write(str[pos]);
     writeln;
     pos:= 0;
     ok:= expr;
     if ok and (pos = length)
        then write('valid')
        else  write('invalid')
     {The condition can fail for one (or both) of two}
     {    reasons. If not ok then there is no valid      }
     { expression beginning at pos. If pos < length  }
     {there may be a valid expression starting at pos }
     {    but it does not occupy the entire string.     }
end {program findexp}.
```

The functions *factor* and *term* are much like *expr* except that they are responsible for recognizing factors and terms, respectively. They also reposition *pos* to the last position of the longest factor or term within the string *str* that they can find.

The code for these routines adheres closely to the definitions given earlier. Each of the routines attempts to satisfy one of the criteria for the entity being recognized. If one of these criteria is satisfied, then *true* is returned. If none of these criteria are satisfied, then *false* is returned.

```
function expr: boolean;
var ok: boolean;
    c: char;
begin {function expr}
    {Look for a term.}
    ok:= term;
    if not ok {no expression exists}
      then expr:= false
      else begin
            {Look at the next symbol.}
            c:= getsymb;
            if c <> '+'
              then begin
                    {We have found the longest expression}
                    {   (a single term).  Reposition pos so   }
                    {      it refers to the last position      }
                    {            of the expression.            }
                    pos:= pos - 1;
                    expr:= true
                  end {then begin}
              else  begin
                    { At this point, we have found a term }
                    { and a plus sign.  We must look for  }
                    {            another term.            }
                    ok:= term;
                    if ok
                      then expr:= true
                      else  expr:= false
                  end {else begin}
          end {else begin}
end {function expr};
```

The routine *term* that recognizes a term is similar, and we present it without comments. Note that the return type of *term* has already been specified as *boolean* and cannot be repeated.

```
function term;
var ok: boolean;
    c: char;
begin {function term}
    ok:= factor;
    if not ok
      then term:= false
```

```
                    else begin
                         c:= getsymb;
                         if c <> '*'
                              then begin
                                        pos:= pos - 1;
                                        term:= true
                                   end {then begin}
                              else  begin
                                        ok:= factor;
                                        if ok
                                             then term:= true
                                             else  term:= false
                                   end {else begin}
                    end {else begin}
          end {function term};
```

The function *factor* recognizes a factor and should now be fairly straight-forward. It uses a function *letter* which returns *true* if its character parameter is a letter and *false* otherwise.

```
          function factor;
          var ok: boolean;
              c: char;
          function letter(c: char): boolean;
                    {body of letter goes here}
          begin {function factor}
               c:= getsymb;
               if c <> '('
                    then {check for a letter}
                         if letter(c)
                              then factor:= true
                              else  factor:= false
                    else begin {the factor is a parenthesized expression}
                              ok:= expr;
                              if not ok
                                   then factor:= false
                                   else begin
                                             c:= getsymb;
                                             if c <> ')'
                                                  then factor:= false
                                                  else  factor:= true
                                        end {else begin}
                         end {else begin}
          end {function factor};
```

All three routines are recursive since each may call itself indirectly. For example, if you trace through the actions of the program *findexp* for the input string '$(A*B+C*D)+(E*(F)+G)$', you will find that each of the routines *expr*, *term*, and *factor* calls on itself.

1. Determine what the following recursive Pascal function computes. Write an iterative function to accomplish the same purpose.

```
function func(n: nonegint): nonegint;
begin
    if n = 0
        then func:= 0
        else func:= n + func(n-1)
end { function func};
```

2. The Pascal expression m **mod** n yields the remainder of m upon division by n. Define the **greatest common divisor** (**gcd**) of two integers x and y by

$$gcd(x,y) = y \qquad\qquad \text{if } y \leqslant x \text{ and } x \textbf{ mod } y = 0$$
$$gcd(x,y) = gcd(y,x) \qquad \text{if } x < y$$
$$gcd(x,y) = gcd(y, x \textbf{ mod } y) \quad \text{otherwise}$$

Write a recursive Pascal function to compute $gcd(x,y)$. Find an iterative method for computing this function.

3. Let $comm(n,k)$ represent the number of different committees of k people that can be formed, given n people to choose from. For example, $comm(4,3) = 4$, since given four people A, B, C, and D there are four possible committees: ABC, ABD, ACD, and BCD. Prove the identity

$$comm(n,k) = comm(n-1,k) + comm(n-1,k-1)$$

Write and test a recursive Pascal program to compute $comm(n,k)$ for $n,k >= 1$.

4. Define a **generalized Fibonacci sequence of $f0$ and $f1$** as the sequence $gfib(f0,f1,0)$, $gfib(f0,f1,1), gfib(f0,f1,2), \ldots$, where

$$gfib(f0,f1,0) = f0$$
$$gfib(f0,f1,1) = f1$$
$$gfib(f0,f1,n) = gfib(f0,f1,n-1) + gfib(f0,f1,n-2) \qquad \text{if } n > 1$$

Write a recursive Pascal function to compute $gfib(f0,f1,n)$. Find an iterative method for computing this function.

5. Write a recursive Pascal function to compute the number of sequences of n binary digits that do not contain two 1s in a row. (*Hint:* Compute how many such sequences exist that start with a 0, and how many exist that start with a 1.)

6. An **order n matrix** is an $n \times n$ array of numbers. For example,

$$(3)$$

is a 1×1 matrix,

$$\begin{pmatrix} 1 & 3 \\ -2 & 8 \end{pmatrix}$$

is a 2 X 2 matrix, and

$$\begin{pmatrix} 1 & 3 & 4 & 6 \\ 2 & -5 & 0 & 8 \\ 3 & 7 & 6 & 4 \\ 2 & 0 & 9 & -1 \end{pmatrix}$$

is a 4 X 4 matrix. Define the **minor** of an element x in a matrix as the submatrix formed by deleting the row and column containing x. In the foregoing example of a 4 X 4 matrix, the minor of the element 7 is the 3 X 3 matrix

$$\begin{pmatrix} 1 & 4 & 6 \\ 2 & 0 & 8 \\ 2 & 9 & -1 \end{pmatrix}$$

Clearly, the order of a minor of any element is 1 less than the order of the original matrix. Denote the minor of an element $a[i,j]$ by $minor(a[i,j])$.

Define the **determinant** of a matrix a (written $det(a)$) recursively as follows:

I. If a is a 1 X 1 matrix (x), then $det(a) = x$.
II. If a is of order greater than 1, compute the determinant of a as follows:
   a. Choose any row or column. For each element $a[i,j]$ in this row or column, form the product.

$$(-1)^{i+j} * a[i,j] * det(minor(a[i,j]))$$

   where i and j are the row and column positions of the element chosen, $a[i,j]$ is the element chosen, $det(minor(a[i,j]))$ is the determinant of the minor of $a[i,j]$.
   b. $det(a)$ = sum of all these products over the chosen row or column. (More concisely, if n is the order of a, then

$$det(a) = \sum_{i=1}^{n} (-1)^{i+j} * a[i,j] * det(minor(a[i,j])), \quad \text{for any } j$$

or

$$det(a) = \sum_{j=1}^{n} (-1)^{i+j} * a[i,j] * det(minor(a[i,j])), \quad \text{for any } i$$

Write a Pascal program that will read in a, print out a in matrix form, and print out $det(a)$, where det is a function that computes the determinant of a matrix.

7. Write a recursive Pascal program to sort an array a as follows:

   (a) Let k be the index of the middle element of the array.
   (b) Sort the elements up to and including $a[k]$.
   (c) Sort the elements past $a[k]$.
   (d) Merge the two subarrays into a single sorted array.

   This method is called a **merge sort**.

8. Show how to transform the following iterative procedure into a recursive procedure. $f(i)$ is a function returning a boolean value based on the value of i, and $g(i)$ is a function that returns a value of the same type as i without changing the value of i.

```
procedure iter(n: ntype);
var i: ntype
function f(k: ntype): boolean;
        {body of f goes here}
function g(k: ntype): ntype;
        {body of g goes here}
begin {procedure iter}
    i:= n;
    while f(i)
        do begin
                {    any group of Pascal statements    }
                { which does not change the value of i}
                i:= g(i)
            end {while...do begin}
end {procedure iter};
```

3. WRITING RECURSIVE PROGRAMS

In the preceding section we saw how to take a recursive definition or algorithm and transform it into a Pascal program. It is a much more difficult task to develop a recursive Pascal solution to a problem specification whose algorithm is not supplied. It is not only the program but also the original definitions and algorithms that must be developed. In general, when faced with the task of writing a program to solve a problem, there is no reason to look for a recursive solution. Most problems can be solved in a straightforward manner using nonrecursive methods. We shall have more to say about these "efficiency" considerations in later sections. However, some problems can be solved logically and most elegantly by recursion. In this section we shall try to identify those problems that can be solved recursively, develop a technique for finding recursive solutions, and present some examples.

Let us reexamine the factorial function. Factorial is probably a prime example of a problem that should not be solved recursively since the iterative solution is so direct and simple. However, let us examine the elements that make the recursive solution work. First, we can recognize a large number of distinct cases to solve. That is, we want to write a program to compute 0!, 1!, 2!, and so on. We can also identify a "trivial" case for which a nonrecursive solution is directly obtainable. This is the case of 0!, which is defined as 1. The next step is to find a method of solving a "complex" case in terms of a "simpler" case. This will allow reduction of a complex problem to a simpler problem. The transformation of the complex case to the simpler case should eventually result in the trivial case. This would mean that the complex case is ultimately defined in terms of the trivial case.

Let us examine what this means when applied to the factorial function.

4! is a more "complex" case than 3!. The transformation that is applied to the number 4 to obtain the number 3 is simply the subtraction of 1. Repeatedly subtracting 1 from 4 eventually results in 0, which is a "trivial" case. Thus, if we are able to define 4! in terms of 3!, and in general n! in terms of $(n-1)$!, we will be able to compute 4! by first working our way down to 0! and then working our way back up to 4! using the definition of n! in terms of $(n-1)$!. In the case of the factorial function we have such a definition, since

$$n! = n*(n-1)!$$

Thus $4! = 4*3! = 4*3*2! = 4*3*2*1! = 4*3*2*1*0! = 4*3*2*1*1 = 24$.

These are the essential ingredients of a recursive routine—being able to define a "complex" case in terms of a "simpler" case and having a directly solvable (nonrecursive) "trivial" case. Once this has been done, one can develop a solution using the assumption that the simpler case has already been solved. The Pascal version of the factorial function assumes that $(n-1)$! is defined and uses that quantity in computing n!.

Let us see how these ideas apply to other examples of the previous sections. In defining $a*b$, the case of $b=1$ is trivial, since in that case, $a*b$ is defined as a. In general, $a*b$ may be defined in terms of $a*(b-1)$ by the definition $a*b = a*(b-1) + a$. Again the complex case is transformed into a simpler case by subtracting one, eventually leading to the trivial case of $b=1$. Here the recursion is based on the second parameter b alone.

In the case of the Fibonacci function, two trivial cases were defined: $fib(0) = 0$ and $fib(1) = 1$. A complex case, $fib(n)$, is then reduced to two simpler cases, $fib(n-1)$ and $fib(n-2)$. It is because of the definition of $fib(n)$ as $fib(n-1) + fib(n-2)$ that two trivial cases directly defined are necessary. $fib(1)$ cannot be defined as $fib(0) + fib(-1)$, because the Fibonacci function is not defined for negative numbers.

The binary search function is an interesting case of recursion. The recursion is based on the number of elements in the array that must be searched. Each time the routine is called recursively, the number of elements to be searched is halved (approximately). The trivial case is the one in which there are either no elements to be searched or the element being searched for is at the middle of the array. If $low>high$, then the first of these two conditions holds and 0 is returned. If $x=a[mid]$, the second condition holds and mid is returned as the answer. In the more complex case of $high-low+1$ elements to be searched, the search is reduced to taking place in one of two subregions.

1. The lower half of the array from low to $mid - 1$.
2. The upper half of the array from $mid + 1$ to $high$.

Thus a complex case (a large area to be searched) is reduced to a simpler case (an area to be searched of approximately half the size of the original area). This eventually reduces to a comparison with a single element ($a[mid]$) or a search within an array of no elements.

The Towers of Hanoi Problem

Thus far we have been looking at recursive definitions and examining how they fit the pattern we have established. Let us now look at a problem that is not specified in terms of recursion and see how we can use recursive techniques to produce a logical and elegant solution. The problem is the "Towers of Hanoi" problem, whose initial setup is shown in Figure 3.3.1. Three pegs, A, B, and C, exist. Five disks of differing diameters are placed on peg A so that a larger disk is always below a smaller disk. The object is to move the five disks to peg C using peg B as auxiliary. Only the top disk on any peg may be moved to any other peg, and a larger disk may never rest on a smaller one. See if you can produce a solution. Indeed, it is not even apparent that a solution exists.

Let us see if we can develop a solution. Instead of focusing our attention on a solution for five disks, let us consider the general case of n disks. Suppose that we had a solution for $n-1$ disks and we could state a solution for n disks in terms of the solution for $n-1$ disks. Then the problem would be solved. This is true because in the trivial case of one disk (continually subtracting 1 from n will eventually produce 1), the solution is simple: merely move the single disk from peg A to peg C. Therefore, we will have developed a recursive solution if we can state a solution for n disks in terms of $n-1$. See if you can find such a relationship. In particular, for the case of five disks, suppose that we knew how to move the top four disks from peg A to another peg according to the rules. How could we then complete the job of moving all five? Recall that there are three pegs available.

Suppose that we could move four disks from peg A to peg C. Then we could just as easily move them to B, using C as auxiliary. This would result in the situation depicted in Figure 3.3.2a. We could then move the largest disk from A to C (Figure 3.3.2b) and finally again apply the solution for four disks to move the four disks from B to C, using the now empty peg A as an auxiliary (Figure 3.3.2c). Thus we may state a recursive solution to the Towers of Hanoi problem as follows:

To move n disks from A to C, using B as auxiliary:

1. If $n=1$, then move the single disk from A to C and stop.
2. Move the top $n-1$ disks from A to B, using C as auxiliary.
3. Move the remaining disk from A to C.
4. Move the $n-1$ disks from B to C, using A as auxiliary.

We are sure that this algorithm will produce a correct solution for any value of n. If $n=1$, step 1 will result in the correct solution. If $n=2$, we know that we already have a solution for $n-1 = 1$, so that steps 2 and 4 will perform correctly. Similarly, when $n=3$, we already have produced a solution for $n-1 = 2$, so that steps 2 and 4 can be performed. In this fashion, we can show that the solution works for $n=1, 2, 3, 4, 5, \ldots$ up to any value for which we desire a solution. Notice that we developed the solution by identifying a trivial case ($n=1$) and a solution for a general complex case (n) in terms of a simpler case ($n-1$).

CHAP. 3: RECURSION

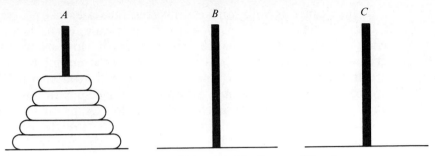

Figure 3.3.1 The initial setup of the Towers of Hanoi.

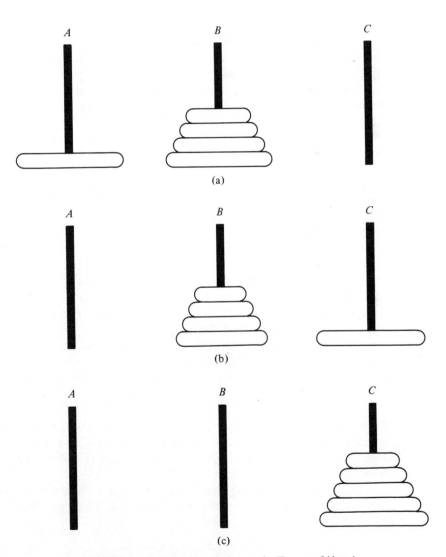

(a)

(b)

(c)

Figure 3.3.2 Recursive solution to the Towers of Hanoi.

Sec. 3: Writing Recursive Programs

How can this solution be converted into a Pascal program? We are no longer dealing with a mathematical function such as factorial, but rather with concrete actions such as "move a disk." How are we to represent such actions in the computer? The problem is not completely specified. What are the inputs to the program? What are its outputs to be? Whenever you are told to write a program, you must receive specific instructions as to exactly what the program is expected to do. A problem statement such as "Solve the Towers of Hanoi problem" is quite insufficient. What is usually meant when such a problem is specified is that not only the program but also the inputs and outputs must be designed, so that they reasonably correspond to the problem description. The design of inputs and outputs is an important phase of a solution and should be given as much attention as the rest of a program. There are two reasons for this. The first is that the user (who must ultimately evaluate and pass judgment on your work) will not see the elegant method you incorporated in your program but will struggle mightily to decipher the output or to adapt his input data to your particular input conventions. The failure to agree early on input and output details has been the cause of much grief to programmers and users alike. The second reason is that a slight change in the input or output format may make the program much simpler to design. Thus the programmer can make his job much easier if he is able to design an input or output format compatible with his algorithm. Of course, these two considerations, convenience to the user and convenience to the programmer, often conflict sharply, and some happy medium must be found. However, the user as well as the programmer must be a full participant in the decisions on input and output formats.

Let us, then, proceed to design the inputs and outputs for this program. The only input needed is the value of n, the number of disks. At least, that may be the programmer's view. The user may want the names of the disks (such as "red," "blue," "green," etc.) and perhaps the names of the pegs (such as "left," "right," and "middle") as well. The programmer can probably convince the user that naming the disks 1, 2, 3, ..., n and the pegs A, B, and C is just as convenient. If necessary, the programmer can write a small function to convert the user's names to his own, and vice versa.

A reasonable form for the output would be a list of statements such as

move disk nnn from peg yyy to peg zzz

where nnn is the number of the disk to be moved and yyy and zzz are the names of the pegs involved. The action to be taken for a solution would be to perform each of the output statements in the order that they appear in the output.

The programmer then decides to write a procedure *towers* (he is purposely vague about the parameters at this point) to print the output shown above. The main program would be

```
program result(input,output);
var n: 1..maxint;
```

```
        begin
            read(n); { read the number of disks }
            towers( parameters)
        end { program result}.
```

Let us assume that the user will be satisfied to name the disks 1, 2, 3, ...,
n and the pegs *A*, *B*, and *C*. What should the parameters to *towers* be?
Clearly, they should include *n*, the number of disks to be moved. This includes not only information about how many disks there are but also what
their names are. The programmer then notices that in the recursive algorithm, he will have to move *n*-1 disks using a recursive call to *towers*. Thus,
on the recursive call, the first parameter to *towers* will be *n*-1. But this implies that the top *n*-1 disks are numbered 1, 2, 3, ..., *n*-1 and that the
smallest disk is numbered 1. This is a good example of programming convenience determining problem representation. There is no a priori reason for
labeling the smallest disk 1; logically, the largest disk could have been labeled
1 and the smallest disk *n*. However, since it leads to a simpler and more
direct program, we will choose to label our disks so that the smallest disk has
the smallest number.

What are the other parameters to *towers*? At first glance, it might appear
that no additional parameters are necessary, since the pegs are named *A*, *B*,
and *C* by default. However, a closer look at the recursive solution leads us to
the realization that on the recursive calls disks will not be moved from *A*
to *C* using *B* as auxiliary, but rather from *A* to *B* using *C* (step 2) or from *B*
to *C* using *A* (step 4). We therefore include three more parameters in *towers*.
The first, *frompeg*, represents the peg from which we are removing disks; the
second, *topeg*, represents the peg to which we will take the disks; and the
third, *auxpeg*, represents the auxiliary peg. This situation is one that is quite
typical of recursive routines; additional parameters are necessary to handle
the recursive call situation. We already saw one example of this in the binary
search program where the parameters *low* and *high* were necessary.

The complete program to solve the Towers of Hanoi problem, closely
following the recursive solution, may be written as follows:

```
program result(input,output);
type posint = 1..maxint;
var n: posint;

procedure towers(n: posint; frompeg,topeg,auxpeg: char);
begin
    { if only one disk, make the move and return }
    if n = 1
        then writeln('move disk 1 from peg ', frompeg, ' to peg ', topeg)
        else begin
                { move top n-1 disks from A to B, using C as }
                {                  auxiliary                 }
                towers(n-1, frompeg, auxpeg, topeg);
                {    move remaining disk from A to C      }
                writeln('move disk ', n, 'from peg ', frompeg, ' to peg ', topeg);
```

```
{   move n-1 disks from B to C, using A as   }
{                auxiliary                   }
          towers(n-1, auxpeg, topeg, frompeg)
    end {else begin}
end {procedure towers};

begin {program result}
    read(n);
    towers(n, 'a', 'c', 'b')
end {program result}.
```

towers is our first example of a recursive procedure as opposed to a function. It is called by using the name of the procedure, exactly as any other procedure would be called. Trace the actions of the foregoing program when it reads the value 5 for *n*. Be careful to keep track of the changing values of the parameters *frompeg*, *auxpeg*, and *topeg*. Verify that it produces the following output:

```
move disk 1  from peg a to peg c
move disk 2  from peg a to peg b
move disk 1  from peg c to peg b
move disk 3  from peg a to peg c
move disk 1  from peg b to peg a
move disk 2  from peg b to peg c
move disk 1  from peg a to peg c
move disk 4  from peg a to peg b
move disk 1  from peg c to peg b
move disk 2  from peg c to peg a
move disk 1  from peg b to peg a
move disk 3  from peg c to peg b
move disk 1  from peg a to peg c
move disk 2  from peg a to peg b
move disk 1  from peg c to peg b
move disk 5  from peg a to peg c
move disk 1  from peg b to peg a
move disk 2  from peg b to peg c
move disk 1  from peg a to peg c
move disk 3  from peg b to peg a
move disk 1  from peg c to peg b
move disk 2  from peg c to peg a
move disk 1  from peg b to peg a
move disk 4  from peg b to peg c
move disk 1  from peg a to peg c
move disk 2  from peg a to peg b
move disk 1  from peg c to peg b
move disk 3  from peg a to peg c
move disk 1  from peg b to peg a
move disk 2  from peg b to peg c
move disk 1  from peg a to peg c
```

Verify that this solution actually works and does not violate any of the rules.

Translation from Prefix to Postfix Using Recursion

Let us examine another problem for which the recursive solution is the most direct and elegant one. This is the problem of converting a prefix expression to postfix. Prefix and postfix notation were discussed in Chapter 2. Briefly, prefix and postfix notations are methods of writing mathematical expressions without parentheses. In prefix notation each operator immediately precedes its operands. In postfix notation each operator immediately follows its operands. To refresh your memory, here are a few conventional (infix) mathematical expressions with their prefix and postfix equivalents:

infix	prefix	postfix
$A+B$	$+AB$	$AB+$
$A+B*C$	$+A*BC$	$ABC*+$
$A*(B+C)$	$*A+BC$	$ABC+*$
$A*B+C$	$+*ABC$	$AB*C+$
$A+B*C+D-E*F$	$-++A*BCD*EF$	$ABC*+D+EF*-$
$(A+B)*(C+D-E)*F$	$**+AB-+CDEF$	$AB+CD+E-*F*$

The most convenient way to define postfix and prefix is by using recursion. Assuming no constants and using only single letters as variables, a prefix expression is a single letter or an operator followed by two prefix expressions. A postfix expression may be similarly defined as a single letter, or as an operator preceded by two postfix expressions. The foregoing definitions assume that all operations are binary (i.e., each requires two operands). Examples of such operations are addition, subtraction, multiplication, division, and exponentiation. It is easy to extend these definitions of prefix and postfix to include unary operations such as negation or factorial, but in the interest of simplicity we will not do so here. Verify that each of the foregoing prefix and postfix expressions are valid by showing that they satisfy the definitions and make sure that you can identify the two operands of each operator.

We will put these recursive definitions to use in a moment, but first let us return to our problem. Given a prefix expression, how can we convert it into a postfix expression? We can immediately identify a trivial case—if a prefix expression consists of only a single variable, that expression is its own postfix equivalent. That is, an expression such as A is valid as both a prefix and a postfix expression.

Now consider a longer prefix string. If we knew how to convert any shorter prefix string to postfix, could we convert this longer prefix string? The answer is yes, with one proviso. Every prefix string longer than a single variable contains an operator, a first operand, and a second operand (remember that we are assuming binary operators only). Assume that we are able to identify the first and second operands, which are necessarily shorter than the original string. We can then convert the long prefix string to postfix by first converting the first operand to postfix, then converting the second operand to postfix and appending it to the end of the first converted operand, and finally appending the initial operator to the end of the resultant string. Thus we have developed a recursive algorithm for converting a prefix string to postfix with the single provision that we must specify a method for identifying the operands in a prefix expression. We can summarize our algorithm as follows:

1. If the prefix string is a single variable, it is its own postfix equivalent.
2. Let *op* be the first operator of the prefix string.
3. Find the first operand *opnd*1 of the string. Convert it to postfix and call it *post*1.
4. Find the second operand *opnd*2 of the string. Convert it to postfix and call it *post*2.
5. Concatenate *post*1, *post*2, and *op*.

In order to manipulate the expressions in this program, it will be necessary to store the initial prefix expression and the final postfix expression as strings of characters. The most direct way to do this is by defining a type *string* (as in Section 1.3) by the following:

```
const strsize = 80;
type string = record
                 ch: packed array [1..strsize] of char;
                 length: 0..strsize
              end;
```

The *length* portion of this record represents the current length of the string, whose characters are stored in the array *ch*. We also define two subrange types:

```
type postype = 1..strsize;
     lentype = 0..strsize;
```

One operation that will be required in this program is that of concatenation. For example, if two strings represented by *a* and *b* of type *string* represent the strings '*abcde*' and '*xyz*', respectively, then the procedure call

concat(a,b,c)

places into *c* (also of type *string*) the string '*abcdexyz*' (i.e., the string consisting of all the elements of *a* followed by all the elements of *b*). We also require a routine *substr*(*s*1,*i*,*j*,*s*2) which sets the string *s*2 to the substring of *s*1 starting at position *i* containing *j* characters. The routines *concat* and *substr* for this implementation of character strings may be found in Section 1.3.

Before transforming the conversion algorithm into a Pascal program, let us examine its inputs and outputs. We wish to write a procedure *convert* which accepts a character string. This string represents a prefix expression in which all variables are single letters and the allowable operators are '+', '−', '*', and '/'. The procedure produces a string which is the postfix equivalent of the prefix parameter.

Assume the existence of a function *find* which accepts a string and a position and returns an integer which is the length of the longest prefix expression contained within the input string which starts at that position. For example, *find*('a+cd',1) returns 1, since 'a' is the longest prefix string starting at the beginning of 'a+cd'. *find*('+*abcd+gh',1) returns 5, since '+*abc' is the longest prefix string starting at the beginning of '+*abcd+gh'. *find*('a+cd',2) returns 3, since '+cd' is the longest prefix string starting at position 2 of 'a+cd'. If no such prefix string exists within the input string starting at the specified position, *find* returns 0. [For example, *find*('*+ab',1) and *find*('+*a−c*d',6) both return 0.] This function is used to identify the first and second operands of a prefix operator. Assuming the existence of the function *find*, a conversion routine may be written as follows. *convert* also calls the function *letter*, which determines if its parameter is a letter.

```
procedure convert(prefix: string; var postfix: string);
var post1,post2,opstr,opnd1,opnd2,temp: string;
    op: char;
    m,n: lentype;
begin
    if prefix.length = 1
        then { check for variable }
            if letter(prefix.ch[1])
                then postfix:= prefix
                else error(' illegal prefix string ')
    else begin
            { The prefix string is longer than a single }
            { character. Extract the operator and the }
            {        two operand lengths.              }
            op:= prefix.ch[1];
            m:= find(prefix, 2);
            n:= find(prefix, m+2);
            if not (op in ['+', '−', '*', '/']) or
                (m = 0) or (n = 0) or (m+n+1 <> prefix.length)
                then error(' illegal prefix string ')
                else begin
                        substr(prefix, 2, m, opnd1);
                        substr(prefix, m+2, n, opnd2);
                        convert(opnd1,post1);
                        convert(opnd2,post2);
                        concat(post1,post2,temp);
```

```
                    opstr.ch[1]:= op;
                    opstr.length:= 1;
                    concat(temp, opstr, postfix)
           end {else begin}
      end {else begin}
end { function convert};
```

Note that several checks have been incorporated into *convert* to ensure that the parameter is a valid prefix string. One of the most difficult classes of errors to detect are those resulting from invalid inputs and the programmer's neglect to check for validity.

We now turn our attention to the function *find*, which accepts a character string and a starting position and returns the length of the longest prefix string which is contained in that input string starting at that position. The word "longest" in this definition is superfluous since there is at most one substring starting at a given position of a given string which is a valid prefix expression. We first show that there is at most one valid prefix expression starting at the beginning of a string. To see this, note that it is trivially true in a string of length 1. Assume that it is true for a short string. Then a long string that contains a prefix expression as an initial substring must begin with either a variable, in which case that variable is the desired substring, or with an operator. Deleting the initial operator, the remaining string is shorter than the original string and can therefore have at most a single initial prefix expression. This expression is the first operand of the initial operator. Similarly, the remaining substring (after deleting the first operand) can have only a single initial substring which is a prefix expression. This expression must be the second operand. Therefore, we have uniquely identified the operator and operands of the prefix expression starting at the first character of an arbitrary string, if such an expression exists. Since there is at most one valid prefix string starting at the beginning of any string, there is at most one such string starting at any position of an arbitrary string. This is obvious when we consider the substring of the given string starting at the given position.

Notice that this proof has given us a recursive method for finding a prefix expression in a string. We now incorporate this method into the function *find*:

```
function find(str: string; position: postype): lentype;
var m, n: lentype;
    first: char;
begin { function find}
    if position > str.length
      then find:= 0
      else begin
              first:= str.ch[position];
              if letter(first)
                then { First character is a letter.  That }
                     {  letter is the desired substring  }
                     find:= 1
```

CHAP. 3: RECURSION

```
              else { otherwise find the }
                  {  two operands   }
                begin
                    m:= find(str, position+1);
                    n:= find(str, position+m+1);
                    if (m = 0) or (n = 0)
                       then find:= 0
                       else find:= m + n + 1
                end {else begin}
          end {else begin}
    end { function find };
```

Make sure that you understand how these routines work by tracing their actions on both valid and invalid prefix expressions. More important, make sure that you understand how they were developed and how logical analysis led to a natural recursive solution that was directly translatable into a Pascal program.

1. Suppose that another provision were added to the Towers of Hanoi problem: that one disk may not rest on another disk which is more than one size larger (e.g., disk 1 may rest only on disk 2 or on the ground, disk 2 may rest only on disk 3 or on the ground, etc.). Why does the solution in the text fail to work? What is faulty about the logic that led to it under the new rules?

2. Prove that the number of moves performed by *towers* in moving n disks equals 2^n-1. Can you find a method of solving the Towers of Hanoi problem in fewer moves? Either find such a method for some n or prove that none exists.

3. Define a postfix and prefix expression to include the possibility of unary operators. Write a program to convert a prefix expression possibly containing the unary negation operator (represented by the symbol '@') to postfix.

4. Rewrite the function *find* in the text so that it is nonrecursive and computes the length of a prefix string by counting the number of operators and single-letter operands.

5. Write a recursive function that accepts a prefix expression consisting of binary operators and single-digit integer operands and returns the value of the expression.

6. Consider the following procedure for converting a prefix expression to postfix. The routine would be called by *convert(prefix,n,postfix)*, where n has been initialized to 1.

```
procedure convert(prefix: string; var n: posint; var postfix: string);
var p1,p2: string;
    c: char;
    len: lentype;
begin
    if n > prefix.length
       then postfix.length:= 0
```

```
            else begin
                    c:= prefix.ch[n];
                    n:= n + 1;
                    if letter(c)
                        then begin
                                postfix.ch[1]:= c;
                                postfix.length:= 1
                            end {then begin}
                        else  begin
                                convert(prefix, n, p1);
                                convert(prefix, n, p2);
                                concat(p1, p2, postfix);
                                len:= postfix.length + 1;
                                postfix.ch[len]:= c;
                                postfix.length:= len
                            end {else begin}
                end {else begin}
            end {procedure convert};
```

Explain how the procedure works. Is it better or worse than the method of the text? What happens if the routine is called with an invalid prefix string as input? Can you incorporate a check for such an invalid string within *convert*? Can you design such a check for the calling program after *convert* has returned? What is the value of *n* after *convert* returns?

7. Develop a recursive method (and program it) to compute the number of different ways in which an integer k can be written as a sum, each of whose operands is less than n.

8. Develop a recursive method (and program it) to print in alphabetical order all possible permutations of the letters stored in an array of size n.

9. Write a recursive Pascal program to find the kth smallest element of an array a of numbers by choosing any element $a[i]$ of a and partitioning a into those elements smaller than, equal to, and greater than $a[i]$.

10. The Eight Queens problem is to place eight queens on a chessboard so that no queen is attacking any other queen. The following is a recursive program to solve the problem. *board* is an 8 × 8 array that represents a chessboard. *board*[i,j] equals *true* if there is a queen at position [i,j], and *false* otherwise. *good(board)* is a function that returns *true* if no two queens on the chessboard are attacking each other, and *false* otherwise. At the end of the program, the status of *board* represents a solution to the problem.

```
program queens(input,output);
var board: array[1..8,1..8] of boolean;
    b: boolean;
    i,j: integer;
```

```
            function try(n: integer): boolean;
            var i: integer;
                ans: boolean;
            begin {function try}
                if n > 8
                    then try:= true
                    else begin
                            ans:= false;
                            i:= 1;
                            while (i <= 8) and (not ans)
                                do begin
                                        board[n,i]:= true;
                                        if good(board) and try(n+1)
                                            then ans:= true
                                            else begin
                                                    board[n,i]:= false;
                                                    i:= i + 1
                                                end {else begin}
                                    end {while...do begin};
                            try:= ans
                        end {else begin}
            end {function try};

            begin {program queens}
                for i:= 1 to 8
                    do for j:= 1 to 8
                            do board[i,j]:= false;
                b:= try(1)
            end {program queens}.
```

The recursive function *try* returns *true* if it is possible, given the *board* at the time
that it is called, to add queens in rows *n* through 8 to achieve a solution. *try* returns
false if there is no solution which has queens at the positions in *board* that already
contain *true*. If *true* is returned, the function also adds queens in rows *n* through 8
to produce a solution. Write the function *good* used above, and verify that the program produces a solution.

[The idea behind the solution is as follows: *board* represents the global situation
during an attempt to find a solution. The next step toward finding a solution is chosen
arbitrarily. Place a queen in the next untried position in row *n* and recursively test
whether it is possible to produce a solution which includes that step. If it is, then
return. If it is not, then backtrack from the attempted next step (*board*[n,i]:=*false*)
and try another possibility. This method is called ***backtracking***.]

11. A 10 × 10 array *maze* of 0s and 1s represent a maze in which a traveler must find a
    path from *maze*[1,1] to *maze*[10,10]. The traveler may move from a square into
    any adjacent square in the same row or column, but may not skip over any squares
    or move diagonally. In addition, the traveler may not move into any square that
    contains a 1. *maze*[1,1] and *maze*[10,10] contain 0s. Write a routine that accepts
    such a *maze* and either prints a message that no path through the maze exists or
    prints a list of positions representing a path from [1,1] to [10,10].

4. SIMULATING RECURSION

In this section we examine more closely some of the mechanisms used to implement recursion so that we can simulate these mechanisms using nonrecursive techniques. This activity is important for several reasons. First, many commonly used programming languages (such as FORTRAN, COBOL, and most machine languages) do not allow recursive programs. Problems such as the Towers of Hanoi and prefix-to-postfix conversion, whose solutions can be derived and stated quite simply using recursive techniques, can be programmed in these languages by simulating the recursive solution using more elementary operations. If we know that the recursive solution is correct (and it is often fairly easy to prove such a solution correct) and we have established techniques for converting a recursive solution to a nonrecursive one, then we can create a correct solution in a nonrecursive language. It is not an uncommon occurrence for a programmer to be able to state a solution to a problem in the form of a recursive algorithm. The ability to generate a nonrecursive solution from this algorithm is indispensable if he is using a compiler that does not support recursion.

Another reason for examining the implementation of recursion is that it will allow us to understand the implications of recursion and some of its hidden pitfalls. While these pitfalls do not exist in mathematical definitions that employ recursion, they seem to be an inevitable accompaniment of an implementation in a real language on a real machine.

Finally, even in a language such as Pascal which does support recursion, a recursive solution to a problem is usually more expensive than a nonrecursive solution, both in terms of time and space. Frequently, this expense is a small price to pay for the logical simplicity and self-documentation of the recursive solution. However, in a production program (such as a compiler, for example) which may be run thousands of times, the recurrent expense is a heavy burden on the system's limited resources. Thus a program may be designed to incorporate a recursive solution in order to reduce the expense of design and certification, and then carefully converted to a nonrecursive version to be put into actual day-to-day use. As we shall see, in performing such a conversion it is often possible to identify parts of the implementation of recursion that are superfluous in a particular application and thereby significantly reduce the amount of work that the program must perform.

Before examining the actions of a recursive routine, let us take a step back and examine the action of a nonrecursive routine. We will then be able to see what mechanisms must be added to support recursion. Before proceeding, we adopt the following convention. Suppose that we have the statement

$$rout(x)$$

where *rout* is defined as a procedure by the statement

$$\textbf{procedure } rout(a: \ldots);$$

x will be referred to as an *argument* (of the calling routine) and a will be referred to as a *parameter* (of the called routine).

What happens when a subroutine is called? The action of calling a subroutine (either a procedure or function) may be divided into three parts:

1. Passing arguments.
2. Allocating and initializing local variables.
3. Transferring control to the subroutine.

Let us examine each of these three steps in turn.

1. Passing arguments.

For a value parameter in Pascal, a copy of the argument is made locally within the procedure and any changes to the parameter are made to that local copy. The effect of this scheme is that the original input argument cannot be altered. In this method, storage for the argument is allocated within the data area of the subroutine.

For *var* parameters in Pascal the rule for transmission is different and we do not consider its effects on recursion here. For a discussion of value and variable parameters, see Section 5 of the Appendix.

2. Allocating and initializing local variables.

After arguments have been passed, the local variables of the subroutine are allocated. These local variables include all those declared directly in the procedure and any temporaries that must be created during the course of execution. For example, in evaluating the expression

$$x + y + z$$

a storage location must be set aside to hold the value of $x+y$ so that z can be added to it. Another storage location must be set aside to hold the value of the entire expression after it has been evaluated. Such locations are called *temporaries*, since they are needed only temporarily during the course of execution. Similarly, in a statement such as

$$x := fact(n)$$

a temporary must be set aside to hold the value of *fact*(n) before that value can be assigned to x.

3. Transferring control to the subroutine.

At this point control may still not be passed to the subroutine because provision has not yet been made for saving the *return address*. If a subroutine is given control, it must eventually restore control to the calling routine by means of a branch. However, it cannot execute that branch unless it knows the location to which it must return. Since this location is within the calling routine and not within the subroutine, the only way that the subroutine can know this address is to have it passed as an argument. This is exactly what happens. Aside from the explicit arguments specified by the programmer, there are also a set of implicit arguments that contain information necessary for the subroutine to execute and return correctly. Chief among these implicit arguments is the return address. The subroutine stores this address within its own data area. When it is ready to return control to the calling program, the subroutine retrieves the return address and branches to that location.

Once the arguments and the return address have been passed, control may be transferred to the subroutine, since everything required has been done to ensure that the subroutine will operate on the appropriate data and then return safely to the calling routine.

Return from a Subroutine

When a subroutine returns, three actions are performed. First, the return address is retrieved and stored in a safe location. Second, the subroutine's data area is freed. This data area contains all local variables (including local copies of arguments), temporaries, and the return address. Finally, a branch is taken to the return address, which had been previously saved. This restores control to the calling program at the point immediately after the instruction that initiated the call. In addition, if the subprogram is a function, the value returned is placed in a secure location from which the calling program may retrieve it. Usually, this location is a hardware register that is set aside for this purpose.

Suppose that a main procedure has called a subroutine b, which has called c, which has in turn called d. This is illustrated in Figure 3.4.1a,

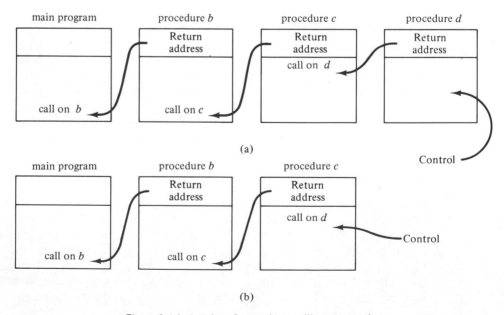

Figure 3.4.1 A series of procedures calling one another.

where we indicate that control currently resides somewhere within d. Within each subroutine, there is a location set aside for the return address. Thus the return address area of d contains the address of the instruction in c immediately following the call to d. Figure 3.4.1b shows the situation immediately following d's return to c. The return address within d has been retrieved and control transferred to that address.

You may have noticed that the string of return addresses forms a stack (i.e., the most recent return address to be added to the chain is the first to be removed). At any point, we can only access the return address from within the subroutine that is currently executing which represents the top of the stack. When the stack is popped (i.e., when the subroutine returns), a new top is revealed within the calling routine. Calling a subroutine has the effect of pushing an element onto the stack and returning pops the stack.

Implementing Recursive Routines

What must be added to this description in the case of a recursive routine? The answer is, surprisingly little. Each time a recursive routine calls itself, an entirely new data area for that particular call must be allocated. As before, this data area contains all parameters, local variables, temporaries, and a return address. The point to remember is that in recursion a data area is associated not with a subroutine alone, but with a particular call to that subroutine. Each call causes a new data area to be allocated, and each reference to an item in the subroutine's data area is to the data area of the most recent call. Similarly, each return causes the current data area to be freed, and the data area allocated immediately prior to the current area becomes current. This behavior, of course, suggests the use of a stack.

Simulation of Factorial

In Section 2, where we described the action of the recursive factorial function, we used a set of stacks to represent the successive allocations of each of the local variables and parameters. These stacks may be thought of as separate stacks, one for each local variable. Alternatively, and closer to reality, we may think of all of these stacks as a single large stack. Each element of this large stack is an entire data area containing subparts representing the individual local variables or parameters. Each time that the recursive routine is called, a new data area is allocated. The parameters within this data area are initialized to refer to the values of their corresponding arguments. The return address within the data area is initialized to the address following the call instruction. Any reference to local variables or parameters are via the current data area. When the recursive routine returns, the returned value (in the case of a function) and the return address are saved, the data area is freed, and a branch to the return address is executed. The calling routine retrieves the returned value (if any), resumes execution, and refers to its own data area, which is now on top of the stack.

Let us now examine how we can simulate the actions of a recursive procedure. We will need a stack of data areas defined by

```
const maxstack = 50;
type stack = record
               top: 0..maxstack;
               item: array[1..maxstack] of dataarea
            end;
```

dataarea is itself a record containing the various items that exist in a data area and must be defined to contain the fields required for the particular routine being simulated.

Since we do not yet know how to manipulate addresses in Pascal, we cannot simulate the mechanism of a call with *var* parameters. Since all of the recursive routines we have looked at in this chapter used value parameters, we do not address the question of *var* parameters for recursive routines at this time.

Let us look at a specific example—the factorial function. We repeat the code for that function:

```
function fact(n: nonegint): posint;
var x: nonegint;
    y: posint;
begin
    if n = 0
       then fact:= 1
       else begin
              x:= n - 1;
              y:= fact(x);
              fact:= n * y
          end {else begin}
end { function fact};
```

How are we to define the data area for this routine? It must contain the parameter *n* and the local variables *x* and *y*. As we shall see, no temporaries are needed. The data area must also contain a return address. In this case, there are two possible points to which we might want to return: the assignment of *fact*(*x*) to *y*, and the main program which called *fact*. Suppose that we had two labels declared by

label 1,2;

and we let the label 2 be the label of a section of code

2: y:= result

within the simulating program. Let the label 1 be the label of a statement

1: fact:= result

This reflects a convention that the variable *result* contains the value to be returned by an invocation of the *fact* function. The return address will be stored as an integer *i* (equal to either 1 or 2). To effect a return from a recursive call, the statement

```
case i of
   1: goto 1;
   2: goto 2
end
```

is executed. Thus, if $i=1$ a return is executed to the main program which called *fact*, and if $i=2$, a return is simulated to the assignment of the returned value to *y* in the previous execution of *fact*. Note that since the labels are not integers (even though they look like integers), we cannot write *goto i*.

Thus the data area stack for this example can be defined as follows:

```
const maxstack = 50;
type  dataarea =
          record
              param: nonegint;
              x: nonegint;
              y: posint;
              retaddr: 1..2
          end;
      stack =
          record
              top: 0..maxstack;
              item: array[1..maxstack] of dataarea
          end;
var s: stack;
```

The field in the data area that contains the simulated parameter is called *param* rather than *n*, to avoid confusion with the parameter *n* passed to the simulating routine. We also declare a current data area to hold the values of the variables in the simulated "current" call on the recursive routine. The declaration is

```
var currarea: dataarea;
```

In addition, we declare a single variable *result* by

```
var result: posint;
```

This variable is used to communicate the returned value of *fact* from one recursive call of *fact* to its caller, and from *fact* to the outside calling routine. Since the elements on the stack of data areas are records and a Pascal function cannot return a record, we cannot use a function *pop* to pop a data area from *stack*. Instead, we must write a procedure *popsub* defined by

```
procedure popsub(var s: stack; var area: dataarea);
```

popsub pops the stack and sets *area* to the popped element. We leave the details as an exercise.

A return from *fact* is simulated by the code

```
                 result:= value to be returned;
                 i:= currarea.retaddr;
                 popsub(stack,currarea);
                 case i of
                    1: goto 1;
                    2: goto 2
                 end;
```

A recursive call on *fact* is simulated by pushing the current data area on the stack, reinitializing the variables *currarea.param* and *currarea.retaddr* to the parameter and return address of this call, respectively, and then transferring control to the start of the simulated routine. Recall that *currarea.x* holds the value of $n-1$ which is to be the new parameter. Recall also that on a recursive call we wish to eventually return to label 2. The code to accomplish this is

```
        push(stack,currarea);
        currarea.param:= s.item[s.top].x;
        currarea.retaddr:= 2;
        goto 10 { 10 is the label of the start of the simulated routine }
```

Of course, the *popsub* and *push* routines must be written so that they pop and push entire records of type *dataarea* rather than simple variables. (Another imposition of the array implementation of stacks is that the variable *currarea.y* must be initialized to some value or an error will result in the *push* routine upon assignment of *currarea.y* to *item*[*top*].*y*.) Notice that in assigning a value to *currarea.param* we reference the top of the stack. In order to keep the array implementation of a stack transparent to the program, we should use a version of the *stacktop* function of Chapter 2 to access the top element of the stack. However, in the interest of simplicity, we do not do this here.

When the simulation first begins, the current area must be initialized so that *currarea.param* equals *n* and *currarea.retaddr* equals 1 (indicating a return to the calling routine). A dummy data area must be pushed onto the stack so that when *popsub* is executed in returning to the main routine, an underflow does not occur. This dummy data area must also be initialized so as not to cause an error in the *push* routine (see the parenthesized comment in the last paragraph). Thus the simulated version of the recursive *fact* routine is as follows:

```
        function simfact(n: nonegint): posint;
        label 1,2,10;
        const maxstack = 50;
        type dataarea =
                record
                   param: nonegint;
```

```
                    x: nonegint;
                    y: posint;
                    retaddr: 1..2
                end;
            stack =
                record
                    top: 0..maxstack;
                    item: array[1..maxstack] of dataarea
                end;
        var i: 1..2;
            result: posint;
            currarea: dataarea;
            s: stack;
        begin {initialization}
            s.top:= 0;
            currarea.param:= 0;
            currarea.x:= 0;
            currarea.y:= 1;
            currarea.retaddr:= 1;
            {   push the dummy data area onto the stack   }
            push(s,currarea);
            {   set the parameter and the return address   }
            { of the current data area to their proper values }
            currarea.param:= n;
            currarea.retaddr:= 1;
    10:     {      this is the beginning of the simulated      }
            {               factorial routine               }
            if currarea.param = 0
                then { simulation of fact:= 1 }
                    begin
                        result:= 1;
                        i:= currarea.retaddr;
                        popsub(s,currarea);
                        case i of
                            1: goto 1;
                            2: goto 2
                        end {case}
                    end {then begin};
            currarea.x:= currarea.param - 1;
            { simulation of recursive call to fact }
            push(s,currarea);
            currarea.param:= s.item[s.top].x;
            currarea.retaddr:= 2;
            goto 10;
```

```
2:  {     This is the point to which we return     }
    {     from the recursive call.  Set currarea.y     }
    {                 to the returned value.           }
    currarea.y:= result;
    {              simulation of fact:= n * y          }
    result:= currarea.param * currarea.y;
    i:= currarea.retaddr;
    popsub(s,currarea);
    case i of
       1: goto 1;
       2: goto 2
    end {case};
1:  { at this point we return to the main routine  }
    simfact:= result
end { function simfact};
```

Trace through the execution of this program for *n*=5 and be sure that you understand what the program does and how it does it.

Notice that no space was reserved in the data area for temporaries, since they need not be saved for later use. The temporary location that holds the value of *n*y* in the original recursive routine is simulated by the temporary for *currarea.param * currarea.y* in the simulating routine. This is not the case in general. For example, if a recursive function *funct* contained a statement such as

$$x:= a*funct(b) + c*funct(d)$$

the temporary for *a*funct*(*b*) must be saved during the recursive call on *funct*(*d*). However, in the example of the factorial function it is not required to stack the temporary.

Improving the Simulated Routine

This leads, naturally, to the question of whether all of the local variables really need to be stacked at all. A variable must be saved on the stack only if its value at the point of initiation of a recursive call must be reused after return from that call. Let us examine whether the variables *n*, *x*, and *y* meet this requirement. Clearly, *n* does have to be stacked. In the statement

$$y:= n * fact(x)$$

the old value of *n* must be used in the multiplication after return from the recursive call on *fact*. However, this is not the case for *x* and *y*. In fact, the value of *y* is not even defined at the point of the recursive call, so clearly it need not be stacked. Similarly, although *x* is defined at the point of call, it is never used again after returning, so why bother saving it?

This point can be illustrated even more sharply by the following realization. If *x* and *y* were not declared within the recursive function *fact*, but rather were declared as global variables, the routine would work just as well. Thus the automatic stacking and unstacking action performed by recursion for the local variables x and y is unnecessary.

Another interesting question to consider is whether the return address is really needed on the stack. Since there is only one textual recursive call to *fact*, there is only one return address within *fact*. The other return address is to the main routine which originally called *fact*. But suppose that a dummy data area had not been stacked upon initialization of the simulation. Then a data area is placed on the stack only in simulating a recursive call. When the stack is popped in returning from a recursive call, that area is removed from the stack. However, when an attempt is made to pop the stack in simulating a return to the main procedure, an underflow will occur. We can test for this underflow by using *popandtest* rather than *popsub*, and when it does occur we can return directly to the outside calling routine rather than through a local label. This means that one of the return addresses can be eliminated. Since this leaves only a single possible return address, it need not be placed on the stack.

Thus the data area has been reduced to contain the parameter alone and the stack may be declared by

```
const maxstack = 50;
type stack =
        record
          top: 0..maxstack;
          param: array[1..maxstack] of nonegint
        end;
var s: stack;
```

The current data area is reduced to a single variable declared by

```
var currparam: nonegint;
```

The program is now quite compact and comprehensible.

```
function simfact(n: nonegint): posint;
label 1,2,10;
const maxstack = 50;
type  stack =
        record
          top: 0..maxstack;
          param: array[1..maxstack] of nonegint
        end;
var s: stack;
    currparam,x: nonegint;
    y,result: posint;
    und: boolean;
begin {initialization}
    s.top:= 0;
    currparam:= n;
```

```
10:  {beginning of the simulated routine}
     if currparam = 0
        then {simulation of fact:= 1}
              begin
                    result:= 1;
                    popandtest(s, currparam, und);
                    if und
                        then { return to main routine }
                              goto 1
                        else {return from recursive call}
                              goto 2
              end {then begin};
     {currparam <> 0}
     x:= currparam - 1;
     {        simulation of recursive call        }
     push(s, currparam);
     currparam:= x;
     goto 10;
2:   {we return to this point from the simulated}
     {                recursive call             }
     y:= result;
     {        simulation of fact:= n * y;        }
     result:= currparam * y;
     popandtest(s, currparam, und);
     if und
        then {return to main routine}
              goto 1
        else {return to recursive call}
              goto 2;
1:   simfact:= result
end {function simfact};
```

Eliminating *goto*s

Although the foregoing program is certainly simpler than the previous one, it is still far from an "ideal" program. If you were to look at the program without having seen its derivation, it is probably doubtful that you could identify it as computing the factorial function. The statements

$$\textbf{goto 10} \quad \text{and} \quad \textbf{goto 2}$$

are particularly irritating, since they interrupt the flow of thought at a time that one might otherwise come to an understanding of what is happening. Let us see if we can transform this program into a still more readable version.

Several transformations are immediately apparent. First, the statements

```
popandtest(s, currparam, und);
if und
    then goto 1
    else goto 2
```

appear twice for the two cases *currparam* = 0 and *currparam* <> 0. The two sections can easily be combined into one. A further observation is that the two variables *x* and *currparam* are assigned values from each other and are never in use simultaneously, so they may be combined and referred to as one variable *x*. A similar statement may be made about the variables *result* and *y*, which may be combined and referred to as the single variable *y*.

Performing these transformations leads to the following version of *simfact*:

```
function simfact(n: nonegint): posint;
label 2,10;
const maxstack = 50;
type  stack =
          record
              top: 0..maxstack;
              param: array[1..maxstack] of nonegint
          end;
var s: stack;
    x: nonegint;
    y: posint;
    und: boolean;
begin {function simfact}
      s.top:= 0;
      x:= n;
10:   if x = 0
          then y:= 1
          else begin
                    push(s, x);
                    x:= x - 1;
                    goto 10
               end {else begin};
2:    popandtest(s,x,und);
      if und
          then simfact:= y
          else begin
                    y:= x * y;
                    goto 2
               end {else begin}
end {function simfact};
```

We are now beginning to approach a readable program. Note that the program consists of two loops:

1. The loop that consists of the entire *if* statement labeled 10. This loop is exited when *x*=0, at which point *y* is set to 1 and execution proceeds to the label 2.

2. The loop that begins at label 2 and ends with the statement *goto 2*. This loop is exited when the stack has been emptied and underflow occurs, at which point a return is executed.

These loops can easily be transformed into explicit *while* loops as follows:

```
{ subtraction loop }
while x <> 0
        do begin
                      push (s,x);
                      x:= x - 1
              end {do begin};
      y:= 1;
      popandtest (s, x, und);
      {multiplication loop}
      while not und
              do begin
                      y:= x * y;
                      popandtest (s, x, und)
              end {do begin};
      simfact:= y
```

Let us examine these two loops more closely. x starts off at the value of the input parameter n and is reduced by one each time that the subtraction loop is repeated. Each time x is set to a new value, the old value of x is saved on the stack. This continues until x is 0. Thus after the first loop has been executed, the stack contains, from top to bottom, the integers 1 to n.

The multiplication loop merely removes each of these values from the stack and sets y to the product of the popped value and the old value of y. Since we know what the stack contains at the start of the multiplication loop, why bother popping the stack? We can use those values directly. We can eliminate the stack and the first loop entirely and replace the multiplication loop with a loop that multiplies y by each of the integers from 1 to n in turn. The resulting program is

```
function simfact (n: nonegint): posint;
var x: nonegint;
    y: posint;
begin {function simfact}
      y:= 1;
      for x:= 1 to n
          do y:= y * x;
      simfact:= y
end {function simfact};
```

But this program is a direct Pascal implementation of the iterative version of the factorial function as presented in Section 1. The only change is that x varies from 1 to n rather than from n to 1.

Simulating the Towers of Hanoi

We have shown that successive transformations of a nonrecursive simulation of a recursive routine may lead to a simpler program for solving a problem. Let us now look at a more complex example of recursion, the Towers of Hanoi problem presented in Section 3. We will simulate its recursion and attempt to simplify the simulation to produce a nonrecursive solution. We present again the recursive procedure of Section 3.

```
procedure towers(n: posint; frompeg,topeg,auxpeg: char);
begin
    if n = 1
        then writeln('move disk 1 from peg ', frompeg, ' to peg ', topeg)
        else begin
                towers(n-1, frompeg, auxpeg, topeg);
                writeln('move disk ', n, ' from peg ', frompeg, ' to peg ', topeg);
                towers(n-1, auxpeg, topeg, frompeg)
            end {else begin}
end {procedure towers};
```

Make sure that you understand the problem and the recursive solution before proceeding.

There are four parameters in this subroutine, each of which is subject to change in a recursive call. Therefore, the data area must contain elements representing all four. There are no local variables. There is a single temporary that is needed to hold the value of $n-1$, but this can be represented by a similar temporary in the simulating program and does not have to be stacked. There are three possible points to which the subroutine returns on various calls: the calling program and the two points following the recursive calls. Therefore, three labels are necessary:

label 1,2,3;

The return address will be encoded as an integer (either 1, 2, or 3) within each data area.

Consider the following nonrecursive simulation of *towers*:

```
procedure simtowers(n: posint; frompeg,topeg,auxpeg: char);
label 1,2,3,10;
const maxstack = 50;
type  dataarea =
        record
          nparam: posint;
          fromparam: char;
          toparam: char;
          auxparam: char;
          retaddr: 1..3
        end;
```

```
          stack =
             record
                top: 0..maxstack;
                item: array[1..maxstack] of dataarea
             end;
      var s: stack;
         currarea: dataarea;
         i: 1..3;
      begin {initialization}
         s.top:= 0;
         currarea.nparam:= 1;
         currarea.fromparam:= ' ';
         currarea.toparam:= ' ';
         currarea.auxparam:= ' ';
         currarea.retaddr:= 1;
         {    push dummy data area onto stack    }
         push(s,currarea);
         {set the parameters and the return address}
         { of the current data area to their proper }
         {                values                    }
         currarea.nparam:= n;
         currarea.fromparam:= frompeg;
         currarea.toparam:= topeg;
         currarea.auxparam:= auxpeg;
         currarea.retaddr:= 1;
 10:    {this is the start of the simulated routine}
         if currarea.nparam = 1
            then with currarea
                 do begin
                       writeln('move disk 1 from peg ', fromparam,
                                                ' to peg ', toparam);
                       i:= retaddr;
                       popsub(s,currarea);
                       case i of
                          1: goto 1;
                          2: goto 2;
                          3: goto 3
                       end {case}
                    end {then with...do begin};
         {      this is the first recursive call      }
         push(s,currarea);
         currarea.nparam:= s.item[s.top].nparam - 1;
         currarea.fromparam:= s.item[s.top].fromparam;
         currarea.toparam:= s.item[s.top].auxparam;
         currarea.auxparam:= s.item[s.top].toparam;
```

```
        currarea.retaddr := 2;
        goto 10;
  2:   {     we return to this point from the     }
        {              first recursive call          }
        writeln('move disk ', currarea.nparam, ' from peg ',
                  currarea.fromparam, ' to peg ', currarea.toparam);
        {     this is the second recursive call     }
        push(s, currarea);
        currarea.nparam := s.item[s.top].nparam - 1;
        currarea.fromparam := s.item[s.top].auxparam;
        currarea.toparam := s.item[s.top].toparam;
        currarea.auxparam := s.item[s.top].fromparam;
        currarea.retaddr := 3;
        goto 10;
  3:   { return to this point from the second   }
        {              recursive call             }
        i := currarea.retaddr;
        popsub(s, currarea);
        case i of
          1: goto 1;
          2: goto 2;
          3: goto 3
        end {case};
  1:   {       return to the calling program        }
  end {procedure simtowers};
```

Let us attempt to simplify the foregoing program. First, notice that three labels were used for return addresses; one for each of the two recursive calls and one for the return to the main program. However, the return to the main program can be signaled by an underflow in the stack, exactly as in the second version of *simfact*. This leaves two return labels. If we could eliminate one more such label it would no longer be necessary to stack the return address, since there would be only one point remaining to which control may be passed if the stack is popped successfully. We focus our attention on the second recursive call and the following segment:

$$\text{towers}(n-1, \text{auxpeg}, \text{topeg}, \text{frompeg})$$
$$\textbf{end}$$

The actions that occur in simulating this call are:

1. Push the current data area, $a1$, onto the stack.
2. Set the parameters in the new current data area, $a2$, to their respective values: $n-1$, *auxpeg*, *topeg*, and *frompeg*.
3. Set the return label in the current data area, $a2$, to the address of the statement immediately following the call.
4. Branch to the beginning of the simulated routine.

After the simulated routine has completed, it is ready to return. The following actions occur:

5. Save the return label, l, from the current data area $a2$.
6. Pop the stack and set the current data area to the popped data area, $a1$.
7. Branch to l.

But l is a label at the keyword *end*. Thus the next step is to pop the stack again and return once more. We never again make use of the information in the current data area $a1$, since it is immediately destroyed by popping the stack as soon as it has been restored. Since there is no reason to use this data area again, there is no reason to save it on the stack in simulating the call. Data need be saved on the stack only if it is to be reused. Therefore, in this case, the call may be simulated simply by:

1. Changing the parameters in the current data area to their respective values.
2. Branching to the beginning of the simulated routine.

When the simulated routine returns, it can return directly to the routine that called the current version. There is no reason to execute a return to the current version, only to return immediately to the previous version. Since there is only one possible return address left, it is unnecessary to keep it in the data area, to be pushed and popped with the rest of the data. Whenever the stack is popped successfully, there is only one address to which a branch can be executed: the statement following the first call. If an underflow is encountered, the routine returns to the calling routine. Since the new values of the variables in the current data area will be obtained from the old value in the current data area, it will be necessary to declare an additional variable *temp* so that values can be interchanged.

Our revised nonrecursive simulation of *towers* follows:

```
procedure simtowers(n: posint; frompeg, topeg, auxpeg: char);
label 1, 2, 10;
const maxstack = 50;
type  dataarea =
          record
            nparam: posint;
            fromparam: char;
            toparam: char;
            auxparam: char
          end;
      stack =
          record
            top: 0..maxstack;
            item: array [1..maxstack] of dataarea
          end;
```

```
var s: stack;
    currarea: dataarea;
    und: boolean;
    temp: char;
begin {initialization}
    s.top:= 0;
    currarea.nparam:= n;
    currarea.fromparam:= frompeg;
    currarea.toparam:= topeg;
    currarea.auxparam:= auxpeg;
10:   {the simulated routine begins here}
    if currarea.nparam = 1
        then with currarea
            do begin
                    writeln('move disk 1 from peg ',
                                    fromparam, ' to peg', toparam);
                    {simulate the return}
                    popandtest(s,currarea,und);
                    if und
                        then goto 1 { return to main routine   }
                        else  goto 2 {go to point after recursive}
                                     {          call          }
                end {with...do begin};
        {simulation of first recursive call}
        push(s,currarea);
        currarea.nparam:= s.item[s.top].nparam - 1;
        currarea.fromparam:= s.item[s.top].fromparam;
        currarea.toparam:= s.item[s.top].auxparam;
        currarea.auxparam:= s.item[s.top].toparam;
        goto 10;
2:    {this is the point of return from the}
      {          first recursive call          }
        writeln('move disk ', currarea.nparam, ' from peg ',
                    currarea.fromparam, ' to peg ', currarea.toparam);
        {simulation of second recursive call}
        currarea.nparam:= currarea.nparam - 1;
        temp:= currarea.fromparam;
        currarea.fromparam:= currarea.auxparam;
        currarea.auxparam:= temp;
        goto 10;
1:    {   return to the calling program   }
end {procedure simtowers};
```

Examining the structure of the program, we see that it can easily be reorganized into a simpler format. We begin from the code appearing at the label 10.

```
und := false;
repeat
    while currarea.nparam <> 1
        do with currarea
            do begin
                push(s, currarea);
                nparam := s.item[s.top].nparam - 1;
                fromparam := s.item[s.top].fromparam;
                toparam := s.item[s.top].auxparam;
                auxparam := s.item[s.top].toparam
            end {do begin};
    writeln('move disk 1 from peg ', currarea.fromparam, ' to peg ',
                                            currarea.toparam);
    popandtest(s, currarea, und);
    if not und
        then with currarea
            do begin
                writeln('move disk ', nparam, ' from peg ',
                                    fromparam, 'to peg ', toparam);
                nparam := nparam - 1;
                temp := fromparam;
                fromparam := auxparam;
                auxparam := temp
            end {with...do begin}
    until und
```

Trace through the actions of this program and see how it reflects the actions of the original recursive version.

EXERCISES

1. Write a nonrecursive simulation of the functions *convert* and *find* presented in Section 3.

2. Write a nonrecursive simulation of the recursive binary search procedure, and transform it into an iterative procedure.

3. Write a nonrecursive simulation of *fib*. Can you transform it into an iterative method?

4. Write nonrecursive simulations of the recursive routines of Sections 2 and 3 and the exercises of those sections.

5. Convert the following recursive program scheme into an iterative version that does not use a stack. $f(n)$ is a function that returns a boolean value based on the value of n, and $g(n)$ is a function that returns a value of the same type as n without modifying n.

```
procedure rec(n: ntype);
begin
    if not f(n)
        then begin
            {    any group of Pascal statements    }
            {which does not change the value of n}
            rec(g(n))
        end {then begin}
end {procedure rec};
```

Generalize your result to the case in which *rec* is a function.

6. Let $f(n)$ be a boolean-valued function and $g(n)$ and $h(n)$ be functions that return a value of the same type as n without modifying n. Let (*stmts*) represent any group of Pascal statements that do not modify the value of n. Show that the recursive program scheme *rec* is equivalent to the iterative scheme *iter*:

```
procedure rec(n: type1);
begin
      if not f(n)
         then begin
                    (stmts);
                    rec(g(n));
                    rec(h(n))
              end {then begin}
end {procedure rec};
```

```
procedure iter(n: type1);
type stack =
        record
          top: 0..100;
          nvalues: array[1..100] of type1
        end;
    var s: stack;
    begin
        s.top:= 0;
        push(s,n);
        while not empty(s)
             do begin
                       n:= pop(s);
                       if not f(n)
                          then begin
                                     (stmts);
                                     push(s,h(n));
                                     push(s,g(n))
                                end {then begin}
                end {while...do begin}
    end {procedure iter};
```

Show that the *if* statements in *iter* can be replaced by the loop:

```
while not f(n)
      do begin
               (stmts)
               push(s,h(n));
               n:= g(n)
        end {while...do begin}
```

Modify the two iterative versions for the case of a recursive function.

5. EFFICIENCY OF RECURSION

In general, a nonrecursive version of a program will execute more efficiently in terms of time and space than a recursive version. This is because the overhead involved in entering and exiting a block is avoided in the nonrecursive version. As we have seen, it is often possible to identify a good number of local variables and temporaries that do not have to be saved and restored through the use of a stack. In a nonrecursive program this needless stacking activity can be eliminated. However, in a recursive procedure, the compiler is usually unable to identify such variables, and they are therefore stacked and unstacked to ensure that no problems arise.

However, we have also seen that sometimes a recursive solution is the most natural and logical way of solving a problem. It is doubtful whether a programmer could have developed the nonrecursive solution to the Towers of Hanoi problem directly from the problem statement. A similar comment may be made about the problem of converting prefix to postfix, where the recursive solution flows directly from the definitions. A nonrecursive solution involving stacks is much more difficult to develop and more prone to error.

Thus we have a conflict between machine efficiency and programmer efficiency. With the cost of programming increasing steadily and the cost of computation decreasing, we have reached the point where in most cases it is not worth a programmer's time to laboriously construct a nonrecursive solution to a problem which is most naturally solved recursively. Of course, an incompetent overly clever programmer may come up with a complicated recursive solution to a simple problem which can be solved directly by non-recursive methods. (An example of this is the factorial function, or even the binary search.) However, if a competent programmer identifies a recursive solution as being the simplest and most straightforward method for solving a particular problem, it is often not worth the time and effort to discover a more efficient method.

However, this is not always the case. If a program is to be run very frequently (often, entire computers are dedicated to continually running the same program), so that increased efficiency in execution speed significantly increases throughput, the extra investment in programming time is worthwhile. Even in such cases, it is probably better to create a nonrecursive version by simulating and transforming the recursive solution than by attempting to create a nonrecursive solution from the problem statement.

To do this most efficiently, what is required is to first write the recursive routine and then its simulated version, including all stacks and temporaries. After this has been done, eliminate all stacks and variables that are super-fluous. The final version is a refinement of the original program, and is certainly more efficient. Clearly, the elimination of each superfluous and redundant operation will improve the efficiency of the resulting program. However, every transformation applied to a program is another opening through which an unanticipated error may creep in.

The ideas and transformations that we have put forward in presenting the factorial function and the Towers of Hanoi can be applied to more complex problems whose nonrecursive solution is not readily apparent. The extent to which a recursive solution (actual or simulated) can be transformed into a direct solution will depend in large measure on the particular problem and the ingenuity of the programmer.

EXERCISES   1. Run the recursive and nonrecursive versions of the factorial function of Sections 2 and 4, and examine how much space and time each requires as n becomes larger.

2. Do the same as in Exercise 1 for the Towers of Hanoi problem.

4 Queues and Lists

This chapter introduces the queue, an important data structure that is often used to simulate real-world situations. The concepts of the stack and queue are then extended to a new structure, the list. Various forms of lists and their associated operations are examined and several applications are presented.

1. THE QUEUE AND ITS SEQUENTIAL REPRESENTATION

A *queue* is an ordered collection of items from which items may be deleted at one end (called the *front* of the queue) and into which items may be inserted at the other end (called the *rear* of the queue).

Figure 4.1.1a illustrates a queue containing three elements, A, B, and C. A is at the front of the queue and C is at the rear. In Figure 4.1.1b, an element has been deleted from the queue. Since elements may be deleted only from the front of the queue, A is removed and B is now at the front. In Figure 4.1.1c, when items D and E are inserted, they must be inserted at the rear of the queue.

Since D has been inserted into the queue before E, it will be removed earlier. The first element inserted into a queue is the first element to be removed. For this reason a queue is sometimes called a *fifo* (first in, first out) list, as opposed to a stack which is a *lifo* (last in, first out) list. Examples of queues abound in the real world. A line at a bank or at a bus stop, and a batch of jobs waiting to be read by a card reader, are familiar examples of queues.

There are three primitive operations that can be applied to a queue. The operation *insert*(q,x) inserts item x at the rear of the queue q. The operation $x:=remove(q)$ deletes the front element from the queue q and sets x to its contents. The third operation, *empty*(q), returns *false* or *true* depending on whether or not the queue contains any elements. The queue in Figure 4.1.1 can be obtained by the following sequence of operations. We assume that the queue is initially empty.

158

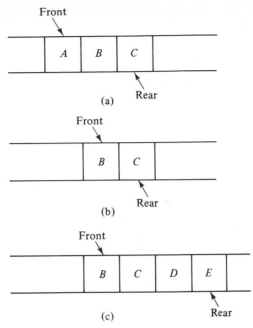

Front

| A | B | C |

Rear

(a)

Front

| B | C |

Rear

(b)

Front

| B | C | D | E |

Rear

(c)

Figure 4.1.1 A queue.

insert (q,A);
insert (q,B);
insert (q,C);   (Figure 4.1.1a)
$x := remove(q)$;   (Figure 4.1.1b; x is set to A)
insert (q,D);
insert (q,E) (Figure 4.1.1c)

The *insert* operation can always be performed since there is no limit to the number of elements a queue may contain. The *remove* operation, however, can be applied only if the queue is nonempty—there is no way to remove an element from a queue that contains no elements. The result of an illegal attempt to remove an element from an empty queue is called *underflow*. The *empty* operation is, of course, always applicable.

How shall a queue be represented in Pascal? An idea that comes immediately to mind is to use an array to hold the elements of the queue, and to use two variables, *front* and *rear*, to hold the positions within the array of the first and last elements of the queue. Thus a queue of integers might be declared by

```
const maxqueue = 100;
type  queue = record
                items: array[1..maxqueue] of integer;
                front,rear: 0..maxqueue
              end;
var   q: queue;
```

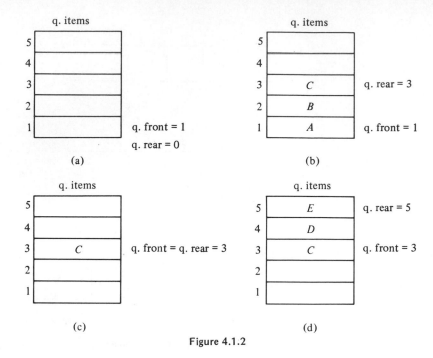

Figure 4.1.2

Of course, using an array to hold a queue introduces the possibility of *overflow* if the queue contains more elements than were allocated for the array. Ignoring the possibility of underflow and overflow for the moment, the operation *insert* (q,x) could be implemented by the statements

$$q.rear := q.rear + 1;$$
$$q.items[q.rear] := x$$

and the operation $x := remove(q)$ could be implemented by

$$x := q.items[q.front];$$
$$q.front := q.front + 1$$

[handwritten annotation: -1? $+1$ correct → front advances as element removed.]

Initially, *q.rear* is set to 0 and *q.front* is set to 1, and the queue is empty whenever *q.rear* < *q.front*. The number of elements in the queue at any time is equal to the value of *q.rear* - *q.front* + 1.

Let us examine what might happen under this representation. Figure 4.1.2 illustrates an array of five elements used to represent a queue (i.e., *maxqueue*=5). Initially (Figure 4.1.2a), the queue is empty. In Figure 4.1.2b items *A*, *B*, and *C* have been inserted. In Figure 4.1.2c two items have been deleted, and in Figure 4.1.2d two new items *D* and *E* have been inserted. The value of *q.front* is 3 and the value of *q.rear* is 5, so that there are only 5–3+1=3 elements in the queue. Since the array contains five elements, there should be room for the queue to expand without the worry of overflow. However, to insert *F* into the queue, *q.rear* must be increased by 1 to 6 and *q.items*[6] must be set to the value *F*. But *q.items* is an array of

CHAP. 4: QUEUES AND LISTS

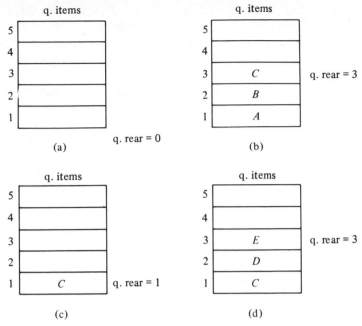

Figure 4.1.3

only five elements, so that the insertion cannot be made. It is possible to reach the absurd situation where the queue is empty, yet no new element can be inserted (see if you can come up with a sequence of insertions and deletions to reach that situation). Clearly, the array representation as outlined above is unacceptable.

One solution is to modify the *remove* operation so that when an item is deleted, the entire queue is shifted to the beginning of the array. The operation $x := remove(q)$ would then be modified (again, ignoring the possibility of underflow) to

```
x:= q.items[1];
for i:= 1 to q.rear - 1
    do q.items[i] := q.items[i+1];
q.rear:= q.rear - 1
```

The field *front* need no longer be specified as part of a queue, because the front of the queue is always at the first element of the array. The empty queue is represented by the queue in which *rear* equals zero. Figure 4.1.3 shows the queue of Figure 4.1.2 under this new representation.

This method, however, is too inefficient to be satisfactory. Each deletion involves moving every remaining element of the queue. If a queue contains 500 or 1000 elements, this is clearly too high a price to pay. Further, the operation of removing an element from a queue logically involves manipulation of only one element—the one currently at the front of the queue. The implementation of that operation should reflect this and should not involve a host of extraneous operations.

Another solution is to treat the array that holds the queue as a circle rather than as a straight line. That is, we imagine the first element of the array as immediately following its last element. This implies that even if the last element is occupied, a new value can be inserted behind it in the first element of the array as long as that first element is empty.

Let us look at an example. Assume that a queue contains three items in positions 3, 4, and 5 of a five-element array. This is the situation of Figure 4.1.2d, reproduced as Figure 4.1.4a. Although the array is not full, the last element of the array is occupied. If an attempt is now made to insert item F into the queue, it can be placed in position 1 of the array, as shown in Figure 4.1.4b. The first item of the queue is in $q.items[3]$, which is fol-

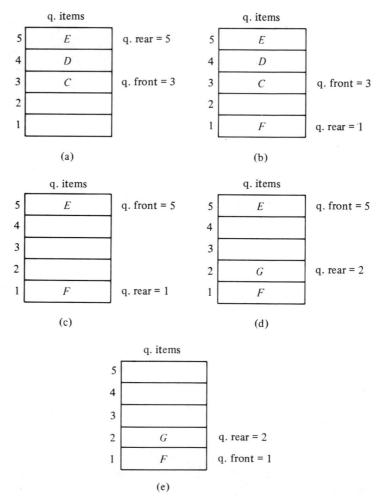

Figure 4.1.4

lowed in the queue by $q.items[4]$, $q.items[5]$, and $q.items[1]$. Figures 4.1.4c–e show the status of the queue as first two items C and D are deleted, then G is inserted, and finally E is deleted.

Unfortunately, it is difficult under this representation to determine when the queue is empty. The condition $q.rear < q.front$ is no longer valid as a test for the empty queue, since Figures 4.1.4b–d all illustrate situations in which the condition is true, yet the queue is not empty.

One way of solving this problem is to establish the convention that the value of $q.front$ is the index of the array element immediately preceding the first element of the queue rather than the index of the first element itself. Thus since $q.rear$ contains the index of the last element of the queue, the condition $q.front = q.rear$ implies that the queue is empty.

A queue of integers may therefore be declared and initialized by

```
const maxqueue = 100;
type  queue = record
                    items: array[1..maxqueue] of integer;
                    front,rear: 1..maxqueue
              end;
var   q: queue;
begin
      q.front:= maxqueue;
      q.rear:= maxqueue
```

Note that $q.front$ and $q.rear$ are initialized to the last index of the array, rather than 0 or 1, because the last element of the array immediately precedes the first one within the queue under this representation. Since $q.rear = q.front$, the queue is initially empty.

The *empty* function may be coded as

```
function empty(q: queue): boolean;
begin
      with q
            do if front = rear
                  then empty:= true
                  else  empty:= false
end {function empty};
```

The operation *remove*(q) may be coded as

```
function remove(var q: queue): integer;
begin
      if empty(q)
            then error('queue underflow')
            else with q
                  do begin
                        if front = maxqueue
                              then front:= 1
                              else  front:= front + 1;
```

```
                        remove:= items[front]
                    end {else with q do begin}
        end {function remove};
```

Note that *q.front* must be updated before an element is extracted.

Of course, often an underflow condition is meaningful and serves as a signal for a new phase of processing. We may wish to use a procedure *remvandtest* that would be declared by

```
        procedure remvandtest(var q: queue; var x: integer; var und: boolean);
```

This routine sets *und* to *false* and *x* to the element removed from the queue if the queue is nonempty and sets *und* to *true* if underflow occurs. The coding of the routine is left to the reader.

The *insert* Operation

The *insert* operation involves taking care of overflow. Overflow occurs when the entire array is occupied by items of the queue and an attempt is made to insert yet another element into the queue. For example, consider the queue of Figure 4.1.5a. There are three elements in the queue: C, D, and E in $q.items[3]$, $q.items[4]$, and $q.items[5]$, respectively. Since the last item of the queue occupies $q.items[5]$, $q.rear$ equals 5. Since the first element of the queue is in $q.items[3]$, $q.front$ equals 2. In Figure 4.1.5b and c, items F and G are inserted into the queue and the value of $q.rear$ is changed accordingly. At that point, the array is full and an attempt to perform any more insertions will cause an overflow. But this is indicated by the fact that $q.front = q.rear$, which is precisely the indication for underflow. It seems that there is no way to distinguish between the empty queue and the full queue under this implementation. Such a situation is clearly unsatisfactory.

One solution is to sacrifice one element of the array and to allow a queue to grow only as large as one less than the size of the array. Thus, if an array of 100 elements is declared as a queue, the queue may have up to 99 members. An attempt to insert a hundredth element into the queue will cause an overflow. The *insert* routine may then be written as follows:

```
        procedure insert(var q: queue; x: integer);
        begin
            with q
                do begin
                        if rear = maxqueue
                            then rear:= 1
                            else rear:= rear + 1;
                        if rear = front
                            then error('queue overflow')
                            else items[rear] := x
                    end {with q do begin}
        end {procedure insert};
```

164   CHAP. 4: QUEUES AND LISTS

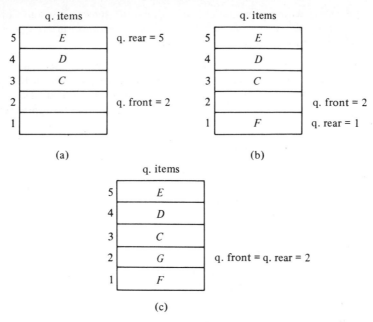

Figure 4.1.5

The test for overflow in *insert* occurs after $q.rear$ has been adjusted, whereas the test for underflow in *remove* occurs immediately upon entering the routine, before $q.front$ is updated.

EXERCISES

1. Write the procedure *remvandtest* (q,x,und), which sets *und* to *false* and x to the item removed from a nonempty queue q, and sets *und* to *true* if the queue is empty.

2. What set of conditions are necessary and sufficient for a sequence of *insert* and *remove* operations on a single empty queue to leave the queue empty without causing an underflow? What set of conditions are necessary and sufficient for such a sequence to leave a nonempty queue unchanged?

3. If an array is not considered circular, the text suggests that each *remove* operation must shift down every remaining element of a queue. An alternative method is to postpone shifting until *rear* equals the last index of the array. When that situation occurs and an attempt is made to insert an element into the queue, the entire queue is shifted down so that the first element of the queue is in the first position of the array. What are the advantages of this method over performing a shift at each *remove* operation? What are the disadvantages? Rewrite the routines *remove*, *insert*, and *empty* using this method.

4. Show how a sequence of insertions and removals from a queue represented by a linear array can cause an overflow to occur upon an attempt to insert an element into an empty queue.

5. We can avoid sacrificing one element of a queue if a field *empty:boolean* is added to the queue representation. Show how this can be done and rewrite the queue manipulation routines under that representation.

6. How would you implement a queue of stacks? A stack of queues? A queue of queues? Write routines to implement the appropriate operations for each of these data structures.

7. Show how to implement a queue of integers in Pascal by using an array *queue* [-1.. 100], where *queue* [-1] is used to indicate the front of the queue, *queue* [0] is used to indicate its rear, and *queue* [1] through *queue* [100] are used to contain the queue elements. Show how to initialize such an array to represent the empty queue and write routines *remove*, *insert*, and *empty* for such an implementation.

8. Show how to implement a queue in Pascal in which each item consists of a variable number of integers.

9. A *deque* is an ordered set of items from which items may be deleted at either end and into which items may be inserted at either end. Call the two ends of a deque *left* and *right*. How can a deque be represented as a Pascal array? Write four Pascal routines,

remvleft, remvright, insrtleft, insrtright

to remove and insert elements at the left and right ends of a deque. Make sure that the routines work properly for the empty deque and that they detect overflow and underflow.

10. Define an **input-restricted deque** as a deque (see Exercise 9) for which only the operations *remvleft*, *remvright*, and *insrtleft* are valid, and an **output-restricted deque** as a deque for which only the operations *remvleft*, *insrtleft*, and *insrtright* are valid. Show how each of these can be used to represent both a stack and a queue.

11. The Scratchemup Parking Garage contains a single lane which can hold up to 10 cars. Cars arrive at the south end of the garage and leave from the north end. If a customer arrives to pick up a car that is not the northernmost, all cars to the north of his car are moved out, his car is driven out, and the other cars are restored in the same order that they were in originally. Whenever a car leaves, all cars to the south are moved forward so that at all times all the empty spaces are in the south part of the garage.

  Write a program that reads a group of input lines. Each line contains an 'a' for arrival or a 'd' for departure, and a license plate number. Cars are assumed to arrive and depart in the order specified by the input. The program should print a message each time that a car arrives or departs. When a car arrives, the message should specify whether or not there is room for the car in the garage. If there is no room for a car, the car waits until there is room or until a departure card is read for the car. When room becomes available, another message should be printed. When a car departs, the message should include the number of times the car was moved within the garage (including the departure itself but not the arrival). This number is 0 if the car departs from the waiting line.

2. LINKED LISTS

What are the drawbacks of using sequential storage to represent stacks and queues? One major drawback is that a fixed amount of storage remains allocated to the stack or queue even when the structure is actually using a smaller amount or possibly no storage at all. Further, no more than that fixed amount of storage may be allocated, thus introducing the possibility of overflow.

Assume that a program uses two stacks implemented in two separate arrays, $s1.items$ and $s2.items$. Further, assume that each of these arrays has 100 elements. Then despite the fact that 200 elements are available for the two stacks, neither can grow beyond 100 items. Even if the first stack contains only 25 items, the second cannot contain more than 100. One solution to this problem is to allocate a single array $items$ of 200 elements. The first stack will occupy $items[1]$, $items[2]$, ..., $items[top1]$, while the second stack will be allocated from the other end of the array, occupying $items[200]$, $items[199]$, ..., $items[top2]$. Thus when one of the stacks is not occupying storage, the other stack may make use of that storage. Of course, two distinct sets of pop, $push$, and $empty$ routines are necessary for the two stacks, since one grows by increasing $top1$ while the other grows by decreasing $top2$.

Unfortunately, although such a scheme allows two stacks to share a common area, no such simple solution exists for three or more stacks or even for two queues. Instead, one must keep track of the tops and bottoms (or fronts and rears) of all the structures sharing a single large array. Each time that the growth of one structure is about to impinge on the storage currently being used by another, all the structures must be shifted within the single array to allow for the growth.

In a sequential representation, the items of a stack or queue are implicitly ordered by the sequential order of storage. Thus, if $q.items[x]$ represents an element of a queue, the next element will be $q.items[x + 1]$ (or if $x = maxqueue$, $q.items[1]$). Suppose that the items of a stack or a queue were explicitly ordered; that is, each item contained within itself the address of the next item. Such an explicit ordering gives rise to a data structure pictured in Figure 4.2.1, which is known as a *linear linked list*. Each item in the list is called a *node* and contains two fields, an *information* field and a *next address* field. The information field holds the actual element on the list. The next address field contains the address of the next node in the list. Such an address, which is used to access a particular node, is known as a *pointer*. The entire linked list is accessed from an external pointer *list*, which points to (contains the address of) the first node in the list. (By an "external" pointer, we mean one that is not included within a

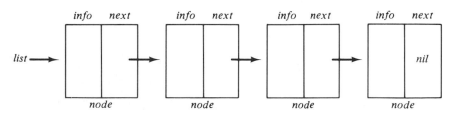

Figure 4.2.1 A linear linked list.

node. Rather its value can be accessed directly by referencing a variable.) The next address field of the last node in the list contains a special value, known as *nil*, which is not a valid address. This *nil pointer* is used to signal the end of a list.

The list with no nodes on it is called the *empty list* or the *nil list*. The value of the external pointer *list* to such a list is the nil pointer. Thus a list can be initialized to the empty list by the operation *list:= nil*.

We now introduce some notation for use in algorithms (but not in Pascal programs). If *p* is a pointer to a node, *node(p)* refers to the node pointed to by *p*, *info(p)* refers to the information portion of that node, and *next(p)* refers to the next address portion and is therefore a pointer. Thus, if *next(p)* is not *nil*, *info(next(p))* refers to the information portion of the node that follows *node(p)* in the list.

Inserting and Removing Nodes from a List

A list is a dynamic data structure. The number of nodes on a list may vary dramatically as elements are inserted and removed. The dynamic nature of a list may be contrasted with the static nature of an array whose size remains constant. For example, suppose that we are given a list of integers, as illustrated in Figure 4.2.2a and we desire to add the integer 6 to the front of that list. That is, we wish to change the list so that it appears as in Figure 4.2.2f.

The first step is to obtain a node in which to house the additional integer. If a list is to grow and shrink, there must be some mechanism for obtaining empty nodes to be added onto the list. Note that, unlike an array, a list does not come with a presupplied set of storage locations into which elements can be placed.

Let us assume the existence of a mechanism for obtaining empty nodes. The operation

$$p:= getnode$$

obtains an empty node and sets the contents of a variable named *p* to the address of that node. This means that *p* is a pointer to this newly allocated node. Figure 4.2.2b illustrates the list and the new node after performing the *getnode* operation. The details of how this operation works will be explained shortly.

The next step is to insert the integer 6 into the *info* portion of the newly allocated node. This is done by the operation

$$info(p):= 6$$

The result of this operation is illustrated in Figure 4.2.2c.

After setting the *info* portion of *node(p)*, it is necessary to set the *next* portion of that node. Since *node(p)* is to be inserted at the front of the list, the node that follows should be the current first node on the list. Since the variable *list* contains the address of that first node, *node(p)* can be added

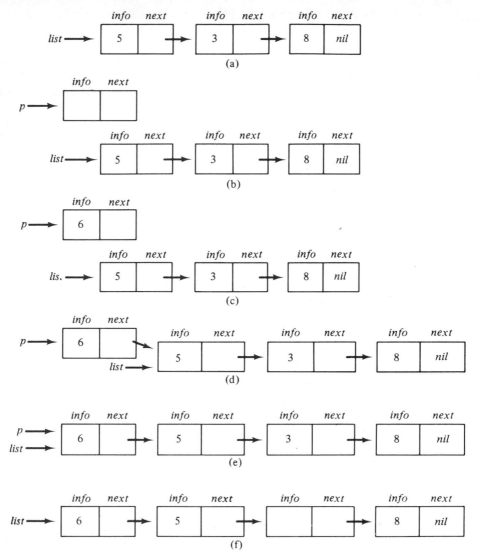

Figure 4.2.2 Adding an element to the front of a list.

to the list by performing the operation

$$next(p) := list$$

This operation places the value of *list* (which is the address of the first node on the list) into the *next* field of *node*(*p*). Figure 4.2.2d illustrates the result of this operation.

At this point, *p* points to the list with the additional item included. However, since *list* is the external pointer to the desired list, its value must be modified to the address of the new first node of the list. This can be done by performing the operation

$$list := p$$

which changes the value of *list* to the value of *p*. Figure 4.2.2e illustrates the result of this operation. Note that Figures 4.2.2e and f are identical except that the value of *p* is not shown in Figure 4.2.2f. This is because *p* is used as an auxiliary variable during the process of modifying the list, but its value is irrelevant to the status of the list before and after the process. Once the foregoing operations have been performed, the value of *p* may be changed without affecting the list.

Putting all the steps together, we have an algorithm for adding the integer 6 to the front of the list *list*:

$$p := getnode;$$
$$info(p) := 6;$$
$$next(p) := list;$$
$$list := p$$

The algorithm can obviously be generalized so that it adds any object *x* to the front of a list *list* by replacing the operation $info(p) := 6$ with $info(p) := x$. Convince yourself that the algorithm works correctly, even if the list is initially empty (*list* = *nil*).

Figure 4.2.3 illustrates the process of removing the first node of a nonempty list and storing the value of its *info* field into a variable *x*. The initial configuration is shown in Figure 4.2.3a and the final configuration is shown in Figure 4.2.3f. The process itself is almost the exact opposite of the process to add a node to the front of a list. To obtain Figure 4.2.3d from Figure 4.2.3a, the following operations (whose actions should be clear) are performed:

$$p := list; \qquad \text{(Figure 4.2.3b)}$$
$$list := next(p); \qquad \text{(Figure 4.2.3c)}$$
$$x := info(p) \qquad \text{(Figure 4.2.3d)}$$

At this point, the algorithm has accomplished what it was supposed to do: the first node has been removed from *list* and *x* has been set to the desired value. However, the algorithm is not yet complete. In Figure 4.2.3d, *p* still points to the node that was formerly first on the list. However, that node is currently useless because it is no longer on the list and its information has been stored in *x*. [The node is not considered to be on the list despite the fact that *next(p)* points to a node on the list, since there is no way to reach *node(p)* from the external pointer *list*.] The variable *p* was used as an auxiliary variable during the process of removing the first node from the list. The starting and ending configurations of the list make no reference to *p*. It is therefore reasonable to expect that *p* will be used for some other purpose in a short while after this operation has been performed. But once the value of *p* is changed, there is no way to access the node at all, since neither an external pointer nor a *next* field contains its address. There-

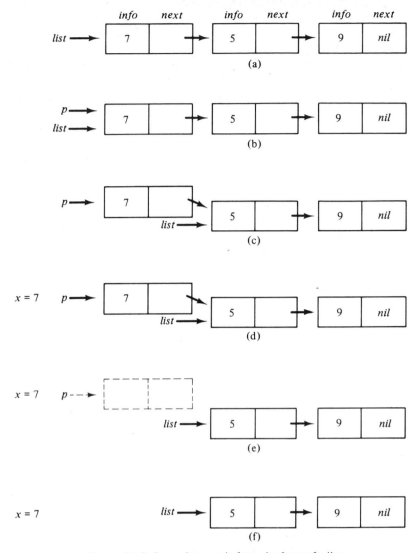

Figure 4.2.3 Removing a node from the front of a list.

fore, the node is currently useless and cannot be reused, yet it is taking up valuable storage.

It would be desirable to have some mechanism for making $node(p)$ available for reuse even if the value of the pointer p is changed. The operation that does this is

$$freenode(p) \quad \text{(Figure 4.2.3e)}$$

Once this operation has been performed, it becomes illegal to reference $node(p)$, since the node is no longer allocated. Since the value of p is a pointer to a node that has been freed, any reference to that value is also illegal.

However, the node might be reallocated and a pointer to it reassigned to p by the operation $p := getnode$. Note that we say that the node "might be" reallocated, since the *getnode* operation returns a pointer to some newly allocated node. There is no guarantee that this new node is the same as the one that has just been freed.

Another way of thinking of *getnode* and *freenode* is that *getnode* creates a new node, whereas *freenode* destroys a node. Under this view, nodes are not used and reused but are rather created and destroyed. We shall say more about the two operations *getnode* and *freenode* and about the concepts they represent in a moment, but first we make the following interesting observation.

Linked Implementation of Stacks

The operation of adding an element to the front of a linked list is quite similar to that of pushing an element onto a stack. In both cases, a new item is added as the only immediately accessible item in a collection. A stack can be accessed only through its top element, and a list can be accessed only from the pointer to its first element. Similarly, the operation of removing the first element from a linked list is analogous to popping a stack. In both cases, the only immediately accessible item of a collection is removed from that collection, and the next item becomes immediately accessible.

Thus we have discovered another way of implementing a stack. A stack may be represented by a linear linked list. The first node of the list is the top of the stack. If an external pointer s points to such a linked list, the operation $push(s,x)$ may be implemented by

$$p := getnode;$$
$$info(p) := x;$$
$$next(p) := s;$$
$$s := p$$

The operation $empty(s)$ is merely a test as to whether s equals *nil*. The operation $x := pop(s)$ is the operation of removing the first node from a nonempty list and signaling underflow if the list is empty:

$$if\ empty(s)$$
$$then\ error('stack\ underflow')$$
$$else\ begin$$
$$p := s;$$
$$s := next(p);$$
$$x := info(p);$$
$$freenode(p)$$
$$end\ \{else\ begin\}$$

Figure 4.2.4a illustrates a stack implemented as a linked list, and Figure 4.2.4b illustrates the same stack after another element has been pushed onto it.

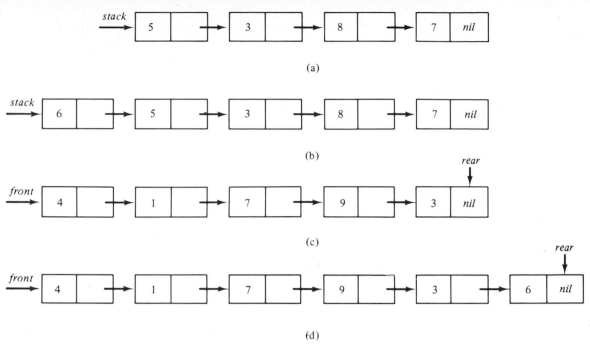

(a)

(b)

(c)

(d)

Figure 4.2.4 A stack and a queue as linked lists.

getnode and *freenode* Operations

We now return to a discussion of the *getnode* and *freenode* operations. In an abstract, idealized world it is possible to postulate an infinite number of unused nodes available for use by abstract algorithms. The *getnode* operation finds one such node and makes it available to the algorithm. Alternatively, the *getnode* operation may be regarded as a machine that manufactures nodes and never breaks down. Thus each time that *getnode* is invoked, it presents its caller with a brand new node, different from all the nodes previously in use.

In such an ideal world, the *freenode* operation would be unnecessary to make a node available for reuse. Why use an old second-hand node when a simple call to *getnode* can produce a new, never-before-used node? The only harm that an unused node can do is to reduce the number of nodes that can possibly be used, but if an infinite supply of nodes is available, such a reduction is meaningless. Therefore, there is never any reason to reuse a node.

Unfortunately, we live in a real world. Computers do not have an infinite amount of storage and cannot manufacture more storage for immediate utilization (at least, not yet). Therefore, there are a finite number of nodes available and it is impossible to use more than that number at any given instant. If it is desired to use more than that number over a given period of time, some nodes must be reused. The function of *freenode* is to make a node that is no longer being used in its current context available for reuse in a different context.

We might think of a finite pool of empty nodes existing initially. This pool cannot be accessed by the programmer, except through the *getnode* and *freenode* operations. *getnode* removes a node from the pool, while *freenode* returns a node to the pool. Since any unused node is as good as any other, it makes no difference which node is retrieved by *getnode* or where within the pool a node is placed by *freenode*.

The most natural form for this pool to take is that of a linked list acting as a stack. The list is linked together by the *next* field in each node. The *getnode* operation removes the first node from this list and makes it available for use. The *freenode* operation adds a node to the front of the list, making it available for reallocation by the next *getnode*. The list of available nodes is called the **available list**.

What happens when the available list is empty? This means that all nodes are currently in use and it is impossible to allocate any more. If a program calls on *getnode* when the available list is empty, then the amount of storage assigned for that program's data structures is too small. Therefore, overflow occurs. This is similar to the situation of a stack implemented in an array overflowing the array bounds.

As long as data structures are abstract, theoretical concepts in a world of infinite space, there is no possibility of overflow. It is only when they are implemented as real objects in a finite area that the possibility of overflow arises.

Let us assume that the external pointer *avail* points to the list of available nodes. Then the operation

$$p := getnode$$

is implemented as follows:

> **if** *avail* = *nil*
> **then** *error*('overflow')
> **else begin**
> > $p := avail;$
> > $avail := next(avail)$
> **end** {else begin}

Since the possibility of overflow is accounted for in the *getnode* operation, it need not be mentioned in the list implementation of *push*. If a stack is about to overflow all available nodes, the statement $p := getnode$ within the *push* operation will result in an overflow.

The implementation of *freenode*(*p*) is straightforward:

> $next(p) := avail;$
> $avail := p$

The advantage of the list implementation of stacks is that all the stacks being used by a program can share the same available list. When a stack needs a node, it can obtain it from the single available list. When a stack no longer needs a node, it returns the node to that same available list. As long as the total amount of space needed by all the stacks at any one time is less than the amount of space initially available to them all, each stack is able to grow and shrink to any size. No space has been preallocated to any single stack and no stack is using space that it does not need. Furthermore, other data structures, such as queues, may also share the same set of nodes.

Linked Implementation of Queues

Let us now examine how to represent a queue as a linked list. Recall that items are deleted from the front of a queue and inserted at the rear. Let the list pointer that points to the first element of a list represent the front of the queue. Another pointer to the last element of the list represents the rear of the queue, as shown in Figure 4.2.4c. Figure 4.2.4d illustrates the same queue after a new item has been inserted.

If we let a queue q consist of a list and two pointers, $q.front$ and $q.rear$, then the operations $empty(q)$ and $x:=remove(q)$ are completely analogous to $empty(s)$ and $x:=pop(s)$, with the pointer $q.front$ replacing s. However, special attention must be paid to the case in which the last element is removed from a queue. In this case, $q.rear$ must also be set to nil, since in an empty queue both $q.front$ and $q.rear$ are nil. The algorithm for $x:=remove(q)$ is therefore as follows:

```
if empty(q)
    then error('queue underflow')
    else with q
        do begin
                p:= front;
                x:= info(p);
                front:= next(p);
                if front = nil
                    then rear:= nil;
                freenode(p);
                remove:= x
        end {else with q do begin}
```

remove function, of linked list

The operation $insert(q,x)$ can be implemented by

```
with q
    do begin
            p:= getnode;
            info(p):= x;
            next(p):= nil;
            if rear = nil
                then front:= p
                else next(rear):= p;
            rear:= p
    end {with q do begin}
```

insert function, of linked list

What are the disadvantages of representing a stack or queue by a linked list? Clearly, a node in a linked list occupies more storage than a corresponding element in an array, since two pieces of information are necessary in a list node for each item (*info* and *next*), whereas only one piece of information is needed in the array implementation. However, the space used for a list node is usually not twice the space used by an array element, since the elements in such a list usually consist of records with many subfields. For example, if each element on a stack were a record occupying 10 words, the addition of an eleventh word to contain a pointer increases the space requirement by only 10%. Further, in many machine languages it is possible to compress information and a pointer into a single word so that there is no space degradation.

Another disadvantage is the additional time that must be spent in managing the available list. Each addition and deletion of an element from a stack or a queue involves a corresponding deletion or addition to the available list.

The advantage of using linked lists is that all the stacks and queues of a program have access to the same free list of nodes. Nodes that are unused by one stack may be used by another, as long as the total number of nodes in use at any one time is not greater than the total number of nodes available.

The Linked List as a Data Structure

Linked lists are important not only as a means of implementing stacks and queues, but as data structures in their own right. An item is accessed in a linked list by traversing the list from its beginning. An array implementation allows access to the nth item in a group using a single operation, while a list implementation requires n operations. It is necessary to pass through each of the first $n-1$ elements before reaching the nth element, because there is no relation between the memory location occupied by an element of a list and its position within that list.

The advantage of a list over an array occurs when it is necessary to insert or delete an element in the middle of a group of other elements. For example, suppose that we wished to insert an element x between the third and fourth elements in an array of size 10 which currently contains seven items. Items 7 through 4 must first be moved one slot and the new element inserted in the newly available position 4. This process is illustrated by Figure 4.2.5a. In this case, insertion of one item involves moving four items in addition to the insertion itself. If the array contained 500 or 1000 elements, a correspondingly larger number of elements would have to be moved. Similarly, to delete an element from an array, all the elements past the element deleted must be moved one position.

On the other hand, if the items are stored as a list, then if p is a pointer to a given element of the list, inserting a new element after *node*(p) involves allocating a node, inserting the information, and adjusting two pointers. The amount of work required is independent of the size of the list. This is illustrated in Figure 4.2.5b.

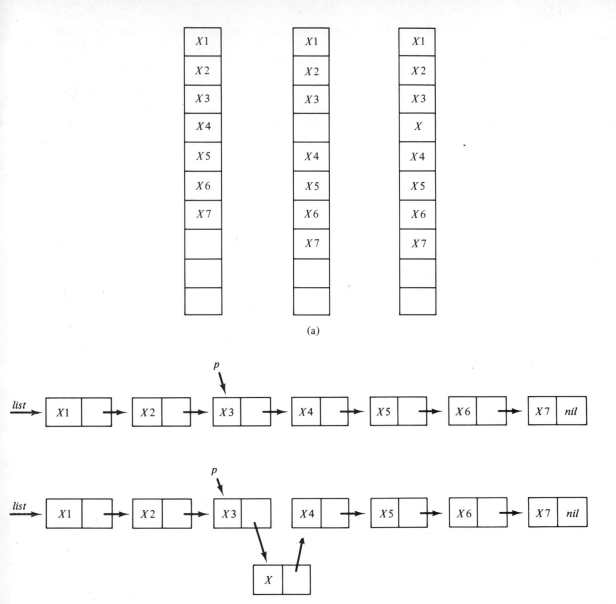

(a)

(b)

Figure 4.2.5

Let *insafter*(*p*,*x*) denote the operation of inserting an item *x* into a list after a node pointed to by *p*. This operation may be implemented as follows:

```
q := getnode;
info(q):= x;
next(q):= next(p);
next(p):= q
```

An item can only be inserted after a given node, not before the node. This is because there is no way to proceed from a given node to its predecessor in a linear list without traversing the list from its beginning. To insert an item before $node(p)$, the *next* field of its predecessor must be changed to point to a newly allocated node. But, given p, there is no way to find that predecessor. However, it is possible to achieve the effect of inserting an element before a given node in a linked list by inserting the element after the node and then switching the contents of the given node and its newly created successor. We leave the details for the reader.

Similarly, to delete a node from a linear list it is insufficient to be given a pointer to that node. This is because the *next* field of the node's predecessor must be changed to point to the node's successor, and there is no direct way of reaching the predecessor of a given node. The best that can be done is to delete a node following a given node. (However, it is possible to save the contents of the following node, delete the following node, and then replace the contents of the given node with the saved information. This achieves the effect of deleting a given node.) Let $delafter(p,x)$ denote the operation of deleting the node following $node(p)$ and assigning its contents to the variable x. This operation may be implemented as follows:

$$q := next(p);$$
$$x := info(q);$$
$$next(p) := next(q);$$
$$freenode(q)$$

The freed node is placed back onto the available list so that it may be reused in the future.

Examples of List Operations

We illustrate these two operations as well as the *push* and *pop* operations for lists with some simple examples. The first example is to delete all occurrences of the number 4 from a list *list*. The list is traversed in a search for nodes that contain 4 in their *info* fields. Each such node must be deleted from the list. But in order to delete a node from a list, its predecessor must be known. For this reason, two pointers, p and q, are used. p is used to traverse the list and q always points to the predecessor of p. The algorithm makes use of the *pop* operation to remove nodes from the beginning of the list, and the *delafter* operation to remove nodes from the middle of the list.

```
q := nil;
p := list;
while p <> nil
     do if info(p) = 4
          then begin
                   p := next(p);    {advance p}
                   if q = nil
                        then {remove the first node of the list}
                             x := pop(list)
```

$$else \text{ \{remove the node following } q\}$$
$$delafter\ (q,x)$$
$$end \text{ \{then begin\}}$$
$$else \text{ \{continue traversing the list\}}$$
$$begin \text{ \{advance } p \text{ and } q\}$$
$$q := p;$$
$$p := next(p)$$
$$end \text{ \{else begin\}}$$

The practice of using two pointers, one following the other, is a common one in working with lists. This technique is used in the next example as well. Assume that a list *list* is ordered so that smaller items precede larger ones. It is desired to insert an item *x* into this list in its proper place. The algorithm to do so makes use of the *push* operation to add a node to the front of the list and the *insafter* operation to add a node in the middle of the list:

$$q := nil;$$
$$p := list;$$
$$while\ (p <> nil)\ and\ (x > info(p))$$
$$do\ begin$$
$$q := p;$$
$$p := next(p)$$
$$end \text{ \{while...do begin\};}$$
$$\text{\{at this point, a node containing } x \text{ must be inserted\}}$$
$$if\ q = nil$$
$$then \text{ \{insert } x \text{ at the head of the list\}}$$
$$push(list,x)$$
$$else\ insafter(q,x)$$

place (list, x)

This is a very common operation and will be denoted by *place (list,x)*.

Lists in Pascal

How can linear lists be represented in Pascal? Since a list is simply a collection of nodes, an array of nodes immediately suggests itself. However, the nodes cannot be ordered by the array ordering; each must contain within itself a pointer to its successor. Thus a group of nodes might be declared as follows:

```
const numnodes = 500;
type  nodeptr = 0..numnodes;
      nodetype = record
                     info: integer;
                     next: nodeptr
                 end;
var   node: array[1..numnodes] of nodetype;
```

In this scheme, a pointer to a node is an integer between 1 and *numnodes* which references a particular element of the array *node*. The nil pointer is represented by the integer 0.

Under this implementation, the Pascal expression $node[p]$ is used to reference $node(p)$, $info(p)$ is referenced by $node[p].info$, and $next(p)$ is referenced by $node[p].next$. nil is represented by 0. Let the variable $list$ represent a pointer to a list. Suppose that $list$ has the value 7. Then $node[7]$ is the first node on the list, so that $node[7].info$ is the first data item on the list. The second node of the list is given by $node[7].next$. Suppose that $node[7].next$ equals 385. Then $node[385].info$ is the second data item on the list and $node[385].next$ points to the third node. The nodes of a list may be scattered throughout the array $node$ in any arbitrary order. Each node carries within itself the address of its successor until the last node in the list, whose $next$ field contains 0, which is the nil pointer. There is no relation between the contents of a node and the pointer to it. The pointer p to a node merely specifies which element of the array $node$ is being referenced; it is $node[p].info$, which represents the information contained within that node.

Figure 4.2.6 illustrates a portion of an array $node$ that contains four linked lists. The list $list1$ starts at $node[17]$ and contains the integers 3, 7,

		info	next
	1	26	0
	2	11	10
	3	5	16
list4 =	4	1	25
list2 =	5	17	1
	6	13	2
	7		
	8	19	19
	9	14	13
	10	4	22
	11		
list3 =	12	31	8
	13	6	3
	14		
	15		
	16	37	24
list1 =	17	3	21
	18		
	19	32	0
	20		
	21	7	9
	22	15	0
	23		
	24	12	0
	25	18	6
	26		
	27		

Figure 4.2.6 An array of nodes containing four linked lists.

14, 6, 5, 37, and 12. The nodes that contain these integers in their *info* fields are scattered throughout the array. The *next* field of each node contains the index within the array of the node containing the next element of the list. The last node on the list is *node* [24] , which contains the integer 12 in its *info* field and the nil pointer (0) in its *next* field to indicate that it is last on the list. Similarly, *list*2 begins at *node* [5] and contains the integers 17 and 26, *list*3 begins at *node* [12] and contains the integers 31, 19, and 32, and *list*4 begins at *node* [4] and contains the integers 1, 18, 13, 11, 4, and 15. The variables *list*1, *list*2, *list*3, and *list*4 are integers (or *nodeptrs*) representing external pointers to the four lists. Thus the fact that the variable *list*2 has the value 5 represents the fact that the list to which it points begins at *node* [5] .

Initially, all nodes are unused, since no lists have yet been formed. Therefore, they must all be placed on the available list. If the global variable *avail*: *nodeptr* is used to point to the available list, we may initially organize that list as follows:

```
avail:= 1;
for i:= 1 to numnodes-1
    do node[i].next:= i + 1;
node[numnodes].next:= 0
```

The 500 nodes are initially linked in their natural order, so that *node* [*i*] points to *node* [*i*+1]. Thus *node* [1] is the first node on the available list, *node* [2] is the second, and so on. *node* [500] is the last node on the list, since *node* [500] .*next* equals 0. There is no reason other than convenience for initially ordering the nodes in this fashion. We could just as well have set *node* [1] .*next* to 500, *node* [500] .*next* to 2, *node* [2] .*next* to 499, and so on, until *node* [250] .*next* is set to 251 and *node* [251] .*next* to 0. The important point is that the ordering is explicit within the nodes themselves and is not implied by some other underlying structure.

For the remaining subroutines in this section, we assume that the variables *node* and *avail* are global and can therefore be used by any routine.

When a node is needed for use in a particular list, it is obtained from the available list. Similarly, when a node is no longer necessary, it is returned to the available list. These two operations are implemented by the Pascal routines *getnode* and *freenode*. *getnode* is a function that removes a node from the available list and returns a pointer to it.

```
function getnode: nodeptr;
begin
    if avail = 0
        then error('list overflow')
        else begin
                getnode:= avail;
                avail:= node[avail].next
            end {else begin}
end {function getnode};
```

If *avail* equals 0 when this function is called, there are no nodes available. This means that the list structures of a particular program have overflowed the available space.

The procedure *freenode* accepts a pointer to a node and returns that node to the available list:

```
procedure freenode(p: nodeptr);
begin
        node[p].next:= avail;
        avail:= p
end {procedure freenode};
```

The primitive operations for lists are straightforward Pascal versions of the corresponding algorithms. The routine *insafter* accepts a pointer p to a node and an item x as parameters. It first ensures that p is not nil and then inserts x into a node following the node pointed to by p.

```
procedure insafter(p: nodeptr; x: integer);
var q: nodeptr;
begin
    if p = 0
        then error('void insertion')
        else begin
                q:= getnode;
                node[q].info:= x;
                node[q].next:= node[p].next;
                node[p].next:= q
            end {else begin}
end {procedure insafter};
```

The routine *delafter*(p,x) deletes the node following *node*(p) and stores its contents in x.

```
procedure delafter(p: nodeptr; var x: integer);
var q: nodeptr;
begin
    if p = 0
        then error('void deletion')
        else if node[p].next = 0
                then error('void deletion')
                else begin
                        q:= node[p].next;
                        x:= node[q].info;
                        node[p].next:= node[q].next;
                        freenode (q)
                    end {else begin}
end {procedure delafter};
```

Before calling *insafter*, we must be sure that p is not nil. Before calling *delafter*, we must be sure that neither p nor *node* [p].*next* is nil.

Queues as Lists in Pascal

We now present Pascal routines for manipulating a queue represented as a linear list, leaving routines for manipulating a stack as exercises for the reader. A queue is represented by a record:

```
type queue = record
                 front: nodeptr;
                 rear: nodeptr
             end;
```

front and *rear* are pointers to the first and last nodes of a queue represented as a list. The empty queue will be represented by *front* and *rear* both equaling 0, the nil pointer. The function *empty* need check only one of these pointers, since in a nonempty queue, neither *front* nor *rear* will be 0.

```
function empty(q: queue): boolean;
begin
    if q.front = 0
        then empty:= true
        else empty:= false
end {function empty};
```

The routine to insert an element into a queue may be written as follows:

```
procedure insert(var q: queue; x: integer);
var p: nodeptr;
begin
    p:= getnode;
    with node[p]
        do begin
                info:= x;
                next:= 0
           end {with...do begin};
    with q
        do begin
                if rear = 0
                    then front:= p
                    else node[rear].next:= p;
                rear:= p
           end {with...do begin}
end {procedure insert};
```

The function *remove*, which deletes the first element from a queue and returns its value, may be written as follows:

```
function remove (var q: queue): integer;
var p: nodeptr;
    x: integer;
begin
      if empty (q)
         then error ('queue underflow')
         else begin
                  p:= q.front;
                  with node [p]
                     do begin
                            x:= info;
                            q.front:= next;
                            if q.front = 0
                               then q.rear:= 0
                     end {with...do begin};
                  freenode (p);
                  remove:= x
         end {else begin}
end {function remove};
```

An Example of a List Operation in Pascal

Let us look at a somewhat more complex list operation implemented in Pascal. We have defined the operation *place* (*list*,*x*), where *list* points to a sorted linear list and *x* is an element to be inserted into its proper position within the list. Ordinarily, the algorithm for performing that operation could be translated directly into Pascal. However, that algorithm contains the line

$$\textit{while } (p <> nil) \textit{ and } (x > info (p))$$

If p is equal to 0 (which is the nil pointer under this Pascal implementation of lists), then *info* (*p*) (i.e., *node* [*p*].*info*) is undefined and a reference to it will cause an error. Thus we want to avoid the evaluation of *node* [*p*] in the case that p equals 0. We assume that we have already implemented the stack operation *push*. The code to implement the *place* operation follows:

```
procedure place (var list: nodeptr; x: integer);
var found: boolean;
    p,q: nodeptr;
begin
      found:= false;
      p:= list;
      q:= 0;
```

```
                    while (p <> 0) and (not found)
                        do if x <= node[p].info
                               then found:= true
                               else begin
                                          q:= p;
                                          p:= node[p].next
                                   end {else begin};
                 if q = 0
                     then {insert x at the head of the list}
                             push(list,x)
                     else insafter(q,x)
            end {procedure place};
```

Note that *list* must be declared as a variable parameter since its value is changed if *x* is inserted at the front of the list using the *push* procedure.

Noninteger Lists

Of course, a node on a list need not represent an integer. For example, to represent a stack of character strings by a linked list, nodes containing character strings in their *info* fields are needed. Such nodes could be defined by

```
type nodetype = record
                    info: packed array[1..100] of char;
                    next: nodeptr
                end;
```

A particular application may call for nodes containing more than one item of information. For example, each student node in a list of students may contain the following information: the student's name, college identification number, address, grade-point index, major, and so on. Nodes for such an application may be defined as follows:

```
type nodetype = record
                    info: record
                              name:    packed array[1..50] of char;
                              id:      packed array[1..9] of char;
                              address: packed array[1..100] of char;
                              gpindex: real;
                              major:   packed array[1..20] of char
                          end;
                    next: nodeptr
                end;
```

A separate set of Pascal routines must be written to manipulate lists containing each type of node.

It is possible to use a variant record to define a node that can hold more than one type of item. For example, a node that can hold either an integer or a character might be defined as follows:

```
type nodetype = record
                    next: nodeptr;
                    case infotype: (ch,int) of
                      ch: (cinfo: char);
                      int: (iinfo: integer)
                end;
```

Note that the *next* field precedes the variant part of the record in the definition because the fixed part of a variant record must always precede the variant part.

Header Nodes

Sometimes it is desirable to keep an extra node at the front of a list. Such a node does not represent an item in the list and is called a *header node* or a *list header*. The *info* portion of such a header node might be unused, as illustrated in Figure 4.2.7a. More often, the *info* portion of such a node could be used to keep global information about the entire list. For example, Figure 4.2.7b illustrates a list in which the *info* portion of the header node contains the number of nodes (not including the header) in the list. In such a data structure more work is needed to add or delete an item from the list, since the count in the header node must be adjusted properly. However, the number of items in the list may be obtained directly from the header node, so that the entire list need not be traversed.

Another example of the use of header nodes is the following. Suppose that a factory assembles machinery out of smaller units. A particular machine (inventory number $A746$) might be composed of a number of different parts (numbers $B841$, $K321$, $A087$, $J492$, $G593$). This assembly could be represented by a list such as the one illustrated in Figure 4.2.7c, where each item on the list represents a component and where the header node represents the entire assembly. The empty list would no longer be represented by the nil pointer, but rather by a list with a single header node, as in Figure 4.2.7d.

Of course, routines such as *empty*, *push*, *pop*, *insert*, and *remove* must be rewritten to account for the presence of a header node. Most of the routines become a bit more complex, but some, like *insert*, become simpler, because an external list pointer is never nil. We leave the rewriting of the routines as an exercise for the reader. The routines *insafter* and *delafter* need not be changed at all. In fact, *insafter* and *delafter* can be used instead of *push* and *pop*, since the first item in such a list appears in the node that follows the header node, rather than in the first node on the list.

If the *info* portion of a node can contain a pointer (as is true in our Pascal implementation of a list of integers where a pointer is represented by an integer), then additional possibilities for the use of a header node present themselves. For example, the *info* portion of a list header might contain a

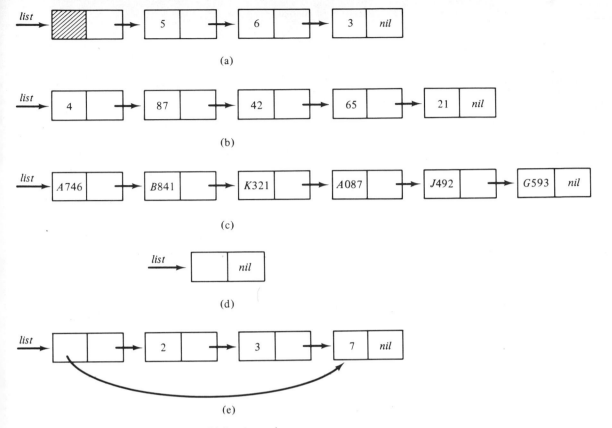

Figure 4.2.7 Lists with header nodes.

pointer to the last node in the list, as in Figure 4.2.7e. Such an implementation would simplify the representation of a queue. Until now, two external pointers, *front* and *rear*, were necessary for a list to represent a queue. However, now only a single external pointer q to the header node of the list is necessary. $next(q)$ would point to the front of the queue and $info(q)$ to its rear.

Another possibility for the use of the *info* portion of a list header is as a pointer to a "current" node in the list during a traversal process. This would eliminate the need for an external pointer during traversal.

It is also possible for header nodes to be declared as variables separate from the array of list nodes. For example, consider the following set of declarations:

```
const numnodes = 500;
type  nodeptr  = 0..numnodes;
      nodetype = record
                    info: char;
                    next: nodeptr
                 end;
```

```
charstr     = record
                    length: integer;
                    firstchar: nodeptr
              end;
var    node: array[1..numnodes] of nodetype;
       s1,s2: charstr;
```

The variables $s1$ and $s2$ of type *charstr* are header nodes for a list of characters. The header contains the number of characters in the list (*length*) and a pointer to the list (*firstchar*). Thus $s1$ and $s2$ represent varying-length character strings. As exercises, you may wish to write routines to concatenate two such character strings or to extract a substring from such a string.

EXERCISES

1. Write a set of routines for implementing several stacks and queues within a single array.

2. What are the advantages and disadvantages of representing a group of items as an array versus a linear linked list?

3. Present four methods of implementing a queue of queues using the list and array implementations of a queue. Write each of the following routines for each implementation:

   $remvq(qq,q)$ which removes a queue from the queue of queues
                         qq and assigns it to q;
   $insrtq(qq,q)$ which adds queue q to qq;
   $remvonq(qq,x)$ which removes an element from the first queue
                         of qq and assigns it to x;
   $insrtonq(qq,x)$ which adds an element x to the first queue on qq.

   Define analogous implementations and operations for a stack of stacks, a stack of queues, and a queue of stacks.

4. Write an algorithm and a Pascal routine to perform each of the following operations:

   (a) Append an element to the end of a list.
   (b) Concatenate two lists.
   (c) Free all the nodes in a list.
   (d) Reverse a list, so that the last element becomes the first, and so on.
   (e) Delete the last element from a list.
   (f) Delete the nth element from a list.
   (g) Combine two ordered lists into a single ordered list.
   (h) Form a list containing the union of the elements of two lists.
   (i) Form a list containing the intersection of the elements of two lists.
   (j) Insert an element after the nth element of a list.
   (k) Delete every second element from a list.
   (l) Place the elements of a list in increasing order.
   (m) Return the sum of the integers in a list.
   (n) Return the number of elements in a list.
   (o) Move $node(p)$ forward n positions in a list.
   (p) Make a copy of a list.

5. Write an algorithm and a Pascal routine to perform each of the operations of Exercise 4 on a group of elements in contiguous positions of an array.

6. Write a Pascal routine to interchange the *m*th and *n*th elements of a list.

7. Write a routine *inssub*(*l1,i1,l2,i2,len*) to insert the elements of list *l2* beginning at the *i2*th element and continuing for *len* elements into the list *l1* beginning at position *i1*. No elements of the list *l1* are to be removed or replaced. If $i1 > length(l1)+1$ [where *length*(*l1*) denotes the number of nodes in the list *l1*], or if $i2+len-1 > length(l2)$, or if $i1 < 1$, or if $i2 < 1$, print an error message. The list *l2* should remain unchanged.

8. Write a Pascal function *search*(*l,x*), which accepts a pointer *l* to a list of integers and an integer *x* and returns a pointer to a node containing *x*, if it exists, and the nil pointer otherwise. Write another function *srchinsrt*(*l,x*), which adds *x* to *l* if it is not found and always returns a pointer to a node containing *x*.

9. Write a Pascal program to read a group of input lines, each containing one word. Print each word that appears in the input and the number of times that it appears.

10. Suppose that a character string is represented by a list of single characters, as described at the end of this section. Write a set of routines to manipulate such lists as follows (where *l1*, *l2*, and *list* are pointers to a header node of a list representing a character string, *str* is a packed array of characters and *i1* and *i2* are integers):

    (a) *convcl*(*str*)   to convert the character string *str* to a list. This function returns a pointer to a header node.

    (b) *convlc*(*list,str*)   to convert a list into a character string.

    (c) *posl*(*l1,l2*)   to perform the *pos* function of Section 1.2 on two character strings represented by lists. This function returns an integer.

    (d) *verifyl*(*l1,l2*)   to determine the first position of the string represented by *l1* which is not contained in the string represented by *l2*. This function returns an integer.

    (e) *substrl*(*l1,i1,i2*)   to perform the *substr* function of Section 1.2 on a character string represented by list *l1* and integers *i1* and *i2*. This function returns a pointer to the header node of a list representing a character string that is the desired substring. The list *l1* remains unchanged.

    (f) *psubstrl*(*l1,i1,i2,l2*)   to perform a pseudo-*substr* assignment to list *l1*. The elements of list *l2* should replace the *i2* elements of *l1* beginning at position *i1*. The list *l2* should remain unchanged.

    (g) *comparel*(*l1,l2*)   to compare two character strings represented by lists. This function returns −1 if the character string represented by *l1* is less than the string represented by *l2*, 0 if they are equal, and 1 if the string represented by *l1* is greater.

One of the most useful applications of queues and linked lists is in *simulation*. A simulation program is one that attempts to model a real-world situation in order to learn something about it. Each object and action in the real situation has its counterpart in the program. If the simulation is accurate, that is, if the program successfully mirrors the real world, then the result of the program should mirror the result of the actions being simulated. Thus it is possible to understand what occurs in the real-world situation without actually observing its occurrence.

Let us look at an example. Consider a bank with four tellers. A customer enters the bank at a specific time $t1$, desiring to conduct a transaction with any teller. The transaction may be expected to take a certain period of time $t2$ before it is completed. If a teller is free, the teller can process the customer's transaction immediately and the customer leaves the bank as soon as the transaction has been completed, at time $t1+t2$. The total time spent in the bank by the customer is exactly equal to the duration of the transaction, $t2$.

However, it is possible that none of the tellers are free; they are all servicing customers who arrived previously. In that case, there is a line waiting at each teller's window. The line for a particular teller may consist of a single person—the one currently transacting his business with the teller, or it may be a very long line. The customer proceeds to the back of the shortest line and waits until all the customers who precede him on the line have completed their transactions and have left the bank. At that time, he may transact his business. The customer leaves the bank at $t2$ time units after he has reached the front of his teller's line. In this case the time spent in the bank is $t2$ plus the time spent waiting on line.

Given such a system, we would like to compute the average time spent by a customer in the bank. One way of doing so is to stand in the bank doorway, ask departing customers the time of their arrival and record the time of their departure, subtract the first from the second, and take the average over all customers. However, this would not be very practical. It would be difficult to ensure that no customer is overlooked leaving the bank. Furthermore, it is doubtful that most customers would remember the exact time of arrival.

Instead, we write a program to simulate the customer actions. Each part of the real-world situation has its analog in the program. Each line input to the program represents a customer. The real-world action of a customer arriving is modeled by an input line being read. As each customer arrives, two facts are known: the time of his arrival and the duration of his transaction (since, at the time of arrival, the customer presumably knows what he wishes to do at the bank). Thus each input line contains two numbers: the time (in minutes since the bank opened) of the customer's arrival and the amount of time (again, in minutes) necessary for his transaction. These input lines are ordered by increasing arrival time. We assume at least one input line.

The four lines in the bank are represented by four queues. Each node of the queues represents a customer waiting on a line, and the node at the front of a queue represents the customer currently being serviced by a teller.

Suppose that at a given instant of time the four lines each contain a specific number of customers. What can happen to alter the status of the lines? Either a new customer enters the bank, in which case one of the lines will have an additional customer, or the first customer on one of the four lines completes his transaction, in which case that line will have one less customer. Thus there are a total of five actions (a customer entering plus four cases of a customer leaving) that can change the status of the lines. Each of these five actions is called an *event*.

The simulation proceeds by finding the next event to occur and effecting the change in the queues that mirrors the change in the lines at the bank due to that event. To keep track of events, the program uses an *event list*. This list contains at most five nodes, each representing the next occurrence of one of the five types of event. Thus the event list contains one node representing the next customer arriving and four nodes representing each of the four customers at the head of a line completing his transaction and leaving the bank. Of course, it is possible that one or more of the lines in the bank are empty, or that the doors of the bank have been closed for the day so that no more customers are arriving. In such cases, the event list contains fewer than five nodes.

An event node representing a customer's arrival is called an *arrival node*, and a node representing a departure is called a *departure node*. At each point in the simulation, it is necessary to know the next event to occur. For this reason, the event list is ordered by increasing time of event occurrence so that the first event node on the list represents the next event to occur.

The first event to occur is the arrival of the first customer. The event list is therefore initialized by reading the first input line and placing an arrival node representing the first customer's arrival on the event list. Initially, of course, all four queues are empty. The simulation then proceeds as follows. The first node is removed from the event list and the changes which that event causes are made to the queues. As we shall soon see, these changes may also cause additional events to be placed on the event list. The process of removing the first node from the event list and effecting the changes that it causes is repeated until the event list is empty.

When an arrival node is removed from the event list, a node representing the arriving customer is placed on the shortest of the queues representing the four lines. If that customer is the only one on his queue, a node representing his departure is also placed on the event list, since he is at the front of his queue. At the same time, the next input line is read and an arrival node representing the next customer to arrive is placed on the event list. Thus there will always be an arrival node on the event list (as long as the input is not exhausted, at which point no more customers arrive), because as soon as one arrival node is removed from the event list, another is added to it.

When a departure node is removed from the event list, the node representing the departing customer is removed from the front of one of the four queues. At that point, the amount of time that the departing customer has spent in the bank is computed and added to a total. At the end of the simulation, this total will be divided by the number of customers to yield the average time spent by a customer. After a customer node has been deleted from the front of its queue, the next customer on the queue (if any) becomes the one being serviced by that teller and a departure node for that next customer is added to the event list.

This process continues until the event list is empty, at which point the average time is computed and printed. Note that the event list itself does not mirror any part of the real-world situation. It is used as part of the program to control the entire process. A simulation such as this one, which proceeds by changing the simulated situation in response to the occurrence of one of several events, is called an *event-driven simulation*.

We now examine the data structures that are necessary for this program. The nodes on the queues represent customers and therefore must contain fields representing the arrival time and the transaction duration, in addition to a *next* field to link the nodes in a list. The nodes on the event list represent events and therefore must contain the time that the event occurs, the type of the event, and any other information associated with that event, as well as a *next* field. Thus it would seem that either a variant record or two separate node pools are needed for the two different types of node. Using a variant record would entail setting and checking the tag field before inserting or using a node. Two different types of node would entail two *getnode* and *freenode* routines and two sets of list manipulation routines. To avoid this cumbersome set of duplicate routines, let us try to use a single type of node for both events and customers.

We can declare such a pool of nodes as follows:

```
const numnodes = 500;
type  nodeptr = 0..numnodes;
      nodeinfo = record
                     time: integer;
                     duration: integer;
                     ntype : 0..4
                 end;
      nodetype = record
                     info: nodeinfo;
                     next: nodeptr
                 end;
var   node: array[1..numnodes] of nodetype;
```

For a customer, *time* is the customer's arrival time and *duration* is the transaction's duration. *ntype* is unused in a customer node. *next* is used as a pointer to link the queue together. For an event node, *time* is used to hold the time of the event's occurrence; *duration* is used for the transaction duration of the arriving customer in an arrival node and is unused in a departure node. *ntype* is an integer between zero and four, depending on whether the event is an arrival (*ntype* = 0) or a departure from line one, two, three, or four (*ntype* = 1, 2, 3, or 4). *next* holds a pointer linking the event list together.

The four queues are declared as an array by the declaration

```
type queue = record
                front: nodeptr;
                rear:  nodeptr;
                num:  integer
             end;
var  q: array[1..4] of queue;
```

The *num* field of a queue contains the number of customers on that queue. The variable *evlist: nodeptr* points to the front of the event list. The variable *tottime: integer* is used to keep track of the total time spent by all customers, and *count: integer* keeps count of the number of customers that have passed through the bank. An auxiliary variable *auxinfo: nodeinfo* is used to store temporarily the information portion of a node.

The main routine declares all the global variables mentioned above, initializes all lists and queues, and repeatedly removes the next node from the event list to drive the simulation until the event list is empty. It calls on the procedure *place(evlist, auxinfo)* to insert a node whose information is given by *auxinfo* in its proper place in the event list. The event list is ordered by increasing value of the *time* field. The main routine also calls on procedure *popsub(evlist, auxinfo)* to remove the first node from the event list and place its information in *auxinfo*. This procedure is equivalent to the function *pop*. However, a Pascal function may not return an array or a record variable such as *auxinfo*. For this reason, we use a procedure *popsub*. These routines must, of course, be suitably modified from the examples given in the preceding section in order to handle this particular type of node.

The main program also calls on procedures *arrive* and *depart*, which effect the changes in the event list and the queues caused by an arrival and a departure. Specifically, procedure *arrive(atime,dur)* reflects the arrival of a customer at time *atime* with a transaction of duration *dur*, and procedure *depart(qindx,dtime)* reflects the departure of the first customer from queue *q[qindx]* at time *dtime*. The coding of these routines will be given shortly.

```
program bank(input,output);
const numnodes = 500;
type  nodeptr   = 0..numnodes;
      nodeinfo  = record
                     time,duration: integer;
                     ntype: 0..4
                  end;
```

```
            nodetype  = record
                          info: nodeinfo;
                          next: nodeptr
                        end;
            queue = record
                          front,rear: nodeptr;
                          num: integer
                        end;
      var   node: array[1..numnodes] of nodetype;
            qindx: 1..4;
            q: array[1..4] of queue;
            evlist,avail,i: nodeptr;
            tottime,count,atime,dtime,dur: integer;
            auxinfo: nodeinfo;
      procedure place(var evlist: nodeptr; auxinfo: nodeinfo);
              { body of place goes here }
      procedure popsub(var evlist: nodeptr; var auxinfo: nodeinfo);
              {body of popsub goes here}
      procedure arrive(atime,dur: integer);
              { body of arrive goes here }
      procedure depart(qindx,dtime: integer);
              { body of depart goes here }
      begin {program bank}
          {initialization}
          evlist:= 0;
          count:= 0;
          tottime:= 0;
          avail:= 1;
          for i:= 1 to numnodes - 1
              do node[i].next:= i + 1;
          node[numnodes].next:= 0;
          for qindx:= 1 to 4
              do with q[qindx]
                      do begin
                              num:= 0;
                              front:= 0;
                              rear:= 0
                      end {with...do begin};
      {read the first input line and initialize the event list}
          with auxinfo
              do begin
                      readln(time,duration);
                      ntype:= 0; {an arrival}
                      place(evlist,auxinfo)
                  end {with...do begin};
```

```
{run the simulation as long as the event list is not empty}
while evlist <> 0
        do begin
                popsub(evlist,auxinfo);
                {check if the next event is an arrival or departure}
                if auxinfo.ntype = 0
                        then begin {an arrival}
                                atime:= auxinfo.time;
                                dur:= auxinfo.duration;
                                arrive(atime,dur)
                        end {then begin}
                        else begin {a departure}
                                qindx:= auxinfo.ntype;
                                dtime:= auxinfo.time;
                                depart(qindx,dtime)
                        end {else begin}
        end {while...do begin};
        writeln('average time is ', tottime/count)
end {program bank}.
```

The procedure *arrive*(*atime*,*dur*) modifies the queues and the event list to reflect a new arrival at time *atime* with a transaction of duration *dur*. It inserts a new customer node at the rear of the shortest queue by calling the procedure *insert*(*qq*, *auxinfo*), which must be suitably modified to handle the type of node in this example and which also must increase the *num* field of the queue *qq* by 1. If the customer is the only one on his queue, a node representing his departure is added to the event list by calling on the procedure *place*(*evlist*,*auxinfo*). Then, the next input line (if any) is read and an arrival node is placed on the event list to replace the arrival that has just been processed. If there is no more input, the procedure returns without adding a new arrival node and the program processes the remaining (departure) nodes on the event list.

```
procedure arrive(atime,dur: integer);
var small: integer;
    i,j: 1..4; {global variables: q, auxinfo, evlist}
procedure insert(var qq: queue; auxinfo: nodeinfo);
    {body of insert goes here}
begin {procedure arrive}
    j:= 1;
    small:= q[1].num;
    for i:= 2 to 4
        do if q[i].num < small
            then begin
                small:= q[i].num;
                j:= i
            end {then begin};
    { Queue j is the shortest.  Insert a new arrival node. }
```

```
              with auxinfo
                  do begin
                          time:= atime;
                          duration:= dur;
                          ntype:= j
                  end {with...do begin};
          insert(q[j],auxinfo);
          { Check if this is the only node on the queue. If it   }
          {is, the customer's departure node must be placed on}
          {                    the event list.                    }
          if q[j].num = 1
            then begin
                        auxinfo.time:= atime + dur;
                        place(evlist,auxinfo)
                end {then begin};
          { If any input remains, read the next input line and   }
          {        place an arrival on the event list.        }
          if not eof(input)
            then with auxinfo
                  do begin
                          readln(time,duration);
                          ntype:= 0;
                          place(evlist,auxinfo)
                  end {then with...do begin}
      end {procedure arrive};
```

The routine *depart(qindx,dtime)* modifies the queue $q[qindx]$ and the event list to reflect the departure of the first customer on the queue at time *dtime*. The customer is removed from his queue by a call to *remove(qq, auxinfo)*, which must be suitably modified to handle the type of node in this example and must also decrement the queue's *num* field by 1. Note that *remove* must be coded as a procedure rather than as a function, since a Pascal function may not return a record. The departure node of the next customer on the queue (if any) replaces the departure node that has just been removed from the event list.

```
        procedure depart(qindx,dtime: integer);
        var p: nodeptr; {global variables: q, auxinfo, tottime, count,}
                  {                    evlist                    }
        procedure remove(var qq: queue; var auxinfo: nodeinfo);
            {body of remove goes here}
        begin {procedure depart}
            remove(q[qindx],auxinfo);
            tottime:= tottime + (dtime - auxinfo.time);
            count:= count + 1;
```

```
                { if there are any more customers on the queue, }
                { place the departure of the next customer onto }
                {the event list after computing its departure time}
                if q[qindx].num > 0
                    then begin
                            p:= q[qindx].front;
                            with auxinfo
                                do begin
                                        time:= dtime + node[p].info.duration;
                                        ntype:= qindx
                                    end {with...do begin};
                                place(evlist,auxinfo)
                        end {then begin}
                end {procedure depart};
```

Simulation programs are rich in their use of list structures. The reader is urged to explore the use of Pascal for simulation and the use of special-purpose simulation languages.

EXERCISES
1. In the bank simulation program of the text, a departure node on the event list represents the same customer as the first node on a customer queue. Is it possible to use a single node for a customer currently being serviced? Rewrite the program of the text so that only a single node is used. Is there any advantage to using two nodes?

2. The program in the text uses the same type of node for both customer and event nodes. Rewrite the program using two different types of nodes for these two purposes. Does this save space?

3. Revise the bank simulation program of the text to determine the average length of the four lines.

4. Modify the bank simulation program to compute the standard deviation of the time spent by a customer in the bank. Write another program which simulates a single line for all four tellers, with the customer at the head of the single line going to the next available teller. Compare the means and standard deviations of the two methods.

5. Modify the bank simulation program so that whenever the length of one line exceeds the length of another by more than two, the last customer on the longest line moves to the rear of the shortest.

6. Write a Pascal program to simulate a simple computer system as follows. Each user has a unique ID and wishes to perform a number of transactions on the computer. However, only one transaction may be processed by the computer at any given moment. Each input line represents a single user and contains the user's ID, followed by a starting time, followed by a series of integers representing the duration of each of his transactions. The input is sorted by increasing starting time, and all times and durations are in seconds. Assume that a user does not request time for a transaction until that user's previous transaction is complete and that the computer accepts transactions on a first come, first served basis. The program should simulate the system and print a message containing the user ID and the time whenever a transaction begins and ends. At the end of the simulation it should print the average waiting time for a transaction. (The waiting time is the amount of time between the time that the transaction was requested and the time it was started.)

7. Many simulations do not simulate events given by input data, but rather generate events according to some probability distribution. The following exercises illustrate how. Most computer installations have a random-number generating function *rand* (x). (The name and parameters of the function vary from installation to installation. *rand* is used as an example only.) x is initialized to a value called a **seed**. The statement $x:=rand(x)$ resets the value of the variable x to a random uniform real number between 0 and 1. By this we mean that if the statement is executed a sufficient number of times and any two equal-length intervals between 0 and 1 are chosen, approximately as many of the successive values of x fall into one interval as into the other. Thus the probability of a value of x falling in an interval of length $l <= 1$ equals l. Find out the name of the random-number generating function at your installation and verify that the above is true.

Given a random-number generator *rand*, consider the following statements:

$$x:= rand(x);$$
$$y:= (b-a)*x + a$$

Show that, given any two equal-sized intervals within the interval from a to b, if the statements are repeated sufficiently often, an approximately equal number of successive values of y fall into each of the two intervals. Show that if a and b are integers, the successive values of y truncated to an integer equal each integer between a and $b-1$ an approximately equal number of times. The variable y is said to be a **uniformly distributed random variable**. What is the average of the values of y in terms of a and b?

Rewrite the bank simulation of the text assuming that the transaction duration is uniformly distributed between 1 and 15. Each input line represents an arriving customer and contains only the time of his arrival. Upon reading an input line, generate a transaction duration for that customer by computing the next value according to the method outlined above.

8. The successive values of y that are generated by the following statements are said to be **normally distributed**. (Actually, they are approximately normally distributed, but the approximation is close enough.)

```
var x: array[1..15] of real;
    sum,y,s,m: real;
    i: integer;
begin
    {statements initializing the values of s, m and }
    {              the array x go here             }
    repeat
      sum:= 0;
      for i:= 1 to 15
        do begin
                x[i] := rand(x[i]);
                sum:= sum + x[i]
            end {for...do begin};
        y:= s*(sum-7.5)/sqrt(1.25) + m;
            {statements which use the value of y go here}
      until {a terminating condition goes here}
end;
```

Verify that the average of the values of y (the mean of the distribution) equals m and that the standard deviation equals s.

A certain factory produces items according to the following process: an item must be assembled and polished. Assembly time is uniformly distributed between 100 and 300 seconds and polishing time is normally distributed with a mean of 20 seconds and a standard deviation of 7 seconds (but values below five are discarded). After an item is assembled, a polishing machine must be used and a worker cannot begin assembling the next item until the item he has just assembled has been polished. There are 10 workers but only one polishing machine. If the machine is not available, workers who have finished assembling their items must wait for it. Compute the average waiting time per item by means of a simulation. Do the same under the assumption of two and three polishing machines.

4. OTHER LIST STRUCTURES

Although a linked linear list is a rather useful data structure, it has several shortcomings. In this section we shall present other methods of organizing a list and show how they can be used to overcome these shortcomings.

Circular Lists

One of the shortcomings of linear lists is that given a pointer p to a node in such a list, we cannot reach any of the nodes that precede $node(p)$. If a list is traversed, the original pointer to the beginning of the list must be preserved in order to be able to reference the list again.

Suppose a small change is made to the structure of a linear list so that the *next* field in the last node contains a pointer back to the first node rather than the nil pointer. Such a list is called a *circular list* and is illustrated in Figure 4.4.1. From any point in such a list it is possible to reach any other point in the list. If we begin at a given node and traverse the entire list, we ultimately end up at the starting point. Note that a circular list does not have a natural "first" or "last" node. We must, therefore, establish a first and last node by convention. One useful convention is to let the external pointer to the circular list point to the last node, and to allow the following node to be the first node, as illustrated in Figure 4.4.2. We also establish the convention that a nil pointer represents an empty circular list.

The Stack as a Circular List

A circular list can be used to represent a stack or a queue. Let *stack* be a pointer to the last node of a circular list, and let us adopt the convention that the first node is the top of the stack. The following is a Pascal procedure to push an integer x onto the stack, assuming a set of *nodes* and an auxiliary routine *getnode* as presented in previous sections. The *push* procedure calls on the function *empty*, which tests whether its parameter is 0.

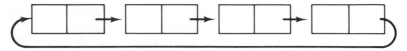

Figure 4.4.1 A circular list.

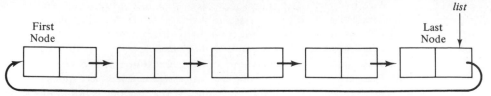

Figure 4.4.2 The first and last nodes of a circular list.

```
procedure push(var stack: nodeptr; x: integer);
var p: nodeptr;
begin
    p:= getnode;
    node[p].info:= x;
    if empty(stack)
       then stack:= p
       else node[p].next:= node[stack].next;
    node[stack].next:= p
end {procedure push};
```

Note that the *push* procedure is slightly more complex for circular lists than it is for linear lists.

The Pascal *pop* function for a stack implemented as a circular list is as follows. It calls the procedure *freenode* introduced earlier.

```
function pop(var stack: nodeptr): integer;
var p: nodeptr;
begin
    if empty(stack)
       then error('stack underflow')
       else begin
                p:= node[stack].next;
                pop:= node[p].info;
                if p = stack
                   then { only one node on the stack }
                       stack:= 0
                   else node[stack].next:= node[p].next;
                freenode(p)
            end {else begin}
end {function pop};
```

The Queue as a Circular List

It is easier to represent a queue as a circular list than as a linear list. As a linear list, a queue is specified by two pointers, one to the front of the list and the other to its rear. However, by using a circular list, a queue may be specified by a single pointer q to that list. *node*[q] is the rear of the queue and the following node is its front. The routine *remove*(q) is identical to *pop*(*stack*) except that all references to *stack* are replaced by q. The Pascal routine *insert* may be coded as follows:

CHAP. 4: QUEUES AND LISTS

```
              procedure insert(var q: nodeptr; x: integer);
              var p: nodeptr;
              begin
                    p:= getnode;
                    node[p].info:= x;
                    if empty(q)
                        then q:= p
                        else node[p].next:= node[q].next;
                    node[q].next:= p;
                    q:= p
              end { procedure insert};
```

Note that this is equivalent to the code

```
                    push(q,x);
                    q:= node[q].next
```

That is, to insert an element into the rear of a circular queue, the element is inserted into the front of the queue and the queue pointer is then advanced one element, so that the new element becomes the rear.

Primitive Operations on Circular Lists

The routine *insafter(p: nodeptr; x: integer)* for a circular list, which inserts a node containing x after *node*[p], is identical to the routine for linear lists as presented in Section 2. Let us now consider the routine *delafter(p: nodeptr; x: integer)*, which deletes the node following *node*[p] and stores its contents in x. Looking at the corresponding routine for linear lists as presented in Section 2, we note one additional consideration in the case of a circular list. Suppose that p points to the only node in the list. In a linear list, *next(p)* is nil in that case, making the deletion invalid. In the case of a circular list, however, *next(p)* points to *node(p)*, so that *node(p)* follows itself. The question is whether or not it is desirable to delete *node(p)* from the list in this case. It is unlikely that we would want to do so, since the operation *delafter* is usually invoked when pointers to each of two nodes are given, one immediately following another and it is desired to delete the second. *delafter* for circular lists is implemented as follows:

```
              procedure delafter(p: nodeptr; var x: integer);
              var q: nodeptr;
              begin
                  if p = 0
                    then { an empty list }
                        error('void deletion')
                    else if p = node[p].next
                            then { the list contains only a single node }
                                error('void deletion')
                            else begin
                                    q:= node[p].next;
```

```
                    x:= node[q].info;
                    node[p].next:= node[q].next;
                    freenode (q)
             end {else begin}
      end {procedure delafter};
```

Note, however, that these routines cannot be used to insert a node following the last node in a circular list or to delete the last node of a circular list. In both cases, the external pointer to the list must be modified to point to the new last node. The routines can be modified to accept *list* as an additional parameter and to change its value when necessary. An alternative is to write separate routines *insend* and *deletelast* for these cases. (*insend* is identical to the *insert* operation for a queue implemented as a circular list.) The calling routine would be responsible for determining which routine to call. We leave the exploration of these possibilities to the reader.

It is also easier to free an entire circular list than to free a linear list. In the case of a linear list, the entire list must be traversed, as one node at a time is returned to the available list. For a circular list, we can write a routine *freelist*, which effectively frees an entire list:

```
             procedure freelist(var list: nodeptr);
             var p: nodeptr;
             begin
                    p:= node[list].next;
                    node[list].next:= avail;
                    avail:= p;
                    list:= 0
             end {procedure freelist};
```

Similarly, we may write a routine *concat(list1,list2)*, which concatenates two lists—that is, it appends the circular list pointed to by *list2* to the end of the circular list pointed to by *list1*:

```
             procedure concat(var list1: nodeptr; list2: nodeptr);
             var p: nodeptr;
             begin
               if list1 = 0
                 then list1:= list2
                 else if list2 <> 0
                      then begin
                             p:= node[list1].next;
                             node[list1].next:= node[list2].next;
                             node[list2].next:= p;
                             list1:= list2
                           end {then begin}
             end {procedure concat};
```

The Josephus Problem

Let us consider a problem that can be solved in a straightforward manner by using a circular list. The problem is known as the Josephus problem and postulates a group of soldiers surrounded by an overwhelming enemy force. There is no hope for victory without reinforcements, but there is only a single horse available for escape. The soldiers agree to a pact to determine which of them is to escape and summon help. They form a circle and a number n is picked from a hat. One of their names is also picked from a hat. Beginning with the soldier whose name is picked, they begin to count clockwise around the circle. When the count reaches n, that solidier is removed from the circle, and the count begins again with the next man. The process continues so that each time the count reaches n, a man is removed from the circle. Once a soldier is removed from the circle, of course, he is no longer counted. The last soldier remaining is to take the horse and escape. The problem is: given a number n, the ordering of the men in the circle, and the man from whom the count begins, to determine the order in which men are eliminated from the circle and which man escapes.

The input to the program is the number n and a list of names that is the clockwise ordering of the men in the circle, beginning with the man from whom the count is to start. The last input line contains the string *'end'*, indicating the end of the input. The program should print the names of the men in the order that they are eliminated and the name of the man who escapes.

For example, suppose that n equals 3 and there are five men named A, B, C, D, and E. We count three men, starting at A, so that C is eliminated first. We then begin at D and count D, E, and back to A, so that A is eliminated next. Then we count B, D, and E (C has already been eliminated) and finally B, D, and B, so that D is the man who escapes.

Clearly, a circular list in which each node represents one man is a natural data structure to use in solving this problem. It is possible to reach any node from any other by counting around the circle. To represent the removal of a man from the circle, his node is deleted from the circular list. Finally, when only one node remains on the list, the result is determined.

An outline of the program might be the following:

```
read(n);
read(name);
while name is not 'end'
    do begin
            insert name on the circular list;
            read(name)
        end {while...do begin};
while there is more than one node on the list
    do begin
            count through n-1 nodes on the list;
            print the name in the nth node;
            delete the nth node
        end {while...do begin};
print the name of the only node on the list
```

We will assume that a set of nodes has been declared in a main program by

```
const numnodes = 500;
type  nametype = packed array[1..30] of char;
      nodeptr  = 0..numnodes;
      nodetype = record
                    info: nametype;
                    next: nodeptr
                 end;
var   node: array[1..numnodes] of nodetype;
```

and that an available list has been initialized. We also assume at least one name in the input. The program uses the routines *insert*, *delafter*, and *freenode*. We also assume the existence of a procedure *readname(var name: nametype)*, which reads a name from the input.

```
procedure josephus;
const endname = 'end
var   name: nametype;
      n,i: integer;
      list: nodeptr;
begin
      read(n);
      list:= 0;
      { read the names, placing each }
      {     at the rear of the list      }
      readname(name);
      while name <> endname
            do begin
                        insert(list,name);
                        readname(name)
                  end {while...do begin};
      { continue counting as long as more }
      { than one node remains on the list }
      while list <> node[list].next
            do begin
                        for i:= 1 to n-1
                           do list:= node[list].next;
                        { node[list].next points }
                        {     to the nth node      }
                        delafter(list,name);
                        writeln(name)
                  end   {while...do begin};
      { print the only name on the }
      {     list and free its node     }
      writeln('the man who escapes is: ', node[list].info);
      freenode(list)
end {procedure josephus};
```

Header Nodes

Suppose that we wish to traverse a circular list. This can be done by repeatedly executing $p:=node[p].next$, where p is initially a pointer to the beginning of the list. However, since the list is circular, we will not know when the entire list has been traversed unless another pointer *list* points to the first node and a test is made for the condition $p = list$.

An alternative method is to place a header node as the first node of a circular list. This list header may be recognized by a special value in its *info* field, which cannot be the valid contents of a list node in the context of the problem, or it may contain a flag marking it as a header. The list can then be traversed using a single pointer, with the traversal halting when the header node is reached. The external pointer to the list is to its header node, as illustrated in Figure 4.4.3. This means that a node cannot easily be added onto the rear of such a circular list, as could be done when the external pointer was to the last node of the list. Of course, it is possible to keep a pointer to the last node of a circular list even when a header node is being used.

If a stationary external pointer to a circular list is present in addition to the pointer used for traversal, the header node need not contain a special code but can be used in much the same way as a header node of a linear list, to contain global information about the list. The end of a traversal would be signaled by the equality of the traversing pointer and the external stationary pointer.

Addition of Long Positive Integers Using Circular Lists

We now present an example of an application that uses circular lists with header nodes. The hardware of most computers allows integers of only a specific maximum length. Suppose that we wish to represent positive integers of arbitrary length and to write a function that returns the sum of two such integers. To add two integers, their digits are traversed from right to left and corresponding digits and a possible carry from the previous digits' sum are added. This suggests representing long integers by storing their digits from right to left in a list so that the first node on the list contains the least significant digit (rightmost) and the last node contains the most significant (leftmost). However, to save space, we will keep five digits in each node. (Some implementations of Pascal may not allow integers to be

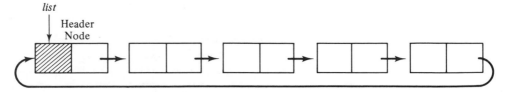

Figure 4.4.3 A circular list with a header node.

as large as 99999. In such implementations, fewer digits must be kept in each node.) We may declare the set of nodes by

```
const numnodes = 500;
type  nodeptr = 0..numnodes;
      nodetype=record
                  info: -1..99999;
                  next: nodeptr
      end;
var node: array[1..numnodes] of nodetype;
```

Since we wish to traverse the lists during the addition but wish to eventually restore the list pointers to their original values, we use circular lists with headers. The header node is distinguished by an *info* value of −1. For example, the integer 459763497210698463 is represented by the list illustrated in Figure 4.4.4.

Now let us write a function *addint* which accepts pointers to two such lists representing integers, creates a list representing the sum of the integers, and returns a pointer to the sum list. Both lists are traversed in parallel and five digits are added at a time. If the sum of two five digit numbers is x, the low-order five digits of x can be extracted by the expression $x \bmod 100000$, which yields the remainder of x on division by 100000. The carry can be computed by the expression $x \operatorname{div} 100000$. When the end of one list is reached, the carry is propagated to the remaining digits of the other list. The function follows and uses the routines *getnode* and *insafter*.

```
function addint(p,q: nodeptr): nodeptr;
const hunthou = 100000;
var   s,pp,qq,r: nodeptr;
      carry: 0..1;
      number: 0..99999;
      total: integer;
begin
      { set pp and qq to the nodes following the headers }
      pp:= node[p].next;
      qq:= node[q].next;
      { set up a header node for the sum }
      s:= getnode;
      node[s].info:= -1;
      node[s].next:= s;
```

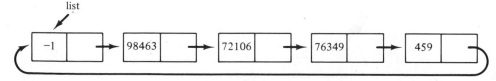

Figure 4.4.4 A large integer as a circular list.

```
                  { initially there is no carry }
       carry:= 0;
       while (node[pp].info <> -1) and (node[qq].info <> -1)
              do begin {traverse the two lists in parallel}
                       { add the info of the two nodes and previous carry }
                       total:= node[pp].info + node[qq].info + carry;
                       { Determine the low order five digits of }
                       {      the sum.  Insert into the list.      }
                       number:= total mod hunthou;
                       insafter(s,number);
                       { determine whether there is a carry }
                       carry:= total div hunthou;
                       s:= node[s].next;      { advance the pointers }
                       pp:= node[pp].next;
                       qq:= node[qq].next
              end {while...do begin};
       { at this point, there may be nodes left in one of the }
       {                   two input lists                    }
       if node[pp].info <> -1
          then r:= pp
          else r:= qq;
       while node[r].info <> -1
              do begin {traverse the remainder of the list}
                       total:= node[r].info + carry;
                       number:= total mod hunthou;
                       insafter(s, number);
                       carry:= total div hunthou;
                       s:= node[s].next;
                       r:= node[r].next
              end {while...do begin};
       { check if there is an extra carry from the first five }
       {                      digits                          }
       if carry = 1
          then begin
                       insafter (s, carry);
                       s:= node[s].next
              end {then begin};
       { s points to the last node in the sum.  next[s] points }
       {            to the header of the sum list.             }
       addint:= node[s].next
end {function addint};
```

Doubly Linked Lists

Although a circularly linked list has advantages over a linear list, it still has
several drawbacks. One cannot traverse such a list backward, nor can a node
be deleted from a circularly linked list given only a pointer to that node. In

cases where these facilities are required, the appropriate data structure is a *doubly linked list*. Each node in such a list contains two pointers, one to its predecessor and another to its successor. In fact, in the context of doubly linked lists, the terms "predecessor" and "successor" are meaningless, since the list is entirely symmetric. Doubly linked lists may be either linear or circular and may or may not contain a header node, as illustrated in Figure 4.4.5.

We may consider the nodes on a doubly linked list to consist of three fields: an *info* field, which contains the information stored in the node, and *left* and *right* fields, which contain pointers to the nodes on either side. We may declare a set of such nodes by

```
const numnodes = 500;
type  nodeptr= 0..numnodes;
         nodetype= record
                         info: integer;
                         left,right: nodeptr
                    end;
var    node: array [1..numnodes] of nodetype;
```

Note that the available list for such a set of nodes need not be doubly linked, since it is not traversed bidirectionally. The available list may be linked together by using either the *left* or *right* pointer. Of course, appropriate *getnode* and *freenode* routines must be written.

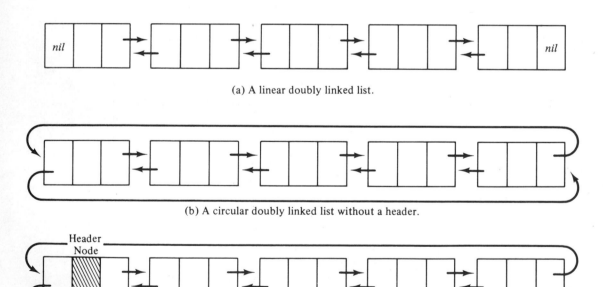

(a) A linear doubly linked list.

(b) A circular doubly linked list without a header.

(c) A circular doubly linked list with a header.

Figure 4.4.5 Doubly linked lists.

We now present routines to operate on doubly linked circular lists. A convenient property of such lists is that if p is a pointer to any node in a doubly linked list, then letting *left(p)* be an abbreviation for *node[p].left*, and *right(p)* an abbreviation for *node[p].right*, we have

$$left(right(p)) = p = right(left(p))$$

One operation that can be performed on doubly linked lists but not on ordinary linked lists is to delete a given node. The following Pascal routine deletes the node pointed to by p from a doubly linked list and stores its contents in x.

```
procedure delete(p: nodeptr; var x: integer);
var r,q: nodeptr;
begin
    if p = 0
        then error('void deletion')
        else begin
                x:= node[p].info;
                q:= node[p].left;
                r:= node[p].right;
                node[q].right:= r;
                node[r].left:= q;
                freenode(p)
            end {else begin}
end { procedure delete};
```

The routine *insertright* inserts a node with information field x to the right of *node[p]* in a doubly linked list.

```
procedure insertright(p: nodeptr; x: integer);
var r,q: nodeptr;
begin
    if p = 0
        then error('void insertion')
        else begin
                q:= getnode;
                node[q].info:= x;
                r:= node[p].right;
                node[r].left:= q;
                node[q].right:= r;
                node[q].left:= p;
                node[p].right:= q
            end {else begin}
end { procedure insertright};
```

A routine *insertleft* to insert a node with information field x to the left of *node[p]* in a doubly linked list is similar and is left as an exercise for the reader.

Addition of Long Integers Using Doubly Linked Lists

As an illustration of the use of doubly linked lists, let us consider extending the implementation of long integers to include negative as well as positive integers. The header node of a circular list representing a long integer will contain an indication of whether the integer is positive or negative. When we wanted to add two positive integers, we traversed the integers from the least significant digit to the most significant. However, to add a positive and a negative integer, the smaller absolute value must be subtracted from the larger absolute value and the result must be given the sign of the integer with the larger absolute value. Thus some method is needed for testing which of two integers represented as circular lists has the larger absolute value.

The first criterion that may be used to identify the integer with the larger absolute value is the length of the integers (assuming that they do not contain leading zeros). Thus we can count the number of nodes in each list, and the list that has more nodes represents the integer with the larger absolute value. However, this count involves an extra traversal of the list. Instead of counting the number of nodes, the count could be kept as part of the header node and referred to as needed.

However, if both lists have the same number of nodes, it is necessary to traverse the lists from the most significant digit to the least significant to determine which number is larger. Note that this traversal is in the opposite direction of the traversal that must be used in actually adding two integers. For this reason, doubly linked lists are used to represent such integers.

Consider the format of the header node. In addition to a right and left pointer, the header must contain the length of the list and an indication of whether the number is positive or negative. These two pieces of information can be combined into a single integer whose absolute value is the length of the list and whose sign is the sign of the number being represented. However, in doing so, the ability to identify the header node by examining the sign of its *info* field is destroyed. When a positive integer was represented as a singly linked circular list, an *info* field of -1 indicated a header node. Under the new representation, however, a header node may contain an *info* field such as 5, which is a valid *info* field for any other node in the list.

There are several ways to remedy this problem. One way is to add another field to each node to indicate whether or not it is a header node. Such a field could be a boolean with the value *true* if the node is a header and *false* if it is not. This means, of course, that each node would require more space. Alternatively, the count could be eliminated from the header node and an *info* field of -1 would indicate a positive number and -2 a negative number. A header node could then be identified by its negative *info* field. However, this would increase the time needed to compare two numbers, since it would be necessary to count the number of nodes in each list. Such space/time trade-offs are very common in computing, and a decision must be made as to which efficiency should be sacrificed and

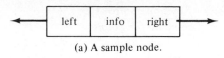

left | info | right

(a) A sample node.

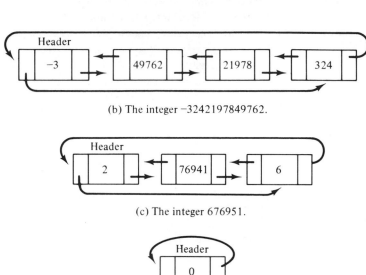

Header

−3 ⇄ 49762 ⇄ 21978 ⇄ 324

(b) The integer −3242197849762.

Header

2 ⇄ 76941 ⇄ 6

(c) The integer 676951.

Header

0

(d) The integer 0.

Figure 4.4.6 Integers as doubly linked lists.

which retained. In our case, we choose yet a third option, which is to retain an external pointer to the list header. A pointer p can be identified as pointing to a header if it is equal to the original external pointer; otherwise, the node to which p points is not a header.

Figure 4.4.6 indicates a sample node and the representation of three integers as doubly linked lists. Note that the least significant digits are to the right of the header and that the counts in the header nodes do not include the header node itself.

Using the representation described above, we present a function *compabs*, which compares the absolute value of two integers represented as doubly linked lists. Its two parameters are pointers to the list headers and it returns a value indicating whether the first has an absolute value less than, greater than, or equal to the second. The type of this value may be defined in the main program as

                                                  FALSE   TRUE

            type comptype= (lessthan, equalto, greaterthan);

    function compabs(p,q: nodeptr): ~~comptype~~; *boolean* ;
    var r,s: nodeptr;
        equal: boolean;

```
            begin {function compabs}
              { compare the counts }
              if abs(node[p].info) > abs(node[q].info)
                then compabs:= greaterthan    true
                else if abs(node[p].info) < abs(node[q].info)
                    then compabs:= lessthan   false
                    else { they are of equal length }
                        begin
                          r:= node[p].left;
                          s:= node[q].left;
                          equal:= true;    define equal boolean,
                                                local to
              { traverse the list from the most significant digits }   procedure
                          while (r <> p) and (equal)
                            do begin
                                if node[r].info > node[s].info
                                  then begin
                                          equal:= false;
                                          compabs:= greaterthan    true
                                      end {then begin};
                                if node[r].info < node[s].info
                                  then begin
                                          equal:= false;
                                          compabs:= lessthan   false
                                      end {then begin};
                                if node[r].info = node[s].info
                                  then begin
                                          r:= node[r].left;
                                          s:= node[s].left
                                      end {then begin}
                            end {while...do begin};
                          if equal
                            then compabs:= equalto   true
                        end {else begin}
            end {function compabs};
```

We are now ready to write a function *addiff*, which accepts two pointers to lists representing long integers of opposite sign, where the absolute value of the first is not less than that of the second, and which returns a pointer to a list representing the sum of the integers. We must, of course, be careful to eliminate leading zeros from the sum. To do this, we keep a pointer *zeroptr* to the first node of a consecutive set of leading zero nodes and a boolean flag *zeroflag*, which is *true* if and only if the last node of the sum generated so far is zero.

In this function p points to the number with the larger absolute value and q points to the number with the smaller absolute value. The values of these variables do not change. Auxiliary variables *pptr* and *qptr* are used to traverse the lists. The sum is formed in a list pointed to by the variable r.

```
function addiff(p,q: nodeptr): nodeptr;
const hunthou = 100000;
var    r,s,zeroptr,pptr,qptr: nodeptr;
       zeroflag: boolean;
       borrow: 0..1;
       diff,count: integer;
begin
     { initialize variables }
     count:= 0;
     borrow:= 0;
     zeroflag:= false;
     { generate a header node for the sum }
     r:= getnode;
     node[r].left:= r;
     node[r].right:= r;
     { traverse the two lists }
     pptr:= node[p].right;
     qptr:= node[q].right;
     while qptr <> q
          do begin
                    diff:= node[pptr].info - borrow - node[qptr].info;
                    if diff >= 0
                       then borrow:= 0
                       else begin
                                   diff:= diff + hunthou;
                                   borrow:= 1
                              end {else begin};
                    { generate a new node and insert it }
                    {    to the left of header in sum    }
                    insertleft(r,diff);
                    count:= count + 1;
                    { test for zero node }
                    if diff = 0
                       then begin
                                   if not zeroflag
                                      then zeroptr:= node[r].left;
                                   zeroflag:= true
                              end {then begin}
                       else zeroflag:= false;
                    pptr:= node[pptr].right;
                    qptr:= node[qptr].right
             end {while...do begin};
     { traverse the remainder of the p list }
     while p <> pptr
          do begin
                    diff:= node[pptr].info - borrow;
```

```
                    if diff >= 0
                        then borrow:= 0
                        else begin
                                diff:= diff + hunthou;
                                `borrow:= 1
                            end {else begin};
                        insertleft(r, diff);
                        count:= count + 1;
                        if diff = 0
                            then begin
                                    if not zeroflag
                                        then zeroptr:= node[r].left;
                                    zeroflag:= true
                                end {then begin}
                            else zeroflag:= false;
                        pptr:= node[pptr].right
                    end {while...do begin};
                if zeroflag { then delete leading zeros }
                    then while zeroptr <> r
                        do begin
                                s:= zeroptr;
                                zeroptr:= node[zeroptr].right;
                                delete(s, diff);
                                count:= count - 1
                            end {while...do begin};
                { insert count and sign into the header }
                if node[p].info > 0
                    then node[r].info:= count
                    else node[r].info:= -count;
                addiff:= r
            end { function addiff };
```

We can also write a function *addsame*, which adds two numbers with like signs. This is very similar to the function *addint* of the previous implementation except that it deals with a doubly linked list and must keep track of the number of nodes in the sum.

Using these routines, we can write a new version of *addint*, which adds two integers represented by doubly linked lists.

```
        function addint(p,q: nodeptr): nodeptr;
        type comptype = (lessthan, equalto, greaterthan);
        { definitions for compabs, addiff and addsame go here }
        begin
            { check if integers are of like sign }
            if node[p].info * node[q].info > 0
                then addint:= addsame(p,q)
```

$$\textbf{else} \; \{ \textit{check which has a larger absolute value} \}$$
$$\textbf{if} \; \text{compabs}(p,q) = \text{greaterthan}$$
$$\textbf{then} \; \text{addint} := \text{addiff}(p,q)$$
$$\textbf{else} \; \text{addint} := \text{addiff}(q,p)$$
$$\textbf{end} \; \{ \textit{function addint} \};$$

EXERCISES

1. Write an algorithm and a Pascal routine to perform each of the operations of Exercise 4.2.4 for circular lists. Which are more efficient on circular lists than on linear lists? Which are less efficient?

2. Rewrite the routine *place* of Section 2 to insert a new item in an ordered circular list.

3. Write a program to solve the Josephus problem by using an array rather than a circular list. Why is a circular list more efficient?

4. Consider the following variation of the Josephus problem. A group of people stand in a circle and each chooses a positive integer. One of their names and a positive integer n are chosen. Starting with the person whose name is chosen, they count around the circle clockwise and eliminate the nth person. The positive integer which that person chose is then used to continue the count. Each time that a person is eliminated, the number the person chose is used to determine the next person eliminated. For example, suppose that the five people are A, B, C, D, and E; they choose integers 3, 4, 6, 2, and 7, respectively; and the integer 2 is initially chosen. Then if we start from A, the order in which people are eliminated from the circle is B, A, E, C, leaving D as the last one in the circle.

   Write a program that reads a group of input lines. Each input line except the first and last contains a name and a positive integer chosen by that person. The order of the names in the data is the clockwise ordering of the people in the circle and the count is to start with the first name in the input. The first input line contains the number of people in the circle. The last input line contains only a single positive integer representing the initial count. The program prints the order in which the people are eliminated from the circle.

5. Write a Pascal function $multpos(p,q)$ to multiply two long positive integers represented by singly linked circular lists.

6. Write a program to print the 100th Fibonacci number.

7. Write algorithms and Pascal routines to perform the operations of Exercise 4.2.4 for doubly linked circular lists. Which are more efficient on doubly linked than on singly linked lists? Which are less efficient?

8. Write a routine *addsame* to add two long integers of the same sign represented by doubly linked lists.

9. Write a Pascal function $multint(p,q)$ to multiply two long integers represented by doubly linked circular lists.

10. How can you represent a polynomial in three variables (x, y, and z) as a circular list? Each node should represent a term and should contain the powers of x, y, and z as well as the coefficient of that term. Write Pascal functions to do the following:

    (a) Add two such polynomials.
    (b) Multiply two such polynomials.

(c) Take the partial derivative of such a polynomial with respect to any of its variables.

(d) Evaluate such a polynomial for given values of x, y, and z.

(e) Divide one such polynomial by another creating a quotient polynomial and a remainder polynomial.

(f) Integrate such a polynomial with respect to any of its variables.

(g) Print the representation of such a polynomial.

(h) Given four such polynomials, $f(x,y,z)$, $g(x,y,z)$, $h(x,y,z)$, and $i(x,y,z)$, compute the polynomial $f(g(x,y,z), h(x,y,z), i(x,y,z))$.

5 Pascal List Processing

This chapter discusses the list processing facilities available in Pascal. Under these techniques, a pointer is the actual address of a portion of storage that can be dynamically allocated and freed. A list can grow and shrink dynamically without tying up valuable storage.

1. IMPLEMENTING LISTS USING DYNAMIC STORAGE

The Need for Dynamic Storage

As we have seen in Chapter 4, the notion of a pointer allows us to build and manipulate linked lists of various types. The concept of a pointer introduces the possibility of assembling a collection of building blocks, called nodes, into flexible structures. By altering the values of pointers, nodes can be attached, detached, and reassembled in patterns that grow and shrink as execution of a program progresses.

In Chapter 4, however, a fixed set of nodes represented by an array and its elements is established for use at the start of execution. A pointer to a node was represented by the relative position of the node within the array. The disadvantage of that approach is twofold. First, the number of nodes that are needed cannot be predicted at the time that a program is written. Usually, the data with which the program is executed determines the number of nodes necessary. Thus no matter how many elements the array of nodes contains, it is always possible that the program will be executed with input that requires a larger number.

The second disadvantage of the array approach is that whatever number of nodes are declared must remain allocated to the program throughout its execution. For example, if 500 nodes of a given type are declared, the amount of storage required for those 500 nodes is reserved for that purpose. If the program actually uses only 100, or even 10, nodes in its execution, the additional nodes are still reserved and their storage cannot be used for any other purpose.

The solution to this problem is to allow nodes that are *dynamic* rather than static. This is, when a node is needed, storage is reserved for it, and when it is no longer needed, the storage is released. Thus the storage for nodes that are no longer in use is available for another purpose. Also, no predefined limit on the number of nodes is established. As long as sufficient storage is available to the job as a whole, part of that storage can be reserved for use as a node.

Pointers in Pascal

The method of access to a node is through a pointer. In the array implementation of Chapter 4, a pointer is simply an index to the array that specifies which of a predefined set of nodes is being accessed. However, if dynamic storage allocation is being used, there is no predefined set of nodes, nor is there a predefined organization among the set of nodes. Therefore, when a portion of storage is reserved for use as a node (i.e., when a node is *allocated*), a method of accessing the node must simultaneously be created. That method of access is a pointer, which may be thought of as the address of the portion of storage allocated to the node.

In Pascal, the type of the node being accessed is part of the type of the pointer. Specifically, we may declare a pointer to an integer by

$$\textbf{var pi: } \uparrow\text{integer;}$$

and a pointer to a real number by

$$\textbf{var pr: } \uparrow\text{real;}$$

The values of *pi* and *pr* will both be addresses, but the value of *pi* must be the address of a portion of storage containing an integer, while the value of *pr* must be the address of a portion of storage containing a real number.

A new kind of variable can be referenced by using a pointer. Given the foregoing declarations of *pi* and *pr*, the constructs *pi*$\uparrow$ and *pr*$\uparrow$ are variables of type *integer* and *real*, respectively. The statement

$$\text{pi}\uparrow := 6$$

is executed in two phases. First, the value of *pi* is used to locate the integer variable *pi*$\uparrow$, and second, the value of that variable is set to 6. Similarly, the statement

$$\text{write (pi}\uparrow\text{)}$$

first uses the value of *pi* to locate the integer variable *pi*$\uparrow$, and then prints the value of that variable.

Note that the statements

$$\text{pi} := 6$$

and

$$\text{write (pi)}$$

are illegal. *pi* is not an integer, but a pointer to an integer, so that it cannot be given an integer value nor can its value be printed. Its sole purpose is to provide access to the integer *pi*↑. *pi*↑ may be thought of as "the variable to which *pi* points."

Allocating and Freeing Dynamic Variables

Once a variable *p* has been declared as a pointer to a specific type of object, it must be possible to dynamically create an object of the specific type and assign its address to *p*. This may be done in Pascal by calling the standard procedure *new*. If *p* is a pointer to an object of type *t*, *new(p)* creates an object of type *t* and assigns its address to *p*. Thus given the declarations

var pi: ↑integer;
pr: ↑real;

executing the statements

new(pi);
new(pr)

dynamically creates the integer variable *pi*↑ and the real variable *pr*↑.

As an example of the use of pointers and the procedure *new*, consider the following statements:

```
1       var p,q: ↑integer;
2           x: integer;
3       begin
4           new(p);
5           p↑:= 3;
6           q:= p;
7           writeln(p↑,q↑);
8           x:= 7;
9           q↑:= x;
10          writeln(p↑,q↑);
11          new(p);
12          p↑:= 5;
13          writeln(p↑,q↑)
14      end;
```

In line 4, an integer variable is created and its address is placed in *p*. Line 5 sets the value of that variable to 3. Line 6 sets *q* to the address of that variable. The assignment statement in line 6 is perfectly valid, since one pointer variable (*q*) is being assigned the value of another (*p*). Figure 5.1.1a illustrates the situation after line 6. Note that at this point, *p*↑ and *q*↑ refer to the same variable. Line 7 therefore prints the contents of this variable (which is 3) twice.

Line 8 sets the value of an *integer* variable, *x*, to 7. Line 9 changes the value of *q*↑ to the value of *x*. However, since *p* and *q* both point to the same

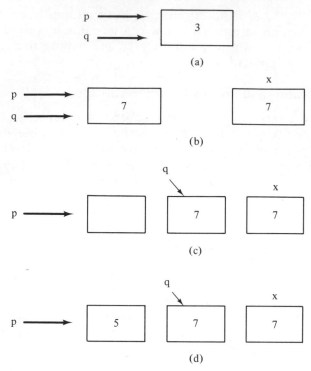

(a)

(b)

(c)

(d)

Figure 5.1.1

variable, $p\uparrow$ and $q\uparrow$ both have values of 7. This is illustrated in Figure 5.1.1b. Line 10 therefore prints the number 7 twice.

Line 11 creates a new integer variable and places its address in p. The results are illustrated in Figure 5.1.1c. $p\uparrow$ now refers to the newly created integer variable, which has not yet been given a value. q has not been changed, so the value of $q\uparrow$ remains 7. Note that $p\uparrow$ does not refer to a single, specific variable. Its value changes as the value of p changes. Line 12 sets the value of this newly created variable to 5, as illustrated in Figure 5.1.1d, and line 13 prints the values 5 and 7.

The procedure *dispose* is used in Pascal to free storage of a dynamically allocated variable. The statement

dispose(p)

makes any future references to the variable $p\uparrow$ illegal (unless, of course, a new value is assigned to p by an assignment statement or by a call to *new*). In most Pascal implementations, calling *dispose*(p) makes the storage occupied by $p\uparrow$ available for reuse, if necessary.

To illustrate the use of the *dispose* procedure, consider the following statements:

```
1    new(p);
2    p↑:= 5;
```

220   CHAP. 5: PASCAL LIST PROCESSING

```
3      new(q);
4      q↑:= 8;
5      dispose(p);
6      p:= q;
7      new(q);
8      q↑:= 6;
9      writeln(p↑,q↑)
```

The values 8 and 6 are printed. Figure 5.1.2a illustrates the situation after line 4, where $p\uparrow$ and $q\uparrow$ have both been allocated and given values. Figure 5.1.2b illustrates the effects of line 5, where the variable to which p points has been freed. Figure 5.1.2c illustrates line 6, where the value of p is changed to point to the variable $q\uparrow$. In line 7, the value of q is changed to point to a newly created variable which is given the value 6 in line 8 (Figure 5.1.2d).

Note that if procedure *new* is called twice in succession with the same parameter, as in

```
new(p);    p↑:= 3;
new(p);    p↑:= 7;
```

the first copy of $p\uparrow$ is lost since its address was not saved. Since the space allocated for these variables can be accessed only through a pointer, unless the pointer to the first variable is saved in another pointer, it will be lost.

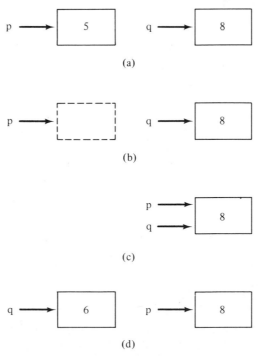

(a)

(b)

(c)

(d)

Figure 5.1.2

In fact, the storage cannot even be freed, because there is no way to reference it in a call to *dispose*. This is an example of a memory location that is allocated but cannot be referenced.

There is a special value that any pointer variable may have, denoted by *nil*. This pointer value does not reference a storage location but denotes the nil pointer, which does not point to anything. The value *nil* may be assigned to any pointer variable p, after which a reference to $p\uparrow$ is illegal. Note that *nil* is a reserved word in Pascal, rather than a predefined identifier such as *true* or *maxint*.

We have noted that a call to *dispose*(p) makes a subsequent reference to $p\uparrow$ illegal. However, the actual effects of a call to *dispose* are not defined by the Pascal language—each implementation of Pascal is free to develop its own version of this procedure. In some Pascal implementations, *dispose* has no effect at all; in others, the storage for $p\uparrow$ is freed, but the value of p is left unchanged. This means that although a reference to $p\uparrow$ becomes illegal, there may be no way of detecting the illegality. The value of p is a valid address and the object at that address of the proper type may be used as the value of $p\uparrow$. p is called a *dangling pointer*. It is the programmer's responsibility never to use such a pointer in a program.

Still other Pascal implementations cause *dispose*(p) to set p to *nil*. In that case a subsequent reference to $p\uparrow$ would be detected as an error, since p no longer points to a valid object. The programmer should determine the effects of the *dispose* procedure in the Pascal implementation that he is using. (Some implementations of Pascal contain a different, nonstandard mechanism for freeing storage, the *mark* and *release* procedures, which are not discussed here.)

One other dangerous feature associated with pointers should be mentioned. If p and q are pointers with the same value, then the variables $p\uparrow$ and $q\uparrow$ are identical. Both $p\uparrow$ and $q\uparrow$ refer to the same object. Thus an assignment to $p\uparrow$ changes the value of $q\uparrow$, despite the fact that neither q nor $q\uparrow$ are explicitly mentioned. It is the programmer's responsibility to keep track of "which pointers are pointing where" and to recognize the occurrence of such implicit results.

Note that when a pointer variable is declared in Pascal, the type of the object to which it points must be specified. A single pointer variable may contain a pointer to only one type of object during a program's execution. For example, if we had declared

var pi: ↑integer;
pc: ↑char;

the statement

pi:= pc

would be illegal, despite the fact that both *pi* and *pc* are pointers. The reason is that the types of *pi* and *pc* are not simply "pointer" but "pointer to an integer" and "pointer to a character," respectively. Since the two variables have different types, it is illegal to assign a value from one to the other.

Linked Lists Using Dynamic Variables

Now that we have the capability of dynamically allocating and freeing a variable, let us see how dynamic variables can be used to implement linked lists. Recall that a linked list consists of a set of nodes, each of which has two fields: an information field and a pointer to the next node in the list. In addition, there is an external pointer to the first node in the list. We will use pointer variables to implement list pointers. Thus we could define the type of a pointer and a node by

$$
\begin{aligned}
&\textbf{type } \text{nodeptr} = \uparrow\text{nodetype;} \\
&\qquad \text{nodetype} = \textbf{record} \\
&\qquad\qquad\qquad \text{info: integer;} \\
&\qquad\qquad\qquad \text{next: nodeptr} \\
&\qquad\qquad \textbf{end;}
\end{aligned}
$$

A node of such type is identical to the nodes of Section 4.2, except that the *next* field is a pointer (containing the address of the next node in the list) rather than an integer (containing the index within an array where the next node in the list is kept). Note that in the definition of a pointer type such as *nodeptr*, Pascal permits a reference to the type to which the pointer points (*nodetype*) before the type pointed to has been defined. This is because it is unnecessary to know the details of that type in order to implement a pointer to it. A pointer is, after all, an address. The storage requirements for an address are the same regardless of the object located at that address.

Let us employ the dynamic allocation features to implement linked lists. Instead of declaring an array to represent an aggregate collection of nodes, a node will be referenced through its pointer. Nodes will be allocated and freed as necessary, and the need for a declared collection of nodes is eliminated.

If we declare

$$\textbf{var } \text{p: nodeptr;}$$

an execution of the statement

$$\text{p:= getnode}$$

should place the address of an available node into *p*. We present the function *getnode*:

```
function getnode: nodeptr;
var p: nodeptr;
begin
    new(p);
    getnode:= p
end {function getnode};
```

Similarly, an execution of the statement

freenode(p)

should return the node whose address is at p to available storage. We present the routine *freenode*. p is declared as a variable parameter in order to have it reset to *nil* under those implementations in which *dispose* sets its argument to *nil*.

```
procedure freenode (var p: nodeptr);
begin
        dispose(p)
end { procedure freenode };
```

The programmer need not be concerned with managing available storage. There is no longer a need for the pointer *avail* (pointing to the first available node) because the system governs the allocating and freeing of nodes and the system keeps track of the first available node. Note also that there is no test in *getnode* for determining whether overflow has occurred. This is because such a condition will be detected during the execution of the *new* function and is system-dependent.

Since the routines *getnode* and *freenode* are so simple under this implementation, they are often replaced by the in-line statements *new(p)* and *dispose(p)*.

The procedures *insafter(p,x)* and *delafter(p,x)* are presented below using the dynamic implementation of a linked list. Assume that *list* is a pointer variable which points to the first node of a list (if any) and is equal to *nil* in the case of an empty list.

```
procedure insafter(p: nodeptr; x: integer);
var q: nodeptr;
begin
    if p = nil
       then error('void insertion')
       else begin
                q:= getnode;
                q↑.info:= x;
                q↑.next:= p↑.next;
                p↑.next:= q
            end {else begin}
end { procedure insafter };

procedure delafter(p: nodeptr; var x: integer);
var q: nodeptr;
begin
    if p = nil
       then error('void deletion')
       else if p↑.next = nil
            then error('void deletion')
```

```
                else begin
                    q:= p↑.next;
                    x:= q↑.info;
                    p↑.next:= q↑.next;
                    freenode(q)
                end {else begin}
        end { procedure delafter};
```

Notice the striking similarity between the foregoing routines and those of the second half of Section 4.2. Both are implementations of the algorithms of the first half of that section. In fact, the only difference between the two versions is in the manner in which the list pointers are specified.

Stacks and queues can also be implemented using this new implementation of linked lists. We leave these as exercises for the reader.

List Operations Using the Dynamic Implementation

We now present several small examples to illustrate some features of list manipulation in Pascal. First, let us write a procedure *insend(list,x)* to insert the element *x* at the end of a list *list*.

```
procedure insend(var list: nodeptr; x: integer);
var p,q: nodeptr;
begin
    p:= getnode;
    p↑.info:= x;
    p↑.next:= nil;
    if list = nil
        then list:= p
        else begin
                { search for the last node }
                q:= list;
                while q↑.next <> nil
                    do q:= q↑.next;
                q↑.next:= p
        end {else begin}
end { procedure insend};
```

We now present a function *search(list,x)*, which returns a pointer to the first occurrence of *x* within the list *list*, and the *nil* pointer if *x* does not occur in the list.

```
function search(list: nodeptr; x: integer): nodeptr;
var p: nodeptr;
    found: boolean;
```

```
begin
    p:= list;
    found:= false;
    while (p <> nil) and (not found)
        do if p↑.info = x
            then found:= true
            else p:= p↑.next;
    search:= p
end {function search};
```

The next routine deletes all nodes whose *info* field contains the value *x*.

```
procedure remvx(var list: nodeptr; x: integer);
var p,q: nodeptr;
    y: integer;
begin
    q:= nil;
    p:= list;
    while p <> nil
        do if p↑.info = x
            then begin
                    p:= p↑.next;
                    if q = nil
                        then { remove first node }
                             {      of the list      }
                            begin
                                freenode(list);
                                list:= p
                            end {then begin}
                        else delafter(q,y)
                end {then begin}
            else { advance to next node of list }
                begin
                    q:= p;
                    p:= p↑.next
                end {else begin}
end {procedure remvx};
```

Allocating and Freeing Variant Records

A node need not contain a simple item such as an integer or character. As we saw in Chapter 4, the *info* field can be an array or a record. In particular, when we wish nodes of several different forms, a variant record can be used. For example, suppose that the elements of a list can be single numbers or pairs of integers. Then we might declare

```
type nodeptr = ↑nodetype;
    nodetype = record
            next: nodeptr;
```

CHAP. 5: PASCAL LIST PROCESSING

```
        case sp: (single,pair) of
            single: (info: integer);
                pair: (info1, info2: integer)
        end;
    var p: nodeptr;
```

A node of this type may be allocated by *new(p)* and freed by *dispose(p)*. When such a node is allocated, enough storage is reserved to hold the largest possible variant of the record—in this case, a pair of integers.

However, suppose we know that the node will only contain a single integer. Then it is wasteful to reserve storage for two integers, since only one is necessary. To assist in conserving storage, Pascal allows another form of the *new* and *dispose* procedures. *new(p,single)* allocates a variable of type *nodetype* with only enough storage in the variant part of the record to contain a single integer; while *new(p,pair)* allocates a *nodetype* variable with enough storage in the variant part to contain two integers. The tag field *sp* is not assigned a value by the call to *new*. Subsequently, the tag field may only be assigned the value specified in the call to *new* and may not be changed. For its entire lifetime, such a record adopts a single one of its variants.

A node created by the *new* function with two arguments must be freed with the *dispose* function using two arguments. *dispose(p,single)* is used to free a record created by *new(p,single)*, while *dispose(p,pair)* is used to free a record created by *new(p,pair)*. Similarly, if a variant record has more than one tag field (in the case of a variant record which contains a field that is itself declared as a variant record), *new* and *dispose* can be called with more than two arguments.

Comparing the Dynamic and Array Implementations of Lists

It is instructive to examine the advantages and disadvantages of the dynamic and array implementations of linked lists. The major disadvantage of the dynamic implementation is that it may be more time-consuming to call upon the system to allocate and free storage than to manipulate a programmer-managed available list. Its major advantage is that a set of nodes is not reserved in advance for use by a particular group of lists. For example, suppose that a program uses two types of lists: lists of integers and lists of characters. Under the array representation, two arrays of fixed size would immediately be allocated. If one group of lists overflows its array, the program cannot continue. Under the dynamic representation, two node types are defined at the outset, but no storage is allocated for variables until needed. As nodes are needed, the system is called upon to provide them. Any storage not used for one type of node may be used for another. Thus as long as sufficient storage is available for the nodes actually present in the lists, no overflow will occur.

Another advantage of the dynamic implementation is that a reference to $p\uparrow$ does not involve the address computation that is necessary in computing the address of *node*[*p*]. To compute the address of *node*[*p*], the contents of *p* must be added to the base address of the array *node*, whereas the address of *p↑* is given by the contents of *p* directly.

Still another advantage of dynamic variables exists in the case of variant records. If an array of nodes is declared, each node must contain enough storage to hold the largest possible variant. By using the *new* and *dispose* procedures with two arguments, each node need contain only as much storage as the particular variant required for that node.

EXERCISES

1. Write a function *binsrch*, which accepts two parameters, an array of pointers to a group of sorted numbers, and a single number. The function should use a binary search (see Section 3.1) to return a pointer to the single number if it is in the group. If the number is not present in the group, return the value **nil**.

2. Consider the following implementation of a stack of integers. Declare and initialize an array of pointers, a dynamic array type, and two variables as follows:

```
type nodeptr = ↑nodetype;
     nodetype = array[1..100] of integer;
var p: array[1..10] of nodeptr;
    i,topptr,topitem: integer;
begin
    topptr:= 0;
    topitem:= 100;
    for i:= 1 to 10
        do p[i]:= nil;
```

   To push an element onto the stack, *topitem* is incremented and the element is inserted into *p*[*topptr*]↑[*topitem*]. If, however, *topitem* equals 100, *topptr* is increased by 1, *new*(*p*[*topptr*]) is called, *topitem* is reset to 1, and the element is inserted into *p*[*topptr*]↑[*topitem*]. The pop operation is implemented analogously.

   Write routines *push*, *pop*, and *empty* for this implementation. What is the maximum number of elements that the stack can hold? How are underflow and overflow signaled? What are the advantages and disadvantages of this implementation of stacks compared to the array implementation of Section 2.2, the list implementation of Section 4.2, and the list implementation of this section?

3. Implement the routines *empty*, *push*, *pop*, and *popandtest* using a dynamic storage implementation of a linked stack.

4. Implement the routines *empty*, *insert*, and *remove* using a dynamic storage implementation of a linked queue.

5. Rewrite the list processing exercises of Sections 4.2 and 4.4 using the dynamic implementation of linked lists. Note any differences in space and time usage between the array and dynamic implementations.

6. Rewrite the bank simulation program of Section 4.3 using the dynamic implementation of linked lists. Note any differences in space and time usage between the two implementations.

7. Write Pascal programs to implement the list operations on circular and doubly linked lists using dynamic storage.

8. Rewrite the solution to the Josephus problem presented in Section 4.4 using the dynamic implementation of circular lists. Note any differences in space and time usage between the two implementations.

9. Rewrite the routines to add long integers presented in Section 4.4 using the dynamic implementation of circular and doubly linked lists. Note any differences in space and time usage between the two implementations.

10. Assume that we wish to form *n* lists, where *n* is a constant. Declare an array *list* of pointers by

```
const n = ... ;
type nodeptr = ↑nodetype;
      nodetype = record
                        info: integer;
                        inext: nodeptr
                 end;
var list: array[1..n] of nodeptr;
```

Read two numbers from each input line, the first number being the list into which the second number is to be placed in ascending order. When there are no more input lines, print out all the lists.

2. AN EXAMPLE: AN AIRLINE RESERVATION SYSTEM

In this section and the next, we consider some examples involving linked allocation that use the dynamic storage implementation of linked lists. The programs could be written equally well using the array representation of Chapter 4. As exercises, you may wish to implement these programs using the methods of Chapter 4.

Consider the problem of programming an airline reservation system. The input consists of two groups of data: a flight control group containing flight data used to initialize the system, followed by a passenger request group containing data on passenger reservations. The flight control group consists of one input line containing a single number (representing the number of flights available that day) followed by a set of input lines (one for each flight) each of which contains a flight number in columns 1 through 3 and the seating capacity for that flight in columns 5 through 7. A sample flight control group is illustrated in Figure 5.2.1a.

Once this flight control group has been read, a separate input line is read for each passenger request for service. The requests may be of three types: reservation, cancellation, or inquiry. The type of each request is indicated by the word *reserve*, *cancel*, or *inquire* beginning in column 1. A request for a reservation or a cancellation is accompanied by a passenger name beginning in column 15 and a flight number beginning in column 50. An inquiry is accompanied by a passenger name only. (We assume that a passenger inquires about all of the flights on a particular journey, but may cancel one

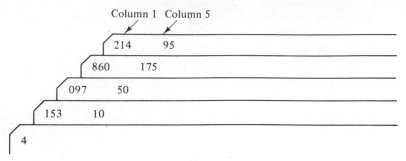

Column 1 Column 5

214   95

860   175

097   50

153   10

4

(a) Flight control group for Airline problem.

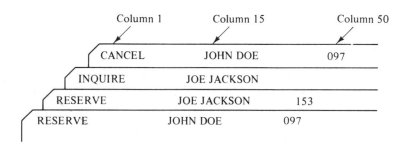

Column 1   Column 15   Column 50

CANCEL   JOHN DOE   097

INQUIRE   JOE JACKSON

RESERVE   JOE JACKSON   153

RESERVE   JOHN DOE   097

(b) Passenger request group for Airline problem.

Figure 5.2.1

particular leg of the journey.) A sample set of data for a passenger request group is shown in Figure 5.2.1b.

We are to write a program that processes these two groups of input. For each passenger service request, a message describing the action taken is to be printed.

Before designing a program, the requirements of the problem must be defined more precisely. In particular, it must be determined what action is to be taken for each of the possible passenger requests. In the case of a reservation, the passenger is to be placed on a flight list for the flight, if the flight is not full. If the flight is full, the passenger is to be placed on a waiting list and will be placed on the flight if there are any cancellations. In the case of a cancellation, the passenger is to be deleted from the flight list if the passenger is currently booked on the flight, and the first passenger from the waiting list (if any) is to be placed on the flight list. If the canceled passenger is on the waiting list, he must be removed from it. Finally, in the case of an inquiry, a list of all flights on which the passenger is booked is to be printed.

Now that we have defined the actions to be taken for the various requests, we may consider the data structures that will be necessary. Clearly, two lists are required for each flight: a list of passengers currently booked on the flight, and a waiting list for the flight. The passenger list has no restrictions as to where a passenger may be inserted or deleted. The waiting list, however, should be a queue, so that if a cancellation occurs, the first person on the waiting list will be the first to be given a seat on the flight. However, we must also have the capability of deleting a passenger from the middle of the waiting list (in case of a cancellation). It will also be necessary to keep a record of the capacity of each flight and of the number of people currently on the flight. We can thus declare the data structures for this program as follows:

```
const numflights = 100; {maximum of 100 flights}
type  nametype = packed array [1..20] of char;
      flightnum: packed array [1..3] of '0'..'9';
      nodeptr = ↑nodetype;
      nodetype = record
                      name: nametype; {     passenger name     }
                      next: nodeptr   {next passenger on the list}
                 end;
      queue = record
                  front: nodeptr;
                  rear: nodeptr
             end;
      flighttype = record
                      fltno: flightnum;  {      flight number     }
                      cpcty: integer;    {     capacity of flight  }
                      count: integer;    {number of people on flight}
                      flthd: nodeptr;    { pointer to first passenger }
                                         {     on the flight list    }
                      waitlist: queue    {  queue for waiting list   }
                 end;
var   flight: array [1..numflights] of flighttype;
```

Before proceeding to the program, let us consider what routines will be required for manipulating the lists. First, it is necessary to be able to locate the index of the record representing the flight within the array *flight* given its flight number. We call the function that does this *find* and leave its coding as an exercise for the reader. The function accepts a flight number as a parameter and returns the index in the array *flight* of the record representing that flight. We will also need the routines *insert* and *remove* to insert and remove an element from a queue. However, we will see shortly that these routines must be somewhat modified. Because elements will be eliminated from positions other than the front of the waiting queues and also from the flight lists, the *delafter* routine will also be required.

The final decision that must be made relates to the structure of the passenger list. Since deletions can be made from either end or from within the list, our choice of a data structure should depend upon the ease with which other operations can be performed. Aside from deleting an element, the only operations needed are insertion and searching for a name within the list. Keeping the list in order by name will make searching more efficient in the case where a name is not present on the list. (Why?) However, keeping a sorted list will reduce the efficiency of every insertion.

We choose to make all insertions at the head of the list. The following additional routines are therefore needed: a procedure *search* (*listhd*, *nam*, *pred*, *found*), which accepts a pointer, *listhd*, to the head of a list, and the name, *nam*, of a passenger. Upon returning, *pred* contains a pointer to the predecessor of the node containing the name *nam* if the name is present in the list, and *found* will be *true*. If *nam* is not present, then *found* will be *false*. A dummy header node is stored at the beginning of each passenger list so that the output parameter *pred* of *search* can be used as an input argument to *delafter* even if the desired node is first on the list. Such a technique is frequently used to make subroutines applicable to special cases. Similarly, a dummy node is stored at the head of each waiting list so that *delafter* may be used to delete the first passenger on the waiting list. This means that the *remove* routine for the queue must be altered, since *front* points to a header node before the actual front of the queue. It is necessary to rewrite *remove* as a procedure rather than as a function, since a Pascal function cannot return a packed array (of type *nametype*). The *empty* function for queues must also be modified to allow for a dummy node. The routine *insafter* is also used. We now present the main program and the procedure for the *cancel* request. The procedures that handle reservations and inquiries are left as exercises for the reader.

```pascal
program airline(input, output);
const numflights = 100;
      nilname = '                    ';
type  nametype = packed array[1..20] of char;
      flightnum = packed array[1..3] of '0'..'9';
      nodeptr = ↑nodetype;
      nodetype = record
                     name: nametype;
                     next: nodeptr
                 end;
      queue = record
                  front: nodeptr;
                  rear: nodeptr
              end;
      flighttype = record
                       fltno: flightnum;
                       cpcty: integer;
                       count: integer;
                       flthd: nodeptr;
                       waitlist: queue
                   end;
```

CHAP. 5: PASCAL LIST PROCESSING

```
var   flight: array [1..numflights] of flighttype;
      i,nflts: 1..numflights; {nflts is the number of flights}
      pred: nodeptr;
      d: '0'..'9';
      j: 1..3;
      c: char;
      command: packed array[1..10] of char;
{The following functions and procedures are defined here:}
{   cancel, delafter, empty, find, inquire, insafter, insert,   }
{              remove, reserve, and search                      }
begin {program airline}
      {initialize variables and lists}
      readln(nflts);
      for i:= 1 to nflts
          do with flight[i]
              do begin
                      for j:= 1 to 3
                          do begin
                                  read(d);
                                  fltno[j] := d
                              end {for...do begin};
                      readln(cpcty);
                      {       flight is initially empty        }
                      count:= 0;
                      { insert dummy node at head of list  }
                      new(pred);
                      flthd:= pred;
                      pred↑.name:= nilname;
                      pred↑.next:= nil;
                      {insert dummy node at front of queue}
                      new(pred);
                      waitlist.front:= pred;
                      waitlist.rear:= pred;
                      pred↑.name:= nilname;
                      pred↑.next:= nil
                  end {with...do begin};
          {process customer requests}
      while not eof
          do begin
                  for i:= 1 to 10
                      do begin
                              read (c);
                              command[i]:= c
                          end {for...do begin};
                  writeln(command);
```

```
                    if command = 'inquire  ' then inquire
                  else if command = 'reserve  ' then reserve
                    else if command = 'cancel   ' then cancel
                      else writeln('invalid command');
               readln
           end {while...do begin}
   end {program airline}.
```

We now present the procedure *cancel*. This procedure utilizes the minor Pascal extension which permits a packed array of a character subrange to appear as an argument to the *writeln* procedure.

```
procedure cancel;
{all variables of airline are global to cancel}
var nam: nametype;
    i: integer;
    flt: flightnum;
    c: char;
    d: '0'..'9';
    pred: nodeptr;
    found: boolean;
begin
    {read the name starting in column 15}
    for i:= 1 to 4
        do read(c);
    for i:= 1 to 20
        do begin
               read(c);
               nam[i] := c
           end {for...do begin};
    {read the flight number starting in column 50}
    for i:= 1 to 15
        do read(c);
    for i:= 1 to 3
        do begin
               read(d);
               flt[i] := d
           end {for...do begin};
    write(nam,' ',flt);
    i:= find(flt);
    if i = 0
       then writeln('invalid flight')
       else with flight[i]
           do begin
                  search(flthd,nam,pred,found);
```

```
          if found
            then begin {remove from flight list}
                    delafter(pred,nam);
                    writeln(nam,' deleted from flight ', fltno);
                    if not empty(waitlist)
                      then begin
                                {remove passenger from}
                                {  queue and place on  }
                                {        flight        }
                              remove(waitlist,nam);
                              insafter(flthd,nam);
                              writeln(nam, ' now booked on flight ', fltno)
                        end {then begin}
                    else count:= count - 1
              end {then begin}
            else begin {cancel passenger from}
                    {      waiting list      }
                  search(waitlist.front,nam,pred,found);
                  if found
                    then begin
                            delafter(pred,nam);
                            writeln(nam, 'deleted from waiting ',
                                             'list of flight ', fltno)
                      end {then begin}
              end {else begin}
          end {with...do begin}
    end {procedure cancel};
```

We leave the coding of the two other major routines, *inquire* and *reserve*, as exercises for the reader. There are more efficient ways of programming the foregoing example so that not so much time is spent in searching for names on lists. Some of these techniques will be examined in Section 9.4.

EXERCISES   1. Write routines *search*, *find*, *insafter*, *remove*, *delafter*, *insert*, *empty*, *inquire*, and *reserve* as called for in the program *airline*.

2. The lists in the airline problem (both passenger lists and queues) each contain a dummy header node. What changes are necessary in the program if no such dummy nodes exist?

3. Modify the airline program to list all the passengers booked or waiting for a given flight upon reading an input line with the command

    fltlist   *flight number*

4. Modify the airline program to accept and process a command *chngcpcty* with a flight number and a quantity. The quantity represents an increase or decrease in the number of seats available on that flight.

5. Write a Pascal routine that accepts a passenger name and cancels all reservations (including those on a waiting list) for that passenger.

6. Assume that each flight has a given ticket price. Modify the data structures and write a routine that will print out a separate bill for each passenger.

7. Redesign the data structures, inputs, and programs of the airline system so that it will include for each passenger an indication of whether he is in the first-class or economy section. Each of these two sections has its own capacity. However, if first class is not full but economy class is, an economy passenger will be placed into first class (at economy prices) until a passenger requests a first-class reservation. Make sure that your system is equitable in handling such questions as the relation among passengers on the waiting list, economy passengers in first class, and requests for cancellations and first-class reservations (i.e., who gets bumped from where to where).

8. Rewrite the example of this section using the array implementation of lists.

3. AN EXAMPLE: SPARSE MATRICES

We now consider a second application of linked lists using dynamic variables. As in the preceding section, the main emphasis is on linked lists. Its implementation using dynamic variables is of secondary importance. As exercises, you may wish to implement the routines presented here using the array method of Chapter 4.

A *matrix* is a two-dimensional array. Figure 5.3.1 illustrates some matrices. Each matrix in that figure is a two-dimensional array with m rows and n columns. The values of m and n for each matrix are shown. Matrices are used in many fields, including mathematics, economics, and computer science. There are a number of recognized operations defined on matrices, some of which will be illustrated in this section and others left as exercises.

Suppose that we are programming a problem whose solution calls for the use of matrices. How can a matrix be represented in memory? The simplest and most obvious answer is, of course, to use a two-dimensional array. For example, we might code

```
const m = ...;
      n = ...;
type  rownum = 1..m;
      colnum = 1..n;
      matrix = array [rownum, colnum] of integer;
var   a: matrix;
```

Storage for a two-dimensional array of m rows and n columns is allocated. Any element in the matrix can be referenced by $a[i,j]$, where i represents the row number and j the column number of the element. Notice that nothing is assumed about the actual contents of the array except that they are integers. $m*n$ is the number of units of storage allocated. We say the matrix is of size m by n (sometimes written as $m \times n$).

The representation of a matrix by an array is certainly satisfactory for small matrices. Very often, however, we deal with a matrix such as the one

$$A = \begin{bmatrix} 5 \end{bmatrix}$$

$$m = 1$$
$$n = 1$$

(a)

$$B = \begin{bmatrix} 1 & 0 & 2 \\ -1 & 4 & 6 \end{bmatrix}$$

$$m = 2$$
$$n = 3$$

(b)

$$C = \begin{bmatrix} 1 & 3 & 7 & 5 \end{bmatrix}$$

$$m = 1$$
$$n = 4$$

(c)

$$D = \begin{bmatrix} 8 & 7 \\ 2 & 5 \\ 1 & 4 \end{bmatrix}$$

$$m = 3$$
$$n = 2$$

(d)

$$E = \begin{bmatrix} 1 & 0 & 0 & 3 & 0 & 0 & 0 & 0 & 0 \\ 0 & 2 & 0 & 0 & 0 & 0 & 0 & 2 & 0 \\ 0 & 0 & 0 & 0 & 0 & 0 & 0 & 0 & 0 \\ 0 & 0 & 0 & 0 & 0 & 0 & 0 & 0 & 0 \\ 0 & 0 & 0 & -1 & 4 & 0 & 0 & 0 & 0 \\ 0 & 0 & 0 & 8 & 0 & 0 & 2 & 0 & 0 \\ 0 & 0 & 0 & 0 & 1 & 0 & 0 & 0 & 0 \end{bmatrix}$$

$$m = 7$$
$$n = 9$$

(e)

Figure 5.3.1 Examples of matrices.

in Figure 5.3.1e, which contains mostly zeros. A matrix that is filled with mostly zeros is called a *sparse* matrix. The actual amount of nonzero data is small compared with the amount of storage set aside for the matrix. Suppose that the matrix of Figure 5.3.1e were 700 by 900 rather than 7 by 9, and the additional entries were all 0. Such a matrix, if represented as a two-dimensional array, would exceed the storage capacity of most computers existing today. Yet since there are only nine nonzero data items in this matrix, surely there must be some method of representing the matrix in fewer than 630,000 units of storage.

Let us see how a sparse matrix can be represented using linked allocation. We will keep in memory a structure containing only those elements which are nonzero, linked to each other in a way that describes their position in the large matrix. If a position of the matrix is represented in the structure, its value is given within a list node. If a position is not represented in the structure, its value is zero. How should this list be organized? One way is as a single linear linked list consisting of all the nonzero elements of the first row, followed by all the nonzero elements of the second row, and so on. Of course, since not every column is represented in a particular row, each node will also include an indication of the column in which the element appears. It will also be necessary to keep an indication of where a particular row ends. (This indication can consist of a special flag in the last node of each row, or an extra node at the end of each row with a zero value field.) This method has the drawback that the entire list would have to be searched each time a particular element is to be accessed. Also, whereas an entire row can be accessed once its first element has been located, accessing a column is an entirely different matter. To access a column, the entire list must be traversed until that column position is encountered in the last row. This is clearly inefficient. In addition, it does not mirror the two-dimensional nature of a matrix, which implies that either a row or a column can be traversed once its first element has been accessed.

One possible solution is to keep a separate list for each row. This would certainly reduce the time necessary to access a particular element, since only a single smaller list (that of the row in question) would have to be searched rather than a list of all the matrix elements. However, the problem of accessing a column remains. Keeping the matrix in column order rather than row order would merely transfer the problem from that of accessing a column to that of accessing a row.

To allow easy access to any row or column of the matrix, we let each nonzero matrix element appear on two lists, one for its row and one for its column. Thus each node contains two pointers, one to the next element in its row and one to the next element in its column. In addition, each node contains fields for the row number, column number, and the value of its element. Thus the type of a node is defined by

```
const m = ...;
       n = ...;
type rownum = 1..m;
     colnum = 1..n;
     nodeptr = ↑nodetype;
     nodetype = record
                   row: rownum;
                   col: colnum;
                   val: integer;
                   nextrow: nodeptr;
                           {to next element in same column}
                   nextcol: nodeptr
                           {  to next element in same row  }
              end;
```

Figure 5.3.2a depicts the fields of a sample node. Figure 5.3.2c illustrates the representation of the matrix of Figure 5.3.2b.

As with any linked list, some method of accessing the first element of each list in the matrix representation is required. This can be done in either of two ways. One method would be to keep two arrays of pointers, *rowfirst*

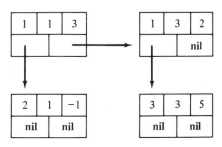

(a) Fields of a sample node.

$$\begin{pmatrix} 3 & 0 & 2 \\ -1 & 0 & 0 \\ 0 & 0 & 5 \end{pmatrix}$$

(b) Matrix in array format.

(c) Matrix using linked allocation.

Figure 5.3.2

and *colfirst*, where *rowfirst* [i] points to the first node in row i and *colfirst* [i] points to the first node in column i.

An alternative method is to keep a dummy column (column 0) containing as many elements as there are rows. Each element in this dummy column points to the first element of its respective row. Similarly, a dummy row (row 0) exists containing as many elements as there are columns. Each element in this dummy row points to the first element of its respective column. Each node in these dummy lists serves as a header node for a row list or a column list. These header nodes may be recognized by a zero value in the column or row field, respectively. Of course, now the types *rownum* and *colnum* must be defined as

type rownum = 0..m;
colnum = 0..n;

Since each row and column has a header, they are kept as circular lists. An external pointer points to a dummy element at row 0, column 0. Figure 5.3.3 illustrates this scheme. Figure 5.3.3a illustrates a 4 × 4 matrix and Figure 5.3.3b illustrates its linked representation. Notice the dummy column on the left and the dummy row on the top, each element of which points to the first nonzero element of a row or column. Since row 1 consists of only zeros, it contains only the dummy node whose *nextcol* field points to itself. Note also that the element pointed to by *a* serves as the "header" node of the matrix. Given *a*, it is possible to reach any node in the matrix.

$$\begin{pmatrix} 0 & 0 & 0 & 0 \\ 0 & 2 & 0 & 3 \\ -2 & 4 & 0 & 0 \\ 0 & 0 & -1 & 8 \end{pmatrix}$$

(a) Matrix using array format.

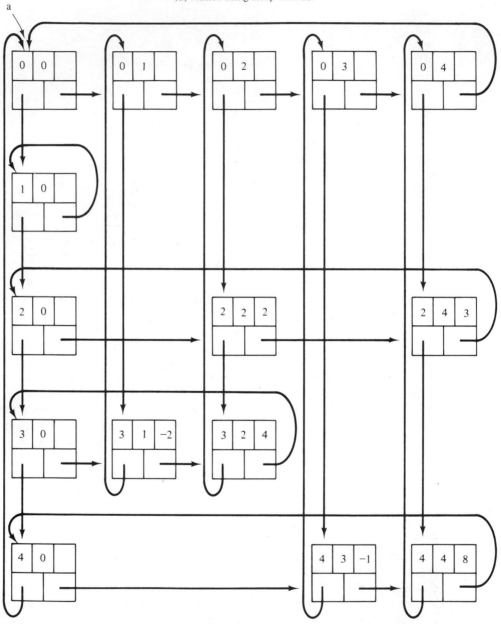

(b) Matrix using linked allocation.

Figure 5.3.3

A structure in which nodes appear on more than one list and contain more than one pointer is called a *multilinked list*.

Before proceeding with some applications of this method, some comments on its use are appropriate. If the matrix of Figure 5.3.3a were to be stored as a two-dimensional array, it would require 16 nodes of storage, each consisting of one field. Using the linked method depicted in Figure 5.3.3b, 16 nodes of storage each consisting of five fields are required. By no stretch of the imagination could this latter method be considered more efficient than the former. Moreover, using the array method, a particular element can be accessed merely by referencing it; to access that same element in the linked method requires a rather elaborate traversal procedure, as we shall see shortly. Thus only where the matrices are very large and sparse (relatively few nonzero entries) is it more efficient to use the linked allocation than the array implementation. All the routines written below are simpler to code when the matrix is stored as an array. Thus, although the methods and examples of this section apply to matrices of any size and any number of nonzero elements, applying them to the wrong types of matrices will seriously affect the speed and storage efficiency of the programs involved.

Let us now consider some transformations on matrices. An *elementary row operation* is defined as one of the following:

1. Multiplying any row by a nonzero constant.
2. Interchanging any two rows.
3. Adding a multiple of one row to another.

We consider each of these three operations in turn, and assume the following routines:

findabove (*a*: *nodeptr*; *r*: *rownum*; *c*: *colnum*): *nodeptr*. This function accepts a pointer *a* to a matrix, a row number *r*, and a column number *c*. The function returns a pointer to the node in column *c* that immediately precedes the position where a node at row *r* and column *c* would be if it were present in the matrix.

insertafter(*p*,*q*: *nodeptr*; *x*: *integer*). This routine inserts a new node with value *x* into the same row as *p*↑ and the same column as *q*↑, immediately following *p*↑ in its row and *q*↑ in its column.

deleteafter(*p*,*q*: *nodeptr*; **var** *x*: *integer*). This routine deletes the node pointed to by both *p*↑.*nextcol* and *q*↑.*nextrow*, and places its value into *x*.

We present the routine *findabove* and leave the coding of the other two as exercises:

```
function findabove(a: nodeptr; r: rownum; c: colnum): nodeptr;
var p,q,z: nodeptr;
begin
    {  find a pointer to the dummy node of column c   }
    p:= a;
```

```
        while p↑.col < c
             do p:= p↑.nextcol;
        {p now points to dummy node of column c.  Advance}
        { p through column c until row r is reached or passed }
        q:= p;
        z:= p↑.nextrow;
        while (p↑.row < r) and (z↑.row <> 0)
             do begin
                      q:= p;
                      p:= p↑.nextrow;
                      z:= p↑.nextrow
                end {while...do begin};
        if p↑.row >= r
          then findabove:= q
          else  findabove:= p
    end {function findabove};
```

1. Multiplying a row by a nonzero constant.

If the array representation is used, the routine is trivial.

```
        procedure mult(var a: matrix; row: rownum; c: integer);
          {multiply row number row by the constant c <> 0}
        var j: colnum;
        begin
             for j = 1 to n
                  do a[row,j] := a[row,j] * c
        end {procedure mult};
```

If the linked representation is used, there are some minor changes necessary in the looping mechanism.

```
        procedure mult2(a: nodeptr; r: rownum; c: integer);
        var above,q: nodeptr;
        begin
             {set above to the element above row r in the dummy column}
             above:= findabove(a,r,0);
             {          set q to the first nonzero entry in row r          }
             q:= above↑.nextrow;
             q:= q↑.nextcol;
             {                 multiply the entire row by c                 }
             while q↑.col > 0
                  do begin
                           q↑.val:= q↑.val * c;
                           q:= q↑.nextcol
                      end {while...do begin}
        end {procedure mult2};
```

Notice that there are no insertions or deletions in *mult2*, since multiplying by a nonzero constant cannot change a nonzero entry to zero, or vice versa. Suppose that we wish to multiply a row by 0. No changes are necessary in *mult* (except that the operation is no longer an elementary row operation). *mult2*, however, must be modified considerably, since an entire row now becomes zero and each of its elements must therefore be removed from the list. We could code *mult0* as follows:

```
procedure mult0(a: nodeptr; r: rownum);
    {c need not be a parameter; we are multiplying by zero}
var above,p,q: nodeptr;
    x: integer;
begin
    above:= findabove(a,r,0);
    q:= above↑.nextrow;
    p:= q↑.nextcol;
    while p↑.col > 0
        do begin
                above:= findabove(a,r,p↑.col);
                deleteafter(q,above,x);
                p:= q↑.nextcol
            end {while...do begin}
end {procedure mult0};
```

Of course, *mult2* and *mult0* could be combined into a single routine.

2. Interchanging two rows.

If a matrix is stored as a two-dimensional array, the routine *int* interchanging two rows is again straightforward:

```
procedure int(var a: matrix; row1,row2: rownum);
var j: colnum;
    hold: integer;
begin
    for j:= 1 to n
        do begin
                hold:= a[row1,j];
                a[row1,j]:= a[row2,j];
                a[row2,j]:= hold
            end {for...do begin}
end {procedure int};
```

Storing the matrix as a multilinked list requires a choice between two options. Nodes in *row1* and *row2* could actually be allocated and freed as necessary so that the interchange is made. A second option is to keep the two rows intact, adjusting the column pointers to reflect the interchange. We select this second option. Since interchanging two rows is a symmetric operation, we will assume, without loss of generality, that *row1* < *row2*.

The rows *row*1 and *row*2 are traversed in parallel. As the algorithm proceeds from one column to the next in each of *row*1 and *row*2, one of three conditions may occur:

a. There is an element in a particular column of *row*2, but the corresponding element in *row*1 is 0. The element must be moved from *row*2 to *row*1.
b. There is an element in a particular column of *row*1, but the corresponding element in *row*2 is 0. The element must be moved from *row*1 to *row*2.
c. There are elements in a particular column of both *row*1 and *row*2. The element of *row*1 must be interchanged with that of *row*2.

Figures 5.3.4a–c depict (for an arbitrary column *j*) the situations after the appropriate action is taken. In Figure 5.3.4a the notation (*row*1=>) means that a nonzero element of *row*1 and column *j* would belong between two elements of column *j* at the point indicated, and similarly for the notation (*row*2=>) in Figure 5.3.4b. (Note that because complete rows are being moved, there is no need to adjust the *nextcol* fields. We begin our loop at the first nonzero column and halt when we reach the dummy column.)

```
procedure int2(a: nodeptr; row1,row2: rownum);
var above1,above2,r1,r2,temp: nodeptr;
    j: colnum;
begin
  r1:= findabove(a,row1,0);
  r1:= r1↑.nextrow;
  r2:= findabove(a,row2,0);
  r2:= r2↑.nextrow;
  repeat
    r1:= r1↑.nextcol;
    r2:= r2↑.nextcol;
    while r1↑.col <> r2↑.col
        do {there is at least one zero}
          if ((r1↑.col < r2↑.col) and (r1↑.col <> 0))
                                    {row1 nonzero, row2 zero}
            or (r2↑.col = 0) {end of row2}
          then begin
              temp:= r1↑.nextrow;
              if (temp↑.row < row2) and (temp↑.row <> 0)
              then begin
                  {r1 and r2 are not adjacent}
                  {move element at r1 to r2.}
                  {     see Figure 5.3.4b     }
```

```
                            j:= r1↑.col;
                            above1:= findabove(a,row1,j);
                            above2:= findabove(a,row2,j);
                            above1↑.nextrow:= r1↑.nextrow;
                            r1↑.nextrow:= above2↑.nextrow;
                            above2↑.nextrow:= r1
                        end {then begin};
                    r1↑.row:= row2;
                    {advance r1 to the next column}
                    r1:= r1↑.nextcol
                end {then begin}
            else  begin
                    j:= r2↑.col;
                    above 1:= findabove(a,row1,j);
                    temp:= above1↑.nextrow;
                    if temp↑.row < row2
                        then begin
                                {r1 and r2 are not adjacent.}
                                {move the element at r2 to }
                                {   r1. see Figure 5.3.4a   }
                                above2:= findabove(a,row2,j);
                                above2↑.nextrow:= r2↑.nextrow;
                                r2↑.nextrow:= above1↑.nextrow;
                                above1↑.nextrow:= r2
                            end {then begin};
                    r2↑.row:= row1;
                    {advance r2 to the next column}
                    r2:= r2↑.nextcol
                end {else begin};
        {at this point, r1 and r2 point to the same column}
        {       swap r1 with r2. see Figure 5.3.4c         }
        j:= r1↑.col;
        above1:= findabove(a,row1,j);
        above2:= findabove(a,row2,j);
        temp:= r2↑.nextrow;
        above1↑.nextrow:= r2;
        if r1↑.nextrow↑.row < row2 {then rows are not adjacent}
            then r2↑.nextrow:= r1↑.nextrow
            else r2↑.nextrow:= r1;
        above2↑.nextrow:= r1;
        r1↑.nextrow:= temp;
        r1↑.row:= row2;
        r2↑.row:= row1
    until r1↑.col = 0
end {procedure int2};
```

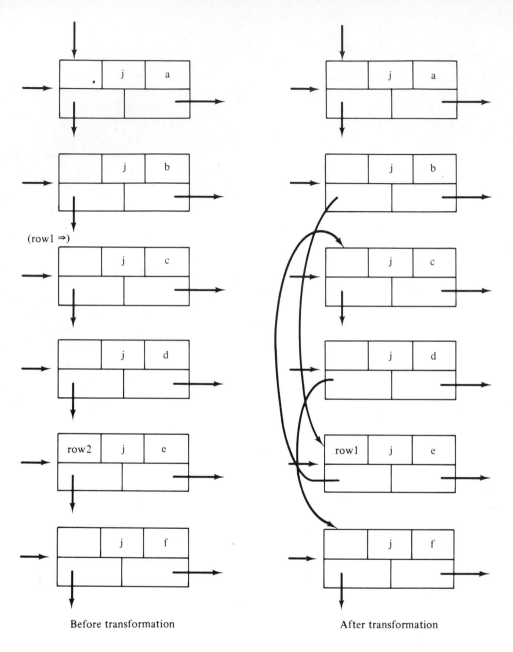

(row1 ⇒)

Before transformation   After transformation

(a) row1 = 0 and row2 ≠ 0.

Figure 5.3.4

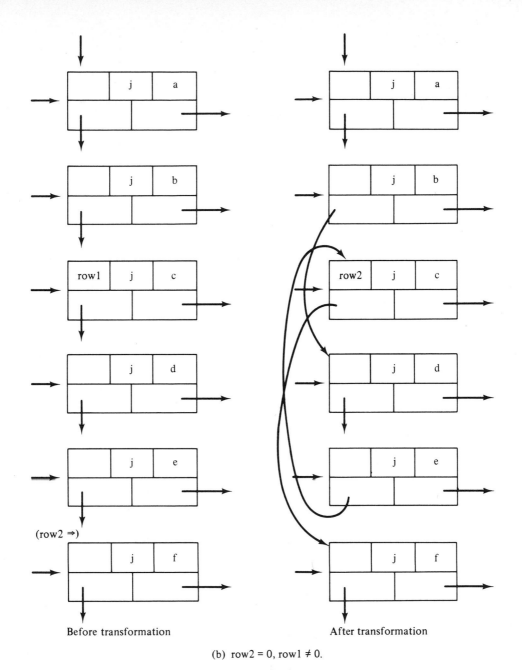

Before transformation   After transformation

(b) row2 = 0, row1 ≠ 0.

Figure 5.3.4 (*cont.*)

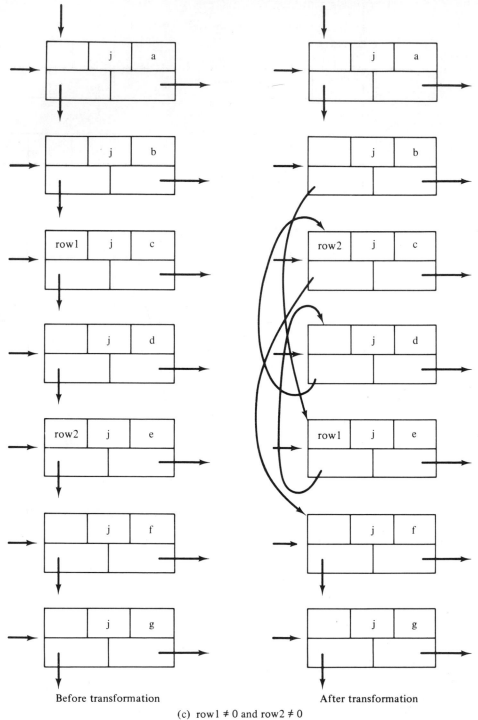

Before transformation

After transformation

(c) row1 ≠ 0 and row2 ≠ 0

Figure 5.3.4 (*cont.*)

3. Adding a multiple of one row to another.

The routine that handles the case where the matrix is stored as an array is straightforward.

```
procedure multiple(var a: matrix; row1,row2: rownum; c: integer);
    {replace row1 by row1 + c*row2}
var j: colnum;
begin
     for j:= 1 to n
         do a[row1,j] := a[row1,j] + c*a[row2,j]
end {procedure multiple};
```

In the case of the matrix stored as a multilinked list, both rows are again traversed in parallel. As each element of *row2* is reached, *r1* is advanced to the corresponding column in *row1*. If such an element exists, its value is adjusted, and if it now becomes zero, it is deleted from the list. If such a column element does not exist, a new node with the appropriate value is created.

```
procedure multiple2(a: nodeptr; row1,row2: rownum; c: integer);
var r1,r2,q,above: nodeptr;
x: integer;
begin
     q:= findabove(a,row1,0);
     r1:= q↑.nextrow;
     r1:= r1↑.nextcol;
     r2:= findabove(a,row2,0);
     r2:= r2↑.nextrow;
     r2:= r2↑.nextcol;
     {traverse row2}
     while r2↑.col > 0
         do begin
             while (r1↑.col < r2↑.col) and (r1↑.col > 0)
                 do begin {corresponding element of row2}
                     {        is zero; advance r1        }
                     q:= r1;
                     r1:= r1↑.nextcol
                 end {while...do begin};
             if r1↑.col = r2↑.col
                 then begin
                     r1↑.val:= r1↑.val + c*r2↑.val;
                     if r1↑.val = 0
                         then begin
                             {delete the node}
                             above:= findabove(a,row1,r1↑.col);
                             deleteafter(q,above,x)
                         end {then begin};
```

```
                        {update r1 and r2}
                        r1:= q↑.nextcol;
                        r2:= r2↑.nextcol
                    end {then begin};
            else begin {insert new element}
                        above:= findabove(a,row1,r2↑.col);
                        insertafter(q,above,r2↑.val*c);
                        q:= q↑.nextcol;
                        r1:= q↑.nextcol;
                        r2:= r2↑.nextcol
                    end {else begin}
            end {while...do begin}
    end {procedure multiple2};
```

EXERCISES

1. Rewrite the routines of this section using the array implementation of linked allocation presented in Chapter 4.

2. Write a routine *linktoarr*(*link*,*arr*) to convert a matrix in linked format pointed to by *link* into its array format *arr*. (*arr* is already of the proper dimension.)
   Write a routine *arrtolink*(*arr*,*link*) to convert a matrix stored as an array *arr* into its linked format. *link* should point to the resultant structure.

3. Write a routine *store*(*a*,*i*,*j*,*x*) to set the element of a matrix at row i and column j to x, where the matrix is represented as a multilinked list pointed to by *a*. Write a function *retrieve*(*a*,*i*,*j*) to return the element at row i and column j in such a matrix.

4. Multiplication of matrices for the array representation is performed by the following routine (*c* is the product of *a* and *b*, where *a* has the same number of columns as *b* has rows):

```
            const m = ...;
                  n = ...;
                  r = ...;
            type amatrix = array[1..m,1..n] of integer;
                  bmatrix = array[1..n,1..r] of integer;
                  cmatrix = array[1..m,1..r] of integer;
            procedure prod(a: amatrix; b: bmatrix; var c: cmatrix);
            var i,j,k: integer;
            begin
                for i:= 1 to m
                    do for j:= 1 to r
                        do begin
                                c[i,j]:= 0;
                                for k:= 1 to n
                                    do c[i,j]:= c[i,j] + a[i,k]*b[k,j]
                            end {for...do begin}
            end {procedure prod};
```

Rewrite this routine using the linked matrix representation.

5. Write a function *det*(*matptr*), which accepts a pointer to a linked list matrix and returns its determinant. (For a definition of the determinant, see Exercise 3.2.6.)

6. Would any harm be done if no dummy node existed in the linked representation of a sparse matrix for a row or column with no elements? Rewrite the elementary row operations and the exercises of this section for this altered representation.

7. Assume that dummy rows and columns did not exist. Instead, assume that there are two arrays *colfirst* and *rowfirst*, as described in the text, and assume that the row and column lists are linear rather than circular. Rewrite the programs in this section under these conditions.

8. Implement the elementary row operations for a matrix that is stored as a single linked list consisting of all the nonzero elements of the first row followed by all the nonzero elements of the second row, and so on, as described in the text. Implement the exercises in this section for this representation.

9. The following questionnaire containing five questions has been completed by a large number of people:

1. Your sex is (1) male (2) female.
2. Your income is (1) below $10,000 (2) $10,000 to $20,000 (3) $20,000 to $30,000 (4) $30,000 to $40,000 (5) above $40,000.
3. Your political affiliation is (1) Democratic (2) Republican (3) Independent.
4. You smoke (1) cigars only (2) pipe only (3) less than one pack of cigarettes a day (4) one to two packs of cigarettes a day (5) more than two packs of cigarettes a day (6) not at all.
5. Your age is (1) below 20 (2) 20 to 29 (3) 30 to 39 (4) 40 to 49 (5) 50 to 59 (6) 60 or above.

The results have been entered on input lines so that the respondent's name appears in columns 1 to 30, and columns 31 to 35 contain five digits representing the respondent's answers to the five questions. Write a program to read such input and create a data structure in which each node containing a name is on five lists, each list representing those people who answered a particular question the same way.

10. Write a routine that accepts a pointer to the data structure created in Exercise 9 and a five-digit code. The code represents a set of answers to the five questions, but a 0 means that we do not care about a particular answer. For example, the code 14020 represents all male pipe smokers who make between $30,000 and $40,000 a year. The routine should print the names of all respondents who have answered the questionnaire according to the code.

6 Trees

In this chapter we focus our attention on a data structure which has been found to be extremely useful in many applications—the tree. We define different forms of this data structure and show how they can be represented in Pascal and how they can be applied to solving a wide variety of problems.

1. BINARY TREES

A *binary tree* is a finite set of elements that is either empty or contains a single element called the *root* of the tree and whose remaining elements are partitioned into two disjoint subsets, each of which is itself a binary tree. These two subsets are called the *left* and *right subtrees* of the original tree. Each element of a binary tree is called a *node* of the tree.

A conventional method of picturing a binary tree is shown in Figure 6.1.1. This tree consists of nine nodes with A as its root. Its left subtree is rooted at B and its right subtree is rooted at C. This is indicated by the two branches emanating from A: to B on the left and to C on the right. The absence of a branch indicates an empty subtree. For example, the left subtree of the binary tree rooted at C and the right subtree of the binary tree rooted at E are both empty. The binary trees rooted at D, G, H, and I have empty right and left subtrees.

Figure 6.1.2 illustrates some structures that are not binary trees. Be sure that you understand why each of them is not a binary tree as defined above.

If $n1$ is the root of a binary tree and $n2$ is the root of its left or right subtree, then $n1$ is said to be the *father* of $n2$ and $n2$ is said to be the *left* or *right son* of $n1$. A node that has no sons (such as D, G, H, or I of Figure 6.1.1) is called a *leaf*. Node $n1$ is an *ancestor* of node $n2$ (and $n2$ is a *descendant* of $n1$) if $n1$ is either the father of $n2$ or the father of some ancestor of $n2$. For example, in the tree of Figure 6.1.1, A is an ancestor of G and H is a descendant of C but E is neither an ancestor nor a descendant of C. A node $n2$ is a *left descendant* of node $n1$ if $n2$ is either the left

252

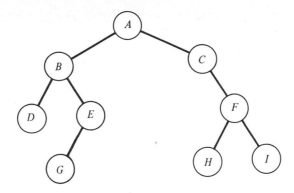

Figure 6.1.1 A binary tree.

son of $n1$ or a descendant of the left son of $n1$. A *right descendant* may be
similarly defined. Two nodes are *brothers* if they are left and right sons of
the same father.

The *level* of a node in a binary tree may be defined as follows. The root
of the tree has level 0 and the level of any other node in the tree is one more
than the level of its father. For example, in the binary tree of Figure 6.1.1,
node E is at level 2 and H is at level 3. A *complete binary tree of level n*
is one in which each node of level n is a leaf and in which each node of level
less than n has nonempty left and right subtrees. Figure 6.1.3 illustrates a
complete binary tree of level 3. (Other texts define the term "complete
binary tree" differently, to refer to a type of tree which we introduce in
Section 4. However, we use this definition consistently in this book.)

One method of viewing a binary tree is to regard each node as having
three elementary fields. *info(node)* references the information which is
stored in a particular node, while *left(node)* and *right(node)* reference
pointers to the roots of the left and right subtrees of the binary tree rooted
at *node*. Of course, if a left or right subtree is empty, the corresponding
pointer is nil.

In constructing a binary tree, the operations *maketree*, *setleft*, and
setright are useful. *maketree(x)* creates a new binary tree consisting of
a single node with information field x and returns a pointer to that node.
An algorithm for this function is the following:

$$p := getnode;$$
$$info(p) := x;$$
$$left(p) := nil;$$
$$right(p) := nil;$$
$$maketree := p$$

setleft(p,x) accepts a pointer p to a binary tree node with no left son. It
creates a new left son of *node(p)* with information field x. An algorithm

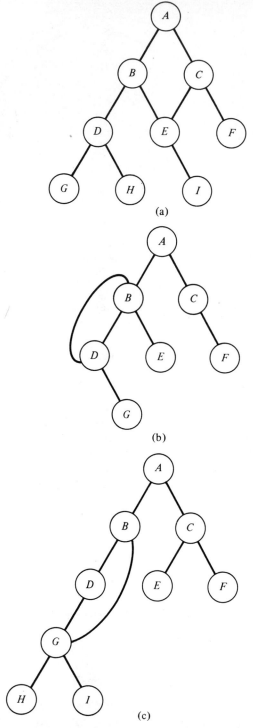

(a)

(b)

(c)

Figure 6.1.2 Structures which are not binary trees.

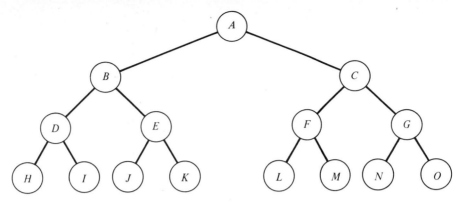

Figure 6.1.3 A complete binary tree of level 3.

for *setleft* follows:

$$
\begin{aligned}
&\textbf{if } left(p) <> nil \\
&\quad \textbf{then } error(\text{'illegal setleft operation'}) \\
&\quad \textbf{else begin} \\
&\qquad\qquad q:=maketree(x); \\
&\qquad\qquad left(p):=q \\
&\quad \textbf{end } \{\text{else begin}\}
\end{aligned}
$$

setright(p,x) is analogous to *setleft* except that it creates a right son of *node(p)*.

Applications of Binary Trees

A binary tree is a useful data structure when two-way decisions must be made at each point in a process. For example, suppose that we wanted to find all duplicates in a list of numbers. One way of doing this is to compare each number with all those that precede it. However, this involves a large number of comparisons. The number of comparisons can be reduced by using a binary tree. The first number is read and placed in a node which is established as the root of a binary tree with empty left and right subtrees. Each successive number in the list is then compared to the number in the root. If it matches, we have a duplicate. If it is smaller, the process is repeated with the left subtree, and if it is larger, the process is repeated with the right subtree. This continues until either a duplicate is found or an empty subtree is reached. In the latter case, the number is placed into a new node at that position in the tree. An algorithm for doing this follows.

$$
\begin{aligned}
&\{\text{ read the first number and insert it into }\} \\
&\{\qquad\quad \text{a single-node binary tree} \qquad\quad\} \\
&read\ (number); \\
&tree := maketree(number); \\
&\textbf{while } \text{there are numbers left in the input} \\
&\quad\textbf{do begin} \\
&\qquad read(number);
\end{aligned}
$$

```
q := tree;
p := tree;
while (number <> info(p)) and (q <> nil)
    do begin
        p := q;
        if number < info(p)
            then q := left(p)
            else q := right(p)
    end;
if number = info(p)
    then print(number, 'is a duplicate')
    else { insert number to the right or left of p }
        if number < info(p)
            then setleft(p, number)
            else setright(p, number)
end {while...do begin}
```

Figure 6.1.4 illustrates the tree that would be constructed from the input

14 15 4 9 7 18 3 5 16 4 20 17 9 14 5

The output would indicate that 4, 9, 14, and 5 are duplicates.

Another common operation is to *traverse* a binary tree, that is, to pass through the tree, enumerating each of its nodes once. We may simply wish to print the contents of each node as we enumerate it, or we may wish to process it in some other fashion. In either case, we speak of *visiting* the nodes of a binary tree.

The order in which the nodes of a linear list are visited in a traversal is clearly from first to last. However, there is no such "natural" linear order for the nodes of a tree. Thus different orderings are used for traversal in different cases. We shall define three of these traversal methods. In each

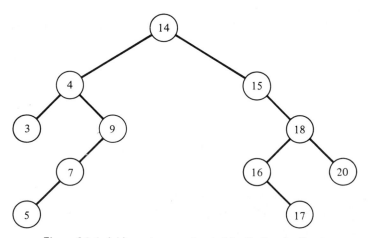

Figure 6.1.4 A binary tree constructed for finding duplicates.

256

of these methods, nothing need be done to traverse an empty binary tree. The methods will all be defined recursively so that traversing a binary tree involves visiting the root and traversing its left and right subtrees. The only difference among the methods is the order in which these three operations are performed.

To traverse a nonempty binary tree in *preorder* (also known as *depth-first order*), we perform the following three operations:

1. Visit the root.
2. Traverse the left subtree in preorder.
3. Traverse the right subtree in preorder.

To traverse a nonempty binary tree in *inorder* or *symmetric order*:

1. Traverse the left subtree in inorder.
2. Visit the root.
3. Traverse the right subtree in inorder.

To traverse a nonempty binary tree in *postorder*:

1. Traverse the left subtree in postorder.
2. Traverse the right subtree in postorder.
3. Visit the root.

Figure 6.1.5 illustrates two binary trees and their traversals in preorder, inorder, and postorder.

Most algorithms or processes that use binary trees proceed in two phases. The first phase builds a binary tree and the second traverses the tree. As an example of such an algorithm, consider the following sorting method. Given a list of numbers in an input file, we wish to print them in ascending order. As we read the numbers, they can be inserted into a binary tree such as the one of Figure 6.1.4. However, unlike the previous algorithm, which was used to find duplicates, duplicate values are also placed in the tree. When a number is compared to the contents of a node in the tree, a left branch is taken if the number is smaller than the contents of the node and a right branch if it is greater than or equal to the contents of the node. Thus, if the input list is

$$14,15,4,9,7,18,3,5,16,4,20,17,9,14,5$$

the binary tree of Figure 6.1.6 is produced. Such a binary tree has the property that the contents of each node in the left subtree of a node n are less than the contents of n, and the contents of each node in the right subtree of n are greater than or equal to the contents of n. Thus, if the tree is traversed in inorder (left, root, right), the numbers are printed in ascending order. (You are asked to prove this as an exercise.) The use of binary trees in sorting and searching will be discussed further in Chapters 8 and 9.

Let us denote the operation of traversing a binary tree in inorder and printing the contents of each of its nodes by *intrav*(*tree*). Then the sorting

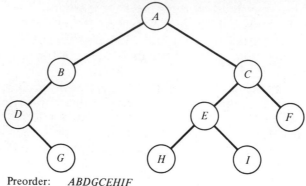

Preorder: *ABDGCEHIF*
Inorder: *DGBAHEICF*
Postorder: *GDBHIEFCA*

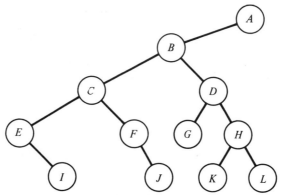

Preorder: *ABCEIFJDGHKL*
Inorder: *EICFJBGDKHLA*
Postorder: *IEJFCGKLHDBA*

Figure 6.1.5 Binary trees and their traversals.

algorithm may be written as follows:

```
read (number);
tree := maketree(number);
while there are numbers left in the input
    do begin
        read (number);
        q := tree;
        while q <> nil
            do begin
                p := q;
                if number < info(p)
                    then q := left(p)
                    else q := right(p)
            end {while...do begin};
```

$$\textbf{if } number < info(p)$$
$$\qquad \textbf{then } setleft(p, number)$$
$$\qquad \textbf{else } setright(p, number)$$
$$\textbf{end } \{\text{while}\ldots\text{do begin}\};$$
$$\{\ \text{ traverse the tree }\ \}$$
$$intrav(tree)$$

As another application of binary trees, consider the following method of representing an expression containing operands and binary operators. The root of such a binary tree contains an operator that is to be applied to the results of evaluating the expressions represented by the left and right subtrees. A node representing an operator has two nonempty subtrees while a node representing an operand has two empty subtrees. Figure 6.1.7 illustrates some expressions and their tree representations. (The character "$" is again used to represent exponentiation.)

Let us see what happens when these binary trees are traversed. Traversing such a tree in preorder means that the operator (the root) will precede its two operands (the subtrees). Thus a preorder traversal should yield the prefix form of the expression. (For definitions of the prefix and postfix forms of an arithmetic expression, see Sections 2.3. and 3.3.) This is indeed

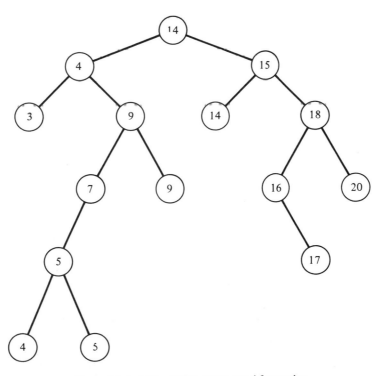

Figure 6.1.6 A binary tree constructed for sorting.

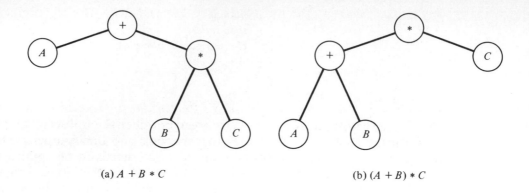

(a) $A + B * C$

(b) $(A + B) * C$

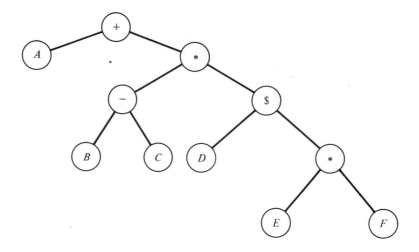

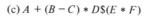

(c) $A + (B - C) * D\$(E * F)$

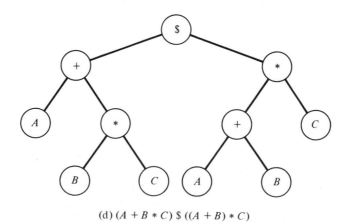

(d) $(A + B * C) \$ ((A + B) * C)$

Figure 6.1.7 Expressions and their binary tree representation.

the case. Traversing the binary trees of Figure 6.1.7 yields the prefix forms

$+A*BC$	(Figure 6.1.7a)
$*+ABC$	(Figure 6.1.7b)
$+A*-BC\$D*EF$	(Figure 6.1.7c)
$\$+A*BC*+ABC$	(Figure 6.1.7d)

Similarly, traversing such a binary tree in postorder places the operator after its two operands, so that a postorder traversal produces the postfix form of the expression. The postorder traversals of the binary trees of Figure 6.1.7 yield the postfix forms

$ABC*+$	(Figure 6.1.7a)
$AB+C*$	(Figure 6.1.7b)
$ABC-DEF*\$*+$	(Figure 6.1.7c)
$ABC*+AB+C*\$$	(Figure 6.1.7d)

What happens when such binary trees are traversed in inorder? Since the root (operator) is visited after the nodes of the left subtree and before the nodes of the right subtree (the two operands), we might expect an inorder traversal to yield the infix form of the expression. Indeed, if the binary tree of Figure 6.1.7a is traversed, the infix expression $A+B*C$ is obtained. However, the binary tree does not contain parentheses since the ordering of the operations is implied by the structure of the tree. Thus an expression whose infix form requires parentheses to override explicitly the conventional precedence rules cannot be retrieved by a simple inorder traversal. The inorder traversals of the trees of Figure 6.1.7 yield the expressions

$A+B*C$	(Figure 6.1.7a)
$A+B*C$	(Figure 6.1.7b)
$A+B-C*D\$E*F$	(Figure 6.1.7c)
$A+B*C\$A+B*C$	(Figure 6.1.7d)

which are correct except for parentheses.

EXERCISES

1. Prove that the root of a binary tree is an ancestor of every node in the tree except itself.

2. Prove that a node of a binary tree has at most one father.

3. How many ancestors does a node at level n in a binary tree have? Prove your answer.

4. What are the maximum number of nodes at level n in a binary tree?

5. Write an algorithm to determine if a binary tree is complete.

6. Two binary trees are *similar* if they are both empty or if they are both nonempty, their left subtrees are similar, and their right subtrees are similar. Write an algorithm that determines if two binary trees are similar.

7. Two binary trees are *mirror similar* if they are both empty or if they are both nonempty and the left subtree of each is mirror similar to the right subtree of the other. Write an algorithm which determines if two binary trees are mirror similar.

8. Write algorithms to determine whether or not one binary tree is similar and mirror similar (see the previous exercises) to some subtree of another.

9. Develop an algorithm to find duplicates in a list of numbers without using a binary tree. If there are n distinct numbers in the list, how many times must two numbers be compared for equality in your algorithm? What if all n numbers are equal?

10. Write an algorithm that accepts a binary tree representing an expression and returns the infix version of the expression which contains only those parentheses that are necessary.

2. BINARY TREE REPRESENTATIONS

In this section we examine various methods of implementing binary trees in Pascal and present routines that build, traverse, and apply binary trees.

As is the case with list nodes, tree nodes may be implemented as array elements or as allocations of a dynamic variable. Each node must contain *info*, *left*, and *right* fields. The *left* and *right* fields of a node point to the roots of its left and right subtrees, respectively. Using the array implementation, we may declare

```
const numnodes = 500;
type  nodeptr = 0..numnodes;
      nodetype = record
                      info: integer;
                      left:  nodeptr;
                      right: nodeptr
                 end;
var   node: array[1..numnodes] of nodetype;
```

and create an available list by

```
var avail,i: nodeptr;
begin
     avail:= 1;
     for i:= 1 to numnodes-1
         do node[i].left:= i+1;
     node[numnodes].left:= 0
end
```

The routines *getnode* and *freenode* are straightforward and are left as exercises. Note that the available list is not a binary tree but a linear list whose nodes are linked together by the *left* field.

Under the array implementation, the following function implements the *maketree* operation, which allocates a node and sets it as the root of a binary tree with empty right and left subtrees:

```
function maketree(x: integer): nodeptr;
var p: nodeptr;
```

```
        begin {function maketree}
            p:= getnode;
            node[p].info:= x;
            node[p].left:= 0;
            node[p].right:= 0;
            maketree:= p
        end {function maketree};
```

The routine *setleft*(p, x) sets a node with contents x as the left son of *node*(p).

```
        procedure setleft (p: nodeptr; x: integer);
        var q: nodeptr;
        begin {procedure setleft}
            if p = 0
                then error('void insertion')
                else if node[p].left <> 0
                        then error('invalid insertion')
                        else begin
                                q:= maketree(x);
                                node[p].left:= q
                            end {else begin}
        end {procedure setleft};
```

The routine *setright*(p, x), which creates a right son of *node*(p) with contents x, is similar and is left as an exercise for the reader.

The following program uses a binary tree to find duplicate numbers in an input file in which each number is on a separate input line. It closely follows the algorithm of Section 1.

```
        program dup (input, output);
        const numnodes = 500;
        type  nodeptr = 0..numnodes;
              nodetype = record
                            info: integer;
                            left: nodeptr;
                            right: nodeptr
                         end;
        var   p,q,i,tree,avail: nodeptr;
              node: array[1..numnodes] of nodetype;
              number: integer;
        begin {program dup}
            avail:= 1;
            for i:= 1 to numnodes-1
                do node[i].left:= i+1;
            node[numnodes].left:= 0;
            readln(number);
            tree:= maketree(number);
```

```
              while not eof
                do begin
                        readln(number);
                        p:= tree;
                        q:= tree;
                        while(number <> node[p].info) and (q <> 0)
                            do begin
                                    p:= q;
                                    if number < node[p].info
                                        then q:= node[p].left
                                        else q:= node[p].right
                                end {while...do begin};
                        if number = node[p].info
                            then writeln(number, ' is a duplicate')
                            else if number < node[p].info
                                    then setleft(p, number)
                                    else setright(p, number)
                end {while...do begin}
        end { program dup}.
```

Alternatively, a node may be defined by:

```
            type nodeptr = ↑nodetype;
                 nodetype = record
                                info:  integer;
                                left:  nodeptr;
                                right: nodeptr
                            end;
```

Under this implementation, an explicit available list is not needed. The routines *getnode* and *freenode* simply allocate and free a copy of the dynamic variable node using the system routines *new* and *dispose*. The *maketree* function may be written as follows:

```
            function maketree (x: integer): nodeptr;
            var p: nodeptr;
            begin { function maketree}
                p:=getnode;
                p↑.info:= x;
                p↑.left:= nil;
                p↑.right:= nil;
                maketree:= p
            end { function maketree};
```

The *setleft* routine is also straightforward.

```
            procedure setleft(p: nodeptr; x: integer);
            var q: nodeptr;
            begin { procedure setleft}
                if p = nil
                    then error('void insertion')
                    else if p↑.left <> nil
                            then error('invalid insertion')
                            else begin
                                    q: = maketree(x);
                                    p↑.left: = q
                                 end {else begin}
            end { procedure setleft};
```

We will use the array implementation in subsequent examples—the dynamic implementation versions are straightforward modifications of the programs we present and we leave them as exercises for the reader.

Binary Tree Traversals in Pascal

We may implement the traversal of binary trees in Pascal by recursive routines that mirror the traversal definitions. The three Pascal routines *pretrav*, *intrav*, and *posttrav* print the contents of a binary tree in preorder, inorder, and postorder, respectively. The parameter to each routine is a pointer to the root node of a binary tree.

```
            procedure pretrav (tree: nodeptr);
            begin
                if tree <> 0
                    then with node[tree]
                            do begin
                                    writeln(info);  { visit the root }
                                    pretrav (left);  { traverse left subtree }
                                    pretrav (right) { traverse right subtree }
                                 end {with...do begin}
            end { procedure pretrav};

            procedure intrav (tree: nodeptr);
            begin
                if tree <> 0
                    then with node[tree]
                            do begin
                                    intrav (left);  { traverse left subtree }
                                    writeln(info); { visit the root }
                                    intrav (right) { traverse right subtree }
                                 end {with...do begin}
            end { procedure intrav};
```

```
procedure posttrav (tree: nodeptr);
begin
      if tree <> 0
        then with node[tree]
              do begin
                        posttrav (left);  { traverse left subtree }
                        posttrav(right);  { traverse right subtree }
                        writeln(info)    { visit the root }
                  end {with...do begin}
      end { procedure posttrav};
```

The reader is invited to simulate the actions of these routines on the trees of Figures 6.1.5 and 6.1.6.

Of course, more efficient routines could be written to perform these traversals which explicitly perform the necessary stacking and unstacking. For example, a nonrecursive routine to traverse a binary tree in inorder may be written as follows:

```
procedure intrav2 (tree: nodeptr);
const maxstack = 100;
type stack = record
                top: 0..maxstack;
                item: array[1..maxstack] of nodeptr
            end;
var  s: stack;
     p: nodeptr;
     {routines pop, push, and empty are inserted here}
begin { procedure intrav2}
     s.top:= 0;
     p:= tree;
     repeat
           { travel down left branches as far as possible }
           {       saving pointers to nodes passed         }
           while p <> 0
              do begin
                       push (s,p);
                       p:= node[p].left
                  end {while...do begin};
           { check if finished }
           if not empty(s)
              then begin { at this point the left subtree is empty }
                       p:= pop(s);
                       writeln(node[p].info); { visit the root }
                       p:= node[p].right       { traverse right subtree }
                  end {then begin}
     until (empty(s)) and (p=0)
end { procedure intrav2};
```

Threaded Binary Trees

Similar nonrecursive routines can be written to implement preorder and postorder traversals. However, since traversing a binary tree is such a common operation, it would be helpful to find a more efficient method to perform the operation. Let us examine the routine *intrav2* to discover why a stack is needed. The stack is popped when p equals the nil pointer (0 under the array implementation). This happens in one of two cases: one case is when the *while* loop is exited after having been executed one or more times. This implies that the program has traveled down left branches until it reached a nil pointer, stacking each node as it was passed. Thus the top element of the stack is the value of p before it became 0. If an auxiliary pointer q is kept one step behind p, the value of q can be used directly and need not be popped.

The other case in which p is 0 is when the *while* loop is skipped entirely. This occurs after reaching a node with an empty right subtree, executing the statement $p := node[p].right$ and returning to repeat the *repeat* loop. At this point, we would have lost our way were it not for the stack whose top points to the node whose left subtree was just traversed. Suppose, however, that instead of a nil pointer, a node with an empty right subtree contained a pointer to the node that would be on top of the stack at that point in the algorithm. Then there would no longer be a need for the stack since the node directly points to its inorder successor. Such a pointer is called a *thread* and must be differentiable from a tree pointer, which is used to link a node to its left or right subtree. Figure 6.2.1 shows the binary trees of Figure 6.1.5 with threads replacing nil pointers in nodes with empty right subtrees. The threads are drawn with dotted lines to differentiate them from tree pointers. Note that the rightmost node in each tree still has a nil right pointer since it has no inorder successor. Such trees are called *right in-threaded* binary trees.

How can threads be represented in the Pascal implementation of binary trees? In the array implementation, a thread can be represented by a negative value of $node[p].right$ whose absolute value is the index in the array *node* of the inorder successor of $node[p]$. The sign of $node[p].right$ indicates whether its absolute value represents a thread (minus) or a pointer to a nonempty subtree (plus). This would necessitate redefining *nodeptr* to accommodate negative pointers by

```
const numnodes= 500;
      negnodes= -500;
type  nodeptr= negnodes..numnodes;
```

Under this implementation, the following routine traverses a right in-threaded binary tree in inorder:

```
procedure intrav3 (tree: nodeptr);
var p,q: nodeptr;
```

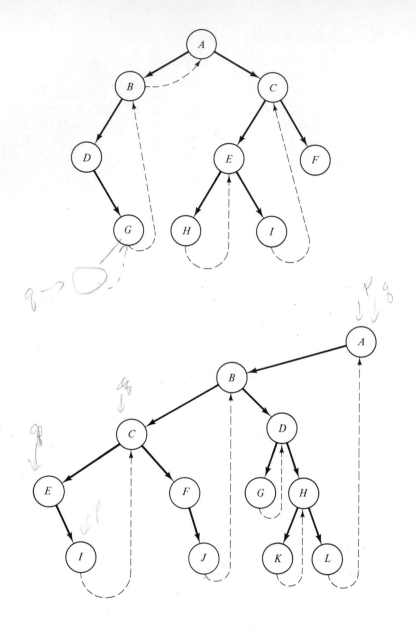

Figure 6.2.1 Right in-threaded binary trees.

```
begin { procedure intrav 3 }
      p:= tree;
      repeat
            { travel down left links keeping q behind p }
            q:= 0;
            while p <> 0
                do begin
                          q:= p;
                          p:= node[p].left
                    end { while...do begin };
            if q <> 0  { check if finished }
               then begin
                          writeln(node[q].info);
                          p:= node[q].right;
                          while p < 0
                                do begin
                                        q:= -p;
                                        writeln(node[q].info);
                                        p:= node[q].right
                                   end {while...do begin}
                    end {then begin}
            { traverse right subtree }
      until q = 0
end { procedure intrav3 };
```

In a right in-threaded binary tree, the inorder successor of any node can be found efficiently. Such a tree can also be constructed in a straightforward manner. The function *maketree* remains unchanged. The routines *setleft* and *setright* follow.

```
procedure setleft (p: nodeptr; x: integer);
var q: nodeptr;
begin
   if p = 0
      then error('void insertion')
      else if node[p].left <> 0
              then error('invalid insertion')
              else begin
                        q:= getnode;
                        node[q].info:= x;
                        node[p].left:= q;
                   { the inorder successor of node[q] is node[p] }
                        node[q].right:= -p;
                        node[q].left:= 0
                   end {else begin}
end { procedure setleft };
```

```
    procedure setright (p: nodeptr; x: integer);
    var q,r: nodeptr;
    begin
        if p=0
            then error('void insertion')
            else if node[p].right > 0
                then error('invalid insertion')
                else begin
                        q:= getnode;
                        node[q].info:= x;
                    { save the inorder successor of node[p] }
                        r:= node[p].right;
                        node[p].right:= q;
                        node[q].left:= 0;
                    { the inorder successor of node[q] is the }
                    {      previous successor of node[p]      }
                        node[q].right:= r
                    end {else begin}
    end { procedure setright};
```

To implement a right in-threaded binary tree under the dynamic implementation for nodes of a binary tree, an extra boolean field must be added
to each node to indicate whether or not its right pointer is a thread. Thus
a node is defined as follows:

```
    type nodeptr = ↑nodetype;
        nodetype = record
                    info:    integer;
                    left:    nodeptr;
                    right:   nodeptr;
                    rthread: boolean { rthread is true if right }
                                      {   is a non-nil thread    }
                end;
```

We present a routine to implement inorder traversal.

```
    procedure intrav4 (tree: nodeptr);
    var p,q: nodeptr;
    begin
        p:= tree;
        repeat
            q:= nil;
            while p <> nil { traverse left branch }
                do begin
                        q:= p;
                        p:= p↑.left
                end;
```

```
                    if q <> nil
                      then begin
                              writeln(q↑.info);
                              p:= q↑.right;
                              while q↑.rthread { back up }
                                 do begin
                                         writeln(p↑.info);
                                         q:= p;
                                         p:= q↑.right
                                    end {while...do begin}
                              end {then begin}
                  until q = nil
              end { procedure intrav4};
```

We leave to the reader to provide appropriate *maketree*, *setleft*, and *setright* routines for right in-threaded binary trees under this implementation.

A *left in-threaded* binary tree may be similarly defined as one in which each nil left pointer is altered to contain a thread to that node's inorder predecessor, and an *in-threaded* binary tree may be defined as a binary tree that is both left in-threaded and right in-threaded. However, left in-threading does not yield the advantages of right in-threading. We may also define right and left *pre-threaded* binary trees in which nil right and left pointers of nodes are replaced by their preorder successors and predecessors, respectively. A right pre-threaded binary tree may be traversed efficiently in preorder without the use of a stack. A right in-threaded binary tree may also be traversed in preorder without the use of a stack. The traversal algorithms are left as exercises for the reader.

Heterogeneous Binary Trees

Often, the nodes of a binary tree do not all contain the same kind of information. For example, in representing a binary expression with constant numerical operands, we may wish to use a binary tree whose leafs contain numbers but whose nonleaf nodes contain characters representing operators. Figure 6.2.2 illustrates such a binary tree. To represent such a tree in Pascal, we may use a variant record to represent the information portion of the node. Of course, each tree node should contain a tag field to indicate the type of object that its *info* field contains.

```
            type infotype = (operand, operator);
                 nodeptr = ↑nodetype;
                 nodetype = record
                         left: nodeptr;
                         right: nodeptr;
                         case tag: infotype of
                              operator: (chinfo: char);
                              operand: (numinfo: real)
                  end;
```

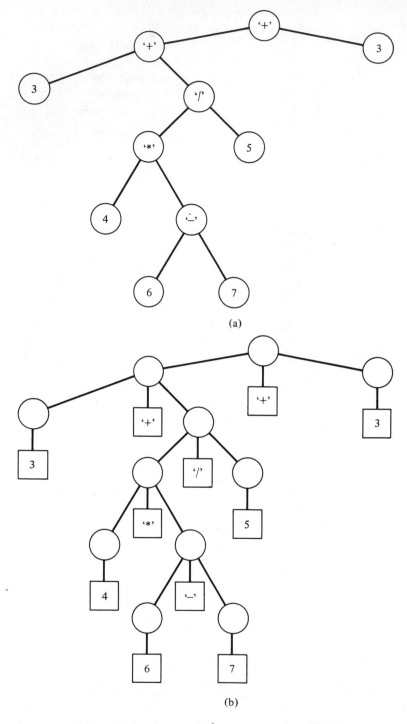

(a)

(b)

Figure 6.2.2 Binary tree representing $3 + 4 * (6 - 7)/5 + 3$.

Let us write a Pascal function *evalbintree* which accepts a pointer to such a tree and returns the value of the expression represented by the tree. The function recursively evaluates the left and right subtrees and then applies the operator of the root to the two results. We use the auxiliary function *oper(symb,opnd1,opnd2)* introduced in Section 2.3. The first parameter of *oper* is a character representing an operator and the last two parameters are real numbers which are two operands. The function *oper* returns a real number which is the result of applying the operator to the two operands. The function *evalbintree* may then be written as follows:

```
function evalbintree (tree: nodeptr): real;
var opnd1,opnd2: real;
    symb: char;
begin
    case tree↑.tag of
        operand: { the expression is a single operand }
                    evalbintree:= tree↑.numinfo;
        operator: begin
                    { evaluate the left subtree }
                    opnd1:= evalbintree(tree↑.left);
                    { evaluate the right subtree }
                    opnd2:= evalbintree(tree↑.right);
                    symb:= tree↑.chinfo; { extract the operator }
                    { apply the operator and return }
                    {            the result           }
                    evalbintree:= oper(symb, opnd1, opnd2)
                end
    end {case}
end { function evalbintree};
```

EXERCISES

1. Write a Pascal function that accepts a pointer to a node and returns *true* if that node is the root of a valid binary tree and *false* otherwise.

2. Write a Pascal function that accepts a pointer to a binary tree and a pointer to a node of the tree and returns the level of the node in the tree.

3. Write a Pascal function (for both the array and dynamic representations) that accepts a pointer to a binary tree and returns a pointer to a new binary tree which is the mirror image of the first (i.e., all left subtrees are now right subtrees, and vice versa).

4. Explain why it is impossible to find the brother of a node, given only a pointer to that node, under the representation of binary trees presented in this section. Write a function *brother(t,p)* that accepts a pointer *t* to a binary tree and a pointer *p* to a node in that tree and returns a pointer to that node's brother in the tree. Show how to add a field to each node in the representation of a binary tree so that it is possible to find a node's brother, given only a pointer to the node.

5. Write a Pascal program to perform the following experiment. Generate 100 random numbers. As each one is generated, insert it into an initially empty binary tree so that all numbers in a left subtree of a node are smaller than the number in the node, which is in turn smaller than the numbers in the right subtree of the node. When all 100 numbers have been inserted, print the level of the leaf with largest level and the level of the leaf with smallest level. Repeat this process 50 times. Print a table with a count of how many of the 50 runs resulted in a difference between the maximum and minimum leaf level of 1, 2, 3, and so on.

6. Write a Pascal function that accepts a pointer to a binary tree and two pointers to nonroot nodes in the tree and returns a pointer to the youngest common ancestor of the two nonroot nodes. What if each node contained a *father* field in addition to *left*, *right*, and *info* fields?

7. Write a Pascal function to create a binary tree given:

   (a) The preorder and inorder traversals of that tree.
   (b) The preorder and postorder traversals of that tree.

   Each function should accept two character strings as parameters. The tree created should contain a single character in each node.

8. How do you account for the similarity between the nonrecursive subroutine for inorder traversal presented in this section and the nonrecursive routine to solve the Towers of Hanoi problem of Section 3.4?

9. An index of a textbook consists of major terms, ordered alphabetically. Each major term is accompanied by a set of page numbers and a set of subterms. The subterms are printed on successive lines after the major term and are arranged alphabetically within the major term. Each subterm is accompanied by a set of page numbers.

   Design a data structure to represent such an index and write a Pascal program to print an index from data as follows. Each input line begins with an 'm' (major term) or an 's' (subterm). An 'm' line contains an 'm' followed by a major term followed by an integer n (possibly zero) followed by n page numbers where the major term appears. An 's' line is similar except that it contains a subterm rather than a major term. The input lines appear in no particular order except that each subterm is considered to be a subterm of the major term that most recently precedes it. There may be many input lines for a single major term or subterm (all page numbers appearing on any line for a particular term should be printed with that term).

   The index should be printed with one term on a line followed by all the pages on which the term appears in ascending order. Subterms should appear in alphabetical order immediately following their major term. Subterms should be indented five columns from the major terms. Major terms should be printed in alphabetical order.

   The set of major terms should be organized as a binary tree. Each node in the tree contains (in addition to left and right pointers and the major term itself) pointers to two other binary trees. One of these represents the set of page numbers in which the major term occurs and the other represents the set of subterms of the major term. Each node on a subterm binary tree contains (in addition to left and right pointers and the subterm) a pointer to a binary tree representing the set of page numbers in which the subterm occurs.

10. Define a ternary tree and extend the concepts of the last two sections to it.

3. OTHER REPRESENTATIONS AND APPLICATIONS—THE HUFFMAN ALGORITHM

There are other representations of binary trees, each suited for the efficient performance of specific operations. In this section and the next, we examine some of these representations and their applications.

Consider the following problem. Suppose that we have an alphabet of n symbols and a long message consisting of symbols from this alphabet. We wish to encode this message as a long bit string (we define a bit to be either 0 or 1) by assigning a bit string code to each symbol of the alphabet and concatenating the individual codes of the symbols making up the message to produce an encoding for the message. For example, suppose that the alphabet consists of the four symbols A, B, C, D and codes are assigned to these symbols as follows:

Symbol	Code
A	010
B	100
C	000
D	111

The message $ABACCDA$ would then be encoded as 010100010000000111010. However, such an encoding would be inefficient since 3 bits are used for each symbol, so that 21 bits are needed to encode the entire message. Suppose that a 2-bit code is assigned to each symbol, as follows:

Symbol	Code
A	00
B	01
C	10
D	11

Then the code for the message would be 00010010101100, which requires only 14 bits. We wish to find a code that minimizes the length of the encoded message.

Let us reexamine the foregoing example. Each of the letters B and D appears only once in the message, whereas the letter A appears three times. Thus, if a code is chosen in which the letter A is assigned a shorter bit string than the letters B and D, the length of the encoded message would be small. This is because the short code (representing the letter A) would appear more frequently than the long code. Indeed, codes can be assigned as follows:

Symbol	Code
A	0
B	110
C	10
D	111

Using this code, the message *ABACCDA* is encoded as 0110010101110, which requires only 13 bits. In very long messages that contain symbols which appear very infrequently, the savings are substantial. Note that the code for one symbol should not be a prefix of the code for another. This must be true if the decoding is to proceed from left to right. If the code for a symbol x, $c(x)$, were a prefix of the code of a symbol y, $c(y)$, then when $c(x)$ is encountered, it is unclear whether $c(x)$ represents the symbol x or whether it is the first part of $c(y)$. In our example the bit string is scanned from left to right. If a 0 is encountered as the first bit, the symbol is an A; otherwise, it is a B, C, or D and the next bit is examined. If the second bit is a 0, the symbol is a C; otherwise, it must be a B or a D and the third bit must be examined. If the third bit is a 0, the symbol is a B; if it is a 1, the symbol is a D. As soon as the first symbol has been identified, the process is repeated, starting at the next bit to find the second symbol.

This suggests a method for developing an optimal encoding scheme given the frequency of occurrence of each symbol in a message. Find the two symbols that appear least frequently. In our example, these are B and D. The last bit of their codes will differentiate between them: 0 for B and 1 for D. Combine these two symbols into the single symbol BD, whose code represents the knowledge that a symbol is either a B or a D. The frequency of occurrence of this new symbol is the sum of the frequencies of its two constituent symbols. Thus the frequency of BD is 2. There are now three symbols: A (frequency 3), C (frequency 2), and BD (frequency 2). Again choose the two symbols with smallest frequency: C and BD. The last bit of their codes will differentiate between them: 0 for C and 1 for BD. The two symbols are then combined into the single symbol CBD with frequency 4. There are now only two symbols remaining: A and CBD. These are combined into the single symbol $ACBD$. The last bits of the codes for A and CBD will differentiate between them: 0 for A and 1 for CBD.

The symbol $ACBD$ now contains the entire alphabet; it is assigned the nil bit string of length 0 as its code. This means that at the start of the decoding, before any bits have been examined, it is certain that any symbol is contained in $ACBD$. The two symbols that comprise $ACBD$ (A and CBD) are assigned the codes 0 and 1, respectively. If a 0 is encountered, the encoded symbol is an A; if a 1 is encountered, it is a C, B, or D. Similarly, the two symbols that constitute CBD (C and BD) are assigned the codes 10 and 11, respectively. The first bit indicates that the symbol is one of the constituents of CBD and the second bit indicates whether it is a C or a BD. The symbols that comprise BD (B and D) are then assigned the codes 110 and 111. By this process, symbols that appear frequently in the message are assigned shorter codes than symbols that appear infrequently.

The action of combining two symbols into one suggests the use of a binary tree. Each nonleaf node of the tree represents a symbol and the leafs represent the symbols of the original alphabet. Figure 6.3.1a shows the binary tree constructed using the preceding example. Each node in the illustration contains a symbol and its frequency. Figure 6.3.1b shows the binary

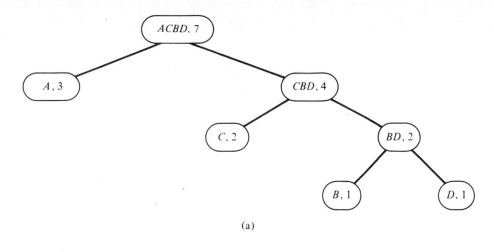

(a)

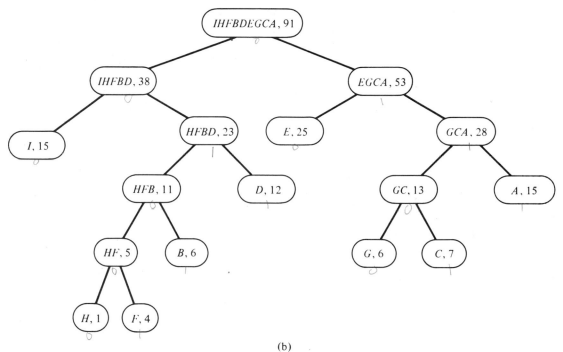

(b)

Symbol	Frequency	Code	Symbol	Frequency	Code	Symbol	Frequency	Code
A	15	111	D	12	011	G	6	1100
B	6	0101	E	25	10	H	1	01000
C	7	1101	F	4	01001	I	15	00

(c)

Figure 6.3.1 Huffman trees.

tree constructed by this method for the alphabet and frequency table of Figure 6.3.1c. Such trees are called *Huffman trees* after the discoverer of this encoding method.

Once the Huffman tree is constructed, the code of any symbol in the alphabet can be determined by starting at the leaf which represents that symbol and climbing up to the root. The code is initialized to nil. Each time that a left branch is climbed, a 0 is appended to the left of the code; each time that a right branch is climbed, a 1 is appended to the left of the code.

Note that in constructing the tree and obtaining the codes, it is only necessary to keep links from each node to its father and an indication of whether each node is a left or right son; links from a father to either of its two sons are unnecessary. Each node contains three fields: *father*, *sontype*, and *freq*. *father* is a pointer to the node's father. If the node is the root, its *father* field is nil. The value of *sontype* is one of the constants *lson* or *rson*, depending on whether the node is a left or right son. *freq* is the frequency of occurrence of the symbol represented by that node. The inputs to the algorithm are *n*, the number of symbols in the original alphabet, and *frequency*, an array of size at least *n* such that *frequency*[*i*] is the relative frequency of the *i*th symbol. The algorithm is to assign values to an array *code* of size at least *n* so that *code*[*i*] contains the code assigned to the *i*th symbol. The algorithm also constructs an array *position* of size at least *n* such that *position*[*i*] points to the node representing the *i*th symbol.

We may outline Huffman's algorithm as follows:

```
        { initialize the set of root nodes }
rootnodes := the empty set;
            { construct a node for each symbol }
for i := 1 to n
    do begin
            p := getnode;
            freq(p) := frequency[i];
            position[i] := p;
            add p to rootnodes
        end {for...do begin};
while rootnodes contains more than one item
    do begin
            p1 := the element in rootnodes with smallest freq value;
            remove p1 from rootnodes;
            p2 := the element in rootnodes with smallest freq value;
            remove p2 from rootnodes;
            {combine p1 and p2 as branches of a single tree}
            p := getnode;
            father(p1) := p;
            sontype(p1) := lson;
            father(p2) := p;
```

```
            sontype(p2):= rson;
            freq(p):= freq(p1) + freq(p2);
            add p to rootnodes
        end {while...do begin};

                { the tree is now constructed; use it to find codes }
        root:= the single element of rootnodes;
        for i:= 1 to n
            do begin
                    p:= position[i];
                    code[i]:= the nil bit string;
                    while p <> root
                        do begin
                        { travel up the tree }
                                if sontype(p) = lson
                                    then code[i]:= 0 followed by code[i]
                                    else code[i]:= 1 followed by code[i];
                                p:= father(p)
                        end {while...do begin}
            end {for...do begin}
```

Note that every nonleaf node in a Huffman tree has nonempty right and left subtrees. Such a tree is called a *strictly binary tree*. The trees used to represent binary expressions in Section 2 are also strictly binary. It can be shown that a strictly binary tree with n leafs has $2n-1$ nodes (this is left as an exercise for the reader). Since the leafs of a Huffman tree represent the symbols of the original alphabet, the total number of nodes in the tree can be computed from the number of symbols in the alphabet. Thus, if there are n symbols in the alphabet, the Huffman tree can be represented by an array of nodes of size $2n-1$.

Unfortunately, Pascal does not permit the size of an array to be determined based on the value of a variable. Thus we must allocate arrays based on the maximum possible symbols (a constant *maxsymbs*) rather than on the actual number of symbols, n. Thus an array of nodes that should be of size $2n-1$ must be declared as being of size $2 * maxsymbs + 1$. This means that some space is wasted. Of course, n itself could be made a constant rather than a variable, but then the program must be changed every time that the number of symbols differs. Other languages do have the capability of declaring an array dynamically during execution, and in such languages, no space would be wasted using an array implementation. Note that in Pascal, the nodes can be represented by dynamic variables without wasting space. However, we present an array implementation.

Let us write a program to encode a message using Huffman's algorithm. Ordinarily, codes are not constructed on the basis of the frequency of the occurrence of characters within a single message, but rather on the basis of their frequency within a whole set of messages, and the same code set is used for each message. For example, if messages consist of English words, the known relative frequency of occurrence of the letters of the alphabet in the English language could be used. Since the code is constructed from right to left, we define a type *codetype* as follows:

```
const maxbits = 50;
      maxbitpos = 51; {maxbits plus one}
type bit = '0'..'1';
     codetype = record
                   bits: array[1..maxbits] of bit;
                   startpos: 1..maxbitpos
                end;
```

maxbits is the maximum number of bits allowed in a code. If a code is nil, then its *startpos* equals *maxbitpos*, which is one more than *maxbits*. Each time that a bit is appended to a code *cd* at the left, *cd.startpos* is decremented by 1 and the bit is inserted in *cd.bits*[*cd.startpos*]. When the array *cd.bits* is completed, the bits of the code are in positions *cd.startpos* through *maxbits* inclusive.

The input to the program consists of the number *n* of symbols in the alphabet followed by a set of *n* pairs, each of which consists of a symbol and its relative frequency. The program constructs a string *alph*, which consists of all the symbols in the alphabet, and an array *code* such that *code*[*i*] is the code assigned to the *i*th symbol in *alph*.

```
program findcode (input, output);
const maxbits = 50;
      maxbitpos = 51;
      maxsymbs = 50;
      maxnodes = 99; {maxnodes equals 2*maxsymbs-1}
type  stype = (lson,rson);
      nodeptr = 0..maxnodes;
      bit = '0'..'1';
      codetype = record
                    bits: array[1..maxbits] of bit;
                    startpos: 1..maxbitpos
                 end;
      nodetype = record
                    freq: integer;
                    father: nodeptr; {father is 0 if a node is in rootnodes}
                    sontype: stype
                 end;
var   alph: array[1..maxsymbs] of char;
      code: array[1..maxsymbs] of codetype;
      nodes: array[1..maxnodes] of nodetype;
      n,i: 0..maxsymbs;
      n1,n2,j,m: nodeptr;
      cd: codetype;
      k: 1..maxbits;
```

```
      symb: char;
      small1,small2: integer;
      begin
            { initialize nodes }
            for j:= 1 to maxnodes
                do begin
                        nodes[j].freq:= 0;
                        nodes[j].father:= 0
                    end { for...do begin };
            for i:= 1 to maxsymbs
                do alph[i]:= ' ';
            { input the alphabet and frequencies }
            readln(n);
            for i:= 1 to n
                do begin
                        readln(symb, nodes[i].freq);
                        alph[i]:= symb
                    end { for...do begin};

            { we now build the trees }
            for m:= n+1 to 2*n-1
                do begin
                    { m is the next available node.  Search all previous }
                    {   nodes for the two root nodes n1 and n2 with    }
                    {              smallest frequencies                 }
                    n1:= 0;
                    n2:= 0;
                    small1:= maxint;
                    small2:= maxint;
                    for j:= 1 to m-1
                        do if nodes[j].father = 0
                            then   {j is a root node}
                            if nodes[j].freq < small1
                            then begin
                                        small2:= small1;
                                        small1:= nodes[j].freq;
                                        n2: = n1;
                                        n1:= j
                                end { then begin }
                            else if nodes[j].freq < small2
                                then begin
                                        small2:= nodes[j].freq;
                                        n2:= j
                                    end;

                    { set n1 to the left subtree of m and }
                    {      n2 to the right subtree        }
```

```
                    nodes[n1].father:= m;
                    nodes[n1].sontype:= lson;
                    nodes[n2].father:= m;
                    nodes[n2].sontype:= rson;
                    nodes[m].freq:= nodes[n1].freq + nodes[n2].freq
              end { for...do begin };
              { extract the codes from the tree }
         for i:= 1 to n
              do begin
                  { initialize code[i] }
                       cd.startpos:= maxbitpos;
                            { travel up the tree }
                       j:= i;
                       while nodes[j].father <> 0
                            do begin
                                    if nodes[j].sontype = lson
                                       then    {left son}
                                            begin
                                               cd.startpos:= cd.startpos - 1;
                                               cd.bits[cd.startpos]:= 0
                                            end
                                       else    {right son}
                                            begin
                                               cd.startpos:= cd.startpos - 1;
                                               cd.bits[cd.startpos]:= 1
                                            end;
                                    j:= nodes[j].father
                            end {while...do begin};
                       code[i]:= cd
              end { for...do begin };
         { print results }
         for i:= 1 to n
              do begin
                       writeln(alph[i], nodes[i].freq, ' ');
                       for k:= code[i].startpos to maxbits
                            do write(code[i].bits[k]);
                       writeln
              end { for...do begin }
    end { program findcode }.
```

The reader is referred to Section 9.4, which suggests further improvements to the foregoing program. We leave to the reader the coding of the
procedure *encode(alph,code,msge,bitcode)*. This procedure accepts the
string *alph* and the array *code* constructed in the foregoing program and a
message *msge* and sets *bitcode* to the bit string encoding of the message.

Given the encoding of a message and the Huffman tree used in constructing the code, the original message can be recovered as follows. Begin at the

root of the tree. Each time that a 0 is encountered, move down a left branch and each time that a 1 is encountered, move down a right branch. Repeat this process until a leaf is encountered. The next character of the original message is the symbol that corresponds to that leaf. See if you can decode 1110100010111011 using the Huffman tree of Figure 6.3.1b.

In order to decode, it is necessary to travel from the root of the tree down to its leafs. This means that instead of an array *father*, two arrays *left* and *right* are needed to hold the left and right sons of a particular node. It is straightforward to construct the arrays *left* and *right* from the arrays *father* and *sontype*. Alternatively, the arrays *left* and *right* can be constructed directly from the frequency information for the symbols of the alphabet using an approach similar to that used in constructing the array *father*. (Of course, if the trees are to be identical, the symbol/frequency pairs must be presented in the same order under the two methods.) We leave these algorithms, as well as the decoding algorithm as exercises for the reader.

This section has illustrated an example using two distinct concepts. The first is that of a strictly binary tree. Such a binary tree is one in which each nonleaf node has both left and right sons. If the number of leafs in such a tree is n, the total number of nodes is $2n-1$. The significance of this fact is that the amount of storage that such a tree needs is known and may be declared in advance.

The other concept is that there are many ways to represent a binary tree. For example, a node could contain pointers to its left and right sons (as in the last section) or a pointer to its father (as in this section) or a pointer to its brother, or any combination of these. It is up to the programmer to select the representation that makes the particular application most efficient in terms of time, space, and ease of programming.

EXERCISES

1. Prove that a strictly binary tree with n leafs contains $2n-1$ nodes.

2. Write a Pascal function that accepts a pointer to a binary tree and returns *true* if the tree is strictly binary and *false* if it is not.

3. Write Pascal routines that convert a strictly binary tree represented by the arrays *father* and *sontype* to its representation using the arrays *left* and *right*, and vice versa.

4. Write a Pascal procedure *encode(alph,code,msge,bitcode)*. The procedure accepts the string *alph* and the array *code* produced by the program *findcode* in the text and a message *msge*. The procedure sets *bitcode* to the Huffman encoding of that message.

5. Write a Pascal procedure *decode(alph,left,right,bitcode,msge)*, where *alph* is the string produced by the program *findcode* in the text, *left* and *right* are arrays used to represent a Huffman tree, and *bitcode* is a bit string. The procedure should set *msge* to the Huffman decoding of *bitcode*.

6. Is it possible to have two different Huffman trees for a set of symbols with given frequencies? Either give an example in which two such trees exist or prove that there is only a single such tree.

7. Given a strictly binary tree with n leafs, let $level(i)$ for i between 1 and n equal the level of the ith leaf. Prove that $\sum_{i=1}^{n} 2^{-level(i)} = 1$.

8. Define a **Fibonacci binary tree of order n** as follows. If $n=0$ or $n=1$, the tree consists of a single node. If $n>1$, the tree consists of a root, with the Fibonacci tree of order $n-1$ as the left subtree and the Fibonacci tree of order $n-2$ as the right subtree.

    (a) Write a Pascal function that returns a pointer to the Fibonacci binary tree of order n.
    (b) Is such a tree strictly binary?
    (c) What is the number of leafs in the Fibonacci tree of order n?
    (d) What is the depth of the Fibonacci tree of order n?

9. Given a binary tree T, its **extension** is defined as the binary tree $e(T)$ formed from T by adding a new node at each nil left and right pointer in T. The new nodes are called **external** nodes and the original nodes are called **internal** nodes. $e(T)$ is called an **extended binary tree**.

    (a) Prove that an extended binary tree is strictly binary.
    (b) If T has n nodes, how many nodes does $e(T)$ have?
    (c) Prove that all leafs in an extended binary tree are external nodes.
    (d) Write a Pascal routine that extends a binary tree T.
    (e) Prove that any strictly binary tree with more than one node is an extension of one and only one binary tree.
    (f) Write a Pascal function that accepts a pointer to a strictly binary tree $T1$ containing more than one node and deletes nodes from $T1$, creating a binary tree $T2$ such that $T1=e(T2)$.
    (g) Show that the complete binary tree of order n is the nth extension of the binary tree consisting of a single node.

10. Given a strictly binary tree T in which the n leafs are labeled as nodes 1 through n, let $level(i)$ be the level of node i and let $freq(i)$ be an integer assigned to node i. Define the **weighted path length** of T as the sum of $freq(i)*level(i)$ over all leafs of T.

    (a) Write a Pascal routine to compute the weighted path length given fields $freq$ and $father$.
    (b) Show that the Huffman tree is the strictly binary tree with minimum weighted path length.

4. THE JOSEPHUS PROBLEM REVISITED

All the representations of binary trees that we have discussed so far specified the links among the nodes explicitly by using either *father* or *left* and *right* fields. For a certain class of strictly binary trees, this explicit specification can be eliminated. Define an *almost complete binary tree* as a strictly binary tree for which there is a nonnegative integer k such that:

1. Every leaf in the tree is at level k or at level $k+1$.
2. If a node in the tree has a right descendant at level $k+1$, then all its left descendants which are leafs are also at level $k+1$.

The binary tree of Figure 6.3.1a is not almost complete since it contains leafs at levels 1, 2, and 3, thus violating condition 1. Similarly, the binary

284

tree of Figure 6.3.1b is not almost complete since it contains leafs at levels
2, 3, 4, and 5. The strictly binary tree of Figure 6.4.1a satisfies condition 1
since every leaf is either at level 2 or at level 3. However, condition 2 is vio-
lated since A has a right descendant at level 3 (J) but also has a left descendant which is a leaf at level 2 (E). The binary tree of Figure 6.4.1b satisfies
both conditions 1 and 2 and is therefore an almost complete binary tree.

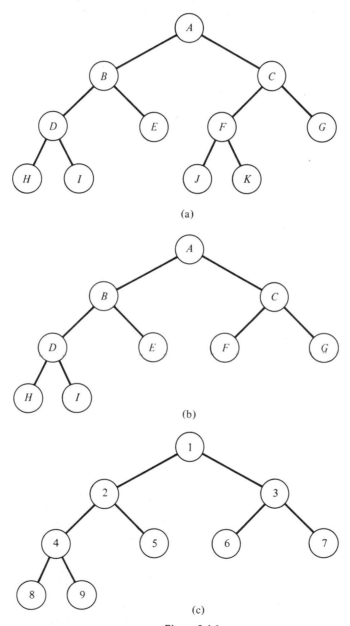

(a)

(b)

(c)

Figure 6.4.1

The nodes of an almost complete binary tree can be numbered in such a way that the number assigned a left son is twice the number assigned its father and the number assigned a right son is one more than twice the number assigned its father. Figure 6.4.1c illustrates the numbering of the nodes of the tree of Figure 6.4.1b. To represent an almost complete binary tree, we do not need *father*, *left*, or *right* links. Instead, node n is the implicit father of nodes $2n$ and $2n+1$. (We should note that many texts refer to such a tree as a "complete binary tree" rather than as an "almost complete binary

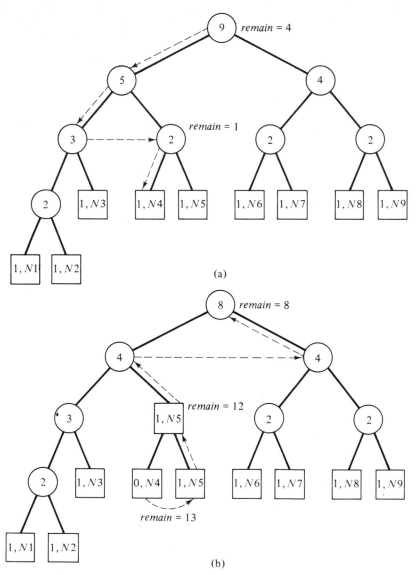

(a)

(b)

Figure 6.4.2 The Josephus problem (*total* = 9, n = 13).

tree." Still other texts use the term "complete" to refer to the concept which we call "strictly binary." We prefer to use the term "complete" as it was introduced in Section 1.)

As an example of the use of such a tree representation, let us reconsider the Josephus problem of Section 4.4. The reader should reread the statement of the problem. The solution presented in that section uses a circular list containing names. Each time that n people are counted, the step

$$\text{list}:= \text{node[list].next}$$

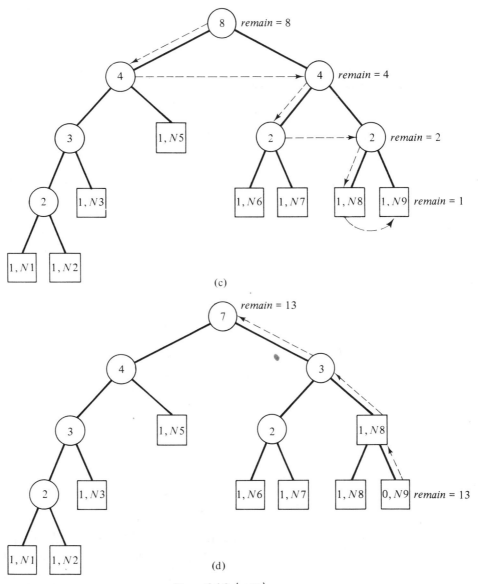

(c)

(d)

Figure 6.4.2 *(cont.)*

is performed $n-1$ times.

We can use an almost complete strictly binary tree to represent the Josephus problem as follows. Let the initial number of people be *total*. Then the binary tree has *total* leafs representing people and therefore $2 * total-1$ nodes. Each node of the tree contains an integer which is the number of leafs in the subtree rooted at that node. In addition, each leaf contains the name of the person whom it represents. Figure 6.4.2a illustrates the initial binary tree for the Josephus problem with *total*=9. (Leafs are shown as squares, nonleafs as circles.) The names are represented by the identifiers $N1$ through $N9$. The dashed arrows in that figure will be explained shortly.

Let n be the number to be counted around the circle in choosing the next person to be eliminated. To illustrate the algorithm we use $n=13$. The process proceeds in two phases. The first phase finds the root of a subtree which is known to contain the leaf representing the next person to be eliminated. Initially, this is the root of the tree. The next phase travels down the tree to find that leaf and eliminates it. Since $n=13$ is greater than the count in the tree root (9), the fourth person in the circle must be found (since counting the first nine only returns us to the beginning). Proceed to the left son of the root. Since the count in that left son (5) is greater than the number which remains to be counted (4), the next person to be eliminated is in that subtree. Again proceed to the left son of that node. Now, however, the count in that left son (3) is less than the number to be counted (4). This means that the next person is not in the left subtree but in the right subtree. Therefore, move to the right subtree and reduce the number remaining to be counted by the number of people represented by the left subtree. Three people have been counted and one person remains to be counted. The left son is a leaf representing the next person to be eliminated. The dashed lines in Figure 6.4.2a represent the path taken to this leaf.

To eliminate this person, reduce the count in that node and all of its ancestors by 1. Also, transfer the name in its right brother to its father. The father now becomes a leaf in the tree, representing the person previously represented by the right son. The new tree is shown in Figure 6.4.2b.

The process executes the first phase and climbs back up the tree. The number of people remaining to be counted is set to n, which is 13. In moving up the tree, it starts at the node representing the person just eliminated, and repeats the following process:

1. At a left son, advance to its right brother.
2. At a right son, subtract the count in that node from the number of people remaining to be counted and move up the tree until a left son is encountered.

Note that the first time this process is executed, the number subtracted from the remaining count will be 0 (if the person just eliminated was in a right son) or 1 (if the person just eliminated was in a left son). The process continues until it reaches either the root of the tree or a left son whose count is greater than the number of people remaining to be counted. At that point, the next person to be eliminated is in the subtree rooted at that node, so the second phase is executed once again.

The dashed lines in Figure 6.4.2b illustrate this process. Figure 6.4.2c and d illustrate the entire process being performed once again. The number of people remaining to be counted is illustrated at certain nodes.

The algorithm for the Josephus problem follows. $count(p)$ is the number of people represented by the subtree rooted at $node(p)$, $father(p)$ is the father of $node(p)$, $left(p)$ is its left son, $rbro(p)$ is its right brother, and $name(p)$ is the name of the person represented by $node(p)$ if it is a leaf. We assume that all of these quantities have been suitably initialized to represent an almost complete binary tree with *total* leaves. *n* represents the number of persons to be counted.

```
                    {  initialization  }
        p := tree;
                    { remain is the number of people remaining to be counted. }
                    {     Eliminate complete traversals of the tree from this     }
                    {                            count.                            }
        remain := (n-1) mod (count(p)) + 1;
        while count(tree) <> 1
            do begin
                    { Repeat the process as long as more than one person }
                    {      remains. At this point, p always points to      }
                    {    a node which is the root of a subtree known to    }
                    {   contain the next person to be eliminated. Move    }
                    {           down the tree to find that person.          }
                while count(p) > 1
                    do begin
                            p := left(p);
                            if remain > count(p)
                                then begin
                                        remain := remain - count(p);
                                        p := rbro(p)
                                end {then begin}
                    end {while count(p)>1 do begin};
                { At this point p points to the next person to be }
                {                   eliminated.                    }
                print(name(p));
                q := p;
                while q <> nil
                    do begin
                            { Reduce the count of each ancestor of p. }
                            count(q) := count(q) - 1;
                            if count(q) = 1
                                then if count(left(q)) = 1
                                    then name(q) := name(left(q))
```

```
              else name(q):= name(right(q));
          q := father(q)
      end {while q <> nil do begin};
  {Reset remain and move up the tree.}
  remain := n;
  if p points to a left son
      then p := rbro(p);
  while (remain > count(p)) and (p <> tree)
      do begin
              remain := remain - count(p);
              while p is a right son
                  do p := father(p);
              if p <> tree
                  then p := rbro(p)
      end {while...do begin};
  if  p = tree
      then remain := (remain - 1) mod count(tree) + 1
  end {while count(tree) <> 1 do begin};
{ At this point count(tree) = 1, so name(tree) is }
{                    the last person.             }
print(name(tree))
```

In implementing this algorithm in Pascal, we can take advantage of the fact that the original tree is almost complete. The tree is represented by two arrays, *count* and *name*, each of size $2*total-1$. A pointer to a node is therefore an integer between 1 and $2*total-1$. The root of the tree will be at position 1, so that $tree=1$. The left son of the node at position p is at position $2*p$, and the right son of the node at position p is at position $2*p+1$. Thus *left(p)* may be translated into $2*p$ and *rbro(p)* into $p+1$. *father(p)* may be computed by p *div* 2. p is a left son if and only if it is a multiple of 2. Thus the test for whether p is a right son is a check whether or not *odd(p)* equals *true*.

To set up the original tree, we must face the problem of initializing the arrays *count* and *name*. Initially, only the leafs have names assigned to them. These leafs occupy positions *total* through $2*total-1$ in the array, so that *name(i)* may be set equal to the nil string for $i<total$. However, in looking at the tree of Figure 6.4.2a we note that the *total* names do not appear sequentially in positions *total* through $2*total-1$. Rather, in that example, the first two names appear in positions 16 and 17 and the remaining names in positions 8 through 15. It can be shown that the leftmost node at level j in an almost complete binary tree occupies position 2^j. Thus if i is the *depth* (maximum level) of such a binary tree, the first names are assigned to positions 2^i through $2*total-1$ and the remainder (if any) to positions *total* through 2^i-1. The maximum level in an almost complete binary tree is the smallest integer j such that 2^j is greater than or equal to the number of leafs.

We may now write a Pascal program to read the number n, which is the count used in eliminating people, and the names of the people in the circle and to print the names of the people in the order in which they are eliminated from the circle. The number *total* of people is initialized in the program as a constant. Note that by representing the number of people (*total*) by a constant rather than by a variable, we assure that no space is wasted in the Pascal arrays. However, the definition of *total* in the program must be changed to produce a solution for a different number of people. The program uses an auxiliary procedure *readstr* to read a name.

```
program josephus (input, output);
const total = 100;
       maxnodes = 199; { maxnodes equals 2*total-1 }
type  nodeptr = 0..maxnodes;
      treenode = record
                    name: packed array[1..20] of char;
                    count: 0..total
                 end;
var   tree: array[1..maxnodes] of treenode;
      i, p, q, twotomax: nodeptr;
      remain,n,j: integer;
    { the routine readstr is inserted here }
begin { program josephus}
      readln(n);
      {        initialize the tree       }
      { find the maximum level - 1 }
      twotomax:= 1;
      while twotomax < total
         do twotomax:= 2*twotomax;
      { assign names and counts }
      for i:= twotomax to 2*total-1
          do with tree[i]
                 do begin
                       readstr(name);
                       count:= 1
                    end {with...do begin};
      for i:= total to twotomax-1
          do with tree[i]
                 do begin
                       readstr(name);
                       count:= 1
                    end { with...do begin };
      { initialize the remaining }
      {         counts            }
      for i:= total-1 downto 1
          do tree[i].count:= tree[2*i].count + tree[2*i+1].count;
```

```
{ follow the algorithm }
p:= 1;
remain:= (n-1) mod tree[p].count + 1;
{repeat as long as more than }
{      one person remains      }
while tree[1].count <> 1
    do begin
                { p points to the root of the subtree }
                {      containing the next person       }
            while tree[p].count > 1
                do begin
                        p:= 2*p;
                        if remain > tree[p].count
                            then begin
                                        remain:= remain - tree[p].count;
                                        p:= p+1
                                    end { then begin }
                    end {while...do begin};
            { p points to the next person to be }
            {             eliminated             }
            writeln(tree[p].name);
            q:= p;
            while q <> 0
                do begin
                        { reduce the count of each ancestor }
                        tree[q].count:= tree[q].count-1;
                        { move up the name of the son of q, }
                        {            if necessary            }
                        if tree[q].count = 1
                            then if tree[2*q].count = 1
                                    then tree[q].name:= tree[2*q].name
                                    else tree[q].name:= tree[2*q+1].name;
                        q:= q div 2
                    end {while q<>0 do begin};
            { reset remain and move up the tree }
            remain:= n;
            if not odd(p)
                then p:= p+1;
            {        p points to a right son        }
            while (remain > tree[p].count) and (p <> 1)
                do begin
                        remain:= remain-tree[p].count;
                        while (odd(p)) and (p <> 1)
                            do p:= p div 2;
                        if p <> 1  {p points to a left son}
                            then p:= p+1
                    end {while...do begin};
```

292   CHAP. 6: TREES

$$\textbf{if } p = 1$$
$$\textbf{then } remain := (remain - 1) \textbf{ mod } tree[p].count + 1$$
$$\textbf{end } \{while \; tree[i].count <> 1 \; do \; begin\};$$
$$writeln(tree[i].name)$$
$$\textbf{end } \{ program \; josephus \}.$$

EXERCISES 1. Write Pascal functions that accept a pointer to a binary tree and return *true* if the tree is:

   (a) Almost complete.
   (b) Complete.

   and *false* if it is not.

2. Prove that the nodes of an almost complete strictly binary tree can be numbered from 1 to $2n-1$ in such a way that the number assigned to the left son of the node numbered i is $2i$ and the number assigned to the right son of the node numbered i is $2i+1$.

3. Prove that the leftmost node at level n in an almost complete binary tree is assigned the number 2^n under the numbering scheme of Exercise 2.

4. Prove that the maximum level in an almost complete binary tree is the smallest integer i such that 2^i is greater than or equal to the number of leafs.

5. If an almost complete binary tree were defined as in the text except that such a tree need not be strictly binary, which of the statements in the previous three exercises would remain true?

6. Prove that the extension (see Exercise 6.3.9) of an almost complete binary tree is almost complete.

7. For what values of n and *total* is the solution to the Josephus problem given in this section faster in execution than the solution given in Section 4.4? Why is this so?

8. Show how to represent a linked list as an almost complete binary tree in which each list element is represented by one tree node. Write a Pascal function to return a pointer to the kth element of such a list.

5. TREES AND THEIR APPLICATIONS

In this section we consider general trees and their representations. We also investigate some of their uses in problem solving.

A *tree* is a finite nonempty set of elements in which one element is called the *root* and the remaining elements are partitioned into $m \geqslant 0$ disjoint subsets, each of which is itself a tree. Each element in a tree is called a *node* of the tree.

Figure 6.5.1 illustrates some trees. Each node may be the root of a tree with zero or more subtrees. A node with no subtrees is a *leaf*. We use the terms *father*, *son*, *ancestor*, *descendant*, and *level* in the same sense that we used them for binary trees. Two nodes that have the same father are *brothers*. We also define the *degree* of a node in a tree as the number of its sons. Thus in Figure 6.5.1a, node C has degree 0 (and is therefore a leaf), node D has

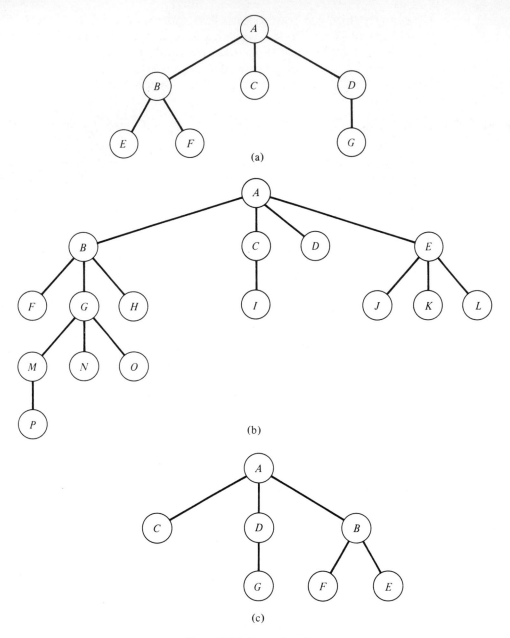

(a)

(b)

(c)

Figure 6.5.1 Examples of trees.

degree 1, node B has degree 2, and node A has degree 3. There is no upper limit on the degree of a node.

Let us compare the trees of Figure 6.5.1a and c. They are equivalent as trees. Each has A as its root and three subtrees. One of those subtrees has root C with no subtrees, another has root D with a single subtree rooted at

G, and the third has root B with two subtrees rooted at E and F. The only difference between the two illustrations is the order in which the subtrees are arranged. The definition of a tree made no distinction among subtrees of a general tree as in the case of a binary tree, where a distinction is made between the left and right subtrees. An *ordered tree* is defined as a tree in which the subtrees of each node form an ordered set. Thus, in an ordered tree, we may speak of the first, second, or last son of a particular node. The first son of a node in an ordered tree is often called the *oldest* son of that node and the last son is called the *youngest*. Although the trees of Figure 6.5.1a and c are equivalent as unordered trees, they are different as ordered trees. In the remainder of this chapter we use the word "tree" to refer to "ordered tree." A *forest* is an ordered set of ordered trees.

The question arises as to whether a binary tree is a tree. Every binary tree except for the empty binary tree is indeed a tree. However, not every tree is binary because a tree node may have more than two sons whereas a binary tree node may not. Even a tree whose nodes have at most two sons is not necessarily a binary tree. This is because an only son in a general tree is not designated as being a "left" or a "right" son, and in a binary tree every son must be either a "left" son or a "right" son. In fact, although a nonempty binary tree is a tree, the designations of left and right have no meaning within the context of a tree (except perhaps to order the two subtrees of those nodes with two sons). A nonempty binary tree is a tree each of whose nodes has a maximum of two subtrees, which have the added designation of "left" or "right."

Pascal Representations of Trees

How can an ordered tree be represented in Pascal? Two alternatives immediately come to mind: an array of tree nodes is declared or a dynamic variable is allocated for each node created. However, what should the structure of each individual node be? In the representation of a binary tree, each node contains an information field and two pointers to its two sons. But how many pointers should a tree node contain? The number of sons of a node is variable and may be as large or as small as desired. If we arbitrarily declare

```
const maxnodes = 500;
      maxsons = 20;
type  ndptr = 0..maxnodes;
      treenode = record
                    info: integer;
                    sons: array[1..maxsons] of ndptr
                 end;
var   node: array[1..maxnodes] of treenode;
```

then we are restricting the number of sons a node may have to a maximum of 20. Although it is true that, in most cases, this will be sufficient, it is inadequate when it is necessary to create dynamically a node with 21 or 100

SON INFO NEXT

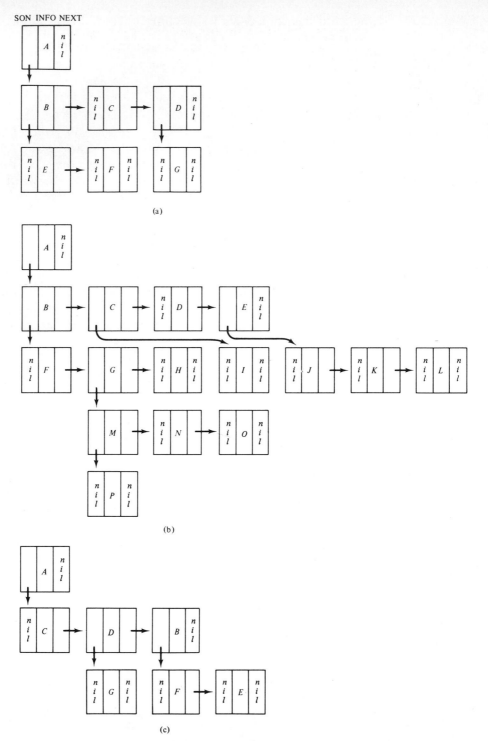

(a)

(b)

(c)

Figure 6.5.2 Tree representations.

sons. Far worse than this remote possibility is the fact that 20 units of storage are reserved for each node in the tree, even though a node may actually have only one or two (or even zero) sons. This is a tremendous waste of space.

One alternative is to link all the sons of a node together in a linear list. Thus the set of available nodes (using the array implementation) might be declared as follows:

```
const maxnodes = 500;
type  ndptr = 0..maxnodes;
        treenode = record
                          info: integer;
                          son: ndptr;
                          next: ndptr
                    end;
      var node: array[1..maxnodes] of treenode;
```

node[*p*].*son* points to the oldest son of *node*[*p*] and *node*[*p*].*next* points to the next younger brother of *node*[*p*]. Alternatively, a node may be declared as a dynamic variable:

```
type ndptr = ↑treenode;
        treenode = record
                          info: integer;
                          son: ndptr;
                          next: ndptr
                    end;
```

Figure 6.5.2 illustrates the representations of the trees of Figure 6.5.1 under these methods.

Note that under this implementation, each tree node contains two pointers, *son* and *next*. If we think of *son* as corresponding to the *left* pointer of a binary tree node and *next* as corresponding to its *right* pointer, this method actually represents a general ordered tree by a binary tree. We may picture this binary tree as the original tree tilted 45 degrees with all father–son links removed except for those between a node and its oldest son, and with links added between each node and its next younger brother. Figure 6.5.3 illustrates the binary trees corresponding to the trees of Figure 6.5.1.

In fact, a binary tree may be used to represent an entire forest since the *next* pointer in the root of a tree can be used to point to the next tree of the forest. Figure 6.5.4 illustrates a forest and its corresponding binary tree.

Tree Traversals

The traversal methods for binary trees induce traversal methods for forests. The preorder, inorder, or postorder traversals of a forest may be defined as the preorder, inorder, or postorder traversals of its corresponding binary

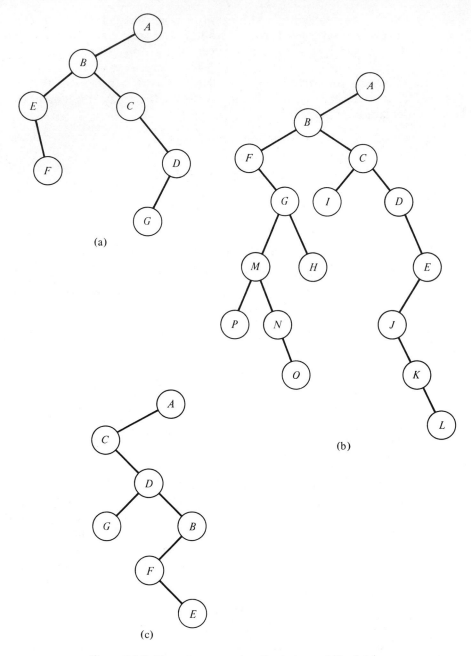

(a)

(b)

(c)

Figure 6.5.3 Binary trees corresponding to trees of Fig. 6.5.1.

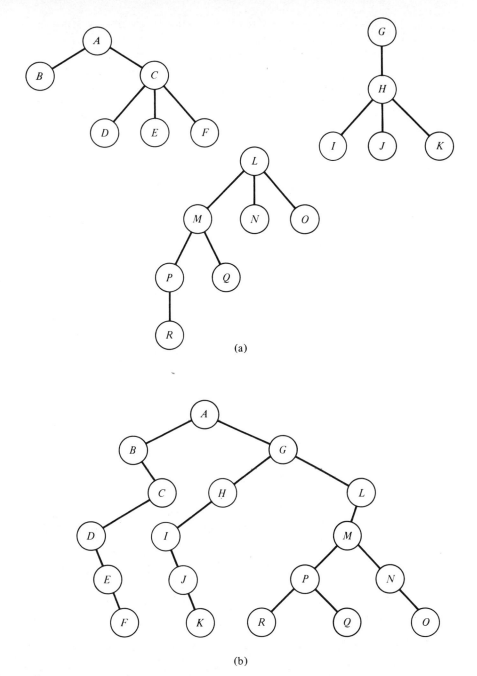

(a)

(b)

Figure 6.5.4 A forest and its corresponding binary tree.

tree. If a forest is represented as a set of dynamic variable nodes with *son* and *next* pointers as given above, a Pascal routine to print out the contents of its nodes in inorder may be written as follows:

```
procedure intrav (p: ndptr);
begin
    if p <> nil
        then with p↑
                do begin
                    intrav(son);
                    writeln(info);
                    intrav(next)
                end {with...do begin}
end { procedure intrav};
```

Routines for preorder and postorder traversals are similar.

These traversals of a forest may also be defined directly as follows:

preorder
1. Visit the root of the first tree in the forest.
2. Traverse in preorder the forest formed by the subtrees of the first tree, if any.
3. Traverse in preorder the forest formed by the remaining trees in the forest, if any.

inorder
1. Traverse in inorder the forest formed by the subtrees of the first tree in the forest, if any.
2. Visit the root of the first tree.
3. Traverse in inorder the forest formed by the remaining trees in the forest, if any.

postorder
1. Traverse in postorder the forest formed by the subtrees of the first tree in the forest, if any.
2. Traverse in postorder the forest formed by the remaining trees in the forest, if any.
3. Visit the root of the first tree in the forest.

The nodes of the forest in Figure 6.4.5a may be listed in preorder as *ABCDEFGHIJKLMPRQNO*, in inorder as *BDEFCAIJKHGRPQMNOL*, and in postorder as *FEDCBKJIHRQPONMLGA*.

General Expressions as Trees

An ordered tree may be used to represent a general expression in much the same way that a binary tree may be used to represent a binary expression. Since a node may have any number of sons, nonleaf nodes need not represent only binary operators but can represent operators with any number of operands. Figure 6.5.5 illustrates two expressions and their tree representations. The symbol "%" is used to represent unary negation to avoid confusing it with binary subtraction, which is represented by a minus sign. A

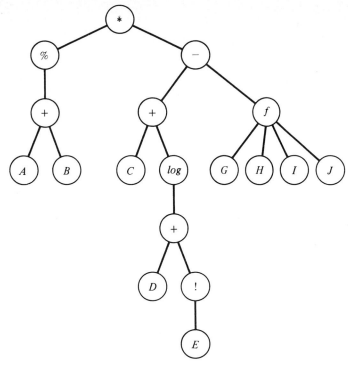

(a) $-(A + B) * (C + log(D + E!) - f(G, H, I, J))$

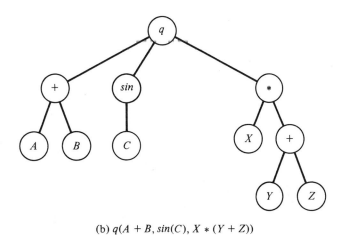

(b) $q(A + B, sin(C), X * (Y + Z))$

Figure 6.5.5 Tree representation of an arithmetic expression.

function reference such as $f(G,H,I,J)$ is viewed as the operator f applied to the operands G, H, I, and J.

A traversal of the trees of Figure 6.5.5 in preorder results in the strings $*\% + A\ B - + C\ log + D\ !\ E\ f\ G\ H\ I\ J$ and $q + A\ B\ sin\ C * X + Y\ Z$, respectively. These are the prefix versions of those two expressions. Thus we see that a preorder traversal of an expression tree produces its prefix expression. Inorder traversal yields the respective strings $A\ B + \%\ C\ D\ E\ !\ +\ log +$ $G\ H\ I\ J\ f - *$ and $A\ B + C\ sin\ X\ Y\ Z + * q$, which are the postfix versions of the two expressions. The fact that an inorder traversal yields a postfix expression might be surprising at first glance. However, the reason for it becomes clear upon examination of the transformation which takes place when a general ordered tree is represented by a binary tree.

Consider an ordered tree in which each node has zero or two sons. Such a tree is shown in Figure 6.5.6a and its binary tree equivalent is shown in Figure 6.5.6b. Traversing the binary tree of Figure 6.5.6b is the same as traversing the ordered tree of Figure 6.5.6a. However, a tree such as the one in Figure 6.5.6a may be considered as a binary tree in its own right rather than as an ordered tree. Thus it is possible to perform a binary tree traversal directly on the tree of Figure 6.5.6a. Beneath that figure are the binary traversals of that tree; beneath Figure 6.5.6b are the binary traversals of the tree in that figure, which are the same as the traversals of the tree of Figure 6.5.6a if it is considered as an ordered tree.

Note that the preorder traversals of the two binary trees are the same. Thus, if a preorder traversal on a binary tree representing a binary expression yields the prefix of the expression, then that traversal on an ordered tree representing a general expression which happens to have only binary operators yields prefix as well. However, the postorder traversals of the two binary trees are not the same. Instead, the inorder traversal of the second (which is the same as the inorder traversal of the first, if it is considered as an ordered tree) is the same as the postorder traversal of the first. Thus, the inorder traversal of an ordered tree representing a binary expression is equivalent to the postorder traversal of the binary tree representing that expression, which yields postfix.

Suppose that it is desired to evaluate an expression whose operands are all numerical constants. Such an expression can be represented in Pascal by a tree whose nodes are defined by

```
type nodetype = (oprtr, opnd);
     ndptr = ↑treenode;
     treenode = record
                    son: ndptr;
                    next: ndptr;
                    case tag: nodetype of
                        oprtr: (operator: packed array [1..10] of char);
                        opnd: (val: real)
                end;
```

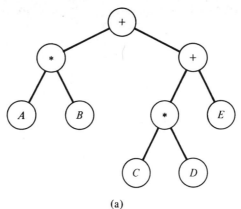

(a)

Preorder: $+ * AB + * CDE$
Inorder: $A * B + C * D + E$
Postorder: $AB * CD * E + +$

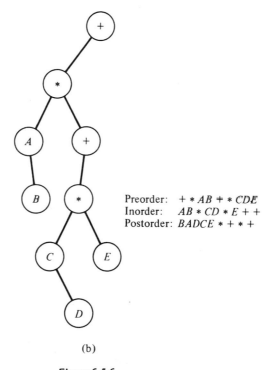

Preorder: $+ * AB + * CDE$
Inorder: $AB * CD * E + +$
Postorder: $BADCE * + * +$

(b)

Figure 6.5.6

The *son* and *next* pointers are used to link together the nodes of a tree as previously illustrated. Since a node may contain information that may be either a number (operand) or a character string (operator), the information portion of the node is the variant portion of the record.

    We wish to write a Pascal function *evaltree*(*p*) which accepts a pointer to such a tree and returns the value of the expression represented by that tree. The routine *evalbintree* presented in Section 2 performs a similar function for binary expressions. *evalbintree* utilizes a function *oper* which accepts an operator symbol and two numerical operands and returns the numerical result of applying the operator to the operands. However, in the case of a general expression, we cannot use such a function, since the number of operands (and hence the number of arguments) varies with the operator. We therefore introduce a new function *apply(p)*, which accepts a pointer to an expression tree which contains a single operator and its numerical operands and returns the result of applying the operator to its operands. For example, the result of calling the function *apply* with parameter *p* pointing to the tree in Figure 6.5.7 is 24. Thus if the root of the tree which is passed to *evaltree* represents an operator, each of its subtrees must be replaced by tree nodes representing the numerical results of their evaluation so that the function *apply* may be called. As the expression is evaluated, the tree nodes representing operands must be freed and operator nodes must be converted to operand nodes.

We present a recursive procedure *replace* which accepts a pointer to an expression tree and replaces the tree with a tree node containing the numerical result of its evaluation.

```
procedure replace (p: ndptr);
var value: real;
    q, r: ndptr;
```

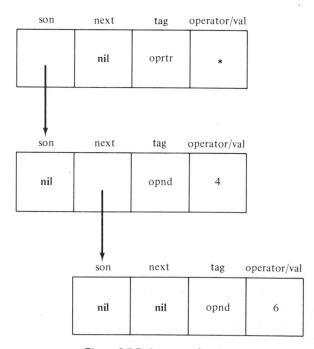

Figure 6.5.7 An expression tree.

```
begin { procedure replace }
    if p↑.tag = oprtr
        { the tree has an operator }
        {          as its root          }
    then begin
            q:= p↑.son;
            while q <> nil
                do begin
                        { replace each of its subtrees }
                        {          by operands          }
                        replace(q);
                        q:= q↑.next
                    end {while...do begin};
            { apply the operator in the root to }
            {    the operands in the subtrees    }
            value:= apply(p);
            { replace the operator by the result }
            p↑.tag:= opnd;
            p↑.val:= value;
            {    free all the subtrees    }
            q:= p↑.son;
            p↑.son:= nil;
            while q <> nil
                do begin
                        r:= q;
                        q:= q↑.next;
                        dispose(r)
                    end {while...do begin}
        end {then begin}
end { procedure replace };
```

The function *evaltree* may now be written as follows:

```
function evaltree (var p: ndptr): real;
var q: ndptr;
begin
    replace(p);
    evaltree:= p↑.val;
    dispose(p)
end { function evaltree };
```

Note that after calling *evaltree(p)* the tree is destroyed and the value of *p* is meaningless. This is a case of a *dangling pointer* in which a pointer variable may contain an address of a variable that has been freed (depending on the action taken by *dispose* for a particular implementation). Pascal programmers who use dynamic variables should be very careful to recognize such pointers and not to use them subsequently.

Other Tree Operations

In constructing a tree, there are several operations which are frequently used. One of these is *setsons*, which accepts a node of a tree that has no sons and a linear list of nodes linked together through the *next* field. *setsons* establishes the nodes in the list as the sons of the node in the tree. The Pascal routine to implement this operation is straightforward (we use the array of nodes implementation).

```
procedure setsons (p, list: ndptr);
       {   p points to a tree node, list to a list   }
       { of nodes linked together through their }
       {                    next fields                    }
begin
    if p = 0
        then error('invalid insertion')
        else if treenode[p].son <> 0
                then error('invalid insertion')
                else node[p].son:= list
end { procedure setsons};
```

Another common operation is *addson(p,x)*, where *p* points to a node in a tree and it is desired to add a node containing *x* as the youngest son of *node(p)*. The Pascal routine to implement *addson* is as follows. The routine calls the auxiliary function *getnode*, which removes a node from the available list and returns a pointer to it.

```
procedure addson (p: ndptr; x: integer);
var q, r: ndptr;
begin
    if p = 0
        then error('invalid insertion')
        else begin
                { the pointer q traverses the list of sons }
                {      of p.  r is one node behind q      }
                r:= 0;
                q:= node[p].son;
                while q <> 0
                    do begin
                            r:= q;
                            q:= node[q].next
                        end;
                { at this point, r points to the youngest }
                {    son of p, or is nil if p has no sons    }
                q:= getnode;
                node[q].info:= x;
                node[q].next:= 0;
```

```
                    if r = 0        {p has no sons}
                        then node[p].son:= q
                        else node[r].next:= q
                    end {else begin}
            end { procedure addson};
```

Note that in order to add a new son to a node, the list of existing sons must be traversed. Since adding a son is a common operation, a representation is often used which makes this operation more efficient. Under this alternative representation, the list of sons is ordered from youngest to oldest rather than vice versa. Thus *son(p)* points to the youngest son of *node(p)*, and *next(p)* points to its next older brother. Under this representation the routine *addson* may be written as follows:

```
procedure addson (p: ndptr; x: integer);
var q: ndptr;
begin
    if p = 0
        then error('invalid insertion')
        else begin
                q:= getnode;
                node[q].info:= x;
                node[q].next:= node[p].son;
                node[p].son:= q
            end
end { procedure addson};
```

Another variation in representing a tree is to allow the *next* field of the last son of a node to point back to its father rather than to contain the nil pointer. This allows a node to be reached from any of its descendants. Of course, there must be an indication within a node as to whether its *next* field points to a brother or a father. This can be accomplished in one of two ways. In the implementation that uses an array of nodes, we can represent a pointer to the father by the negative of the subscript of the father node. An alternative method, which can be used both in the array and dynamic implementation, is to add another field to *treenode* to indicate whether the next field points to a brother or to the father. These two methods are similar to the methods used to represent threads in binary trees.

Alternatively, a *father* field can be included in each node so that it is possible to proceed directly from a node to its father without having to first traverse a possibly long list of brothers.

EXERCISES 1. How many trees exist with n nodes?

2. How many trees exist with n nodes and maximum level m?

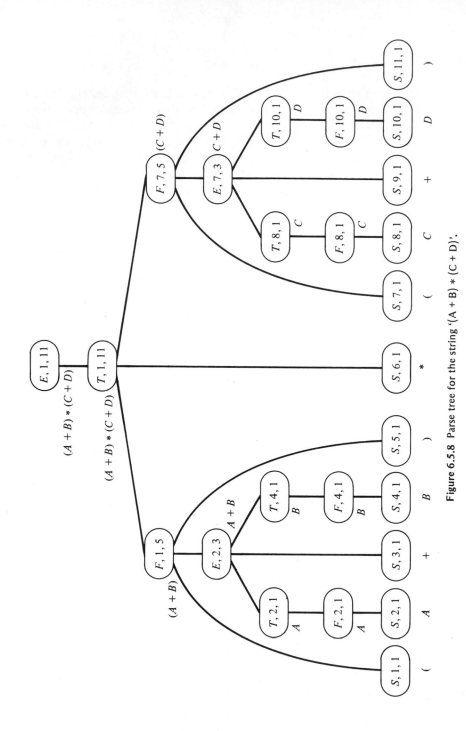

Figure 6.5.8 Parse tree for the string '(A + B) * (C + D)'.

3. Prove that if m pointer fields are set aside in each node of a general tree to point to a maximum of m sons, and if the number of nodes in the tree is n, then the number of nil son pointer fields is $n(m-1)+1$.

4. If a forest is represented by a binary tree as in the text, show that the number of nil right links is 1 greater than the number of nonleafs of the forest.

5. Define the **breadth-first order** of the nodes of a general tree as the root followed by all nodes on level 1, followed by all nodes on level 2, and so on. Within each level, the nodes should be ordered so that children of the same father appear in the same order as they appear in the tree, and if $n1$ and $n2$ have different fathers, $n1$ appears before $n2$ if the father of $n1$ appears before the father of $n2$. Extend the definition to a forest. Write a Pascal program to traverse a forest represented as a binary tree in breadth-first order.

6. Consider the following method of transforming a general tree gt into a strictly binary tree bt. Each node of gt is represented by a leaf of bt. If gt consists of a single node, then bt consists of a single node. Otherwise, bt consists of a new root node and a left subtree lt and a right subtree rt. lt is the strictly binary tree formed recursively from the oldest subtree of gt, and rt is the strictly binary tree formed recursively from gt without its oldest subtree. Write a Pascal routine to convert a general tree into a strictly binary tree.

7. Write a Pascal function *compute* which accepts a pointer to a tree representing an expression with constant operands and returns the result of evaluating the expression without destroying the tree.

8. Write a Pascal program to convert an infix expression into an expression tree. Assume that all nonbinary operators precede their operands. Let the input expression be represented as follows. An operand is represented by the character 'n' followed by a number, an operator by the character 't' followed by a character string representing the operator, and a function by the character 'f' followed by the name of the function.

9. Consider the definition of an expression, term, and factor given at the end of Section 3.2. Given a string of letters, plus signs, asterisks, and parentheses which form a valid expression, a **parse tree** can be formed for the string. Such a tree is illustrated in Figure 6.5.8 for the string $(A+B)*(C+D)$. Each node in such a tree represents a substring and contains a letter (E for expression, T for term, F for factor, or S for symbol) and two integers. The first is the position within the input string where the substring represented by that node begins and the second is the length of the substring. (The substring represented by each node is shown below that node in the figure.) The leafs are all S nodes and represent single symbols of the original input. The root of the tree must be an E node. The sons of any non-S node n represent the substrings that make up the grammatical object represented by n.
   Write a Pascal routine that accepts such a string and constructs a parse tree for it.

6. AN EXAMPLE: GAME TREES

One application of trees is to game playing by computer. We illustrate this application by writing a Pascal program to determine the "best" move in tic-tac-toe from a given board position. Assume that there is a function *evaluate* which accepts a board position and an indication of a player (X or

O) and returns a numerical value which represents how "good" the position seems to be for that player (the larger the value returned by *evaluate*, the better the position). Of course, a winning position yields the largest possible value and a losing position yields the smallest. An example of such an evaluation function for tic-tac-toe is the number of rows, columns, and diagonals remaining open for one player minus the number remaining open for his opponent (except that the value 9 would be returned for a position that wins and −9 for a position that loses). This function does not "look ahead" to consider any possible board positions that might result from the current position—it merely evaluates a static board position.

Given a board position, the best next move could be determined by considering all possible moves and resulting positions. That move that results in the board position with the highest evaluation should be selected. However, such an analysis does not necessarily yield the best move, as can be seen from Figure 6.6.1. This figure illustrates a position and the five possible moves which X can make from that position. Applying the evaluation function described above to the five resulting positions yields the values shown. Four moves yield the same maximum evaluation, although three of them are distinctly inferior to the fourth. (The fourth position yields a certain victory for X while the other three can be drawn by O.) In fact, the move that yields the smallest evaluation is as good or better than the moves that yield a higher evaluation. The foregoing static evaluation function is not good enough to predict the outcome of the game. Although a better evaluation function could easily be produced for the game of tic-tac-toe (even if it were by the brute-force method of listing all positions and the appropriate response), most games are too complex for static evaluators to determine the best response.

Suppose that it were possible to look ahead several moves. Then the choice of a move could be improved considerably. Define the *look ahead level* as the number of future moves to be considered. Starting at any position, it is possible to construct a tree of the possible board positions that may result from each move. Such a tree is called a *game tree*. The game tree for the opening tic-tac-toe position with a look ahead level of 2 is illustrated in Figure 6.6.2. (Actually, other positions do exist but, because

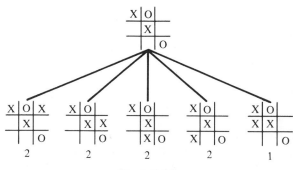

Figure 6.6.1

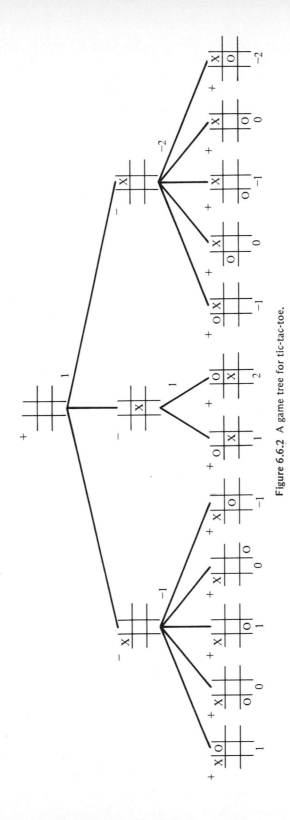

Figure 6.6.2 A game tree for tic-tac-toe.

of symmetry considerations, these are effectively the same as the positions shown.) Note that the maximum level (called the *depth*) of the nodes in such a tree is equal to the look-ahead level.

Let us designate the player who must move at the root's game position as *plus* and the opponent as *minus*. We attempt to find the best move for plus from the root's game position. The remaining nodes of the tree may be designated as *plus nodes* or *minus nodes* depending upon which player must move from that node's position. Each node of Figure 6.6.2 is marked as a plus or minus node.

Suppose that the game positions of all the sons of a plus node have been evaluated for player plus. Then clearly, plus should choose the move that yields the maximum evaluation. Thus the value of a plus node to player plus is the maximum of the values of its sons. On the other hand, once plus has moved, minus will select the move that yields the minimum evaluation for player plus. Thus the value of a minus node to player plus is the minimum of the values of its sons.

Therefore, in order to decide the best move for player plus from the root, the positions in the leafs must be evaluated for player plus using a static evaluation function. These values are then moved up the game tree by assigning to each plus node the maximum of its sons' values and to each minus node the minimum of its sons' values on the assumption that minus will select the move that is worst for plus. The value assigned to each node of Figure 6.6.2 by this process is indicated in that figure immediately below the node. The move that plus should select, given the board position in the root node, is the one that maximizes its value. Thus the opening move for X should be the middle square, as illustrated in Figure 6.6.2. Figure 6.6.3 illustrates the determination of O's best reply. Note that the designation of

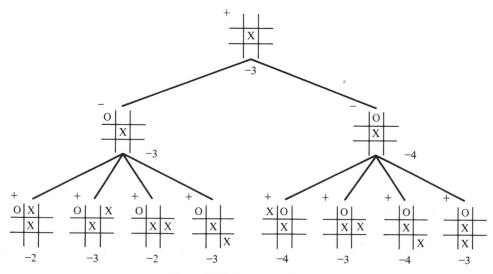

Figure 6.6.3 Computing 0's reply.

"plus" and "minus" depends on whose move is being calculated. Thus in Figure 6.6.2, *X* is designated as plus, while in Figure 6.6.3, *O* is designated as plus. In applying the static evaluation function to a board position, the value of the position to whichever player is designated as plus is computed. This method is called the *minimax* method because, as the tree is climbed, the maximum and minimum functions are applied alternately.

The best move for a player from a given position may be determined by first constructing the game tree and applying a static evaluation function to the leafs. These values are then moved up the tree by applying the minimum and maximum at minus and plus nodes, respectively. Each node of the game tree must include a representation of the board and an indication of whether the node is a plus node or a minus node. An array of nodes is therefore declared by

```
const numnodes = 500;
type  nodeptr = 0..numnodes;
      boxtype = (xval, oval, blank);
      boardtype = array[1..3, 1..3] of boxtype;
      playertype = xval..oval;
      turntype = (plus, minus);
      nodetype = record
                    board: boardtype;
                    turn:  turntype;
                    son:   nodeptr;
                    next:  nodeptr
                 end;
var node: array[1..numnodes] of nodetype;
```

node[*p*].*board*[*i,j*] has the value *xval*, *oval*, or *blank*, depending on whether the square in row *i* and column *j* of *node*[*p*] is occupied by either of the players or is unoccupied. *node*[*p*].*turn* has the value *plus* or *minus*, depending on whether *node*[*p*] is a plus or a minus node, respectively. The remaining two fields of a node are used to position the node within the tree. *node*[*p*].*son* points to the oldest son of *node*[*p*], while *node*[*p*].*next* points to its next younger brother. We assume that the foregoing declaration is global, that an available list of nodes has been established and appropriate *getnode* and *freenode* routines have been written.

The Pascal procedure· *nextmove*(*brd*, *player*, *looklevel*, *newbrd*) computes the best next move. *brd* is a 3 by 3 array representing the current board position; *player* is *xval* or *oval*, depending on whose move is being computed (note that in tic-tac-toe the value of *player* could be computed from *brd*, so that this parameter is not strictly necessary); and *looklevel* is the look-ahead level used in constructing the tree. *newbrd* is an output parameter which represents the best board position that can be achieved by *player* from position *brd*. *nextmove* uses two auxiliary routines, *buildtree* and *bestbranch*. The function *buildtree* builds the game tree and returns a pointer to its root. The procedure *bestbranch* computes the value of two output parameters: *best*, which is a pointer to the tree node representing the best move, and *value*, which is the evaluation of that move using the minimax technique.

```
procedure nextmove (brd: boardtype; looklevel: integer;
                              player: playertype; var newbrd: boardtype);
var tree,best: nodeptr;
    value: integer;
begin
      tree:= buildtree(brd,looklevel);
      bestbranch(tree, player, best, value);
      newbrd:= node[best].board
end { procedure nextmove};
```

The function *buildtree* returns a pointer to the root of a game tree. It uses the auxiliary function *getnode*, which removes a node from the available list and returns a pointer to it. It also uses a routine *expand(p,plevel,depth)* in which *p* is a pointer to a node in a game tree, *plevel* is its level, and *depth* is the depth of the game tree that is to be constructed. *expand* produces the subtree rooted at *p* to the proper depth.

```
function buildtree (brd: boardtype; looklevel: integer): nodeptr;
var tree: nodeptr;
begin
      {create the root of the tree and initialize it}
      tree:= getnode;
      node[tree].board:= brd;
      {the root is a plus node by definition}
      node[tree].turn:= plus;
      node[tree].son:= 0;
      node[tree].next:= 0;
      {create the rest of the game tree}
      expand(tree, 0, looklevel);
      buildtree:= tree
end { function buildtree};
```

expand may be implemented by generating all board positions that may be obtained from the board position of *node[p]* and establishing them as the sons of *p* in the game tree. *expand* then repeatedly calls itself using each of these sons successively as its first parameter until the desired depth is reached. *expand* uses an auxiliary function *generate*, which accepts a board position *brd* and returns a pointer to a list of nodes containing the board positions that can be obtained from *brd*. This list is linked together by the *next* field. We leave the coding of *generate* as an exercise for the reader.

```
procedure expand (p: nodeptr; plevel, depth: integer);
var q: nodeptr;
```

```
begin { procedure expand }
    if plevel < depth
        then begin
                { p is not at the maximum level }
                q:= generate(node[p].board);
                node[p].son:= q;
                while q <> 0  { traverse the list of nodes }
                    do begin
                            if node[p].turn = plus
                                then node[q].turn:= minus
                                else node[q].turn:= plus;
                            node[q].son:= 0;
                            expand(q, plevel+1, depth);
                            q:= node[q].next
                    end {while...do begin}
            end {then begin}
    end { procedure expand };
```

Once the game tree has been created, *bestbranch* evaluates the nodes of the tree. When a pointer to a leaf is passed to *bestbranch*, it calls a function *evaluate*, which statically evaluates the board position of that leaf for the player whose move we are determining. The coding of *evaluate* is left as an exercise. When a pointer to a nonleaf is passed to *bestbranch*, the routine calls itself recursively on each of its sons and then assigns the maximum of its sons' values to the nonleaf if it is a plus node, and the minimum if it is a minus node. *bestbranch* also keeps track of which son yielded this minimum or maximum value.

If $node[p].turn$ is *minus*, then $node[p]$ is a minus node and it is to be assigned the minimum of the values assigned to its sons. If, however, $node[p].turn$ is *plus*, $node[p]$ is a plus node and its value should be the maximum of the values assigned to the sons of $node[p]$. If $min(x,y)$ is the minimum of x and y and $max(x,y)$ is their maximum, then $min(x,y)=-max(-x,-y)$ (you are invited to prove this as a trivial exercise). Thus the correct maximum or minimum can be found as follows. In the case of a plus node, compute the maximum; in the case of a minus node, compute the maximum of the negatives of the values and then reverse the sign of the result. These ideas are incorporated into *bestbranch*. The output parameters *best* and *value* are, respectively, a pointer to that son of the tree's root which maximizes its value and the value of that son which has now been assigned to the root.

```
procedure bestbranch (nd: nodeptr; player: playertype;
                                var best: nodeptr; var value: integer);
    var p,pbest: nodeptr;
        val: integer;
```

```
begin { procedure bestbranch}
    if node[nd].son = 0
        then begin { nd is a leaf }
                    value:= evaluate(node[nd].board, player);
                    best:= nd
            end {then begin}
        else begin
            { the node is not a leaf, traverse the list of sons }
                p:= node[nd].son;
                bestbranch(p, player, best, value);
                best:= p;
                if node[nd].turn = minus
                    then value:= -value;
                p:= node[p].next;
                while p <> 0
                    do begin
                            bestbranch(p, player, pbest, val);
                            if node[nd].turn = minus
                                then val:= - val;
                            if val > value
                                then begin
                                        value:= val;
                                        best:= p
                                    end {then begin};
                            p:= node[p].next
                        end {while...do begin};
                if node[nd].turn = minus
                    then value:= -value
            end {else begin}
    end { procedure bestbranch};
```

1. Examine the routines of this section and determine whether all the parameters are actually necessary. How would you revise the parameter lists?

2. Write the Pascal routines *generate* and *evaluate* as described in the text.

3. Rewrite the programs of this and the preceding sections under the implementation in which each tree node includes a field *father* that contains a pointer to its father. Under which implementation are they more efficient?

4. Write nonrecursive versions of the routines *expand* and *bestbranch* given in the text.

5. Modify the routine *bestbranch* in the text so that the nodes of the tree are freed after they are no longer needed.

6. Combine the processes of building the game tree and evaluating its nodes into a single process so that the entire game tree need not exist at any one time and nodes are freed when no longer necessary.

7. Modify the program of Exercise 6 so that if the evaluation of a minus node is greater than the minimum of the values of its father's older brothers, the program does not bother expanding that minus node's younger brothers, and if the evaluation of a plus node is less than the maximum of the values of its father's older brothers, the program does not bother expanding that plus node's younger brothers. This method is called the *alpha-beta minimax* method. Explain why it is correct.

8. The game of *kalah* is played as follows: Two players each have seven holes, six of which are called *pits* and the seventh a *kalah*. These are arranged according to the following diagram:

Player 1

```
K P P P P P P
  P P P P P P K
```

Player 2

Initially, there are six stones in each pit and no stones in either kalah, so that the opening position looks like this:

```
0 6 6 6 6 6 6
  6 6 6 6 6 6 0
```

The players alternate turns, each turn consisting of one or more moves. To make a move, a player chooses one of his nonempty pits. The stones are removed from that pit and are distributed counterclockwise into the pits and into that player's kalah (the opponent's kalah is skipped), one stone per hole, until there are no stones remaining. For example, if player 1 moves first, a possible opening move might result in the following board position:

```
1 7 7 7 7 7 0
  6 6 6 6 6 6 0
```

If a player's last stone lands in his own kalah, the player gets another move. If the last stone lands in one of his own pits which is empty, that stone and the stones in the opponent's pit directly opposite are removed and placed in the player's kalah. The game ends when either player has no stones remaining in his pits. At that point, all of the stones in his opponent's pits are placed in the opponent's kalah and the game ends. The player with the most stones in his kalah is the winner.

Write a program that accepts a kalah board position and an indication of whose turn it is and produces that player's best move.

9. How would you modify the ideas of the tic-tac-toe program to compute the best move in a game that contains an element of chance, such as backgammon?

10. Why have computers been programmed to play perfect tic-tac-toe but not perfect chess or checkers?

11. The game of *nim* is played as follows. Some number of sticks are placed in a pile. Two players alternate in removing either one or two sticks from the pile. The player to remove the last stick is the loser. Write a Pascal procedure to determine the best move in nim.

7 Graphs and Their Applications

In this chapter we consider a new data structure, the graph. We define some of the terms associated with graphs and show how to implement them in Pascal. We also present several applications of graphs.

1. GRAPHS

A *graph* consists of a set of *nodes* (or *vertices*) and a set of *arcs*. Each arc in a graph is specified by a pair of nodes. Figure 7.1.1a illustrates a graph. The set of nodes is {*A*,*B*,*C*,*D*,*E*,*F*,*G*,*H*} and the set of arcs is {(*A*,*B*),(*A*,*D*), (*A*,*C*),(*C*,*D*),(*C*,*F*),(*E*,*G*),(*A*,*A*)}. If the pairs of nodes that make up the arcs are ordered pairs, the graph is said to be a *directed graph* (or *digraph*). Figure 7.1.1b, c, and d illustrate three digraphs. The arrows between nodes represent arcs. The head of each arrow represents the second node in the ordered pair of nodes making up an arc, while the tail of each arrow represents the first node in the pair. The set of arcs for the graph of Figure 7.1.1b is {⟨*A*,*B*⟩,⟨*A*,*C*⟩,⟨*A*,*D*⟩,⟨*C*,*D*⟩,⟨*F*,*C*⟩,⟨*E*,*G*⟩,⟨*A*,*A*⟩}. We use parentheses to indicate an unordered pair and angled brackets to indicate an ordered pair. In the remainder of this chapter we restrict our attention to digraphs.

Note that a graph need not be a tree (Figure 7.1.1a, b, and d) but that a tree must be a graph (Figure 7.1.1c). Note also that a node need not have any arcs associated with it (node *H* in Figure 7.1.1a and b).

A node *n* is *incident* to an arc *x* if *n* is one of the two nodes in the ordered pair of nodes that comprise *x*. (We also say that *x* is incident to *n*.) The *degree* of a node is the number of arcs incident to it. The *indegree* of a node *n* is the number of arcs that have *n* as the head and the *outdegree* of *n* is the number of arcs that have *n* as the tail. For example, node *A* in Figure 7.1.1d has indegree 1, outdegree 2, and degree 3. A node *n* is *adjacent* to a node *m* if there is an arc from *m* to *n*.

A *relation R* on a set *A* is a set of ordered pairs of elements of *A*. If ⟨*x*,*y*⟩ is a member of a relation *R*, then *x* is said to be *related* to *y* in *R*. For example, if *A* = {3,5,6,8,10,17}, then the set *R* = {⟨3,10⟩,⟨5,6⟩,⟨5,8⟩,

318

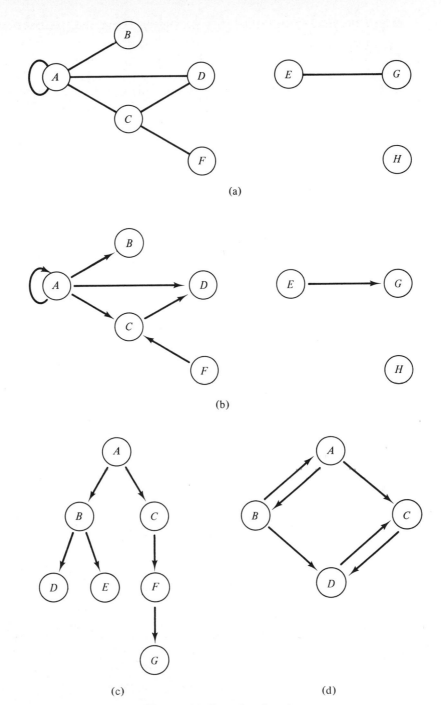

(a)

(b)

(c)   (d)

Figure 7.1.1 Examples of graphs.

$\langle 6,17 \rangle, \langle 8,17 \rangle, \langle 10,17 \rangle\}$ is a relation on A. The relation R may be described by saying that x is related to y if x is less than y and the remainder obtained by dividing y by x is odd. $\langle 8,17 \rangle$ is a member of this relation since 8 is smaller than 17 and the remainder on dividing 17 by 8 is 1, which is odd. A relation may be represented by a graph in which the nodes represent the underlying set and the arcs represent the ordered pairs of the relation. Figure 7.1.2a illustrates the graph representing the foregoing relation. A number may be associated with each arc of a graph as in Figure 7.1.2b. In that figure, the number associated with each arc is the remainder obtained by

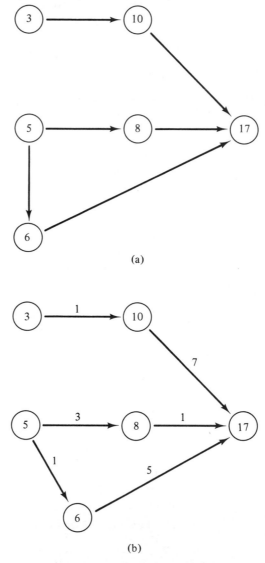

(a)

(b)

Figure 7.1.2 Relations and graphs.

CHAP. 7: GRAPHS AND THEIR APPLICATIONS

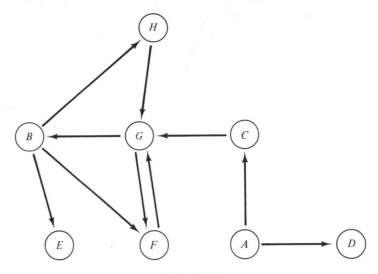

Figure 7.1.3

dividing the integer at the head of the arc by the integer at the tail. Such a graph, in which a number is associated with each arc, is called a *weighted graph* or a *network*. The number associated with an arc is called its *weight*.

We identify several primitive operations which are useful in dealing with graphs. The operation *join* (a,b) adds an arc from node a to node b if one does not already exist. *joinwt* (a,b,x) adds an arc from a to b with weight x in a weighted graph. *remv* (a,b) and *remvwt* (a,b,x) remove an arc from a to b if one exists (*remvwt* also sets x to its weight). Although we may also want to add or delete nodes from a graph, we postpone a disucssion of these possibilities until a later section. The function *adjacent* (a,b) returns *true* if b is adjacent to a, and *false* otherwise.

A *path of length k* from node a to node b is defined as a sequence of $k+1$ nodes $n_1, n_2, \ldots, n_{k+1}$ such that $n_1 = a$, $n_{k+1} = b$, and *adjacent* (n_i, n_{i+1}) is *true* for all i between 1 and k. If for some integer k, a path of length k exists between a and b, there is a *path* from a to b. A path from a node to itself is called a *cycle*. If a graph contains a cycle, it is *cyclic*; otherwise it is *acyclic*.

Consider the graph of Figure 7.1.3. There is a path of length 1 from A to C, two paths of length 2 from B to G, and a path of length 3 from A to F. There is no path from B to C. There are cycles from B to B, from F to F, and from H to H. Be sure that you can find all paths of length less than 9 and all cycles in the figure.

An Application of Graphs

We now consider an example. We wish to read one input line containing four integers, followed by any number of input lines with two integers each. The first integer on the first line, n, represents a number of cities which for simplicity are numbered from 1 to n. The second and third integers on that line are between 1 and *n* and represent two cities, *A* and *B*. It is desired to travel from city *A* to city *B* using exactly *nr* roads, where *nr* is the fourth integer on the first input line. Each subsequent input line contains two integers representing two cities. This indicates that there is a road from the first city to the second. The problem is to determine whether there is a path of required length by which one can travel from city *A* to city *B*.

A plan for solution is the following. Create a graph with the cities as nodes and the roads as arcs. To find a path of length *nr* from node *A* to node *B*, look for a node *C* such that an arc exists from *A* to *C* and a path of length *nr*-1 exists from *C* to *B*. If these conditions are satisfied for some node *C*, the desired path exists. If the conditions are not satisfied for any node *C*, the desired path does not exist. The algorithm uses an auxiliary recursive function *findpath* (*k*,*a*,*b*). This function returns *true* if there is a path of length *k* from *A* to *B* and *false* otherwise. The algorithms for the program and the function follow:

```
read (n);      {number of cities}
create n nodes and label them from 1 to n;
read (a,b);      {      seek path from a to b      }
read (nr);      {desired number of roads to take}
while there is more input
    do begin
            readln(city1, city2);
            join(city1, city2)
        end {while...do begin};
if findpath (nr,a,b)
    then write ('a path exists from ', a, ' to ', b, ' in ',nr, ' steps')
    else write ('no path exists from ',a, ' to ', b,' in ',nr, ' steps')
```

The algorithm for the function *findpath* (*k*,*a*,*b*) follows:

```
if k=1
    then {search for a path of length 1}
        if adjacent (a, b)
            then findpath := true
            else findpath := false
    else begin
            findpath := false; {assume that no path exists}
            for c := 1 to n
                do if adjacent (a, c)
                        then if findpath (k-1, c, b)
                                then findpath := true
        end {else begin}
```

Although the foregoing algorithm is a solution to the problem, it has several deficiencies. Many paths are investigated several times during the recursive process. Also, although the algorithm must actually check each possible path, the final result merely ascertains whether a desired path exists; it does not produce the path itself. More likely than not, it is desirable to find the arcs of the path in addition to knowing whether or not a path exists. Also, the algorithm does not test for the existence of a path regardless of length; it only tests for a path of specific length. We explore solutions to some of these problems later in this chapter and in the exercises.

Pascal Representation of Graphs

Let us now turn to the question of representing graphs in Pascal. Suppose that the number of nodes in the graph is constant (i.e., arcs may be added or deleted but nodes may not). A graph with 50 nodes could then be declared as follows:

```
const maxnodes = 50;
type  nodeptr = 1..maxnodes;
      arc = record
              adj: boolean;
              { information associated with each arc }
            end;
      node = record
              {information associated with each node}
             end;
      graph = record
                nodes: array[nodeptr] of node;
                arcs: array[nodeptr,nodeptr] of arc
              end;
var   g: graph;
```

Each node of the graph is represented by an integer between 1 and *maxnodes* and the array field *nodes* represents the appropriate information assigned to each node. The array field *arcs* is a two-dimensional array representing every possible ordered pair of nodes. The value of $g.arcs[i,j].adj$ is either *true* or *false*, depending upon whether or not node j is adjacent to node i. The two-dimensional array $g.arcs[nodeptr,nodeptr].adj$ is called an *adjacency matrix*. In the case of a weighted graph, information can also be assigned to each arc.

Frequently, the nodes of a graph are numbered from 1 to *maxnodes* and no information is assigned to them. Also, we may be interested in the existence of arcs but not in any weights or other information about them. In such cases the graph could be declared simply by

```
const maxnodes = 50;
type  nodeptr = 1..maxnodes;
      adjmatrix = array[nodeptr,nodeptr] of boolean;
var   adj: adjmatrix;
```

In effect, the graph is totally described by its adjacency matrix. We present the code for the primitive operations described above in the case where a graph is described by its adjacency matrix.

```
procedure join (var adj: adjmatrix; node1,node2: nodeptr);
begin {add an arc from node1 to node2}
     adj[node1, node2] := true
end {procedure join};

procedure remv (var adj: adjmatrix; node1, node2: nodeptr);
begin {delete arc from node1 to node2 if one exists}
     adj[node1, node2] := false
end {procedure remv};

function adjacent (adj: adjmatrix; node1, node2: nodeptr): boolean;
begin {test whether there is an arc from node1 to node2}
     if adj[node1, node2]
       then adjacent:= true
       else adjacent:= false
end {function adjacent};
```

A weighted graph with a fixed number of nodes may be declared by

```
type arc = record
              adj: boolean;
              weight: integer
           end;
     arcs = array[nodeptr,nodeptr] of arc;
var  g: arcs;
```

The routine *joinwt*, which adds an arc from *node*1 to *node*2 with a given weight *wt*, may be coded as follows:

```
procedure joinwt (var g: arcs; node1,node2: nodeptr; wt: integer);
begin
     g[node1, node2].adj:= true;
     g[node1, node2].weight:= wt
end {procedure joinwt};
```

The routine *remvwt* is left to the reader as an exercise.

Transitive Closure

Let us assume that a graph is completely described by its adjacency matrix, *adj* (i.e., no data is associated with the nodes and the graph is not weighted). Consider the logical expression $adj[i,k]$ *and* $adj[k,j]$. Its value is *true* if and only if the values of both $adj[i,k]$ and $adj[k,j]$ are *true*, which implies that there is an arc from node i to node k and an arc from node k to node j. Thus $adj[i,k]$ *and* $adj[k,j]$ equals *true* if and only if there is a path of length two from i to j passing through k.

Now consider the expression

$$(adj[i,1] \textbf{ and } adj[1,j]) \textbf{ or } (adj[i,2] \textbf{ and } adj[2,j])$$
$$\textbf{or}\ldots\textbf{or}\ (adj[i,maxnodes] \textbf{ and } adj[maxnodes,j])$$

The value of this expression is *true* only if there is a path of length two from node i to node j either through node 1 or through node 2, . . . , or through node *maxnodes*. This is the same as saying that the expression evaluates to *true* if and only if there is some path of length two from node i to node j. Consider an array adj_2 such that $adj_2[i,j]$ is the value of the foregoing expression. adj_2 is called the ***path matrix of length 2***. $adj_2[i,j]$ indicates whether or not there is a path of length two between i and j. [If you are familiar with matrix multiplication, you should realize that adj_2 is the product of *adj* with itself, with numerical multiplication replaced by conjunction (the ***and*** operation) and addition replaced by disjunction (the ***or*** operation).] adj_2 is said to be the ***boolean product*** of *adj* with itself.

Figure 7.1.4 illustrates this process. Figure 7.1.4a depicts a graph and its adjacency matrix in which *true* is represented by 1 and *false* is represented by 0. Figure 7.1.4b is the boolean product of that matrix with itself and thus is the path matrix of length two for the graph. Convince yourself that a 1 appears in row i, column j of the matrix of Figure 7.1.4b if and only if there is a path of length two from node i to node j in the graph.

Similarly, define adj_3, the path matrix of length three, as the boolean product of adj_2 with *adj*. $adj_3[i,j]$ equals *true* if and only if there is a path

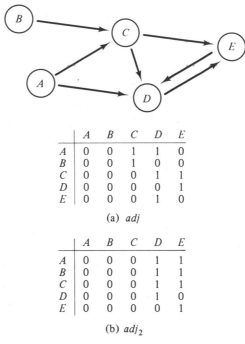

	A	B	C	D	E
A	0	0	1	1	0
B	0	0	1	0	0
C	0	0	0	1	1
D	0	0	0	0	1
E	0	0	0	1	0

(a) *adj*

	A	B	C	D	E
A	0	0	0	1	1
B	0	0	0	1	1
C	0	0	0	1	1
D	0	0	0	1	0
E	0	0	0	0	1

(b) adj_2

Figure 7.1.4

	A	B	C	D	E
A	0	0	0	1	1
B	0	0	0	1	1
C	0	0	0	1	1
D	0	0	0	0	1
E	0	0	0	1	0

(a) adj_3

	A	B	C	D	E
A	0	0	0	1	1
B	0	0	0	1	1
C	0	0	0	1	1
D	0	0	0	1	0
E	0	0	0	0	1

(b) adj_4

Figure 7.1.5

of length three from i to j. In general, to compute the path matrix of length l, form the boolean product of the path matrix of length $l-1$ with the adjacency matrix. Figure 7.1.5 illustrates the matrices adj_3 and adj_4 of the graph in Figure 7.1.4a.

Assume that we want to know whether a path of length three or less exists between two nodes of a graph. If such a path exists between nodes i and j, it must be of length one, two, or three. If there is a path of length three or less between nodes i and j, the value of

$$adj[i,j] \ or \ adj_2[i,j] \ or \ adj_3[i,j]$$

must be *true*. Figure 7.1.6 shows the matrix formed by *or*ing the matrices adj, adj_2, and adj_3. This matrix contains the value *true* (represented by the value 1 in the figure) in row i, column j, if and only if there is a path of length three or less from node i to node j.

Suppose that we wish to construct a matrix *path* such that *path*$[i,j]$ equals *true* if and only if there is some path from node i to node j (of any length). Clearly,

$$path[i,j] = adj[i,j] \ or \ adj_2[i,j] \ or \ ...$$

	A	B	C	D	E
A	0	0	1	1	1
B	0	0	1	1	1
C	0	0	0	1	1
D	0	0	0	1	1
E	0	0	0	1	1

Figure 7.1.6

Unfortunately, this equation cannot be used in computing *path*, since the process that it describes is an infinite one. However, if the graph has *n* nodes, it must true that

$$path[i,j] = adj[i,j] \text{ or } adj_2[i,j] \text{ or } \ldots \text{ or } adj_n[i,j] .$$

This is because if there is a path of length $m > n$ from i to j such as $i, i_2, i_3, \ldots,$ i_m, j, there must be another path from i to j of length less than or equal to n. To see this, note that since there are only n nodes in the graph, at least one node k must appear in the path twice. The path from i to j can be shortened by removing the cycle from k to k. This process is repeated until no two nodes in the path (except possibly i and j) are equal and therefore the path is of length n or less. Figure 7.1.7 illustrates the matrix *path* for the graph of Figure 7.1.4a. The matrix *path* is often called the ***transitive closure*** of the matrix *adj*.

We may write a Pascal routine that accepts an adjacency matrix *adj*, and computes its transitive closure *path*. This routine uses an auxiliary routine *prod*(*a*,*b*,*c*), which sets the array *c* equal to the boolean product of *a* and *b*.

```
procedure transclose (adj: adjmatrix; var path: adjmatrix);
var i,j,k: nodeptr;
      newprod,adjprod: adjmatrix;
begin
      adjprod:= adj;
      path:= adj;
      for i:= 1 to maxnodes - 1
            {i represents the number of times adj has}
            {    been multiplied by itself to obtain    }
            { adjprod. At this point path represents }
            {        all paths of length i or less        }
      do begin
            prod(adjprod, adj, newprod);
            for j:= 1 to maxnodes
                do for k:= 1 to maxnodes
                    do path[j,k] := path[j,k] or newprod[j,k] ;
            adjprod:= newprod
      end {for...do begin}
end {procedure transclose};
```

	A	B	C	D	E
A	0	0	1	1	1
B	0	0	1	1	1
C	0	0	0	1	1
D	0	0	0	1	1
E	0	0	0	1	1

Figure 7.1.7 *path = adj or adj_2 or adj_3 or adj_4 or adj_5.*

The routine *prod* may be written as follows:

```
procedure prod (a, b: adjmatrix; var c: adjmatrix);
var val: boolean;
    i, j, k: integer;
begin
    for i:= 1 to maxnodes {pass through rows}
        do for j:= 1 to maxnodes {pass through columns}
            do begin {compute c[i,j]}
                val:= false;
                for k:= 1 to maxnodes
                    do val:= val or (a[i,k] and b[k,j]);
                c[i,j] := val
            end {for...do begin}
end {procedure prod};
```

Warshall's Algorithm

The method described above is quite inefficient. Let us see if a more efficient method to compute *path* can be produced. Let us define the matrix $path_k$ such that $path_k[i,j]$ equals *true* if and only if there is a path from node i to node j which does not pass through any nodes numbered higher than k (except, possibly, for i and j themselves). How can the value of $path_{k+1}[i,j]$ be obtained from $path_k$? Clearly, for any i and j such that $path_k[i,j]=true$, $path_{k+1}[i,j]$ must equal *true* (why?). The only situation in which $path_{k+1}[i,j]$ can equal *true* while $path_k[i,j]$ equals *false* is if there is a path from i to j passing through node $k+1$ but there is no path from i to j passing through only nodes 1 through k. But this means that there must be a path from i to $k+1$ passing through only nodes 1 through k and a similar path from $k+1$ to j. Thus $path_{k+1}[i,j]=true$ if and only if one of the following two conditions holds:

1. $path_k[i,j]=true$ or
2. $path_k[i,k+1]=true$ and $path_k[k+1,j]=true$.

This means that $path_{k+1}[i,j]$ equals $path_k[i,j]$ *or* $(path_k[i,k+1]$ *and* $path_k[k+1,j])$. An algorithm to obtain the matrix $path_k$ from the matrix $path_{k-1}$ based on this observation follows:

```
for i:= 1 to maxnodes
    do for j:= 1 to maxnodes
        do pathₖ[i,j] := pathₖ₋₁[i,j] or (pathₖ₋₁[i,k] and pathₖ₋₁[k,j])
```

This may be logically simplified and made more efficient as follows:

```
pathₖ:= pathₖ₋₁;
for i:= 1 to maxnodes
    do if pathₖ₋₁(i,k)
        then for j:= 1 to maxnodes
            do pathₖ[i,j] := pathₖ₋₁[i,j] or pathₖ₋₁[k,j]
```

Clearly, $path_0[i,j]=adj$ since the only way to go from node i to node j without passing through any other nodes is to go directly from i to j. Further, $path_{maxnodes}[i,j]=path[i,j]$ since if a path may pass through any nodes numbered from 1 to *maxnodes*, then any path from node i to node j may be selected. The following Pascal routine may therefore be used to compute the transitive closure.

```
procedure transclose (adj: adjmatrix; var path: adjmatrix);
var i,j,k: nodeptr;
begin
        path:= adj; { path starts off as adj}
        for k:= 1 to maxnodes
            do for i:= 1 to maxnodes
                    do if path[i,k]
                        then for j:= 1 to maxnodes
                                do path[i,j] := path[i,j] or path[k,j]
    end {procedure transclose};
```

This method of finding the transitive closure is often called *Warshall's Algorithm*, after its discoverer.

EXERCISES

1. For the graph of Figure 7.1.1:

   (a) Find its adjacency matrix.
   (b) Find its path matrix using powers of the adjacency matrix.
   (c) Find its path matrix using Warshall's Algorithm.

2. Draw a digraph to correspond to each of the following relations on the integers from 1 to 12:

   (a) x is related to y if $x-y$ is evenly divisible by 3.
   (b) x is related to y if $x+10*y < x*y$.
   (c) x is related to y if the remainder on division of x by y is 2.

   Compute the adjacency and path matrices for each of these relations.

3. A node $n1$ is **reachable** from a node $n2$ in a graph if $n1$ equals $n2$ or there is a path from $n2$ to $n1$. Write a Pascal function $reach(adj,i,j)$ which accepts an adjacency matrix and two integers and determines if the jth node in the digraph is reachable from the ith node.

4. Write Pascal routines which, given an adjacency matrix and two nodes of a graph, compute:

   (a) The number of paths of a given length existing between them.
   (b) The total number of paths existing between them.

5. A relation on a set S (and its corresponding digraph) is **reflexive** if every element of S is related to itself.

   (a) What must be true of a digraph if it represents a reflexive relation?
   (b) Give an example of a reflexive relation and draw its corresponding digraph.

(c) What must be true of the adjacency matrix of a reflexive digraph?

(d) Write a Pascal routine that accepts an adjacency matrix and determines if the digraph represents a reflexive relation.

6. A relation on a set S (and its corresponding digraph) is *irreflexive* if no element of S is related to itself.

(a) What must be true of a digraph if it represents an irreflexive relation?

(b) Give an example of an irreflexive relation and draw its corresponding digraph.

(c) Does there exist a relation that is neither reflexive nor irreflexive? (See Exercise 5.)

(d) What must be true of the adjacency matrix of an irreflexive digraph?

(e) Write a Pascal routine that accepts an adjacency matrix and determines if the digraph it represents is irreflexive.

7. A relation on a set S (and its corresponding digraph) is *symmetric* if for any two elements x and y in S such that x is related to y, y is also related to x.

(a) What must be true of a digraph if it represents a symmetric relation?

(b) Give an example of a symmetric relation and draw its digraph.

(c) What must be true of the adjacency matrix of a symmetric digraph?

(d) Write a Pascal routine that accepts an adjacency matrix and determines if the digraph it represents is symmetric.

8. A relation on a set S (and its corresponding digraph) is *antisymmetric* if for any two distinct elements x and y in S such that x is related to y, y is not related to x.

(a) What must be true of a digraph if it represents an antisymmetric relation?

(b) Give an example of an antisymmetric relation and its digraph.

(c) Does there exist a relation that is both symmetric and antisymmetric? (See Exercise 7.)

(d) What must be true of the adjacency matrix of an antisymmetric digraph?

(e) Write a Pascal routine that accepts an adjacency matrix and determines if the digraph it represents is antisymmetric.

9. A relation on a set S (and its corresponding digraph and adjacency matrix) is *transitive* if for any three elements x, y, and z in S, if x is related to y and y is related to z, then x is related to z.

(a) What must be true of a digraph if it represents a transitive relation?

(b) Give an example of a transitive relation and draw its digraph.

(c) What must be true of the boolean product of the adjacency matrix of a transitive digraph with itself?

(d) Write a Pascal routine that accepts an adjacency matrix and determines if the digraph it represents is transitive.

(e) Prove that the transitive closure of any digraph is transitive.

(f) Prove that the smallest transitive digraph which includes all nodes and arcs of a given digraph is the transitive closure of that digraph.

10. Given a digraph, prove that it is possible to renumber its nodes so that the resultant adjacency matrix is lower triangular (see Exercise 1.2.8) if and only if the digraph is acyclic. Write a Pascal program *lowtri*(*adj,ltadj,perm*) which accepts an adjacency matrix *adj* of an acyclic graph and creates a lower triangular adjacency matrix *ltadj* which represents the same graph. *perm* is a one-dimensional array such that *perm*[i] is set to the new number assigned to the node that was numbered i in the matrix *adj*.

2. A FLOW PROBLEM

In this section we consider a real-world problem and illustrate a solution that uses a weighted graph. There are a number of formulations of this problem whose solutions carry over to a wide range of applications. We present one such formulation here and refer the reader to the literature for alternative versions.

Assume a water pipe system as in Figure 7.2.1a. Each arc represents a pipe and the number above each arc represents the capacity of that pipe in gallons per minute. The nodes represent points at which pipes are joined and water is transferred from one pipe to another. Two nodes, S and T, are designated as a *source* of water and a *user* of water (or a *sink*), respectively. This means that water originating at S must be carried through the pipe system to T. Water may flow through a pipe in only one direction (pressure-sensitive valves may be used to prevent water from flowing backward) and there are no pipes entering S or leaving T. Thus a weighted directed graph, as in Figure 7.2.1a, is an ideal data structure to model the situation.

We would like to maximize the amount of water flowing from the source to the sink. Although the source may be able to produce water at a prodigious rate and the sink may be able to consume water at a comparable rate, the pipe system may not have the capacity to carry it all from the source to the sink. Thus the limiting factor of the entire system is the pipe capacity. Many other real-world problems are similar in nature. The system could be an electrical network, a railway system, a communications network, or any other distribution system in which one wants to maximize the amount of an item being delivered from one point to another.

Define a *capacity function*, $c(a,b)$, where a and b are nodes, as follows. If *adjacent*(a,b) (i.e., if there is a pipe from a to b), then $c(a,b)$ is the capacity of the pipe from a to b. If there is no pipe from a to b, then $c(a,b)=0$. At any point in the operation of the system, a given amount of water (possibly 0) flows through each pipe. Define a *flow function*, $f(a,b)$, where a and b are nodes, as 0 if b is not adjacent to a, and as the amount of water flowing through the pipe from a to b otherwise. Clearly, $f(a,b) \geqslant 0$ for all nodes a and b. Furthermore, $f(a,b) \leqslant c(a,b)$ for all nodes a and b since a pipe may not carry more water than its capacity. Let v be the amount of water that flows through the system from S to T. Then the amount of water leaving S through all pipes equals the amount of water entering T through all pipes and both these amounts equal v. This can be stated by the equality

$$\sum_{x \in nodes} f(S, x) = v = \sum_{x \in nodes} f(x, T)$$

No node other than S can produce water and no node other than T can absorb water. Thus the amount of water leaving any node other than S or T is equal to the amount of water entering that node. This can be stated by

$$\sum_{y \in nodes} f(x,y) = \sum_{y \in nodes} f(y,x) \qquad \text{for all nodes } x \neq S, T$$

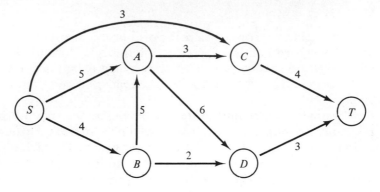

(a) A flow problem.

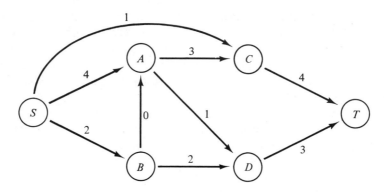

(b) A flow function.

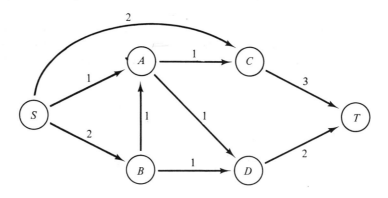

(c) A flow function.

Figure 7.2.1

Define the *inflow* of a node x as the total flow entering x and the *outflow* as the total flow leaving x. The conditions above may be rewritten as

$$outflow(S) = inflow(T) = v$$
$$inflow(x) \;\; = outflow(x) \quad \text{for all } x \neq S, T$$

Several flow functions may exist for a given graph and capacity function. Figure 7.2.1b and c illustrate two possible flow functions for the graph of Figure 7.2.1a. Make sure that you understand why both of them are valid flow functions and why both satisfy the foregoing equations and inequalities.

We wish to find a flow function that maximizes the value of v, the amount of water going from S to T. Such a flow function is called *optimal*. Clearly, the flow function of Figure 7.2.1b is better than the one of Figure 7.2.1c, since v equals 7 in the former but only 5 in the latter. See if you can find a flow function that is better than the one of Figure 7.2.1b.

One valid flow function can be achieved by setting $f(a,b)$ to 0 for all nodes a and b. Of course, this flow function is least optimal since no water flows from S to T. Given a flow function, it can be improved so that the flow from S to T is increased. However, the improved version must satisfy all the conditions for a valid flow function. In particular, if the flow entering any node (except for S or T) is increased or decreased, the flow leaving that node must be increased or decreased correspondingly. The strategy for producing an optimal flow function is to begin with the zero flow function and to successively improve upon it until an optimal flow function is produced.

Improving a Flow Function

Given a flow function f, there are two ways to improve upon it. One way consists of finding a path $S = x_1, x_2, \ldots, x_n = T$ from S to T such that the flow along each arc in the path is strictly less than the capacity [i.e., $f(x_{k-1}, x_k) < c(x_{k-1}, x_k)$ for all k between 2 and n]. The flow can be increased on each arc in such a path by the minimum value of $c(x_{k-1}, x_k) - f(x_{k-1}, x_k)$ for all k between 2 and n [so that when the flow has been increased along the entire path there is at least one arc $\langle x_{k-1}, x_k \rangle$ in the path for which $f(x_{k-1}, x_k) = c(x_{k-1}, x_k)$ and through which the flow may not be increased].

This may be illustrated by the graph of Figure 7.2.2a, which gives the capacity and the current flow, respectively, for each arc. There are two paths from S to T with positive flow [(S,A,C,T) and (S,B,D,T)]. However, each of these paths contains one arc ($\langle A,C \rangle$ and $\langle B,D \rangle$) in which the flow equals the capacity. Thus the flow along these paths may not be improved. However, the path (S,A,D,T) is such that the capacity of each arc in the path is greater than its current flow. The maximum amount by which the flow can be increased along this path is 1, since the flow along arc $\langle D,T \rangle$ cannot exceed 3. The resulting flow function is shown in Figure 7.2.2b. The total flow from S to T has been increased from 5 to 6. To see that the

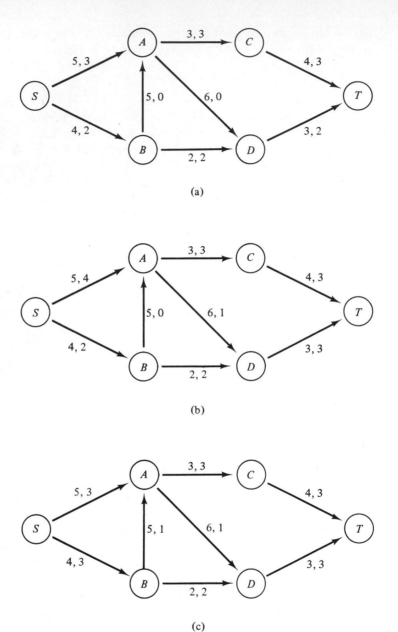

(a)

(b)

(c)

Figure 7.2.2 Increasing the flow in a graph.

result is still a valid flow function, note that for each node (except T) whose inflow is increased, the outflow is increased by the same amount.

Are there any other paths whose flow can be improved? In this example, you should satisfy yourself that there are not. However, given the graph of Figure 7.2.2a, we could have chosen to improve the path (S,B,A,D,T). The resulting flow function is illustrated in Figure 7.2.2c. This function also provides for a net flow of 6 from S to T and is therefore neither better nor worse than the flow function of Figure 7.2.2b.

Even if there is no path whose flow may be improved, there may be another method of improving the net flow from the source to the sink. This is illustrated by Figure 7.2.3. In Figure 7.2.3a there is no path from S to T whose flow may be improved. But if the flow from X to Y is reduced, the flow from X to T can be increased. To compensate for the decrease in the inflow of Y, the flow from S to Y could be increased, thereby increasing the net flow from S to T. The flow from X to Y can be redirected to T as shown in Figure 7.2.3b, and the net flow from S to T can thereby be increased from 4 to 7.

We may generalize this second method as follows. Suppose that there is a path from S to some node y, a path from some node x to T, and a path from x to y with positive flow. Then the flow along the path from x to y may be reduced and the flows from x to T and from S to y may be increased by the same amount. This amount is the minimum of the flow from x to y and the differences between capacity and flow in the paths from S to y and x to T.

These two methods may be combined by proceeding through the graph from S to T as follows. The amount of water emanating from S toward T can

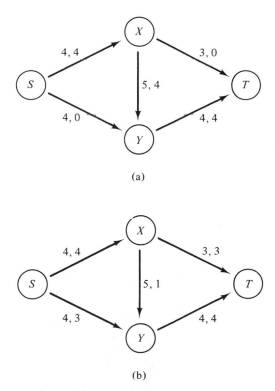

(a)

(b)

Figure 7.2.3 Increasing the flow in a graph.

be increased by any amount (since we have assumed no limit on the amount that can be produced by the source) only if the pipes from S to T can carry the increase. Suppose that the pipe capacity from S to x allows the amount of water entering x to be increased by an amount a. If the pipe capacity to carry the increase from x to T exists, then the increase can be made. Then if a node y is adjacent to x (i.e., there is an arc $\langle x,y \rangle$), the amount of water emanating from y toward T can be increased by the minimum of a and the unused capacity of arc $\langle x,y \rangle$. This is an application of the first method. Similarly, if node x is adjacent to some node y (i.e., there is an arc $\langle y,x \rangle$), then the amount of water emanating from y toward T can be increased by the minimum of a and the existing flow from y to x. This can be done by reducing the flow from y to x, as in the second method. Proceeding in this fashion from S to T, the amount by which the flow to T may be increased can be determined.

Define a *semipath* from S to T as a sequence of nodes $S = x_1, x_2, \ldots, x_n = T$ such that, for all $1 < i \leqslant n$, either $\langle x_{i-1}, x_i \rangle$ or $\langle x_i, x_{i-1} \rangle$ is an arc. Using the foregoing technique, we may describe an algorithm to discover a semipath from S to T such that the flow to each node in the semipath may be increased. This is done by building upon already discovered partial semipaths from S. If the last node in a discovered partial semipath from S is a, the algorithm considers extending it to any node b such that either $\langle a,b \rangle$ or $\langle b,a \rangle$ is an arc. The partial semipath is extended to b only if the extension can be made in such a way that the inflow to b can be increased. Once a partial semipath has been extended to a node b, that node is removed from consideration as an extension of some other partial semipath. (This is because at this point we are trying to discover a single semipath from S to T.) The algorithm, of course, keeps track of the amount by which the inflow to b may be increased and whether its increase is due to considerations of the arc $\langle a,b \rangle$ or $\langle b,a \rangle$.

This process continues until some partial semipath from S has been completed by extending it to T. The algorithm then proceeds backward along the semipath, adjusting all flows until S is reached. (This will be illustrated shortly with an example.) The entire process is then repeated in an attempt to discover yet another such semipath from S to T. When no partial semipath may be successfully extended, the flow cannot be increased and the existing flow is optimal. (You are asked to prove this as an exercise.)

AN EXAMPLE

Let us illustrate this process with an example. Consider the arcs and capacities of the weighted graph of Figure 7.2.4. We begin by assuming a flow of 0 and attempt to discover an optimal flow. Figure 7.2.4a illustrates the initial situation. The two numbers next to each arc represent the capacity and current flow, respectively. We may extend a semipath from S to (S,X) and (S,Z), respectively. The flow from S to X may be increased by 4 and the flow from S to Z may be increased by 6. The semipath (S,X) may be extended to (S,X,W) and (S,X,Y) with corresponding increases of flow to W

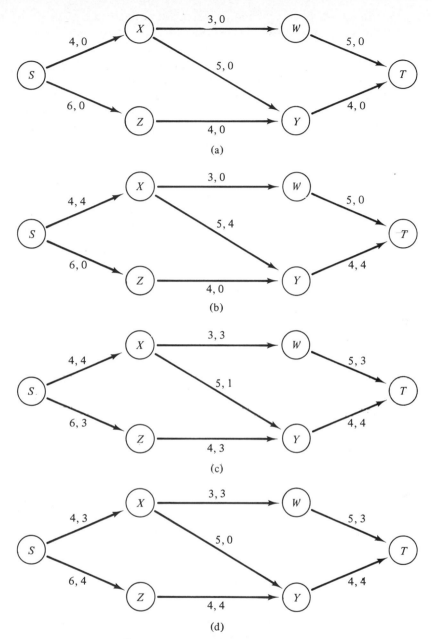

Figure 7.2.4 Producing an optimum flow.

and Y of 3 and 4, respectively. The semipath (S,X,Y) may be extended to (S,X,Y,T) with an increase of flow to T of 4. [Note that at this point we could have chosen to extend (S,X,W) to (S,X,W,T). Similarly, we could have extended (S,Z) to (S,Z,Y) rather than (S,X) to (S,X,W) and (S,X,Y). These decisions are arbitrary.]

Since we have reached T by the semipath (S,X,Y,T) with a net increase of 4, we increase the flow along each forward arc of the semipath by this amount. The results are depicted in Figure 7.2.4b.

We now repeat the foregoing process with the flow of Figure 7.2.4b. (S) may be extended to (S,Z) only since the flow in arc $\langle S,X \rangle$ is already at capacity. The net increase to Z through this semipath is 6. (S,Z) may be extended to (S,Z,Y), yielding a net increase of 4 to Y. (S,Z,Y) cannot be extended to (S,Z,Y,T) since the flow in arc $\langle Y,T \rangle$ is at capacity. However, it can be extended to (S,Z,Y,X) with a net increase to node X of 4. Note that since this semipath includes a backward arc $\langle Y,X \rangle$, it implies a reduction in the flow from X to Y of 4. The semipath (S,Z,Y,X) may be extended to (S,Z,Y,X,W) with a net increase of 3 (the unused capacity of $\langle X,W \rangle$) to W. This semipath may then be extended to (S,Z,Y,X,W,T) with a net increase of 3 in the flow to T. Since we have reached T with an increase of 3, we proceed backward along this semipath. Since $\langle W,T \rangle$ and $\langle X,W \rangle$ are forward arcs, their flow may each be increased by 3. Since $\langle Y,X \rangle$ is a backward arc, the flow along $\langle X,Y \rangle$ is reduced by 3. Since $\langle Z,Y \rangle$ and $\langle S,Z \rangle$ are forward arcs, their flow may be increased by 3. This results in the flow shown in Figure 7.2.4c.

We then attempt to repeat the process. (S) may be extended to (S,Z) with an increase of 3 to Z, (S,Z) may be extended to (S,Z,Y) with an increase of 1 to Y, and (S,Z,Y) may be extended to (S,Z,Y,X) with an increase of 1 to X. However, since arcs $\langle S,X \rangle$, $\langle Y,T \rangle$, and $\langle X,W \rangle$ are at capacity, no semipath may be extended further and an optimum flow has been found. Note that this optimum flow need not be unique. Figure 7.2.4d illustrates another optimum flow for the same graph, which was obtained from Figure 7.2.4a by considering the semipaths (S,X,W,T) and (S,Z,Y,T).

The Algorithm and Program

Given a weighted graph (an adjacency matrix and a capacity matrix) with a source S and a sink T, the algorithm to produce an optimum flow function for that graph may be outlined as follows:

1. initialize the flow function to 0 at each arc;
2. *cannotimprove*:= *false*;
3. **repeat**
4.   attempt to find a semipath from S to T which increases the flow to T by $x > 0$;
5.   **if** a semipath cannot be found
           then *cannotimprove*:= *true*
6.   **else** increase the flow to each node (except S) in the semipath by x
7. **until** *cannotimprove*

Of course, the heart of the algorithm lies in line 4. Once a node has been placed on a partial semipath, it can no longer be used to extend a different semipath. Thus the algorithm uses a boolean array *onpath* such that *onpath* [*node*] indicates whether or not *node* is on some semipath. It also needs an indication of which nodes are at the ends of partial semipaths so that such partial semipaths can be extended by adding adjacent nodes. *endpath* [*node*] indicates whether or not *node* is at the end of a partial semipath. For each node on a semipath the algorithm must keep track of what node precedes it on that semipath and the direction of the arc. *precede*[*node*] points to the node that precedes *node* on its semipath, and *forward*[*node*] has the value *true* if and only if the arc is from *precede*[*node*] to *node*. *improve*[*node*] indicates the amount by which the flow to *node* may be increased along its semipath. The algorithm that attempts to find a semipath from S to T along which the flow may be increased may be written as follows. (We assume that $c[a,b]$ is the capacity of the pipe from a to b and that $f[a,b]$ is the current flow from a to b.)

```
set endpath[node], onpath[node] to false for all nodes;
endpath[S]:= true;
onpath[S]:= true;
   { compute maximum flow from S which pipes can carry }
improve[S] := sum of c[S,node] over all nodes node;
while (not onpath[T]) and (there exists a node nd such that endpath[nd])
      do begin
                  endpath[nd]:= false;
                  while there exists a node i such that
                              (not onpath[i]) and (f[nd,i]<c[nd,i]) and (adjacent(nd,i))
                  {  the flow from nd to i may be increased  }
                  {          place i on the semipath          }
                     do begin
                              onpath[i]:= true;
                              endpath[i]:= true;
                              precede[i]:= nd;
                              forward[i]:= true;
                              x:= c[nd,i] - f[nd,i];
                              if improve[nd]<x
                                 then improve[i]:= improve[nd]
                                 else improve[i]:= x
                     end {while there exists...do begin};

            while there exists a node i such that
                              (not onpath[i]) and (f[i,nd]>0) and (adjacent(i,nd))
            {  the flow from i to nd may be decreased  }
            {          place i on the semipath          }
               do begin
                        onpath[i]:= true;
                        endpath[i]:= true;
                        precede[i]:= nd;
                        forward[i]:= false;
```

$$\textbf{if } improve[nd] < f[i,nd]$$
$$\textbf{then } improve[i] := improve[nd]$$
$$\textbf{else } improve[i] := f[i,nd]$$
$$\textbf{end } \{\text{while there exists...do begin}\}$$
$$\textbf{end } \{\text{while (not } onpath[T])\text{...do begin}\};$$

$$\textbf{if } onpath[T] \textbf{ then } \text{we have found a semipath from } S \text{ to } T$$
$$\textbf{else } \text{the flow is already optimum};$$

Once a semipath from S to T has been found, the flow may be increased along that semipath (line 6 above) by the following algorithm:

$$x := improve[T];$$
$$nd := T;$$
$$\textbf{while } nd <> S$$
$$\quad \textbf{do begin}$$
$$\qquad pred := precede[nd];$$
$$\qquad \textbf{if } forward[nd] \textbf{ then } f[pred,nd] := f[pred,nd] + x$$
$$\qquad\qquad\qquad\qquad \textbf{else } f[nd,pred] := f[nd,pred] - x;$$
$$\qquad nd := pred$$
$$\quad \textbf{end } \{\text{while...do begin}\}$$

This method of solving the flow problem is known as the *Ford–Fulkerson algorithm* after its discoverers.

Let us now convert these algorithms into a Pascal procedure $maxflow(cap,s,t,flow,totflow)$. cap is an input parameter representing a capacity function defined on a weighted graph whose type $capfunct$ is defined by

```
const maxnodes = 50;
type  nodeptr = 1..maxnodes;
      capfunct = array[nodeptr,nodeptr] of integer;
```

s and t are input parameters representing the source and sink, $flow$ is an output parameter representing the maximum flow function, and $totflow$ is the amount of flow from s to t under the flow function $flow$.

The previous algorithms may be converted easily into Pascal programs. Three boolean arrays, $endpath$, $forward$, and $onpath$; one integer array, $improve$; and an array $precede$ of $nodeptrs$ are required. (In some nonstandard Pascal implementations, $forward$ is a reserved word and may not be used as a variable identifier.) The question of whether j is adjacent to i can be answered by checking whether or not $cap[i,j]=0$.

We present the routine here as a straightforward implementation of the algorithms. any is a function that accepts a boolean array and returns *true* if any element of the array is *true*. If none of the elements of the array is *true*, then any returns *false*. We leave its coding as an exercise.

```
procedure maxflow (cap: capfunct; s,t: nodeptr; var flow: capfunct; var totflow: integer);
var pred, nd, i: nodeptr;
    x: integer;
```

```
precede: array[nodeptr] of nodeptr;
improve: array[nodeptr] of integer;
endpath, forward, onpath: array[nodeptr] of boolean;
{insert the function any here}
begin {procedure maxflow}
   for nd:= 1 to maxnodes
       do for i:= 1 to maxnodes
              do flow[nd,i]:= 0;
   totflow:= 0;
   repeat
       {attempt to find a semipath from s to t}
       for nd:= 1 to maxnodes
           do begin
                      endpath[nd]:= false;
                      onpath[nd]:= false
              end {for...do begin};
       endpath[s]:= true;
       onpath[s]:= true;
       improve[s]:= maxint;
       {we assume that s can provide infinite flow}
       while (not onpath[t]) and (any(endpath))
           do begin
                      {attempt to extend an existing path}
                      nd:= 1;
                      while not endpath[nd]
                          do nd:= nd + 1;
                      endpath[nd]:= false;
                      for i:= 1 to maxnodes
                          do begin
                              if (flow[nd,i] < cap[nd,i]) and (not onpath[i])
                                 then begin
                                         onpath[i]:= true;
                                         endpath[i]:= true;
                                         precede[i]:= nd;  ·
                                         forward[nd]:= true;
                                         x:= cap[nd,i] - flow[nd,i];
                                         if improve[nd]<x
                                            then improve[i]:= improve[nd]
                                            else improve[i]:= x
                                      end {then begin};
                              if (flow[i,nd] > 0) and (not onpath[i])
                                 then begin
                                         onpath[i]:= true;
                                         endpath[i]:= true;
                                         precede[i]:= nd;
                                         forward[nd]:= false;
```

```
                              if improve[nd] < flow[i,nd]
                                then improve[i]:= improve[nd]
                                else improve[i]:= flow[i,nd]
                           end {then begin}
                        end { for...do begin}
                  end {while...do begin};
            if onpath[t]
               then { flow on semipath to t can be increased }
                  begin
                     x:= improve[t];
                     totflow:= totflow + x;
                     nd:= t;
                     while nd <> s
                        do begin { travel back along path }
                           pred:= precede[nd];
                           if forward[pred]
                              then { increase flow from pred }
                                 flow[pred,nd]:= flow[pred,nd]+x
                              else { decrease flow to pred }
                                 flow[nd,pred]:= flow[nd,pred]-x;
                           nd:= pred
                        end {while...do begin}
                  end {then begin}
         until not onpath[t]
end { procedure maxflow};
```

For large graphs with many nodes, the arrays *improve* and *endpath* may be prohibitively expensive in terms of space. Furthermore, a search through all nodes to find one such that *endpath*[*nd*] = *true* may be very inefficient in terms of time. An alternative solution might be to note that the value of *improve* is required only for those nodes *nd* such that *endpath*[*nd*]=*true*. Those graph nodes which are at the end of semipaths may be kept in a list whose nodes are defined by

```
                  const maxnodes = 100;
                  type  nodeptr = 0..maxnodes;
                        listnode = record
                                graphnode: nodeptr;
                                improve: integer;
                                next: nodeptr
                           end;
```

When a node that is at the end of a semipath is required, remove the first element from the list. We can similarly dispense with the array *precede* by maintaining a separate list of nodes for each semipath. However, this suggestion is of dubious value since almost all nodes will be on some semipath.

You are invited to write the routine *maxflow* as an exercise using these suggestions to save time and space.

EXERCISES
1. Find the maximum flows for the graphs in Figure 7.2.1 using the Ford–Fulkerson method (the capacities are shown next to the arcs).

2. Given a graph and a capacity function as in this section, define a *cut* as any set of nodes x containing S but not T. Define the *capacity of the cut x* as the sum of the capacities of all the arcs leaving the set x minus the sum of the capacities of all the arcs entering x.

   (a) Show that for any flow function f, the value of the total flow v is less than or equal to the capacity of any cut.
   (b) Show that equality in part (a) is achieved when the flow is maximum and the cut has minimum capacity.

3. Prove that the Ford–Fulkerson algorithm produces an optimum flow function.

4. Rewrite the routine *maxflow* using a linked list to contain nodes at the end of semi-paths, as suggested in the text.

5. Assume that in addition to a capacity function, there is also a cost function, *cost*. $cost(a,b)$ is the cost of each unit of flow from node a to node b. Modify the program of the text to produce the flow function that maximizes the total flow from source to sink at the lowest cost (i.e., if there are two flow functions, both of which produce the same maximum flow, choose the one with the least cost.)

6. Assuming a cost function as in Exercise 5, write a program to produce the maximum cheapest flow: that is, a flow function such that the total flow divided by the cost of the flow is greatest.

7. A *probabilistic* directed graph is one in which a probability function associates a probability with each arc. The sum of the probabilities of all arcs emanating from any node is 1. Consider an acyclic probabilistic digraph representing a tunnel system. A person is placed at one node in the tunnel. At each node, the person chooses to take a particular arc to another node with probability given by the probability function. Write a program to compute the probability that the person passes through each node of the graph. What if the graph were cyclic?

8. Write a Pascal program that reads the following information about an electrical network:

   (a) n, the number of wires in the network.
   (b) The amount of current entering through the first wire and leaving through the nth.
   (c) The resistance of each of the wires 2 through $n-1$.
   (d) A set of ordered pairs $\langle i,j \rangle$ indicating that wire i is connected to wire j and that electricity flows through wire i to wire j.

   The program should compute the amount of current flowing through each of wires 2 through $n-1$ by applying Kirchhoff's law and Ohm's law. Kirchhoff's law states that the amount of current flowing into a junction equals the amount leaving a junction. Ohm's law states that if two paths exist between two junctions, the sums of the currents times the resistances over all wires in each of the two paths are equal.

3. THE LINKED REPRESENTATION OF GRAPHS

The adjacency matrix representation of a graph is frequently inadequate because it requires advance knowledge of the number of nodes. If a graph must be constructed in the course of solving a problem, or if it must be dynamically updated as the program proceeds, a new matrix must be created for each addition or deletion of a node. This is prohibitively inefficient, especially in a real-world situation where a graph may have 100 or more nodes. Further, even if a graph has very few arcs so that the adjacency matrix (and the weight matrix for a weighted graph) is sparse, space must be reserved for every possible arc between two nodes whether or not such an arc exists. If the graph contains n nodes, a total of n^2 locations must be used.

As you might expect, the remedy is to use a linked structure, allocating and freeing nodes from an available pool. This is similar to the methods used to represent dynamic binary and general trees. In the linked representation of trees, each allocated node corresponds to a tree node. This is possible because each tree node is the son of only one other tree node and is therefore contained in only a single list of sons. However, in a graph an arc may exist between any two graph nodes. It is possible to keep an adjacency list for every node in a graph (such a list contains all nodes adjacent to a given node) and a node might find itself on many different adjacency lists (one for each node to which it is adjacent). But this requires that each allocated node contain a variable number of pointers, depending on the number of nodes to which it is adjacent. This solution is clearly impractical, as we saw in attempting to represent general trees with nodes containing pointers to each of its sons.

An alternative is to construct a multilinked structure in the following way. The nodes of the graph (hereafter referred to as *graph nodes*) are represented by a linked list of *header nodes*. Each such header node contains three fields: *info*, *nextnode*, and *arcptr*. If p points to a header node representing a graph node a, then *info*(p) contains any information associated with graph node a. *nextnode*(p) is a pointer to the header node representing the next graph node, if any. Each header node is at the head of a list of nodes of a second type called *list nodes*. This list is called the *adjacency list*. Each node on an adjacency list represents an arc of the graph. *arcptr*(p) points to the adjacency list of nodes representing the arcs emanating from the graph node a.

Each adjacency list node contains two fields: *ndptr* and *nextarc*. If q points to a list node representing an arc $\langle A,B \rangle$, *ndptr*(q) is a pointer to the header node representing the graph node B. *nextarc*(q) points to a list node representing the next arc emanating from graph node A, if any. Each list node is contained in a single adjacency list representing all arcs emanating from a given graph node. The term *allocated nodes* is used to refer to both header and list nodes of a multilinked structure representing a graph. We also refer to an adjacency list node as an *arc node*.

Figure 7.3.1 illustrates this representation. If each graph node carries

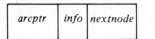

A sample header node representing a graph node.　　A sample list node representing an arc.

(a)

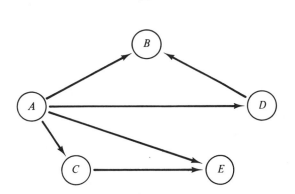

(b) A graph.

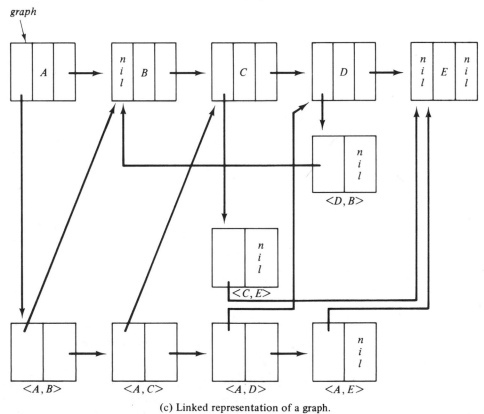

(c) Linked representation of a graph.

Figure 7.3.1　Linked representation of a graph.

some information but (since the graph is not weighted) the arcs do not, then two types of allocated nodes are needed: one for header nodes (graph nodes) and the other for adjacency list nodes (arcs). These are illustrated in Figure 7.3.1a. Each header node contains an *info* field and two pointers. The first of these is to the adjacency list of arcs emanating from the graph node, and the second is to the next header node in the graph. Each arc node contains two pointers, one to the next arc node in the adjacency list and the other to the header node representing the graph node that terminates the arc. Figure 7.3.1b depicts a graph and 7.3.1c its linked representation.

Note that header nodes and list nodes have different formats and must be represented by different Pascal types. This necessitates either keeping two distinct available lists or defining a single variant type. Even in the case of a weighted graph in which each list node contains an *info* field to hold the weight of an arc, two different types may be necessary if the information in the header nodes is not an integer. However, for simplicity we make the assumption that both header and list nodes have the same format and contain two pointers and a single-integer information field. These nodes are declared using the array implementation by

```
const maxnodes = 500;
type  nodeptr = 0..maxnodes;
      nodetype = record
                     info: integer;
                     point: nodeptr;
                     next: nodeptr
                 end;
var   node: array[1..maxnodes] of nodetype;
```

In the case of a header node, *node*[*p*] represents a graph node *A*, *node*[*p*].*info* represents the information associated with the graph node *A*, *node*[*p*].*next* points to the next graph node, and *node*[*p*].*point* points to the first list node representing an arc emanating from *A*. In the case of a list node, *node*[*p*] represents an arc ⟨*A*,*B*⟩, *node*[*p*].*info* represents the weight of the arc, *node*[*p*].*next* points to the next arc emanating from *A*, and *node*[*p*].*point* points to the header node representing the graph node *B*.

Using the dynamic implementation, the nodes may be defined by

```
type nodeptr = ↑nodetype;
     nodetype = record
                    info: integer;
                    point: nodeptr;
                    next: nodeptr
                end;
```

We use the array implementation in the remainder of this section and assume the existence of routines *getnode* and *freenode*.

We now present the implementation of the primitive graph operations using the linked representation. The operation *joinwt*(*p*,*q*,*wt*) accepts two pointers p and q to two header nodes and creates an arc between them with weight wt. If an arc already exists between them, that arc's weight is set to wt.

```
procedure joinwt (p, q: nodeptr; wt: integer);
var r, r2: nodeptr;
    found: boolean;
begin
    {search the list of arcs emanating from node[p] }
    {              for an arc to node[q]            }
    found:= false;
    r2:= 0;
    r:= node[p].point;
    while (r <> 0) and (not found)
      do if node[r].point = q
          then begin {node[r] represents an arc from}
                    {      node[p] to node[q]        }
                  node[r].info:= wt;
                  found:= true
              end {then begin}
          else {keep looking}
              begin
                  r2:= r;
                  r:= node[r].next
              end {else begin};
    if not found
      then {an arc from node[p] to node[q] does not}
          {   exist; such an arc must be created.   }
          begin
              r:= getnode;
              node[r].point:= q;
              node[r].next:= 0;
              node[r].info:= wt;
              if r2 = 0
                  then node[p].point:= r
                  else  node[r2].next:= r
          end {then begin}
end {procedure joinwt};
```

We leave the implementation of the operation *join* for an unweighted graph as an exercise for the reader. The operation *remv(p,q)* accepts pointers to two header nodes and removes the arc between them, if one exists.

```
procedure remv (p, q: nodeptr);
var r, r2: nodeptr;
    deleted: boolean;
```

```
begin {procedure remv}
    deleted:= false;
    r2:= 0;
    r:= node[p].point;
    while (r <> 0) and (not deleted)
        do if node[r].point = q
            then {r points to an arc from node[p]}
                 {            to node[q]            }
                begin
                    if r2 = 0
                        then node[p].point:= node[r].next
                        else node[r2].next:= node[r].next;
                    freenode(r);
                    deleted:= true
                end {then begin}
            else {continue searching}
                begin
                    r2:= r;
                    r:= node[r].next
                end {else begin}
            {if no arc has been found, then no action}
            {            need be taken            }
end {procedure remv};
```

We leave the implementation of the operation $remvwt(p,q,x)$, which sets x to the weight of the arc $\langle p,q \rangle$ in a weighted graph and then removes the arc from the graph as an exercise for the reader.

The function $adjacent(p,q)$ accepts pointers to two header nodes and determines whether $node(q)$ is adjacent to $node(p)$.

```
function adjacent (p, q: nodeptr): boolean;
var r: nodeptr;
    found: boolean;
begin
    r:= node[p].point;
    found:= false; {assume no arc exits}
    while (r <> 0) and (not found)
        do if node[r].point = q
            then found:= true {an arc is found}
            else r:= node[r].next;
    adjacent:= found
end {function adjacent};
```

Another useful function is $findnode(graph,x)$, which returns a pointer to a header node with information field x if such a header node exists, and returns the nil pointer otherwise.

```
function findnode (graph: nodeptr; x: integer): nodeptr;
var p: nodeptr;
    found: boolean;
begin
    p:= graph;
    found:= false;
    while (p <> 0) and (not found)
        do begin
                if node[p].info = x
                    then begin
                                findnode:= p;
                                found:= true
                        end {then begin}
                    else  p:= node[p].next
            end {while...do begin};
        if not found
            then findnode:= 0
end {function findnode};
```

The function *addnode*(*graph*,*x*) adds a node with information field *x* to a graph and returns a pointer to that node.

```
function addnode (var graph: nodeptr; x: integer): nodeptr;
var p: nodeptr;
begin
    p:= getnode;
    node[p].info:= x;
    node[p].point:= 0;
    node[p].next:= graph;
    graph:= p;
    addnode:= p
end {function addnode};
```

The reader should be aware of another important difference between the adjacency matrix representation and the linked representation of graphs. Implicit in the matrix representation is the ability to traverse a row or column of the matrix. Traversing a row is equivalent to identifying all arcs emanating from a given node. This can be done efficiently in the linked representation by traversing the list of arc nodes starting at a given header node. Traversing a column of an adjacency matrix, however, is equivalent to identifying all arcs that terminate at a given node; there is no corresponding method for accomplishing this under the linked representation. Of course, the linked representation could be modified to include two lists emanating from each header node: one for the arcs emanating from the graph node and the other for the arcs terminating at the graph node. However, this would require allocating two nodes for each arc, thus increasing the complexity of adding or deleting an arc. Alternatively, each arc node could be placed on two lists. In this case, an arc node would contain four pointers: one to the next arc emanating from the same node, one to the next arc terminating at the same node, one to the header node at which it terminates, and one to the header node from which it emanates. A header node would contain three pointers: one to the next header node, one to the list of arcs emanating from it, and one to the list of arcs terminating at it. The programmer must, of course, choose from among these representations by examining the needs of the specific problem and considering both time and storage efficiency. We invite the reader to write a routine *remvnode* (*graph*,*p*) which removes a header node pointed to by *p* from a graph pointed to by *graph* using the various graph representations that we have outlined above. Of course, when a node is removed from a graph, all arcs emanating and terminating at that node must also be removed. In the linked representation that we have presented there is no easy way of removing a node from a graph since the arcs terminating at the node cannot be obtained directly.

It would also be instructive for the reader to compare and contrast the methods outlined for representing a graph with the methods outlined in Section 5.3 for representing a sparse matrix.

An Application to Scheduling

Let us now consider an application using the linked representation of graphs. Suppose that a chef in a diner receives an order for a fried egg. The job of frying an egg can be decomposed into a number of distinct subtasks:

Get egg	Crack egg	Get grease
Grease pan	Heat grease	Pour egg into pan
Wait until egg is done		Remove egg

Some of these tasks must precede others (e.g., "get egg" must precede "crack egg"). Others may be done simultaneously (e.g., "get egg" and "heat grease"). The chef wishes to provide the quickest service possible and is assumed to have an unlimited number of assistants. The problem is to assign tasks to the assistants so as to complete the job in the least possible time.

Although this example may seem frivolous, it is typical of many real-world scheduling problems. A computer system may wish to schedule jobs to minimize turnaround time; a compiler may wish to schedule machine language operations to minimize execution time; a plant manager may wish to organize an assembly line to minimize production time; and so on. All of these problems are closely related and can be solved by the use of graphs.

Let us represent this problem as a graph. Each node of the graph represents a subtask and each arc $\langle x,y \rangle$ represents the requirement that subtask y cannot be performed until subtask x has been completed. This graph G is shown in Figure 7.3.2.

Consider the transitive closure of G. The transitive closure is the graph T such that $\langle x,y \rangle$ is an arc of T if and only if there is a path from x to y in G. This transitive closure is shown in Figure 7.3.3.

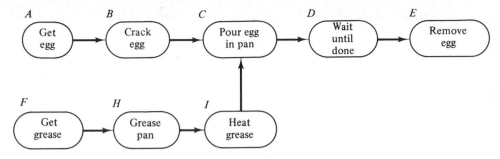

Figure 7.3.2 The graph G.

In the graph T, an arc exists from node x to node y if and only if subtask x must be performed before subtask y. Note that neither G nor T can contain a cycle, since if a cycle from node x to itself existed, then subtask x could not be performed until after subtask x had been completed. This is clearly an impossible situation in the context of the problem.

Since G does not contain a cycle, there must be at least one node in G which has no predecessors. To see this, suppose that every node in the graph did have a predecessor. In particular, let us choose a node z that has a predecessor y. y cannot equal z or the graph would have a cycle from z to itself. Since every node has a predecessor, y must also have a predecessor x which is not equal to either y or z. Continuing in this fashion, a sequence of distinct nodes

$$z, y, x, w, v, u, \dots$$

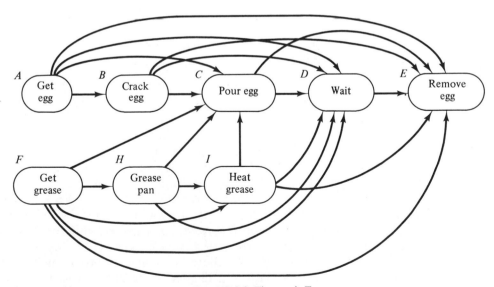

Figure 7.3.3 The graph T.

is obtained. If any two nodes in this sequence were equal, a cycle would exist from that node to itself. However, the graph contains only a finite number of nodes, so that eventually, two of the nodes must be equal. This is a contradiction. Thus there must be at least one node without a predecessor.

In the graphs of Figures 7.3.2 and 7.3.3, the nodes A and F do not have predecessors. Since they have no predecessors, the subtasks which they represent may be performed immediately and simultaneously without waiting for any other subtasks to be completed. Every other subtask must wait until at least one of these is completed. Once these two subtasks have been performed, their nodes and incident arcs can be removed from the graph. Note that the resulting graph does not contain any cycles since nodes and arcs have been removed from a graph that originally contained no cycles. Therefore, the resulting graph must also contain at least one node with no predecessors. In the example, B and H are two such nodes. Thus the subtasks B and H may be performed simultaneously in the second time period.

Continuing in this fashion we find that the minimum time in which the egg can be fried is six time periods (assuming that every subtask takes exactly one time period) and that a maximum of two assistants need be employed, as follows:

Time period	Assistant 1	Assistant 2
1	Get egg	Get grease
2	Crack egg	Grease pan
3	Heat grease	
4	Pour egg into pan	
5	Wait until done	
6	Remove egg	

This process can be outlined as follows: ·

1. Read the precedences and construct the graph.
2. Use the graph to determine subtasks that can be done simultaneously.

Let us refine each of these two steps. Two crucial decisions must be made in refining step 1. The first is to decide the format of the input; the second is to decide on the representation of the graph. Clearly, the input must contain indications of which subtasks must precede others. The most convenient way to represent these requirements is by ordered pairs of subtasks; each input line contains the names of two subtasks, where the first subtask on a line must precede the second. Of course, the data must be valid in the sense that no subtask may precede itself (no cycles are permitted in the graph). Only those precedences that are implied by the data and the transitive closure of the resulting graph are assumed to hold. A subtask may be represented by a character string such as '*get egg*' or by a number. We choose to represent subtasks by character strings in order that the input data reflect the real-world situation as closely as possible. If the number of subtasks at the start of execution is known, an adjacency matrix where each element is initialized to *false* could be used to represent the graph. As each precedence is read, *true* could be inserted in the matrix at an appropriate position. However, let us assume that this information is unavailable at the start of execution and that it is necessary to provide for an arbitrary number of nodes. For this reason the linked representation of a graph is used.

What information should be kept with each node of the graph? Clearly, the name of the subtask that the node represents is needed for output purposes. This name will be kept as a packed array of characters. The remaining information depends on how the graph is used. This will become apparent only after step 2 is refined. Here is a good example of how the various parts of a program outline interact with each other to produce a single unit.

Step 2 can be refined into the following algorithm:

while the graph is not empty
    do begin
            determine which nodes have no predecessors;
            output this group of nodes with an indication that
                  they can be performed simultaneously in the next time period;
            remove these nodes and their incident arcs from the graph
    end;

How can it be determined which nodes have no predecessors? One method is to maintain a *count* field in each node containing the number of nodes that precede it. Note that we are not interested in which nodes precede a given node—only in how many. If the *count* of a node is 0, that node is known to have no predecessors and may be placed on an output list. Each time a node x is output, its adjacency list of arcs must be traversed and the *count* field decremented in every node adjacent to x. During each simulated time period, the list of nodes remaining in the graph is traversed, in a search for those whose *count* field is 0 and which may now be output. Thus the refinement of step 2 may be rewritten as follows:

period := 0;
while *graph* <> *nil*
    do begin
            period := *period*+1;
            outp := *nil*; {initialize the output list to empty}
            {traverse the graph, searching for nodes which may}
            {   be placed on the output list   }
            p := *graph*;
            while *p* <> *nil*
                do begin
                      if *count* (*p*) = 0
                        then remove *node* (*p*) from the list of graph nodes
                                and place it on the output list;
                    set *p* to the next graph node
                end {while *p*<>*nil* do begin};

```
     if outp = nil
        then error — every node in the graph has a predecessor
                                    and therefore the graph contains a cycle;
        {traverse the output list}
     p := outp;
     while p <> nil
        do begin
                print (info (p));
                traverse the list of arcs emanating from node (p),
                      reducing the count of each terminating node by one.
                            Free each arc node as it is encountered;
                r := next node in output list;
                free node (p);
                p := r
        end {while p<>nil do begin}
  end {while graph<>nil do begin}
```

Note that it is possible to delete nodes from the linked representation in this example efficiently only because the only nodes deleted are those with no predecessors. Thus deleted nodes have no arcs terminating in them.

The Pascal Program

At this point in the refinement of step 2, we can indicate the structure of the nodes that we shall need. The header nodes which represent graph nodes contain the following fields:

info	holds the name of the subtask represented by this node.
count	holds the number of predecessors of this graph node.
arcptr	a pointer to the list of arcs emanating from this node.
nextnode	a pointer to the next node in the graph or in the output list.

Each list node representing an arc contains two pointers:

nodeptr	a pointer to its terminating node.
nextarc	a pointer to the next arc in the adjacency list.

Thus two types of nodes are required—one to represent graph nodes and one to represent arcs. Using the array representation of lists, these may be declared by

```
const maxgraph = 500;
      maxarc = 500;
type  graphpointer = 0..maxgraph;
      arcpointer = 0..maxarc;
      task = packed array[1..20] of char;
      graphtype = record
                     info: task;
                     count: integer;
```

```
                    arcptr: arcpointer;
                    nextnode: graphpointer
              end;
        arctype = record
                    nodeptr: graphpointer;
                    nextarc: arcpointer
              end;
var     graphnode: array[1..maxgraph] of graphtype;
        arc: array[1..maxarc] of arctype;
```

An alternative would be to use a single array of variant records, but we choose to use two different record types.

Of course, there are two available lists (pointed to by *availnode* and *availarc*) and two sets of routines (*getnode*, *freenode* and *getarc*, *freearc*) to allocate and free allocated nodes. We also assume the existence of a function *find(graph,inf)*, which searches a list of graph nodes pointed to by *graph* for one such node whose *info* field equals *inf*. If no such graph node exists, *find* allocates a new graph node *nd* and sets *graphnode[nd].info* to *inf*, *graphnode[nd].count* to 0, and *graphnode[nd].arcptr* to 0. *find* then adds *nd* to the list of graph nodes. In either case, *find* returns a pointer to the graph node containing *inf*. If the list of graph nodes is empty before a call to *find*, *find* places a single node on the list. The routine *join* described above is also used. Finally, a procedure *readstr* is used to read a string of characters.

We may now write a Pascal scheduling program:

```
program schedule (input, output);
const maxgraph = 500;
      maxarc = 500;
type  graphpointer = 0..maxgraph;
      arcpointer = 0..maxarc;
      task = packed array[1..20] of char;
      graphtype = record
                      info: task;
                      count: integer;
                      arcptr: arcpointer;
                      nextnode: graphpointer
                  end;
      arctype = record;
                      nodeptr: graphpointer;
                      nextarc: arcpointer
                  end;
var   graphnode: array[1..maxgraph] of graphtype;
      arc: array[1..maxarc] of arctype;
      p, q, r, outp, graph, availnode: graphpointer;
      availarc, s, t: arcpointer;
```

```
                    period: integer;
                    inf1, inf2: task;
                    {insert routines readstr, find, join, freearc, freenode here}
        begin        { program schedule }
                    { initialize the available lists }
                    for p:= 1 to maxgraph-1
                        do graphnode[p].nextnode:= p+1;
                    graphnode[maxgraph].nextnode:= 0;
                    availnode:= 1;
                    for s:= 1 to maxarc-1
                        do arc [s].nextarc:= s+1;
                    arc[maxarc].nextarc:= 0;
                    availarc:= 1;
                    { initialize the count field in each graph node }
                    for p:= 1 to maxgraph
                        do graphnode[p].count:= 0;
                    { construct the graph }
                    graph:= 0;
                    while not eof
                        do begin
                                { read a precedence and place arc representing }
                                {                 it into the graph            }
                                readstr(inf1);
                                readstr(inf2);
                                readln;
                                p:= find(graph,inf1);
                                q:= find(graph,inf2);
                                join(p, q);
                                { increment the count of the terminal node }
                                graphnode[q].count:= graphnode[q].count+1
                        end {while...do begin}
                    { the graph has been constructed }

                    {                 step 2                 }
                    period:= 0;
                    while graph <> 0
                        do begin
                                period:= period+1;
                                outp:= 0;
                                p:= graph;
                                q:= 0;
                                {                 traverse the graph            }
                                { q remains one node behind p during traversal }
                                while p <> 0
                                    do begin
                                            r:= graphnode[p].nextnode;
```

```
                    if graphnode[p].count = 0
                        then {remove graphnode[p] from the graph}
                            begin
                                if q = 0
                                    then graph:= r
                                    else graphnode[q].nextnode:=r;
                                { place graphnode[p] on the }
                                {          output list           }
                                graphnode[p].nextnode:= outp;
                                outp:= p
                            end {then begin}
                        else q:= p;
                    p:= r
                end {while p<>0 do begin};
            if outp = 0
                then error('error in input—graph contains a cycle');
            writeln;
            writeln('period ', period);
                { traverse the output list }
            p:= outp;
            while p <> 0
                do begin
                        writeln(graphnode[p].info);
                        {traverse the arcs emanating from}
                        {             node[p]            }
                        s:= graphnode[p].arcptr;
                        while s <> 0
                            do begin
                                    r:= arc[s].nodeptr;
                                    graphnode[r].count:= graphnode[r].count-1;
                                    t:= arc[s].nextarc;
                                    freearc(s);
                                    s:= t
                                end {while s<>0 do begin};
                        r:= graphnode[p].nextnode;
                        freenode(p);
                        p:= r
                end {while p<>0 do begin}
        end {while graph<>0 do begin}
end {program schedule}.
```

Improving the Program

Although the foregoing program is correct, it is highly inefficient. See if you can spot the reason for this before reading further. Consider the fact that, in a typical real-world situation, there may be hundreds of subtasks, yet no more than three or four of them can be preformed in a single time period. Thus the entire job may require 100 or more time periods to complete. This means that the loop following the comment {*step 2*} is repeated many times. Each time it is repeated, the entire list of 100 graph nodes (on the average) must be traversed in order to locate the few whose *count* field is 0. (This average of 100 assumes that the graph initially has 200 nodes. Justify this estimate as an exercise.) This is very inefficient.

As each time period is simulated, those nodes whose subtasks can be performed in the next time period can be identified. This can be done when the *count* in a node is reduced by 1 and the *count* becomes 0. At that point, why not remove the node from the list of graph nodes and place it on a new list of those nodes that can be output in the next time period? Then, in the next time period, this new list can be traversed to produce the output, so that the entire graph need not be searched for nodes with a *count* field of 0.

The reader is encouraged at this point to discover the reason for not using this seemingly simple system. Once you have discovered the problem, you are encouraged to find a solution.

Consider the method that would be used to remove a node from the list of graph nodes. Since this list is a linked linear list, we cannot remove a node from it unless we have a pointer to its predecessor on the list. However, when we identify a node with zero count from the arc which it terminates, we have a pointer only to that node itself and not to its predecessor on the list of graph nodes. To reach the predecessor, we have to traverse the list from its beginning, which is the source of the original inefficiency.

There are several possible solutions to this problem. One possible solution is deferred to Section 9.4.2, at which point we will have introduced the concepts necessary for its implementation. Another solution, which the thoughtful reader should have discovered, is to link the graph nodes in a doubly linked list rather than in a singly linked linear list, so that a node's predecessor may be reached directly from the node itself instead of through a traversal of the entire list from its beginning.

Although the graph nodes are linked in a doubly linked list, the output list may remain a singly linked linear list, since it actually behaves like a stack, for which a linear list is sufficient. After performing step 1, which creates the graph, the doubly linked list of graph nodes is traversed once in order to initialize the output list to contain those graph nodes which initially have no predecessors. As each time period is subsequently simulated, the output list created in the previous time period is traversed, the subtask represented by each node in the list is output, the counts in the graph nodes adjacent to each node in the output list are reduced, and if the count in an adjacent node becomes zero, that adjacent node is placed in the output list for the next period. This means that two output lists are needed: one for the current period, which was created in the previous period and is now being traversed; and one that is being created in the current period and will be traversed in the next.

The refinement of step 2 under this implementation may be outlined as follows:

```
            { traverse the list of graph nodes and place all those }
            {  nodes with zero count on the initial output list   }
p:= graph;
outp:= nil;
while p <> nil
   do begin
            q:= nextnode(p);
            if count(p) = 0
               then begin
                        remove node(p) from the graph list;
                        place node(p) on the output list
                    end;
            p:= q
       end {while...do begin};
        { simulate the time periods }
period:= 0;
while outp <> nil
   do begin
            period:= period+1;
            print(period);
                { initialize the next period's output list }
            nextout:= nil;
                { traverse the output list }
            p:= outp;
            while p <> nil
               do begin
                        print (info(p));
                        { traverse the list of arcs emanating from }
                        {                node(p)                   }
                        r:= arcptr(p);
                        while r <> nil
                           do begin
                                    s:= nextarc(r);
                                    { reduce count in terminating }
                                    {            node             }
                                    t:= nodeptr(r);
                                    count(t):= count(t)-1;
                                    if count(t) = 0
                                       then begin
                                                remove node(t) from the graph;
                                            { add node(t) to the next outlist }
                                                nextnode(t):= nextout;
                                                nextout:= t
                                            end {then begin};
```

$$freearc(r);$$
$$r := s$$
end {while $r <> nil$ do begin};
$$q := nextnode(p);$$
$$freenode(p);$$
$$p := q$$
end {while $p <> nil$ do begin};
$$outp := nextout$$
end {while $outp <> nil$ do begin};
if $graph <> nil$
   then error—there is a cycle in the graph

In order to accommodate the pointers of the doubly linked list, the graph nodes must include an extra field *backnode* containing a pointer to the previous graph node in the list. Thus *graphnode* is declared by

```
type graphtype = record
              info: task;
              count: integer;
              arcptr: arcpointer;
              backnode: graphpointer;
              nextnode: graphpointer
            end;
var   graphnode: array[1..maxgraph] of graphtype;
```

The available list of graph nodes and the two output lists need not be doubly linked, so that the contents of *backnode* are irrelevant for nodes on these lists. The procedure *find* must be suitably modified to accommodate doubly linked lists. The routines *join* and *readstr* are also used. Having dispensed with these preliminaries, we may write a Pascal scheduling program as follows:

```
program schedule (input, output);
const maxgraph = 500;
      maxarc = 500;
type  graphpointer = 0..maxgraph;
      arcpointer = 0..maxarc;
      task = packed array[1..20] of char;
      graphtype = record
              info: task;
              count: integer;
              arcptr: arcpointer;
              backnode: graphpointer;
              nextnode: graphpointer
            end;
      arctype = record
              nodeptr: graphpointer;
              nextarc: arcpointer
            end;
```

```
var     graphnode: array[1..maxgraph] of graphtype;
        arc: array[1..maxarc] of arctype;
        availnode,p,q,r,t,v,w,graph,outp,nextout: graphpointer;
        availarc,pp,s: arcpointer;
        inf1, inf2: task;
        period: integer;
      {insert routines readstr, find, join, freearc, freenode here}
begin
        { initialize the available lists }
        for p:= 1 to maxgraph-1
            do graphnode[p].nextnode:= p+1;
        graphnode[maxgraph].nextnode:= 0;
        availnode:= 1;
        for pp:= 1 to maxarc-1
            do arc[pp].nextarc:= pp+1;
        arc[maxarc].nextarc:= 0;
        availarc:= 1;
        for p:= 1 to maxgraph
            do graphnode[p].count:= 0;
                { construct the graph }
        graph:= 0;
        while not eof
          do begin
                    readstr(inf1);
                    readstr(inf2);
                    readln;
                      {    the function find adjusts all necessary    }
                      { forward and backward pointers in adding a }
                      {  graph node with info field inf1 or inf2 to  }
                      {    the doubly linked list of graphnodes.    }
                    p:= find(graph, inf1);
                    q:= find(graph, inf2);
                    join(p, q);
                    graphnode[q].count:= graphnode[q] count+1
              end {while...do begin};
        { step 2: traverse the list of graph nodes and place  }
        { all graph nodes with zero count on the output list }
        p:= graph;
        outp:= 0;
        while p <> 0
            do begin
                    q:= graphnode[p].nextnode;
                    if graphnode[p].count = 0
                        then begin
                              { remove graphnode[p] from the graph list }
                                r:= graphnode[p].backnode;
```

```
                              if q <> 0
                                  then graphnode[q].backnode:= r;
                              if r <> 0
                                  then graphnode[r].nextnode:= q
                                  else graph:= q;
                          { place graphnode[p] on the output list }
                              graphnode[p].nextnode:= outp;
                              outp:= p
                          end {then begin};
                  p:= q
              end {while...do begin};

              { simulate the time periods }
period:= 0;
while outp <> 0
    do begin
              period:= period+1;
              writeln('period ', period);
              { initialize the next output list and traverse }
              nextout:= 0;
              p:= outp;
              while p <> 0
                  do begin
                              writeln(graphnode[p].info);
                      { traverse arcs emanating from graphnode[p] }
                              pp:= graphnode[p].arcptr;
                          while pp <> 0
                              do begin
                                      s:= arc[pp].nextarc;
                          { reduce the count in the terminating node }
                                      t:= arc[pp].nodeptr;
                                      graphnode[t].count:= graphnode[t].count−1;
                                      if graphnode[t].count = 0
                                          then begin
                                      { once the subtask represented by graphnode[p] }
                                      { has been performed, the subtask represented  }
                                      {      by graphnode[t] may be performed         }
                                      {   remove graphnode[t] from the graph list     }
                                                  v:= graphnode[t].nextnode;
                                                  w:= graphnode[t].backnode;
                                                  if v <> 0
                                                      then graphnode[v].backnode:=w;
                                                  if w <> 0
                                                      then graphnode[w].nextnode:=v
                                                      else graph:= v;
                                              { place graphnode[t] on the output list}
```

```
                        graphnode[t].nextnode:= nextout;
                        nextout:= t
                     end {then begin};
                  freearc(pp);
                  pp:= s
               end {while pp<>0 do begin};
               { continue traversing the output list }
               q:= graphnode[p].nextnode;
               freenode(p);
               p:= q
            end {while p<>0 do begin};
            { reset the output list for the next period }
            outp:= nextout
         end {while outp<>0 do begin};
      if graph <> 0
         then error('error in input—graph contains a cycle')
   end { program schedule }.
```

EXERCISES

1. Implement a graph using linked lists so that each header node heads two lists: one containing the arcs emanating from the graph node and the other containing the arcs terminating at the graph node.

2. Implement a graph so that the lists of header nodes and arc nodes are circular.

3. Implement a graph using an adjacency matrix represented by the sparse matrix techniques of Section 5.3.

4. Implement a graph using a list of adjacency lists. Under this representation, a graph of n nodes consists of n header nodes, each containing an integer from 1 to n and a pointer. The pointer is to a list of list nodes each of which contains the node number of a node adjacent to the node represented by the header node.

5. There may be more than one way to organize a set of subtasks in a minimum number of time periods. For example, the subtasks in Figure 7.3.2 may be completed in six time periods by one of three different methods:

Period	Method 1	Method 2	Method 3
1	A, F	F	A, F
2	B, H	A, H	H
3	I	B, I	B, I
4	C	C	C
5	D	D	D
6	E	E	E

Write a program which will generate all possible methods of organizing the subtasks in the minimum number of time periods.

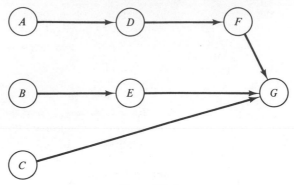

Figure 7.3.4

6. Consider the graph of Figure 7.3.4. The program *schedule* outputs the following organization of tasks:

Time	Subtasks
1	A, B, C
2	D, E
3	F
4	G

This requires three assistants (for time period 1). Can you find a method of organizing the subtasks so that only two assistants are required at any time period, yet the entire job can be accomplished in the same four time periods? Write a program which organizes subtasks so that a minimum number of assistants are needed to complete the entire job in the minimum number of time periods.

7. If there is only one worker available, it will take k time periods to complete the entire job, where k is the number of subtasks. Write a program to list a valid order in which the worker can perform the tasks. Note that this program is simpler than *schedule*, since an output list is not needed; as soon as the *count* field reaches 0, the task may be output. The process of converting a set of precedences into a single linear list in which no later element precedes an earlier one is called a ***topological sort***.

8. A ***PERT network*** is a weighted acyclic directed graph in which each arc represents an activity and its weight represents the time needed to perform that activity. If arcs $\langle a,b \rangle$ and $\langle b,c \rangle$ exist in the network, then the activity represented by arc $\langle a,b \rangle$ must be completed before the activity represented by $\langle b,c \rangle$ can be started. Each node x of the network represents a time at which all activities represented by arcs terminating at x can be completed.

   (a) Write a Pascal routine that accepts a representation of such a network and assigns to each node x the earliest time that all activities terminating in that node can be completed. Call this quantity $et(x)$. [*Hint:* Assign time 0 to all nodes with no predecessors. If all predecessors of a node x have been assigned times, then $et(x)$ is the maximum over all predecessors of the sum of the time assigned to a predecessor and the weight of the arc from that predecessor to x.]

CHAP. 7: GRAPHS AND THEIR APPLICATIONS

(b) Given the assignment of times in part (a), write a Pascal routine that assigns to each node x the latest time that all activities terminating in x can be completed without delaying the completion of all the activities. Call this quantity $lt(x)$. [*Hint:* Assign time $et(x)$ to all nodes x with no successors. If all successors of a node x have been assigned times, then $lt(x)$ is the minimum over all successors of the difference between the time assigned to a successor and the weight of the arc from x to the successor.]

(c) Prove that there is at least one path in the graph from a node with no predecessors to a node with no successors such that $et(x)=lt(x)$ for every node x on the path. Such a path is called a ***critical path***.

(d) Explain the significance of a critical path by showing that reducing the time of the activities along every critical path reduces the earliest time by which the entire job can be completed.

(e) Write a Pascal routine to find all critical paths in a PERT network.

(f) Find the critical paths in the networks of Figure 7.3.5.

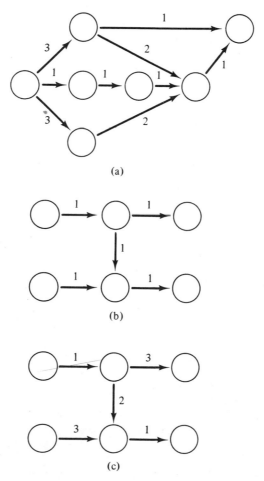

(a)

(b)

(c)

Figure 7.3.5 Some PERT networks.

9. Write a Pascal program that accepts a representation of a PERT network as given in Exercise 8 and computes the earliest time in which the entire job can be finished if as many activities as possible may be performed in parallel. The program should also print the starting and ending time of each activity in the network. Write another Pascal program to schedule the activities so that the entire job can be completed at the earliest possible time subject to the constraint that at most m activities can be performed in parallel.

8 Sorting

Sorting and searching are among the most common programming processes. In the first section of this chapter we discuss some of the overall considerations involved in sorting. In the remainder of the chapter we discuss some of the more common sorting techniques. In Chapter 9 we discuss searching and some applications.

1. GENERAL BACKGROUND

The concept of an ordered set of elements is one that has considerable impact on our daily lives. Consider, for example, the process of finding a telephone number in a telephone directory. This process, called a *search*, is simplified considerably by the fact that the names in the directory are listed in alphabetical order. Consider the trouble you might have in attempting to locate a telephone number if the names were listed in the order in which the customers placed their phone orders with the telephone company. In such a case, the names might as well have been entered in random order. Since the entries are sorted in alphabetical rather than in chronological order, the process of searching is simplified. Or consider the case of someone searching for a book in a library. Because the books are shelved in a specific order (Library of Congress, Dewey System, etc.), each book is assigned a specific position relative to the others and can be retrieved in a reasonable amount of time (if it is there). Or consider a set of numbers sorted sequentially in a computer's memory. As we shall see in Chapter 9, it is usually easier to find a particular element of that set if the numbers are sorted. In general, a set of items is kept sorted either to produce a report (to simplify manual retrieval of information, as in a telephone book or a library shelf) or to make machine access to data more efficient.

We now present some basic terminology. A *file of size n* is a sequence of n items $r(1), r(2), \ldots, r(n)$. Each item in the file is called a *record*. (The terms file and record are not being used here as Pascal terminology to refer to specific data structures. Rather, they are being used in a more general sense.) A *key*, $k(i)$, is associated with each record $r(i)$. The key is usually (but not always) a subfield of the entire record. The file is said to be *sorted on the key* if $i<j$ implies that $k(i)$ precedes $k(j)$ in some ordering on the keys. In the example of the telephone book, the file consists of all the entries in the book. Each entry is a record. The key upon which the file is sorted is the name field of the record. Each record also contains fields for an address and a telephone number.

A sort can be classified as being *internal* if the records that it is sorting are in main memory, or *external* if some of the records that it is sorting are in auxiliary storage. We restrict our attention to internal sorts.

It is possible for two records in a file to have the same key. A sorting technique is called *stable* if for all records i and j such that $k(i)=k(j)$, if $r(i)$ precedes $r(j)$ in the original file, then $r(i)$ precedes $r(j)$ in the sorted file.

A sort takes place either on the records themselves or on an auxiliary table of pointers (called *sorting by address*). For example, consider Figure 8.1.1a in which a file of five records is shown. If the file is sorted in increasing order on the numeric key shown, the resulting file is as shown in Figure 8.1.1b. In this case the actual records themselves have been sorted.

Suppose, however, that the amount of data stored in each of the records in the file of Figure 8.1.1a is so large that the overhead involved in moving the actual data is prohibitive. In this case an auxiliary table of pointers may be used so that these pointers are moved instead of the actual data. This is shown in Figure 8.1.2. The table in the center is the file and the table at the left is the initial table of pointers. The entry in position j in the table of pointers points to record j. During the sorting process, the entries in the pointer table are adjusted so that the final table is as shown at the right. Originally, the first pointer was to the first entry in the file; upon completion the first pointer is to the fourth entry in the table. Note that none of the original file entries are moved. In most of the programs in this chapter

	Key	Other fields			
Record 1	4	DDD		1	AAA
Record 2	2	BBB		2	BBB
Record 3	1	AAA		3	CCC
Record 4	5	EEE		4	DDD
Record 5	3	CCC		5	EEE
		File			File

(a) Original file.   (b) Sorted file.

Figure 8.1.1 Sorting actual records.

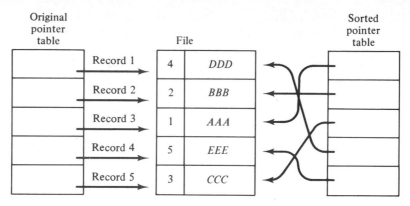

Figure 8.1.2 Sorting by using an auxiliary table of pointers.

we illustrate techniques of sorting actual records. The extension of these techniques to sorting by address is straightforward and will be left as an exercise for the reader.

Because of the relationship between sorting and searching, the first question to ask in any application is whether or not it pays to sort. Sometimes, there is less work involved in searching a set of elements for a particular one than to first sort the entire set and then to extract the desired element. On the other hand, if frequent use of the file is required for the purpose of retrieving specific elements, it might be more efficient to sort the file. This is because the overhead of successive searches may far exceed the overhead involved in first sorting the file and subsequently retrieving elements from the sorted file. Thus it cannot be said that it is more efficient either to sort or not to sort. The programmer must make a decision based on individual circumstances. Once a decision to sort has been made, other decisions must be made, including what is to be sorted and what methods are to be used. There is no one sorting method that is universally superior to all others. The programmer must carefully examine the problem and the desired results before deciding these very important questions.

Efficiency Considerations

As we shall see in this chapter, there are a great number of methods that can be used to sort a file. The programmer must be aware of several interrelated efficiency considerations to choose intelligently which sorting method is most appropriate to the particular problem. Three of the most important of these considerations include the length of time that must be spent by the programmer in coding a particular sorting program, the amount of machine time necessary for running the program and the amount of space necessary for the program.

If a file is small, sophisticated sorting techniques designed to minimize space and time requirements are usually worse or only marginally better in achieving efficiencies than are simpler, generally less efficient methods.

Similarly, if a particular sorting program is to be run only once and there is sufficient machine time and space in which to run it, it would be ludicrous for a programmer to spend days investigating the best methods of obtaining the last ounce of efficiency. In such cases, the amount of time that must be spent by the programmer is properly the overriding consideration in determining which sorting method to use. However, a strong word of caution must be inserted. Programming time is never a valid excuse for using an incorrect program. A sort that is run only once may be able to afford the luxury of an inefficient technique, but it cannot afford an incorrect one. The presumably sorted data may be used in an application in which the assumption of ordered data is crucial.

A programmer must be able to recognize the fact that a particular sort is inefficient and must be able to justify its use in a particular situation. Too often, programmers take the easy way out and code an inefficient sort which is then incorporated into a larger system in which the sort is a key component. The designers and planners of the system are then surprised at the inadequacy of their creation. To maximize his or her own efficiency, a programmer must be knowledgeable of a wide range of sorting techniques and be cognizant of the advantages and disadvantages of each, so that when the need for a sort arises he or she can supply the one that is most appropriate for the particular situation.

This brings us to the other two efficiency considerations: time and space. As in most computer applications, the programmer must often optimize one of these at the expense of the other. In considering the time necessary to sort a file of size n, we do not concern ourselves with actual time units, as these will vary from one machine to another, from one program to another, and from one set of data to another. Rather, we are interested in the change in the amount of time required to sort a file induced by a change in the file size n. Let us see if we can make this concept more precise. We say that y is *proportional* to x if multiplying x by a constant multiplies y by that same constant. Thus if y is proportional to x, doubling x will double y and multiplying x by 10 multiplies y by 10. Similarly, if y is proportional to x^2, then doubling x multiplies y by 4 and multiplying x by 10 multiplies y by 100.

There are two ways to determine the time requirements of a sort, neither of which yields results that are applicable to all cases. One method is to go through a sometimes intricate and involved mathematical analysis of various cases (e.g., best case, worst case, average case). The result of this analysis is usually a formula giving the average time required for a particular sort as a function of the file size n. Suppose that such a mathematical analysis on a particular sorting program results in the conclusion that the program takes $.01n^2 + 10n$ time units to execute. Figure 8.1.3 shows the time needed by the sort for various values of n. You will notice that for small values of n, the quantity $10n$ overwhelms the quantity $.01n^2$. This is because the difference between n^2 and n is small for small values of n and is more than compensated for by the difference between 10 and .01. Thus for small values

n	$a = 0.01n^2$	$b = 10n$	$a + b$	$\dfrac{(a + b)}{n^2}$
10	1	100	101	1.01
50	25	500	525	0.21
100	100	1,000	1,100	0.11
500	2,500	5,000	7,500	0.03
1,000	10,000	10,000	20,000	0.02
5,000	250,000	50,000	300,000	0.01
10,000	1,000,000	100,000	1,100,000	0.01
50,000	25,000,000	500,000	25,500,000	0.01
100,000	100,000,000	1,000,000	101,000,000	0.01
500,000	2,500,000,000	5,000,000	2,505,000,000	0.01

Figure 8.1.3

of n, an increase in n by a factor of 2 (e.g., from 50 to 100) increases the time needed for sorting by approximately that same factor of 2 (from 525 to 1100). Similarly, an increase in n by a factor of 5 (e.g., from 10 to 50) increases the sorting time by approximately 5 (from 101 to 525). However, as n becomes larger, the difference between n^2 and n increases so quickly that it eventually more than makes up for the difference between 10 and .01. Thus when n equals 1000, the two terms contribute equally to the amount of time needed by the program. As n becomes even larger, the term $.01n^2$ overwhelms the term $10n$ and the contribution of the term $10n$ becomes almost insignificant. Thus for large values of n, an increase in n by a factor of 2 (e.g., from 50,000 to 100,000) causes an increase in sorting time of approximately 4 (from 25.5 million to 101 million) and an increase in n by a factor of 5 (e.g., from 10,000 to 50,000) increases the sorting time by approximately a factor of 25 (from 1.1 million to 25.5 million). Indeed, as n becomes larger and larger, the sorting time becomes more and more closely proportional to n^2, as is clearly illustrated by the last column of Figure 8.1.3. Because of this, we say that the time for the sort is on the *order of* n^2, written $O(n^2)$. Thus for large n the time required by the sort is almost proportional to n^2. Of course, for small values of n, the sort may exhibit drastically different behavior (as in Figure 8.1.3), a situation that must be taken into account in analyzing its efficiency.

Using this concept of the order of a sort, we can compare various sorting techniques and classify them as being "good" or "bad" in specific cases. One might hope to discover the "optimal" sort, which is $O(n)$; unfortunately, however, it can be shown that no such sort exists. Most of the classical sorts we shall consider have time requirements that range from $O(n \log n)$ to $O(n^2)$. (You are asked to show as an exercise that the base of the logarithm is irrelevant in determining the order of the sort.) In the former, multiplying the file size by 100 will multiply the sorting time by less than 200 (if the base of the logarithm is 10); in the latter, multiplying the file size by 100 multiplies the sorting time by a factor of 10,000. Figure 8.1.4 shows the comparison of $n \log n$ with n^2 for a range of values of n. It can be seen from the figure that for large n, as n increases, n^2 increases at a much more rapid

n	$n \log_{10} n$	n^2
1×10^1	1.0×10^1	1.0×10^2
5×10^1	8.5×10^1	2.5×10^3
1×10^2	2.0×10^2	1.0×10^4
5×10^2	1.3×10^3	2.5×10^5
1×10^3	3.0×10^3	1.0×10^6
5×10^3	1.8×10^4	2.5×10^7
1×10^4	4.0×10^4	1.0×10^8
5×10^4	2.3×10^5	2.5×10^9
1×10^5	5.0×10^5	1.0×10^{10}
5×10^5	2.8×10^6	2.5×10^{11}
1×10^6	6.0×10^6	1.0×10^{12}
5×10^6	3.3×10^7	2.5×10^{13}
1×10^7	7.0×10^7	1.0×10^{14}

Figure 8.1.4 A comparison of $n \log n$ and n^3 for various value of n.

rate than $n \log n$. However, a sort should not be selected simply because it is $O(n \log n)$. The relation of the file size n and the other terms comprising the actual sorting time must be known. In particular, terms that play an insignificant role for large n may play a very dominant role for small n. All of these considerations must be taken into account before an intelligent sort selection can be made.

A second method of determining time requirements of a sorting technique is to actually run the program and measure its efficiency (either by measuring absolute time units or the number of operations performed). In order to use such results, the test must be run on "many" sample files. Even when such statistics have been gathered, the application of that sort to a specific file need not yield results that follow the general pattern. Peculiar attributes of the file in question may make the sorting speed deviate significantly. In the sorts of the subsequent sections we shall give an intuitive explanation as to why a particular sort is classified as $O(n^2)$ or $O(n \log n)$; we leave mathematical analysis and sophisticated testing of empirical data as exercises for the ambitious reader.

In most cases, the time needed by a sort depends upon the original sequence of the data. For some sorts, input data that is almost in sorted order can be completely sorted in time $O(n)$, whereas input data in reverse order needs time $O(n^2)$. For other sorts the time required is $O(n \log n)$ regardless of the original order of the data. Thus, if we have some knowledge about the original data, we can make a more intelligent decision as to which sorting method to select. On the other hand, if we have no such knowledge, we may wish to select a sort based on the worst possible case or based on the "average" case. In any event, the only general comment that can be made about sorting techniques is that there is no "best" general sorting technique. The choice of a sort must, of necessity, depend on the specific circumstances.

Once a particular sorting technique has been selected, the programmer should try to make the program as efficient as possible. In many programming applications it is often necessary to sacrifice effiency for the sake of clarity. With sorting, the situation is usually the opposite. Once a sorting program has been written and tested, the programmer's chief goal is to improve its speed, even if it becomes less readable. The reason for this is that a sort may account for the major part of a program's efficiency, so that any improvement in sorting time significantly affects overall efficiency. Another reason is that a sort is often used quite frequently, so that a small improvement in its execution speed saves a great deal of computer time. It is usually a good idea to remove subroutine calls, especially from inner loops, and to replace them with the code of the subroutine in line, since the call-return mechanism of a language can be prohibitively expensive in terms of time. In many of the programs we do not do this, so as not to obfuscate the intent of the program with huge blocks of code. But before using the following programs on large files the reader would do well to replace subroutine calls with code in line.

Space constraints are usually less important than time considerations. One of the reasons for this is that for most sorting programs the amount of space needed is closer to $O(n)$ than to $O(n^2)$. A second reason is that if more space is required, it can almost always be found in auxiliary storage. Of course the usual relationship between time and space holds for sorting algorithms (i.e., those programs that require less time usually require more space, and vice versa).

In the remaining sections we investigate some of the more popular sorting techniques and indicate some of their advantages and disadvantages.

EXERCISES

1. Choose any sorting technique you are familiar with.

   (a) Write a program for the sort.
   (b) Is the sort stable?
   (c) Determine the time requirements of the sort as a function of the file size, both mathematically and empirically.
   (d) What is the order of the sort?
   (e) At what file size does the most dominant term begin to overshadow the others?

2. Show that if a sort is $O(n \log_2 n)$, it is also $O(n \log_{10} n)$, and vice versa.

3. Suppose that a time requirement is given by the formula $an^2 + bn \log_2 n$, where a and b are constants. Answer the following questions by both proving your results mathematically and writing a program to empirically validate the results.

   (a) For what values of n (expressed in terms of a and b) does the first term dominate the second?
   (b) For what value of n (expressed in terms of a and b) are the two terms equal?
   (c) For what values of n (expressed in terms of a and b) does the second term dominate the first?

4. Show that any process which sorts a file can be extended to find all duplicates in the file.

5. Consider a Pascal subroutine $sort(x,n)$ to sort the first n elements of an array x. What are the relative advantages and disadvantages of leaving x as a parameter or of making it a global variable?

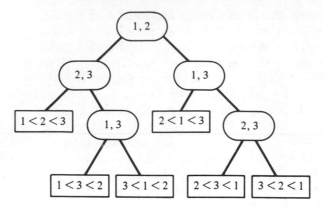

Figure 8.1.5 A decision tree for a file of 3 elements.

6. A *sort decision tree* is a binary tree that represents a sorting method based on comparisons. Figure 8.1.5 illustrates such a decision tree for a file of three elements. Each nonleaf of such a tree represents a comparison between two elements. Each leaf represents a completely sorted file. A left branch from a nonleaf indicates that the first key found was smaller than the second; a right branch indicates that it was larger. (We assume that all the elements in the file have distinct keys.) For example, the tree of Figure 8.1.5 represents a sort on three elements $x[1]$, $x[2]$, $x[3]$, which proceeds as follows:

Compare $x[1]$ to $x[2]$. If $x[1]<x[2]$, then compare $x[2]$ with $x[3]$, and if $x[2]<x[3]$, then the sorted order of the file is $x[1]$, $x[2]$, $x[3]$; otherwise, if $x[1]<x[3]$, the sorted order is $x[1]$, $x[3]$, $x[2]$, and if $x[1]>x[3]$, then the sorted order is $x[3]$, $x[1]$, $x[2]$. If $x[1]>x[2]$, then proceed in a similar fashion down the right subtree.

   (a) Show that a sort decision tree which never makes a redundant comparison (i.e., never compares $x[i]$ and $x[j]$ if the relationship between $x[i]$ and $x[j]$ is known) has $n!$ leafs.

   (b) Show that the depth of such a decision tree is at least $\log_2(n!)$.

   (c) Show that $n! \geqslant (n/2)^{n/2}$, so that the depth of such a tree is $O(n \log n)$.

   (d) Explain why this proves that any sorting method which uses comparisons on a file of size n must make at least $O(n \log n)$ comparisons.

7. Given a sort decision tree for a file as in Exercise 6, show that if the file contains some equal elements, the result of applying the tree to the file (where either a left or right branch is taken whenever two elements are equal) is a sorted file.

8. Extend the concept of the binary decision tree of the previous exercises to a ternary tree which includes the possibility of equality. It is desired to determine which elements of the file are equal, in addition to the order of the distinct elements of the file. How many comparisons are necessary?

9. Show that if k is the smallest integer greater than or equal to $n + \log_2 n - 2$, then k comparisons are necessary and sufficient to find the largest and second largest elements of a set of n distinct elements.

10. How many comparisons are necessary to find the largest and smallest of a set of n distinct elements?

2. EXCHANGE SORTS

Bubble Sort

The first sort we present is probably the most widely known among beginning students of programming—the *bubble sort*. One of the characteristics of this sort is that it is easy to understand and program. Yet, of all the sorts that we shall consider, it is probably the least efficient.

In each of the subsequent examples, x is an array of integers of which the first n are to be sorted so that $x[i] \leqslant x[j]$ for $1 \leqslant i < j \leqslant n$. It is straightforward to extend this simple format to one that is used in sorting n records, each with a subfield key k.

The basic idea underlying the bubble sort is to pass through the file sequentially several times. Each pass consists of comparing each element in the file with its successor ($x[i]$ with $x[i+1]$) and interchanging the two elements if they are not in proper order. Consider the following file:

$$25 \quad 57 \quad 48 \quad 37 \quad 12 \quad 92 \quad 86 \quad 33$$

The following comparisons are made on the first pass:

$x[1]$ with $x[2]$	(25 with 57)	no interchange
$x[2]$ with $x[3]$	(57 with 48)	interchange
$x[3]$ with $x[4]$	(57 with 37)	interchange
$x[4]$ with $x[5]$	(57 with 12)	interchange
$x[5]$ with $x[6]$	(57 with 92)	no interchange
$x[6]$ with $x[7]$	(92 with 86)	interchange
$x[7]$ with $x[8]$	(92 with 33)	interchange

Thus, after the first pass, the file is in the order

$$25 \quad 48 \quad 37 \quad 12 \quad 57 \quad 86 \quad 33 \quad 92$$

Notice that after this first pass, the largest element (in this case 92) is in its proper position within the array. In general, $x[n-i+1]$ will be in its proper position after iteration i. The method is called the bubble sort because each number slowly "bubbles" up to its proper position. After the second pass the file is

$$25 \quad 37 \quad 12 \quad 48 \quad 57 \quad 33 \quad 86 \quad 92$$

Notice that 86 has now found its way to the second highest position. Since each iteration places a new element into its proper position, a file of n elements requires no more than $n-1$ iterations.

The complete set of iterations is illustrated on the top of the next page.

On the basis of this discussion we could proceed to code the bubble sort. However, there are some obvious improvements to the method. First, since all of the elements in positions greater than or equal to $n-i+1$ are already in proper position after iteration i, they need not be compared in succeeding iterations. Thus on the first pass $n-1$ comparisons are made, on the second pass $n-2$ comparisons, and on the $(n-1)$th pass only one comparison is made

iteration 0 (original file)	25	57	48	37	12	92	86	33
iteration 1		25	48	37	12	57	86	33	92
iteration 2		25	37	12	48	57	33	86	92
iteration 3		25	12	37	48	33	57	86	92
iteration 4		12	25	37	33	48	57	86	92
iteration 5		12	25	33	37	48	57	86	92
iteration 6		12	25	33	37	48	57	86	92
iteration 7		12	25	33	37	48	57	86	92

(between $x[1]$ and $x[2]$). Therefore, the process speeds up as it proceeds through successive passes.

We have shown that $n-1$ passes are sufficient to sort a file of size n. However, in the above sample file of eight elements, the file was sorted after five iterations, making the last two iterations unnecessary. To eliminate unnecessary passes we must be able to detect the fact that the file is already sorted. But this is a simple task since in a sorted file, no interchanges are made on any pass. By keeping a record of whether or not any interchanges are made in a given pass it can be determined whether any further passes are necessary. Under this method, if the file can be sorted in fewer than $n-1$ passes, the final pass makes no interchanges.

Using these improvements, we present the routine *bubble*, which accepts two parameters, x and n. We assume the following global declarations:

```
const numelts = 100;
      abovelts = 101; { numelts plus one }
type arraytype = array[1..numelts] of integer;
     aptr = 1..numelts;
     aptr2 = 0..abovelts;
var x: arraytype;
    n: aptr;
```

x is an array of integers and n is an integer representing the number of elements to be sorted. (n may be less than the upper bound of x.) The type *aptr2* is defined because sorting algorithms often need auxiliary variables, whose value can sometimes be 0 or one more than the number of elements being sorted. (For an alternative method of implementing sorting algorithms as Pascal programs, see Section 5 of the Appendix.)

```
procedure bubble(var x: arraytype; n: aptr);
var pass,j: aptr;
    intchnge: boolean;
    hold: integer;
begin { procedure bubble}
    intchnge:= true;
    pass:= 1;
```

CHAP. 8: SORTING

```
while (pass <= n-1) and (intchnge)
         {        outer loop controls the number of passes          }
    do begin
             intchnge:= false;  {    initially no interchanges    }
                                {  have been made on this pass  }
         for j:= 1 to n-pass
             { inner loop governs each individual pass }
             do if x[j] > x[j+1]  { elements out of order }
                then begin
                             { an interchange is necessary }
                         intchnge:= true;
                         hold:= x[j];
                         x[j]:= x[j+1];
                         x[j+1]:= hold
                  end {then begin};
         pass:= pass+1
    end {while...do begin}
end { procedure bubble};
```

What can be said about the efficiency of the bubble sort? In the case of a sort that does not include the two improvements outlined above, the analysis is simple. There are $n-1$ passes and $n-1$ comparisons on each pass. Thus the total number of comparisons is $(n-1)*(n-1)=n^2-2n+1$, which is $O(n^2)$. Of course, the number of interchanges depends on the original order of the file. However, the number of interchanges cannot be greater than the number of comparisons. It is probable that the number of interchanges rather than the number of comparisons take up the most time in the algorithm's execution.

Let us see how the improvements that we introduced affect the speed of the bubble sort. The number of comparisons on iteration i is $n-i$. Thus, if there are k iterations, the total number of comparisons is $(n-1)+(n-2)+(n-3)+\cdots+(n-k)$, which equals $(2kn-k^2-k)/2$. It can be shown that the average number of iterations, k, is $O(n)$, so that the entire formula is still $O(n^2)$, although the constant multiplier is smaller than before. However, there is additional overhead involved in testing and initializing the boolean variable *intchnge* (once per pass) and setting it to *true* (once for every interchange).

The only redeeming features of the bubble sort are that it requires little additional space (one memory location to hold the temporary value for interchanging) and that it is $O(n)$ in the case that the file is completely sorted (or almost completely sorted). This follows from the observation that only one pass of $n-1$ comparisons (and no interchanges) is necessary to establish that a sorted file is sorted.

There are some other ways to improve the bubble sort. One of these is to observe that the number of passes necessary before the file is sorted is the largest distance by which a number must move towards the beginning of the array. In our example, for instance, 33 starts at position 8 in the array and ultimately finds its way to position 3 after five iterations. The bubble sort can be speeded up by having successive passes go in opposite directions, so that the number of passes is reduced. This version is left as an exercise.

Quicksort

The next sort we consider is the *partition exchange sort* (or *quicksort*). Let x be an array and n the number of elements in the array to be sorted. Choose an element a from a specific position within the array (e.g., a can be chosen as the first element so that $a=x[1]$). Suppose that the elements of x are rearranged so that a is placed into position j and the following conditions hold:

1. Each of the elements in positions 1 through $j-1$ is less than or equal to a.
2. Each of the elements in positions $j+1$ through n is greater than or equal to a.

Notice that if these two conditions hold for a particular a and j, then a remains in position j when the array is completely sorted. (You are asked to prove this fact as an exercise.) If the process is repeated with the subarrays $x[1]$ through $x[j-1]$ and $x[j+1]$ through $x[n]$ and any subarrays created by the process in successive iterations, the final result is a sorted file.

Let us illustrate the quicksort with an example. If an initial array is given as

$$25 \quad 57 \quad 48 \quad 37 \quad 12 \quad 92 \quad 86 \quad 33$$

and the first element (25) is placed in its proper position, the resulting array is

$$12 \quad 25 \quad 57 \quad 48 \quad 37 \quad 92 \quad 86 \quad 33$$

At this point, 25 is in its proper position in the array ($x[2]$), each element below that position (12) is less than or equal to 25, and each element above that position (57, 48, 37, 92, 86 and 33) is greater than or equal to 25. Since 25 is in its final position, the original problem has been decomposed into the problem of sorting the two subarrays

$$(12) \quad \text{and} \quad (57 \ 48 \ 37 \ 92 \ 86 \ 33)$$

Nothing need be done to sort the first of these subarrays; a file of one element is already sorted. To sort the second subarray the process is repeated and the subarray is further subdivided. The entire array may now be viewed as

$$12 \quad 25 \quad (57 \quad 48 \quad 37 \quad 92 \quad 86 \quad 33)$$

where parentheses enclose the subarrays that are yet to be sorted. Repeating the process on the subarray $x[3]$ through $x[8]$ yields

$$12 \quad 25 \quad (48 \quad 37 \quad 33) \quad 57 \quad (92 \quad 86)$$

and further repetitions yield

12	25	(37	33)	48	57	(92	86)
12	25	(33)	37	48	57	(92	86)
12	25	33	37	48	57	(92	86)
12	25	33	37	48	57	(86)	92
12	25	33	37	48	57	86	92

Note that the final array is sorted.

By this time you should have noticed that the quicksort may be defined most conveniently as a recursive procedure. We may outline an algorithm $quick(lb,ub)$ to sort all elements in an array x between $x[lb]$ and $x[ub]$ (lb is the lower bound, ub the upper bound) as follows:

```
if lb < ub
    then begin                { if lb ⩾ ub, then array is   }
                              { sorted and return to calling }
                              {          procedure           }
          rearrange(lb,ub,j);
                              { rearrange the elements of the }
                              { subarray such that one of the }
                              {  elements (possibly x[lb]) is }
                              {  now at x[j] (j is an output  }
                              {       parameter) and:         }
                              {  1. x[i]⩽x[j] for lb⩽i<j      }
                              {  2. x[i]⩾x[j] for j<i⩽ub      }
                              {    x[j] is now at its final   }
                              {             position          }
          quick(lb,j-1);
                              {  sort the subarray between    }
                              {      x[lb] and x[j-1]         }
          quick(j+1,ub)
                              {  sort the subarray between    }
                              {      x[j+1] and x[ub]         }
    end {then begin}
```

The only remaining problem is to describe a mechanism to implement *rearrange*, which allows a specific element to find its proper position with respect to the others in the subarray. Note that the way in which this rearrangement is implemented is irrelevant to the sorting method. All that is required by the sort is that the elements are partitioned properly. In the example above, the elements in each of the two subfiles remain in the same relative order as they appear in the original file. However, such a rearrangement method is relatively inefficient. (Why?)

One way to effect a rearrangement efficiently is the following. Let $a = x[lb]$ be the element whose final position is sought. (There is no appreciable efficiency gained by selecting the first element of the subarray as the one that is inserted into its proper position; it merely makes some of the programs easier to code.) Two pointers, *up* and *down*, are initialized to the upper and lower bounds of the subarray, respectively. At any point during execution, each element in a position above *up* is greater than or equal to *a*, and each element in a position below *down* is less than or equal to *a*. The two pointers *up* and *down* are alternately moved toward each other. Execution begins by decreasing the pointer *up* one position at a time until $x[up] < a$. At that point $x[up]$ and $x[down]$ are interchanged. (Note that at that point the value of $x[up]$ is *a*.) The algorithm then proceeds in the opposite direction and increments the pointer *down* one position at a time until $x[down] > a$. When this happens, $x[up]$ and $x[down]$ are interchanged and scanning resumes in the opposite direction. (Note that after this interchange the value of $x[down]$ is *a*.) The process halts when $up = down$, at which point $j = up$, $x[j] = a$ and each element in a position above j is greater than or equal to $x[j]$ and each element in a position below j is less than or equal to $x[j]$.

We illustrate this process on the sample file, showing the positions of *up* and *down* as they are adjusted. The direction of the scan is indicated by an arrow at the pointer being moved. An asterisk indicates that an interchange is made.

$a = x[lb] = 25$

```
down                                              ←up
 25    57    48    37    12    92    86    33

down                                  ←up
 25    57    48    37    12    92    86    33

down                            ←up
 25    57    48    37    12    92    86    33

down                            up
 25    57    48    37    12    92    86    33        *

down→                           up
 12    57    48    37    25    92    86    33

       down                     up
 12    57    48    37    25    92    86    33        *

       down                ←up
 12    25    48    37    57    92    86    33

       down          ←up
 12    25    48    37    57    92    86    33

       down   ←up
 12    25    48    37    57    92    86    33

       down=up
 12    25    48    37    57    92    86    33
```

At this point 25 is in its proper position (position 2) and every element to its left is less than or equal to 25 and every element to its right is greater than or equal to 25. We could now proceed to sort the two subarrays (12) and (48 37 57 92 86 33) by applying the same method.

An algorithm to implement *rearrange* is as follows (*lb* and *ub* are input parameters, and *j* is an output parameter):

```
a:= x[lb]                        { a is the element whose final }
                                 {      position is sought      }
j:= lb;                          {   j will be set to the final }
                                 {        position of a         }
up:= ub;
down:= lb;
repeat
  while (up > down) and (x[up] ⩾ a)
       do up:= up-1;
  j:= up;
  if up <> down
    then begin
              interchange x[up] and x[down];
              while (down < up) and (x[down] ⩽ a)
                  do down:= down+1;
              j:= down;
              if down <> up
                then interchange x[down] and x[up]
         end {then begin}
until up = down
```

Before writing a procedure to implement *rearrange*, there is one improvement that can be made. Each time *x[up]* and *x[down]* are interchanged, *a* is inserted into a new position which is only temporary if an additional interchange is necessary. Instead of actually inserting *a* into this position, let us simply remember the position in a variable *j* (which we must do anyway). Should additional "interchanges" be necessary, the new element can be inserted into *x[j]* and *j* is set to the former position of this element. Before returning we must, of course, insert *a* into *x[j]*.

We assume the global definitions of the types *arraytype*, *aptr*, and *aptr2*, as well as the global declarations of the variables *x* and *n*, as given above.

A program for *rearrange* follows:

```
procedure rearrange(lb,ub: aptr2; var j: aptr);
var up,down: aptr;
    a: integer;
begin { procedure rearrange}
    a:= x[lb];
    j:= lb;
    up:= ub;
    down:= lb;
```

```
    repeat
        while (up > down) and (x[up] >= a) {move down the array}
            do up:= up-1;
        j:= up;
        if up <> down
            then begin
                    x[down]:= x[up];
                        { move up the array }
                        while (down < up) and (x[down] <= a)
                            do down:= down+1;
                        j:= down;
                        if down <> up
                            then x[up]:= x[down]
                end {then begin}
    until down = up;
    x[j]:= a
end { procedure rearrange};
```

[handwritten margin note: what about x[up] <= x[down]? not needed, since x[down] saved as a]

The routine can be made slightly more efficient by eliminating some of the redundant tests. You are asked to do this as an exercise.

We may now code a program to implement the quicksort. As in the case of *bubble*, the parameters are the array x and the number of elements of x we wish to sort, n. Since the algorithm requires the sorting of two subarrays, we write an internal recursive routine *quick* whose parameters are the lower and upper bounds of the array between which we wish to sort.

```
procedure quicksrt(var x: arraytype;  n: aptr);
procedure quick(lb,ub: aptr2);
var j: aptr;
            { the procedure rearrange goes here }
begin { procedure quick}
    if lb < ub
        then begin
                rearrange(lb,ub,j);
                quick(lb,j-1);
                quick(j+1,ub)
            end {then begin}
end { procedure quick};

begin { procedure quicksrt}
    quick(1,n)
end { procedure quicksrt};
```

Improving the Program

Although the preceding programs are concise in terms of what they accomplish and how they do it, the overhead of subroutine calls (especially recursive subroutine calls) should be avoided in programs such as sorts in which execution efficiency is a significant consideration. The recursive calls to *quick* can easily be eliminated by using a stack as in Chapter 3. Once *rearrange* has been executed, the current parameters to *quick* are no longer needed, except in computing the arguments to the two subsequent recursive calls. Thus instead of stacking the current parameters upon each recursive call, we can compute and stack the new parameters for each of the two recursive calls. Under this approach, the stack at any point contains the lower and upper bounds of all subarrays that must yet be sorted. Furthermore, since the second recursive call immediately precedes the return to the calling program (as in the Towers of Hanoi problem) it may be eliminated entirely and replaced with a branch. Finally, since the order in which the two recursive calls are made is irrelevant in this problem, we elect in each case to stack the larger subarray and process the smaller subarray immediately. As an exercise you are asked to show that this keeps the size of the stack to a minimum. With these improvements in mind, we code the routine *quick2*:

```
procedure quick2(var x: arraytype;  n: aptr);
type stackitem = record
                   lb: aptr2;
                   ub: aptr2
                 end;
     stack = record
               top: 0..numelts;
               item: array[1..numelts] of stackitem
             end;
var s: stack;
    newbnds: stackitem;
    i,j: aptr;
{the routines rearrange, push, popsub, and empty go here}
begin { procedure quick2}
    s.top:= 0;
    with newbnds
        do begin
            lb:= 1;
            ub:= n;
            push(s,newbnds);
            {    repeat as long as there are    }
            { unsorted subarrays on the stack }
            while not empty(s)
                do begin
                    popsub(s,newbnds);
                    while ub > lb
                        do begin
                            { process next subarray }
                            rearrange(lb,ub,j);
```

```
                              {    stack the larger    }
                              {        subarray        }
                          if j - lb > ub - j
                              {  stack first subarray   }
                                then begin
                                        i:= ub;
                                        ub:= j - 1;
                                        push(s,newbnds);
                                        { process second subarray }
                                        lb:= j + 1;
                                        ub:= i
                                    end {then begin}
                                 { stack second subarray }
                                else begin
                                        i:= lb;
                                        lb:= j + 1;
                                        push(s,newbnds);
                                        { process first subarray }
                                        lb:= i;
                                        ub:= j - 1
                                    end {else begin}
                             end {while ub > lb do begin}
                        end {while not empty(s) do begin}
                end {with...do begin}
          end {procedure quick2};
```

How efficient is the quicksort? Assume that the file size n is a power of 2, say $n=2^m$, so that $m = \log_2 n$. Assume also that the proper position for $x[lb]$ always turns out to be the exact middle of the subarray. In that case there will be approximately n comparisons (actually $n-1$) on the first pass, after which the file is split into two subfiles each of size $n/2$ approximately. For each of these two files there are approximately $n/2$ comparisons and a total of four files each of size $n/4$ are formed. Each of these files requires $n/4$ comparisons, yielding a total of $n/8$ subfiles. After halving the subfiles m times, there are n files of size 1. Thus the total number of comparisons for the entire sort is approximately

$$n + 2(n/2) + 4(n/4) + 8(n/8) + \cdots + n(n/n)$$

or

$$n + n + n + n + \cdots + n \quad (m \text{ terms})$$

comparisons. There are m terms because the file is subdivided m times. Thus the total number of comparisons is $O(nm)$ or $O(n\log n)$ (recall that $m=\log_2 n$). Thus, if these properties describe the file, the quicksort is $O(n\log n)$, which is relatively efficient.

This analysis assumes that the original array and all the resulting sub-arrays are unsorted, so that $x[lb]$ always finds its proper position at the middle of the subarray. Suppose that these conditions do not hold and that the original array is sorted (or almost sorted). If, for example, $x[lb]$ is in its correct position, the original file is split into subfiles of sizes 0 and $n-1$. If this process continues, a total of $n-1$ subfiles are sorted, the first of size n, the second of size $n-1$, the third of size $n-2$, and so on. Assuming k comparisons for a file of size k, the total number of comparisons to sort the entire file is

$$n + (n-1) + (n-2) + \cdots + 2$$

which is $O(n^2)$. Similarly, if the original file is sorted in descending order, the final position of $x[lb]$ is ub and the file is again split into two subfiles, which are heavily unbalanced (sizes $n-1$ and 0). Thus the quicksort has the seemingly absurd property that it works best for files that are completely unsorted and worst for files that are completely sorted. The situation is precisely the opposite for the bubble sort, which works best for sorted files and worst for unsorted files.

The analysis for the case where the file size is not an integral power of 2 is similar but slightly more complex; the results, however, remain the same. It can be shown, however, that on the average (over all files of size n), the quicksort makes $O(n \log n)$ comparisons.

The space requirements for the quicksort depend upon the number of nested recursive calls or on the size of the stack. Clearly, the stack can never grow larger than the number of elements in the original file. How much smaller than n the stack grows depends upon the number of subfiles generated and on their sizes. The size of the stack can be somewhat contained by always stacking the larger of the two subarrays and applying the routine to the smaller of the two. This guarantees that all smaller subarrays are subdivided before larger subarrays, giving the net effect of having fewer elements on the stack at any given time. The reasons for this is that a smaller subarray can be divided fewer times than a larger subarray. Of course, the larger subarray will ultimately be processed and subdivided, but this will occur after the smaller subarrays have been sorted.

EXERCISES

1. Prove that the number of passes necessary in the bubble sort of the text before the file is in sorted order (not including the last pass, which detects the fact that the file is sorted) equals the largest distance by which an element must move from a larger index to a smaller index.

2. Rewrite the program *bubble* so that successive passes go in opposite directions.

3. Prove that in the sort of Exercise 2, if two elements are not interchanged during two consecutive passes in opposite directions, they are in their final position.

4. A sort by **counting** is performed as follows. Declare an array *count* and set *count*[i] to the number of elements which are less than or equal to $x[i]$. Then place $x[i]$ in position *count*[i] of an output array. (However, beware of the possibility of equal elements.) Write a routine to sort an array x of size n using this method.

5. Assume that a file contains integers between a and b, with many numbers repeated several times. A *distribution sort* proceeds as follows. Declare *number*: *array*[$a..b$] *of integer* and set *number*[i] to the number of times that integer i appears in the file, and then reset the values in the file appropriately. Write a routine to sort an array x of size n containing integers between a and b by this method.

6. The *odd–even transposition sort* proceeds as follows. Pass through the file several times. On the first pass, compare $x[i]$ with $x[i+1]$ for all odd i. On the second pass, compare $x[i]$ with $x[i+1]$ for all even i. Each time that $x[i] > x[i+1]$, interchange the two. Continue alternating in this fashion until the file is sorted.

(a) What is the condition for the sort's termination?
(b) Write a Pascal routine to implement the sort.
(c) What is the sort's efficiency on the average?

7. Rewrite the program for the quicksort by starting with the recursive version and applying the methods of Chapter 3 to produce a nonrecursive version.

8. Modify the quicksort program of the text so that if a subarray is small, the bubble sort is used. Determine, by actual computer runs, how small the subarray should be so that this mixed strategy will be more efficient than an ordinary quicksort.

9. Modify *rearrange* so that the middle value of $x[lb]$, $x[ub]$, and $x[(ub+lb)$ *div* $2]$ is used to partition the array. In what cases is the quicksort using this method more efficient than the version of the text? In what cases is it less efficient?

10. Evaluate the efficiency of each of the following sorting methods with respect to time and space considerations:

(a) The bubble sort using $n-1$ passes in which every pass goes through all the elements of the file.
(b) The bubble sort in which each pass makes one fewer comparison than the previous pass.
(c) The bubble sort of the text, modified as in Exercise 2.
(d) The counting sort of Exercise 4.
(e) The distribution sort of Exercise 5.
(f) The odd–even transposition sort of Exercise 6.
(g) The quicksort as modified in Exercise 8.
(h) The quicksort as modified in Exercise 9.

11. (a) Rewrite the routines for the bubble sort and the quicksort as presented in the text and the sorts of Exercise 10 so that a record is kept of the actual number of comparisons and the actual number of interchanges made.
(b) Write a random-number generator (or use an existing one if your installation has one) that generates integers between 0 and 9999.
(c) Using the generator of part (b), generate several files of size 10, size 100, and size 1000. Apply the sorting routines of part (a) to measure the time requirements for each of the sorts on each of the files.
(d) Measure the results of part (c) against the theoretical values presented in this section. Do they agree? If not, explain. In particular, rearrange the files so that they are completely sorted and in reverse order and see how the sorts behave with these inputs.

3. SELECTION AND TREE SORTING

Straight Selection Sort

A *selection sort* is one in which successive elements are selected from the file and placed in their proper position. The following program is an example of a *straight selection sort*. The largest number is first placed in the nth position, the next largest is placed in position $n-1$, and so on.

```
procedure select(var x: arraytype; n: aptr);
var i,j,indx: aptr;
    large: integer;
begin { procedure select}
    for i:= n downto 2
        do begin
                { place the largest number of x[1] through }
                {    x[i] into large and its index into indx   }
                large:= x[1];
                indx:= 1;
                for j:= 2 to i
                    do if x[j] > large
                            then begin
                                    large:= x[j];
                                    indx:= j
                                end {then begin}
                {         place large into position i          }
                x[indx]:= x[i];
                x[i]:= large
            end { for,,,do begin}
end { procedure select};
```

This sort is also known as the *push-down* sort.

Analysis of the straight selection sort is straightforward. The first pass makes $n-1$ comparisons, the second pass makes $n-2$, and so on. Therefore, there is a total of

$$(n-1) + (n-2) + (n-3) + \cdots + 1 = n(n-1)/2$$

comparisons, which is $O(n^2)$. The number of interchanges is always $n-1$ (unless a test is added to prevent the interchanging of an element with itself). There is little additional storage required (except to hold a few temporary variables). The sort may therefore be categorized as $O(n^2)$, although it is faster than the bubble sort. There is no improvement if the input file is completely sorted or unsorted because the testing proceeds to completion without regard to the makeup of the file. Despite the fact that it is simple to code, it is unlikely that the straight selection sort would be used on any files except those for which n is small.

Binary Tree Sorts

In the remainder of this section we illustrate several selection sorts that utilize binary trees. Before we do that, however, let us analyze the binary tree sort of Section 6.1. The reader is advised to review that sort before proceeding.

The method involves scanning each element of the input file and placing it into its proper position in a binary tree. To find the proper position of an element y, a left or right branch is taken at each node, depending upon whether y is less than the element in the node or greater than or equal to it. Once each input element is in its proper position in the tree, the sorted file can be retrieved by an inorder traversal of the tree. We present the algorithm for this sort, modifying it to accommodate the input as a preexisting array.

```
{ establish the first element as a root }
tree:= maketree(x[1]);
{ repeat for each successive element }
for i:= 2 to n
    do begin
        y:= x[i];
        p:= tree;
        { travel down the tree until a leaf is reached }
        while p <> nil
            do begin
                q:= p;
                if y < info(p)
                    then p:= left(p)
                    else p:= right(p)
            end {while...do begin};
        if y < info(q)
            then setleft(q,y)
            else setright(q,y)
    end {for...do begin};
{ the tree is built, traverse it in inorder }
intrav(tree)
```

To convert this algorithm into a procedure to sort an array, it is necessary to revise *intrav* so that visiting a node involves placing the contents of the node into the next position of the original array.

The relative efficiency of this method depends on the original order of the data. If the original array is completely sorted (or sorted in reverse order), the resulting tree appears as a sequence of only right (or left) links, as in Figure 8.3.1. In this case the insertion of the first node requires no comparisons, the second node requires two comparisons, the third node three comparisons, and so on. Thus the total number of comparisons is

$$2 + 3 + \cdots + n = n(n + 1)/2 - 1$$

which is $O(n^2)$.

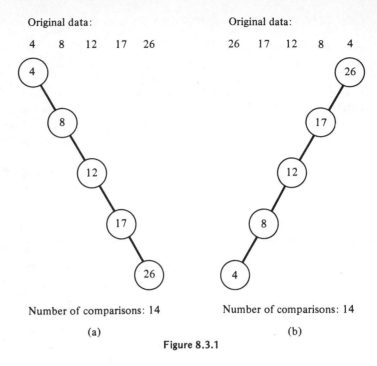

Original data:

4   8   12   17   26

4
8
12
17
26

Number of comparisons: 14

(a)

Original data:

26   17   12   8   4

26
17
12
8
4

Number of comparisons: 14

(b)

Figure 8.3.1

On the other hand, if the data in the original array are organized so that approximately half the numbers following any given number a in the array are less than a and half are greater than a, trees such as those in Figure 8.3.2 result. In such a case, the depth of the resulting binary tree is the smallest integer d greater than or equal to $\log_2(n+1)-1$. The number of nodes at any level l (except possibly for the last) is 2^l and the number of comparisons necessary to place a node at level l (except when $l=0$) is $l+1$. Thus the total

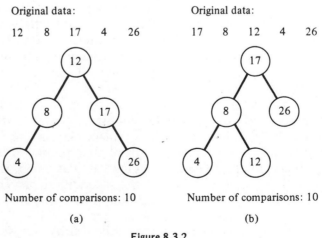

Original data:

12   8   17   4   26

12
8   17
4   26

Number of comparisons: 10

(a)

Original data:

17   8   12   4   26

17
8   26
4   12

Number of comparisons: 10

(b)

Figure 8.3.2

number of comparisons is between

$$d + \sum_{l=1}^{d-1} 2^l(l+1) \quad \text{and} \quad \sum_{l=1}^{d} 2^l(l+1)$$

It can be shown (mathematically inclined readers might be interested in proving this fact as an exercise) that the resulting sums are $O(n \log n)$.

Of course, once the tree has been created, time is expended in traversing it. (Note that if the tree is threaded as it is created, the traversal time is sharply reduced.)

This sort requires that one tree node be reserved for each array element. Depending on the method used to implement the tree, space may be required for tree pointers and threads, if any.

Tournament Sort

The next tree sort we consider is frequently called the *tournament sort*, because its actions mirror those of a tournament where participants play each other to determine the best player. (This sort is also called the *tree selection sort*.) Consider a tournament that determines the best player from the set {Ed, Gail, Keith, George, Jack, Pat, Barbara, Frank}. The outcome of the tournament can be represented by a binary tree as in Figure 8.3.3. Each leaf of the tree represents a player in the tournament. Each nonleaf node represents the results of a game between the players represented by its two sons. In Figure 8.3.3a it is clear that Gail is the tournament champion.

But suppose that it is also desired to determine the second-best player. Pat is not necessarily the second-best player, despite the fact that he played Gail in the championship game. To determine the second-best player, it would be necessary for Keith (who lost to Gail in the quarter-finals) to play George (who lost to Gail in the semifinals) and the winner of that match to play Pat.

Let us indicate that a player has been declared a winner by placing an asterisk in the leaf node corresponding to that player. Clearly, if a node is marked with an asterisk, its player does not participate in any future runoffs. If both sons of a node contain an asterisk, then those sons both represent players who have completed the tournament, and therefore the father node is also marked with an asterisk and no longer participates in any further runoffs. If only one son of a node is marked with an asterisk, the player represented by the other son is moved up to the father node. For example, when the leaf containing Gail in Figure 8.3.3a is marked with an asterisk, the name Keith is moved up to replace Gail in the father of that leaf. The tournament is then replayed from that point, with George playing Keith (George wins) and George playing Pat (Pat wins), thus yielding the tree of Figure 8.3.3b. Pat is indeed the second-best player. This process may be continued (Figure 8.3.3c illustrates that George is third-best) until all the nodes of the tree are marked with asterisks.

The same technique is used in the tournament sort. Each of the original

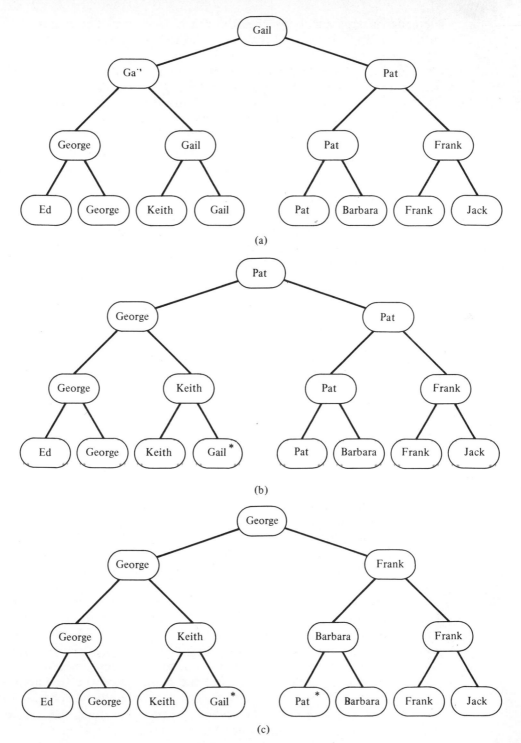

(a)

(b)

(c)

Figure 8.3.3 A tournament.

elements is assigned to a leaf node of a binary tree. The tree is constructed in bottom-up fashion from the leaf nodes to the root as follows. Choose two leaf nodes and establish them as the sons of a newly created father node. The content of the father node is set to the larger of the two numbers represented by its sons. This process is repeated until either one or zero leafs remain. If one remains, move the node itself up to the previous level. Now repeat this process with the newly created father nodes (plus the possible node that had no partner in the previous repetition) until the largest number is placed in the root node of a binary tree whose leafs contains all the numbers of the original file. The contents of this root node may then be output as the largest element. The leaf node containing the value at the root is then replaced by a number smaller than any in the original file (this corresponds to marking it with an asterisk). The contents of all its ancestors are then recomputed from the leafs to the root. This process is repeated until all the original elements have been output.

Figure 8.3.4a shows the initial tree using the file presented in Section 2:

25   57   48   37   12   92   86   33

After 92 is output, the tree is transformed as in Figure 8.3.4b, where 92 has been replaced by –1 and 86 is moved up to the root position. Note that it is necessary to recompute the contents of those nodes which were ancestors of the original leaf node which contained 92. Figure 8.3.4c shows the tree after 57 has moved up to the root. Note that –1 is used as the smallest value in this example because the numbers being sorted are all positive. The reader is asked to complete the process until all the elements of the original file have been output.

Before writing a program to implement the tournament sort, we must decide how to implement the tree in Pascal. The linked representation of Section 6.2 could be used. The efficiency of the program can be improved by using the representation of Section 6.4, in which an almost complete binary tree is represented as an array. In this representation, if index i references a node, then $left(i)$ is referenced by index $2*i$, $right(i)$ is referenced by $2*i+1$, and $father(i)$ is referenced by $i \ div \ 2$. To simplify the coding, we use a complete binary tree. In such a tree, only those nodes at the maximum level are leafs. Such a tree with eight leafs is illustrated in Figure 8.3.4. In general, the number of leafs in a complete binary tree is a power of 2. If the original file is of size n which is not a power of 2, then the number of leafs is the smallest power of 2 greater than n and the extra leafs are initialized to a value smaller than all values in the file to be sorted. In the ensuing program, which assumes a file of integers, this value is $-maxint$, which is the smallest integer allowed in a particular Pascal implementation.

A second question concerns what the contents of the tree nodes should be. Suppose that we allow the tree nodes to contain the actual items to be sorted, as in Figure 8.3.4. Then when the root is output, the leaf node corresponding to that root element must be replaced by a very small number and the contents of all its ancestors must be readjusted. But to locate the

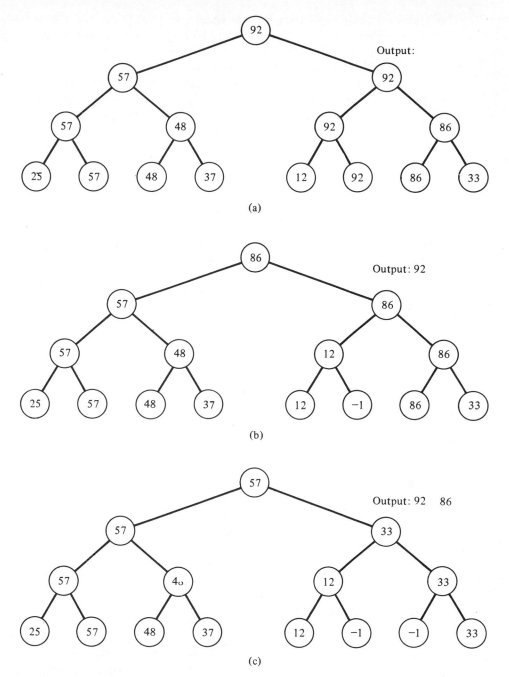

(a)

(b)

(c)

Figure 8.3.4

leaf node corresponding to the root, given only the root, it is necessary to travel from the root down to the leaf, making a comparison at each level. Furthermore, this process must be repeated for each new root node. It would certainly be more efficient if it were possible to proceed directly from the root to the leaf that corresponds to its contents. We therefore construct the complete binary tree in the following way. Each leaf contains an element of the original array. Each nonleaf node contains the index of the leaf node corresponding to the array element that the nonleaf node represents. If the content of a leaf node i, $tree[i]$, is moved up to a nonleaf node j, then $tree[j]$ is set to i (the index in the tree of the leaf node corresponding to the element) rather than $tree[i]$ (the actual element itself). The content of a nonleaf node (which is the index of the appropriate leaf node) is subsequently moved up the tree directly. Thus, if i is a leaf node, then $tree[i]$ contains the actual element that node i represents; if i is a nonleaf node, then $tree[i]$ references the index of a leaf node and hence $tree[tree[i]]$ references the actual element that node i represents.

For example, the array $tree$ representing the tree of Figure 8.3.4a is initialized as follows. (Nodes 8 through 15 are leafs; nodes 1 through 7 are nonleafs.)

i	$tree(i)$
1	13
2	9
3	13
4	9
5	10
6	13
7	14
8	25
9	57
10	48
11	37
12	12
13	92
14	86
15	33

We may now code our program as follows:

```
procedure tourn(var x: arraytype; n: aptr);
          {    size is the number of leafs necessary in the    }
          {      complete binary tree. size is equal to the    }
          {    smallest power of 2 greater than n. treesize    }
          { is the number of nodes and is equal to 2*size-1. }
  const size = 128; { smallest power of 2 greater than numelts }
        treesize = 255;
  type   treeptr = 0..treesize;
```

```
                var tree: array[1..treesize] of integer;
                    k: aptr;
                    i: treeptr;
                procedure initialize;
                            { body of initialize goes here }
                procedure readjust(var i: treeptr);
                            { body of readjust goes here }
                begin { procedure tourn}
                    initialize; { creates initial tree }
                                { as described in text }
                    { now that the tree is constructed, repeatedly place }
                    { the element represented by the root in the next }
                    { lower position in the array x and readjust the tree }
                    for k:= n downto 2
                        do begin
                            i:= tree[1]; { i is the index of the leaf node }
                                        { corresponding to the root }
                            x[k]:= tree[i]; { place element referenced }
                                        { by root in position k }
                            tree[i]:= -maxint;
                            readjust(i)    { readjust tree based on }
                                        { new contents of tree[i] }
                        end { for...do begin}
                    x[1]:= tree[tree[1]]
                end { procedure tourn};
```

We now present the routines *initialize* and *readjust*. Note that the level directly above the leafs must be treated differently than the other levels.

```
                procedure initialize;
                var j: integer;
                    k: aptr;
                begin { procedure initialize}
                    {        initialize leafs of tree        }
                    j:= 1;
                    while j <= n
                        do begin
                            tree[size+j-1]:= x[j];
                            j:= j+1
                        end {while...do begin};
                    {    initialize remaining leafs    }
                    for j:= size+j-1 to 2*size-1
                        do tree[j]:= -maxint;
                    { compute upper levels of the tree }
                    {    the level directly above the    }
                    {     leafs is treated separately     }
                    j:= size;
```

```
            while j <= 2*size-1
                do begin
                        if tree[j] >= tree[j+1]
                            then tree[j div 2]:= j
                            else tree[j div 2]:= j+1;
                        j:= j+2
                    end {while...do begin};
            k:= size div 2;
            while k > 1
                do begin {next level}
                        j:= k;
                        while j <= 2*k-1
                            do begin
                                    if tree[tree[j]] >= tree[tree[j+1]]
                                        then tree[j div 2]:= tree[j]
                                        else tree[j div 2]:= tree[j+1];
                                    j:= j+2
                                end {while j <= 2*k-1 do begin};
                        k:= k div 2
                    end {while k>1 do begin}
    end { procedure initialize};


procedure readjust(var i: treeptr);
var j: treeptr;
begin { procedure readjust}
        { now that tree[i] has a new value (-maxint) }
        {         we readjust all its ancestors.         }
        {             adjust the father node             }
        if odd(i)
            then tree[i div 2]:= i-1
            else tree[i div 2]:= i+1;
        {             advance to the root             }
        i:= i div 2;
        while i > 1
            do begin
                    { j is the brother of i }
                    if odd(i)
                        then j:= i-1
                        else j:= i+1;
                    if tree[tree[i]] > tree[tree[j]]
                        then tree[i div 2]:= tree[i]
                        else tree[i div 2]:= tree[j];
                    i:= i div 2
                end {while...do begin}
    end { procedure readjust};
```

Measuring the time and space requirements of this sort is straightforward. Observe that after the initial tree has been created and the root has been output, d comparisons are required to readjust the tree and move a new element to the root position, where d is the depth of the tree. Since d is approximately $\log_2(n+1)$ and $n-1$ adjustments must be made to the tree, the number of comparisons is approximately $(n-1)\log_2(n+1)$, which is $O(n\log n)$. Of course, comparisons are made in creating the initial tree, but the number of such comparisons is $O(n)$ and is therefore dominated by the $O(n\log n)$ term.

The space requirements, in addition to temporary values, are the 2*$size$ memory units reserved for the array $tree$, where $size$ is the smallest integral power of 2 which is greater than or equal to n. Since n is not a constant, we must use its constant upper bound, $numelts$, to determine the size of the static Pascal arrays. Since we insisted on a complete binary tree in this program, there may be some wasted space if, for example, the value of $numelts$ is 33 or 129. Of course, if a linked implementation of trees is used, additional space is required for the links.

Heapsort

Although the foregoing program appears to be relatively efficient in all cases, it does have a serious shortcoming, which is easy to remove. The upper levels of the tree contain pointers, whereas the actual data are kept only at the lowest level. Because of this, considerable work is involved in bringing an element from the leaf to the root. Much of this work is unnecessary in the later stages of the sort when most of the leafs (and indirectly, many of the upper levels) contain the value $-maxint$, causing unnecessary comparisons to be made.

This drawback is remedied by the *heapsort*. In this sort, only one node is reserved for each of the elements in the original file. This serves to eliminate the large amount of space allocated in the tournament sort and the redundant comparisons of the later stages of that sort. In fact, the original array x is used as a workspace for the sort, so that extra space is required only for temporary variables.

Define a *heap of size n* as an almost complete binary tree of n nodes such that the content of each node is less than or equal to the content of its father. [Recall that the definition of an almost complete binary tree in Section 6.4 requires such a tree to be strictly binary. If this requirement is dropped, an almost complete binary tree containing an even number of nodes exists. However, there would then be a nonleaf in the tree which has no right son (i.e., there is an i for which $2*i+1$ is outside the array bounds). In the remainder of this section, the initial array x which is to be sorted may contain an even number of elements. Thus, an almost complete binary tree need not be strictly binary, and it is necessary to ensure that all array references are within bounds.] If the array implementation of an almost complete binary tree is used, as was done in the implementation of the tournament sort, this condition reduces to the inequality

$$info[j] \leqslant info[j \ div \ 2] \qquad for \ 1 \leqslant (j \ div \ 2) < j \leqslant n$$

It is clear from this definition of a heap that the root of the tree (or the first element of the array) is the largest element in the heap. Assuming that the routine *createheap*(i) creates a heap of size i consisting of the first i elements of the array x, a sorting method could be implemented as follows:

```
for i:= n downto 2
    do begin
            createheap(i);
            interchange x[1] and x[i]
        end {for...do begin}
```

As we shall see, however, it is not necessary to create the entire heap anew on each iteration; we can readjust the heap that was created on the previous iteration so that it remains a heap even after the interchange. Thus the heap-sort consists of the following algorithm.

```
createheap(n);
for i:= n downto 2
    do begin
            interchange x[1] and x[i];
            create a heap of order i−1 by readjusting the position of x[1]
        end {for...do begin}
```

We must consider two problems: how to create the original heap and how to adjust the intermediate heaps. To create the original heap, start with a heap of size 1 consisting of $x[1]$ alone and try to create a heap of size 2 consisting of $x[1]$ and $x[2]$. This can be accomplished quite easily by interchanging $x[2]$ and $x[1]$ if $x[1]$ is less than $x[2]$. In general, in order to create a heap of size i by inserting node i into an existing heap of size $i-1$, compare node i with its father. If node i is greater, interchange the two and reset i to point to the father. Repeat this process until the content of the father of node i is greater than or equal to the content of node i or until i is the root of the heap. Thus an algorithm to create a heap of order k may be written as follows:

```
for node:= 2 to k
    do begin
            { insert x[node] into heap }
            i:= node;
            j:= i div 2; { j is father of i }
            while (i is not the root) and (x[j] ≤ x[i])
                do begin
                        interchange x[i] and x[j];
                        i:= j; { advance up the tree }
```

$$j := i \ div \ 2 \ \{ \ j \text{ is father of } i \ \}$$
$$\textbf{end} \ \{ \text{while...do begin} \}$$
$$\textbf{end} \ \{ \text{for...do begin} \}$$

To solve the second problem of finding the proper place for $x[1]$ in a tree that satisfies the requirements of a heap (except for the root), initialize i to 1 and repeatedly interchange the content of node i with the content of the larger of its two sons as long as its content is not larger than those of both its sons, resetting i to point to the larger son. The algorithm to readjust the heap of order k may be written as follows:

$$i := 1;$$
$$\{ \text{ compute the larger of } i\text{'s two sons and place in } j \ \}$$
$$j := 2;$$
$$\textbf{if} \ (k \geqslant 3) \ \textbf{and} \ (x[3] > x[2])$$
$$\quad \textbf{then} \ j := 3;$$
$$\textbf{while} \ (j \leqslant k) \ \textbf{and} \ (x[j] > x[i])$$
$$\quad \textbf{do begin}$$
$$\qquad \text{interchange } x[i] \text{ and } x[j];$$
$$\qquad i := j;$$
$$\qquad j := 2 * i; \ \{ \ j := \text{larger of } i\text{'s sons} \ \}$$
$$\qquad \textbf{if} \ j+1 \leqslant k$$
$$\qquad \quad \textbf{then if} \ x[j+1] > x[j]$$
$$\qquad \qquad \textbf{then} \ j := j + 1$$
$$\quad \textbf{end} \ \{ \text{while...do begin} \}$$

The last *if* statement reads

$$\textbf{if} \ j+1 \leqslant k$$
$$\quad \textbf{then if} \ x[j+1] > x[j]$$
$$\qquad \textbf{then} \ j := j + 1$$

rather than

$$\textbf{if} \ (j+1 \leqslant k) \ \textbf{and} \ (x[j+1] > x[j])$$
$$\quad \textbf{then} \ j := j + 1$$

because we must ensure that the references to $x[j+1]$ and $x[j]$ are within array bounds.

Figure 8.3.5 illustrates the creation of a heap of size 8 from the original file:

$$25 \quad 57 \quad 48 \quad 37 \quad 12 \quad 92 \quad 86 \quad 33$$

The dotted lines in that figure indicate that two elements are interchanged.

Figure 8.3.6 illustrates the adjustment of the heap as $x[1]$ is moved to its proper position in the original array, until all the elements of the heap are processed. Note that after an element has been "removed" from the heap, it retains its position in the array; it is merely ignored in subsequent processing. Note also that the transformations in Figure 8.3.6 illustrate a tournament in which, after an element is inserted into a father node, the

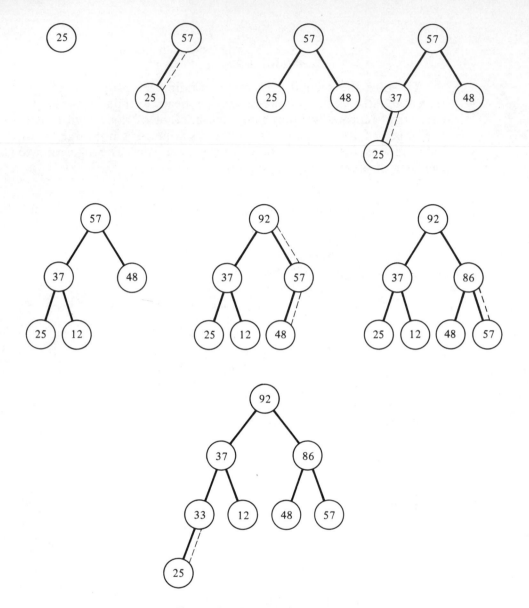

Figure 8.3.5 Creating a heap of size 8.

sons below it advance up the tree to take their proper position. This eliminates the redundant nodes and the redundant tests of the tournament sort.

In the program below we implement the heapsort. The statements of the program mirror the description above except that not all the interchanges called for are made immediately. The value whose correct position is being sought is kept in a temporary variable y. Advances up or down the tree are made by adjusting pointers.

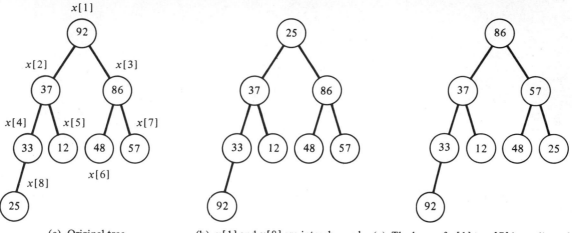

(a) Original tree.   (b) $x[1]$ and $x[8]$ are interchanged.   (c) The heap of $x[1]$ to $x[7]$ is readjusted.

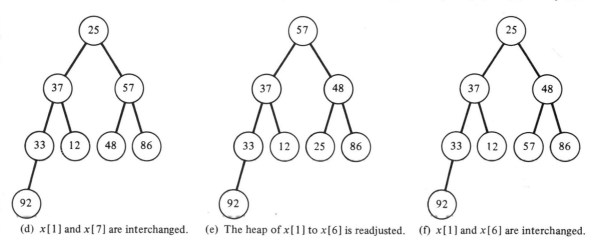

(d) $x[1]$ and $x[7]$ are interchanged.   (e) The heap of $x[1]$ to $x[6]$ is readjusted.   (f) $x[1]$ and $x[6]$ are interchanged.

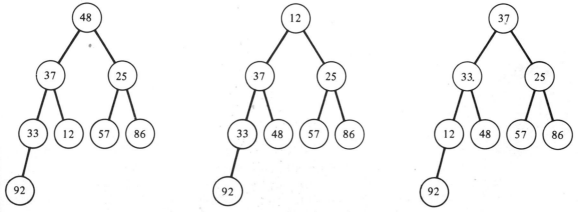

(g) The heap of $x[1]$ to $x[5]$ is readjusted.   (h) $x[1]$ and $x[5]$ are interchanged.   (i) The heap of $x[1]$ to $x[4]$ is readjusted.

Figure 8.3.6 Adjusting a heap.

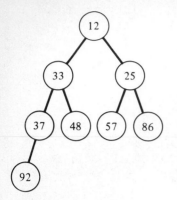

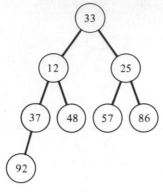

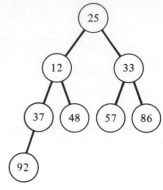

(j) $x[1]$ and $x[4]$ are interchanged.   (k) The heap of $x[1]$ to $x[3]$ is readjusted.   (l) $x[1]$ and $x[3]$ are interchanged.

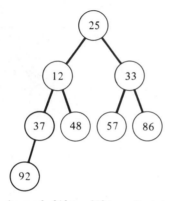

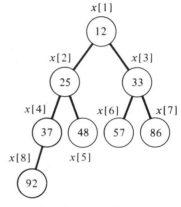

(m) The heap of $x[1]$ to $x[2]$ is readjusted.   (n) $x[1]$ and $x[2]$ are interchanged. The array is sorted.

Figure 8.3.6 (cont.)

We present the program to implement the heapsort. n is assumed to be greater than or equal to 3.

```
procedure heap(var x: arraytype; n: aptr);
label 10, 11;
var i,j,k,y: integer;
begin { procedure heap}
        { create initial heap }
    for k:= 2 to n
        do begin
                { insert x[k] into existing heap of size k-1 }
                i:= k;
                y:= x[k];
                j:= i div 2;
        while j > 0
```

CHAP. 8: SORTING

```
                    do begin
                        if y <= x[j]
                            then goto 10;
                        x[i]:= x[j];
                        i:= j;
                        j:= i div 2
                    end {while...do begin};
10:             x[i]:= y
        end { for...do begin};
        { We remove x[1] and place it in its proper position }
        {        in the array. We then adjust the heap.       }
    for k:= n downto 2
        do begin
            y:= x[k];
            x[k]:= x[1];
            {       Readjust the heap of order k-1.       }
            {Move y down the heap for proper position. }
            i:= 1;
            j:= 2;
            if (x[3] > x[2]) and (k-1 >= 3)
                then j:= 3;
            {              j is the larger son of i              }
            {                 in the heap of size k-1            }
            while j <= k-1
                do begin
                    if x[j] <= y
                        then goto 11;
                    x[i]:= x[j];
                    i:= j;
                    j:= 2 * i;
                    if j+1 <= k-1
                        then if x[j+1] > x[j]
                                then j:= j + 1
                end {while...do begin};
11:             x[i]:= y
        end { for...do begin}
    end { procedure heap};
```

To analyze the heapsort, note that a complete binary tree with n nodes (where n is one less than a power of 2) has $\log_2(n+1)$ levels. Thus, if each element in the array were a leaf, requiring it to be filtered through the entire tree both while creating and adjusting the heap, the sort would still be $O(n\log n)$. However, clearly not every element must pass through the entire tree. Thus while the sort is $O(n\log n)$, the multipliers are not as large as those for the tournament sort. The worst case for the heapsort is $O(n\log n)$; but it is not very efficient for small n. (Why?) The space requirement for the heapsort is only one additional variable to hold the temporary for switching, provided that the array implementation of an almost complete binary tree is used.

1. Explain why the straight selection sort is more efficient than the bubble sort.

2. Consider the following *quadratic selection sort*. Divide the n elements of the file into k groups of k elements each, where $k = \sqrt{n}$. Find the largest element of each group and insert it into an auxiliary array. Find the largest of the elements in the array. This is the largest element of the file. Then replace this element in the array by the next largest element of the group from which it came. Again find the largest element of the array. This is the second largest element of the file. Repeat the process until the file has been sorted. Write a Pascal routine to implement a quadratic selection sort as efficiently as possible.

3. Rewrite the tournament sort of this section using linked allocation to store the binary tree.

4. Modify the routines of the tournament sort so that nonleafs as well as leafs contain the actual elements of the original file. When the content of the root is output, move down the tree to find the leaf whose ancestors must be modified.

5. Modify the routine *readjust* of the tournament sort so that when the content of a leaf is set to $-maxint$, the content of its brother (rather than the index of its brother) is moved up the tree. [Note that under this modification, a nonleaf may contain the index of a nonleaf. For example, the array *tree* for the tree of Figure 8.3.4c would be as follows (-1 is used instead of $-maxint$):

i	1	2	3	4	5	6	7	8	9	10	11	12	13	14	15
$tree[i]$	9	9	7	9	10	12	33	25	57	48	37	12	-1	-1	33

tree[6] and *tree*[7] both contain actual values and *tree*[3] contains the index of a nonleaf.] Why is this method more efficient?

6. Modify the tournament sort in the following ways. When the initial tree is created and the content of a leaf node is moved up, the content of the leaf is immediately changed to $-maxint$. When the content of a nonleaf is moved up, the winner between its two sons is moved up to take its place. Each time that the root of the tree is output, move up its largest son, then move up the largest son of that son, and so on, until the value $-maxint$ is moved up.

7. Use the technique of the tournament sort to merge n input files, each of which is sorted in ascending order, into a single output file, as follows. The tree is maintained so that the key represented by each node is the smaller of the keys of its two sons. Each leaf is designated as an input area for a single file. An auxiliary routine $inp(i)$ reads the next input value from the ith input file into the appropriate leaf. When all the elements of file i have been input, $inp(i)$ returns *maxint*. An auxiliary routine *writeroot* outputs the element in the tree root into the output file. Each node of the tree contains an element and the input file number from which the element came. An element is contained in only a single node of the tree at any time. When an element is moved from a node *nd* to its father, another element is moved from below to *nd*. When an element is moved up from a leaf, the routine *inp* is called with the appropriate parameter to read a new input value into the leaf.

8. Define an *almost complete ternary tree* as a tree in which every node has at most three sons and such that the nodes can be numbered from 1 to n so that the sons of $node[i]$ are $node[3*i-1]$, $node[3*i]$ and $node[3*i+1]$. Define a *ternary heap* as an almost complete ternary tree in which the content of each node is greater than or equal to the contents of all its descendants. Write a sorting routine similar to the heapsort except that it uses a ternary heap.

9. Write a routine *combine*(x) that accepts an array x in which the subtrees rooted at $x[2]$ and $x[3]$ are heaps and which modifies the array x so that it represents a single heap.

4. INSERTION SORTS

Simple Insertion Sort

An *insertion sort* is one that sorts a set of records by inserting records into an existing sorted file. An example of a simple insertion sort is the following procedure:

```
procedure insert(var x: arraytype; n: aptr);
var k: aptr;
    i: aptr2;
    y: integer;
    found: boolean;
begin { procedure insert}
        { Initially x[1] may be thought of as a sorted }
        { file of one element. After each repetition }
        {  of the following loop, the elements x[1]   }
        {         through x[k] are in order.          }
      for k:= 2 to n
          do begin
                  { insert x[k] into the sorted file }
                  y:= x[k];
                  {  Move down one position all  }
                  {    numbers greater than y.    }
                  i:= k-1;
                  found:= false;
                  while (i >= 1) and (not found)
                      do if y < x[i]
                          then begin
                                  x[i+1]:= x[i];
                                  i:= i-1
                              end
                          else found:= true;
                  {   insert y at proper position   }
                  x[i+1]:= y
              end { for...do begin}
  end { procedure insert};
```

If the initial file is sorted, only one comparison is made on each pass so that the sort is $O(n)$. If the file is initially sorted in the reverse order, the sort is $O(n^2)$, since the total number of comparisons is

$$(n - 1) + (n - 2) + \cdots + 3 + 2 + 1 = (n - 1)*n/2$$

which is $O(n^2)$. However, the simple insertion sort is still usually better than the bubble sort. The closer the file is to sorted order, the more efficient the simple insertion sort becomes. The average number of comparisons in the simple insertion sort (by considering all possible permutations of the input array) is also $O(n^2)$. The space requirements for the sort consist of only one temporary variable, y.

The speed of the sort can be improved somewhat by using a binary search (see Sections 3.1, 3.2, and 9.1) to find the proper position for $x[k]$ in the sorted file $x[1], \ldots, x[k-1]$. This reduces the number of comparisons from $O(n^2)$ to $O(n \log n)$. However, even if the correct position i for $x[k]$ is found in $O(n \log n)$ steps, each of the elements $x[i+1], \ldots, x[k-1]$ must be moved one position. This latter operation performed n times requires $O(n^2)$ replacements. Unfortunately, therefore, the binary search technique does not significantly improve the overall time requirements of the sort.

Another improvement to the simple insertion sort can be made by using *list insertion*. In this method there is an array *link* of pointers, one for each of the original array elements. Initially, $link[i]=i+1$ for $1 \leqslant i < n$ and $link[n]=0$. Thus the array may be thought of as a linear list pointed to by an external pointer *first* initialized to one. To insert the kth element the linked list is traversed until the proper position for $x[k]$ is found or until the end of the list is reached. At that point $x[k]$ can be inserted into the list by merely adjusting the list pointers without shifting any elements in the array. This reduces the time required for insertion but not the time required for searching for the proper position. The space requirements are also increased because of the extra *link* array. The number of comparisons is still $O(n^2)$, although the number of replacements in the *link* array is $O(n)$. You are asked to code both the binary insertion sort and the list insertion sort as exercises.

Shell Sort

More significant improvement can be achieved by using the *shell sort* (or *diminishing increment sort*), named after its discoverer. This method sorts separate subfiles of the original file. These subfiles contain every kth element of the original file. The value of k is called an *increment*. For example, if k is 5, the subfile consisting of $x[1], x[6], x[11], \ldots$ is first sorted. Five subfiles, each containing one-fifth of the elements of the original file, are sorted in this manner. These are (reading across) shown on the top of page 407. In general, the ith element of the jth subfile is $x[(i-1)*5+j]$. If a different increment k is chosen, the k subfiles are divided so that the ith element of the jth subfile is $x[(i-1)*k+j]$.

subfile 1	→	$x[1]$	$x[6]$	$x[11]$	$\cdots$
subfile 2	→	$x[2]$	$x[7]$	$x[12]$	$\cdots$
subfile 3	→	$x[3]$	$x[8]$	$x[13]$	$\cdots$
subfile 4	→	$x[4]$	$x[9]$	$x[14]$	$\cdots$
subfile 5	→	$x[5]$	$x[10]$	$x[15]$	$\cdots$

After the first k subfiles are sorted (usually by simple insertion), a new smaller value of k is chosen and the file is again partitioned into a new set of subfiles. Each of these larger subfiles is sorted and the process is repeated yet again with an even smaller value of k. Eventually, the value of k is set to 1 so that the subfile consisting of the entire file is sorted. A decreasing sequence of increments is fixed at the start of the entire process. The last value in this sequence must be 1.

For example, if the original file is

$$25 \quad 57 \quad 48 \quad 37 \quad 12 \quad 92 \quad 86 \quad 33$$

and the sequence (5, 3, 1) is chosen, the following subfiles are sorted on each iteration.

> first iteration (increment = 5)
> $(x[1], x[6])$
> $(x[2], x[7])$
> $(x[3], x[8])$
> $(x[4])$
> $(x[5])$
>
> second iteration (increment = 3)
> $(x[1], x[4], x[7])$
> $(x[2], x[5], x[8])$
> $(x[3], x[6])$
>
> third iteration (increment = 1)
> $(x[1], x[2], x[3], x[4], x[5], x[6], x[7], x[8])$

Figure 8.4.1 illustrates the shell sort on this sample file. The lines underneath each array join individual elements of the separate subfiles. Each of the subfiles is sorted using the simple insertion sort.

We present below a routine to implement the shell sort. In addition to the standard parameters x and n, it requires an array *incrmnts* containing the diminishing increments of the sort. The type definition for the array *incrmnts* is given by

```
type incrarray =
    record
        numinc: 1..numelts;
        incrmnts: array[1..numelts] of aptr
    end;
```

```
    procedure shell(var x: arraytype; n: aptr; inc: incrarray);
    var j,span: aptr;
        incr,y,k: integer;
        found: boolean;
    begin { procedure shell}
        for incr:= 1 to inc.numinc
            do begin
                span:= inc.incrmnts[incr]; { span is the size  }
                                           { of the increment }
                for j:= span+1 to n
                    do begin
                        { insert element x[j] into its proper }
                        {      position within its subfile      }
                        y:= x[j];
                        k:= j - span;
                        found:= false;
                        while (k >= 1) and (not found)
                            do if y < x[k]
                                then begin
                                    x[k+span]:= x[k];
                                    k:= k-span
                                end
                                else found:= true;
                        x[k+span]:= y
                    end { for...do begin}
            end { for...do begin}
    end { procedure shell};
```

Be sure that you can trace the actions of this program on the sample file of Figure 8.4.1. Notice that on the last iteration, where *span* equals 1, the sort reduces to a simple insertion.

The idea behind the shell sort is a simple one. We have already noted that the simple insertion sort is highly efficient on a file that is in almost sorted order. It is also important to realize that when the file size n is small, an $O(n^2)$ sort is often more efficient than an $O(n \log n)$ sort. The reason for this is that $O(n^2)$ sorts are generally quite simple to program and involve very few actions other than comparisons and replacements on each pass. Because of this low overhead, the constant of proportionality is rather small. An $O(n \log n)$ sort is generally quite complex and employs a large number of extra operations on each pass in order to reduce the work of subsequent passes. Thus its constant of proportionality is larger. When n is large, n^2 overwhelms $n \log n$ so that the constants of proportionality do not play a major role in determining the faster sort. However, when n is small, n^2 is not much larger than $n \log n$, so that a large difference in those constants often causes an $O(n^2)$ sort to be faster.

Since the first increment used by the shell sort is large, the individual subfiles are quite small, so that the simple insertion sorts on those subfiles

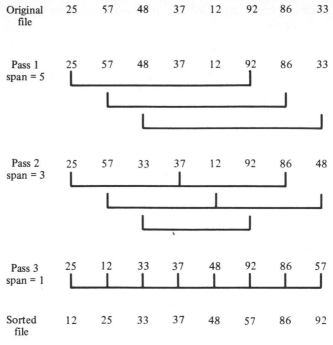

Figure 8.4.1

are fairly fast. Each sort of a subfile causes the entire file to be more nearly sorted. Thus, although successive passes of the shell sort use smaller increments and therefore deal with larger subfiles, those subfiles are almost sorted due to the actions of previous passes. Thus the insertion sorts on those subfiles are also quite efficient. In this connection, it is significant to note that if a file is partially sorted using an increment k and is subsequently partially sorted using an increment j, the file remains partially sorted on the increment k. That is, subsequent partial sorts do not disturb earlier ones.

The efficiency analysis of the shell sort is mathematically involved and beyond the scope of this book. The actual time requirements for a specific sort depends upon the number of elements in the array *incrmnts* and on their actual values. It has been shown that the order of the shell sort can be approximated by $O(n(\log n)^2)$ if an appropriate sequence of increments is used. One requirement that is intuitively clear is that the elements of *incrmnts* should be relatively prime (i.e., have no common divisors other than 1). You are asked to show, as an exercise, why this is so. This guarantees that successive iterations intermingle subfiles so that the entire file is indeed almost sorted when *span* equals 1 on the last iteration.

Address Calculation Sort

As a final example of sorting by insertion, consider the following technique, called sorting by *address calculation* (sometimes called sorting by *hashing*). In this method a function f is applied to each key. The result of this function determines into which of several subfiles the record is to be placed. The function should have the property that if $x < y$, then $f(x) < f(y)$. Thus all the records in one subfile will have keys that are less than the keys of the records in another subfile. An item is placed into a subfile in correct sequence by using any sorting method; simple insertion is usually used. After all the items of the original file have been placed into subfiles, the subfiles may be concatenated to produce the sorted result.

For example, consider again the sample file:

$$25 \quad 57 \quad 48 \quad 37 \quad 12 \quad 92 \quad 86 \quad 33$$

Let us create 10 subfiles, one for each of the 10 possible first digits. Initially, each of these subfiles is empty. An array of pointers $f[0..9]$ is declared, where $f[i]$ points to the first element in the file whose first digit is i. After scanning the first element (25), it is placed into the file headed $f[2]$. Each of the subfiles is maintained as a sorted linked list of the original array elements. After processing each of the elements in the original file, the subfiles appear as shown in Figure 8.4.2.

We present a procedure to implement the address calculation sort. The routine assumes an array of two-digit numbers and uses the first digit of

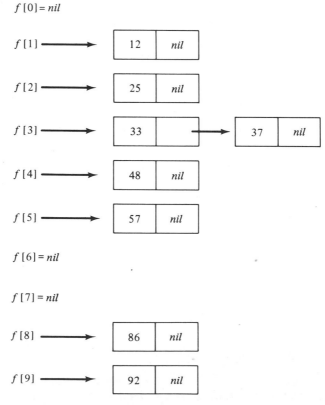

Figure 8.4.2 Address calculation sort.

each number to assign that number to a subfile. The routine uses the procedure *place(list, x)* to insert an integer x into its proper position in the ordered list *list*.

```
procedure addr(var x: arraytype; n: aptr);
type nodetype = record
                    info: integer;
                    next: aptr2
                end;
var node: array[1..numelts] of nodetype;
    f: array[0..9] of aptr;
    q: aptr;
    first, i, j, p, avail: aptr2;
    y: integer;
begin { procedure addr}
    { initialize available list }
    avail:= 1;
    for i:= 1 to n-1
        do node[i].next:= i+1;
    node[n].next:= 0;
    for i:= 0 to 9
        do f[i]:= 0; { initialize pointers }
    for i:= 1 to n
        do begin
                { we successively insert each element into its }
                {     respective subfile using list insertion    }
                y:= x[i];
                first:= y div 10; {    find the first digit of   }
                                   {      a two-digit number       }
                {          insert into proper linked list        }
                place(f[first], y)
                {    place inserts y into its proper position  }
                {    in the linked list pointed to by f[first]  }
            end { for...do begin};
    { copy numbers back into the array x }
    i:= 0;
    for j:= 0 to 9
        do begin
                p:= f[j];
                while p <> 0
                    do begin
                            i:= i+1;
                            x[i]:= node[p].info;
                            p:= node[p].next
                        end {while...do begin}
            end { for...do begin}
end { procedure addr};
```

The space requirements of the address calculation sort are approximately $2*numelts$ (used by the array *node*) plus some header nodes and temporary variables. Note that if the original data is given in the form of a linked list rather than as a sequential array, it is not necessary to maintain both the array x and the linked structure *node*.

To evaluate the time requirements for the sort, note the following. If the n original elements are approximately uniformly distributed over the m subfiles and the value of n/m is approximately 1, the time of the sort is nearly $O(n)$, since the function assigns each element to its proper file and little extra work is required to place the element within the subfile itself. On the other hand, if n/m is much larger than 1, or if the original file is not uniformly distributed over the m subfiles, significant work is required to insert an element into its proper subfile and the time is therefore closer to $O(n^2)$.

EXERCISES
1. The *two-way insertion sort* is a modification of the simple insertion sort as follows. A separate output array of size *numelts* is set aside. This output array acts as a circular structure as in Section 4.1. $x[1]$ is placed into the middle element of the array. Once a contiguous group of elements are in the array, room for a new element is made by shifting all smaller elements one step to the left or all larger elements one step to the right. Which of these shifts is performed depends on which would cause the smallest amount of shifting. Write a routine to implement this technique.

2. The *merge insertion sort* proceeds as follows:

   Step 1: For all odd i between 1 and $n-1$, compare $x[i]$ with $x[i+1]$. Place the larger in the next position of an array *large* and the smaller in the next position of an array *small*. If n is odd, place $x[n]$ in the last position of the array *small*. (*large* is of size n *div* 2; *small* is of size n *div* 2 or n *div* 2 + 1, depending on whether n is even or odd.)

   Step 2: Sort the array *large* using merge insertion recursively. Whenever an element $large[j]$ is moved to $large[k]$, $small[j]$ is also moved to $small[k]$. (At the end of this step, $large[i] \leqslant large[i+1]$ for all i less than n *div* 2 and $small[i] \leqslant large[i]$ for all i less than or equal to n *div* 2.)

   Step 3: Copy $small[1]$ and all the elements of *large* into $x[1]$ through $x[n$ *div* $2 + 1]$.

   Step 4: Define the integer $int(i)$ as $(2^{i+1} + (-1)^i)$ *div* 3. Beginning with $i=1$ and proceeding by 1 while $int(i) \leqslant n$ *div* 2 + 1, insert the elements $small[int(i+1)]$ down to $small[int(i)+1]$ into x in turn using binary insertion. (For example, if $n=20$, then the successive values of *int* are $int(1)=1$, $int(2)=3$, $int(3)=5$, $int(4)=11$, which equals n *div* 2 + 1. Thus the elements of *small* are inserted in the following order: $small[3]$, $small[2]$; then $small[5]$, $small[4]$; then $small[10]$, $small[9]$, $small[8]$, $small[7]$, $small[6]$. In this example, there is no $small[11]$.)

   Write a Pascal procedure to implement this sort.

3. Modify the quicksort of Section 2 so that it uses a simple insertion sort when a subfile is below some size s. Determine by experiments what value of s should be used for maximum efficiency.

412   CHAP. 8: SORTING

4. Prove that if a file is partially sorted using an increment j in the shell sort, it remains partially sorted on that increment even after it is partially sorted on another increment, k.

5. Explain why it is desirable to choose all the increments of the shell sort so that they are relatively prime.

6. What is the number (in terms of file size n) of comparisons and interchanges performed by each of the sorting methods below for the following files?

   (1) A sorted file.
   (2) A file that is sorted in reverse order (i.e., from largest to smallest).
   (3) A file in which the elements $x[1]$, $x[3]$, $x[5]$, ... are the smallest elements and are in sorted order and in which the elements $x[2]$, $x[4]$, $x[6]$, ... are the largest elements and are in reverse sorted order (i.e., $x[1]$ is the smallest, $x[2]$ is the largest, $x[3]$ is next to smallest, $x[4]$ is the next to the largest, etc.).
   (4) A file in which $x[1]$ through $x[n \ div \ 2]$ are the smallest elements and are sorted and in which $x[n \ div \ 2 + 1]$ through $x[n]$ are the largest elements and are in reverse-sorted order.
   (5) A file in which $x[1]$, $x[3]$, $x[5]$, ... are the smallest elements in sorted order and in which $x[2]$, $x[4]$, $x[6]$, ... are the largest elements in sorted order.

   (a) The simple insertion sort.
   (b) The insertion sort using a binary search.
   (c) The list insertion sort.
   (d) The two-way insertion sort of Exercise 1.
   (e) The merge insertion sort of Exercise 2.
   (f) The shell sort using increments 2 and 1.
   (g) The shell sort using increments 3, 2, and 1.
   (h) The shell sort using increments 8, 4, 2, and 1.
   (i) The shell sort using increments 7, 5, 3, and 1.
   (j) The address calculation sort presented in the text.

7. Under what circumstances would you recommend the use of each of the following sorts over the others?

   (a) The shell sort of this section.
   (b) The heapsort of Section 3.
   (c) The quicksort of Section 2.

8. Determine which of the following sorts is most efficient:

   (a) The simple insertion sort of this section.
   (b) The straight selection sort of Section 3.
   (c) The bubble sort of Section 2.

5. MERGE AND RADIX SORTS

Merge Sorts

Merging is the process of combining two or more sorted files into a third sorted file. An example of a procedure that accepts two sorted arrays a and *b* of *an* and *bn* elements, respectively, and merges them into a third array *c* containing *cn* elements is the following:

```
procedure mergearr(a,b: arraytype; var c; arraytype; an,bn: aptr; var cn: aptr);
        {merge arrays a and b into array c}
var apoint,bpoint,cpoint: aptr2;
begin {procedure mergearr}
    if an+bn > numelts
        then error('too many elements to be merged')
        else begin
                cn:= an+bn;
                {apoint and bpoint are indicators of how}
                {far we are in arrays a and b, respectively}
                apoint:= 1;
                bpoint:= 1;
                cpoint:= 1;
                while (apoint <= an) and (bpoint <= bn)
                    do begin
                            if a[apoint] < b[bpoint]
                                then begin
                                        c[cpoint] := a[apoint];
                                        apoint:= apoint + 1
                                    end {then begin}
                                else begin
                                        c[cpoint] := b[bpoint];
                                        bpoint:= bpoint + 1
                                    end {else begin};
                            cpoint:= cpoint + 1
                        end {while...do begin};
                {copy any remaining elements}
                while apoint <= an
                    do begin
                            {copy remaining elements from a}
                            c[cpoint] := a[apoint];
                            cpoint:= cpoint + 1;
                            apoint:= apoint + 1
                        end {while...do begin};
                while bpoint <= bn
                    do begin
                            {copy remaining elements from b}
                            c[cpoint] := b[bpoint];
                            cpoint:= cpoint + 1;
                            bpoint:= bpoint + 1
                        end {while...do begin}
            end {else begin}
end {procedure mergearr};
```

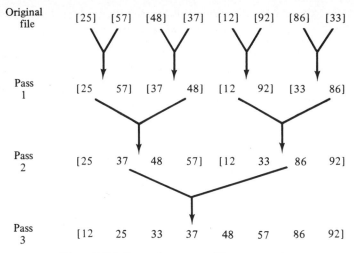

Original
file $\qquad$ [25] [57] [48] [37] [12] [92] [86] [33]

Pass
1 $\qquad$ [25   57] [37   48] [12   92] [33   86]

Pass
2 $\qquad$ [25   37   48   57] [12   33   86   92]

Pass
3 $\qquad$ [12   25   33   37   48   57   86   92]

Figure 8.5.1 Successive passes of the merge sort.

We can use this technique to sort a file in the following way. Divide the file into n subfiles of size 1 and merge adjacent (disjoint) pairs of files. We then have approximately $n/2$ files of size 2. Repeat this process until there is only one file remaining of size n. Figure 8.5.1 illustrates how this process operates on a sample file. Each individual file is contained in brackets.

We present a procedure to implement the foregoing description of a *straight merge sort*. An auxiliary array *aux* of size *numelts* is required to hold the results of merging two subarrays of x. The variable *size* is used to control the size of the subarrays being merged. Since at any time the two files being merged are both subarrays of x, lower and upper bounds are required to indicate the subfiles of x being merged. *lb*1 and *ub*1 represent the lower and upper bounds of the first file and *lb*2 and *ub*2 represent the lower and upper bounds of the second file, respectively. i and j are used to reference elements of the source files being merged and k indexes the destination file. The procedure follows:

```
procedure msort(var x: arraytype; n: aptr);
var aux: arraytype;
    lb2,ub1,ub2: aptr;
    lb1,i,j,k: aptr2;
    size: integer;
begin {procedure msort}
    size:= 1; {merge files of size 1}
    while size < n
        do begin
            lb1:= 1; {initialize lower bound of first file}
            k:= 1;   {  k is index for auxiliary array  }
```

```
while lb1+size <= n
        {check if there are two files to merge}
        do begin
                {compute remaining indices}
                lb2 := lb1 + size;
                ub1 := lb2 - 1;
                if lb2+size-1 > n
                    then ub2 := n
                    else ub2 := lb2 + size - 1;
                {proceed through the two subfiles}
                i := lb1;
                j := lb2;
                while (i <= ub1) and (j <= ub2)
                    do begin
                            {enter smaller into}
                            {   the array aux   }
                            if x[i] <= x[j]
                                then begin
                                            aux[k] := x[i];
                                            i := i + 1
                                    end {then begin}
                                else begin
                                            aux[k] := x[j];
                                            j := j + 1
                                    end {else begin};
                            k := k+1
                    end   {while...do begin};
                {  At this point one of the subfiles  }
                {  has been exhausted.  Insert any  }
                {remaining portions of the other file}
                while i <= ub1
                    do begin
                            aux[k] := x[i];
                            i := i + 1;
                            k := k + 1
                    end {while...do begin};
                while j <= ub2
                    do begin
                            aux[k] := x[j];
                            j := j + 1;
                            k := k + 1
                    end {while...do begin};
                {advance lb1 to start of next pair}
                {               of files               }
                lb1 := ub2 + 1
    end {while...do begin};
```

```
        {copy any remaining single file}
        i:= lb1;
        while k <= n
              do begin
                          aux[k] := x[i];
                          k:= k + 1;
                          i:= i + 1
                    end {while...do begin};
              {adjust x and size}
              for k:= 1 to n
                  do x[k] := aux[k];
              size:= size * 2
        end {while...do begin}
  end {procedure msort};
```

There is one deficiency in this procedure, which is easily remedied if the program is to be practical for sorting large arrays. Instead of merging each set of files into the auxiliary array *aux* and then recopying the array *aux* into *x*, alternate merges can be performed from *x* to *aux* and from *aux* to *x*. We leave this modification as an exercise for the reader.

The time required for the sort is $O(n \log n)$, since there are obviously no more than log *n* passes. The sort does, however, require an auxiliary array *aux* into which the merged files can be stored.

There are two modifications of the foregoing procedure which can result in more efficient sorting. The first of these is the *natural merge*. In the straight merge, the files all had the same size (except perhaps for the last file). We can, however, exploit any order that may already exist among the elements and let the files be defined as the longest subarrays of increasing elements. You are asked to code such a procedure as an exercise.

The second modification uses linked allocation instead of sequential allocation. By adding a single pointer field to each record, the need for the second array *aux* can be eliminated. This can be done by explicitly linking together each input and output subfile. The modification can be applied to both the straight merge and the natural merge. You are asked to implement these in the exercises.

Radix Sort

The next sorting method that we consider is called the *radix sort*. This sort is based on the values of the actual digits in the positional representations of the numbers being sorted. For example, the number 235 in decimal notation is written with a 2 in the hundreds position, a 3 in the tens position, and a 5 in the units position. The larger of two such three-digit integers can be determined as follows. Start at the most significant digit and advance through the least significant digits as long as the corresponding digits in the two numbers match. The number with the larger digit in the first position in which the digits of the two numbers do not match is the larger of the two numbers. Of course, if all the digits of both numbers match, the numbers are equal.

We can write a sorting routine based on this method. Using the decimal base, for example, the numbers can be sorted into 10 groups based on their most significant digit. (For simplicity, we assume that all the numbers have the same number of digits by padding with leading zeros, if necessary.) Thus every element in the "0" group is less than every element in the "1" group which is less than every element in the "2" group, and so on. We can then sort within the individual groups based on the next significant digit. We repeat this process until each subgroup has been subdivided, so that the least significant digits are sorted. At this point the original file is sorted. This method is sometimes called the *radix-exchange sort*; its coding is left as an exercise for the reader.

Let us now consider an alternative to the method described above. It is apparent from our discussion that considerable bookkeeping is involved in

Original file

| | 25 | 57 | 48 | 37 | 12 | 92 | 86 | 33 |

Queues based on least significant digit.

	Front	Rear
queue [0]		
queue [1]		
queue [2]	12	92
queue [3]	33	
queue [4]		
queue [5]	25	
queue [6]	86	
queue [7]	57	37
queue [8]	48	
queue [9]		

After first pass:

| | 12 | 92 | 33 | 25 | 86 | 57 | 37 | 48 |

Queues based on most significant digit.

	Front	Rear
queue [0]		
queue [1]	12	
queue [2]	25	
queue [3]	33	37
queue [4]	48	
queue [5]	57	
queue [6]		
queue [7]		
queue [8]	86	
queue [9]	92	

Sorted file: 12   25   33   37   48   57   86   92

Figure 8.5.2 Illustration of the radix sort.

constantly subdividing files and distributing their contents into subfiles based on particular digits. It would certainly be easier if we could process the entire file as a whole rather than deal with many individual files.

Suppose that we perform the following actions on the file for each digit, beginning with the least significant digit and ending with the most significant digit. Take each number in the order in which it appears in the file and place it into one of 10 queues, depending on the value of the digit currently being processed. Then, starting with the queue of numbers with a 0 digit and ending with the queue of numbers with a 9 digit, return the numbers to the original file in the order in which they were placed onto the queue. When these actions have been performed for each digit, starting with the least significant and ending with the most significant, the file is sorted. This sorting method is called the *radix sort*.

Notice that this scheme sorts on the least significant digit first. This allows processing of the entire file without subdividing the files and keeping track of where each subfile begins and ends. Figure 8.5.2 illustrates this sort on the sample file

$$25 \quad 57 \quad 48 \quad 37 \quad 12 \quad 92 \quad 86 \quad 33$$

Be sure that you can follow the actions depicted in the two passes of Figure 8.5.2.

We can therefore outline an algorithm to sort in the foregoing fashion as follows:

```
for k := least significant digit to most significant digit
    do begin
        for i := 1 to n
            do begin
                y := x[i];
                j := kth digit of y;
                place y at rear of queue[j]
            end {for...do begin};
        for qu := 0 to 9
            do place elements of queue[qu] in next sequential positions of x
    end {for...do begin}
```

We now present a program that implements this sort on four-digit numbers. In order to save a considerable amount of work in processing the queues (especially in the step where we return the queue elements to the original file), we write the program using linked allocation. If the initial input to the subroutine is an array, that input is first converted into a linear linked list; if the original input is already in linked format, this step is not necessary and, in fact, space is saved. This is the same situation as in the program *addr* (address calculation sort) of Section 4. Again, as in previous programs, we do not make any internal calls to subroutines but rather perform their actions in place.

```
procedure radix(var x: arraytype; n: aptr);
const m = 4; {number of digits}
type nodetype = record
                        info: integer;
                        next: aptr2
                    end;
var node: array[1..numelts] of nodetype;
    front: array[0..10] of aptr2;
    rear: array[0..9] of aptr2;
    p: aptr;
    first,q,i,j: aptr2;
    y,expon,k: integer;
begin {procedure radix}
    {initialize linked list}
    for i:= 1 to n-1
        do begin
                    node[i].info:= x[i];
                    node[i].next:= i+1
            end {for...do begin};
    node[n].info:= x[n];
    node[n].next:= 0;
    first:= 1; {first is head of linked list}
    for k:= 1 to m
        {m is the number of digits in the numbers}
        do begin
                    for i:= 0 to 9
                        do rear[i]:= 0;
                    for i:= 0 to 10
                        do front[i]:= 0; {initialize queues}
                    {process each element on the list}
                    while first <> 0
                        do begin
                                    p:= first;
                                    first:= node[first].next;
                                    y:= node[p].info;
                                    {extract kth digit}
                                    expon:= 1;
                                    for i:= 1 to k-1
                                        do expon:= expon * 10;
                                    j:= (y div expon) mod 10;
                                    {insert y into queue[j]}
                                    q:= rear[j];
                                    if q = 0
                                        then front[j]:= p
                                        else node[q].next:= p;
```

```
                          rear[j] := p
                    end {while...do begin};
              { At this point each record is in }
              {its proper queue based on digit}
              { k.  We now form a single list  }
              { from all the queue elements.  }
              {     Find the first element.     }
              j := 0;
              while (j <= 9) and (front[j] = 0)
                    do j := j+1;
              first := front[j];
              {   link up remaining queues   }
              while j <= 9
                    {check if finished}
                    do begin
                            {find next element}
                            i := j+1;
                            while (i <= 9) and (front[i] = 0)
                                  do i := i + 1;
                            if i <= 9
                               then begin
                                       p := i;
                                       node[rear[j]].next := front[i]
                                    end {then begin};
                            j := i
                    end {while...do begin};
              node[rear[p]].next := 0
           end {for...do begin};
        {copy back to original array}
        for i := 1 to n
           do begin
                   x[i] := node[first].info;
                   first := node[first].next
              end {for...do begin}
   end {procedure radix};
```

The time requirements for the radix sorting method clearly depend on
the number of digits (m) and the number of elements in the file (n). Since
the outer loop *for* $k := 1$ *to* m *do...* is traversed m times (once for each digit)
and the inner loop n times (once for each element in the file), the sort is
approximately $O(m*n)$. Thus the sort is reasonably efficient if the number
of digits in the keys is not too large. The sort does, however, require space
to store pointers to the fronts and rears of the queues in addition to an extra
field in each record to be used as a pointer in the linked lists. If the number
of digits is large, it is sometimes more efficient to sort the file by first apply-

ing the radix sort to the most significant digits and then using simple insertion on the rearranged file. In cases where most of the records in the file
have differing most significant digits, this process eliminates wasteful passes
on the least significant digits.

EXERCISES

1. Write a routine $merge(x, lb1, ub1, ub2)$ which assumes that $x[lb1]$ through $x[ub1]$ and
   $x[ub1+1]$ through $x[ub2]$ are sorted and which merges the two into $x[lb1]$ through
   $x[ub2]$.

2. Consider the following recursive version of the merge sort, which uses the routine
   $merge$ of Exercise 1. It is called by the statement $msort2(x,1,n)$. Rewrite the routine
   by eliminating recursion and simplifying. How does the resulting routine differ from
   the one given in the text?

   ```
   procedure msort2(var x: arraytype; lb,ub: aptr);
   var mid: aptr;
   begin
         if lb <> ub
            then begin
                        mid := (ub+lb) div 2;
                        msort2(x, lb, mid);
                        msort2(x, mid+1, ub);
                        merge(x, lb, mid, ub)
                  end {then begin}
   end {procedure msort2};
   ```

3. Let $a(l1, l2)$ be the average number of comparisons necessary to merge two sorted
   arrays of length $l1$ and $l2$, respectively, where the elements of the arrays are chosen at
   random from among $l1+l2$ elements.

   (a) What are the values of $a(l1, 0)$ and $a(0, l2)$?
   (b) Show that for $l1>0$ and $l2>0$, $a(l1, l2)$ is equal to $(l1/(l1+l2))*(1+a(l1-1,l2)) +
       (l2/(l1+l2))*(1+a(l1,l2-1))$. (*Hint:* Express the average number of comparisons
       in terms of the average number of comparisons after the first comparison.)
   (c) Show that $a(l1, l2)$ equals $(l1*l2*(l1+l2+2))/((l1+1)*(l2+1))$.
   (d) Verify the formula in part (c) for two arrays, one of size 2 and one of size 1.

4. Consider the following method of merging two arrays a and b into c. Perform a binary
   search for $b[1]$ in the array a. If $b[1]$ is between $a[i]$ and $a[i+1]$, output $a[1]$
   through $a[i]$ to the array c, then output $b[1]$ to the array c. Next, perform a binary
   search for $b[2]$ in the subarray $a[i+1]$ to $a[la]$ (where la is the number of elements in
   the array a) and repeat the output process. Repeat this procedure for every element
   of the array b.

   (a) Write a Pascal routine to implement this method.
   (b) In which cases is this method more efficient than the method given in the text?
       In which cases is it less efficient?

5. Consider the following method (called **binary merging**) of merging two sorted arrays
   a and b into c. Let la and lb be the number of elements of a and b, respectively, and
   assume that $la \geqslant lb$. Divide a into $lb+1$ approximately equal subarrays. Compare $b[1]$
   with the smallest element of the second subarray of a. If $b[1]$ is smaller, then find

$a[i]$ such that $a[i] \leqslant b[1] \leqslant a[i+1]$ by a binary search in the first subarray. Output all elements of the first subarray up to and including $a[i]$ into c, and then output $b[1]$ into c. Repeat this process with $b[2]$, $b[3]$, ..., $b[j]$, where $b[j]$ is found to be larger than the smallest element of the second subarray. Output all remaining elements of the first subarray and the first element of the second subarray into c. Then compare $b[j]$ to the smallest element of the third subarray of a, and so on.

    (a) Write a program to implement the binary merge.
    (b) Show that if $la=lb$, the binary merge acts like the merge described in the text.
    (c) Show that if $lb=1$, the binary merge acts like the merge of Exercise 4.

6. Determine the number of comparisons (as a function of n and m) that are performed in merging two ordered files a and b of sizes n and m, respectively, by each of the merge methods below on each of the following sets of ordered files:

    (1) $m=n$ and $a[i] < b[i] < a[i+1]$ for all i.
    (2) $m=n$ and $a[n] < b[1]$.
    (3) $m=n$ and $a[n \; div \; 2] < b[1] < b[m] < a[(n \; div \; 2)+1]$.
    (4) $n=2m$ and $a[i] < b[i] < a[i+1]$ for all i between 1 and m.
    (5) $n=2m$ and $a[m+i] < b[i] < a[m+i+1]$ for all i between 1 and m.
    (6) $n=2m$ and $a[2i] < b[i] < a[2i+1]$ for all i between 1 and m.
    (7) $m=1$ and $b[1] = a[n \; div \; 2]$.
    (8) $m=1$ and $b[1] < a[1]$.
    (9) $m=1$ and $a[n] < b[1]$.

    (a) The merge method presented in the text.
    (b) The merge of Exercise 4.
    (c) The binary merge of Exercise 5.

7. Generate two random sorted files of size 100 and merge them by each of the methods of Exercise 6, keeping track of the number of comparisons made. Do the same for two files of size 10 and two files of size 1000. Repeat the experiment 10 times. What do the results indicate about the average efficiency of the merge methods?

8. Write a routine that sorts a file by first applying the radix sort to the most significant r digits (where r is a given constant) and then uses simple insertion to sort the entire file. This eliminates excessive passes on low-order digits that may not be necessary.

9. Write a program that prints all sets of six positive integers $a1$, $a2$, $a3$, $a4$, $a5$, and $a6$ such that

$$a1 \leqslant a2 \leqslant a3 \leqslant 20$$

$$a1 < a4 \leqslant a5 \leqslant a6 \leqslant 20$$

and the sum of the squares of $a1$, $a2$, and $a3$ equals the sum of the squares of $a4$, $a5$, and $a6$. (*Hint:* Generate all possible sums of squares, and use a sorting procedure to find duplicates.)

9 Searching

In this chapter we consider various methods of searching through large amounts of data to find a particular piece of information. As we shall see, certain methods of organizing data make the search process more efficient. Since searching is such a common task in computing, a knowledge of these methods goes a long way toward making a good programmer.

1. BASIC SEARCH TECHNIQUES

Before we consider specific search techniques, let us define some terms. A *table* or a *file* is a group of elements, each of which is called a *record*. (We are using the terms "file" and "record" in their general sense. They should not be confused with the same terms as they refer to specific Pascal constructs.) Associated with each record is a *key* which is used to differentiate among different records. The association between a record and its key may be simple or complex. In the simplest form, the key is contained within the record at a specific offset from the start of the record. Such a key is called an *internal key* or an *embedded key*. In other cases, there is a separate table of keys which includes pointers to the records. Such keys are called *external*. For every file there is at least one set of keys (possibly more) that is unique (i.e., no two records have the same key value). Such a key is called a *primary key*. For example, if the file is stored as an array, the index within the array of an element is a unique external key for that element. However, since any field or combination of fields of a record can serve as the key in a particular application, keys need not always be unique. For example, in a file of names and addresses, if the state is used as the key for a particular search, it will probably not be unique, because there may be two records with the same state in the file. Such a key is called a *secondary key*. Some of the algorithms that we present assume unique keys; others allow for multiple keys. When adopting an algorithm for a particular application the programmer should know whether the keys are unique and make sure that the algorithm selected is appropriate.

424

A *search algorithm* is an algorithm that accepts an argument a and tries to find a record whose key is a. The algorithm may return the entire record or, more commonly, it may return a pointer to that record. It is possible that the search for a particular argument in a table is unsuccessful; that is, there is no record in the table with that argument as its key. In such a case, the algorithm may return a special "nil record" or a nil pointer. Very often, if a search is unsuccessful, it may be desirable to add a new record with the argument as its key. An algorithm that does this is called a *search and insertion algorithm*. A successful search is often called a *retrieval*.

In some cases it is desirable to insert a record with primary key *key* into a file without first searching for another record with the same key. Such a situation could arise if it has already been determined that no such record already exists in the file. In subsequent discussions we investigate and comment upon the relative efficiency of various algorithms. In such cases, the reader should note whether the comments refer to a search, to an insertion, or to a search and insertion.

Note that we have said nothing about the manner in which the table or file is organized. It may be an array of records, a linked list, a tree, or even a graph. Because different search techniques may be suitable for different table organizations, a table is often designed with a specific search technique in mind. The table may be contained completely in memory, completely in auxiliary storage, or it may be divided between the two. Clearly, different search techniques are necessary under these different assumptions. Searches in which the entire table is constantly in main memory are called *internal searches*, while those in which most of the table is kept in auxiliary storage are called *external searches*. As with sorting, we discuss only internal searching, and leave it to the reader to investigate the extremely important topic of external searching.

Algorithmic Notation

Most of the techniques presented in this chapter will be presented as algorithms rather than as Pascal programs. The reason for this is that a table may be presented in a wide variety of ways. For example, a table (keys plus records) organized as an array might be declared by

```
const tablesize = 1000;
type keytype = ...;
     rectype = ...;
     element = record
                   k: keytype;
                   r: rectype
               end;
var table: array[1..tablesize] of element;
```

or it might be declared as two separate arrays:

```
var k: array[1..tablesize] of keytype;
    r: array[1..tablesize] of rectype;
```

In the first case, the *i*th key would be referenced as *table*[*i*].*k*; in the second case, as *k*[*i*]:

Similarly, for a table organized as a list, either the array representation of a list or the dynamic representation of a list could be used. In the former case the key of the record pointed to by a pointer *p* would be referenced as *node*[*p*].*k*; in the latter case, as *p*↑.*k*.

However, the techniques for searching these tables are very similar. Thus to free ourselves from the necessity of choosing a specific representation, we adopt the algorithmic convention of referencing the *i*th key in an array as $k(i)$ and the key of the record pointed to by *p* in a linked structure as $k(p)$. Similarly, we reference the corresponding record as $r(i)$ or $r(p)$. In this way we can focus on details of technique rather than details of implementation.

Sequential Searching

The simplest form of a search is the *sequential search*. This search is applicable to a table that is organized either as an array or as a linked list. Let us assume that *k* is an array of *n* keys and *r* an array of records such that $k(i)$ is the key of $r(i)$. Let us also assume that *key* is a search argument. We wish to set the variable (or function identifier) *search* to the smallest integer *i* such that $k(i)=key$ if such an *i* exists and zero otherwise. The algorithm for doing this is as follows:

> *found* := *false*;
> *i* := 1;
> *while* ($i \leqslant n$) *and* (*not found*)
>   *do if key* = k(i)
>   *then begin*
>   *search* := *i*;
>   *found* := *true*
>   *end*
>   *else i* := *i*+1;
> *if not found*
>   *then search* := 0

The algorithm examines each key in turn; upon finding one that matches the search argument, its index (which acts as a pointer to its record) is returned. If no match is found, 0 is returned.

This algorithm can easily be modified to add a record *rec* with key *key* to the table if *key* is not already in the table. The last *if* statement is modified to read

> *if not found*
>   *then begin*
>   *n* := *n*+1;   { increase the table size }
>   *k*(*n*) := *key*; { insert the new key and }
>   *r*(*n*) := *rec*; {   record   }
>   *search* := *n*
>   *end*

Note that if insertions are made using only the revised algorithm, then no two records can have the same key. When this algorithm is implemented in Pascal, we must ensure that increasing n by 1 does not make its value go beyond the upper bound of the array. To use such a *sequential insertion search* on an array, sufficient storage must have been previously allocated for the array.

Storing a table as a linked list has the advantage that the size of the table can be increased dynamically as needed. Let us assume that the table is organized as a linear linked list pointed to by *table* and linked by a pointer field *next*. Then assuming k, r, *key*, and *rec* as before, the sequential insertion search for a linked list may be written as follows:

```
found := false;
q := nil;
p := table;
while (p <> nil) and (not found)
     do if k(p) = key
          then begin
                      search := p;
                      found := true
               end {then begin}
          else begin
                      q := p;
                      p := next(p)
               end {else begin};
if not found
    then begin { insert a new node }
               s := getnode;
               k(s) := key;
               r(s) := rec;
               next(s) := nil;
               if q = nil
                  then table := s
                  else next(q) := s;
               search := s
          end {then begin}
```

Another advantage of storing a table as a linked list rather than an array is that it is easier to delete a record from a linked list. Deleting an element from an array requires moving half the elements in the array on the average. (Why?)

One method of improving the efficiency of deleting a record from an array is to add a boolean field *flag(i)* to each record. Initially, when there is no record in position i, *flag(i)* is off. When a record is inserted at position i, the flag is turned on. When the record at position i is deleted, its flag is turned off. New records are inserted at the end of the array. If there are a substantial number of insertions, all the space in the array is soon exhausted.

If an attempt is made to insert a new record when there is no more room in the array, the array is condensed by overwriting all records whose flags are off. This yields an array that contains all valid records at the beginning, and room for new records at the end. The new record may then be inserted.

There is another method that avoids the necessity of periodically condensing the array but also entails lowered efficiency in individual insertions. In this method an insertion involves traversing the array sequentially, looking for a record that has been flagged as deleted. The new record is inserted over the first record whose flag is off. Yet another method is to link together all flagged records. This does not require any extra space because the information content of a deleted record is irrelevant and can therefore be overwritten by a pointer to the next deleted record. This available list of records can be maintained as a stack to make insertion more efficient. However, if an insertion is performed only after a search, then no efficiency gains result from these methods, because the entire table must be searched for an existing record with the same key. We leave the development of these ideas into algorithms and programs as exercises for the reader.

Efficiency of Sequential Searching

How efficient is a sequential search? Let us examine the number of comparisons that must be made by a sequential search in searching for a given key. If we assume no insertions or deletions, so that we are searching through a table of constant size n, then the number of comparisons depends on where the record with the argument key appears in the table. If the record is the first one in the table, only one comparison is performed; if the record is the last one in the table, n comparisons are necessary. If it is equally likely for the argument to appear at any given table position, a successful search will take (on the average) $(n+1)/2$ comparisons, and an unsuccessful search will take n comparisons. In any case, the number of comparisons is $O(n)$.

However, it is usually the case that some arguments are presented to the search algorithm more often than others. For example, in the files of a college registrar, the records of a senior who is applying for transcripts for graduate school or of a freshman whose high school average is being updated are more likely to be called for than are those of the average sophomore and junior. Similarly, the records of scofflaws and tax cheats are more likely to be retrieved from the files of a motor vehicle bureau or the Internal Revenue Service than those of a law-abiding citizen. (As we shall see later, these examples are unrealistic because it is unlikely that a sequential search would be used for such large files; but for the moment, let us assume that a sequential search is being used.) Then, if frequently accessed records are placed at the beginning of the file, the average number of comparisons is sharply reduced, because the most commonly accessed records take the least amount of time to retrieve.

Let us assume that $p(i)$ is the probability that record i is retrieved. [$p(i)$ is a number between 0 and 1 such that if m retrievals are made from the file, $m*p(i)$ of them will be from $r(i)$.] Let us also assume that $p(1)+p(2)+\cdots+p(n)=1$, so that there is no possibility that an argument key is missing from the table. Then the average number of comparisons that are made in searching for a record is

$$p(1) + 2p(2) + 3p(3) + \cdots + np(n)$$

Clearly, this number is minimized if

$$p(1) \geqslant p(2) \geqslant p(3) \geqslant \cdots \geqslant p(n)$$

(Why?) Thus, given a large stable file, reordering the file in order of decreasing probability of retrieval achieves a greater degree of efficiency each time the file is searched. Of course, this method implies that an extra field p is kept with each record, which gives the probability of accessing that record; or that p can be computed based on some other information in each record.

Reordering a List for Maximum Search Efficiency

If many insertions and deletions are to be performed on a table, a list structure is preferable to an array. However, even in a list, it would be better to maintain the relationship

$$p(1) \geqslant p(2) \geqslant \cdots \geqslant p(n)$$

to provide for efficient sequential searching. This can be done most easily if a new item is inserted into the list at its proper place. This means that if *prob* is the probability that a record with a given key will be the search argument, that record should be inserted between records $r(i)$ and $r(i+1)$, where i is such that

$$p(i) \geqslant \text{prob} \geqslant p(i+1)$$

Unfortunately, the probabilities $p(i)$ are rarely known in advance. Although it is usual for certain records to be retrieved more often than others, it is almost impossible to identify those records in advance. Also, the probability that a given record will be retrieved may change over time. To use the example of the college registrar given earlier, a student begins as a freshman (high probability of retrieval) and then becomes a sophomore and a junior (low probability) before becoming a senior (high probability). Thus it would be helpful to have an algorithm which would continually reorder the table so that more frequently accessed records would drift to the front while less frequently accessed records would drift to the back.

There are several search methods that accomplish this. One of them is known as the *move-to-front* method and is efficient only for a table that is organized as a list. In this method, whenever a search is successful (i.e., when the argument is found to match the key of a given record), the retrieved record is removed from its current location in the list and is placed at the head of the list. Another method is the *transposition* method, in which a successfully retrieved record is interchanged with the record that immediately precedes it. We present an algorithm to implement the transposition method on a table stored as a linked list. The algorithm returns a pointer to the retrieved record, or the nil pointer if the record is not found. As before, *key* is the search argument and *k* and *r* are the tables of keys and records. *table* is a pointer to the first node of the list.

```
found := false;
p := table;
q := nil; { q is one step behind p }
s := nil; { s is two steps behind p }
while (p <> nil) and (not found)
    do if k(p) = key
        then begin { we have found the record. transpose }
                    {  the records pointed to by p and q   }
                if q <> nil
                    then begin
                                next(q) := next(p);
                                next(p) := q;
                                if s = nil
                                    then table := p
                                    else next(s) := p
                         end {then begin};
                found := true;
                search := p
             end {then begin}
        else begin
                s := q;
                q := p;
                p := next(p)
             end {else begin};
    if not found
        then search := nil
```

We leave the implementation of the transposition method for an array and the move-to-front method as exercises for the reader.

Both of these methods are based on the observed phenomenon that a record that has been retrieved is likely to be retrieved again. By advancing such records toward the front of the table, subsequent retrievals are more efficient. The rationale behind the move-to-front method is that since the record is likely to be retrieved again, it should be placed at the position within the table at which such retrieval will be most efficient. However, the counterargument for the transposition method is that a single retrieval does not yet imply that the record will be retrieved frequently; placing it at the front of the table reduces search efficiency for all the other records that formerly preceded it. By advancing a record only one position each time that it is retrieved, we ensure that it will advance to the front of the list only if it is retrieved frequently. Indeed, it has been shown that, in general, the transposition method is more efficient than the move-to-front method.

Another advantage of the transposition method over the move-to-front method is that it can be applied efficiently to tables stored in array form as well as to list structured tables. Transposing two elements in an array is a rather efficient operation, whereas moving an element from the middle of an array to its front involves (on the average) moving half the array. (However, in this case the average number of moves is not as large, because the element to be moved most often comes from the initial portion of the array.)

Searching an Ordered Table

If the table is stored in ascending or descending order of the record keys, there are several techniques that can be used to improve the efficiency of searching. This is especially true if the table is of fixed size. One immediately obvious advantage in searching a sorted file over searching an unsorted file is in the case that the argument key is absent from the file. In the case of an unsorted file, n comparisons are needed to detect this fact. In the case of a sorted file, assuming that the argument keys are uniformly distributed over the range of keys in the file, only $n/2$ comparisons (on the average) are needed. This is because we know that a given key is missing from a file that is sorted in ascending order of keys as soon as we encounter a key in the file which is greater than the argument.

Suppose that it is possible to collect a large number of retrieval requests before any of them are processed. For example, in many applications a response to a request for information may be deferred to the next day. In such a case, all requests on a specific day may be collected and the actual searching may be done overnight, when no new requests are coming in. If both the table and the list of requests are sorted, the sequential search can proceed through both concurrently. Thus it is not necessary to search through the entire table for each retrieval request. In fact, if there are many such requests uniformly distributed over the entire table, each request will require only a few lookups (if the number of requests is less than the number of table entries) or perhaps only a single comparison (if the number of requests is greater than the number of table entries). In such situations sequential searching is probably the best method to use.

Because of the simplicity and efficiency of sequential processing on sorted files, it may be worthwhile to sort a file before searching for keys in it. This is especially true in the situation described in the preceding paragraph, where we are dealing with a "master" file and a large "transaction" file of requests for searches.

The Indexed Sequential Search

There is another technique to improve search efficiency for a sorted file, but it involves an increase in the amount of space required. This method is called the *indexed sequential* search method. An auxiliary table, called an *index*, is set aside in addition to the sorted file itself. Each element in the index consists of a key *kindex* and a pointer to the record in the file that corresponds to *kindex*. The elements in the index, as well as the elements in the file, must be sorted on the key. If the index is one-eighth the size of the file, then every eighth record of the file is represented in the index. This is illustrated by Figure 9.1.1.

The algorithm used for searching an indexed sequential file is straightforward. Let *r*, *k*, and *key* be defined as before; let *kindex* be an array of the keys in the index; and let *pindex* be the array of pointers within the index to the actual records in the file. We assume that the file is stored as an array, that *n* is the size of the file, and that *indxsze* is the size of the index.

```
found := false;
i := 1;
while (i ≤ indxsze) and (not found)
      do if kindex(i) > key
            then found := true
            else i := i+1;
if i = 1
   then lowlim := 1
   else lowlim := pindex(i-1);
if found
   then hilim := pindex(i)-1
   else hilim := n;
{ search the table between positions lowlim and hilim }
j := lowlim;
found := false;
while (j ≤ hilim) and (not found)
      do if k(j) = key
            then found := true
            else j := j+1;
if found
   then search := j
   else search := 0
```

Note that in the case of multiple records with the same key, the foregoing algorithm does not necessarily return a pointer to the first such record in the table.

The real advantage of the indexed sequential method is that the items in the table can be examined sequentially if all the records in the file must be accessed, yet the search time for a particular item is sharply reduced. A sequential search is performed on the smaller index rather than on the larger table. Once the correct index has been found, a second sequential search is performed on a small portion of the record table itself.

The use of an index is applicable to a sorted table stored as a linked list, as well as to one stored as an array. Use of a linked list implies a larger space overhead for pointers, although insertions and deletions can be performed much more readily.

432   CHAP. 9: SEARCHING

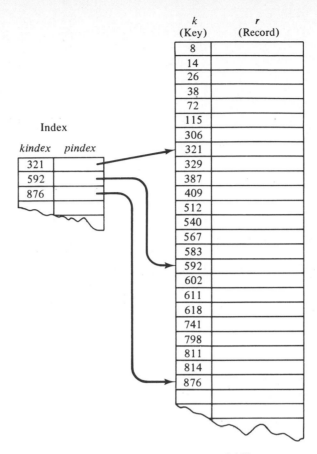

Figure 9.1.1 An indexed sequential file.

If the table is so large that even the use of an index does not achieve sufficient efficiency (either because the index is large in order to reduce sequential searching in the table, or because the index is small so that adjacent keys in the index are far from each other in the table), then a secondary index can be used. The secondary index acts as an index to the primary index, which points to entries in the sequential table. This is illustrated in Figure 9.1.2.

Deletions from an indexed sequential table can be made most easily by flagging deleted entries. In sequential searching through the table, deleted entries are ignored. Note that if an element is deleted, then even if its key is in the index, nothing need be done to the index; only the original table entry is flagged.

Insertion into an indexed sequential table is more difficult because there may not be room between two already existing table entries, thus necessitating a shift in a large number of table elements. However, if a nearby item has been flagged as deleted in the table, only a few items need be shifted and the deleted item can be overwritten. This may, in turn, necessitate alteration

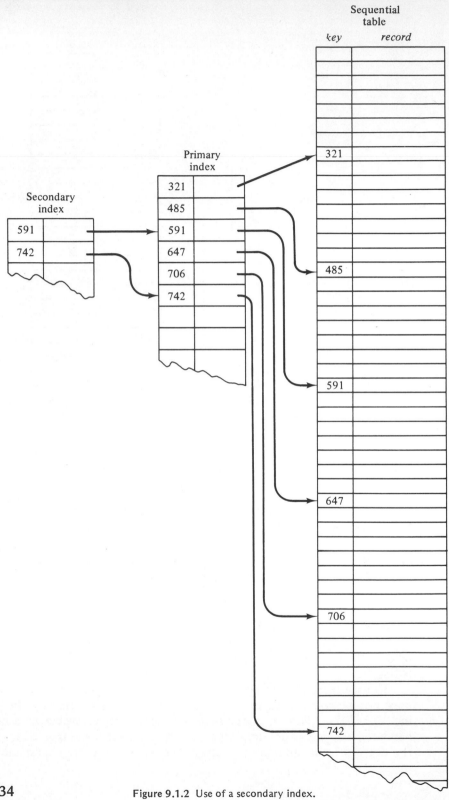

Sequential
table

key   record

Secondary   Primary
index   index

321

591   321
742   485
           591
           647
           706
           742

321

485

591

647

706

742

Figure 9.1.2 Use of a secondary index.

of the index if an item pointed to by an index element is shifted. An alternative method is to keep an overflow area at some other location and link together any inserted records. However, this would require an extra pointer field in each record of the original table. You are asked to explore these possibilities as an exercise.

The Binary Search

The most efficient method of searching a sequential table without the use of auxiliary indices or tables is the binary search. You should be familiar with this search technique from Sections 3.1 and 3.2. Basically, the argument is compared with the key of the middle element of the table. If they are equal, the search ends successfully; otherwise, either the upper or lower half of the table must be searched in a similar manner.

In Chapter 3 it was noted that the binary search can best be defined recursively. As a result, a recursive definition, a recursive algorithm, and a recursive program were presented for the binary search. However, the large overhead that is associated with recursion makes it inappropriate for use in practical situations in which efficiency is a prime consideration. We therefore present the following nonrecursive version of the binary search algorithm:

$$
\begin{aligned}
&found := false; \\
&low := 1; \\
&hi := n; \\
&\textbf{while } (low \leqslant hi) \textbf{ and } (\textbf{not } found) \\
&\quad \textbf{do begin} \\
&\qquad\qquad mid := (low + hi) \textbf{ div } 2; \\
&\qquad\qquad \textbf{if } key = k(mid) \\
&\qquad\qquad\quad \textbf{then } found := true \\
&\qquad\qquad\quad \textbf{else if } key < k(mid) \\
&\qquad\qquad\qquad\qquad \textbf{then } hi := mid - 1 \\
&\qquad\qquad\qquad\qquad \textbf{else } low := mid + 1 \\
&\qquad \textbf{end } \{while...do\ begin\}; \\
&\textbf{if } found \\
&\quad \textbf{then } search := mid \\
&\quad \textbf{else } search := 0
\end{aligned}
$$

Each comparison in the binary search reduces the number of possible candidates by a factor of 2. Thus the maximum number of key comparisons that will be made is approximately $\log_2 n$. [Actually, it is $2\log_2 n$, since in Pascal two key comparisons are made each time through the loop: $key = k(mid)$ and $key < k(mid)$. However, in an assembly language or in FORTRAN using an arithmetic IF statement, only one comparison is made. An optimizing Pascal compiler should be able to eliminate the extra comparison.] Thus we may say that the binary search algorithm is $O(\log n)$.

Note that the binary search may be used in conjunction with the indexed sequential table organization mentioned earlier. Instead of searching the index sequentially, a binary search can be used. The binary search can also be used in searching the main table once two boundary records are identified. However, the size of this table segment is likely to be sufficiently small that a binary search is no more advantageous than a sequential search.

Unfortunately, the binary search algorithm can only be used if the table is stored as an array. This is because it makes use of the fact that the indices of array elements are consecutive integers. For this reason the binary search is practically useless in situations where there are many insertions or deletions, so that an array structure is inappropriate.

EXERCISES

1. Modify the search and insertion algorithms of this section so that they become update algorithms. If an algorithm finds an i such that $key=k(i)$, change the value of $r(i)$ to rec.

2. Implement the sequential search and the sequential search and insertion algorithms in Pascal for both arrays and linked lists.

3. Compare the efficiency of searching an ordered sequential table of size n and searching an unordered table of the same size for the key key:
    (a) If no record with key key is present.
    (b) If one record with key key is present and only one is sought.
    (c) If more than one record with key key is present and it is desired to find only the first one.
    (d) If more than one record with key key is present and it is desired to find them all.

4. Assume that an ordered table is stored as a circular list with two external pointers: $table$ and $other$. $table$ always points to the node containing the record with the smallest key. $other$ is initially equal to $table$, but is reset each time a search is performed to point to the record that is retrieved. If a search is unsuccessful, $other$ is reset to $table$. Write a Pascal function $search(table,other,key)$ which implements this method and returns a pointer to a retrieved record or a nil pointer if the search is unsuccessful. Explain how keeping the pointer $other$ can reduce the average number of comparisons in a search.

5. Consider an ordered table implemented as an array or as a doubly linked list so that the table can be searched sequentially either backward or forward. Assume that a single pointer p points to the last record successfully retrieved. The search always begins at the record pointed to by p but may proceed in either direction. Write a function $search(table,p,key)$ for the case of an array and a doubly linked list to retrieve a record with key key and to modify p accordingly. Prove that the numbers of key comparisons in both the successful and unsuccessful cases are the same as in the method of Exercise 4, where the table may be scanned in only one direction but the scanning process may start at one of two points.

6. Consider a programmer who writes the following code:

$$\text{if } c_1 \text{ then}$$
$$\quad \text{if } c_2 \text{ then}$$
$$\quad\quad \text{if } c_3 \text{ then}$$
$$\quad\quad\quad \cdots$$
$$\quad\quad\quad\quad \text{if } c_n \text{ then } \{ \textit{statement} \}$$

where c_i is a condition that is either true or false. Note that rearranging the conditions in a different order results in an equivalent program, since the { statement } is executed only if all the c_i are true. Assume that $time(i)$ is the time needed to evaluate condition c_i and that $prob(i)$ is the probability that condition c_i is true. In what order should the conditions be arranged to make the program most efficient?

7. Modify the indexed sequential search so that in the case of multiple records with the same key, it returns the first such record in the table.

8. Consider the following Pascal implementation of an indexed sequential file:

```
const indxsize = 100;
      tablesize = 1000;
type  indxtype = record
                     kindex: integer;
                     pindex: 1..tablesize
                 end;
      tabletype = record
                     k: integer;
                     r: integer;
                     flag: boolean
                  end;
var   isfile : record
                  indx: array [1..indxsize] of indxtype;
                  table: array [1..tablesize] of tabletype
               end;
```

Write a Pascal routine *create(isfile)* that initializes such a file from input data. Each input line contains a key and a record. The input is sorted in ascending key order. Each index entry corresponds to 10 table entries. *flag* is set to *true* in an occupied table entry and to *false* in an unoccupied entry. Two of every 10 table entries are left unoccupied, to allow for future growth.

9. Given an indexed sequential file as in Exercise 8, write a Pascal routine *search(isfile,key)* to print the record in the file with key *key* if it is present and an indication that the record is missing if no record with that key exists. (How can you ensure that an unsuccessful search is as efficient as possible?) Also, write routines *insert(isfile,key,rec)* to insert a record *rec* with key *key* and *delete(isfile,key)* to delete the record with key *key*.

10. Consider the following version of the binary search, which assumes a special element $k(0)$ which is smaller than every possible key:

```
mid:= (n+1) div 2;
len:= n div 2;
finish := false;
while (key <> k(mid)) and (not finish)
    do begin
            if key < k(mid)
               then mid:= mid - (len + 1) div 2
               else mid:= mid + (len + 1) div 2;
            if len = 1
               then finish:= true
               else len:= len div 2
    end {while...do begin};
```

$$\textbf{if } key = k(mid)$$
$$\quad\textbf{then } search := mid$$
$$\quad\textbf{else } search := 0$$

Prove that this algorithm is correct. What are the advantages and/or disadvantages of this method over the method presented in the text?

11. The following search algorithm on a sorted array is known as the *Fibonaccian search* because of its use of Fibonacci numbers. (For a definition of Fibonacci numbers and the *fib* function, see Section 3.1.)

```
j := 1;
while fib(j) < n + 1
     do j := j + 1;
mid := n - fib(j-2) + 1;
f1 := fib(j - 2);
f2 := fib(j - 3);
finish := false;
while (key <> k(mid)) and (not finish)
     do if (mid ≤ 0) or (key > k(mid))
          then if f1 = 1
                    then finish := true
                    else begin
                              mid := mid + f2;
                              f1 := f1 - f2;
                              f2 := f2 - f1
                         end {else begin}
          else if f2 = 0
                    then finish := true
                    else begin
                              mid := mid - f2;
                              t := f1 - f2;
                              f1 := f2;
                              f2 := t
                         end {else begin};
if finish
     then search := 0
     else search := mid
```

Explain how this algorithm works. Compare the number of key comparisons with the number used by the binary search. Modify the initial portion of this algorithm so that it computes the Fibonacci numbers efficiently, rather than looking them up in a table or computing each anew.

12. Modify the binary search of the text so that in the case of an unsuccessful search, it returns the index i such that $k(i) < key < k(i+1)$. If $key < k(1)$, then it returns 0, and if $key > k(n)$, it returns n. Do the same for the searches of Exercises 10 and 11.

2. TREE SEARCHING

In Section 1 we discussed search operations on a file that is organized either as an array or as a list. In this section we consider several ways of organizing files as trees and some associated searching algorithms.

In Sections 6.1 and 8.3 we presented a method of using a binary tree to store a file in order to make sorting the file more efficient. In that method, all the left descendants of a node with key *key* have keys that are less than *key*, and all the right descendants have keys that are greater than or equal to *key*. The inorder traversal of such a binary tree yields the file in ascending key order.

Such a tree may also be used as a binary search tree. Using binary tree notation, the algorithm for searching for the key *key* in such a tree is as follows. (We assume that each node contains four fields: k, which holds the record's key value; r, which holds the record itself; and *left* and *right*, which are pointers to the subtrees.)

> *found* := *false*;
> p := *tree*;
> **while** ($p <> nil$) **and** (**not** *found*)
>   **do if** *key* = $k(p)$
>   **then** *found* := *true*
>   **else if** *key* $< k(p)$
>   **then** p := *left*(p)
>   **else** p := *right*(p);
> **if** *found*
>   **then** *search* := p
>   **else** *search* := *nil*

Note that the binary search of Section 1 actually uses a sorted array as an implicit binary search tree. The middle element of the array can be thought of as the root of the tree, the lower half of the array (all of whose elements are less than the middle element) can be considered the left subtree, and the upper half (all of whose elements are greater than the middle element) can be considered the right subtree.

A sorted array can be produced from a binary search tree by traversing the tree in inorder and inserting each element sequentially into the array as it is visited. On the other hand, there are many binary search trees which correspond to a given sorted array. Viewing the middle element of the array as the root of a tree and viewing the remaining elements recursively as left and right subtrees produces a relatively balanced binary search tree (Figure 9.2.1a). Viewing the first element of the array as the root of a tree and each successive element as the right son of its predecessor produces a very unbalanced binary tree (Figure 9.2.1b).

The advantage of using a binary search tree over an array is that a tree enables search, insertion, and deletion operations to be performed efficiently. If an array is used, an insertion or deletion requires that approximately half of the elements of the array be moved. (Why?) Insertion or deletion in a search tree, on the other hand, requires that only a few pointers must be adjusted.

Inserting into a Binary Search Tree

The following algorithm searches such a binary tree and inserts a new record into the tree if the search is unsuccessful. (We assume the existence of a

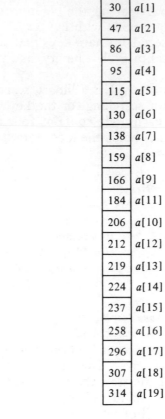

30	$a[1]$
47	$a[2]$
86	$a[3]$
95	$a[4]$
115	$a[5]$
130	$a[6]$
138	$a[7]$
159	$a[8]$
166	$a[9]$
184	$a[11]$
206	$a[10]$
212	$a[12]$
219	$a[13]$
224	$a[14]$
237	$a[15]$
258	$a[16]$
296	$a[17]$
307	$a[18]$
314	$a[19]$

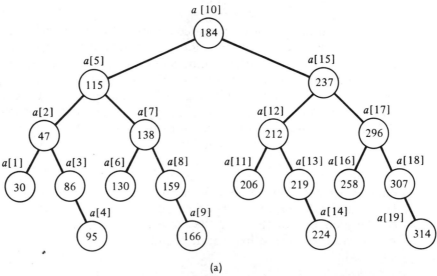

(a)

Figure 9.2.1 A sorted array and two of its binary tree representations.

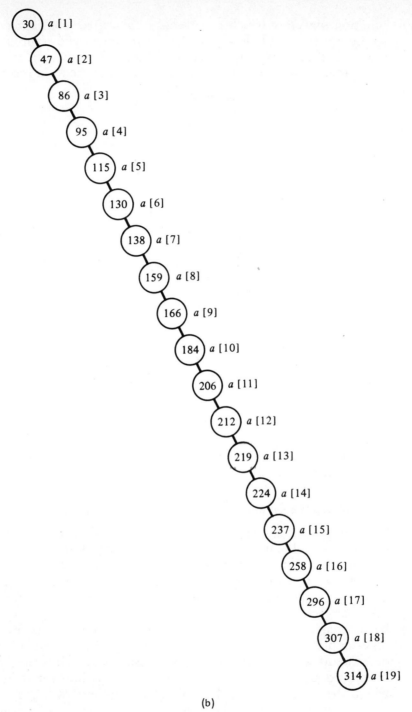

(b)

Figure 9.2.1 (cont.)

function *maketree* which constructs a binary tree consisting of a single node whose information field is passed as an argument and returns a pointer to the tree. This function is described in Section 6.1. However, in the version used here, we assume that *maketree* accepts two arguments, a record and a key.)

```
found := false;
q := nil;
p := tree;
while (p <> nil) and (not found)
    do if key = k(p)
        then found := true
        else begin
                q := p;
                if key < k(p)
                    then p := left(p)
                    else p := right(p)
            end {else begin};
    if not found
        then begin
                p := maketree(rec,key);
                if q = nil
                    then tree := p
                    else if key < k(q)
                            then left(q) := p
                            else right(q) := p
            end {then begin};
    search := p
```

Note that after a new record is inserted, the tree retains the property of being sorted in an inorder traversal.

Deleting from a Binary Search Tree

We now present an algorithm that deletes a node with key *key* from a binary search tree and leaves the tree as a binary search tree. There are three cases to consider. If the node to be deleted has no sons, it may be deleted without further adjustment to the tree. This is illustrated in Figure 9.2.2a. If the node to be deleted has only one subtree, its only son can be moved up to take its place. This is illustrated in Figure 9.2.2b. If, however, the node p to be deleted has two subtrees, its inorder successor s (or predecessor) must take its place. The inorder successor cannot have a left subtree (since a left descendant would be the inorder successor of p). Thus the right son of s can be moved up to take the place of s. This is illustrated in Figure 9.2.2c, where the node with key 12 replaces the node with key 11 and is replaced, in turn, by the node with key 13.

In the following algorithm, if no node with key *key* exists in the tree, the tree is left unchanged.

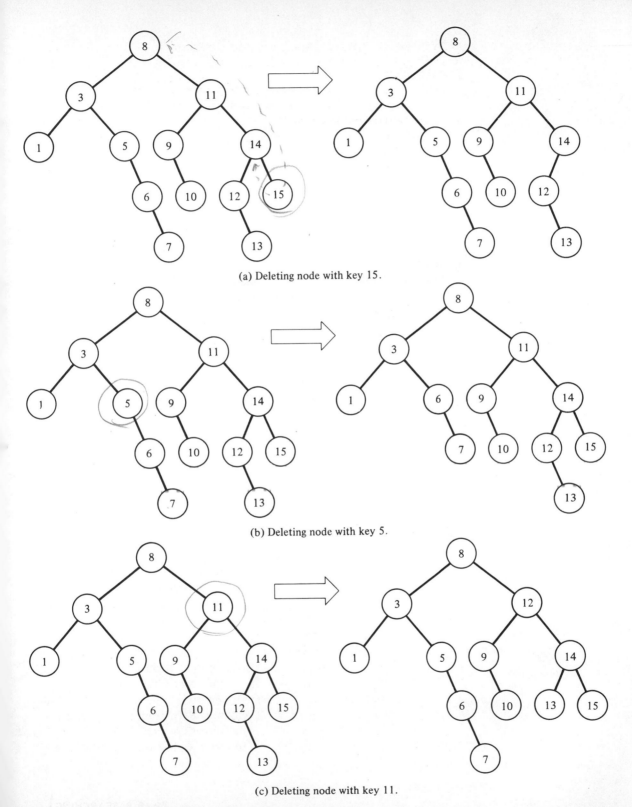

(a) Deleting node with key 15.

(b) Deleting node with key 5.

(c) Deleting node with key 11.

Figure 9.2.2 Deleting nodes from a binary search tree.

```
p := tree;
q := nil;
found := false;
{ search for the node with key key. set p to point to }
{          the node and q to its father, if any          }
while (p <> nil) and (not found)
     do if k(p) = key
          then found := true
          else begin
                    q := p;
                    if key < k(p)
                       then p := left(p)
                       else p := right(p)
               end {else begin};
if found
   then begin  { set v to point to the node which will }
               {          replace node(p)               }
          if left(p) = nil
             then v := right(p)
             else if right(p) = nil
                     then v := left(p)
                     else { node(p) has two sons; set v }
                          { to the inorder successor of  }
                          { p, and t to the father of v  }
                          begin
                             t := p;
                             v := right(p);
                             s := left(v); { s is the left }
                                           {   son of v   }
                             while s <> nil
                                do begin
                                      t := v;
                                      v := s;
                                      s := left(v)
                                   end {while...do begin};
                          { at this point, v is the }
                          { inorder successor of p  }
                          if t <> p
                             then begin
                                     { p is not the father of v }
                                     {      and v=left(t)        }
                                     left(t) := right(v);
                                     { remove node(v) from }
                                     { its current position }
                                     { to take the place of }
                                     {        node(p)        }
```

444   CHAP. 9: SEARCHING

$$right(v) := right(p)$$
$$\textbf{end} \{\text{then begin}\};$$
$$left(v) := left(p)$$
$$\textbf{end} \{\text{else begin}\};$$

{ insert $node(v)$ into the position formerly occupied }
{   by $node(p)$ }

$\textbf{if } q = nil$
   $\textbf{then } \{ \ node(p) \text{ was the root of the tree } \}$
      $tree := v$
   $\textbf{else if } p = left(q)$
       $\textbf{then } left(q) := v$
       $\textbf{else } right(q) := v;$
 $freenode(p)$
$\textbf{end} \{\text{then begin}\}$

Efficiency of Binary Tree Search

As we have already seen in Section 8.3 (see Figures 8.3.1 and 8.3.2), the time required to search a binary search tree varies between $O(n)$ and $O(\log n)$ depending on the structure of the tree. If elements are inserted into the tree by the insertion algorithm presented above, the structure of the tree depends on the order in which the records are inserted. If the records are inserted in sorted (or reverse) order, the resulting tree will contain all nil left (or right) links so that the tree search reduces to a sequential search. If, however, the records are inserted so that half the records inserted after any given record r with key k have keys smaller than k and half have keys greater than k, a balanced tree is achieved in which approximately $\log_2 n$ key comparisons are sufficient to retrieve an element. (Again, it should be noted that examining a node in our insertion algorithm requires two comparisons: one for equality and the other for less than. However, in machine language and in some compilers, these can be combined into a single comparison.)

If the records are presented in random order (i.e., any permutation of the n elements is equally likely), balanced trees will result more often than not, so that on the average, search time will remain $O(\log n)$. However, the constant of proportionality will be greater on the average than in the specific case of an evenly balanced tree.

All of the preceding assumes that it is equally likely for the search argument to equal any key in the table. However, in actual practice it is usually the case that some records are retrieved very often, some moderately often, and some are almost never retrieved. Suppose that records are inserted into the tree so that a more commonly accessed record precedes one that is not so frequently accessed. Then the most frequently retrieved records will be nearer the root of the tree, so that the average successful search time will be reduced. (Of course, this assumes that reordering the keys in order of reduced frequency of access does not seriously unbalance the binary tree, since if it did, the reduced number of comparisons for the most frequently accessed records might be offset by the increased number of comparisons for the vast majority of records.)

If the elements to be retrieved form a constant set, with no insertions or deletions, it may pay to set up a binary search tree which makes subsequent searches more efficient. For example, consider the binary search trees of Figure 9.2.3. Both the trees of Figure 9.2.3a and b contain three elements $K1$, $K2$, and $K3$, where $K1 < K2 < K3$, and are valid binary search trees for that set. However, a retrieval of $K3$ requires two comparisons in Figure 9.2.3a but requires only one comparison in Figure 9.2.3b. Of course, there are still other valid binary search trees for this set of keys.

The number of key comparisons necessary to retrieve a record is equal to the level of that record in the binary search tree plus one. Thus a retrieval of $K2$ requires one comparison in the tree of Figure 9.2.3a but requires three comparisons in the tree of Figure 9.2.3b. An unsuccessful search for an argument lying immediately between two keys a and b requires as many key comparisons as the maximum number of comparisons required by successful searches for either a or b. (Why?) This is equal to one plus the maximum of the levels of a or b. For example, a search for a key lying between $K2$ and $K3$ requires two key comparisons in Figure 9.2.3a and three comparisons in Figure 9.2.3b, while a search for a key greater than $K3$ requires two comparisons in Figure 9.2.3a, but only one comparison in Figure 9.2.3b.

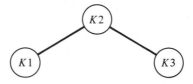

(a) Expected number of comparisons:
$2p1 + p2 + 2p3 + 2q0 + 2q1 + 2q2 + 2q3$

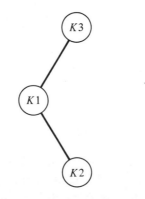

(b) Expected number of comparisons:
$2p1 + 3p2 + p3 + 2q0 + 3q1 + 3q2 + q3$

Figure 9.2.3 Two binary search trees.

Suppose $p1$, $p2$, and $p3$ are the probabilities that the search argument equals $K1$, $K2$, and $K3$, respectively. Suppose also that $q0$ is the probability that the search argument is less than $K1$, $q1$ is the probability that it is between $K1$ and $K2$, $q2$ is the probability that it is between $K2$ and $K3$, and $q3$ is the probability that it is greater than $K3$. Then $p1+p2+p3+q0+q1+q2+q3 = 1$. The *expected number* of comparisons in a search is the sum of the probabilities that the argument has a given value times the number of comparisons required to retrieve that value, where the sum is taken over all possible search argument values. For example, the expected number of comparisons in searching the tree of Figure 9.2.3a is

$$2p1 + p2 + 2p3 + 2q0 + 2q1 + 2q2 + 2q3$$

and the expected number of comparisons in searching the tree of Figure 9.2.3b is

$$2p1 + 3p2 + p3 + 2q0 + 3q1 + 3q2 + q3$$

This expected number of comparisons can be used as a measure of how "good" a particular binary search tree is for a given set of keys and a given set of probabilities. Thus for the probabilities listed below on the left, the tree of Figure 9.2.3a is more efficient; for the probabilities listed on the right, the tree of Figure 9.2.3b is more efficient.

$p1 = .1$	$p1 = .1$
$p2 = .3$	$p2 = .1$
$p3 = .1$	$p3 = .3$
$q0 = .1$	$q0 = .1$
$q1 = .2$	$q1 = .1$
$q2 = .1$	$q2 = .1$
$q3 = .1$	$q3 = .2$

Expected number for 9.2.3a = 1.7 Expected number for 9.2.3a = 1.9
Expected number for 9.2.3b = 2.4 Expected number for 9.2.3b = 1.8

A binary search tree that minimizes the expected number of comparisons for a given set of keys and probabilities is called *optimum*. Although an algorithm to produce such a tree may be very expensive, the tree that it produces yields efficiencies in all subsequent searches. Unfortunately, however, it is rare that the probabilities of the search arguments are known in advance.

Balanced Trees

As noted above, if the probability of searching for a key in a table is the same for all keys, a balanced binary tree yields the most efficient search. Unfortunately, the search and insertion algorithm presented above does not ensure that the tree remains balanced—the degree of balance is dependent on the order in which keys are inserted into the tree. We would like to have an efficient search and insertion algorithm which maintains the search tree as a balanced binary tree.

Let us first define more precisely the notion of a "balanced" tree. The *height* of a binary tree is the maximum level of its leafs (this is also sometimes known as the *depth* of the tree). For convenience, the height of a nil tree is defined as – 1. A *balanced binary tree* (sometimes called an *AVL tree*) is a binary tree in which the heights of the two subtrees of every node never differ by more than one. The *balance* of a node in a binary tree is defined as

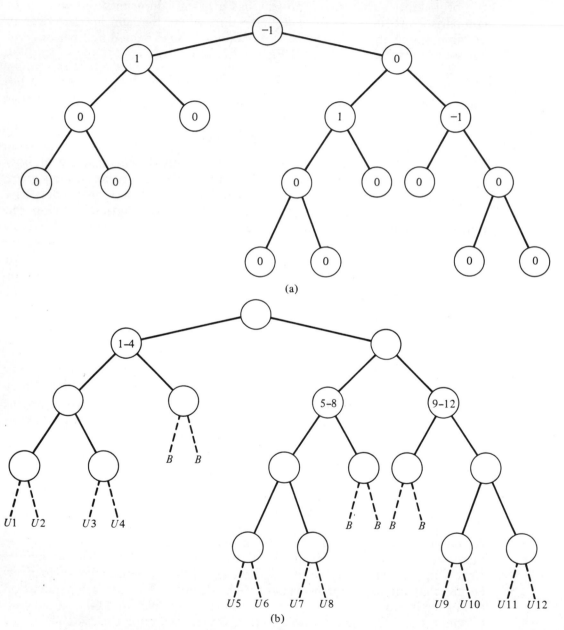

(a)

(b)

Figure 9.2.4 A balanced binary tree and possible additions.

the height of its left subtree minus the height of its right subtree. Figure 9.2.4a illustrates a balanced binary tree. Each node in a balanced binary tree has a balance of 1, -1, or 0, depending on whether the height of its left subtree is greater than, less than, or equal to the height of its right subtree. The balance of each node is indicated in Figure 9.2.4a.

Suppose that we are given a balanced binary tree and use the search and insertion algorithm above to insert a new node p into the tree. Then the resulting tree may or may not remain balanced. Figure 9.2.4b illustrates all possible insertions that may be made to the tree of Figure 9.2.4a. Each insertion that yields a balanced tree is indicated by a B. The unbalanced insertions are indicated by a U and are numbered from 1 to 12. It is easy to see that the tree becomes unbalanced only if the newly inserted node is a left descendant of a node which previously had a balance of 1 (this occurs in cases $U1$ through $U8$ in Figure 9.2.4b) or if it is a right descendant of a node which previously had a balance of -1 (cases $U9$ through $U12$). In Figure 9.2.4b, the youngest ancestor that becomes unbalanced in each insertion is indicated by the numbers contained in three of the nodes.

Let us examine further the subtree rooted at the youngest ancestor to become unbalanced as a result of an insertion. We illustrate the case where the balance of this subtree was previously 1, leaving the other case to the reader. Figure 9.2.5 illustrates this case. Let us call the unbalanced node A. Since A had a balance of 1, its left subtree was nonnil; we may therefore designate its left son as B. Since A is the youngest ancestor of the new node to become unbalanced, node B must have had a balance of 0. (You are asked to prove this fact as an exercise.) Thus node B must have had (before the insertion) left and right subtrees of equal height n (where possibly $n = -1$). Since the balance of A was 1, the right subtree of A must also have been of height n.

There are now two cases to consider, illustrated by Figure 9.2.5a and b. In Figure 9.2.5a the newly created node is inserted into the left subtree of B, changing the balance of B to 1 and the balance of A to 2. In Figure 9.2.5b the newly created node is inserted into the right subtree of B, changing the balance of B to -1 and the balance of A to 2. To maintain a balanced tree, it is necessary to perform a transformation on the tree so that:

1. The inorder traversal of the transformed tree is the same as for the original tree (i.e., the transformed tree remains a binary search tree).
2. The transformed tree is balanced.

Consider the trees of Figure 9.2.6a and b. The tree of Figure 9.2.6b is said to be a *right rotation* of the tree rooted at A of Figure 9.2.6a. Similarly, the tree of Figure 9.2.6c is said to be a *left rotation* of the tree rooted at A of Figure 9.2.6a.

An algorithm to implement a left rotation of a subtree rooted at p is as follows:

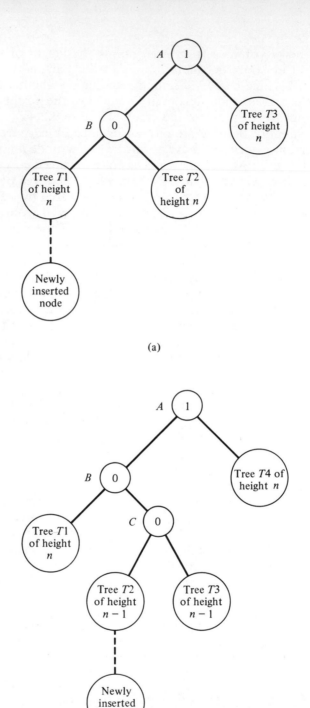

(a)

(b)

Figure 9.2.5 Initial insertion; all balances are prior to insertion.

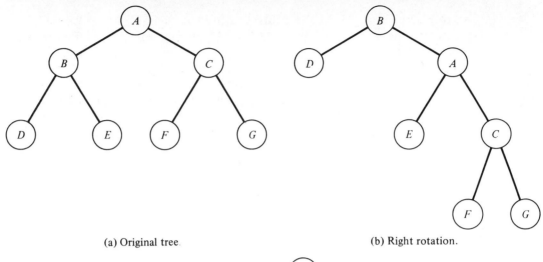

(a) Original tree.　　　　　　　　　　　　　　　(b) Right rotation.

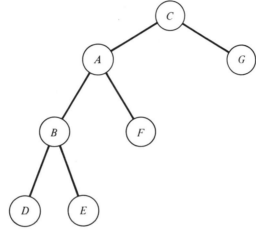

(c) Left rotation.

Figure 9.2.6 Simple rotation on a tree.

$$q := right(p);$$
$$hold := left(q);$$
$$left(q) := p;$$
$$right(p) := hold$$

Let us call this operation *leftrotation(p)*. *rightrotation(p)* may be defined similarly. Of course, in any rotation the value of the pointer to the root of the subtree being rotated must be changed to point to the new root. (In the case of the left rotation above, this new root is *q*.) Note that the order of the nodes in an inorder traversal is preserved under both right and left rotations. It therefore follows that any number of rotations (left or right) can be performed on an unbalanced tree in order to obtain a balanced tree, without disturbing the order of the nodes in an inorder traversal.

Let us now return to the trees of Figure 9.2.5. Suppose that a right rotation is performed on the subtree rooted at A in Figure 9.2.5a. The resulting tree is shown in Figure 9.2.7a. Note that the tree of Figure 9.2.7a yields the same inorder traversal as that of Figure 9.2.5a and is also balanced. Also, since the height of the subtree of Figure 9.2.5a was $n+2$ before the insertion and the height of the subtree of Figure 9.2.7a is $n+2$ with the inserted node, the balance of each ancestor of node A remains undisturbed. Thus, replacing the subtree of Figure 9.2.5a with its right rotation of Figure 9.2.7a guarantees that a balanced binary search tree is maintained.

Let us now turn to the tree of Figure 9.2.5b, where the newly created node is inserted into the right subtree of B. Let C be the right son of B. (There are three cases: C may be the newly inserted node in which case $n = -1$, or the newly inserted node may be in the left or right subtree of C. Figure 9.2.5b illustrates the case where it is in the left subtree; the analysis

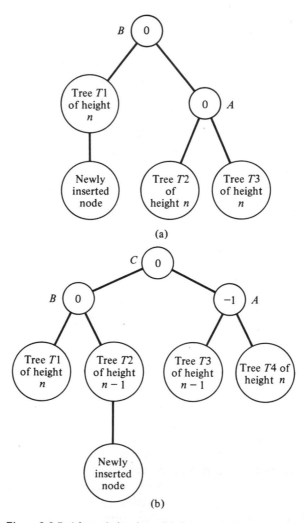

Figure 9.2.7 After rebalancing; all balances are after insertion.

CHAP. 9: SEARCHING

of the other cases is analogous.) Suppose that a left rotation on the subtree rooted at B is followed by a right rotation on the subtree rooted at A. Figure 9.2.7b illustrates the resulting tree. Verify that the inorder traversals of the two trees are the same and that the tree of Figure 9.2.7b is balanced. The height of the tree in Figure 9.2.7b is $n+2$, which is the same as the height of the tree in Figure 9.2.5b before the insertion, so that the balance in all ancestors of A is unchanged. Therefore, by replacing the tree of Figure 9.2.5b with that of Figure 9.2.7b whenever it occurs after insertion, a balanced search tree is maintained.

Let us now present an algorithm to search and insert into a nonempty balanced binary tree. Each node of the tree contains five fields: k and r, which hold the key and record, respectively; *left* and *right*, which are pointers to the left and right subtrees, respectively; and *bal*, whose value is 1, -1, or 0, depending on the node's balance. In the first part of the algorithm, if the desired key is not already in the tree, a new node is inserted into the binary search tree without regard to balance. This first phase also keeps track of the youngest ancestor, *ya*, which may become unbalanced upon insertion. The algorithm makes use of the function *maketree* described above and routines *rightrotation* and *leftrotation*, which accept a pointer to the root of a subtree and perform the desired rotation.

```
{   part I:  search and insert into the binary tree   }
s := nil;
p := tree;
v := nil;
ya := p;
        { ya points to the youngest ancestor which may }
        { become unbalanced. v points to the father of }
        {         ya, and s points to the father of p      }
found := false;
while ( p <> nil ) and ( not found )
      do if key = k(p)
            then found := true
            else begin
                     if key < k(p)
                        then q := left(p)
                        else q := right(p);
                     if q <> nil
                        then if bal(q) <> 0
                                 then begin
                                          v := p;
                                          ya := q
                                      end {then begin};
                     s := p;
                     p := q
                 end {else begin};
```

```
if found
    then search := p
    else begin { insert a new record }
                q := maketree(rec,key);
                bal(q):= 0;
                if key < k(s)
                    then left(s):= q
                    else right(s):= q;
                { the balance in all nodes between node(ya) and }
                {          node(q) must be changed from 0          }
                if key < k(ya)
                    then p := left(ya)
                    else p := right(ya);
                s := p;
                while p <> q
                    do if key < k(p)
                            then begin
                                    bal(p):= 1;
                                    p := left(p)
                            end {then begin}
                            else  begin
                                    bal(p):= -1;
                                    p := right(p)
                            end {else begin};


        {   part II:  ascertain whether or not the tree is unbalanced.   }
        {    If it is, q is the newly inserted node, ya is its youngest   }
        {    unbalanced ancestor, v is the father of ya and s is the      }
        {          son of ya in the direction of the imbalance.           }
    if key < k(ya)
        then imbal:= 1
        else imbal:= -1;
    if bal(ya) = 0
        then {   Another level has been added to the tree.   }
             {              The tree remains balanced          }
            bal(ya):= imbal
        else if bal(ya) <> imbal
                then {   The added node has been placed in   }
                     {      the opposite direction of the      }
                     { imbalance.  The tree remains balanced }
                     bal(ya):= 0
                else begin


        {    part III:  the additional node has unbalanced the tree.   }
        {       Rebalance it by performing the required rotations       }
        {       and then adjust the balances of the nodes involved      }
    if bal(s) = imbal
```

454   CHAP. 9: SEARCHING

```
then begin {    ya and s have been unbalanced in the same      }
          { direction; see Figure 9.2.5a where ya=A and s=B }
             p:= s;
             if imbal = 1
                then rightrotation(ya)
                else leftrotation(ya);
             bal(ya):= 0;
             bal(s):= 0
       end {then begin}
else  begin {    ya and s are unbalanced in opposite  }
            {        directions; see Figure 9.2.5b       }
          if imbal = 1
             then begin
                        p:= right(s);
                        leftrotation(s);
                        left(ya):= p;
                        rightrotation(ya)
                   end {then begin}
             else  begin
                        p:= left(s);
                        right(ya):= p;
                        rightrotation(s);
                        leftrotation(ya)
                   end {else begin};
          {    adjust bal field for involved nodes    }
          if bal(p) = 0
             then begin  { p was the inserted node }
                        bal(ya):= 0;
                        bal(s):= 0
                   end {then begin}
             else if bal(p) = imbal
                     then begin { see Figures 9.2.5b and 9.2.7b }
                               bal(ya):= -imbal;
                               bal(s):= 0
                          end {then begin}
                     else  begin { see Figures 9.2.5b and 9.2.7b }
                               { but the new node was inserted }
                               {            into T3            }
                               bal(ya):= 0;
                               bal(s):= imbal
                          end {else begin};
          bal(p):= 0
       end {else begin};
{ adjust the pointer to the rotated subtree }
if v = nil
   then tree:= p
   else if ya = right(v)
```

then $right(v):= p$
else $left(v):= p$
  end {else begin *part III*};
  $search := q$
end {if *found*...else begin}

  The algorithm to delete a node from a balanced binary search tree while maintaining its balance is even more complex and is left as an exercise.

Digital Search Trees

Another method of using trees to expedite searching is to form a general tree based on the symbols of which the keys are comprised. For example, if the keys are integers, each digit position determines one of 10 possible sons of a given node. A forest representing one such set of keys is illustrated in Figure 9.2.8. If the keys consist of alphabetic characters, each letter of the alphabet determines a branch in the tree. Note that every leaf node contains the special symbol *eok*, which represents the end of a key. Such a leaf node must also contain a pointer to the record that is being stored.

  If a forest is represented by a binary tree, as in Section 6.5, each node of the binary tree contains three fields: *symbol*, which contains a symbol of the key; *son*, which is a pointer to the node's oldest son in the original tree; and *brother*, which is a pointer to the node's next younger brother in the original tree. The first tree in the forest is pointed to by an external pointer *tree*, and the roots of the other trees in the forest are linked together in a linear list by the *brother* field. The *son* field of a leaf in the original forest points to a record; the concatenation of all the *symbol*s in the original forest in the path of nodes from the root to the leaf is the key of the record. We make two further stipulations, which will speed up the search and insertion process for such a tree. Each list of bothers is arranged in the binary tree in ascending order of the *symbol* field. The symbol *eok* is considered to be larger than any other.

  Using this binary tree representation, we may present an algorithm to search and insert into such a nonempty *digital tree*. As usual, *key* is the key for which we are searching and *rec* is the record that we wish to insert if *key* is not found. We also let *key(i)* be the *i*th symbol of the key. If the key has n symbols, we also assume that $key(n+1)$ equals *eok*. The algorithm uses the *getnode* operation to allocate a new tree node when necessary. We assume that *recptr* is a pointer to a node containing the record *rec* to be inserted. The algorithm sets *search* to the pointer to the record that is being sought. The algorithm uses an auxiliary function *insert*, whose algorithm is also given below.

  $p := tree;$
  $father := nil;$ { *father* is the father of p }
  $found := false;$
  $i := 1;$
  while not *found*
    do begin { search for the *i*th symbol in the key }
      $q := nil;$ { q points to the older brother of p }

Keys
180
185
1867
195
207
217
2174
21749
217493
226
27
274
278
279
2796
281
284
285
286
287
288
294
307
768

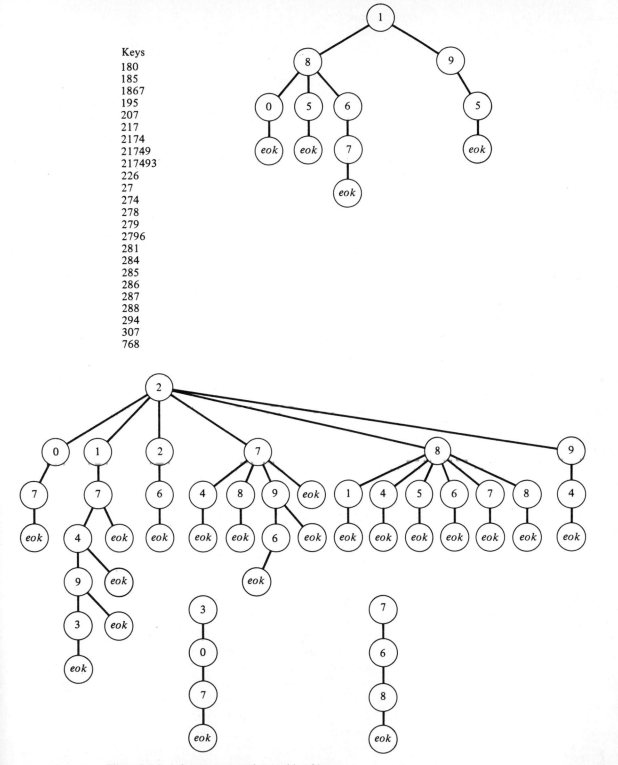

Figure 9.2.8 A forest representing a table of keys.

```
            past := false;
            while (p <> nil) and (not past)
                do if symbol(p) ⩾ key(i)
                    then past := true
                    else begin
                            q := p;
                            p := brother(p)
                         end {else begin};
        found := true;
        if (p = nil) or (symbol(p) > key(i))
            then search := insert {       insert the record       }
            else if key(i) = eok
                    then search := son(p) { found the record }
                    else begin {  continue searching for the  }
                             {           next symbol           }
                            father := p;
                            p := son(p);
                            found := false;
                            i := i + 1
                         end {else begin}
    end {while...do begin}
```

The algorithm for *insert* is as follows:

```
            { insert the ith symbol of the key }
            s := getnode;
            symbol(s) := key(i);
            brother(s) := p;
            if tree = nil
                then tree := s
                else if q <> nil
                        then brother(q) := s
                        else if father = nil
                                then tree := s
                                else son(father) := s;
            { insert the remaining symbols of the key }
            j := i;
            while key(j) <> eok
                do begin
                        father := s;
                        s := getnode;
                        symbol(s) := key(j+1);
                        son(father) := s;
                        brother(s) := nil;
                        j := j + 1
                   end {while...do begin};
        son(s) := recptr;
        insert := recptr
```

Note that by keeping the table of keys as a general tree, we need search only a small list of sons to find whether a given symbol appears at a given position within the keys of the table. However, it is possible to make the tree even smaller by eliminating those nodes from which only a single leaf can be reached. For example, in the keys of Figure 9.2.8, once the symbol '7' is recognized, the only key that can possibly match is 768. Similarly, upon recognizing the two symbols '1' and '9', the only matching key is 195. Thus the forest of Figure 9.2.8 can be abbreviated to the one of Figure 9.2.9. In that figure, a box indicates a key and a circle indicates a tree node. A dashed line is used to indicate a pointer from a tree node to a key.

There are some significant differences between the trees of Figures 9.2.8 and 9.2.9. In Figure 9.2.8, a path from a root to a leaf represents an entire key; thus there is no need to repeat the key itself. In Figure 9.2.9, however, a key may be recognized only by its first few symbols. In those cases where the search is made for a key that is known to be in the table, then upon finding a leaf the record corresponding to that key can be accessed. If, however, as is more likely, it is not known whether the key is present in the table, it must be confirmed that the key is indeed correct. Thus the entire key must be kept in the record as well. Furthermore, a leaf node in the tree of Figure 9.2.8 can be recognized because its contents are *eok*. Thus its *son* pointer can be used to point to the record which that leaf represents. However, a leaf node of Figure 9.2.9 may contain any symbol. Thus to use the *son* pointer of a leaf to point to the record, an extra boolean field is required in each node to indicate whether or not the node is a leaf. We leave the representation of the forest of Figure 9.2.9 and the implementation of a search-and-insert algorithm for it as an exercise for the reader.

The tree representation of a table of keys is efficient when each node has relatively few sons. For example, in Figure 9.2.9 only one node has as many as six (out of a possible 10) sons, whereas most nodes have only one, two, or three sons. Thus the process of searching through the list of sons to match the next symbol in the key is relatively efficient. However, if the set of keys is *dense* within the set of all possible keys (i.e., if almost any possible combination of symbols actually appears as a key), most nodes will have a large number of sons and the cost of the search process becomes prohibitive.

Tries

A modification of the digital tree proves to be quite efficient when the set of keys in the table is dense. Instead of storing the table as a tree, the table is stored as a two-dimensional array. Each row of the array represents one of the possible symbols that may appear in the key, and each column represents a node in a digital tree. Each entry in the array is a pointer to either another column in the array or to a key and its record. In searching for a key *key*, *key*(1) is used to index the first column of the array. The entry that is found at row *key*(1) and column 1 is either a pointer to a key and record, in which case there is only one key in the table that begins with the symbol *key*(1); or it is a pointer to another column of the array, say

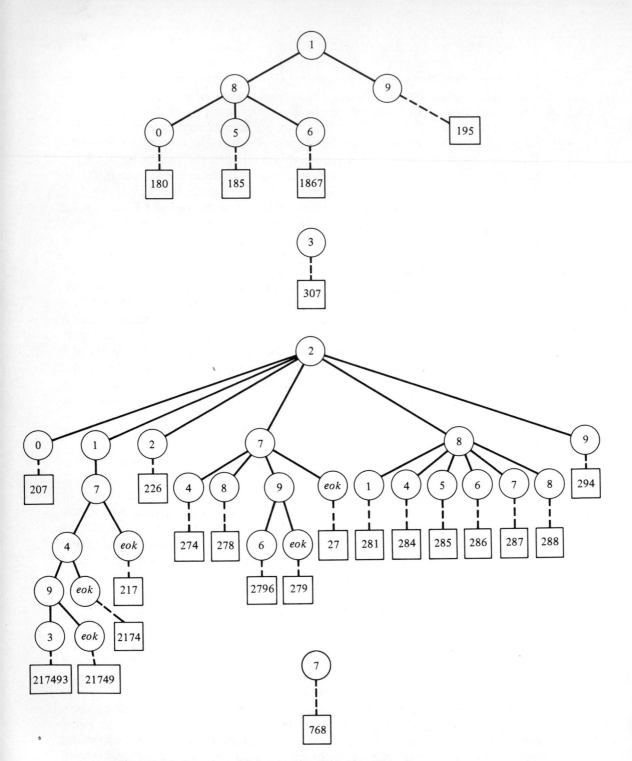

Figure 9.2.9 A condensed forest representing a table of keys.

	1	2	3	4	5	6	7	8	9	10	11	12	13	14
0			180	207										
1	(2)			(5)							281			
2	(4)			226										
3	307							217493						
4						(7)			274		284			
5			185								285			
6			1867							2796	286			
7	768			(9)	(6)						287			
8		(3)		(11)					278		288			
9		195		294			(8)		(10)					
eok						217	2174	21749	27	279				

Figure 9.2.10 A trie.

column j. Column j represents all keys in the table that begin with $key(1)$. $key(2)$ is used to index column j to determine either the only key in the table beginning with $key(1)$ and $key(2)$, or the column representing all keys in the table beginning with those two symbols. Similarly, each column in the array represents the set of all keys that begin with the same initial symbols. Such an array is called a *trie* (from the word re*trie*val).

Figure 9.2.10 illustrates a trie containing the keys of Figures 9.2.8 and 9.2.9. A pointer to a key and its corresponding record is indicated by an unparenthesized number which is the actual key, and a pointer to a column is indicated by a parenthesized number. In an actual implementation, an extra boolean field would be required to differentiate between these two types of pointers.

For example, suppose that a search is to be made for a record whose key is 274, in the trie of Figure 9.2.10. In this case, $key(1)=2$, $key(2)=7$, and $key(3)=4$. $key(1)$ is used to index column 1. Row 2 of column 1 points to column 4; thus column 4 represents all keys whose first character is 2. $key(2)$ is then used to index column 4. Row 7 of column 4 points to column 9; thus column 9 represents all keys whose first two characters are 2 and 7, respectively. $key(3)$ is then used to index column 9, in which row 4 contains the key 274. At this point the search is successful. Actually, since the array that forms the trie is dynamic (columns must be added as new records are inserted), a trie is best implemented as a general tree in which each node has a fixed number of sons. Each node of the general tree represents a column of the trie.

You will note that the trie of Figure 9.2.10 contains a large amount of unused space. This is because the set of keys in this example is not dense, so there are many digits at many positions which do not appear in a key.

If the set of keys is dense, most of the entries in the trie will be filled. The reason a trie is so efficient is that for each symbol of the key only a single table lookup need be performed rather than a list traversal.

EXERCISES

1. Write an efficient insertion algorithm for a binary search tree to insert a new record whose key is known not to exist in the tree.

2. Show that it is possible to obtain a binary search tree in which only a single leaf exists even if the elements of the tree are not inserted in strictly ascending or descending order.

3. Verify by simulation that if records are presented to the binary tree search and insertion algorithm in random order, the number of key comparisons will be $O(\log n)$.

4. Prove that every n-node binary search tree is not equally likely (assuming that items are inserted in random order), and that balanced trees are more probable than are straight-line trees.

5. Write an algorithm to delete a node from a binary tree which replaces the node with its inorder predecessor rather than its inorder successor.

6. Suppose that the node type of a binary search tree is defined as follows:

    type nodetype = **record**
                 k,r: integer;
                 left,right: nodeptr
        end;

    The k and r fields contain the key and record of the node; *left* and *right* are pointers to the node's sons. Write a Pascal function *sinsert(tree,key,rec)* to search and insert a record *rec* with key *key* into a binary search tree pointed to by *tree*.

7. Write a Pascal function *sdelete(tree,key)* to search and delete a record with key *key* from a binary search tree implemented as in Exercise 6. If such a record is found, the function returns the value of its r field; if it is not found, the function returns 0.

8. Write a Pascal routine *delete(tree,key1,key2)* to delete all records with keys between *key*1 and *key*2 (inclusive) from a binary search tree whose nodes are declared as in the previous exercises.

9. Consider the search trees of Figure 9.2.11.

    (a) How many permutations of the integers 1 through 7 would produce the binary search trees of Figure 9.2.11a, b, and c, respectively?
    (b) How many permutations of the integers 1 through 7 would produce binary search trees which are similar to the trees of Figure 9.2.11a, b, and c, respectively? (See Exercise 6.1.6.)
    (c) How many permutations of the integers 1 through 7 would produce binary search trees with the same number of nodes at each level as the trees of Figure 9.2.11a, b, and c, respectively?
    (d) Find an assignment of probabilities to the first seven positive integers as search arguments which makes each of the trees of Figure 9.2.11a, b, and c optimum.

CHAP. 9: SEARCHING

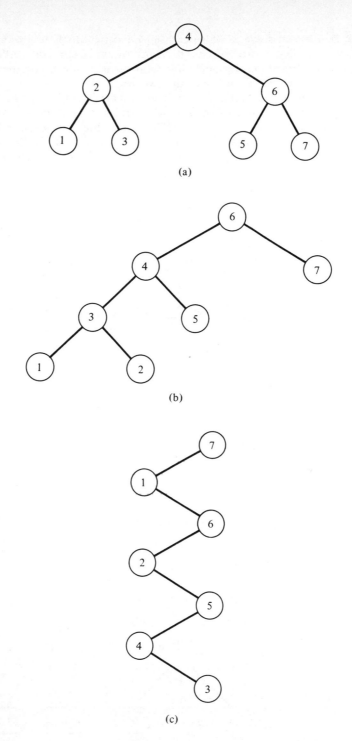

(a)

(b)

(c)

Figure 9.2.11

10. A **3-2 tree** is one in which each node has two or three sons and contains either one or two keys. If a node has two sons, it contains one key. All keys in its left subtree are less than that key and all keys in its right subtree are greater than that key. If a node has three sons, it contains two keys. All keys in its left subtree are less than its left key, which is less than all keys in its middle subtree. All keys in its middle subtree are less than its right key, which is less than all keys in its right subtree. Figure 9.2.12a illustrates such a tree. (The two or three subtrees of a leaf are all nil.)

A key is inserted into such a tree as follows. First, find the leaf into which the key would be inserted if there were no limit to the number of keys to a node. For

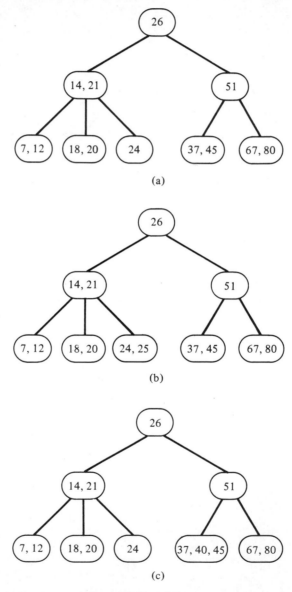

Figure 9.2.12 A 3-2 tree.

example, Figure 9.2.12b illustrates the key 25 inserted into a leaf, and Figure 9.2.12c illustrates the key 40 inserted into a leaf. The tree of Figure 9.2.12b is a valid 3-2 tree, so that the key 25 has been properly inserted. Figure 9.2.12c is not a valid 3-2 tree, since one node contains three keys. In this case, the insertion process continues by moving the middle one of the three keys into the father node and splitting the other two keys into two separate nodes, as shown in Figure 9.2.12d. Since the resulting tree is a 3-2 tree, the insertion process terminates. Figure 9.2.12e illustrates the 3-2 tree that finally results from an insertion of the key 16 into the tree of Figure 9.2.12d, and Figure 9.2.12f illustrates the tree that results from an insertion of the key 85 into the tree of Figure 9.2.12e.

Develop a Pascal implementation of 3-2 trees and write search and insertion and deletion algorithms for them.

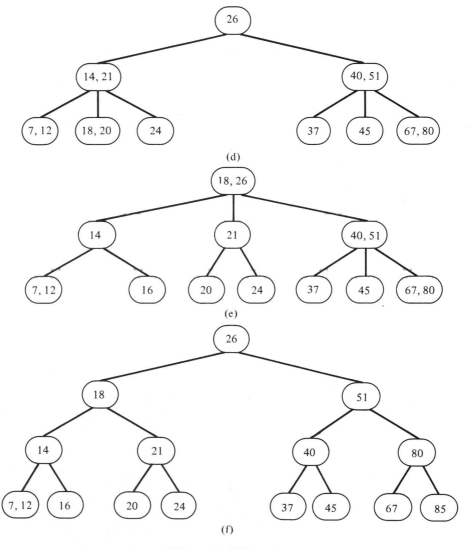

(d)

(e)

(f)

Figure 9.2.12 (cont.)

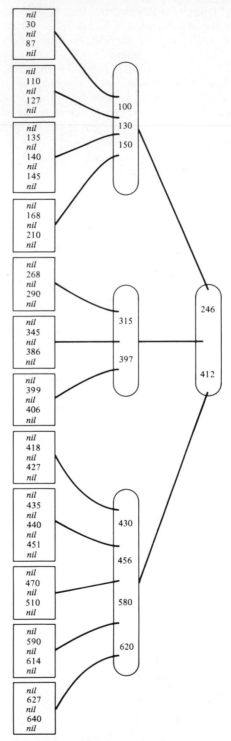

Figure 9.2.13 A B-tree of order 5.

11. A **B-tree of order** *m* is a generalization of the 3-2 trees of Exercise 10. Such a tree is defined as a general tree that satisfies the following properties:

(1) Each node contains at most $m-1$ keys.
(2) Each node except for the root contains at least $(m \ div \ 2) - 1$ keys.
(3) The root has at least two sons, unless it is a leaf.
(4) All leafs are on the same level.
(5) A nonleaf node with n keys has $n+1$ sons.

Figure 9.2.13 illustrates a B-tree of order 5. Note that each node may be thought of as an ordered set

$$(p_1, k_1, p_2, k_2, ..., k_{n-1}, p_n)$$

where p_i is a pointer (possibly nil, if the node is a leaf) and k_i is a key. All keys in the node pointed to by p_i are between k_{i-1} and k_i, and $k_1 < k_2 < \cdots < k_{n-1}$ within each node.

(a) Develop an algorithm to search and insert into a B-tree of order m.
(b) Convert your algorithm in part (a) into a Pascal program.
(c) Why are B-trees particularly useful in external searching?

3. HASHING

In the preceding two sections we assumed that the record being sought is stored in a table and that it is necessary to pass through some number of keys before finding the desired one. The organization of the file (sequential, indexed sequential, binary tree, etc.) and the order in which the keys are inserted determine the number of keys that must be inspected before obtaining the desired one. Obviously, the efficient search techniques are those that minimize the number of these comparisons. Optimally, we would like to have a table organization in which there are no unnecessary comparisons. Let us see if such a table organization is feasible.

If each key is to be retrieved in a single access, the location of the record within the table can depend only upon the key; it may not depend upon the locations of other keys as in a tree. The most efficient way to organize such a table is as an array (i.e., each record is stored at a specific offset from the base address of the table). If the record keys are integers, the keys themselves can be used as indices to the array.

Let us consider an example of such a system. Suppose that a manufacturing company has an inventory file consisting of 100 parts, each part having a unique two-digit part number. Then the obvious way to store this file is to declare an array:

var part: **array**[0..99] **of** parttype;

where *part* [*i*] represents the record whose part number is *i*. In this situation, the part numbers are keys which are used as indices to the array. Even if the company stocks fewer than 100 parts, the same structure can be used to maintain the inventory file (provided that the keys are still two digits). Although many locations in *part* correspond to nonexistent keys, this waste is offset by the advantage of direct access to each of the existent parts.

Unfortunately, however, such a system is not always practical. For example, suppose that the company has an inventory file of more than 100 items and the key to each record is a seven-digit part number. To use direct indexing using the entire seven-digit key, an array of 100 million elements would be required. This clearly wastes an unacceptably large amount of space because it is extremely unlikely that a company stocks more than a few thousand parts.

What is necessary is some method of converting a key into an integer within a limited range. Ideally, no two keys should be converted into the same integer. Unfortunately, such an ideal method usually does not exist. Let us attempt to develop methods that come close to the ideal, and determine what action to take when the ideal is not achieved.

Let us reconsider the example of a company with an inventory file in which each record is keyed by a seven-digit part number. Suppose that the company has fewer than 1000 parts and there is only a single record for each part. Then an array of 1000 elements is sufficient to contain the entire file. The array is indexed by an integer between 0 and 999 inclusive. The last three digits of the part number are used as the index for that part's record in the array. This is illustrated in Figure 9.3.1. Note that two keys which are relatively close to each other numerically, such as 4618396 and 4618996, may be farther from each other in the table than two keys that are widely separated numerically, such as 0000991 and 9846995. This is because only the last three digits of the key are used in determining the position of a record.

A function that transforms a key into a table index is called a *hash function*. If h is a hash function and *key* is a key, then $h(key)$ is called the *hash* of *key* and is the index at which a record with key *key* should be placed. The hash function in the example above is $h(key) = key \bmod 1000$. The values that h produces should cover the entire set of indices in the table. For example, the function $x \bmod 1000$ can produce any integer between 0 and 999, depending upon the value of x. As we shall see shortly, it is a good idea for the table size to be somewhat larger than the number of records that are to be inserted. This is illustrated in Figure 9.3.1, where several positions in the table are unused.

The foregoing method has one flaw. Suppose that two keys $k1$ and $k2$ are such that $h(k1) = h(k2)$. Then when a record with key $k1$ is entered into the table, it is inserted at position $h(k1)$. But when $k2$ is hashed, the position obtained is the same as where the record with key $k1$ is stored. Clearly, two records cannot occupy the same position. Such a situation is called a *hash collision* or a *hash clash*. A hash clash occurs in the inventory example of Figure 9.3.1 if a record with key 0596397 is added to the table. We will explore shortly how to resolve such a situation. However, it should be noted that a good hash function is one that minimizes collisions and spreads the records uniformly throughout the table. That is why it is desirable to have the array size larger than the number of actual records. The larger the range of the hash function, the less likely it is that two keys will yield the same

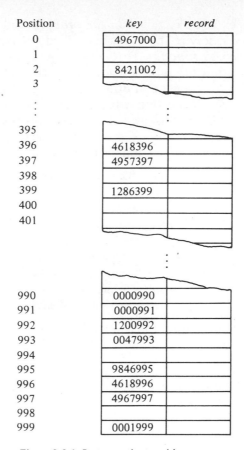

Position	key	record
0	4967000	
1		
2	8421002	
3		
⋮		
395		
396	4618396	
397	4957397	
398		
399	1286399	
400		
401		
⋮		
990	0000990	
991	0000991	
992	1200992	
993	0047993	
994		
995	9846995	
996	4618996	
997	4967997	
998		
999	0001999	

Figure 9.3.1 Part records stored in an array.

hash value. Of course, this involves a space/time trade-off. Leaving empty spaces in the array is inefficient in terms of space; but it reduces the necessity of resolving hash clashes and is therefore more efficient in terms of time.

Resolving Hash Clashes by Open Addressing

Let us consider what would happen if it was desired to enter a new part number 0596397 into the table of Figure 9.3.1. Using the hash function *key mod* 1000, we find that $h(0596397) = 397$ and that the record for that part belongs in position 397 of the array. However, position 397 is already occupied because the record with key 4957397 is in that position. Therefore, the record with key 0596397 must be inserted elsewhere in the table.

The simplest method of resolving hash clashes is to place the record in the next available position in the array. In Figure 9.3.1, for example, since position 397 is already occupied, the record with key 0596397 is placed in location 398, which is still open. Once that record has been inserted, another record, which hashes to either 397 (such as 8764397) or 398 (such as 2194398), is inserted at the next available position, which is 400.

This technique is called *linear probing* and is an example of a general method for resolving hash clashes called *rehashing* or *open addressing*. In general, a *rehash function*, *rh*, accepts one array index and produces another. If array location *h(key)* is already occupied by a record with a different key, *rh* is applied to the value of *h(key)* to find another location where the record may be placed. If position *rh(h(key))* is also occupied, it, too, is rehashed to see if *rh(rh(h(key)))* is available. This process continues until an empty location is found. Thus we may write a search and insertion function using hashing as follows. We assume the following declarations:

```
const maxtable = ...; { one less than the table size }
type keytype = ...;    {      type of a key        }
     rectype = ...;    {      type of a record     }
     entry = record
               k: keytype;
               r: rectype
             end;
     index = 0..maxtable;
var table = array[index] of entry;
```

We also assume a hash function *h(key:keytype):index* and a rehash function *rh(i:index):index*. The special value *nilkey* is used to indicate an empty record.

```
function search(key: keytype; rec: rectype): index;
var i: index;
begin
    i:= h(key); { hash the key }
    while (table[i].k <> key) and (table[i].k <> nilkey)
        do i:= rh(i); { rehash }
    if table[i].k = nilkey
       then begin { insert the record into the empty position }
               table[i].k:= key;
               table[i].r:= rec
            end {then begin};
    search:= i
end { function search};
```

In the example of Figure 9.3.1, *h(key)* is the function *key mod* 1000 and *rh(i)* is the function *(i+1) mod* 1000 (i.e., the rehash of any index is the next sequential position in the array, except that the rehash of 999 is 0).

Let us examine the algorithm more closely to see if we can determine the properties of a "good" rehash function. In particular, we focus our attention on the loop, because the number of iterations determines the efficiency of the search. The loop can be exited in one of two ways: either *i* is set to a value such that *table[i].k* equals *key* (in which case the record is found); or *i* is set to a value such that *table[i].k* equals *nilkey* (in which case an empty position is found and the record may be inserted).

470

It may happen, however, that the loop executes forever. There are two possible reasons for this. First, the table may be full, so that it is impossible to insert any new records. This situation can be detected by keeping a count of the number of records in the table. When the count is equal to the table size, no additional insertions are attempted.

However, it is possible for the algorithm to loop infinitely even if there are some (or even many) empty positions. Suppose, for example, that the function $rh(i) = (i+2) \ mod \ 1000$ is used as a rehash function. Then any key that hashes into an odd integer rehashes into successive odd integers, and any key that hashes into an even integer rehashes into successive even integers. Consider the situation in which all the odd positions of the table are occupied and all the even ones are empty. Despite the fact that half the positions of the array are empty, it is impossible to insert a new record whose key hashes into an odd integer. Of course, it is unlikely that all the odd positions are occupied while none of the even positions are. However, if the rehash function $rh(i) = (i+200) \ mod \ 1000$ is used, each key can be placed in only one of five places [since $x \ mod \ 1000 = (x+1000) \ mod \ 1000$] and it is quite possible for these five places to be full while much of the table is empty.

One property of a good rehash function is that for any index i, the successive rehashes $rh(i)$, $rh(rh(i))$, ... cover as many of the integers between 0 and *maxtable* as possible (ideally, all of them). The rehash function $rh(i) = (i+1) \ mod \ 1000$ has this property. In fact, any function $rh(i) = (i+c) \ mod \ m$, where m is the number of elements in the table (note that $m = maxtable + 1$) and c is a constant value such that c and m are relatively prime (i.e., they cannot both be divided evenly by a single integer other than 1), produce successive values which cover the entire table. You are invited to confirm this fact by choosing some examples; the proof is left as an exercise.

There is another measure of the suitability of a rehash function. Consider the case of the linear rehash. Assuming that the hash function produces indices which are uniformly distributed over the interval 0 through *maxtable* [i.e., it is equally likely that $h(key)$ is any particular integer in that range], then initially when the entire array is empty it is equally likely that a random record will be placed at any given empty position within the array. However, once entries have been inserted and several hash clashes have been resolved, this is no longer true. For example, in Figure 9.3.1 it is five times as likely for a record to be inserted at position 994 than at position 401. This is because any record whose key hashes into 990, 991, 992, 993, or 994 will be placed in 994, while only a record whose key hashes into 401 will be placed in that location. This phenomenon, where two keys that hash into different values compete with each other in successive rehashes, is called *clustering*.

The same phenomenon occurs in the case of the rehash function $rh(i) = (i+c) \ mod \ (maxtable+1)$. For example, if *maxtable* = 999, c = 21 and positions 10, 31, 52, 73, and 94 are all occupied, any record whose key is any one of these five integers will be placed at location 115. In fact, any rehash function that depends solely upon the index to be rehashed causes clustering.

One way to eliminate clustering is to use *double hashing*, which involves the use of two hash functions, $h1(key)$ and $h2(key)$. $h1$, which is known as the *primary* hash function, is first used to determine the position at which the record should be placed. If that position is occupied, the rehash function $rh(i) = (i+h2(key)) \bmod (maxtable+1)$ is used successively until an empty location is found. As long as $h2(key1)$ does not equal $h2(key2)$, records with keys $key1$ and $key2$ do not compete for the same set of locations. This is true despite the possibility that $h1(key1)$ may indeed equal $h1(key2)$. The rehash function depends not only on the index to be rehashed but also on the original key. Note that the value $h2(key)$ does not have to be recomputed for each rehash—it need be computed only once for each key that must be rehashed. Optimally, therefore, one should choose functions $h1$ and $h2$ which distribute the hashes and rehashes uniformly over the interval 0 to *maxtable* and also minimize clustering. Such functions are not always easy to find.

Another approach is to allow the rehash function to depend on the number of times that the function is applied to a particular hash value. In this approach, the function rh is a function of two arguments. $rh(i,j)$ yields the rehash of the integer i if the key is being rehashed for the jth time. One example is $rh(i,j) = (i+j) \bmod (maxtable+1)$. The first rehash yields $rh1 = rh(h(key),1) = (h(key)+1) \bmod (maxtable+1)$, the second yields $rh2 = (rh1+2) \bmod (maxtable+1)$, the third yields $rh3 = (rh2+3) \bmod (maxtable+1)$, and so on.

Resolving Hash Clashes by Chaining

There are several reasons why rehashing may not be an adequate method to deal with hash clashes. First, it assumes a fixed table size m. If the number of records grows beyond m, it is impossible to insert them without allocating a larger table and recomputing the hash values of the keys of all records already in the table using a new hash function. Furthermore, it is difficult to delete a record from such a table. For example, suppose that record $r1$ is at position p. To add a record $r2$ whose key $k2$ hashes into p, it must be inserted into the first free position from among $rh(p), rh(rh(p)), \ldots$. Suppose that $r1$ is then deleted, so that position p becomes empty. A subsequent search for record $r2$ begins at position $h(k2)$, which is p. But since that position is now empty, the search process may erroneously conclude that record $r2$ is absent from the table.

One possible solution to this problem is to mark a deleted record as "deleted" rather than "empty" and to continue searching whenever a "deleted" position is encountered in the course of a search. But this is possible only if there are a small number of deletions; otherwise, an unsuccessful search would require a search through the entire table because most positions will be marked "deleted" rather than "empty."

Another method of resolving hash clashes is called *chaining* and involves keeping a linked list of all records whose keys hash into the same value. Suppose that the hash function produces values between 0 and $m-1$. Then an array of header nodes of size *m*, called *buckets*, is declared. *bucket*[*i*] points to the list of all records whose keys hash into *i*. In searching for a record, the list head that occupies position *i* in the bucket array is accessed and the list that it initiates is traversed. If the record is not found, it is inserted at the end of the list. Figure 9.3.2 illustrates chaining. We assume a 10-element array and that the hash function is *key mod* 10. The keys in that figure are presented in the order

75 66 42 192 91 40 49 87 67 16 417 130 372 227

We may write a search and insertion function with chaining using a hash function *h* and a bucket array *bucket*, and nodes which contain three fields: *k* for the key. *r* for the record, and *next* as a pointer to the next node in the list.

```
function search(key: keytype; rec: rectype): nodeptr;
var i: index;
     p,q,s: nodeptr;
     found: boolean;
begin
     found:= false;
     i:= h(key);
     q:= nil;
     p:= bucket[i];
     while (p <> nil) and (not found)
          do if p↑.k = key
               then found:= true
               else begin
                         q:= p;
                         p:= p↑.next
                    end {else begin};
     if found
        then search:= p
        else begin { insert a new record }
                 s:= getnode;
                 s↑.k:= key;
                 s↑.r:= rec;
                 s↑.next:= nil;
                 if q = nil
                    then bucket[i]:= s
                    else q↑.next:= s;
                 search:= s
             end {else begin}
end { function search};
```

Deleting a node from a table that is constructed by hashing and chaining involves simply removing a node from a linked list. A deleted node has no effect on the efficiency of the search algorithm; the algorithm continues

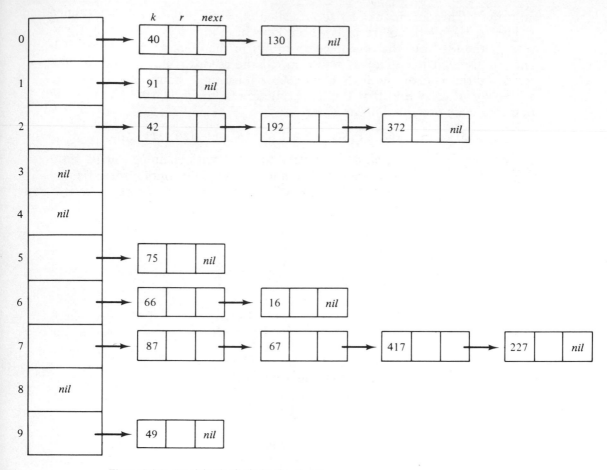

Figure 9.3.2 Resolving hash clashes by chaining.

as though the node had never been inserted. Note that the lists may be reordered dynamically for more efficient searching by the methods of Section 9.1.

The primary disadvantage of chaining is the extra space that is required for buckets and pointers. However, the initial array is usually smaller in schemes that use chaining than in those that use rehashing. This is because under chaining it is less catastrophic if the entire array becomes full—it is always possible to allocate more nodes and add them to the various lists. Of course, if the lists become very long, the whole purpose of hashing—direct addressing and resultant search efficiency—is defeated.

Choosing a Hash Function

Let us now turn to the question of how to choose a good hash function. Clearly, the function should produce as few hash clashes as possible; that is, it should spread the keys uniformly over the possible array indices. Of course, unless the keys are known in advance, it cannot be determined whether a particular hash function will disperse them properly. However, although it is rare to know the keys before selecting a hash function, it is fairly common to know some properties of the keys which will affect their dispersal.

For example, the most common hash function (which we have used in the examples of this section) uses the *division method*, in which an integer key is divided by the table size and the remainder is taken as the hash value. This is the hash function $h(key) = key \bmod (maxtable + 1)$. Suppose, however, that $maxtable + 1$ equals 1000 and that all the keys end in the same three digits (e.g., the last three digits of a part number might represent a plant number, and the program is being written for that plant). Then the remainder on dividing by 1000 will yield the same value for all the keys, so that a hash clash will occur for each record except the first. Clearly, given such a collection of keys, a different hash function should be used.

It has been found that the best results with the division method are achieved when the table size m (which equals $maxtable + 1$) is prime (i.e., m is not divisible by any positive integer other than 1 and m.)

In another hash function, known as the *midsquare method*, the key is multiplied by itself and the middle few digits (the exact number depends on the number of digits allowed in the index) of the square are used as the index. If the square is considered as a decimal number, the table size must be a power of 10, whereas if it is considered as a binary number, the table size must be a power of 2. The *folding method* breaks up a key into several segments which are added or exclusive *or*ed together to form a hash value. For example, suppose that the internal bit string representation of a key is 010111001010110 and that 5 bits are allowed in the index. The three bit strings 01011, 10010, and 10110 are exclusive *or*ed to produce 01111, which is 15 as a binary integer. (The *exclusive or* of two bits is 1 if the two bits are different, and 0 if they are the same.)

There are many other hash functions, each with its own advantages and disadvantages, depending on the set of keys to be hashed. One consideration in choosing a hash function is efficiency of calculation; it does no good to be able to find an object on the first try if that try takes longer than several tries in an alternative method.

If the keys are not integers, they must be converted into integers before applying one of the foregoing hash functions. There are several ways to do this. For example, for a character string the internal bit representation of each character can be interpreted as a binary number. One disadvantage of this is that the bit representations of all the letters or digits tend to be very similar on most computers. If the keys consist of letters alone, the index of each letter in the alphabet can be used to create an integer. Thus the first letter of the alphabet (*a*) is represented by the digits 01 and the fourteenth (*n*) is represented by the digits 14. The key '*hello*' is represented by the integer 0805121215. Once an integer representation of a character string exists, the folding method can be used to reduce it to manageable size.

EXERCISES   1. Write a Pascal function *search(table,key)* which searches a hash table for a record with key *key*. The function accepts an integer key and a table declared by

type elemtype = **record**

k: keytype;

r: rectype;

flag: boolean

end;

var table: **array**[0..maxtable] of elemtype;

table[*i*].*k* and *table*[*i*].*r* are the *i*th key and record, respectively. *table*[*i*].*flag* equals *false* if the *i*th table position is empty and *true* if it is occupied. The function returns an integer in the range 0..*maxtable* if a record with key *key* is present in the table. If no such record exists, the function returns −1. Assume the existence of a hashing routine, *h(key)*, and a rehashing routine *rh(index)*, which both produce integers in the range 0..*maxtable*.

2. Write a Pascal function *sinsert(table,key,rec)* to search and insert into a hash table as in Exercise 1.

3. Develop a mechanism for detecting when all possible rehash positions of a given key have been searched. Incorporate this method into the Pascal routines *search* and *sinsert* of the previous exercises.

4. Consider a double hashing method using primary hash function *h1(key)* and rehash function *rh(index)=m* **mod** (*index+h2(key)*). Assume that *h2(key)* is relatively prime to *m* for any key *key*. Develop a search algorithm and an algorithm to insert a record whose key is known not to exist in the table so that the keys at successive rehashes of a single key are in ascending order. The insertion algorithm may rearrange records previously inserted into the table. Can you combine these algorithms into a search and insertion algorithm?

5. Suppose that a key is equally likely to be any integer between *a* and *b*. Suppose that the midsquare hash method is used to produce an integer between 0 and 2^{k-1}. Is the result equally likely to be any integer within that range? Why?

6. Given a hash function *h(key)* for a table of size *m*, write a Pascal simulation program to determine each of the following quantities after .8*m* random keys have been generated. The keys should be random six-digit integers.

   (1) The percentage of integers between 0 and *m*−1 that do not equal *h(key)* for any generated key.
   (2) The percentage of integers between 0 and *m*−1 that equal *h(key)* for more than one generated key.
   (3) The maximum number of keys that hash into a single value between 0 and *m*−1.
   (4) The average number of keys that hash into values between 0 and *m*−1, not including those values into which no key hashes.

   Run the program to test the uniformity of each of the following hash functions:

   (a) *h(key)* = *key* **mod** *m* for *m* a prime.
   (b) *h(key)* = *key* **mod** *m* for *m* a power of 2.
   (c) The folding method, using exclusive *or* to produce 5-bit indices, where *m*=32.
   (d) The midsquare method, using decimal arithmetic to produce four-digit indices, where *m*=10000.

476

7. If a hash table contains m positions and n records currently occupy the table, the **load factor** is defined as n/m. Show that if a hash function uniformly distributes keys over the m positions of the table and if lf is the load factor of the table, then $(n-1)*lf/2$ of the n keys in the table collided upon insertion with a previously entered key.

8. Assume that n random positions of an m-element hash table are occupied, using hash and rehash functions which are equally likely to produce any index in the table. What is the average number of comparisons needed to insert a new element in terms of m and n? Explain why linear probing does not satisfy this condition.

4. EXAMPLES AND APPLICATIONS

In this section we reexamine several problems that were programmed in preceding chapters to see how the search techniques of this chapter can be applied to make the solutions more efficient. We examine some trade-offs in time and space among various solutions and show how searching plays an important role in problem solving.

Example 9.4.1: The Huffman Algorithm

Our first example is the Huffman algorithm of Section 6.3. Readers are asked to reread that section to refamiliarize themselves with the problem and the solution presented therein.

We focus our attention on the program *findcode*, especially on the loop that searches for the nodes with smallest *freq* value, controlled by the code *for m:= n+1 to 2*n-1*. The nodes of a strictly binary tree with n leafs are represented by the integers between 1 and $2*n-1$. The field *father* in a node contains a pointer to the father of the node in the tree, the field *sontype* indicates whether the node is a left or right son, and the field *freq* contains the information associated with the node.

We begin with *nodes*[*i*].*freq* defined for i between 1 and n and with *nodes*[*i*].*father* equal to 0 for all i. That is, we are given frequencies for the original symbols each of which is a root of its own single-element binary tree. These nodes are to be combined into a single binary tree. The unoccupied nodes (from $n+1$ through $2*n-1$) are thought of as an available list of nodes. The algorithm proceeds through this available list in sequence, setting each node as the father of two previously allocated nodes.

In choosing two previously allocated nodes to set as the sons of a newly allocated node, the algorithm searches for the two nodes without fathers with the smallest *freq* values. We now reproduce the section of code that accomplishes this. m is the index of the newly allocated node. $n1$ and $n2$ point to the two nodes that are found by the search process.

```
n1 := 0;
n2 := 0;
small1 := maxint;
small2 := maxint;
```

```
for j:= 1 to m-1
    do if nodes[j].father = 0
        then {j is a root node}
            if nodes[j].freq < small1
                then begin
                        small2:= small1;
                        small1:= nodes[j].freq;
                        n2:= n1;
                        n1:= j
                    end {then begin}
                else if nodes[j].freq < small2
                    then begin
                            small2:= nodes[j].freq;
                            n2:= j
                        end {then begin}
```

Once the two nodes $n1$ and $n2$ are identified, they are set as the sons of node m by the code:

```
nodes[n1].father:= m;
nodes[n1].sontype:= lson;
nodes[n2].father:= m;
nodes[n2].sontype:= rson;
nodes[m].freq:= nodes[n1].freq + nodes[n2].freq
```

The search process is inefficient because each time a new node is allocated, all the previous nodes must be examined in searching for the two root nodes with the smallest frequency.

The first improvement that can be made is to keep a separate list of root nodes (i.e., nodes m such that *nodes* [m] *.father* = 0). If this is done, we need not search through all allocated nodes—only through those which have no father. Also, the test for whether *nodes*[m].*father* equals 0 can be eliminated from the loop. These benefits are not without disadvantages: extra space is required for the pointers that link together the list of root nodes, and extra time is required to add or delete an element from this list. These are the general disadvantages that must be faced in moving from an array to a list representation: in an array, elements are ordered implicitly, whereas in a list they must be linked explicitly. (However, in this case it is possible to use the *father* field of all root nodes to link together the list. In the interest of clarity, we do not pursue this possibility here but leave it as an exercise for the reader.)

Thus we may add a field *nextroot* to the type *nodetype* as follows:

```
type nodetype = record
                    freq: integer;
                    father: nodeptr;
                    sontype: stype;
                    nextroot: nodeptr
                end;
```

We also include a new variable *firstroot* declared by

var firstroot: nodeptr;

nodes[*m*].*nextroot* is undefined if *m* is not a root node. If *m* is a root node, *nodes*[*m*].*nextroot* is the next root node after *m* on the list of root nodes. If *m* is the last root node on the list, *nodes*[*m*].*nextroot* equals 0. *firstroot* is the index of the first root node on the list. These variables are initialized as follows:

```
firstroot := 1;
for j := 1 to n-1
      do nodes[j].nextroot := j+1;
nodes[n].nextroot := 0;
```

The search may then be rewritten as follows. *kk* remains one step behind *j* in traversing the list of root nodes. *k*1 and *k*2 are set to the nodes immediately preceding *n*1 and *n*2, respectively, on the list of root nodes.

```
n1 := 0;
n2 := 0;
k1 := 0;
k2 := 0;
kk := 0;
small1 := maxint;
small2 := maxint;
j := firstroot;
while j <> 0 {traverse the list of rootnodes}
      do begin
            if nodes[j].freq < small1
               then begin
                       small2 := small1;
                       small1 := nodes[j].freq;
                       n2 := n1;
                       n1 := j;
                       k2 := k1;
                       k1 := kk
                    end {then begin}
               else if nodes[j].freq < small2
                  then begin
                          small2 := nodes[j].freq;
                          n2 := j;
                          k2 := kk
                       end {then begin};
            kk := j;
            j := nodes[j].nextroot
      end {while...do begin}
```

The code to remove nodes *n*1 and *n*2 from the list of root nodes, insert them into the binary tree, and insert the new root node *m* into the list of root nodes becomes more complex. The following code performs these tasks, inserting *m* in place of *n*2 and removing *n*1 from the list entirely.

```
{insert m into the binary tree}
nodes[n1].father:= m;
nodes[n1].sontype:= lson;
nodes[n2].father:= m;
nodes[n2].sontype:= rson;
nodes[m].freq:= nodes[n1].freq + nodes[n2].freq;

{replace n2 in the list of rootnodes by m}
nodes[m].nextroot:= nodes[n2].nextroot;
if k2 = 0
    then firstroot:= m
    else nodes[k2].nextroot:= m;
{remove n1 from the list of rootnodes}
if nodes[m].nextroot = n1
    then k1:= m;
if k1 = 0
    then firstroot:= nodes[n1]nextroot
    else nodes[k1].nextroot:= nodes[n1].nextroot
```

This code can be simplified somewhat and made more efficient if the list of root nodes is maintained as a circular list. We leave this implementation as an exercise for the reader.

Further efficiency will be realized if the list of root nodes is kept sorted, ordered by increasing values of the *freq* field. Then the search for the two nodes of smallest frequency is eliminated—they are the first two nodes on the list. Thus the entire search loop can be replaced by the two statements

```
n1:= firstroot;
n2:= nodes[n1].nextroot
```

However, to keep the list sorted, the *n* original symbols must first be sorted using one of the sorting techniques of Chapter 8. Also, each time a new node *m* is inserted into the list of root nodes, it must be inserted into its proper position. The code to insert *m* into the binary tree and the root node list therefore becomes

```
{insert m into the binary tree}
nodes[n1].father:= m;
nodes[n1].sontype:= lson;
nodes[n2].father:= m;
nodes[n2].sontype:= rson;
nodes[m].freq:= nodes[n1].freq + nodes[n2].freq;
frq:= nodes[m].freq;
{remove n1 and n2 from the root node list and}
{              insert m into that list              }
firstroot:= nodes[n2].nextroot;
```

```
                    kk:= 0;
                    j:= firstroot;
                    found:= false;
                    while (j<>0) and (not found)
                        do if nodes[j].freq >= frq
                            then found:= true
                            else begin
                                    kk:= j;
                                    j:= nodes[j].nextroot
                            end {else begin};
                    if kk = 0
                        then firstroot:= m
                        else nodes[kk].nextroot:= m;
                    nodes[m].nextroot:= j
```

Thus the search process has been moved from the first step (finding the two nodes with lowest frequency) to the second (inserting a new node into its proper place). However, in the second step it is not necessary to search through the entire list of root nodes, but rather only until the proper position for the new node is found. Whether or not this is appreciably faster depends on the initial distribution of frequencies. For example, if the initial frequencies are successive integers starting at n, then the first new root node allocated will have to be placed at the end of the list. In most cases, however, the search time is reduced by a factor of 2.

This saving must be weighed against the cost of initially sorting the n original symbols, which may be quite expensive. As n becomes larger and the saving in search time becomes more worthwhile, the cost of sorting increases. We leave to the reader to determine which method is more efficient for various values of n.

EXERCISES
1. Rewrite the program implementing the Huffman algorithm with the list of root nodes kept as an unordered circular list.

2. Implement the Huffman algorithm using an ordered list of root nodes and various sort techniques of Chapter 8 to initially create the ordered list.

3. How does the efficiency of the implementations in Exercise 2 vary depending upon the distribution of initial frequencies? Can you find a distribution of initial frequencies so that a newly allocated node is always placed at the end of the root node list? Can you find a distribution so that a newly allocated node is always placed at the front of the list? Explain.

4. Modify the Huffman algorithm so that the *father* field is used to link together all root nodes. The *nextroot* field is no longer necessary.

Example 9.4.2: A Scheduling Problem

Our next example of the application of search techniques is the scheduling problem of Section 7.3. Again, you should reread that section to refamiliarize yourself with the problem and the solutions that were presented therein.

The primary search problem of the scheduling algorithm is to search through the nodes of a graph represented by a linked data structure. This search takes place at two distinct points in the solution presented in Section 7.3. (We are now focusing our attention on the first solution presented in Section 7.3, in which a singly linked list is used for the graph nodes. This solution is presented in that section as the Pascal program named *schedule*.)

1. When the program reads a precedence relationship indicating that task *inf*1 must be performed before task *inf*2, an arc must be drawn from *inf*1 to *inf*2. All the nodes in the graph must be searched for nodes with contents *inf*1 and *inf*2, respectively. If no nodes with contents *inf*1 or *inf*2 exist, they must be allocated and added to the list of graph nodes. This search and insertion is performed by the function *find*, which is called twice from within the loop beginning *while not eof*. (Actually, an immediate saving in efficiency would result if the list of graph nodes were traversed only once for each pair of input tasks to search for both *inf*1 and *inf*2 simultaneously.)

2. In the output phase of the program (the loop beginning with *while graph <> 0*), the entire list of graph nodes must be searched during each time period to find those nodes whose *count* field is 0. These nodes are removed from the graph and placed on another list, from which they are subsequently printed. As noted in Section 7.3, the only reason this search is necessary is because a node cannot be removed from a singly linked list without a pointer to its predecessor. This prevents us from placing a node on the output list when its count is reduced to 0, because at that time we have only a pointer to the node itself and not to its predecessor. One way to eliminate this search, as noted in Section 7.3, is to keep the list of graph nodes as a doubly linked list so that a node contains a pointer to its predecessor as well as to its successor.

A careful analysis of the program *schedule* yields the interesting observation that there is no reason whatever to keep the graph nodes in a list except to perform the two searches listed above. The list of graph nodes is never traversed for any reason other than to search for particular nodes at one of these two points. But since searching an unordered linear list is very inefficient, another way of organizing the graph nodes should improve the search efficiency significantly with no adverse effect to the remainder of the program.

What data structure shall we use to represent the graph nodes? In adding new nodes to the graph (point 1 above), it must be possible to access a graph node from the character string which names the task that it represents. Thus the *info* portion of the graph node acts as the key to the record, which is the node itself. The most direct way to access a node from its key is by using a hash function. If a hashing method is to be used, we must determine how we shall handle hash clashes. This consideration leads directly to the issue of the number of graph nodes that are to be allowed. If hash clashes are resolved by rehashing, the number of graph nodes is limited to the number of positions in the hash table. On the other hand, if collisions are resolved by chaining, an unlimited number of graph nodes is permitted.

Since the array implementation was used in Section 7.3, we will adhere to that implementation and use rehashing to resolve collisions. Thus the set of graph nodes is declared by

```
const maxgraph = 499;
      maxarc = 500;
      niltask = '                    ';
type  graphpointer = 0..maxgraph;
      arcpointer = 1..maxarc;
      task = packed array[1..20] of char;
      graphtype = record
                info: task;            {     name of task      }
                count: integer;        {number of predecessors}
                arcptr: arcpointer;    {  pointer to list of arcs  }
                nextnode: graphpointer {  used to link together  }
                                       {     the output list      }
          end;
var   graphnode[0..maxgraph] of graphtype;
```

Note that since the graph nodes are not linked together on a list, the pointer *nextnode* in each graph node is not used until the node is placed in an output list.

We assume the existence of a hash function *hash* that transforms a character string into an integer between 0 and *maxgraph* and a rehash function *rehash* that accepts an integer in the same range and returns an integer in that range. Then the function *find* can be written to search and insert a node into the graph as follows:

```
function find(inf: task): graphpointer;
var   i,j: graphpointer;
      found: boolean;
begin
      i:= hash (inf);
      if graphnode[i].info = niltask
         then graphnode[i].info:= inf;
      if graphnode[i].info = inf
         then find:= i
         else begin
                j:= rehash (i);
                found:= false;
```

```
                    while (j <> i) and (not found)
                        do begin
                                if graphnode[j].info = niltask
                                    then graphnode[j].info:= inf;
                                if graphnode[j].info = inf
                                    then begin
                                                found:= true;
                                                find:= j
                                            end {then begin}
                                    else j:= rehash (j)
                            end {while...do begin};
                    if not found
                        then error ('error—table size exceeded')
                end {else begin}
        end {function find};
```

By using this *find* function, the input loop can be rewritten with very few changes from the way it appears in Section 7.3.

By representing a graph using a hash table, the first search problem has been solved. Let us see how we can solve the second. We first note that when a node is identified as a candidate for output (i.e., when its *count* field becomes 0), it can be placed on the output list; however, it is no longer necessary to remove it from the list of graph nodes because there is no list of graph nodes. Since the input phase and the output phase of the program are separate and no new nodes are added in the course of processing, it is unnecessary to delete any nodes from the hash table. (If it were necessary to delete nodes, chaining would be preferable to rehashing as the method for resolving hash clashes.) Thus our second problem, which was the necessity to traverse the entire set of graph nodes in order to remove a particular node, does not exist.

We may therefore write a revised version of the scheduling program as follows:

```
        program schedule(input,output);
        const maxgraph = 499;
                maxarc = 500;
                niltask = '                    ';
        type    graphpointer = 0..maxgraph;
                arcpointer = 1..maxarc;
                task = packed array[1..20] of char;
                graphtype = record
                                info: task;
                                count: integer;
                                arcptr: arcpointer;
                                nextnode: graphpointer
                            end;
                arctype  =  record
                                nodeptr: graphpointer;
                                nextarc: arcpointer
```

```
                                    end;
        var    graphnode: array[0..maxgraph] of graphtype;
               arc: array[1..maxarc] of arctype;
               p,q,t,outp,nextout: graphpointer;
               availarc,r,s: arcpointer;
               period: integer;
               int1,int2: task;
        begin {program schedule}
               for p:= 0 to maxgraph
                   do begin
                              graphnode[p].info:= niltask;
                              graphnode[p].count:= 0
                       end {for...do begin};
               for s:= 1 to maxarc-1
                   do arc[s].nextarc:= s+1;
               arc[maxarc].nextarc:= 0;
               availarc:= 1;
               while not eof
                       do begin
                              readstr (inf1);
                              readstr (inf2);
                              readln;
                              p:= find (inf1);
                              q:= find (inf2);
                              join (p,q);
                              graphnode[q].count:= graphnode[q].count + 1
                          end {while...do begin};
               {The graph has been constructed. Traverse the}
               {    hash table and place all graph nodes with     }
               {         zero count on the output list.            }
               outp:= 0;
               for p:= 0 to maxgraph
                   do if graphnode[p].info <> niltask
                       then if graphnode[p].count = 0
                               then begin
                                          graphnode[p].nextnode:= outp;
                                          outp:= p
                                     end {then begin};
               {simulate the time periods}
               period:= 0;
               while outp <> 0
                   do begin
                          period:= period + 1;
                          writeln ('period: ', period);
                          {initialize output list for next period}
                          nextout:= 0;
```

```
            {traverse the output list}
            p:= outp;
            while p <> 0
                do begin
                        writeln (graphnode[p].info);
                        r:= graphnode[p].arcptr;
                        {traverse the list of arcs}
                        while r <> 0
                            do begin
                                    s:= arc[r].nextarc;
                                    t:= arc[r].nodeptr;
                                    graphnode[t].count:=graphnode[t].count-1;
                                    if graphnode[t].count = 0
                                        then begin
                                                {place graphnode[t] on the}
                                                { next period's output list  }
                                                graphnode[t].nextnode:=nextout;
                                                nextout:= t
                                            end {then begin};
                                    freearc (r);
                                    r:= s
                                end {while r <> 0 do begin};
                        {continue traversing the output list}
                        p:= graphnode[p].nextnode
                    end {while p <> 0 do begin};
            {reset output line for the next time period}
            outp:= nextout
        end {while outp <> 0 do begin}
    end {program schedule}.
```

Two points should be noted in passing. Because the list of graph nodes has been eliminated, it is no longer possible to test for cycles. Further, if chaining is used to resolve hash clashes, the list of all graph nodes whose contents hash into the same value must be linked together by their *nextnode* field. Thus we again have the problem of removing a graph node from a list before inserting it into the output list. This can be solved by using doubly linked lists as indicated in Section 7.3 or by adding another field to each node, as in Exercise 3 below. An alternative method is to traverse the list of all nodes hashing to the same value from the initial hash bucket. This list should be relatively short and therefore would not involve the same overhead as a search through the entire list of graph nodes.

EXERCISES   1. Rewrite the program *schedule* of Section 7.3 so that the two list traversals represented by calls to the function *find* in the input loop are combined into a single traversal represented by in-line code.

2. Rewrite the program *schedule* using the dynamic implementation of lists and chaining to resolve hash clashes.

CHAP. 9: SEARCHING

3. One possible solution to the problem of traversing the list of graph nodes to find those whose *count* field is 0 is to add another field *outnext* to each graph node and use it to link together nodes on the *outp* list. This makes it unnecessary to remove a node from the graph list in order to place it on the output list. Implement this solution as a Pascal program.

4. Modify the program *schedule* in this section so that it detects cycles in the original graph.

Example 9.4.3:   An Airline Reservation System

Our next example is the application of search techniques to the airline reservation system of Section 5.2. Before we proceed with the example, a word of caution is necessary. Because a real-world reservation system must store huge quantities of information, the data is usually kept in an external file system. Thus such a system must be programmed using external search techniques which are not discussed in this book. Furthermore, a large portion of such a system consists of systems programs to handle remote terminals accessing the common data base. That type of programming is also beyond the scope of this book.

In this section we concern ourselves with the problem presented in Section 5.2. The reader is urged to review that section before proceeding. The program is to read two groups of input—a flight control group containing flight numbers and capacities, and a group of requests. A request may be one of three types: a reservation, a cancellation, or an inquiry. A reservation request specifies a passenger name and a flight number. The passenger is to be placed on the passenger list for that flight if there is room available; if not, the passenger is placed at the rear of a waiting queue. A cancellation request also specifies a name and a flight number. The passenger is to be removed from the passenger list or the waiting list for the flight in question. An inquiry specifies a passenger name only. The program is to print a list of all flights on which the passenger is either booked or waiting. Let us also assume that we wish to be able to print the passenger list and the waiting list for a particular flight.

In the program of Section 5.2, each flight was represented as an array element containing pointers to two linked lists of passenger names, one representing the passenger list for that flight and the other representing the waiting list for that flight. Let us see what searches are required by this data organization to service our requests.

For a reservation request, a sequential search must be performed on the array of flights and then the name must be added to a passenger list or a waiting queue. The sequential array search (which is performed by the function *find* in Section 5.2) is inefficient, but not overly so if the number of flights is small. To improve the speed of the search, the flights could be stored in an array sorted by flight number, allowing the use of a binary search. The insertion into the appropriate list is a single operation that involves no searching. Thus the reservation operation can be said to be moderately efficient under the organization of Section 5.2.

For a cancellation request, a sequential search must be performed through the array of flights and then one or two sequential searches must be performed through the passenger list and the waiting list. These sequential searches are fairly inefficient.

An inquiry is the most inefficient operation under the organization of Section 5.2. A sequential search through every single passenger list and many waiting lists must be performed in searching for a particular name.

To print the passenger list and waiting list for a particular flight, the array of flights must be searched sequentially and the two lists traversed. Thus any implementation of this operation is fairly efficient, because the list traversals are part of the problem specification.

We would like to develop data structures that will improve the efficiency of a cancellation and an inquiry. To eliminate the sequential array search for a flight number, the table of flights may be kept as a binary search tree, as described in Section 2. Whether or not the tree should be balanced depends upon the number of flights, the order in which they appear in the input, and the frequency with which searches are made for a particular flight. The question here is whether the efficiency of searching a balanced tree is worth the extra work involved in inserting elements into such a tree. If there are n flights, keeping them as a tree rather than as an array reduces the search time from $O(n)$ to $O(\log n)$. We leave the coding of the main program (which inserts the flights into the tree) and a function $treesearch(tree:flightptr;$ $flt:flightnum):flightptr$ (which returns a pointer to the node that represents flight flt in the tree pointed to by $tree$) for the reader as exercises.

What information should each flight node contain? Surprisingly, the same information is needed as in Section 5.2, with the addition of left and right tree pointers. (If a balanced binary tree is used, a field containing the balance is also needed.) It is still necessary to have a passenger list emanating from each flight node, so that the list may be traversed in constructing a passenger roster. However, since cancellations involve accessing a passenger node through the passenger name, the passenger list must be doubly linked to make it possible to delete a passenger node given only a pointer to that node. Similarly, it is necessary to have doubly linked waiting lists which must be organized as queues so that the first passenger placed on the waiting list will be the first to get a seat in case of a cancellation. An indication of the capacity and current passenger count on each flight is also needed. In keeping with the program of Section 5.2, we use the dynamic variable implementation of lists. Thus we may define a flight node by

```
type flightnum = packed array[1..3] of '0'..'9';
     flightptr = ↑flighttype;
     flighttype = record
                    fltno: flightnum;    { flight number }
                    cpcty: integer;      { capacity }
                    count: integer;      { number of passengers }
                    flthd: passptr;      { pointer to passenger list }
                    waitlist: queue;     { queue for waiting list }
```

```
            right: flightptr;        { tree pointers }
            left: flightptr
        end;
```

Of course, we must suitably define the types *passptr* and *queue* within the program.

To make cancellations and inquiries more efficient, it must be possible to access a passenger node directly from the passenger name rather than by traversing a passenger list. To do this, the entire passenger list is kept as a hash table. Since it must be possible to remove passengers from a passenger list in case of a cancellation, and since it is not known how many passengers there will be, hash clashes are resolved by chaining rather than by rehashing.

Each passenger node contains the passenger name as well as three pointers: one to the next node on the same passenger list, one to the previous node on the same passenger list, and one to the next node that hashes into the same value. It is also necessary to keep an indication in the passenger node of which flight list a particular passenger is associated with and whether that passenger is booked or waiting for that flight. This is necessary so that when making an inquiry of the flights that a particular passenger is on, the appropriate messages can be printed directly from the passenger node. Note that this information is unnecessary if a passenger node is accessed only through a flight node rather then directly through its hash. We may therefore define a passenger node by

```
type nametype = packed array[1..20] of char;
     passptr = ↑passtype;
     passtype = record
                 name: nametype;   { passenger name }
                 fltnum: flightnum; { flight number }
                 booked: boolean;  { true if booked, false if waiting }
                 nextpass: passptr; { for passenger lists }
                 prevpass: passptr;
                 nexthash: passptr  { for hash clashes }
              end;
```

Actually, there is much more information associated with each passenger, such as address, phone number, diet, and so on, but we ignore these details here.

Our next decision is one that is crucial in many searching applications—choosing a key for our records. We use the passenger name as the key. Applying a hash function *hash* to a passenger name yields an index of a bucket array. The entry at that index is a pointer to a list of passenger nodes (linked together by the *nexthash* field) all of whose passenger names hashed into the same index. When a search is made for a specific passenger name on a specific flight (as in a cancellation), the passenger name is hashed and this list is traversed, searching for the entry for that particular name. All reservations for a given passenger are on the same list. This means that there may be multiple records with the same key, which almost guarantees that hash clashes will occur. Thus the cancellation operation is somewhat inefficient because the chain must be searched sequentially. (The same inefficiency occurs when information is requested about a specific passenger on a specific flight.)

The solution to this inefficiency is to combine the passenger name field and the flight number as a single key. Then, when searching for a specific passenger on a specific flight, the combination can be hashed directly. However, in the present situation, such an extended key is impractical. In handling an inquiry for the list of all flights for a given passenger, it would be highly inefficient to combine the given passenger name with every possible flight number to produce a set of keys for hashing. Rather, the passenger name alone is hashed to access a list of all the flights on which the name appears (this list might also contain extraneous nodes representing other passengers whose names happen to hash into the same value, but these nodes can be skipped). The number of flights on which an average passenger is booked is small enough so that in the case of a cancellation, it does not present an overhead significant enough to outweigh the alternative overhead in case of inquiry. This illustrates a general phenomenon in choosing a search key: placing more information in a key makes it easier to find a very specific item but more difficult to satisfy a general query.

Let us now examine the bucket table. The number of entries in this table should be slightly larger (about 10%) than the number of passenger names kept at any one time. This avoids long lists of names hashing into the same index while reducing storage requirements. The size of the table should also be a prime number, since it has been found that taking a remainder upon division by a prime yields a good distribution of hash values. We arbitrarily assume approximately 900 passenger names (this is very small for a real system) and declare the bucket table by

```
var table: array[0..1008] of passptr;
```

We now present two of the routines that satisfy service requests, leaving the main program and the other routines for the reader as exercises. The first routine, *cancel*, accepts a passenger name and a flight number and removes the passenger's reservation from that flight. We assume the following global declarations:

```
const maxhash = 1008;
type flightnum = packed array[1..3] of '0'..'9';
     nametype = packed array[1..20] of char;
     passptr = ↑passtype;
     passtype = record
               name: nametype;   { passenger name }
               fltnum: flightnum; { flight number }
               booked: boolean;   { true if booked, false if waiting }
               nextpass: passptr;  { for passenger lists }
```

```
                    prevpass: passptr;
                    nexthash: passptr   { for hash clashes }
                end;
        queue = record
                    front: passptr;
                    rear: passptr
                end;
        flightptr = ↑flighttype;
        flighttype = record
                    fltno: flightnum; { flight number }
                    cpcty: integer;   { capacity }
                    count: integer;   { number of passengers }
                    flthd: passptr;   { pointer to passenger list }
                    waitlist: queue;  { queue for waiting list }
                    right: flightptr; { tree pointers }
                    left: flightptr
                end;
    var  table: array[0..maxhash] of passptr;
```

We also assume the functions *hash* and *treesearch* described above and the existence of an auxiliary list manipulation routine *delete(fptr, p)* which accepts two pointers, the first to a flight node and the second to a passenger node, and deletes the passenger node from either the passenger list or the waiting queue (depending on the value of $p\uparrow.booked$) emanating from the flight node without freeing the node.

```
procedure cancel (nam: nametype;  flt: flightnum);
var   p,q,r: passptr;
      fptr: flightptr;
      h: 0..maxhash;
      found: boolean;
begin { procedure cancel }
      fptr:= treesearch(tree, flt); { find the flight node }
      if fptr = nil                 { no such flight }
        then writeln('illegal flight number')
        else begin
              { hash the passenger name and search the hash list }
              h:= hash(nam);
              q:= nil;
              p:= table[h];
              found:= false;
              while (p <> nil) and (not found)
                  do if (p↑.name = nam) and (p↑.fltnum = flt)
                      then found:= true
                      else begin
                              q:= p;
                              p:= p↑.nexthash
                          end {else begin};
```

```
            if not found
               then writeln('no such passenger for that flight')
               else begin
                      { at this point p points }
                      { to the passenger node }
                      { remove p↑ from the hash list }
                      if q = nil
                         then table[h]:= p↑.nexthash
                         else q↑.nexthash:= p↑.nexthash;
                      {    remove p↑ from the    }
                      { passenger or waiting list }
                      delete(fptr, p);
                      if p↑.booked
                         then begin
                                 { the node was on }
                                 { the passenger list }
                                 writeln(nam, ' deleted from flight ', flt);
                                 q:= fptr↑.waitlist.front;
                                 if q <> nil
                                    then begin
                                    {  remove first passenger  }
                                    { from waiting queue and }
                                    {    insert into passenger    }
                                    {           list           }
                                          delete(fptr, q);
                                          q↑.booked:= true;
                                          r:= fptr↑.flthd;
                                          fptr↑.flthd:= q;
                                          q↑.prevpass:= nil;
                                          q↑.nextpass:= r;
                                          if r <> nil
                                             then r↑.prevpass:= q;
                                          writeln(q↑.name, ' now booked on flight ', flt)
                                       end {then begin}
                                    else
                                       { no one is waiting }
                                       fptr↑.count:= fptr↑.count - 1
                              end {then begin}
                         else
                              { the node was on }
                              { the waiting list }
                              writeln(name, ' deleted from waiting list of flight ', flt);
                      dispose(p)
                   end {else begin}
            end {else begin}
      end { procedure cancel};
```

The next routine we present is for an inquiry. We wish to list all flights on which a given passenger name appears. It is straightforward.

```
procedure inquire (nam: nametype);
var  p: passptr;
     h: 0..maxhash;
begin { procedure inquire }
     writeln(nam, ' found on following flights:');
     h:= hash(nam);
     p:= table[h];
     while p <> nil
          do begin
                  if nam = p↑.name
                     then if p↑.booked
                               then writeln('booked on ', p↑.fltnum)
                               else writeln('waiting for ', p↑.fltnum);
                  p:= p↑.nexthash
          end {while...do begin};
     writeln('end of list')
end { procedure inquire};
```

EXERCISES

1. Write a Pascal program that reads a flight control group as in Section 5.2 and builds a binary search tree of flight nodes. Modify your routine to build a balanced binary tree.

2. Write a Pascal function *treesearch* as described in the text.

3. Write the routine *delete* described in the text.

4. Write a Pascal program that accepts a passenger name and cancels all reservations and waiting-list entries for that passenger. What field would you change in the passenger node to make this operation more efficient? Rewrite the routines of this section under the changed representation.

5. Write a Pascal routine that accepts a passenger name and flight number and reserves a seat for the passenger on the flight or puts the person on the waiting list if the flight is full.

6. Do the exercises of Section 5.2 for the data structure representations of this section.

Appendix

This appendix is a compendium of information on Pascal that students may not have seen in an introductory course and which is important in a data structures context. These topics were originally included in the text (primarily in Chapter 1). In the interest of identifying these topics and allowing the familiar or rushed reader to skip them on a first reading, we have placed them in this appendix. The topics are not related to one another and can be covered individually in any order, or assigned as independent reading when convenient.

1. SCALAR DATA TYPES IN PASCAL

The Pascal language contains four basic data types: *integer*, *real*, *boolean*, and *char*. In most computers, these four types are native to the machine's hardware. Section 1.1 describes how integers, reals, and characters can be implemented in hardware. A boolean variable can be implemented by a single bit which has the value 1 to represent *true* and 0 to represent *false*.

There are two other kinds of scalar types in Pascal. (A *scalar* type is a type whose variables each contain only a single value, as opposed to arrays, records, or sets, which are composed of several values.) The first is the *enumeration type*, in which the programmer specifies a set of identifiers as the possible values of objects of the type being defined. For example, the declaration

type fruittype = (apple, orange, pear, banana);

defines an enumeration type *fruittype*. An object of this type can have one of the four constant values *apple*, *orange*, *pear*, *banana*. If we then declare

var fruit: fruittype;

then *fruit* is an object of this type and the assignment statement

fruit:= pear

494

sets *fruit* to one of the four allowable values. The statement

if fruit = orange then...

tests whether the value of *fruit* is another of these allowable values. An object of an enumeration type has one of several specifically defined values. Enumeration types are useful for representing any of a myriad of real-world concepts (such as colors, days of the week, job titles, etc.) using names that are meaningful in the context (such as "red," "Tuesday," "foreman") instead of representing them by some artificial construct (such as using the integer 1 to represent red, 2 to represent blue, etc.).

Because enumeration types are not native to the hardware of any computer, a set of routines must exist to implement these types and the Pascal operations defined on them. These routines are already present in the software of the Pascal system, so that the Pascal programmer need understand only the Pascal definitions of such data types and need not worry about implementation details. It is, nevertheless, instructive to consider the subject of implementation.

How are enumeration data types implemented? The simplest method is by assigning consecutive integers, beginning with 0, to each value of an enumeration type. For example, in the case of *fruittype* defined above, *apple* is represented by 0, *orange* by 1, *pear* by 2, and *banana* by 3. Thus the assignment statement

fruit:= pear

places the integer value 2 into the storage location named *fruit*, and the statement

if fruit = orange then...

tests whether the contents of that storage location represent the integer 1.

However, the programmer need not be concerned with these implementation details. As far as he or she is concerned, the value of the variable *fruit* can only be *apple*, *orange*, *pear*, or *banana*.

The second Pascal scalar type that is not one of the four basic types is the *subrange type*. For any scalar type *t* except *real*, it is possible to define a new type as a subrange of the values of *t*. For example, consider the following subrange-type definitions:

type digit = 0..9;
grade = 'a'..'f';
newfruit = apple..pear;

Each of these types represents a subset of the values of its parent type. Thus *digit* represents the set of *integer* values 0, 1, 2, 3, 4, 5, 6, 7, 8, and 9; *grade* represents the set of *char* values 'a', 'b', 'c', 'd', 'e', and 'f' (assuming that no other characters exist between 'a' and 'f' in the character representation of the particular computer being used; this is true of almost every computer in existence); and *newfruit* represents the set of *fruittype* values *apple*, *orange*, and *pear*.

A subrange type may be used for two reasons. The first is that the programmer may know that a certain variable can assume values only from a given range. By declaring this range explicitly using a subrange type, the machine can check that all values assigned to the variable are indeed within the specified range. In this way, the computer is able to detect a very common programming error.

The second reason for using a subrange type is to save space. A variable of type *integer* uses as many bits as is necessary to represent the largest integer under that particular Pascal implementation. (This largest integer is the value of the standard constant identifier *maxint*.) However, a variable whose range of possible values is smaller need not use as many bits.

The scalar types, excluding the type *real*, are known as **ordinal types**. For any ordinal type, the standard function *ord* yields the position of a value within the set of values allowed by the type. For example, *ord* (*pear*) is 2, while *ord* (*banana*) is 3, since the first value of an enumeration type is considered to be at position 0. If x is a character, *ord* (x) is an integer representation of that character. One of the rules of Pascal is that the characters '0' through '9' must be represented by successive integers, so that *ord*(x)−*ord*('0') for any digit character x yields the numeric value of that digit. However, the values of *ord* ('a'), *ord* ('b'), and so on, need not be successive integers, although it must be true that *ord* ('a') < *ord* ('b') < *ord* ('c'), and so on. The function *chr*(x), where x is an integer, yields the character c such that $x = ord(c)$. If x is an integer, *ord* (x) equals x. If a value is a member of a subrange type, applying the *ord* function to it yields its position within the host type rather than the subrange type.

Two other functions defined on ordinal types are *pred* and *succ*. *pred* (x) is the predecessor of x within its host type, and *succ* (x) is the successor of x. These functions are not applicable to extreme values of a given type, so that *succ* (*maxint*) or *pred* (*apple*) are undefined.

2. USING ONE-DIMENSIONAL ARRAYS

Beginning students often have difficulty in determining when a one-dimensional array is required. In general, a one-dimensional array is used when it is necessary to keep a large number of items in memory and reference all the items in a uniform manner. Let us see how these two requirements apply to practical situations.

Suppose that we wish to read 100 integers, find their average, and determine by how much each integer deviates from that average. The following program accomplishes this:

```
program aver (input, output);
const numelts = 100;
type index = 1..numelts;
```

```
var num: array [index] of integer;        {array of numbers}
    i: index;
    total: integer;              {   sum of the numbers   }
    avg: real;                   { average of the numbers }
    diff: real;                  {difference between each}
                                 {number and the average}
begin
    total:= 0;
    for i:= 1 to numelts
        do begin {read the numbers into the array and add them}
                read(num[i]);
                total:= total + num[i]
            end {for...do begin};
        {compute the average}
        avg:= total/numelts;
        {print heading}
        writeln('number ', ' difference');
        {print each number and its difference}
        for i:= 1 to numelts
            do begin
                    diff:= num[i] - avg;
                    writeln(num[i], diff)
                end {for...do begin};
        writeln('average is: ', avg)
    end {program aver}.
```

This program uses two groups of 100 numbers. The first group is the set of input integers and is represented by the array *num*; the second group is the set of differences that are the successive values assigned to the variable *diff* in the second loop. The question arises as to why an array is used to hold all the values of the first group simultaneously, but only a single variable is used to hold one value of the second group at a time.

The answer is quite simple. Each difference is computed and printed and is never needed again. Thus the variable *diff* can be reused for the difference of the next integer and the average. However, the original integers which are the values of the array *num* must all be kept in memory. Although each can be added into *total* as it is input, it must be retained until after the average is computed in order for the program to compute the difference between it and the average. Therefore, an array is used.

Of course, 100 separate variables could have been used to hold the integers. The advantage of an array, however, is that it allows the programmer to declare only a single identifier and yet obtain a large amount of space. Furthermore, in conjunction with the *for* loop, it also allows the programmer to reference each element of the group in a uniform manner instead of forcing him to code a statement such as

read(num1, num2, num3, ..., num99, num100)

A particular element of an array may be retrieved through its index. For example, suppose that a company is using a program in which an array is declared by

var sales: **array** [1960..1979] **of** real;

The array will hold sales figures for a 20-year period. Suppose that each line input to the program contains a year and a sales figure for that year and it is desired to read the sales figure into the appropriate element of the array. This can be accomplished by executing the statement

read(yr, sales[yr])

within a loop. In this statement, a particular element of the array is accessed directly by using its index. Consider the situation if 20 variables s1960, s1961,..., s1979 had been declared. Then even after executing *read* (*yr*) to set *yr* to the integer representing the year, the sales figure could not be read into the proper variable without coding something like

if yr = 1960 **then** read(s1960);
if yr = 1961 **then** read(s1961);

.

.

.

if yr = 1979 **then** read(s1979)

This is bad enough with 20 elements—imagine the inconvenience if there were a hundred or a thousand.

3. PACKED ARRAYS

The usual implementation of arrays often leads to a large waste of storage space. For example, consider an array of characters implemented on a computer whose byte size is 8 and whose word size is 32. That is, a single character is represented by eight bits, but the unit of storage most commonly accessed by the set of hardware instructions on the machine is 32 bits. A Pascal character variable on such a machine is often implemented by reserving an entire 32-bit word, although only the last 8-bit byte of the word is used to contain the character. The reason for doing this is that on this machine it is faster and simpler to manipulate an entire word than a single byte. Thus we are willing to forgo some space efficiency in the interests of time efficiency.

But consider what happens when an array of 100 characters is declared. Instead of reserving 100 bytes, 100 words or 400 bytes are reserved. Although we might have been willing to put up with 3 bytes of unused space in implementing a single character, we may not be willing to waste 300 bytes. The situation is even worse in the case of an array of booleans. Only a single bit is required to hold the value *true* or *false*, but an entire word might be reserved for each element of the array, leading to a waste of over 95% of the storage used.

For this reason, Pascal permits the declaration of a *packed array*. For example, a 100-element character array may be declared by

var ch: packed array[1..100] of char;

In implementing this array on our sample computer, Pascal may pack four elements into each word. Thus the entire array will occupy 25, rather than 100, words. Similarly, an array declared by

var b: packed array[1..256] of boolean;

might occupy only eight words, rather than 256. Of course, a price is paid for the space efficiency obtained by the packing process. Each access to an element of an array now involves locating the word containing the element and extracting the element from that word. If every element of an array is accessed in turn, this can be a very expensive time overhead. For example, $ch[1]$, $ch[2]$, $ch[3]$, and $ch[4]$ might all be kept in the same computer word. When $ch[1]$ is accessed, that word is located and the first byte is extracted. Then $ch[2]$ is accessed, so the same word is located again and the second byte is extracted. The process is repeated for $ch[3]$ and $ch[4]$. It would be much more economical if the word were "unpacked" all at once; that is, the single word is located and its four bytes extracted and saved for later use in a single operation.

To realize this time savings for accessing consecutive elements of an array, Pascal provides two standard procedures: *pack* and *unpack*. Let t be a type identifier, let a be an array declared by

var a: array[m..n] of t;

and let b be a packed array declared by

var b: packed array[p..q] of t;

where m, n, p, and q are integer constants such that $n-m \geqslant q-p$. Then $pack(a,i,b)$ is equivalent to the statement

for j:= p to q
do b[j] := a[j-p+i]

and $unpack(b,a,i)$ is equivalent to the statement

for j:= p to q
do a[j-p+i] := b[j]

That is, $pack(a,i,b)$ sets the elements of the packed array b to consecutive elements of the unpacked array a beginning with the ith element of a. Similarly, $unpack(b,a,i)$ sets the elements of the unpacked array a beginning with a's ith element to the consecutive elements of the packed array b until the elements of b are exhausted.

Packed arrays can be used in the same way as unpacked arrays. Whether or not a given array is packed does not affect the meaning of a program; it affects only its efficiency. The only restriction is that an element of a packed array cannot be passed as a variable parameter to a function or procedure. Note that this means that if *a* is a packed array of characters, the call *read* (*a* [*i*]) may be invalid since it involves passing an element of a packed array as a variable parameter. You should check whether this is true for your Pascal compiler. If it is, you can use the two statements *read* (*cb*); *a* [*i*] := *cb* instead.

Many versions of Pascal implement any array of characters or booleans as a packed array to save space. For example, in a machine in which a byte can be accessed as easily as a word, there is no advantage to keeping one character per word. Several characters can be packed in a word, and each can be accessed quickly. In such a version, there is no advantage to the Pascal programmer in explicitly declaring a character array to be packed. Other versions of Pascal ignore any packed declarations completely and implement all arrays as unpacked. The option of using unpacked and packed arrays to implement time-efficient and space-efficient alternative methods of representing arrays is available to any Pascal implementor as part of the language. However, the compiler designer is free to ignore the option as long as the meaning of Pascal programs is preserved. Thus it is important for the programmer to determine exactly how the compiler treats packed and unpacked arrays and to program accordingly. Some nonstandard versions of Pascal that do not differentiate between the implementations of packed and unpacked arrays do not include the procedures *pack* and *unpack*. An example of such a version is UCSD Pascal.

4. ARRAYS AS PARAMETERS

A parameter of a Pascal procedure or function must be declared with a type identifier. This type identifier can be a basic type (such as *integer* or *char*) or it may have been previously defined. For example, the following procedure headings are invalid:

> **procedure** proc(i: 1..10);

> **procedure** proc2(a: **array** [1..10] **of** integer);

Instead, we can define

> **type** index = 1..10;
> atype = **array** [index] **of** integer;

and write

> **procedure** proc(i: index);

> **procedure** proc2(a: atype);

In Pascal, the upper and lower bounds of an array are part of its type and must be specified at the time the program is written. An array parameter must have its type explicitly declared, so that a procedure can accept only one type of array with fixed upper and lower bounds. For example, consider the following function to compute the average of the elements of an array:

```
        const alength = 100;
        type atype = array[1..alength] of real;

        function avg(a: atype): real;
        var i: 1..alength;
            sum: real;
        begin
            sum:= 0;
            for i:= 1 to alength
                do sum:= sum + a[i];
            avg:= sum/alength
        end {function avg};
```

The function can compute only the average of 100 numbers; a different function is needed to compute the average of a 10- or 50-element array. Of course, since we used the constant *alength* consistently for the array size, it is easy to modify the program to work on a smaller or larger array by simply modifying the constant definition. However, the same function can never be applied to arrays of different sizes in the same program. This is considered to be one of the major drawbacks of the Pascal language. (Some new proposals for a Pascal standard suggest that this restriction be relaxed. See the end of Section 5 for a discussion of one of these proposals.) Other languages allow the size of an array parameter to be determined at the time a procedure is called, and that size can vary from one call to another. The reason for this restriction in Pascal is efficiency. It is easier to implement the parameter passing and access mechanism if the size of the array is known at the time the program is compiled.

What, then, should the Pascal programmer do if he or she requires a procedure to accept different-sized groups of elements at different points in the program? One solution is to write several versions of the procedure, one for each size needed. This is highly impractical, for several reasons. First, the work of writing the different versions and compiling a longer program is excessive. Second, each size array will have its own type. Therefore, a separate array variable must be declared for each group of elements to be passed. This wastes an unacceptable amount of storage.

A far better solution is to reserve an array large enough to hold the largest group of elements and include an additional parameter to indicate the number of elements being passed in this particular call. For example, the following function averages a varying-sized group of elements. A type identifier for the array's index type is defined by

```
        type index = 1..alength;
```

The function itself can be written as follows:

```
function avg2(a: atype; n: index): real;
var i: index;
    sum: real;
begin
    sum:= 0;
    for i:= 1 to n
        do sum:= sum + a[i];
    avg2:= sum/n
end {function avg2};
```

The second parameter, n, specifies the number of elements of the array to be averaged. Another proposed solution to this problem is discussed at the end of Section 5.

If the number of elements needed in a particular situation depends on the input, the Pascal programmer must estimate the maximum number that will ever be required and declare an array of that size. If the program is used repetitively in a production environment, it will eventually be presented with input for which the estimate is not large enough and will fail. On the other hand, in most cases the estimate is a gross exaggeration and all the extra space in the array is wasted. Unfortunately, there is no remedy for this situation in Pascal, because the language does not allow the size of an array to be determined dynamically during execution. In such a case, a programmer should use a linked list (as presented in Chapters 4 and 5) instead of an array.

5. VALUE AND VARIABLE PARAMETERS

When one procedure calls another, information is passed between the two through parameters. The parameters that appear in the calling procedure are called *actual parameters* or *arguments*; those that appear in the heading of the called procedure are called *formal parameters*, or simply *parameters*. There are two methods of passing data as parameters in Pascal: as *value parameters* or as *variable parameters*. An argument to a value parameter may be any expression, including a constant, a variable, an arithmetic expression, an array, or an array element. The argument is evaluated before the procedure is called, and the resulting value is used by the called procedure as the initial value of the formal parameter. Any change in the value of the formal parameter within the called procedure does not affect the value of any other variable in the program. Thus a value parameter is a local variable of the called procedure. Its purpose is to input a value to the procedure.

A variable parameter is identified by the keyword *var* preceding its declaration in the procedure heading. An argument passed to a variable parameter must be a variable; it cannot be constant or an arithmetic expression. However, the argument may be an array variable or an element of an unpacked array. (As previously noted, an element of a packed array may not be passed as a variable parameter.) The formal parameter references the same memory location as the argument. Thus any change in the formal

502   APPENDIX

parameter in the called procedure represents a change in the variable argument being passed. A variable parameter may serve to input a value to the called procedure (e.g., if its value is used but never changed), or to output a value from the called procedure to the calling procedure (e.g., if its value is set by the called procedure), or to both input and output a value (e.g., if its value is used by the called procedure and then changed by it). Note that an argument passed to a variable parameter need not have been initialized before the procedure is called if the purpose of the procedure is simply to set the value of its variable parameter. However, an argument passed to a value parameter must have been initialized before the call.

Generally, a value parameter is used when it is desired to simply input a value to a procedure. The benefit of using a value parameter rather than a variable parameter in such a situation is that the argument being passed is protected against change by the called procedure. If some fact is known about the value of the argument before the call (e.g., that its value is positive), that fact remains true about its value after the call, regardless of the actions of the called routine.

If a routine computes a single scalar value, the routine can be written as a function returning that value rather than as a procedure that places the value in a variable parameter. However, if a routine computes more than one value, it is stylistically preferable to pass two variable parameters and code the routine as a procedure rather than to use a function returning one value and assigning the other value to a variable parameter.

Since an array cannot be returned as the value of a function, it should be passed as a variable parameter to a procedure if it is being initialized or modified. Even when an array is not being modified but serves only as input to a computation, it is often a good idea to pass it as a variable rather than a value parameter. The reason for this is efficiency. In order to ensure that the value of the argument to a value parameter is not changed, that value is copied into a new portion of memory reserved for the value parameter. In the case of a scalar value, the time needed for the copying and the extra space needed for the copy are negligible. In addition, access to a value parameter is usually faster than access to a variable parameter. (This is because the address of the copy used to access a value parameter can be determined at compile time or load time, whereas the address of the variable passed to a variable parameter varies from call to call and must be determined at execution time.) However, copying an entire array may take quite a bit of time, and the extra space needed for another copy of an array may be considerable. Therefore, in the interest of efficiency, it is often a good idea to pass an array as a variable parameter.

As of this writing, there is a proposal to add a new kind of variable array parameter to the Pascal language standard. This proposal would allow the same function or procedure to operate on arrays of different sizes. The new kind of parameter, called a *conformant array parameter*, is best illustrated by an example. The following function returns the average of any integer array whose index type is a subrange of the type *integer*.

```
function avg3 (var a: array [low..high: integer] of integer): real;
var i: integer;
    sum: real;
begin
    sum:=0;
    for i:= low to high
        do sum:= sum + a[i];
    avg3:= sum/(high-low+1)
end {function avg3};
```

Suppose the main program contained the declaration

```
var x: array [1..10] of integer;
    y: array [1..100] of integer;
    z: array [-100..100] of integer;
    i: integer;
    xav, yav, zav: real;
```

and the statements

```
for i:= 1 to 10
    do read(x[i]);
for i:= 1 to 100
    do read (y[i]);
for i:= -100 to 100
    do read(z[i]);
xav:= avg3 (x);
yav:= avg3 (y);
zav:= avg3 (z);
writeln (xav, yav, zav)
```

The first three statements read 10 numbers into the array x, 100 numbers into the array y, and 201 numbers into the array z. When *avg3* is called with argument x, the identifiers *low* and *high* denote the lower and upper bounds of the array x. That is, *low* equals 1 and *high* equals 10. Thus the *for* loop in the function adds the 10 values of the array x. When *avg3* is called with the argument y, the identifiers *low* and *high* denote the bounds of the array y and, therefore, equal 1 and 100 respectively. *avg3* returns the average of the 100 elements of y. Similarly, when *avg3* is called with argument z, *low* equals -100, *high* equals 100 and *avg3* returns the average of the 201 elements of z.

Under the current proposal, a conformant array parameter may not be a value parameter even if the array is not modified by the called routine. It is not known at this writing when or whether this proposal will be adopted as part of standard Pascal.

The programs of the text that could best take advantage of this feature are the sorting routines of Chapter 8. In Section 8.2, we introduced conventions for the sorting routines of that chapter. The constant *numelts* was the size of the largest array to be sorted. An array passed to a sorting routine was declared to be of type *array* [1..*numelts*] *of integer*. A smaller group of elements could be sorted by specifying a parameter *n* between 1 and *numelts* to the sorting routine which would sort the elements in positions 1 through *n*. The disadvantages of this approach are obvious. If an array is logically of size *n*, there should be no reason that it must be declared to be of size *numelts* or copied into the first *n* elements of a different array. Using a conformant array parameter, we can eliminate *n* as a parameter. For example, the bubble sort of Section 8.2 could be coded as follows:

```
procedure bubble(var x: array[low..high: integer] of integer);
var pass,j,hold: integer;
    intchange: boolean;
begin {procedure bubble}
    intchange:= true;
    pass:= low;
    while (pass < high) and (intchange)
        do begin
            intchange:= false;
            for j:= low to high-pass+low-1
                do if x[j] > x[j+1]
                    then begin
                        intchange:= true;
                        hold:= x[j];
                        x[j]:= x[j+1];
                        x[j+1]:= hold
                    end {then begin};
            pass:= pass + 1
        end {while...do begin}
end {procedure bubble};
```

6. RECORDS IN PASCAL

In this section we review some highlights of records in Pascal. A record is a group of items in which each item is identified by its own *field identifier*. For example, consider the following type definition:

```
type nametype = record
                first: packed array[1..10] of char;
                midinit: char;
                last: packed array[1..20] of char
            end;
```

This definition creates a record type *nametype* containing three fields of different types: *first*, *midinit*, and *last*. Two of the fields are arrays of characters; the third is a single character.

Once a record type has been defined, a variable of that type may be declared. For example, we may declare

```
var sname,ename: nametype;
```

sname and *ename* are both variables of type *nametype*. Each consists of an array of characters representing a first name, a single character representing a ·middle initial, and an array of characters representing a last name. We could have specified the record type directly in the variable declaration as follows:

```
var sname,ename: record
                first: packed array [1..10] of char;
                midinit: char;
                last: packed array [1..20] of char
            end;
```

However, it is recommended that a type identifier be declared for each record type. This simplifies the declaration of several variables with the same record type. It also enables a record type to appear in the parameter list of a function or procedure, where only a type identifier is permitted.

Once a variable has been declared as a record, each item (or *field*) within that variable may be accessed by specifying the variable name and the item's field identifier separated by a period. Thus the statement

```
write (sname.first)
```

can be used to print the first name in the record *sname*, while the statement

```
ename.midinit:= 'm'
```

can be used to set the middle initial in the record *ename* to the letter *m*. If a field of a record is an array, a subscript may be used to access a particular element of the array, as in

```
for i:= 1 to 20
    do sname.last [i] := ename.last [i]
```

Note that this statement is equivalent to the statement

```
sname.last:= ename.last
```

Two records of the same type may participate in an assignment, as in

```
sname:= ename
```

which is equivalent to

```
sname.first:= ename.first;
sname.midinit:= ename.midinit;
sname.last:= ename.last
```

However, a record (as a whole) may not participate in any other operation. Thus, if a record type *r* consisted of three integer fields, it is not possible to add the three fields of one variable of that type to the corresponding fields of another variable of that type in a single statement. Instead, each field of the two variables must be added separately.

A record type may be a (value or variable) parameter to a procedure or function. For example, the following function prints a name in a neat format and returns the number of characters printed.

```
function writename(name: nametype): integer;
var count,i: integer;
begin
    writeln;
    count:= 0;
    for i:= 1 to 10
        do if name.first[i] <> ' '
            then begin
                    write(name.first[i]);
                    count:= count+1
                end {then begin};
    write(' ');
    count:= count + 1;
    if name.midinit <> ' '
        then begin
                write(name.midinit, '.', ' ');
                count:= count + 3
            end {then begin};
    for i:= 1 to 20
        do if name.last[i] <> ' '
            then begin
                    write(name.last[i]);
                    count:= count + 1
                end {then begin};
    writename:= count
end {function writename};
```

The following table illustrates the effects of the statement $x:=writename$ (*sname*) on two different values of *sname*:

value of *sname.first*:	'allen '	'carl '
value of *sname.midinit*:	'j'	' '
value of *sname.last*:	'schreier '	'markowitz '
printed output:	allen j. schreier	carl markowitz
value of x:	17	14

Similarly, the statement $x:=writename$ (*ename*) would print the values of *ename*'s fields and assign the number of characters printed to x.

Although a record type may appear as the type of a parameter, it may not appear as the type of the value returned by a function. Thus a function header such as

```
function transname(name: nametype): nametype;
```

is invalid. Instead, the function should be transformed into a procedure with a variable parameter, as in

> **procedure** transname(inname: nametype; **var** outname: nametype);

A field of a record type may be declared using any other type, including another record type. For example, given the definition of *nametype* above and the following type definition of *addrtype*

> **type** addrtype = **record**
>> straddr: **packed array** [1..40] **of** char;
>> city: **packed array** [1..10] **of** char;
>> state: **packed array** [1..2] **of** char;
>> zip: **packed array** [1..5] **of** '0'..'9'
>
> **end**;

we may define a new type *nmadtype* by

> **type** nmadtype = **record**
>> name: nametype;
>> address: addrtype
>
> **end**;

If we declare two variables

> **var** nmad1,nmad2: nmadtype;

then the following are examples of valid statements:

> nmad1 := nmad2;
> nmad1.name := nmad2.name;
> nmad1.address.zip := nmad2.address.zip;
> nmad1.name.first := nmad2.name.city

As a further example, we may define two record types, describing an employee and a student, respectively:

> **type** employee = **record**
>> nameaddr: nmadtype;
>> position: **record**
>>> deptno: **packed array** [1..3] **of** '0'..'9';
>>> jobtitle: **packed array** [1..20] **of** char
>>
>> **end**;
>> salary: real;
>> numdep: integer; {*number of dependents*}
>> hplan: boolean;   { *is employee a health* }
>>   {   *plan member?*   }
>> datehired: **record**
>>> month: 1..12;
>>> day: 1..31;
>>> year: 1900..2000
>>
>> **end**
>
> **end**;

```
            student = record
                       nmad: nmadtype;
                       gpindx: real;        {    grade point index    }
                       credits: integer;    {number of credits earned}
                       dateadm: record   {      date admitted        }
                                   month: 1..12;
                                   day: 1..31;
                                   year: 1900..2000
                                end
            end;
        var e: employee;
            s: student;
```

A statement to give a 10% raise to an employee if his grade-point index as a student is above 3.0 is the following:

```
        if (e.nameaddr.name.first = s.nmad.name.first) and
           (e.nameaddr.name.midinit = s.nmad.name.midinit) and
           (e.nameaddr.name.last = s.nmad.name.last)
        then if s.gpindx > 3.0
                then e.salary:= 1.10 * e.salary
```

This statement first ensures that the employee record and the student record refer to the same person by comparing their names. Note that we cannot simply write

```
        if e.nmaddr.name = s.nmad.name
           then...
```

since two records cannot be compared for equality in a single operation in Pascal.

Note the redefinition of a date record as a subrecord of both the student and employee record types. As previously mentioned, if we had earlier defined a date type by

```
        type datetype = record
                          month: 1..12;
                          day: 1..31;
                          year: 1900..2000
                        end;
```

both the fields *datehired* and *dateadm* could have been declared as being of type *datetype*.

You may have noticed that we used two different type identifiers *nameaddr* and *nmad* for the name/address fields of the *employee* and *student* records, respectively. It is not necessary to do so and the same identifier can be reused, as we shall see in Section 8. In fact, the identifiers *month*, *day* and *year* are used in two contexts, within the field *datehired* of *employee* and *dateadm* of *student*.

7. ARRAYS OF RECORDS

We have already seen that a field of a record may be an array or another record. Similarly, a record type may serve as the base type of an array.

For example, if the types *employee* and *student* are defined as above, we can declare two arrays of employee and student records as follows:

```
var e: array[1..100] of employee;
    s: array[1..100] of student;
```

The salary of the fourteenth employee is referenced by $e[14].salary$, and his last name is referenced by $e[14].nameaddr.name.last$. Similarly, the admission year of the first student is $s[1].dateadm.year$.

As a further example, we present a procedure used at the start of a new year to give a 10% raise to all employees with more than 10 years seniority and a 5% raise to all others. First, we must define a new type:

```
type empset = array[1..100] of employee;
```

The procedure now follows:

```
procedure raise(var e: empset);
const thisyear = ...;
var i: 1..100;
begin
    for i:= 1 to 100
        do if e[i].datehired.year < thisyear - 10
            then e[i].salary:= 1.10 * e[i].salary
            else e[i].salary:= 1.05 * e[i].salary
end {procedure raise};
```

As another example, suppose that we add an additional field, *sindex*, to the definition of the *employee* record type. This field contains an integer between 1 and 100 and indicates the student record (in the array *s*) of the particular employee. Let us declare *sindex* (within the *employee* record) as follows:

```
type employee = record
            nameaddr: nmadtype;
                    ...
            datehired: ...;
            sindex: 1..100
        end;
```

The number of credits earned by employee *i* when he was a student can then be referenced by $s[e[i].sindex].credits$.

The following function can be used to give a 10% raise to all employees whose grade-point index was above 3.0 as a student and to return the number of such employees. Note that we no longer have to compare an employee name to a student name to ascertain that their records represent the same person (although those names should be equal if they do). Instead, the field *sindex* can be used directly to access the appropriate student record for an employee. We assume the two type definitions that precede the function:

```
type empset = array[1..100] of employee;
     stset = array[1..100] of student;
function raise2(var e: empset; s: stset): integer;
var j,i,count: 0..100;
begin
    count:= 0;
    for i:= 1 to 100
        do begin
                j:= e[i].sindex;
                if s[j].gpindx > 3.0
                    then begin
                            count:= count + 1;
                            e[i].salary:= 1.10 * e[i].salary
                         end {then begin}
           end {for...do begin};
    raise2:= count
end {function raise2};
```

Very often, a large array of records is used to contain an important data table for a particular application. There is generally only one table for each such array-of-record type. The student table *s* and the employee table *e* of the previous discussion are good examples of such data tables. In such cases, the unique tables are often used as global variables rather than as parameters, with a large number of procedures and functions accessing them. This increases efficiency by eliminating the overhead of parameter passing, especially if the tables are value parameters. We could easily rewrite the function *raise2* above to access *s* and *e* as global variables rather than as parameters by simply changing the function header to

```
function raise2: integer;
```

The body of the function need not be changed, assuming that the tables *s* and *e* are declared in the outer program.

8. SCOPE OF IDENTIFIERS

There are many different kinds of identifiers in Pascal. Constant identifiers and type identifiers are defined by constant and type definitions beginning with the keywords *const* and *type*, respectively. Variable identifiers, procedure identifiers, and function identifiers are declared by variable, procedure, and function declarations beginning with the keywords *var*, *procedure*, and *function*, respectively. Labels are declared by label declarations beginning with the keyword *label*. Parameter identifiers are declared in a function or procedure heading.

The *scope* of a definition or declaration (sometimes called the scope of an identifier or label) is that part of the program text in which an occurrence of the identifier (or label) refers to the same object as in the definition or declaration. The scope of all the identifiers listed above is the block in which the identifier (or label) was defined or declared. (By a *block*, we mean a program, function, or procedure.) However, if the identifier (or label) is redefined or redeclared in an inner block, the inner block is excluded from the scope of the definition or declaration in the outer block. An identifier defined or declared in a block is called *local* to that block. An identifier defined or declared in an outer block and not redefined or redeclared in an inner block is called *global* to the inner block. (Note that a procedure or function name is considered to be declared in the surrounding block, whereas parameter identifiers are considered to be declared in the procedure or function block. The type identifiers used to declare parameters and the returned value of a function are occurrences of identifiers that must have been defined in a surrounding block.) An identifier used as a constant, type, variable, parameter, function, or procedure may not be defined or declared twice within a single block.

To illustrate these rules, consider the following program.

```
 1 program sample;
 2 var i: integer;
 3 procedure proc1;
 4 var i: integer;
 5 procedure proc2;
        {no declaration of i in proc2}
 6 begin {procedure proc2}
 7     i:= i + 2
 8 end {procedure proc2};

 9 begin {procedure proc1}
10     i:= 0;
11     proc2;
12     writeln(i)
13 end {procedure proc1};

14 procedure proc3;
        {no declaration of i in proc3}
15 procedure proc4;
16 var i: integer;
17 begin {procedure proc4}
18     i:= 4
19 end {procedure proc4};

20 begin {procedure proc3}
21     i:= i + 3;
22     writeln(i);
23     proc4;
24     writeln(i)
25 end {procedure proc3};
```

```
26  begin {program sample}
27       i:= 12;
28       proc1;
29       writeln(i);
30       proc3;
31       writeln(i)
32  end {program sample}.
```

The identifier *i* is declared in three places in this program: once in the main program *sample*, once in the procedure *proc*1, and once in the procedure *proc*4. Since the identifier is not declared twice in the same block, the declarations are valid.

Let us determine the scope of each of the three declarations. The *i* declared in the program *sample* (line 2) includes the heading and body of that program (lines 1–2, 26–32) in its scope. Since *i* is redeclared in procedure *proc*1 (line 4), all of that procedure (lines 3–13) is excluded from the scope of the first declaration. Since *proc*3 does not include a redeclaration of *i*, and *sample* includes *proc*3 between its opening and closing statements, the header and body of *proc*3 (lines 14, 20–25) are included in the scope of the first declaration. *proc*4, however, does include a declaration of *i* (line 16), so that it (lines 15–19) is excluded from the scope of the first declaration. Thus the scope of *i* declared in line 2 is lines 1–2, 14, 20–25, and 26–32.

The scope of the second *i*, declared in line 4, may similarly be determined as the entire *proc*1 (lines 3–13). The scope of the third *i*, declared in line 16, is all of *proc*4 (lines 15–19).

Let us see what happens when *sample* is executed. Execution begins with line 27, where the *i* declared in line 2 is initialized to 12. In line 28, *proc*1 is called. This transfers execution to the body of *proc*1 at line 10. However, before the body of *proc*1 is executed, the local variables of the procedure are **allocated**. By this we mean that new memory space is set aside for variables declared in *proc*1 (such as *i* in line 4). Any references to *i* are now to the local variable declared in line 4 rather than the variable declared in line 2. Since memory has just been allocated to this variable, it must be initialized. This is done in line 10, where *i* is set to 0. Note that it would be illegal to use the value of *i* in line 10 without initializing it. Note, also, that the assignment of line 10 does not change the value of the *i* declared in line 2, which retains the value 12. There is no way to reference this value within the body of *proc*1 since *i* is redeclared.

In line 11, *proc*2 is called. *i* is not redeclared in *proc*2, so that any references to *i* in the body of *proc*2 are to the *i* declared in the surrounding block (*proc*1). Thus line 7 increases the value of that *i* from 0 to 2. Line 12 then prints the value 2. *proc*1 then returns and line 29 is executed next. The *i* in that line is the *i* declared in line 2 whose value is 12 (from line 27). Thus line 29 prints 12. Line 30 calls *proc*3. *i* is not redeclared in *proc*3, so that the *i* in line 21 is the *i* declared in the surrounding block (*sample*) whose value was 12. Line 21 changes this value to 15 and line 22 prints this value.

Line 24 calls *proc*4. Since *i* is redeclared in this procedure (line 16), a new memory location is allocated and must be initialized before it can be used. This is done in line 18, but the value assigned is never used, since *proc*4 returns immediately. At line 24, the value of *i* declared in line 2 is printed. This value is 15. Line 31 prints this value once again.

Note that *proc*2 and *proc*4 cannot be called from the body of the main program (lines 26–32). This is because *proc*2 is declared by its appearance in line 5, which is interior to *proc*1. Thus the identifier *proc*2 is local to *proc*1 and cannot be referenced outside *proc*1. Similarly, *proc*4 is declared inside *proc*3 and cannot be referenced outside *proc*3. Note that it would be legal for *proc*1 to call *proc*3 (or vice versa) because the identifier *proc*3 is declared in *sample* and so is global to *proc*1.

Field identifiers of a record, however, have different scope rules from other kinds of identifiers. A field identifier *f* may only appear following a variable of the record type in which the field identifier was declared.

For example, suppose that we define two record types and declare a variable as follows:

```
type date = record
                month: 1..12;
                day: 1..31;
                year: 1900..2000
            end;
     person = record
                name: packed array [1..30] of char;
                birthday: date
            end;
var x: person;
```

A reference to *x.name* is valid because *x* was declared as a *person* and *name* is declared within the type definition of *person*. Similarly, a reference to *x.birthday.day* is valid because *birthday* is declared within the type definition of *person*, *birthday* is declared with the type identifier *date*, and *day* is declared in the type definition of *date*. A reference to *x.month* is invalid because *month* was not declared within the definition of *person* (which is the type of *x*). A reference to *name* alone is invalid because a reference to a field identifier must be preceded by a record variable. Similarly, references to *x.date* and *person.name* are invalid.

Because a field identifier must be preceded by a variable of the proper type, no ambiguity can arise from the multiple declaration of a field identifier within the same block. For example, consider the following series of definitions and declarations:

```
type date = record
                month: 1..12;
                day: 1..31;
                year: 1900..2000
            end;
```

```
            person = record
                       name: packed array[1..30] of char;
                       birthday: date;
                       mother: record
                                    name: packed array[1..30] of char;
                                    birthday: date
                                end
                   end;
            daytype = (sun, mon, tues, wed, thurs, fri, sat);
            monthtype = (jan, feb, mar, apr, may, jun, jul, aug, sep, oct, nov, dec);
            newdate = record
                       day: daytype;
                       month: monthtype;
                       mday: 1..31
                   end;
        var day: daytype;
            month: monthtype;
            x: person;
            d: date;
            dd: newdate;
```

These type definitions and variable declarations are perfectly valid. This is
true despite the fact that four identifiers (*month*, *day*, *name*, *birthday*) are
declared more than once. The reason for this is that in any occurrence of
these identifiers, it is clear which declaration is applicable. Let us see why
this is true.

  month and *day* are each declared three times, once as a field identifier
in the record type *date*, once as a field identifier in the record type *newdate*,
and once as a variable. When either identifier is used, it is clear from the
context which one of these three is meant. If *month* or *day* appears by itself, it is a variable identifier, since a field identifier may appear only after
a variable of the appropriate record type. In a reference to *d.month* or
d.day, the identifier *month* or *day* is a field identifier and the reference is
to a field of type 1..12 or 1..31, respectively, within the record variable *d*
of type *date*. In a reference to *dd.month* or *dd.day*, the identifier is also a
field identifier, but the reference is now to a field of type *daytype* and
monthtype, respectively, within the record variable *dd* of type *newdate*.
Note that it would be invalid to name both the first and third fields of the
record type *newdate* with the identifier *day*, since there would then be no
way to distinguish between those fields of a record variable of type *newdate*,
such as *dd*. Therefore, the third field of *newdate* is named *mday*.

  name and *birthday* are both declared twice as field identifiers. Again,
no ambiguity can arise. If either *name* or *birthday* appears immediately following a record variable of type *person* (as in *x.name*), it references the first
or second field of that record variable. However, if it appears after the field
identifier *mother* (as in *x.mother.name*), it refers to the first or second subfield of the third field of the record variable.

Make sure that you can identify each of the following references: *x.birthday.day*, *d.month*, *x.mother.birthday.month*.

9. THE *with* STATEMENT

It is often tedious for a Pascal programmer to specify the record variable each time that he or she wishes to select a field of that record. Often, a programmer is working with a specific record and is selecting several fields within that record in several different statements. To make such references shorter, Pascal contains a *with* statement. The form of this statement is

with *rv* **do** *s*

where *rv* is a record variable and *s* is any Pascal statement. *s* is usually a compound statement. Within *s*, a field identifier declared in the record type of *rv* can be used as a variable identifier as though it were preceded by *rv*. For example, given the set of declarations presented in Section 8, the statement

with x.birthday
    do read (month,day,year)

is equivalent to

read (x.birthday.month, x.birthday.day, x.birthday.year)

and is also equivalent to

with x
    do read (birthday.month, birthday.day, birthday.year)

As another example, if we wish to initialize *x* (of type *person*) with the name John Smith, birthday May 13, 1950, and mother named Jean Smith, with birthday June 15, 1925, we can use the following *with* statement:

```
with x
    do begin
          name:= 'john smith                 ';
          with birthday
              do begin
                    month:= 5;
                    day:= 13;
                    year:= 1950
                 end {with birthday do begin};
          with mother
              do begin
                    name:= 'jean smith                 ';
                    birthday.month:= 6;
                    birthday.day:= 15;
                    birthday.year:= 1925
                 end {with mother do begin}
       end {with x do begin}
```

This last example illustrates an important point about *with* statements and the scope of field identifiers. As previously noted, the scope of a field identifier of a record type *rt* is restricted to the positions in the program text which immediately follow a variable of type *rt*. The effect of a *with* statement is to broaden this scope to include the entire substatement following the symbol *do* in the *with* statement. Thus it is legal to reference the field identifiers *name*, *birthday*, and *mother* within the scope of *with x do*... without preceding them with the name of the record variable *x*. It is understood that the reference to *name* is *x.name*. Similarly, the statement *with birthday do*... is equivalent to *with x.birthday do*.... Within this statement, references to *month*, *day*, and *year* are to *x.birthday.month*, *x.birthday.day*, and *x.birthday.year*. This is true despite the fact that *month* and *day* may have been also declared as variables within the same block. The reason for this is simple. Although a reference to *day* or *month* outside the *with* statement is to the variable identifier, the *with* statement opens a new scope for these identifiers (because they appear as field identifiers within the record type, *date*, of the record variable *x.birthday*) in much the same way that a function or procedure block opens a new scope for identifiers declared within that block. The innermost scope for an identifier is always the effective scope for a reference within that scope.

Within the *with* statement *with mother do*..., the identifier *name* refers to *x.mother.name*, while outside that statement (but within *with x do*...), *name* refers to *x.name*. Again, the inner *with* statement opens a new scope for *name* which overrides the scope opened by the outer *with*.

Of course, it is valid to include variables which are not fields of the record variable *rv* within the scope of a *with* statement. For example, assume the following type definition and variable declarations:

```
type pair = record
                first: integer;
                second: integer
            end;
     var x,y: pair;
         i: integer;
```

The following *with* statement can be used to switch the fields of *x* and set the fields of *y* to the sum and product of the fields of *x*.

```
with x
    do begin
            i:= first;
            first:= second;
            second:= i;
            y.first:= first + second;
            y.second:= first * second
        end
```

The *with* statement

> with *rv1*,*rv2* do *s*

is equivalent to

> with *rv1* do with *rv2* do *s*

As many record variables as you wish may appear after the keyword *with*, and each succeeding variable opens a new scope. For example, given the earlier declarations, the statement

```
with d,dd
    do begin
            year:= 1980;
            mday:= 20
    end
```

is equivalent to the statement

```
begin
    d.year:= 1980;
    dd.mday:= 20
end
```

It is also equivalent to

```
with d,dd
    do begin
            mday:= 20;
            year:= 1980
    end
```

However, the following two statements are not equivalent and one of them is invalid. Make sure that you understand why.

```
with d,dd                      with dd,d
    do begin                       do begin
            month:= 6;                     month:= 6;
            day:= 13;                      day:= 13;
            year:= 1936;                   year:= 1936;
            mday:= 14                      mday:= 14
    end                            end
```

Caution should be used in dealing with the scoping rules of *with* statements. Some nonstandard Pascal implementations do not follow these scoping rules faithfully, and users of such implementations should be alert for violations.

There is one restriction on the use of *with* statements, which we illustrate with the following example. Assume the following declarations:

```
type pair = record
                first: integer;
                second: integer
            end;
var a: array[1..10] of pair;
    i,x: integer;
```

Assume that the array *a* and integer *x* have been initialized and that we wish to print the *second* field of every array element whose *first* field equals *x*. A correct way to do this is

```
for i:= 1 to 10
    do with a[i]
        do if x = first
            then writeln(second)
```

An incorrect way is the following:

```
i:= 1;
with a[i]
    do while i <= 10
        do begin
            if x = first
                then writeln(second);
            i:= i+1
        end
```

The record variable in the *with* header is determined at the time that the *with* statement is entered and cannot be changed during its execution. In the second example above, *i* equals 1 when the *with* statement is entered, so that the record variable of the *with* statement is $a[1]$. Despite the fact that *i* is changed within the statement, all references to *first* and *second* are to $a[1].first$ and $a[1].second$, not to $a[i].first$ and $a[i].second$. However, in the first example, execution of the entire *with* statement is repeated 10 times. After each execution, control leaves the *with* statement and re-enters it with a new value of *i*. Thus the record variable $a[i]$ is redetermined using the current value of *i* each time that the *with* statement is executed.

10. EFFICIENCY OF RECORD ACCESS

The *with* statement can be used to make references to record components more efficient. For example, consider the following definition and declaration

```
type rectype = record
                field1: integer;
                field2: real;
                field3: packed array[1..10] of char
            end;
var rr: array[1..20] of rectype;
```

Suppose that we wished to set the characters in the array $rr[10].field3$ to the last 10 characters of an array *a* declared by

```
var a: array[1..100] of char;
```

One way of doing this is to use the *for* statement

```
for i:= 1 to 10
    do rr[10].field3[i]:= a[90+i]
```

The address of *rr*[10] must be computed 10 times. However, if we use a *with* statement

```
with rr[10]
    do for i:= 1 to 10
        do field3[i]:= a[90+i]
```

the address of *rr*[10] need be computed only once. As another example of using the *with* statement to promote efficiency, consider the following program segment:

```
type string = record
                length: 0..100;
                ch: packed array[1..100] of char
              end;
     student = record
                 name: string;
                 address: string
               end;
var s: student;
    i: integer;
    c: char;
begin
    read(c);
    i:= 1;
    while (c <> ' ') and (i <= 100)
        do begin
            s.name.ch[i]:= c;
            read(c);
            i:= i + 1
        end {while...do begin};
    s.name.length:= i - 1;
    ...
```

This segment reads the characters of a student's name until a terminating blank is read. The statements in the body of the segment can be rewritten as a *with* statement:

```
begin
    with s.name
        do begin
            read(c);
            i:= 1;
            while (c <> ' ') and (i <= 100)
                do begin
                    ch[i]:= c;
                    read(c);
```

$$i := i + 1$$
$$\textbf{end} \ \{while...do \ begin\};$$
$$length := i - 1$$
$$\textbf{end} \ \{with...do \ begin\};$$
...

In the latter version, the address of *s.name* need be computed only once, whereas in the previous version it must be recomputed each time that a statement involving *s.name* is executed.

(More advanced students may note, however, that the address of *s.name* can actually be computed at compile time rather than at execution time. If this is done by the compiler, the first version involves two compile-time address computations for the two textual appearances of *s.name*, whereas the latter version involves only one such computation. This is hardly a major savings. Similarly, in the previous example, a "smart" compiler might compute the address of *rr*[10] only once at compile time, even if the *with* statement were not used. If, however, *rr*[10] were replaced by *rr*[*j*], the address of *rr*[*j*] would have to be computed at execution time. But even then, a "supersmart" compiler could recognize that since *j* is not changed in the *for* loop, the address of *rr*[*j*] need be computed only once for each execution of the entire loop. However, it should be recognized that one of the primary advantages of Pascal over other languages is that it permits the programmer to write efficient programs, even without the benefit of "supersmart" compilers.

Note also that the *with* statement improves efficiency even when an array of records or a record of records is not being used. Even in a statement such as

$$\textbf{for} \ i := 1 \ \textbf{to} \ 10$$
$$\textbf{do} \ r.field3[i] := a[i]$$

the computation of the base address of *r.field3* is done by loading the base address of *r* into a register and adding the constant offset of *field3* to the contents of that register. The load and add are performed 10 times. However, if the statement were rewritten as

$$\textbf{with} \ r$$
$$\textbf{do for} \ i := 1 \ \textbf{to} \ 10$$
$$\textbf{do} \ field3[i] := a[i]$$

then the base address of *r* can be loaded into a register once and only the addition need be performed 10 times. Nine load operations are eliminated.)

11. PACKED RECORDS

Another method of increasing efficiency is to decrease the space requirements of a record. A record type may be defined as packed in much the same way as an array. Defining a type as a packed record means that the

Pascal system should attempt to minimize the space requirements for that record. For example, a packed record type and variable may be defined and declared by

```
type packrec = packed record
                      field1: char;
                      field2: char;
                      field3: char
                 end;
    var r: packrec;
```

Ordinarily, if the record were not packed, *r* would consist of enough space to hold 3 *char* variables. Although a character can be represented by a single byte, a character variable may cause an entire word to be allocated. (Recall that a word is a group of bytes.) Thus, if the record were not packed, three words would be used for *r*. However, since the record is packed, the three characters in *r* may be packed into a single word.

There are several points to be noted about packed records. First, the space efficiency that may result from declaring a record packed may come at the expense of time efficiency in accessing a component. In the example above, a reference to *r.field*2 involves extracting the relevant byte from the packed word, whereas if the record were not packed, the extraction would be unnecessary.

Second, a compiler may or may not implement a space savings for a packed record. The packed declaration merely allows the compiler to make such a saving (even at the expense of lowering access time) if it can. It does not guarantee that such a saving is realizable. Some compilers may already implement a space saving for all records, even without the *packed* prefix, so the use of the prefix is irrelevant.

Third, the presence or absence of the prefix *packed* does not alter the meaning of a program. Its only effect is on the program's efficiency. The only exception to this rule is that a component of a packed type may not appear in a function or procedure call as the actual parameter corresponding to a *var* formal parameter.

12. FILES OF RECORDS

One extremely important application of records is to input/output. Much computing revolves around the use of sequential external files. These files contain a sequence of records on some external storage medium, such as a disk or a tape. The records in the file are usually ordered on some field. For example, a school may maintain a file of student records ordered by student name or i.d. number, and a company might maintain a file of employee records ordered by employee number. If *rt* is a record type, a file of records of type *rt* may be declared by a declaration such as

```
var f: file of rt;
```

A file is used as an input or an output file. An input file is one that is read by the program, whereas an output file is written by the program. Initially, an input file must be positioned to its beginning by a call to the standard procedure *reset(f)*. Once an input file *f* of type *file of rt* has been reset, it can be read by the statement

$$read(f,r)$$

where *r* is of type *rt*. Each such statement sets *r* to the value of the next record of the file and advances the file one record. Several records may be read from a file in a single statement such as

$$read(f,r1,r2,r3)$$

which is equivalent to

$$read(f,r1);$$
$$read(f,r2);$$
$$read(f,r3)$$

After the last record of an input file has been read, the value of the standard boolean function *eof(f)* becomes *true* and a call on the procedure *read* produces an error. Before all the records of *f* have been read, *eof(f)* is *false*.

An output file must be initialized as a new file by a call to the standard procedure *rewrite(f)*. Once an output file *f* of type *file of rt* has been initialized, a record *r* of type *rt* can be added to the end of file *f* by the statement

$$write(f,r)$$

Several records may be written to a file in a single statement such as

$$write(f,r1,r2,r3)$$

If a program references an external file, the name of the file must appear in the program header. For example, the header

program merge(f,g,h);

would be used if the program accesses files *f*, *g*, and *h*. Of course, *f*, *g*, and *h* must be declared as files within the program.

There are two standard files *input* and *output*, which are the system input and output files, respectively. Both of these are text files; that is, files of characters divided into lines. If a call to *read* does not include a file name as an argument, it references the file *input* by default. If a call to *write* does not include a file name as an argument, it references the file *output* by default. These two files should not be declared in the program, but must appear in the program header. These files need not be initialized by *reset* and *rewrite*. More information on these files, as well as text files in general, may be found in an introductory Pascal text.

As an example of the use of external sequential files, consider the following situation. A student grade record at a college consists of a nine-digit student number, the student's numerical high school average, and the number of credits of As, Bs, Cs, Ds, and Fs that the student has earned. The grade-point index for a student is defined as 4 times the number of A credits the student has earned plus 3 times the number of B credits plus 2 times the number of C credits plus the number of D credits, all divided by the total number of credits (including the F credits). Thus the grade-point index is a real number between 0 and 4.

The college maintains a file of student records, one per student, ordered by increasing student number. This file is updated periodically, using a nonempty group of input transactions. There are three types of transactions, types A, G, and D. Each input line contains a letter ('a', 'g', or 'd') in its first column and a student number in columns 2 through 10. An A line indicates an admission. Columns 11 through 15 of an A line contain the student's high school average, and all columns past 16 are blank. A G line indicates a new grade. Column 11 of a G line contains the letter grade ('a', 'b', 'c', 'd', or 'f'), columns 12 through 15 contain the number of credits, and all columns past 16 are blank. A D line indicates a discharge and contains blanks from columns 11 on. The lines in the transaction input are also ordered by increasing student number. Only one type of transaction may appear for any one student. If the transaction type is A or D, only a single input line may appear for the student, but many G transactions may appear.

We would like to read the student file and the transaction input, produce an updated student file reflecting the transactions, and print an appropriate message for each student whose record has been updated. The following program does this. The input student file is called *stin*, and the output student file is called *stout*. We use three procedures, *updatea*, *updateg*, and *updated*, to perform the updates and output required for each of three types of transaction. We assume the minor Pascal extension which allows a packed array of a character subrange as an argument to the *writeln* procedure.

```
program update(stin,stout,input,output);
type grade = (f,d,c,b,a);
     gradelett = 'a'..'f';
     digit = '0'..'9';
     numtype = packed array[1..9] of digit;
     strec = record
               stnum: numtype;
               hsavg: real;
               numcr: array[grade] of real
             end;
var i: integer;
    student: strec;
    trnum: numtype;
    trans: char;
    stin,stout: file of strec;
    dig: digit;
```

```pascal
lastdel: boolean { indicates if the last element }
                 { of the file has been deleted }

function gpi(st: strec): real;
{ this function computes the grade point index of a student }
var totcr,total: real;
    gr: grade;
begin
    totcr:= 0;
    total:= 0;
    for gr:= f to a
        do begin
                totcr:= totcr + st.numcr[gr];
                total:= total + ord(gr) * st.numcr[gr]
            end { for...do begin};
    if totcr:= 0
      then writeln('error in gpi, no credits earned')
      else gpi:= total/totcr
end { function gpi};



procedure updatea;
var st: strec;
begin
    if trnum = student.stnum
      then writeln('admission error ', trnum, ' already a student');
    if trnum < student.stnum
      then with st
              do begin
                    stnum:= trnum;
                    read(hsavg);
                    for gr:= f to a
                        do numcr[gr]:= 0;
                    write(stout,st);
                    writeln(trnum, ' admitted with average ', hsavg)
                 end {with...do begin};
    if (trnum > student.stnum) and (eof(stin))
      then with student
              do begin
                    write(stout,student);
                    stnum:= trnum;
                    read(hsavg);
                    for gr:= f to a
                        do numcr[gr]:= 0;
                    writeln(trnum, ' admitted with average ', hsavg)
                 end {with...do begin}
end { procedure updatea};
```

```pascal
    procedure updateg;
    var lett: gradelett;
        i: integer;
        cr: real;
        gr: grade;
    begin
        if trnum <> student.stnum
            then writeln('error grade, no student ', trnum)
            else begin
                        read(lett, cr);
                        case lett of
                            'a': gr:= a;
                            'b': gr:= b;
                            'c': gr:= c;
                            'd': gr:= d;
                            'f': gr:= f
                        end {case};
                        with student
                            do numcr[gr]:= numcr[gr] + cr;
                        writeln(trnum, ' now has a grade point index of ', gpi(student))
                end {else begin}
    end { procedure updateg};

    procedure updated;
    begin
        if trnum = student.stnum
            then begin
                        writeln('discharging ',trnum, ' with grade point index ', gpi(student));
                        if not eof(stin)
                            then read(stin, student)
                            else lastdel:= true
                end {then begin}
            else writeln('discharge error, no student ',trnum)
    end { procedure updated};

    begin { program update}
        reset(stin);
        rewrite(stout);
        read(stin,student);
        repeat
                lastdel:= false;
                read(trans);
                for i:= 1 to 9
                    do begin
                                read(dig);
                                trnum[i]:= dig
                        end { for...do begin};
```

```
          while (trnum > student.stnum) and (not eof(stin))
              do begin
                        write(stout,student);
                        read(stin,student)
                  end {while...do begin};
          case trans of
              'a': updatea;
              'g': updateg;
              'd': updated
          end {case};
          readln
      until eof(input);

      while (not eof(stin))
          do begin
                    write(stout,student);
                    read(stin,student)
              end {while...do begin};
      if not lastdel
        then write(stout,student)
  end { program update}.
```

This program is quite complex, particularly in the way it deals with the last student record, once *eof(stin)* becomes *true*. Mimic its actions using sample student files and transaction input to understand it better.

We have merely touched on the topic of files in Pascal, since the study and use of files deserves an entire book in itself. For more details, see other Pascal texts and manuals. The actual use and implementation of files vary from installation to installation.

Bibliography and References

The following bibliography is in no way complete. However, it is an attempt to list a large number of sources and references for further reading. Following each entry is a list of the sections of this book to which the entry applies. If the letter A appears in this list, then the entry is a general reference to the topic of algorithms and their development and efficiency; if the letter D appears, then the entry is a general reference to the topic of data structures, their implementations and applications. Such entries are relevant to most of the topics discussed in this book and are, therefore, not categorized further. If the letter P appears after an entry, then the entry is a general reference to the Pascal language. Other entries contain either an integer, in which case they are relevant to an entire chapter, or a section number (of the form X.X), in which case they are relevant to a particular section.

ACKERMAN, A. F.: "Quadratic Search for Hash Tables of Size p^n," *Comm. ACM*, **17** (3), Mar. 1974. (9.3)

ADDYMAN, A. M.: "A Draft Proposal for Pascal," *SIGPLAN Notices*, **15** (4) Apr. 1980. (P)

ADELSON-VELSKII, G. M. and E. M. LANDIS: "An Algorithm for the Organization of Information," *Dokl. Akad. Nauk SSSR, Mathemat*, **146** (2): 263–66, 1962. (9.2)

AHO, A., J. HOPCROFT and J. ULLMAN: *The Design and Analysis of Computer Algorithms*, Addison-Wesley, Reading, Mass., 1974. (A)

AHO, A. V., J. E. HOPCROFT, and J. D. ULLMAN: "On Finding Lowest Common Ancestors in Trees," *SIAM J. COMP.*, **5** (1), Mar. 1976. (6)

ALAGIC, S. and M. A. ARBIB: *The Design of Well-Structured and Correct Programs*, Springer-Verlag, New York, 1978. (P, A)

AMBLE, O. and D. E. KNUTH: "Ordered Hash Tables," *Computer J.*, **18**: 135–42, 1975. (9.3)

ANDERSON, M. R. and M. G. ANDERSON: "Comments on Perfect Hashing Functions: A Single Probe Retrieving Method for Static Sets," *Comm. ACM*, **22** (2), Feb. 1979. (9.3)

AUGENSTEIN, M. and A. TENENBAUM: "A Lesson in Recursion and Structured Programming," *SIGCSE Bulletin*, **8** (1): 17–23, Feb. 1976. (3.4)

AUGENSTEIN, M. and A. TENENBAUM: "Program Efficiency and Data Structures," *SIGCSE Bulletin*, **9** (3): 21–37, Aug. 1977. (4.4, 6.4)

528

AUGENSTEIN, M. J. and A. M. TENENBAUM: *Data Structures and PL/I Programming*, Prentice-Hall, Englewood Cliffs, N. J., 1979. **(D)**

AUSLANDER, M. A. and H. R. STRONG: "Systematic Recursion Removal," *Comm. ACM*, **21** (2), Feb. 1978. **(3.4)**

BAASE, S.: *Computer Algorithms: Introduction to Design and Analysis*, Addison-Wesley, Reading, Mass., 1978. **(A)**

BAER, J. L. and B. SCHWAB: "A Comparison of Tree-Balancing Algorithms," *Comm. ACM*, **20** (5), May 1977. **(9.2)**

BARRON, D. W.: *Recursive Techniques in Programming*, American-Elsevier, New York, 1968. **(3)**

BATAGELJ, V.: "The Quadratic Hash Method When the Table Size is Not a Prime Number," *Comm. ACM*, **18** (4), Apr. 1975. **(9.3)**

BAYER, R.: "Binary B-trees for Virtual Memory," *Proc. 1971 ACM SIGFIDET Workshop:* 219–35. ACM, New York. **(9.2)**

BAYER, R.: "Symmetric Binary B-Trees: Data Structure and Maintenance Algorithms," *Acta Informatica*, **1** (4): 290–306, 1972. **(9.2)**

BAYER, R. and C. McCREIGHT: "Organization and Maintenance of Large Ordered Indexes," *Acta Informatica*, **1** (3): 173–89, 1972. **(9.2)**

BAYER, R. and J. METZGER: "On Encipherment of Search Trees and Random Access Files," *ACM Trans. Database Syst.*, **1** (1): 37–52, Mar. 1976. **(9.2)**

BAYER, R. and K. UNTERAUER: "Prefix B-trees," *ACM Trans. Database Syst.*, **2** (1): 11–26, Mar. 1977. **(9.2)**

BAYS, C.: "A Note on When to Chain Overflow Items Within a Direct-Access Table," *Comm. ACM*, **16** (1), Jan. 1973. **(9.3)**

BELL, J. R.: "The Quadratic Quotient Method: A Hash Code Eliminating Secondary Clustering," *Comm. ACM*, **13** (2), Feb. 1970. **(9.3)**

BELL, J. R. and C. H. KAMAN: "The Linear Quotient Hash Code," *Comm. ACM*, **13** (11), Nov. 1970. **(9.3)**

BELLMAN, R.: *Dynamic Programming*, Princeton University Press, Princeton, N. J., 1957. **(A)**

BENTLEY, J. L.: "Multidimensional Binary Search Trees Used for Associative Searching," *Comm. ACM*, **18** (9), Sept. 1975. **(9.2)**

BENTLEY, J. L.: "Decomposable Searching Problems," *Inf. Proc. Letters*, **8** (5), Jun. 1979. **(9)**

BENTLEY, J. L.: "Multidimensional Divide and Conquer," *Comm. ACM*, **23** (4), Apr. 1980. **(3, 9)**

BENTLEY, J. L. and J. H. FRIEDMAN: "Algorithms and Data Structures for Range Searching," *ACM Computing Surveys*, **11** (4), Dec. 1979. **(9)**

BENTLEY, J. L. and D. F. STANAT: "Analysis of Range Searches in Quad Trees," *Inf. Proc. Letters*, **3** (6), Jul. 1975. **(6, 9.2)**

BERGE, C.: *Graphs and Hypergraphs*, North-Holland, Amsterdam, 1973. **(7)**

BERGE, C.: *Theory of Graphs and its Applications*, Methuen Press, 1962. **(7)**

BERZTISS, A. T.: *Data Structures, Theory and Practice, 2d ed.*, Academic Press, New York, 1977. **(D)**

BIRD, R. S.: "Improving Programs by the Introduction of Recursion," *Comm. ACM*, **20** (11), Nov. 1977. **(3.4)**

BIRD, R. S.: "Notes on Recursion Elimination," *Comm. ACM*, **20** (6), Jun. 1977.   (3.4)

BITNER, J. R.: "Heuristics that Dynamically Alter Data Structures to Decrease their Access Time," Ph.D. Thesis, University of Illinois, Urbana, Ill., 1976.   (9.1, 9.2)

BITNER, J. R.: "Heuristics that Dynamically Organize Data Structures," *SIAM Journal of Computing*, **8** (1), Feb. 1979.   (9.1, 9.2)

BITNER, J. R. and E. M. REINGOLD: "Backtrack Programming Techniques," *Comm. ACM.*, **18**: 651–56, 1975.   (3.3)

BLUM, M., R. W. FLOYD, V. PRATT, R. L. RIVEST, and R. E. TARJAN: "Time Bounds for Selection," *J. Comput. Sys. Sci.*, **7**: 448–61, 1973.   (8.3)

BOOTHROYD, J.: "Algorithm 201 (Shellsort)," *Comm. ACM*, **6**: 445, 1963.   (8.4)

BOOTHROYD, J.: "Sort of a Section of the Elements of an Array by Determining the Rank of Each Element: Algorithm 25," *Compr. J.*, **10**, Nov. 1967.   (8.2)

BOWLES, K. L.: *Microcomputer Problem Solving Using Pascal*, Springer-Verlag, New York, 1977.   **(P)**

BRENT, R. P.: "Reducing the Retrieval Time of Scatter Storage Techniques," *Comm. ACM*, **16** (2), Feb. 1973.   (9.3)

BRILLINGER, P. C. and D. J. COHEN: *Introduction to Data Structures and Non-numeric Computation*, Prentice-Hall, Englewood Cliffs, N.J., 1972.   **(D)**

BROWN, M.: "A Storage Scheme for Height-Balanced Trees," *Inf. Proc. Lett.*, **7** (5): 231–32, Aug. 1978.   (9.2)

BRUNO, J. and E. G. COFFMAN: "Nearly Optimal Binary Search Trees," *Proc. IFIP Congress 71*: 99–103, North-Holland, Amsterdam, 1972.   (9.2)

BSI DPS/13/4 WORKING GROUP: "The BSI/ISO Working Draft of Standard Pascal," *Pascal News* (14), Jan. 1979, and *Software Practice and Experience*, **9** (5), May 1979.   **(P)**

BURGE, W. H.: "A Correspondence Between Two Sorting Methods," *IBM Research Report RC 6395*, Thomas J. Watson Research Center, Yorktown Heights, N. Y., 1977.   (8.3)

BURSTALL, R. M. and J. DARLINGTON: "A Transformation System for Developing Recursive Programs," *Journal of the ACM*, **24** (1), Jan. 1977.   (3.3, 3.4)

CARTER, J. L. and M. N. WEGMAN: "Universal Classes of Hash Functions," *IBM Research Report RC 6495*, Thomas J. Watson Research Center, Yorktown Heights, N. Y., 1977.   (9.3)

CHERRY, G. W.: *Pascal Programming Structures, An Introduction to Systematic Programming*, Reston Publishing Co., Reston, Va., 1980.   **(P)**

CICHELLI, R. J.: "Minimal Perfect Hash Functions Made Simple," *Comm. ACM*, **23** (1), Jan. 1980.   (9.3)

CLAMPETT, H.: "Randomized Binary Searching With Tree Structures," *Comm. ACM*, **7** (3): 163–65, Mar. 1964.   (9.2)

COLEMAN, D.: *A Structured Programming Approach to Data*, Macmillan, London, 1978.   **(P, D)**

COMER, D.: "A Note on Median Split Trees," *ACM Trans. Prog. Lang. and Sys.*, **2** (1), Jan. 1980.   (9.2)

COMER, D.: "The Ubiquitous B-Tree," *ACM Computing Surveys*, **11** (2), Jun. 1979.   (9.2)

CONDICT, M.: "The Pascal Dynamic Array Controversy and a Method for Enforcing Global Assertions," *SIGPLAN Notices*, **12** (11), Nov. 1977.   (1.2)

CONRADI, R.: "Further Critical Comments on Pascal, Particularly as a Systems Programming Language," *SIGPLAN Notices*, **11** (11), Nov. 1976.   **(P)**

CONWAY, R. W., D. GRIES, and E. C. ZIMMERMAN: *A Primer on Pascal*, Winthrop, Cambridge, Mass., 1976.   **(P)**

DANTZIG, G. B. and D. R. FULKERSON: "On the Max-flow Min-cut Theorem of Networks in Linear Inequalities and Related Systems," *Annals of Math. Study 38:* 215–21, Princeton University Press, Princeton, N. J., 1956.   **(7.2)**

DAVIS, H: *Pascal Handbook* (3 vols), dilithium Press, Forest Grove, Or., 1980.   **(P)**

DEO, N.: *Graph Theory with Applications to Engineering and Computer Science*, Prentice-Hall, Englewood Cliffs, N. J., 1974.   **(7)**

D'IMPERIO, M. E.: "Data Structures and their Representation in Storage," *Annual Review in Automatic Programming*, **5**: 1–75, Pergamon Press, Elmsford, N. Y., 1969.   **(D)**

DOBKIN, D. and R. J. LIPTON: "Multidimensional Search Problems," *SIAM J. of Computing*, **5** (2), Jun. 1976.   **(9)**

DRISCOLL, J. R. and Y. E. LIEN: "A Selective Traversal Algorithm for Binary Search Trees," *Comm. ACM*, **21** (6), Jun. 1978.   **(6.1, 6.2, 9.2)**

EARLSON, I. M.: "Sherlock Holmes and Charles Babbage," *Creative Computing*, **3** (4): 106–13, Jul.–Aug. 1977.   **(3.3)**

EDMONDS, J. and R. M. KARP: "Theoretical Improvements in Algorithmic Efficiency for Network Flow Problem," *Journal of the ACM*, **19**: 248–64, 1972.   **(7.2)**

ELSON, M.: *Data Structures*, Science Research Associates, Palo Alto, Ca., 1975.   **(D)**

EVEN, S.: *Graph Algorithms*, Computer Science Press, Potomac, Md., 1978.   **(7)**

EVEN, S. and R. E. TARJAN: "Network Flow and Testing Graph Connectivity," *SIAM J. of Computing*, **4** (4), Dec. 1975.   **(7.2)**

FILLMORE, J. P. and S. G. WILLIAMSON: "On Backtracking: A Combinatorial Description of the Algorithm," *SIAM J. of Computing*, **3** (1), Mar. 1974.   **(3)**

FINDLAY, W. and D. WATT: *Pascal: An Introduction to Methodical Programming*, Computer Science Press, Potomac, Md., 1978.   **(P)**

FINKEL, R. A. and J. L. BENTLEY: "Quad Trees: A Data Structure for Retrieval on Composite Keys," *Acta Informatica*, **4**: 1–9, 1975.   **(6, 9.2)**

FISHMAN, G. S.: *Concepts and Methods in Discrete Event Digital Simulation*, Wiley, New York, 1973.   **(4.3)**

FLORES, I.: *Computer Sorting*, Prentice-Hall, Englewood Cliffs, N. J., 1969.   **(8)**

FLORES, I.: *Data Structure and Management*, Prentice-Hall, Englewood Cliffs, N. J., 1970.   **(D)**

FLORES, I. and G. MADPIS: "Average Binary Search Lengths for Dense Ordered Lists," *Comm. ACM*, **14** (9), Sept. 1971.   **(9.1)**

FLOYD, R. W.: "Algorithm 245 (Treesort3)," *Comm. ACM.*, **7**: 701, 1964.   **(8.3)**

FLOYD, R. W. and R. L. RIVEST: "Algorithm 489 (Select)," *Comm. ACM*, **18** (3): 173, Mar. 1975.   **(8.3)**

FLOYD, R. W. and R. L. RIVEST: "Expected Time Bounds for Selection," *Comm. ACM*, **18** (3), Mar. 1975.   **(8.3)**

FORD, L. R. and D. R. FULKERSON: *Flows in Networks*, Princeton University Press, Princeton, N. J., 1972. (7.2)

FORD, L. R. and S. M. JOHNSON: "A Tournament Problem," *Amer. Math. Monthly*, **66**: 387–89, 1975. (8.3)

FOSTER, C. C.: "A Generalization of AVL Trees," *Comm. ACM*, **16** (8), Aug. 1973. (9.2)

FRANTA, W. R. and K. MALY: "A Comparison of Heaps and the TL Structure for the Simulation Event Set." *Comm. ACM*, **21** (10), Oct. 1978. (4.3, 8.3)

FRANTA, W. R. and K. MALY: "An Efficient Data Structure for the Simulation Event Set," *Comm. ACM*, **20** (8), Aug. 1977. (4.3)

FRAZER, W. D. and A. C. McKELLAR: "Samplesort: A Sampling Approach to Minimal Storage Tree Sorting," *J. ACM*, **17** (3), Jul. 1970. (8.3)

FULKERSON, D. R.: "Flow Networks and Combinatorial Operations Research," *Amer. Math. Monthly*, **73**: 115, 1966. (7.2)

GALIL, Z. and N. MEGIDDO: "A Fast Selection Algorithm and the Problem of Optimum Distribution of Effort," *Journal of the ACM*, **26** (1), Jan. 1979. (8.2)

GAREY, M. R.: "Optimal Binary Search Trees With Restricted Maximal Depth," *SIAM J. Comp*, **2**: 101–10, 1974. (9.2)

GARSIA, A. M. and M. L. WACHS: "A New Algorithm for Minimum Cost Binary Trees," *SIAM J. Comp.*, **6** (4), Dec. 1977. (9.2)

GHOSH, S. P. and V. Y. LUM: "Analysis of Collisions when Hashing by Division," *Inf. Syst.*, **1**: 15–22, 1975. (9.3)

GOLOMB, S. W. and L. D. BAUMERT: "Backtrack Programming," *J. ACM*, **12**: 516, 1965. (3)

GONNET, G. H.: "Heaps Applied to Event Driven Mechanisms," *Comm. ACM*, **19** (7), Jul. 1976. (4.3, 8.3)

GONNET, G. H. and J. I. MUNRO: "Efficient Ordering of Hash Tables," *SIAM J. Comp.*, **8** (3), Aug. 1979. (9.3)

GONNET, G. H. and L. D. ROGERS: "The Interpolation-Sequential Search Algorithm," *Inf. Proc. Lett.*, **6**: 136–39, 1977. (9.1)

GONNET, G. H., L. D. ROGERS, and J. A. GEORGE: "An Algorithmic and Complexity Analysis of Interpolation Search," *Acta Informatica*, **13** (1): 39–52, 1980. (9.1)

GOODMAN, S. E. and S. T. HEDETNIEMI: *Introduction to the Design and Analysis of Algorithms*, McGraw-Hill, New York, 1977. (A, 3)

GORDON, G.: *System Simulation*, Prentice-Hall, Englewood Cliffs, N. J., 1969. (4.3)

GOTLIEB, C. C. and L. R. GOTLIEB: *Data Types and Structures*, Prentice-Hall, Englewood Cliffs, N. J., 1978. (D)

GRAHAM, N.: *Introduction to Pascal*, West Publishing Co., St. Paul, Minn., 1980. (P)

GRIES, D.: *Compiler Construction for Digital Computers*, Wiley, New York, 1971. (3.2, 3.4, 9.3)

GROGONO, P.: *Programming in Pascal*, Addison-Wesley, Reading, Mass., 1978. (P)

GUIBAS, L. J.: "The Analysis of Hashing Techniques that Exhibit K-ary Clustering," *Journal of the ACM*, **25**: 544–55, 1978. (9.3)

GUIBAS, L., E. McCREIGHT, M. PLASS and J. ROBERTS: "A New Representation for Linear Lists," *Proc. 9th ACM Symp. Theory of Comp.*: 49–60, New York, 1977. (9.2)

GUIBAS, L. J. and E. SZEMEREDI: "The Analysis of Double Hashing," *J. Comp. Sys. Sci.*, **16**: 226–74, 1978. **(9.3)**

HABERMANN, A. N.: "Critical Comments on the Programming Language Pascal," *Acta Informatica*, **3** (1), 1973. **(P)**

HARARY, F.: *Graph Theory*, Addison-Wesley, Boston, 1969. **(7)**

HARRISON, M. C.: *Data Structures and Programming*, Scott-Foresman, Glenville, Ill., 1973. **(D)**

HELD, G. and M. STONEBRAKER: "B-trees Re-examined," *Comm. ACM*, **21** (2): 139–43, Feb. 1978. **(9.2)**

HIRSCHBERG, D. S.: "An Insertion Technique for One-sided Height-Balanced Trees," *Comm. ACM*, **19** (8), Aug. 1976. **(9.2)**

HOARE, C. A. R.: "Partition, Algorithm 63; Quicksort, Algorithm 64; Find, Algorithm 65," *Comm. ACM*, **4** (7), Jul. 1961. **(8.2)**

HOARE, C. A. R.: "Quicksort," *Comp. J.*, **5**: 10–15, 1962. **(8.2)**

HOARE, C. A. R. and N. WIRTH: "An Axiomatic Definition of the Programming Language Pascal," *Acta Informatica*, **2** (4), 1973. **(P)**

HOLT, R. C. and J. N. P. HUME: *Programming Standard Pascal*, Reston Publishing Co., Reston, Va., 1980. **(P)**

HOPGOOD, F. R. A. and J. DAVENPORT: "The Quadratic Hash Method Where the Table Size is a Power of 2," *Comptr. J.*, **15** (4), 1972. **(9.3)**

HOROWITZ, E. and S. SAHNI: *Algorithms: Design and Analysis*, Computer Science Press, Potomac, Md., 1977. **(A)**

HOROWITZ, E. and S. SAHNI: *Fundamentals of Data Structures*, Computer Science Press, Woodland Hills, Calif., 1975. **(D)**

HU, T. C. and A. C. TUCKER: "Optimum Computer Search Trees," *SIAM J. Appl. Math.*, **21**: 514–32, 1971. **(9.2)**

HUFFMAN, D.: "A Method for the Construction of Minimum Redundance Codes," *Proc. IRE*, **40**, 1952. **(6.3)**

HWANG, F. K. and S. LIN: "A Simple Algorithm for Merging Two Disjoint Linearly Ordered Sets," *SIAM J. Comp.*, **1**: 31–39 1972. **(8.5)**

ITAI, A.: "Optimal Alphabetic Trees," *SIAM J. Comp.*, **5** (1), Mar. 1976. **(9.2)**

ITAI, A. and Y. SHILOACH: "Maximum Flow in Planar Networks," *SIAM J. Comp.*, **8** (2), May 1979. **(7.2)**

JACOBI, C.: "Dynamic Array Parameters," *Pascal User's Group Newsletter*, (5), Sept. 1976. **(1.2)**

JENSEN, K. and N. WIRTH: *Pascal User Manual and Report, 2d ed.*, Springer-Verlag, New York, 1974. **(P)**

JONASSEN, A. and O. DAHL: "Analysis of an Algorithm for Priority Queue Administration," *BIT*, **15**: 409–22, 1975. **(6)**

KARLTON, P. L., S. H. FULLER, R. E. SCROGGS, and E. B. KACHLER: "Performance of Height-Balanced Trees," *Comm. ACM*, **19** (1): 23–28, Jan. 1976. **(9.2)**

KERNIGHAN, B. and P. J. PLAUGER: *Software Tools*, Addison-Wesley, Reading, Mass., 1976. **(8)**

KIEBURTZ, R. B.: *Structured Programming and Problem-Solving with Pascal*, Prentice-Hall, Englewood Cliffs, N. J. 1978. **(P)**

KITTLITZ, E. N.: "Another Proposal for Variable Size Arrays in Pascal," *SIGPLAN Notices*, **12** (1), Jan. 1977.   **(1.2)**

KLEINROCK, L.: *Queuing Systems*, Wiley, 1975.   **(4.3)**

KNOTT, G. O.: "Hashing Functions," *Computer Journal*, **18**, Aug. 1975.   **(9.3)**

KNUTH, D. E.: *Fundamental Algorithms, 2d ed.*, Addison-Wesley, Reading, Mass., 1973.   **(D, A)**

KNUTH, D. E.: "Optimum Binary Search Trees," *Acta Informatica*, **1**: 14–25, 1971.   **(9.2)**

KNUTH, D. E.: *Sorting and Searching*, Addison-Wesley, Reading, Mass., 1973.   **(8, 9)**

KNUTH, D. E.: "Structured Programming with Goto Statements," *ACM Computing Surveys*, **6** (4): 261, Dec. 1974.   **(3.4, 8.2)**

KORFHAGE, R. R.: *Discrete Computational Structures*, Academic Press, New York, 1974.   **(7.1)**

KOSARAJU, S. R.: "Insertions and Deletions in One-Sided Height Balanced Trees," *Comm. ACM*, **21** (3), Mar. 1978.   **(9.2)**

LECARME, O. and P. DESJARDINS: "More Comments on the Programming Language Pascal," *Acta Informatica*, **4**: 231–43, 1975.   **(P)**

LECARME, O. and P. DESJARDINS: "Reply to a Paper by A. N. Habermann on the Programming Language Pascal," *SIGPLAN Notices*, **9** (10), Oct. 1974.   **(P)**

LEWIS, T. G. and M. Z. SMITH: *Applying Data Structures*, Houghton Mifflin, Boston, 1976.   **(D)**

LIFFICK, B. W.: *The BYTE Book of Pascal*, BYTE Publications, Peterborough, N. H., 1979.   **(P)**

LOCKYER, K. G.: *Critical Path Analysis: Problem and Solutions*, Pitman, London, 1966.   **(7.3)**

LOCKYER, K. G.: *An Introduction to Critical Data Analysis*, Pitman, London, 1964.   **(7.3)**

LOESER, R.: "Some Performance Tests of 'Quicksort' and Descendants," *Comm. ACM*, **17** (3), Mar. 1974.   **(8.2)**

LUCCIO, F. and L. PAGLI: "On the Height of Height-Balanced Trees," *IEEE Trans. Comptrs.*, **c-25** (1), Jan. 1976.   **(9.2)**

LUCCIO, F. and L. PAGLI: "Power Trees," *Comm. ACM*, **21** (11), Nov. 1978.   **(9.2)**

LUM, U. Y.: "General Performance Analysis of Key-to-Address Transformation Methods Using an Abstract File Concept," *Comm. ACM*, **16** (10): 603, Oct. 1973.   **(9.3)**

LUM, U. Y. and P. S. T. YUEN: "Additional Results on Key-to-address Transform Techniques: A Fundamental Performance Study on Large Existing Formatted Files," *Comm. ACM*, **15** (11): 996, Nov. 1972.   **(9.3)**

LUM, U. Y., P. S. T. YUEN and M. DODD: "Key-to-address Transform Techniques: A Fundamental Performance Study on Large Existing Formatted Files," *Comm. ACM*, **14**: 228, 1971.   **(9.3)**

LYON, G.: "Packed Scatter Tables," *Comm. ACM*, **21** (10), Oct. 1978.   **(9.3)**

MacLENNAN, B. J.: "A Note on Dynamic Arrays in Pascal," *SIGPLAN Notices*, **10** (9), Sept. 1975.   **(1.2)**

MALY, K.: "Compressed Tries," *Comm. ACM*, **19** (7), Jul. 1976.   **(9.2)**

MANNA, Z. and A. SHAMIR: "The Optimal Approach to Recursive Programs," *Comm. ACM*, **20** (11), Nov. 1977.   **(3.4)**

MARTIN, W.: "Sorting," *Comp. Surveys*, **3** (4): 147, 1971.   **(8)**

MAURER, H. A.: *Data Structures and Programming Techniques*, Prentice-Hall, Englewood Cliffs, N. J., 1977. **(D)**

MAURER, H. A. and T. OTTMANN: "Tree Structures for Set Manipulation Problems," in *Mathematical Foundations of Computer Science*, J. Gruska (ed.), Springer-Verlag, New York, 1977. **(6)**

MAURER, H. A., T. OTTMANN and H. W. SIX: "Implementing Dictionaries Using Binary Trees of Very Small Height," *Inform. Proc. Letters*, 5: 11–14, 1976. **(9.2)**

MAURER, H. A. and M. R. WILLIAMS: *A Collection of Programming Problems and Techniques*, Prentice-Hall, Englewood Cliffs, N. J., 1972. **(A)**

MAURER, W. D.: "An Improved Hash Code for Scatter Storage," *Comm. ACM*, **11** (1), Jan. 1968. **(9.3)**

MAURER, W. and T. LEWIS: "Hash Table Methods," *Comp. Surveys*, **7** (1): 5–19, Mar. 1975. **(9.3)**

McCABE, J.: "On Serial Files with Relocatable Records," *Operations Research*, **12**: 609–18, 1965. **(9.1)**

MEHLHORN, K.: "Dynamic Binary Search," *SIAM J. Comp.*, **8** (2), May 1979. **(9.2)**

MEHLHORN, K.: "Nearly Optimal Binary Search Trees," *Acta Informatica*, 5: 287–95, 1975. **(9.2)**

MILLER, R., N. PIPPENGER, A. ROSENBERG and L. SNYDER: "Optimal 2-3 Trees," *IBM Research Rep. RC 6505*, Thomas J. Watson Research Center, Yorktown Heights, N. Y., 1977. **(9.2)**

MORRIS, R.: "Scatter Storage Techniques," *Comm. ACM*, **11** (1): 38–44, Jan. 1968. **(9.3)**

MORRIS, R.: "Some Theorems on Sorting," *SIAM J. Appl. Math.*, **17** (1), Jan. 1969. **(8)**

MUNRO, I.: "Efficient Determination of the Transitive Closure of a Directed Graph," *Inf. Proc. Letters*, 1: 56, 1971–72. **(7.1)**

MUNRO, I. and P. M. SPIRA: "Sorting and Searching in Multisets," *SIAM J. Comp.*, 5 (1), Mar. 1976. **(8, 9)**

MUNRO, J. I. and H. SUWANDA: Implicit Data Structures, *Eleventh Symposium on the Theory of Computing*, Assoc. for Comp. Mach, 1979. **(9)**

NIEVERGELT, J.: "Binary Search Trees and File Organization," *ACM Computing Surveys*, 6 (3), Sept. 1974. **(9.2)**

NIEVERGELT, J., J. C. FARRAR and E. M. REINGOLD: *Computer Approaches to Mathematical Problems*, Prentice-Hall, Englewood Cliffs, N. J., 1974. **(A)**

NIEVERGELT, J. and E. M. REINGOLD: "Binary Search Trees of Bounded Balance," *SIAM J. Comp.*, 2: 33, 1973. **(9.2)**

NIEVERGELT, J. and C. K. WONG: "On Binary Search Trees," *Proc. IFIP Congress 71*: 91–98, North-Holland, Amsterdam, 1972. **(9.2)**

NIJENHUIS, A. and H. S. WILF: *Combinatorial Algorithms*, Academic Press, New York, 1975. **(A)**

NILSSON, N.: *Problem-solving Methods in Artificial Intelligence*, McGraw-Hill, New York, 1971. **(6.6)**

O'NEIL, P. E. and E. J. O'NEIL: "A Fast Expected Time Algorithm for Boolean Matrix Multiplication and Transitive Closure," *Information and Control*, 22: 132–38, 1973. **(7.1)**

ORE, O.: *Graphs and their Uses*, Random House and the L. W. Singer Co., New York, 1963. **(7)**

ORE, O.: *Theory of Graphs*, **38**, American Mathematical Society, Providence, R. I., 1962. **(7)**

OTTMANN, T. and D. WOOD: "Deletion in One-Sided Height-Balanced Search Trees," *Int. J. Comp. Math.*, 6 (4): 265–71, 1978. (9.2)

OTTMANN, T., H. SIX and D. WOOD: "Right Brother Trees," *Comm. ACM*, **21** (9), Sept. 1978. (6)

PAGE, E. S. and L. B. WILSON: *Information Representation and Manipulation in a Computer*, Cambridge University Press, London, 1973. (D)

PAPADIMITRIOU, C. H. and P. A. BERNSTEIN: "On the Performance of Balanced Hashing Functions when the Keys are not Equiprobable," *ACM Trans. Prog. Lang. and Sys.*, **2** (1), Jan. 1980. (9.3)

PASCAL USER'S GROUP: *Pascal News* (1-), Pascal User's Group, Atlanta, Ga., 1974-. (P)

PERL, Y., A. ITAI, and H. AVNI: "Interpolation Search—A Log Log N Search," *Comm. ACM*, **21**: 550–57, 1978. (9.1)

PERL, Y. and E. M. REINGOLD: "Understanding the Complexity of Interpolation Search," *Inf. Proc. Lett.*, **6**: 219–21, 1977. (9.1)

PETERSON, J. L.: "On the Formatting of Pascal Programs," *SIGPLAN Notices*, **12** (12), Dec. 1977. (P)

PETERSON, W. W.: "Addressing for Random-Access Storage," *IBM J. Res. and Dev.*, **1**: 130–46, 1957. (9.3)

PFALTZ, J. L.: *Computer Data Structures*, McGraw-Hill, New York, 1977. (D)

POHL, I.: "A Sorting Problem and its Complexity," *Comm. ACM*, **15** (6), Jun. 1972. (8.1)

POKROVSKY, S.: "Formal Types and their Application to Dynamic Arrays in Pascal," *SIGPLAN Notices*, **11** (10), Oct. 1976. (1.2)

POLYA, G.: *How to Solve it*, Doubleday, Garden City, N. Y., 1957. (A)

POOCH, U. W. and A. NIEDER: "A Survey of Indexing Techniques for Sparse Matrices," *Computer Surveys*, **15**: 109, 1973. (5.3)

PRATT, T. W.: *Programming Languages: Design and Implementation*, Prentice-Hall, Englewood Cliffs, N. J., 1975. (1.2, 1.3, 2.3, 3.2, 3.4)

PRICE, C.: "Table Lookup Techniques," *ACM Comp. Surveys*, **3** (2): 49–65, 1971. (9)

RADKE, C. E.: "The Use of Quadratic Residue Research," *Comm. ACM*, **13** (2), Feb. 1970. (9.3)

RAIHA, K. and S. H. ZWEBEN: "An Optimal Insertion Algorithm for One-Sided Height-Balanced Binary Search Trees," *Comm. ACM*, **22** (9), Sept. 1979. (9.2)

REINGOLD, E. M., J. NIEVERGELT, and N. DEO: *Combinatorial Algorithms: Theory and Practice*, Prentice-Hall, Englewood Cliffs, N. J., 1977. (8)

REYNOLDS, J. C.: "Reasoning About Arrays," *Comm. ACM*, **22** (5), May 1979. (1.2)

RICH, R. P.: *Internal Sorting Methods Illustrated with PL/I Programs*, Prentice-Hall, Englewood Cliffs, N. J., 1972. (8)

RIVEST, R. L.: Optimal Arrangement of Keys in a Hash Table," *Journal of the ACM*, **25**: 200–209, 1978. (9.3)

RIVEST, R.: "On Self-organizing Sequential Search Heuristics," *Comm. ACM*, **19** (2), Feb. 1976. (9.1)

RIVEST, R. L. and D. E. KNUTH: "Bibliography 26: Computer Sorting," *Computing Reviews*, **13**: 283, 1972. (8)

ROSENBERG, A. and L. SNYDER: "Minimal Comparison 2-3 Trees," *SIAM J. Comput.*, **7** (4): 465–80, Nov. 1978. (9.2)

SANTORO, N.: "Full Table Search by Polynomial Functions," *Inform. Proc. Letters*, **5**, Aug. 1976. (9.3)

SAXE, J. B. and J. L. BENTLEY: "Transforming Static Data Structures to Dynamic Structures," *Research Report cmu-cs-79-141*, Carnegie-Mellon University, Pittsburgh, 1979. (9)

SCHNEIDER, G. M., S. W. WEINGART and D. M. PERLMAN: *An Introduction to Programming and Problem-Solving with Pascal*, Wiley, New York, 1978. (P)

SCOWEN, R. S.: "Quicksort: Algorithm 271." *Comm. ACM*, **8** (11), Nov. 1965. (8.2)

SEDGEWICK, R.: "The Analysis of Quicksort Programs," *Acta Informatica*, 7: 327–55, 1977. (8.2)

SEDGEWICK, R.: "Data Movement in Odd-Even Merging," *SIAM J. Comp.*, **7** (3), Aug. 1978. (8.2)

SEDGEWICK, R.: "Implementing Quicksort Programs," *Comm. ACM*, **21** (10), Oct. 1978. (8.2)

SEDGEWICK, R.: "Permutation Generation Methods," *ACM Computing Surveys*, **9** (2): 137, Jun. 1977. (3.3)

SEDGEWICK, R.: "Quicksort," *Report no. STAN-CS-75-492*, Dept. of Computer Science, Stanford University, Stanford, Ca., May 1975. (8.2)

SEVERANCE, D. G.: "Identifier Search Mechanisms: A Survey and Generalized Model," *Computing Surveys*, 6 (3): 175–94, Sept. 1974. (9)

SHEIL, B. A.: "Median Split Trees: A Fast Technique for Frequently Occurring Keys," *Comm. ACM*, **21** (11), Nov. 1978. (9.2)

SHELL, D. L.: "A High Speed Sorting Procedure," *Comm. ACM*, **2** (7), Jul. 1959. (8.4)

SHNEIDERMAN, B.: "Jump Searching: A Fast Sequential Search Technique," *Comm. ACM*, **21** (10), Oct. 1978). (9.1)

SHNEIDERMAN, B.: "A Model for Optimizing Indexed File Structures," *Int. J. Comptr. and Inform. Sci.*, **3** (1), 1974. (9.1)

SHNEIDERMAN, B.: "Polynomial Search," *Software-Practice and Experience*, 3: 5–8, 1973. (9.1)

SINGLETON, R. C.: "An Efficient Algorithm for Sorting with Minimal Storage: Algorithm 347," *Comm. ACM*, **12** (3), Mar. 1969. (8.2)

SPRUGNOLI, R.: "Perfect Hashing Functions: A Single Probe Retrieving Method for Static Sets," *Comm. ACM*, **20** (11), Nov. 1977. (9.3)

STANAT, D. F. and D. F. McALLISTER: *Discrete Mathematics in Computer Science*, Prentice-Hall, Englewood Cliffs, N. J., 1977. (7.1)

STEENSGAARD-MADSEN, J.: "More on Dynamic Arrays in Pascal," *SIGPLAN Notices*, **11** (5), May 1976. (1.2)

STEPHENSON, C. J.: "A Method for Constructing Binary Search Trees by Making Insertions at the Root," *IBM Research Report RC6298*, Thomas J. Watson Research Center, Yorktown Heights, N. Y. 1976. (9.2)

STONE, H.: *Introduction to Computer Organization and Data Structures*, McGraw-Hill, New York, 1972. (1.1)

TANNER, R. M.: "Minimean Merging and Sorting: An Algorithm," *SIAM J. Comp.*, **7** (1), Feb. 1978. (8.5)

TARJAN, R. E. and A. C. YAO: "Storing a Sparse Table," *Comm. ACM*, **22** (11), Nov. 1979. (9.2)

TENENBAUM, A.: "Simulations of Dynamic Sequential Search Algorithms," *Comm. ACM*, **21** (9), Sept. 1978. **(9.1)**

TREMBLAY, J. P. and R. P. MANOHAR: *Discrete Mathematical Structures with Applications to Computer Science*, McGraw-Hill, New York, 1975. **(7.1)**

TREMBLAY, J. P. and P. G. SORENSON: *An Introduction to Data Structures with Applications*, McGraw-Hill, New York, 1976. **(D)**

ULRICH, E. G.: "Event Manipulation for Discrete Simulations Requiring Large Numbers of Events," *Comm. ACM*, **21** (9), Sept. 1978. **(4.3)**

VAN EMDEN, M. H.: "Increasing Efficiency of Quicksort," *Comm. ACM*, **13**: 563–67, 1970. **(8.2)**

VAUCHER, J. G. and P. DURAL: "A Comparison of Simulation Event List Algorithms," *Comm. ACM*, **18** (4), Apr. 1975. **(4.3)**

VUILLEMIN, J.: "A Data Structure for Manipulating Priority Queues," *Comm. ACM*, **21** (4), Apr. 1978. **(6.5)**

VUILLEMIN, J.: "A Unifying Look at Data Structures," *Comm. ACM*, **23** (4), Apr. 1980. **(D, A)**

WAITE, W. M.: *Implementing Software for Non-numeric Applications*, Prentice-Hall, Englewood Cliffs, N. J., 1973. **(D)**

WALKER, W. A. and C. C. GOTLIEB: "A Top-Down Algorithm for Constructing Nearly Optimal Lexicographic Trees," in *Graph Theory and Computing*, R. Read (ed.), Academic Press, New York, 1972. **(9.2)**

WARREN, H. S.: "A Modification of Warshall's Algorithm for the Transitive Closure of Binary Relations," *Comm. ACM*, **18** (4), April 1975. **(7.1)**

WARSHALL, S.: "A Theorem on Boolean Matrices," *J. ACM*, **9** (1): 11, 1962. **(7.1)**

WEBSTER, C. A. G.: *Introduction to Pascal*, Hayden Publishing, Rochelle Park, N. J., 1976. **(P)**

WEIDE, B.: "A Survey of Analysis Techniques for Discrete Algorithms," *ACM Computing Surveys*, **9** (4), Dec. 1977. **(A)**

WELSH, J. and J. ELDER: *Introduction to Pascal*, Prentice-Hall, Englewood Cliffs, N. J., 1980. **(P)**

WELSH, J., W. J. SNEERINGER and C. A. R. HOARE: "Ambiguities and Insecurities in Pascal," *Software-Practice and Experience*, **7**, 1977. **(P)**

WICHMANN, B. A.: "Ackermann's Function: A Study in the Efficiency of Calling Procedures," *BIT*, **16**: 103–10, 1976. **(3)**

WICHMANN, B. A.: "How to Call Procedures, or Second Thoughts on Ackermann's Function," *Software-Practice and Experience*, **7**: 317–29, 1977. **(3)**

WICHMANN, B. A. and A. H. J. SALE: "A Pascal Processor Validation Suite," *Pascal News* (16), Oct. 1979 **(P)**

WICKELGREN, W. A.: *How to Solve Problems: Elements of a Theory of Problems and Problem Solving*, Freeman, San Francisco, 1974. **(A)**

WILLIAMS, J. W. J.: "Algorithm 232 (Heapsort)," *Comm. ACM*, **7**: 347–48, 1964. **(8.3)**

WILSON, I. P. and A. M. ADDYMAN: *A Practical Introduction to Pascal*, MacMillan Press, London, 1978. **(P)**

WIRTH, N.: *Algorithms + Data Structures = Programs*, Prentice-Hall, Englewood Cliffs, N. J., 1976. **(P, D)**

WIRTH, N.: "Comment on A Note on Dynamic Arrays in Pascal," *SIGPLAN Notices*, **11** (1), Jan. 1976. **(1.2)**

WIRTH, N.: "The Programming Language Pascal," *Acta Informatica*, **1** (1), 1971. **(P)**

WIRTH, N.: *Systematic Programming: An Introduction*, Prentice-Hall, Englewood Cliffs, N. J., 1973. **(P, A)**

WYMAN, F. P.: "Improved Event-Scanning Mechanisms for Discrete Event Simulation," *Comm. ACM*, **18** (6), Jun. 1975. **(4.3)**

YAO, A.: "On Random 2-3 Trees," *Acta Informatica*, **9** (2): 159–70, 1978. **(9.2)**

YAO, A. C. and F. F. YAO: "The Complexity of Searching an Ordered Random Table," *Proc. Symp. on Foundations of Comp. Sci.*: 173–76, Houston. 1976. **(9.1)**

ZADEH, N.: "Theoretical Efficiency of the Edmonds-Karp Algorithm for Computing Maximal Flows," *Journal of the ACM*, **19**: 184–92, 1972. **(7.2)**

ZWEBEN, S. H. and M. A. McDONALD: "An Optimal Method for Deletion in One-Sided Height-Balanced Trees," *Comm. ACM*, **21** (6), Jun. 1978. **(9.2)**

Index

540

local variable, 106–7, 109, 139, 140, 144, 149, 156, 502, 512, 513
long integer, 205–7, 210–15
look-ahead level, 310
lower bound, 16, 28
lower-triangular array, 40, 330

machine language, 136, 176, 445
maketree, 253, 262, 264, 269, 271, 453, 454
mantissa, 4
mark, 222
matrix, 236–51
maximum flow, 343
maxint, 479, 496
maze, 135
median, 38
merge, 404, 413–17, 422–23
merge insertion sort, 412, 413
merge sort, 121, 413–17, 422–23
midsquare hash method, 475, 476
minimax method, 313–17
minus node, 312, 313, 315, 317
mirror similar, 261–62
mode, 38
modularization, 68
move, 9
move-to-front method, 429–31
movevar, 10
multi-dimensional array, 30–32
multilinked list, 241
multiplication of matrices, 250

natural merge, 417
nesting depth, 61
network, 321
new, 219, 220, 221, 223, 224, 227, 264
next, 168, 180
nil, 168, 222, 225, 228
nil list, 168
nil pointer, 168, 179
nim, 317
node, 167, 168, 179, 180, 217–23, 252, 293, 318, 320, 322, 324, 326, 327, 331, 335, 336, 342, 344, 477–81, 482
normally distributed, 198

odd-even transposition sort, 386
offset, 46
Ohm's law, 343
one dimensional array, 16–26, 496–98
ones-complement notation, 3–4
O notation, 371–73
open addressing, 469
oper, 80, 83, 273, 304
operand, 9, 11, 76, 259, 302, 303, 304, 309
operator, 76, 259, 271, 300, 302, 303, 304, 309

opnd, 81, 83, 89
optimal flow, 333
optimizing compiler, 435
optimum binary search tree, 447, 462
optimum flow, 338, 343
ord, 18, 27, 29, 496
order, 371–73
ordered pair, 318, 323, 352
ordered tree, 295
ordinal type, 16, 496
order *n* matrix, 120
outdegree, 318
outer block, 512
outflow, 333
output file, 523
output-restricted deque, 166
overflow, 71–72, 75, 160, 164, 165, 167, 174
overflow area, 435
overlay, 51

pack, 499
packed array, 18, 22, 40, 498–500, 502, 504
packed record, 521–22
parameter, 137, 139, 500–5, 507, 511, 512
parenthesis count, 61
parse tree, 309
partial derivative, 216
partition exchange sort (*see* quicksort)
path, 322, 323, 325, 326–29, 333, 334, 335, 342, 343
path matrix, 325, 329
PERT network, 364–66
place, 179, 184–85, 193, 195, 411
plus node, 312, 313, 315, 317
pointer, 167, 176, 179, 186, 217, 218–23, 305, 309, 344, 346, 348, 358
polynomial, 215–16
pop, 60, 65, 68–70, 72, 167, 172, 178, 186, 200, 228
popandtest, 70, 72, 145, 228
popsub, 74, 141, 142, 193
postfix, 76–95, 129–33, 261, 302
postorder, 257, 261, 265, 267, 274, 297–302
posttrav 265, 266
precedence, 76–77, 85, 86, 88, 261, 352, 356
pred, 496
prefix, 76–78, 93–94, 129–33, 259, 261, 302
preorder, 257, 259, 265, 267, 271, 274, 297–302
prethreaded binary tree, 271
pretrav, 265
primary hash, 472
primary key, 424–25
probabilistic directed graph, 343
procedure, 500–5, 507, 511, 512
proportional, 370